CAMPAIGN • 262

MANZIKERT 1071

The breaking of Byzantium

DAVID NICOLLE ILLUSTRATED BY CHRISTA HOOK
Series editor Marcus Cowper

First published in Great Britain in 2013 by Osprey Publishing,
Midland House, West Way, Botley, Oxford OX2 0PH, UK
43-01 21st Street, Suite 220B, Long Island City, NY 11101, USA
E-mail: info@ospreypublishing.com

© 2013 Osprey Publishing Ltd

OSPREY PUBLISHING IS PART OF THE OSPREY GROUP.

All rights reserved. Apart from any fair dealing for the purpose of private study, research, criticism or review, as permitted under the Copyright, Designs and Patents Act, 1988, no part of this publication may be reproduced, stored in a retrieval system, or transmitted in any form or by any means, electronic, electrical, chemical, mechanical, optical, photocopying, recording or otherwise, without the prior written permission of the copyright owner. Enquiries should be addressed to the Publishers.

A CIP catalogue record for this book is available from the British Library.

ISBN: 978 1 78096 503 1
E-book ISBN: 978 1 78096 504 8
E-pub ISBN: 978 1 78096 505 5

Editorial by Ilios Publishing Ltd, Oxford, UK (www.iliospublishing.com)
Index by Fionbar Lyons
Typeset in Myriad Pro and Sabon
Maps by Bounford.com
3D bird's-eye view by The Black Spot
Battlescene illustrations by Christa Hook
Originated by PDQ Media, Bungay, UK
Printed in China through Worldprint Ltd.

15 16 17   10 9 8 7 6 5 4 3 2

DEDICATION

For Carole and Robert Hillenbrand

ARTIST'S NOTE

Readers may care to note that the original paintings from which the colour plates in this book were prepared are available for private sale. The Publishers retain all reproduction copyright whatsoever. All enquiries should be addressed to:

Scorpio Gallery, 158 Mill Road, Hailsham, East Sussex, BN27 2SH, UK
scorpiopaintings@btinternet.com

The Publishers regret that they can enter into no correspondence upon this matter.

THE WOODLAND TRUST

Osprey Publishing are supporting the Woodland Trust, the UK's leading woodland conservation charity, by funding the dedication of trees.

CONTENTS

ORIGINS OF THE CAMPAIGN 5
A revival of Byzantine power • The rise of the Saljuqs •
Romanos Diogenes fights back

CHRONOLOGY 19

OPPOSING COMMANDERS 21
Byzantine commanders • Saljuq commanders

OPPOSING FORCES 25
Byzantine forces • Saljuq forces

OPPOSING PLANS 29
The Byzantine plan • The Saljuq plan

THE CAMPAIGN 32
Alp Arslan invades Syria • Romanos assembles an army and marches east •
Alp Arslan's supposed 'flight' from Aleppo • The armies approach •
Byzantine defeat and Byzantine success • Confrontation, negotiation
and battle • The captive Emperor

AFTERMATH 90
Romanos returns • The death of Alp Arslan • The fall of Anatolia

THE BATTLEFIELDS TODAY 93

FURTHER READING 94

INDEX 95

Empires, nomads and merchants

ORIGINS OF THE CAMPAIGN

The battle of Manzikert in 1071 is widely regarded as one of the most significant turning points in medieval history. More recently, some historians have downgraded its importance, noting that it was not the defeat of a Byzantine army by a Saljuq Islamic army which opened the Byzantine Empire to Turkish conquest, but the Byzantine civil war that followed that defeat. Meanwhile western historians still tend to present the battle of Manzikert as the culmination of a Turco-Islamic assault upon the Byzantine bulwark of a Christian world struggling for survival against an Islamic threat. The reality was far more complex.

Byzantine civilization had its roots in both the Graeco-Roman and Early Christian pasts. Its people believed themselves to be under divine protection while their leaders were doing God's work in this world. As a result, their Orthodox Christianity was central to their identity. Referring to themselves as Romaioi or Romans and their state as the New or Second Rome, the Byzantines' clear sense of superiority annoyed several of their neighbours. Many foreign peoples who had been forcibly settled within the Empire by earlier Byzantine emperors had, by the 11th century, been Byzantinized. Only on the peripheries did non-Greek-speaking, non-Orthodox Christian peoples predominate numerically. In the east these included Armenians, Syriacs, Kurds, Arabs, Georgians and perhaps Laz.

Meanwhile the Byzantine Empire's relations with its western neighbours had a profound impact on the events leading up to the battle of Manzikert,

1 Sicily under local *qadis* (judges).
2 Mirdasids.*
3 Mazyadids.*
4 Marwanids, Saljuq vassal since 1056. **S**
5 'Uqaylids.*
6 Numayrids (probably changed allegiance from Fatimid to 'Abbasid Caliphate in 1060).
7 Qarmati (Shi'a but not recognising Fatimid Caliphate).*
8 Ibadi Imams (Saljuqs apparently controlled the Omani coast after 1054).
9 Sharwan Shahs.
10 Hashimids.
11 Musafirids (Shi'a but vassals of Saljuq Sultanate).*
12 Rawwadids (Saljuq vassals since 1054). **S**
13 Shaddadids (Saljuq vassals since reign of Tughril Beg). **S**
14 Buwayhids (Shi'a but not recognising the Fatimid Caliphate).*
15 'Annazids. **S** (probably)
16 Kakuyids (Saljuq vassals since 1051). **S**
17 Bawandids (Shi'a but recognising Saljuq overlordship). **S**
18 Ziyarids (Saljuq vassals probably since c.1041). **S**
19 Western Qarakhanids.
20 Eastern Qarakhanids.
21 Qarakhanids of Farghana (suzereinty varying between the Eastern and Western Qarakhanids.
22 Maliks (vassals of Ghaznawids).
23 Ghaznawids.
24 Khusdar (vassals of Ghaznawids).
25 Makran (in revolt against Ghaznawids since 1029).
26 Ghurids (vassals of Ghaznawids).
27 Volga Bulgars.

Other Christian states
A Georgia. +
B Armenian Lori-Tashir.

S vassal of Saljuqs
* Shi'a or normally supporting the Fatimid Caliphate
+ vassal of the Byzantine Empire

In the 11th century Christians were a substantial community within the Islamic regions bordering the Byzantine Empire. Today they are a small minority but several medieval monasteries and churches still exist, including the Tahira Church at Qaraqush, near Mosul. (Author's photograph)

The carvings on an Armenian church on Aght'amar Island in Lake Van date from a century before the battle of Manzikert, but they shed light on the costume and equipment of this region when it was ruled by independent Armenian kings. (Author's photograph)

and even more so on the events that followed. Although the Great Schism between the eastern Orthodox and the western Catholic Churches dates from the year 1054, it was as yet merely a theological dispute between senior churchmen. Indeed westerners were widely admired in Byzantium for their simple piety and military prowess, being widely welcomed as military recruits.

The events surrounding the battle of Manzikert focused upon the eastern part of the Byzantine Empire, in what is now Turkey. Here the Byzantine authorities continued the long-standing Romano-Byzantine policy of forcible population movement as a means of strengthening the Empire's defence. Hence, between the 7th and 11th centuries, large numbers of people had been brought in from Europe, the Middle East and the Eurasian Steppes. In other cases unreliable elements had been moved out of Anatolia, for example, to Thrace where there was already a substantial Armenian community.

In many cases these transfers had a religious motivation, the Imperial government being particularly concerned about perceived heresy in vulnerable frontier regions bordering the Islamic world. On the other hand minor theological differences were usually tolerated, if only because their followers numbered millions. For example, in the 10th and 11th centuries Monophysites who maintained that Jesus Christ had 'one nature which was both human and divine', included the Armenian and the largely Arabic-speaking Syriac Churches. In contrast the Nestorian Church, which maintained that Jesus Christ had 'two natures, one human and one divine' remained unacceptable. Instead Nestorians found sanctuary under Islamic rule where their doctrines were closer to those of Muslims, who regarded Jesus as a 'divinely inspired man' – in other words a prophet.

The persecution of more extreme heresies continued. They included the Paulician sect, which was brutally suppressed by the Byzantine authorities before briefly reappearing in the Eastern Euphrates Valley where the Manzikert campaign would later be fought. At the start of the 11th century a related sect called the T'ondrakeci was still recorded, many of its surviving remnants fleeing to Islamic territory where some of its followers, the supposedly 'sun worshipping' Areworik' fought for Damascus during the 12th century.

Armenians were, of course, central to the story of the battle of Manzikert. Early medieval Armenian society was not urbanized and the existing towns were Greek foundations, which, after being used as Roman garrison centres, had flourished under early Islamic rule. These and newly established towns had attracted Muslim settlers as well as garrisons, almost all under the control of Arab *amirs* rather than an Armenian *naxarar* aristocracy who were themselves vassals of the 'Abbasid Caliph in Baghdad. Amongst these new centres were Manzikert, Ahlat, Archech [Erçiş] and Perkri [Muradiye], which would feature in the events around 1071.

During this prolonged period of Islamic domination, Armenians had sometimes fought in support of their Muslim overlords, or in support of the Byzantine Empire, or in attempts to regain Armenian independence. Their homeland straddled the mountainous frontier between the Byzantine and early medieval Islamic worlds, a frontier which remained largely unchanged from the 8th to 10th centuries. Here the frontier zone has been described as a virtually depopulated no man's land rather than a line on a map. It generally followed the crests of hills but was also defined by the possession of fortresses while the main population centres generally lay at some distance on either side.

The wealth of Arab–Christian communities in the 11th century Marwanid amirate of Mayyafariqin and Diyarbakr was reflected in the decoration of some churches. This wall mosaic in the Monastery of Mar Gabriel, near Mardin, is a survival from the early medieval period. (Author's photograph)

Lake Urmia in north-western Iran lay in a broad, fertile region, then called Azarbayjan, where armies traditionally mustered before a campaign. (Author's photograph)

On the Islamic side a system of frontier provinces known as *thughur* had developed, characterized by a strongly militarized, *jihad*-orientated Muslim population. When Caliphal authority fragmented, small but strong and sometimes quite prosperous local Muslim amirates had emerged, some of Arab origin, some of mixed Arab-Armenian heritage, others Kurdish. In most places, however, Muslims were outnumbered by local Christian communities though the latter, mostly being adherents of non-Orthodox, non-Greek churches, tended to support their Muslim overlords or at least to remain neutral in Muslim struggles against the Byzantine Empire.

Meanwhile the Muslim world was wracked by a schism between the Sunni and Shi'a strands of Islam, largely resulting from differing views of authority within the Islamic community. It was reflected in local power struggles between neighbouring *amirs* as well as a wider confrontation between the Sunni 'Abbasid Caliphate in Baghdad and the Shi'a Fatimid Caliphate in Cairo. During the first half of the 11th century it also looked as if the Shi'a would triumph – but then the Saljuq Turks appeared on the scene and changed everything.

THE REVIVAL OF BYZANTINE POWER

By the 11th century Byzantine views of Islam had changed. Muslims ceased to be just another form of heretic, instead becoming God's instrument to punish Christians who were not behaving or believing correctly. Meanwhile, similarities between local Christian and Muslim military elites were remarkable in the eastern frontier regions. Two Armenian kingdoms had also been established under 'Abbasid suzerainty, Bagratids to the north and Artsruni to the south, while the main Arab–Armenian amirates lay north of Lake Van.

Almost all became targets of Byzantine expansion in the 10th century. Eventually only the Marwanid amirate clung to a few outposts north of Lake Van while the Shaddadids survived as a precarious outpost of Islamic rule south of the Caucasus. Unable to profit from the fall of their Muslim rivals, most of the small Christian Armenian states had similarly fallen victim to Byzantine annexation. Only the tiny kingdoms of Tasir-Joraget, Siwnik' and some even smaller principalities, remained more or less independent.

The Byzantine defensive structure

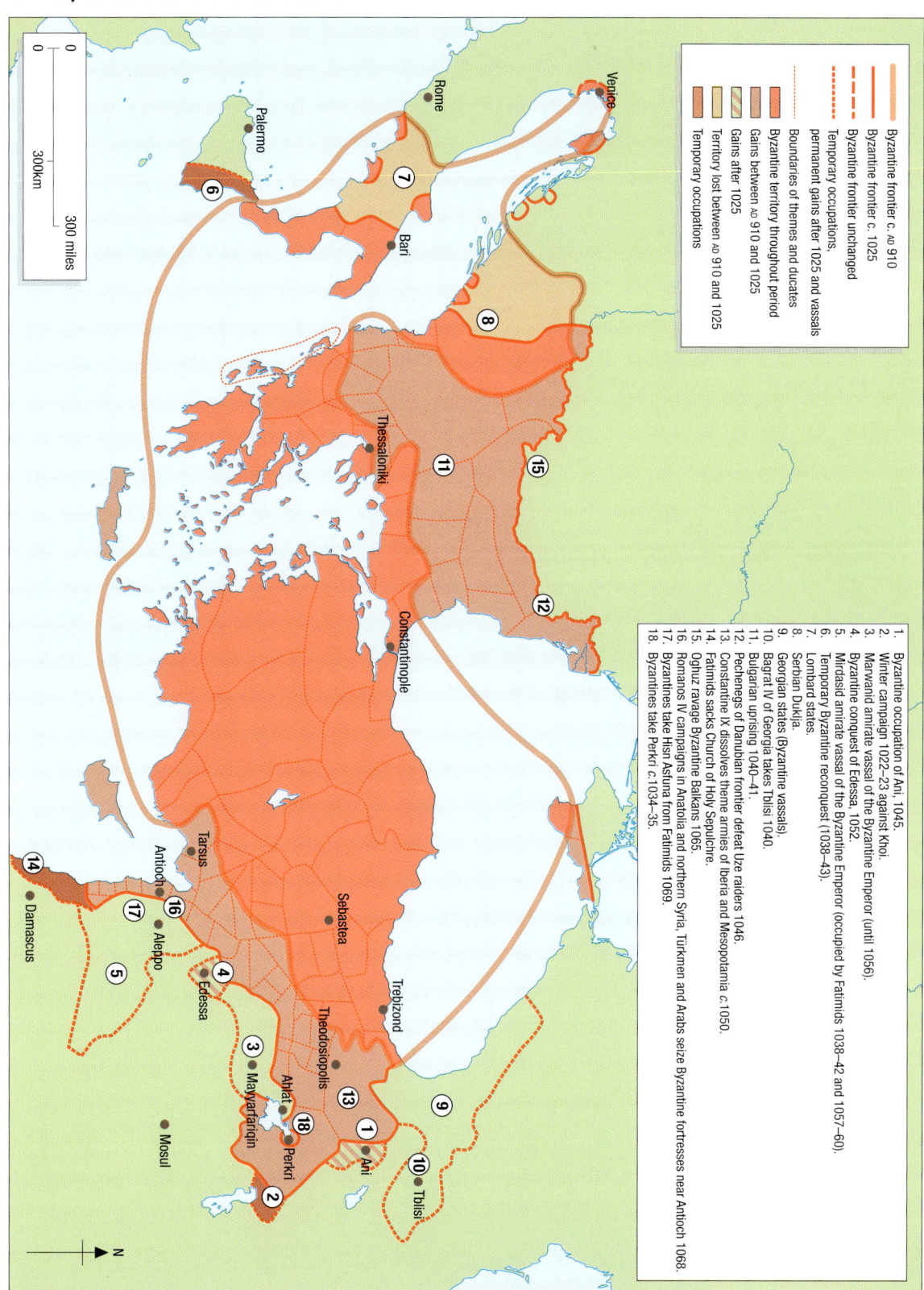

Legend:
- Byzantine frontier c. AD 910
- Byzantine frontier c. 1025
- Byzantine frontier unchanged
- Temporary occupations, permanent gains after 1025 and vassals
- Boundaries of themes and ducates
- Byzantine territory throughout period
- Gains between AD 910 and 1025
- Gains after 1025
- Territory lost between AD 910 and 1025
- Temporary occupations

1. Byzantine occupation of Ani, 1045.
2. Winter campaign 1022–23 against Khoi.
3. Marwanid amirate vassal of the Byzantine Emperor (until 1056).
4. Byzantine conquest of Edessa, 1052.
5. Mirdasid amirate vassal of the Byzantine Emperor (occupied by Fatimids 1038–42 and 1057–60).
6. Temporary Byzantine reconquest (1038–43).
7. Lombard states.
8. Serbian Duklja.
9. Georgian states (Byzantine vassals).
10. Bagrat IV of Georgia takes Tbilisi 1040.
11. Bulgarian uprising 1040–41.
12. Pechenegs of Danubian frontier defeat Uze raiders 1046.
13. Constantine IX dissolves theme armies of Iberia and Mesopotamia c.1050.
14. Fatimids sacks Church of Holy Sepulchre.
15. Oghuz ravage Byzantine Balkans 1065.
16. Romanos IV campaigns in Anatolia and northern Syria, Türkmen and Arabs seize Byzantine fortresses near Antioch 1068.
17. Byzantines take Hisn Asfuna from Fatimids 1069.
18. Byzantines take Perkri c.1034–35.

Such expansionism was seen by the Byzantines as necessary self-defence or the regaining of lands lost to Islam centuries earlier. Furthermore, the region around Lake Van was of key strategic importance. During the 11th century the most important fortified towns on the northern side of the lake were Ahlat, Altzike, Archech and Perkri with Manzikert dominating their hinterland. Rising on the eastern shore of the lake was the citadel of Van while the rugged southern shore was backed by almost inaccessible mountains inhabited by Kurdish tribes who resisted outside interference. To the south-east stood the citadel of Bitlis beyond which was the fertile Tigris Valley, heartland of the still powerful Marwanid amirate.

Annexation of this region therefore seemed to offer Byzantium a significant strategic gain. However, Armenian loyalty to the Byzantine Empire remained at best fragile. To the west the descendants of Armenians forcibly relocated generations earlier had been substantially 'Byzantinized' though remaining members of a different church. Elsewhere the majority of Armenians remained unassimilated, unsupportive and occasionally hostile to the Empire. Indeed, Byzantine chronicles frequently complained that Armenians were unreliable, proud, secretive and separate while Armenian chronicles complained about 'perverse, duplicitous and effeminate Greeks'. The situation was further complicated by the inability of the Armenians and Georgians to form firm alliances against their common rivals – be they Byzantine or Muslim.

Then there were the Kurds. Always present but only occasionally appearing in a leading role, the fragmented Kurdish tribes of the 11th century were not, however, the tribes of the pre-Islamic era. There had been great changes with a restructuring of Kurdish society, conversion to Islam and considerable intermarriage with the conquering Arabs. Nevertheless, several Kurdish tribal leaders had taken over from declining Arab amirates by the early 11th century, the existing Arab civil and military elites transferring their allegiance to these new rulers at a time when Islam was on the defensive against a resurgent Byzantium.

The Byzantine government was aware of the security problems caused by tension between differing Christian churches. Hence they tried – with notable lack of success – to win over the Monophysite Armenians and Syriacs. This in turn often made Armenians and Syriacs complain of 'Greek' bullying. Meanwhile, the military importance of the area meant that many elite mercenary units were stationed there, including many Normans from southern Italy.

By and large the Muslims of these conquered regions could remain only if they converted to Christianity. More often substantial communities were expelled as refugees, eager for revenge. The inhabitants of several lost frontier towns claimed descent from *ghazis*, the religiously motivated frontier warriors of the early years of Islamic rule. Sometimes migrating only a short distance to a nearby Muslim frontier town, they remained a militarized and *jihad*-orientated presence in this volatile region.

For Byzantium, over-extended ambition soon resulted in significant defeats, notably in Syria and Egypt. The Empire now ruled over a large non-Orthodox Christian population and 11th-century emperors faced mounting problems, especially in the Balkans. Yet in the east the Byzantines still faced no significant rivals. In fact historians have traditionally regarded the period from the great Byzantine victories of the 10th century until the disaster of Manzikert as one of military negligence and unjustified overconfidence.

There does indeed seem to have been complacency in the Empire's emphasis on administrative reforms rather than strong defence. Constantine IX is particularly blamed for actions such as his dissolution of *theme* or regional armies facing friendly Georgia and the fragmented Muslim amirates of south-eastern Anatolia.

Similarly the Byzantine annexation of most of Armenia has been criticized as removing a defensive belt, which had worked quite well, and replacing it with something that failed. On the other hand, for several years these measures seemed effective. Around Lake Van, the frontier between Byzantine and Muslim territory remained stable; the Persian chronicler Nasir-i Khusraw, who visited this region in 1046, regarded Marwanid-ruled Ahlat as the frontier between Muslims and Armenians, noting that Arabic, Persian and Armenian were all spoken there. Beyond that frontier the Byzantine garrisons remained scattered and somewhat isolated, though their vulnerability had yet to be demonstrated.

THE RISE OF THE SALJUQS

Amongst many misconceptions about the Turkish cultures of Central and Inner Asia is the idea that the Turks roamed a 'sea of grass' where they fought their endless internecine wars, constructed ephemeral states and occasionally attacked or overran their more civilized neighbours. In reality the steppe grasslands that maintained the Turks' nomadic lifestyle were often surrounded by agricultural river valleys, metal-rich mountains, dense forest to the north and deserts to the south. Furthermore, nomad invasions of their settled neighbours were usually a result of actions by settled states, which had disrupted the affairs of steppe societies.

Nor were tribal loyalties within steppe societies as straightforward as is often assumed. Tribal families tended to support those who were seen as favouring their economic interests, and when common interests failed, fragmentation resulted, as would be seen throughout Saljuq history. Nor were all the Turkish-speakers of these regions nomads, for they also included town or village dwellers, and settled agriculturalists. This was particularly true of Semirechye, on the southern side of Lake Balkhash, which featured prominently in the first decades of Saljuq history.

A Byzantine carved ivory panel showing Joshua accepting the submission of Gibeon, probably made in the 11th century. (Victoria and Albert Museum, inv. A.542–1910, London. Author's photograph)

Much of the Great Mosque in Isfahan dates from the 11th- and 12th-century Saljuq era. (Author's photograph)

The indigenous religious beliefs of the Turks are said to have centred upon a single god, represented as the Blue Sky, plus a strong belief in magic and a veneration of ancestors associated with totemic animals, above all, the grey wolf. The first external belief system to have had a widespread impact is believed to have been Buddhism while Manicheism entered the arena between the mid-8th and early 10th centuries. During the early medieval period there was almost a 'conversion race' between Nestorian Christians and Manicheians seeking to convert the peoples of Inner Asia. However, it was the spread of Islam that underpinned the rise of the Saljuqs; much of the Islamic missionary work amongst nomadic Turkish tribes being undertaken by *sufi* dervishes who were often unorthodox in their beliefs and practices.

A part of the Oghuz people, known as the Toquz-Oghuz, was ruled by a Manichean elite, which nevertheless included many Christians, Buddhists and Muslims. Around AD 940 'heathen Turks', who were probably early Qarakhanids, seized Balasaghun, the main town of Semirechye. The ruling elite of the Qarakhanids then became Muslim in the mid-10th century, resulting in the first Turkish Islamic state in history, and it was from the fringes of this Qarakhanid state that the Saljuqs emerged.

The origins of the Saljuqs are nevertheless shrouded in legend. They claimed descent from Saljuq Ibn Duqaq who came to Jend (now Qyzyl-Orda), one of the main Oghuz towns, and converted to Islam before the local Yabghu or Oghuz ruler did so. By taking control of Jend, Saljuq enabled the Muslim population to stop paying tribute to the still pagan Yabghu. This, it was said, began the hostility between most Oghuz and Saljuqs.

Saljuq campaigns and battles
1. Ghaznawids defeat Saljuqs near Bukhara 1025.
2. Türkmen migrations into Khurasan 1027–35.
3. Türkmen raids into Iran, Azarbayjan and Khwarazm 1031–34.
4. Saljuqs defeat Ghaznawids near Nisa 1035.
5. Battle between Ghaznawids and Saljuqs at Serakhs 1038.
6. 1040 Nishapur seized by Tughril Beg 1040.
7. 1040 Saljuqs defeat Ghaznawids at Dandanaqan 1040.
8. Saljuq advance from Nishapur to Hamadan 1040–42.
9. Saljuq invasion of northern Iraq 1042; Arab tribes defeat Turks at Tal Afar.
10. Saljuqs defeat Shah Malik Barani at Kath 1043.
11. Saljuqs expell the Oghuz Yabghu from Khwarazm and Jend 1043–44.
12. Saljuqs of Kirman take control of Omani coast c.1054.
13. Tughril Beg occupies Baghdad 1055.
14. Defeat of rebellion by Musa Yabgu, Saljuq governor of Harat 1064.
15. Alp Arslan campaigns against Kipchaks and Türkmen 1065.
16. Alp Arslan attacks Türkmen 1066.
17. Alp Arslan defeats rebellion by his brother Kawurd 1067.
18. Defeat of further rebellion by Kawurd and Fazluya 1068–69.

Other events
19. Georgian Christians and Muslim *amir* of Tblisi join forces against Shaddadids 1030.
20. Oghuz Turks plunder Maragheh and massacre Kurds 1037; Oghuz flee south of Lake Van 1040/41.
21. Shah Malik Ibn 'Ali of the Oghuz Yabghu seizes Khwarazm from Ghaznawids 1041.
22. Fatimids execute many local militia in Aleppo 1060.
23. Prolonged famine in Egypt 1062–67; struggle for power between the Fatimid Caliph and army commander Nasir al-Dawla Ibn Hamdan until early 1074.
24. Badr al-Jamali, Fatimid governor in Syria, attempts pro-Fatimid change of ruler in Aleppo 1064.
25. 'Uqaylids take Rahba 1064.
26. Saljuqs unsuccessfully intervene in Marwanid *amirate* 1065/66.
27. Fatimids install garrison at Hisn Afuna 1066/67.
28. Türkmen and Arabs seize Byzantine fortresses near Antioch 1068.
29. Rioting between Turks and Arabs in Aleppo 1070.
30. Sharif of Mecca transfers recognition from Fatimid to 'Abbasid Caliph and accepts Saljuq protection 1070.
31. Conquest of Syrian and Palestinian interior from Fatimids by Türkmen under Atsiz Ibn Uvaq 1071–76.

The rise of the Saljuqs

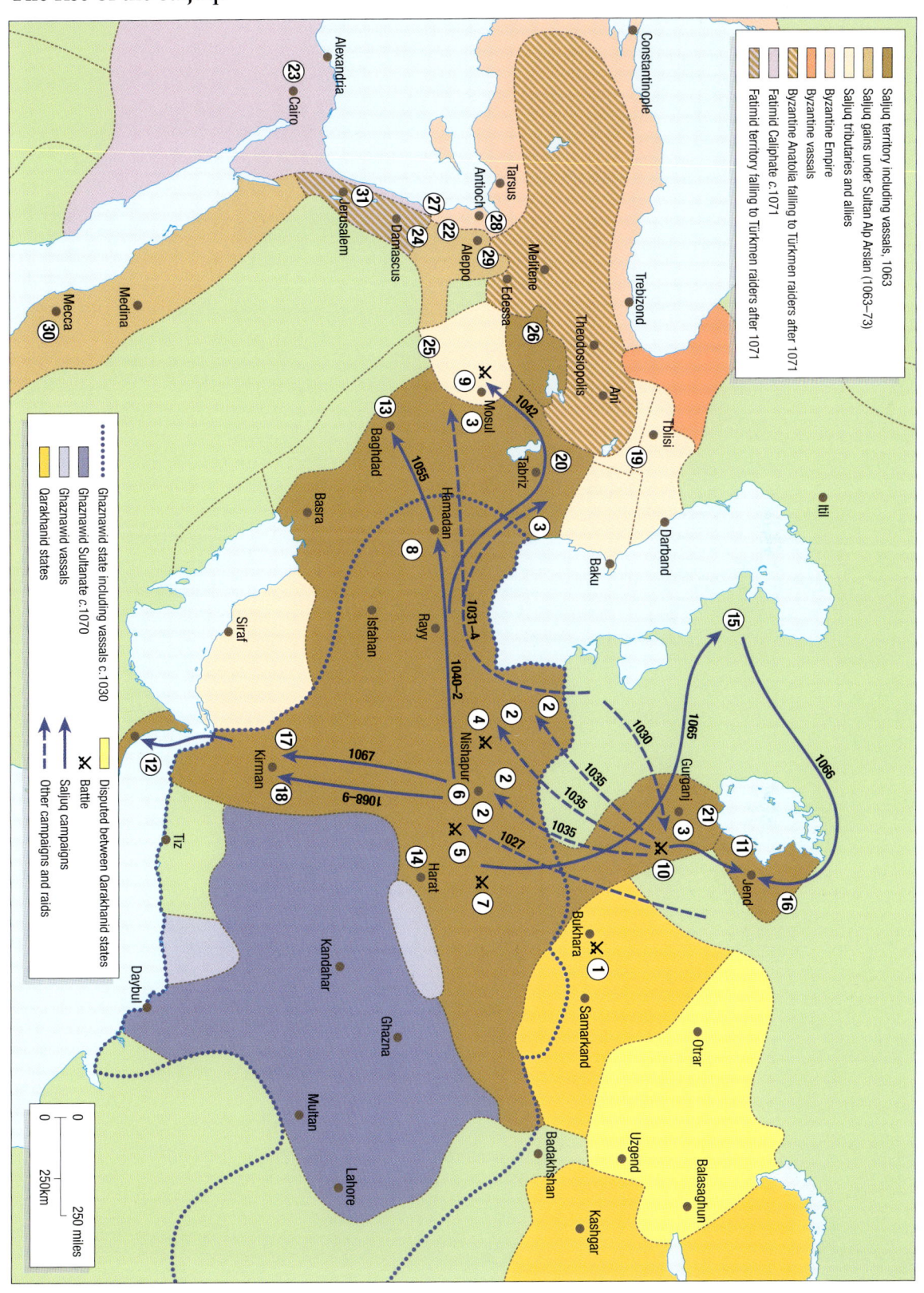

A gold coin from the reign of Romanos IV, the Emperor being at Christ's right hand, Empress Eudocia being at Christ's left hand. (Bibliothèque Nationale, Cabinet des Medailles, Paris)

Other accounts maintain that the Saljuq family and its followers were allowed to live on the frontier of the huge Samanid amirate, in the mid-regions of the Syr Darya River, during the later 10th century. This was on condition they defend it against their pagan Oghuz cousins. What is clear is that, under the loose leadership of the Saljuq family, substantial numbers of Turkish tribal groups crossed the Syr Darya early in the 11th century, then spread into Transoxania, eastern Iran and Afghanistan. Most were those Oghuz (Arabic 'Ghuzz') who converted to Islam while retaining their original tribal framework and nomadic pastoral lifestyle and were known as Türkmen. Their loyalty to the Saljuqs depended entirely upon the latter's military success. The Saljuqs thus headed a substantial tribal migration, which for a while dominated the eastern Islamic world and Middle East. The number of people involved remains unknown but it has been suggested that 16,000 Türkmen warriors fought for the Saljuqs at the early battle of Dandanaqan in 1040.

While the early Saljuqs pressed south and west, other Oghuz migrated westwards, north of the Black Sea until they reached the Byzantine frontier in the Balkans. The Saljuqs' original rivals, the now Muslim Oghuz principality of Jend, lasted about half a century. Then, three years after their victory at Dandanaqan, the Saljuqs returned to expel the Yabghu Shah Malik from Khwarazm and Jend. As the Islamic historian Clifford Bosworth wrote: 'The division of authority and the strong rivalry of the two families within the Oghuz thus ended with the triumph of Saljuq Ibn Duqaq's two grandsons Toghril [Tughril] Beg and Chaghri [Çağri] Beg and the inauguration of the Great Saljuq empire.'[1]

The Saljuqs' first conquests were achieved by traditional nomadic methods of threatening to destroy trade and agriculture. They also decisively defeated their Ghaznawid rivals on the battlefield. The Saljuq family's newfound authority was then legitimized by the Sunni 'Abbasid Caliph who already saw them as a potent ally against his Shi'a rivals. In western Iran and Iraq the Saljuq's main adversaries were indeed the Shi'a but fractured Buwayhid dynasty. But as the Saljuqs' opponents changed, and as their own realm expanded, the victor modified their traditional military and political systems. Their success in doing so influenced the history of the Middle East and beyond for centuries.

In fact the Saljuq Sultans adopted Iranian or Islamic forms of both government and military organization. Herein, perhaps, lay the roots of the Byzantine failure to realize that, in facing a full-scale Saljuq army, they were not fighting a tribal horde of Turkish nomads but one which combined the strengths of both early Islamic and Central Asian Turkish military traditions. Meanwhile, the interests of predatory Türkmen and Saljuq Sultans were diverging. In order to avoid conflict, large numbers of Türkmen moved to Azarbayjan, which already had a Turkish minority. It also possessed a relatively cool climate and ample pasture to maintain the Türkmen's flocks. In addition it was far enough from the centres of Saljuq authority to allow a large measure of autonomy and it lay on the frontier of Islam, facing lands that offered great opportunities to raid – in the name of Islam.

---

1 Bosworth, C. E., 'The Origins of the Seljuqs', in C. Lange and S. Mecit (eds.), *The Seljuqs: Politics, Society and Culture* (Edinburgh 2011) 18.

...NES FIGHTS BACK

...Constantine Dukas in 1067 his widow, the ...olitissa, chose Romanos Diogenes to be her ...ould invigorate Byzantine efforts to defeat the ...kmen raids. To do this the new Emperor not ...lian' or 'bureaucratic' faction at court, whose ...eep, but also the previous Emperor's brother, ...John Dukas would oppose Romanos Diogenes ...er than focus upon this latent opposition, the ...expected of him and turned to deal with ...

...ign of 1068 started when Emperor Romanos ...In April Afşin, a senior Saljuq leader who, ...killing a colleague, had been campaigning ...e territory since 1066, besieged Antioch. ...n, Afşin joined forces with another Saljuq ...raid deep into Anatolia, plundering ...n himself had led his army into Georgia ...Mulk and his senior commander, Sav-...ieved, however, news of the death of the ...r rebellion in southern Iran obliged the ...

...led his army towards Syria but before ...rned that raiders were operating to the ...army at Sebastea, Romanos advanced ...troops. The raiders fled, whereupon the ...marched south again. Byzantine forces ravaged the countryside around Aleppo until they were bought off, whereupon Romanos seized the strategic fortress of Manbij (Hieropolis to the Byzantines). The *amir* Mahmud of Aleppo harried the Byzantine reserves with the help of local Türkmen, defeating a Byzantine force sent to rescue them. Emperor Romanos fell back to besiege Aleppo but, short of supplies and in danger of encirclement, the Byzantine army retreated northwards, trying but failing to intercept Turkish forces under Afşin as they returned from sacking Amorium.

Following this somewhat limited success, Romanos IV prepared for new operations. Meanwhile a Norman mercenary from southern Italy, Robert Crispin, who had been sent to combat Türkmen raiders operating in north-eastern Anatolia, turned upon local Byzantine tax collectors because they refused to provide what Crispin considered necessary to feed his troops. Around the same time Romanos IV set off on another Eastern campaign which achieved no more than the first, being characterized by complex strategic manoeuvring by both Byzantines and Turks.

Perhaps pondering that much more would be needed to defeat this rash of Türkmen raiding, Romanos IV made his way back to the Byzantine capital late in 1069. Even the news that Byzantine forces in Antioch briefly took Hisn Asfuna in central Syria from a local Fatimid garrison is unlikely to have raised spirits at a time when friendly relations with the Fatimid Caliphate would have been a

Carved stone statue from the Ukrainian steppes, probably dating from the 11th or 12th century and apparently showing a Turkish chieftain in Byzantine military costume. (State Historical Museum, Moscow)

strategic benefit. Emperor Romanos did not himself take the field in 1070, instead delegating the defence of Anatolia to Manuel Comnenus while he focused on political problems at court. Manuel established his headquarters at Caesarea in Cappadocia but moved to Sebastea because Türkmen raiders were so active in the Pontic Mountains. Another Türkmen force, largely of the Yavuki tribe and commanded by Erigsen Ibn Yunus Yabgu Ibn Saljuq who had married Alp Arslan's sister Gevher Hatun, then crossed the mountains from north-western Syria to raid Cappadocia.

Looking across the Bosporos towards Istanbul, once the Byzantine Imperial capital of Constantinople. (Fred Nicolle photograph)

Caught between these two enemies, Manuel Comnenus was ordered by Emperor Romanos to attack those from the Aleppo region. He did so but was defeated and captured by Erigsen Ibn Yunus. Accepting the reality of the situation, some local Armenian leaders make peace with Erigsen, thus enabling him to lead his small army westward, though in so doing these Armenians earned the hatred of local Greeks. Apparently against Alp Arslan's orders, Erigsen reached Chonae where his troops sacked the important Byzantine Church of St Michael the Archangel.

1. Bagrat IV of Georgia conquers *amirate* of Tblisi, 1040.
2. Oghuz Türkmen flee south of Lake Van 1040–41.
3. Türkmen raiders defeat Armenians in Vaspourakan, 1042.
4. Gagik II and Grigor Pahlavuni defeat Türkmen raiders at Bjni, 1042/43.
5. Turks attack Ani, 1045.
6. Hasan Ibn Musa Yabgu defeated by Byzantines at river Zab, 1046.
7. Saljuqs under Ibrahim Yinal attack Vagharshaven 1047.
8. Saljuqs under Ibrahim Yinal head towards Ganja but retreat in face of counter-move by Bagrat IV's Byzantine allies, 1048.
9. Sultan Tughril Beg sends Ibrahim Yinal and Kütalmiş against Byzantine forces, sacking Arzen 1048.
10. Saljuqs defeat combined Byzantine-Georgian army at Kapetron, September 1048.
11. Georgian civil war between Bagrat IV and Liparit IV obliges Bagrat to flee to Constantinople, 1050.
12. Bagrat IV returns to Georgia, 1053.
13. Saljuqs, Armenian rulers, Georgian Prince of Kakhetia and exiled *amir* of Tblisi, attack Bagrat IV, 1053.
14. Saljuqs sack Kars, 1053.
15. Tughril Beg imposes Saljuq suzereinty on the Rawwadids and Shaddadids, 1054.
16. Toghril unsuccessfully besieges Manzikert, threatens Theodosiopolis and attacks Paipert, 1054.
17. Türkmen raid Colonia, 1057.
18. Türkmen raid Murat river area, 1057–58; sack Melitene, 1058.
19. Türkmen sack Sebastea, 1059, remaining in eastern Anatolia until 1060.
20. Alp Arslan ravages Georgia in 1060 and subsequent years.
21. Alp Arslan captures Ani, 1064.
22. Fatimid governor in Damascus tries to engineer pro-Fatimid coup in Aleppo, 1064.
23. 'Uqaylids take Rahba, 1064.
24. Türkmen attack Kars, 1065.
25. Saljuqs intervene in Marwanid *amirate*, 1065/66.
26. Alp Arslan sends Gümüş-Tekin and Bekçioğlu Afşin with Türkmen raiders, 1066, taking fortresses between the Murat Su and Tigris rivers; on returning to Ahlat, Afşin kills Gümüş-Tekin.
27. Fleeing Alp Arslan's wrath, Afşin heads towards Antioch.
28. Fatimids install garrison at Hisn Asfuna.
29. Alp Arslan imposes Saljuq suzereinty over the Shirwan Shahs, 1067.
30. Afşin attacks Caesarea, 1067.
31. Afşin besieges Antioch, 1067.
32. Receiving Alp Arslan's pardon, Afşin accepts tribute from Antioch; with Ahmad-Shah he raids deep into Anatolia, plundering Amorium, 1068.
33. Türkmen and Arabs seize Byzantine fortresses near Antioch, 1068.
34. Alp Arslan campaigns in Georgia, 1068.
35. Romanos IV campaigns in Anatolia, 1068.
36. Romanos IV raids northern Syria, 1068.
37. Romanos IV returns to Constantinople, January 1069.
38. Local Byzantine forces take Hisn Asfuna, 1069.
39. Romanos IV starts campaign in spring 1069, divided army, sends Manuel Comnenus to strengthen Sebastea, Philaretus to strengthen Melitene, and himself intends to retake fortresses between Euphrates and Tigris.
40. Romanos IV defeats Saljuq garrison from Ahlat near Larissa.
41. Crispin rebels in Colonia and defeats Imperial force.
42. Romanos IV heads north to Colonia, Crispin submits and is pardoned, summer 1069.
43. Afşin defeats Philaretus outside Melitene, summer 1069.
44. Philaretus flees to Harput.
45. Afşin sacks Iconium.
46. Romanos IV attempts to cut Afşin's escape
47. Afşin crosses mountains and escapes to Aleppo.
48. Byzantine *dux* of Antioch fails to cut Afşin's escape.

The approaching cataclysm

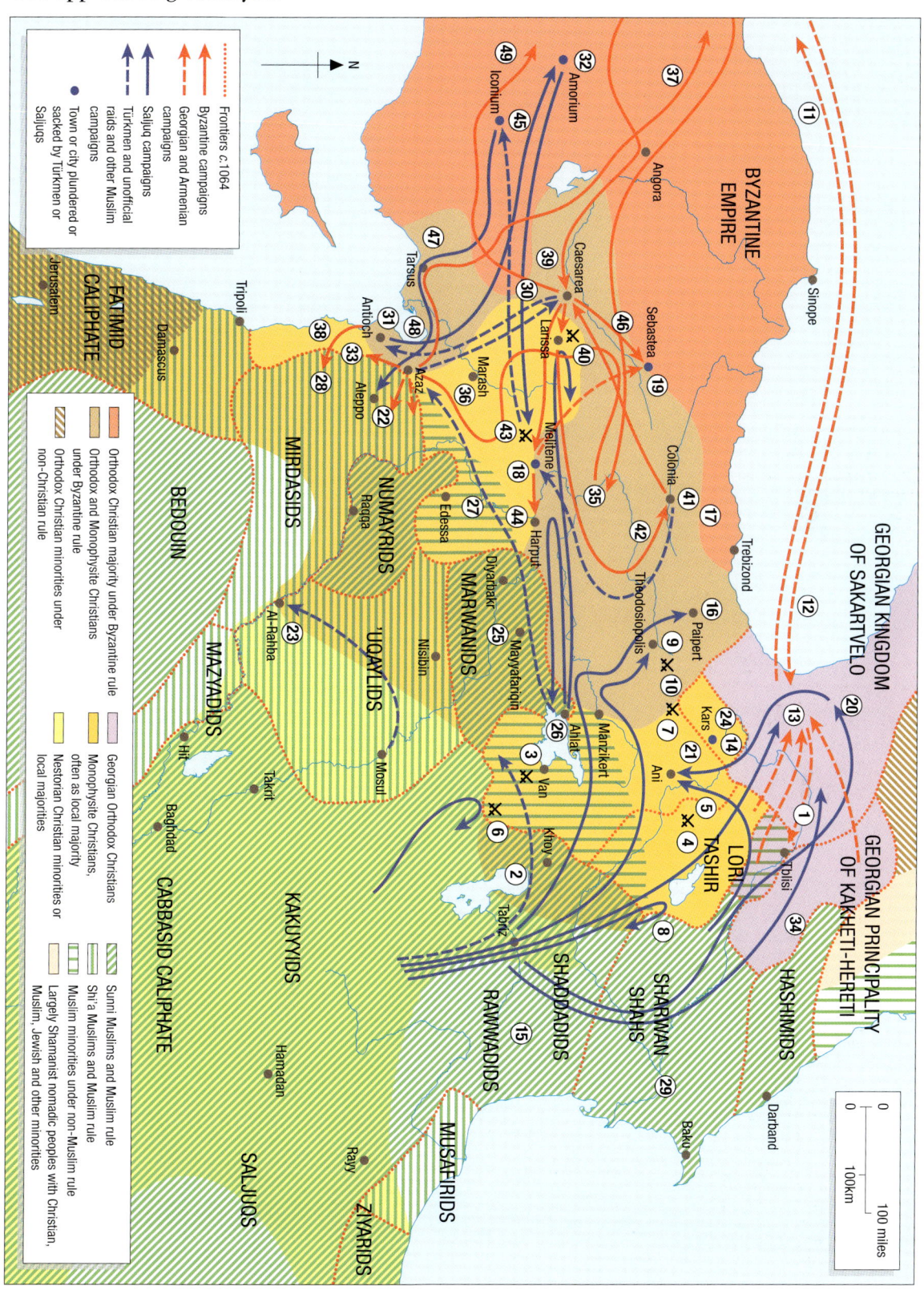

The Ahlat Gate in the massive fortifications of Diyarbakr, which were regarded as the strongest in the medieval Middle East. (Author's photograph)

So Alp Arslan sent another force under Afşin to demand Erigsen's return. The latter, who had already been pardoned by the Sultan for taking part in a rebellion in Kirman a year earlier, was instead persuaded by his captive, Manuel Comnenus, to enter Imperial service. Arriving outside Constantinople with Manuel Comnenus and other senior Byzantine prisoners, the Turkish turncoat was given the rank of *proedrus*. Afşin also approached Constantinople but when Emperor Romanos refused to hand over Erigsen he withdrew, getting trapped by winter snows in the Taurus Mountains. Not until spring 1071 did Afşin make it back to Azarbayjan. Despite his best efforts, Emperor Romanos had made almost no headway against Türkmen raiders, while Alp Arslan was still focused upon Saljuq ambitions within the Islamic Middle East with no apparent intention of taking on the mighty Byzantine Empire.

CHRONOLOGY

1016–27	Byzantine ban on trade with Fatimids.
1022–23	Winter campaign by Byzantine Emperor Basil II against Khoy (north-western Iran).
1028	Türkmen enter Azarbayjan.
1030	Georgia and *amir* of Tbilisi clash with Shaddadids.
1037	Oghuz plunder Maragheh, massacre Kurds.
1040	Bagrat IV of Georgia takes Tbilisi; death of King John-Smbat III of Ani; Saljuqs defeat Ghaznawids at Dandanaqan.
1040–01	Oghuz flee from Azarbayjan to south of Lake Van.
1042	Armenian leaders resist Türkmen raids with mixed success.
1043–04	Saljuqs expel the Oghuz Yabghu from Khwarazm.
1045	Abdication of Gagik II of Ani; Türkmen attack Ani.
1046	Hasan Ibn Musa Yabgu, oldest member of the Saljuq family, defeated by Byzantines at Zab River; Pechenegs of Byzantine frontier zone on Danube, defeat Uzes.
1047	Türkmen attack Vagharshaven.
1048–49	Saljuqs under Ibrahim Yinal move against Ganja in Georgia but are forced back by Byzantine countermove; Türkmen attack Mananaghi district of western Armenia, defeat Byzantines and capture Georgian Prince Liparit.
c.1050	Emperor Constantine IX dissolves some eastern provincial armies.
1053	Türkmen sack Kars; Armenians defeat raiders in Surmani area.
1054	Rawwadids and Shaddadids of Azarbayjan and Arran accept Saljuq suzerainty; Saljuq Sultan Tughril Beg unsuccessfully besieges Manzikert; Türkmen attack Baiburt; Byzantine humiliation of Fatimid envoy in Constantinople results in Fatimids sacking Church of Holy Sepulchre in Jerusalem.
1055	Byzantines abandon alliance with Fatimid Caliphate and agree that Saljuq Sultan's name is mentioned in congregational prayers in Constantinople mosque.
1056–57	Norman mercenary Hervé Phrangopoulos temporarily deserts to Türkman.
1057	Türkmen attack Melitene and Colonia.
1058	Türkmen sack Melitene.
1059	Türkmen sack Sebastea.

1060	Alp Arslan ravages wide area of Georgia; Fatimids execute many local militia in Aleppo.
1062–67	Prolonged famine in Egypt.
1064	Alp Arslan captures Ani; Badr al-Jamali, Fatimid governor in Syria, tries to engineer pro-Fatimid coup in Aleppo; defeat of rebellion by senior Saljuq, Musa Yabgu of Harat; 'Uqaylid ruler of Mosul takes Rahba on the Euphrates.
1065	Alp Arslan campaigns against Kipchaks and Türkmen in Central Asia; Türkmen attack Kars; Saljuqs unsuccessfully intervene in amirate of Mayyafariqin; Oghuz ravage Byzantine Balkans.
1066	Gümüş-Tekin and Bekçioğlu Afşin sieze Byzantine fortresses between Murat and Tigris rivers; Afşin kills Gümüş-Tekin and flees into Anatolia.
1066–67	Fatimids install garrison at Hisn Asfuna.
1067	Alp Arslan defeats rebellion by his brother Kawurd in Kirman, also imposes suzerainty over Shirwan-Shah of Shirwan; Türkmen under Afşin attack Caesarea.
1068	Alp Arslan campaigns in Georgia; Emperor Romanos campaigns in Anatolia and northern Syria; Türkmen and Arabs seize Byzantine fortresses near Antioch.
1068–89	Defeat of further rebellion by Kawurd and Fazluya in Kirman.
1069	Romanos campaigns in Anatolia; Byzantines take Hisn Asfuna from Fatimids; Manuel Comnenus is captured by Türkmen.
1070	Manuel Comnenus returns to Constantinople with his erstwhile captor; Saljuq force under Afşin reaches Sea of Marmara; Sharif of Mecca transfers recognition from Fatimid to 'Abbasid Caliph and accepts Saljuq protection; Alp Arslan invades Byzantine Armenia, taking Archech and Manzikert; Alp Arslan sends Nizam al-Din to Mayyafariqin in attempt to heal quarrel between Marwanid leaders Nasir Ibn Ahmad and Sa'id Ibn Ahmad; Alp Arslan leads army via Mayyafariqin and Diyarbakr to Edessa which he besieges.
1071	Alp Arslan abandons siege of Edessa and marches against Aleppo, arriving January or February; rival embassies from the Fatimid Caliph and the Fatimid *wazir* Nasir al-Dawla seek a Byzantine alliance; Romanos IV prepares a major campaign during the winter, mustering troops in late February and March; Byzantine army marches to the Sangarius River where it is reorganized, April and May; Byzantine army marches via Sebastea to Theodosiopolis, arriving late June; Alp Arslan learns that Emperor Romanos is marching east so abandons siege of Aleppo, 26 April; Alp Arslan dismisses most of his army (probably at Diyarbakr) then leads *askar* of 4,000 *mamluks* across mountains to Khoy, recruiting Kurdish troops on the way; Nizam al-Mulk musters a new Saljuq army; Alp Arslan advances towards Lake Van early in August; Emperor Romanos sends a substantial force to take control of the Ahlat area while himself heading for Manzikert which falls on 23 August; on same day the Byzantine army outside Ahlat is defeated and flees to Muş; Alp Arslan makes camp at the northern edge of the Süphan Dağ; Emperor Romanos is defeated and captured at battle of Manzikert, 26 August; Alp Arslan releases Romanos after eight days then returns to Azarbayjan; reappearance of Emperor Romanos triggers civil war in Byzantine Empire.
1072	Romanos is defeated, is blinded on 29 June and dies soon after; Alp Arslan campaigns against rebels in Transoxania but is assassinated, dying on 24 November and is succeeded by his son Malik Shah.

OPPOSING COMMANDERS

BYZANTINE COMMANDERS

Romanos Diogenes came from an important Byzantine aristocratic family whose powerbase was in Cappadocia, in central Anatolia. After earning a good military reputation against Pechenegs and others in the Balkans, his career almost came to an end when he was convicted of plotting against the widowed Empress Eudocia in 1067. She, however, recognized that Romanos had both talent and drive, so not only pardoned him but also selected him as her husband and co-ruler during the minority of her young son, the future Emperor Michael VII Dukas. Enthroned as Emperor Romanos IV, his task was to deal with various threats to the Empire's frontiers. Nevertheless he continued to face significant political opposition and was overthrown while briefly held captive by the Saljuq Sultan after the battle of Manzikert. Romanos IV tried to regain the throne but was defeated and died as a result of being blinded by the victors.

Nikephoros Bryennios (known as The Elder to distinguish him from the chronicler Nikephoros Bryennios The Younger) came from a minor Byzantine aristocratic family, the son of a general also named Nikephoros Bryennios. Nikephoros Bryennios The Elder became a field commander and was widely considered one of the best tacticians in the Byzantine army. As one of the few Byzantine commanders emerging from the Manzikert campaign with any credit, he was made *dux* of Bulgaria. Deciding that the new Emperor Michael VII was incapable of reversing a continuing Byzantine collapse, Nikephoros Bryennios attempted to seize the Imperial throne. When this Bryennios was defeated, he was blinded but, unlike Emperor Romanos IV, he survived the punishment and became an adviser to Emperor Alexios Komnenos.

An engraved bronze dish showing an enthroned ruler, dating from the 11th century and probably made for the Ghaznawid or early Saljuq court. (Metropolitan Museum of Art, inv. 1971.42, New York. Author's photograph)

The mountains south-east of Lake Van through which Alp Arslan led his *askar* of 4,000 men in the winter of 1070–71. (Author's photograph)

Andronikos Dukas was described as brave and well versed in military strategy but 'ill-disposed' towards the Emperor Romanos IV. As a member of the powerful Dukas family, which supplied the Byzantine Empire with several Emperors, Andronikos was a first cousin of Emperor Michael VII who took the Imperial throne in the aftermath of Manzikert. As much a politician as a military commander, he was at the heart of the intrigues that swirled around the Imperial throne. Defeated by the rebel Norman mercenary, Roussel de Bailleul, Andronikos Dukas was released so that his wounds could be properly treated, eventually dying in 1077.

Theodore Alyates was a senior Cappadocian soldier, though almost nothing seems to be known about his career before the Manzikert campaign. After escaping from that disaster with his Cappadocian units largely intact, Theodore Alyates remained loyal to Emperor Romanos IV during the latter's attempt to regain the throne. However, Theodore Alyates was himself defeated, imprisoned and blinded at Dokeia.

Nikephoros Basilakes was a senior Byzantine soldier of Armenian origin who was *dux* of Theodosioupolis on the eve of the Manzikert campaign. Renowned for courage, but also impetuosity, he was captured at the start of that battle. Subsequently released by the Sultan, Nikephoros Basilakes eventually replaced Nikephoros Bryennios as *dux* of Dyrrhachium in Albania. Like many other senior Byzantine commanders during this troubled period, he rebelled, was defeated and blinded.

Roussel de Bailleul was one of the most successful Norman mercenaries who sought their fortunes in the Byzantine Empire. After earning a reputation as a good commander under Robert Guiscard in southern Italy and Sicily, he proved his worth in the Balkans, being sent to Anatolia where he was given command of the corps of elite Norman mercenaries. In the chaotic aftermath of Manzikert, Roussel de Bailleul successfully defended Kastamoni [Kastamonou] but his tendency to act independently of both Byzantines and Turks was seen as a threat. Proclaimed a rebel by Emperor Michael VII he was captured by Alexios Comnenos (the future Emperor Alexios) but released on the orders of Michael VII. Sent against the rebel Nikephoros Bryennios in the Balkans, Roussel died soon after.

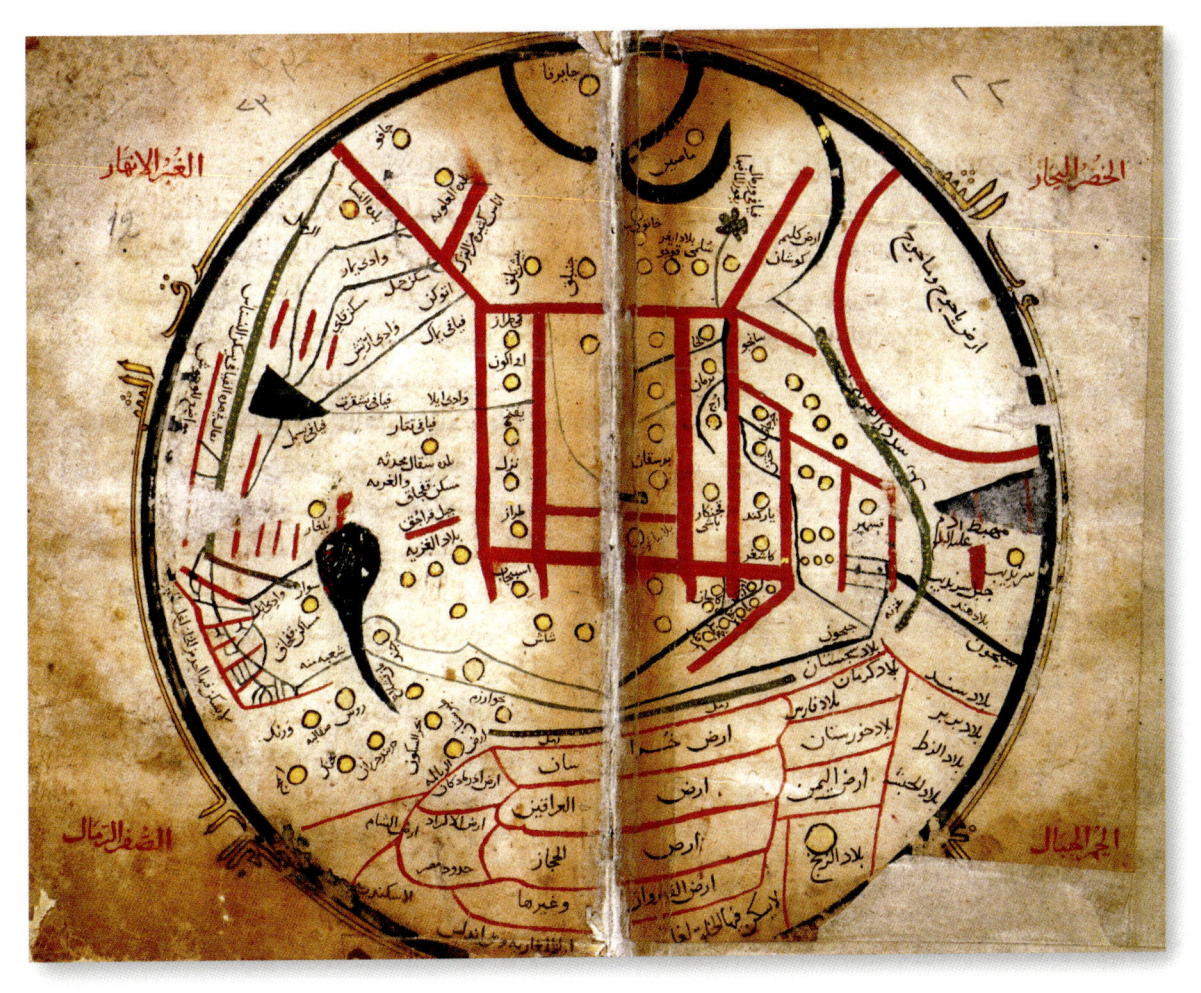

A map of the Turkish peoples and their neighbours in the Diwan Lughat al-Turk *by Mahmud al-Kashgari, written in 1076 (Milet Genel Kütüphanesi, Ms. Ali Emeri, Arabi no. 4189 ff.22–23, Istanbul)*

SALJUQ COMMANDERS

Muhammad Ibn Da'ud Çağri 'Adud al-Dawla Abu Shuja' Alp Arslan took over the Khurasan and Khwarazm when his father, Çağri Beg died around 1058. When Sultan Tughril died in 1063, both Muhammad Ibn Da'ud and his uncle, Kütalmiş, refused to accept the throne going to Muhammad Ibn Da'ud's brother Sulayman. After defeating Kütalmiş and several other rivals, Muhammad Ibn Da'ud took control. Generally referred to as Alp Arslan or 'Heroic Lion' and being a courageous, skilful commander, Alp Arslan was not an orthodox pious Muslim, but drank wine like so many of the Turkish elite at that time. Nevertheless, Alp Arslan's success as a ruler, his conquests and his unexpected defeat of the Byzantine Emperor at Manzikert in 1071, meant that he became a great Islamic hero.

The title **Nizam al-Mulk**, meaning 'good order of the state', was given to Abu 'Ali al-Hasan al-Tusi, a Persian scholar and politician who served as senior *wazir* or minister to the Saljuq Sultans Alp Arslan and his son Malik Shah. Born around 1018, he is said to have studied at Nishapur. After fleeing the Saljuq conquest and finding service under the rival Ghaznawids, Nizam al-Mulk attached himself to Alp Arslan's father Çağri Beg. From there he moved to the service of Alp Arslan who was then governor of eastern Khurasan. It was the start of a close working relationship, which continued

Inside the medieval old city of Edessa, now called Urfa. (Author's photograph)

when Alp Arslan became Saljuq Sultan. Apart from being a highly effective and loyal administrator, Nizam al-Mulk also wrote the *Siyasatnama*, a remarkable treatise on the art of government.

Sav-Tekin was a eunuch in Alp Arslan's service and although little is known about him, he was originally a slave. Rising to be Alp Arslan's senior officer, probably commanding the elite *ghulams*, Sav-Tekin was campaigning in Georgia alongside the *wazir* Nizam al-Mulk in 1068. It seems likely, though unconfirmed, that he was the eunuch and military commander whose troops supposedly included the 'puny' *ghulam* of Byzantine Greek origin who captured Emperor Romanos IV at the battle of Manzikert. Identified as *Tarang* in the Byzantine chronicles – probably a corruption of the senior Persian military title of *sarhang* – Sav-Tekin may have been through the long training and education outlined in Nizam al-Mulk's *Siyasatnama*. Early in 1095 Sav-Tekin served as governor of the town and citadel of Damascus under Alp Arslan's son Tutuş but two years later Sav-Tekin's ambitions got the better of him and he was executed by a rival, Zahir al-Din Tugtakin.

The name Afşin was originally a princely title given to the rulers of Ushrusana in Central Asia during the 7th–8th centuries AD. However, little is known about the early career of the Türkman tribal leader **Afşin Ibn Bakği Beg**. Playing a significant role before and during the Manzikert campaign, Afşin Ibn Bakği clearly had a volatile temper, resulting in excessive cruelty to his enemies and his own occasional disgrace. The fact that Alp Arslan pardoned him after he had killed a fellow Turkish commander suggests that Afşin's services were too useful to lose. He subsequently served as a commander under Alp Arslan's son Tutuş during the Saljuq conquest of Syria in the later 1070s, where he earned a terrifying reputation because of the devastation his men wrought between Aleppo and Ma'arrat al-Nu'man. However, Afşin fled when Sultan Tutuş had another Türkman leader murdered.

OPPOSING FORCES

BYZANTINE FORCES

By the 1060s the Byzantine army, though currently in one of its weaker phases, nevertheless had a long and proud heritage. Its basic structure appears to have remained little changed for centuries, with each *tourma* brigade supposedly consisting of three to five *droungoi* battalions, themselves theoretically consisting of five *banda* companies of 200 to 400 men. The *bandon* remained the basic tactical unit for both cavalry and infantry. The cavalry included heavily armed lancers and light cavalry armed with bows or javelins. The quality of training and equipment may have declined since the 10th century, but confidence is said to have remained high, especially when it came to ranged battle against an enemy who stood to fight.

The territorial military structure had undoubtedly been modified in recent decades, with the three military provinces, *ducates* or *katepanates* on the eastern frontier now being Chaldia in the north-east, Mesopotamia east of the Anti-Taurus mountains, and Antioch closer to the Mediterranean coast. A detailed study of the Byzantine army during this period has estimated that there were around 10,000 in Iberia, 5,000 in Vaspourakan, 3,200 in Mesopotamia, 3,000 in Taron, 12,000 in Derzene, Chozanum, Arsamosata, Charpezicium and Melitene taken together, plus a further 12,000 in other smaller military provinces.[2]

Despite the chroniclers' emphasis on the political struggle between military and civilian or bureaucratic elites, the gap between these sections of Byzantine society was not so wide; intermarriage being common. It would be similarly misleading to equate the 'great families' of the 11th-century Byzantine Empire with a western European form of entrenched territorial aristocracy. Instead, the most powerful of these established families were more like extended clans, some of which believed they had as much right to the Imperial throne as any other 'great family' currently ruling the Empire.

The ceramics made at Nishapur in eastern Iran from the 9th to 11th centuries were often decorated with stylized figures like this armoured cavalryman, clearly showing the military equipment of the period. (Royal Ontario Museum, Toronto. Author's photograph)

[2] Treadgold, W., *Byzantium and its Army, 284–1081* (Stanford, 1995) 83.

After the Saljuq Turks conquered the old Romano-Byzantine citadel of Theodosiopolis, now Erzurum, they added some fine buildings including the Hatuniye Gunbat funerary tower. (Author's photograph)

In the Byzantine Empire military obligations had traditionally been individual rather than feudal, devolving upon leaders of families, which were also obliged to supply 'their' soldier with his equipment. Possession of land had been a secondary consideration, though this had begun to change during the 10th century when military obligations started to be shared between groups of families, largely because cavalry service was increasingly expensive. Such costs almost certainly reflected the fact that, by the time of the Manzikert campaign, the traditional light cavalry *stradioti* of the Byzantine frontier regions had declined, though they would later be revived. The chronicles also suggest that indigenous Byzantine horse archers had become rare, resulting in a need to hire foreigners.

On the other hand the traditional Byzantine system of command and control remained effective and there may have been an increase in the use of different forms of military flag since Late Roman times. The Byzantine defeat outside Manzikert may, in fact, demonstrate how its commanders still had a notable ability to manoeuvre small bodies of troops whereas they had difficulty with larger forces. Above all, however, Manzikert would highlight failures in Byzantine morale and discipline.

While it is clear that the Imperial authorities put significant effort into maintaining a system of major roads for military and administrative reasons, these mainly ran between the north-west and south-east. There had also been a revival of interest in the theoretical aspects of warfare since the mid-10th century, perhaps resulting from greater confidence following the defensive attitudes that had prevailed earlier. Nevertheless, events showed that this offensive strategy brought with it defensive vulnerabilities.

The Empire now relied upon a thinly stretched chain of small border *themes*, each centred upon a fortress, manned by a small garrison and controlled by a *strategos* or governor. In practice, however, many smaller fortifications were maintained in a condition ready to be garrisoned, but not actually housing garrisons, though the major frontier cities were properly manned. Theoretically the new *themes* were under the control of regional military units called *ducates* or *katepanates*, which were themselves under a senior field officer with the title of *dux* or *katepan* headquartered in a key frontier fortress with a substantial garrison. In practice *theme* forces had shrunk during the 10th century, with the emphasis shifting to a more centralized army. In certain important areas the Byzantine Empire had also handed much military control to powerful local leaders, some of whom would prove unreliable.

'The Betrayal of Christ' in an Armenian Gospel dating from the 11th century. (Matenadaran Library, Ms. 9974, Yerevan)

SALJUQ FORCES

Alp Arslan's army in 1071 was not a simple horde of Türkmen tribal warriors, nor was it entirely Turkish. On the other hand it was not one of those professional armies that had characterized the more powerful of previous Middle Eastern states. Alp Arslan's was a mixed force consisting of assorted tribal or volunteer elements around an elite corps of professional *ghulams* of supposed slave origin.

The early Saljuq army had largely been of Türkmen tribesmen following their own chieftains. Equipped and maintained at their own expense, they maintained themselves on campaign from their own family resources to which they might hope to add booty. Ordinary tribal warriors did not receive regular payment, though their leaders may have done so, if only in terms of gifts from a ruler who wanted to retain their loyalty.

What most set the Türkmen apart from existing professional Middle Eastern armies was their fluid system of authority and loyalty. Amongst these Turks a tribal *khan* or leader's position was either acknowledged – or not – by the men of his tribe. Acceptance depended upon his being part of a suitable aristocratic family as well as showing himself capable of leadership. Significantly, a *khan* could expect to be obeyed in war, whereas in peacetime his interference in the everyday affairs of the tribesmen would not be welcomed.

Once established as rulers of the ancient civilization of Iran, the Saljuqs were surrounded by a court structure in which rank and status were paramount, yet the Sultan was not so powerful that he could afford to neglect the interests and sensibilities of tribal and clan leaders, nor of powerful individuals whose loyalty was maintained through favours, titles and gifts. During this period the Saljuq court was also remarkably mobile, moving across huge distances and as a result the Saljuq Sultans ruled 'from the saddle'

The road along the north shore of Lake Van has to cross a rugged promontory east of Adilcevaz, probably marking the frontier between Byzantine and Marwanid territory. (Author's photograph)

as did so many medieval Western European rulers, but unlike the Emperors of Byzantium who ruled through a massive bureaucracy centred upon Constantinople.

This old system of limited government worked well during the initial phases of Saljuq conquest, but once the Saljuqs found themselves in control of a largely settled and substantially urbanized realm which included an array of different languages and traditions, they had little choice but to turn to established Persian-Islamic forms of centralized and bureaucratic government. This would have a profound impact upon their armies, which soon needed a permanent, professional and paid, central force – in other words an *askar*. For centuries such *askars* had relied upon *ghulam* soldiers, supposedly recruited from slaves, though current research suggests that the origins of such men were more complicated than had previously been thought. The most highly prized of such *ghulams* were Turks from the steppes, though they included others. The origin of the Saljuq version of this venerable military system was around the time of the taking of Baghdad, only 16 or so years before the Manzikert campaign.

Saljuq *ghulams* eventually numbered between 10,000 and 15,000 troops, modelled upon the army of the rival Ghaznawid dynasty. Some of its earliest members may have been ex-members of that Ghaznawid army while including others 'mopped up' from different states overthrown or absorbed by the Saljuqs as they marched westward. Such a permanent professional army required a 'tail' of support forces and administrators, and it was here that Persian-speaking bureaucrats played a major role. The unruliness and frequent disaffection of the Türkmen further contributed to the Saljuq rulers increasingly turning to the existing Iranian minor aristocracy, the *dihqans*, to help govern their state.

The archaic but nevertheless prestigious military and administrative ideals that lay behind this tradition can be seen in the military advice which Nizam al-Mulk included in his *Siyasatnama*. Nevertheless, this presented an ideal rather than a current reality. For example, it is unclear whether Saljuq rulers were willing to adopt Nizam al-Mulk's recommendation for a multi-ethnic army in which Iranians, especially Daylami infantry from the north of the country, would counterbalance the need to rely overmuch on Turks. Arabs and Kurds had been enlisted in substantial numbers by the Saljuqs' Buwayid predecessors, but their role in Saljuq armies seems to have been temporary, as volunteers or auxiliaries. The resulting armies varied in size and could vary from 40,000 to a supposed 100,000 for major expeditions during the great era of Saljuq conquests. Later Saljuq armies were assessed at around 10,000 to 15,000 men.

OPPOSING PLANS

The Manzikert campaign provides an example of how the fluidity of medieval international politics could lead to even greater fluidity in medieval military planning.

THE BYZANTINE PLAN

Following the limited results of his 1069 campaign, Romanos IV rejected defeatist advice to abandon the Empire's recent gains and fall back in defence of Anatolia, probably believing that the existing fortresses and provincial garrisons were in no state to serve as a front line. It was probably then that the Emperor decided to launch an offensive in 1071, thus giving the Empire time to get ready. Even a devaluation of Byzantine coinage seemed worthwhile if it helped these military preparations.

Romanos' primary military objective was to rid the Empire of Türkmen raiding by reimposing effective Byzantine control over Armenia as an effective frontier zone, perhaps mirroring the situation around Antioch and Edessa where the Byzantine military position remained strong. There were also political considerations, chief amongst which was to consolidate his own position through military success. Whether the Emperor Romanos IV Diogenes also hoped to establish a Diogenes Imperial dynasty to replace the previous Dukas dynasty is more debatable.

Nevertheless, the Byzantine army would be campaigning in regions where agriculture had declined over recent decades, where food supplies for men and animals would make huge demands upon the army's logistical support. The noted historian

This remarkably well-preserved wall painting comes from a ruined palace in Nishapur and dates from around the 10th–early 11th century. (Archaeological Museum, Tehran. Author's photograph)

Hisn Kayfa, now Hasankayf, was a major fortified city in the Marwanid amirate, which played a major role in the events of 1070–71. (Author's photograph)

of medieval warfare, John Haldon, has suggested that roads in this part of the Empire were no longer suitable for wheeled transport and hence armies had to rely upon baggage animals. The resulting requirement for a huge number of such animals meant that an army moving east would denude a broad area even before it entered regions which had suffered decades of warfare and raiding.[3]

The frontier barrier which Romanos and his advisers envisaged would mean retaking the strategic area north of Lake Van and even if it proved impossible to stop Türkmen raiding entirely, the recently installed Saljuqs could be evicted and the Sultan stopped from consolidating his hold on Byzantine territory.

Key to this plan were the fortified towns and citadels of Manzikert (retaken by Alp Arslan in 1070) and Ahlat which would give the Byzantines command of the Upper Euphrates (Murat) Valley. Furthermore, they might enable the Byzantine army to press farther east, even retaking the province of Vaspourakan. If the Saljuq army could also be defeated, so much the better. However, it is not clear that the Emperor Romanos envisaged challenging the Sultan Alp Arslan in battle.

THE SALJUQ PLAN

During 1070 Saljuq Sultan Alp Arslan, his *wazir* Nizam al-Mulk and senior military commanders planned, prepared and began the execution of an ambitious military campaign. Its aim was to draw the autonomous Kurdish and Arab amirates in the Jazira and northern Syria into the Saljuq sphere

---

[3] Haldon, J., 'La logistique de Mantzikert', in Barthélemy, D. and Cheynet, J-C. (eds.), *Guerre et Société au Moyen Age, Byzance-Occident (VIIIe-XIIIe siècle)* (Paris, 2010) 16–22.

Malekan is an irrigated area on the south-eastern side of Lake Urmia which produced the spring pasture essential for the mustering of a largely mounted army. (Author's photograph)

through diplomacy or war. This would pave the way for a campaign against the Fatimid Caliphate's remaining garrisons in Syria. The Byzantine Empire featured in this inter-Muslim warfare only as a source of potential distraction. However, those Türkmen tribes who continued to raid Byzantium were rarely under Saljuq control though the Sultanate was usually blamed for their activities.

Alp Arslan may have made a serious strategic error in believing that, following the feeble Byzantine reactions in recent years, he could afford to let Byzantines and Türkmen sort matters out between themselves. Consequently, the campaign launched by Romanos at the start of 1071 caught Alp Arslan by surprise. The latter's genius was shown in the way he responded, abandoning his initial plan and developing a new one; doing so while withdrawing in haste from northern Syria to Azarbayjan. Much of the credit for the execution of this new plan must go to Nizam al-Mulk, and for later 11th-century Sunni Islam the Turkish Sultan and his Persian *wazir* would truly be a 'dream team'.

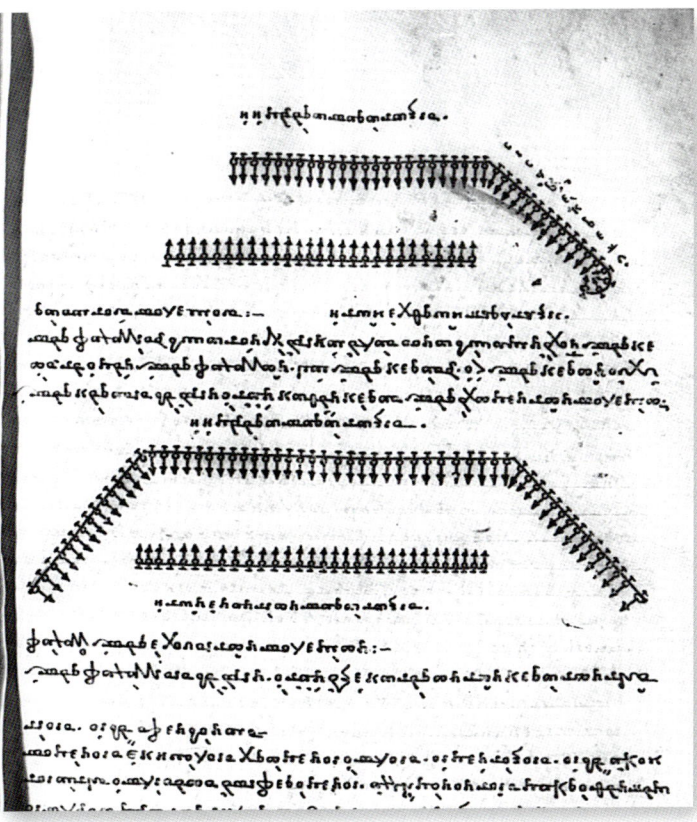

A page from a Byzantine military manual written in the 11th century, explaining various battlefield manoeuvres. (Bibliothèque Nationale, Ms. Grec. 2442, Paris)

THE CAMPAIGN

ALP ARSLAN INVADES SYRIA

Medieval fascination with omens recalls the tendency of modern historians and journalists to be wise after the event. Matthew of Edessa was typical in drawing attention to a presumed comet seen in the sky during 1070–71, recording: 'many said that it was the same omen which had appeared before and after which much bloodshed had occurred... So this was the beginning of the second devastation and final destruction of our country by the wicked Turkish forces, because our sins had increased and spread'.[4]

Meanwhile Egypt was still suffering the effects of a prolonged famine, which would appear to have been one of the worst in the country's history. When people were reduced to cannibalism, a lack of horses, mules and asses would seem a minor matter. But, even if Bar Hebraeus exaggerated when claiming that only three horses were left in the country and those belonged to the Fatimid Caliph, such a situation obviously had serious military repercussions. Meanwhile the Fatimid Caliph's *wazir* Nasir al-Dawla Ibn Hamdan may have lost his job but he retained considerable power. So his suggestion to Alp Arslan that the Sultan seize the opportunity to overthrow the Shi'a Caliphate was taken seriously – if more cautiously than Nasir al-Dawla wished.

In fact Alp Arslan decided to strengthen the Saljuq position along the Byzantine frontier before invading nominally Fatimid Syria. Religiously and politically his position was also strengthened when, in 1070, the *sharif* or dominant figure in Mecca, Muhammad Ibn Abi Hashim, informed Alp Arslan that the *khutba* in this, Islam's most sacred place, was now being proclaimed in the name of the 'Abbasid Caliph and Saljuq Sultan, rather than that of the Shi'a Fatimid Caliph. It was welcome news, which Alp Arslan tried to consolidate by allotting the *sharif* a generous pension. An embassy from the 'Abbasid Caliph also convinced the *amir* of Aleppo to have the *khutba* read in his name, though there is no accompanying recognition of Saljuq suzerainty.

In 1070 Alp Arslan first marched west and retook Manzikert. According to some sources he released its garrison but according to others the garrison had already fled. Alp Arslan's troops also retook Archech where, according to Bar Hebraeus, the Byzantine garrison was treated more harshly. Both these

---

[4] Matthew of Edessa (tr. Dostourian, A.E.), *Armenia and the Crusades, tenth to twelfth centuries: The Chronicle of Matthew of Edessa* (New York, 1993) sect. 55.

fortified towns might have been handed back to nominal Marwanid authority as represented by the governor of Ahlat, but were clearly given Saljuq garrisons.

The Saljuq army then proceeded towards the Upper Tigris Valley, the heartland of the Marwanid amirate, on the way to its main objective of Byzantine-ruled Edessa. The situation in the Jazira and Syria was currently fluid and Alp Arslan was not the only leader attempting to strengthen his position. In 463 AH (1070/1) 'Ali Ibn 'Uqail, the governor of Tyre and Safad, having revolted against the Fatimid Caliphate, was attacked by Badr al-Jamali the Fatimid governor of Syria who was, nevertheless, virtually confined to the coast having lost control of Damascus to the Ibn Manzu clan. 'Ali responded by engaging Qaralu, a recently arrived Türkman tribal leader, who in turn attacked Badr al-Jamali. It was into this complex but promising situation that Alp Arslan planned to launch his major anti-Fatimid campaign.

A carving high on the 10th-century Armenian Church on Aght'amar Island shows a horse archer shooting at a wild animal. His costume, appearance and equipment reflect the strong eastern influence in medieval Armenia. (Author's photograph)

At first things went well for the Sultan who had sent his *wazir*, Nizam al-Mulk, to Mayyafariqin, which was one of two centres of Marwanid authority in the Tigris Valley. According to the *Chronicle of Mayyafariqin* by Ibn al-Azraq al-Fariqi, 'He [Nizam al-Mulk] came on the occasion of Alp Arslan's campaign against the Greeks in 463 AH [9 October 1070–29 September 1071]. The Amir [Nasir al-Dawla] was alarmed; he entertained

In the mid-11th century the massive citadel of Bitlis, south-west of Lake Van was a key defensive position for the Marwanid amirate. (Author's photograph)

the *wazir* sumptuously; and two of his sisters and his wife implored the good offices of their powerful guest, who assured them that he would turn their brother from an Amir into a Sultan.'

In so saying Nizam al-Mulk exceeded his authority because Nasir al-Dawla's demoted brother Sa'id was under the impression that he had been promised Alp Arslan's support. Sa'id may have been correct because other sources maintain that, in his fear, Nasir al-Dawla made additional tax demands upon his subjects, enabling him to offer 100,000 dinars to Alp Arslan on his arrival. This, according to some Muslim sources, the Sultan returned, stating, 'he did not want the peasants' money'. The *Chronicle of Mayyafariqin* went on to describe how the Marwanid *amir* was 'received by Alp Arslan with much favour'. Unfortunately Nizam al-Mulk's over-eager promise remained a problem because there could be only one Sultan – Alp Arslan himself – so Nizam suggested that Nasir be given the title of *Sultan al-Umara*, chief of the *amirs* and thus senior amongst those petty rulers who had accepted Saljuq suzerainty.

This bowl, made in Nishapur, probably in the 10th century, shows a fully armoured cavalryman wearing a long-sleeved mail hauberk with a mail coif over his head and wielding a war axe. (Reza Abbasi Museum, Tehran. Author's photograph)

A stream runs close to the southern wall of Manzikert, now Malazgirt, but is almost clogged with rubbish as this is a poor part of town. (Author's photograph)

Unfortunately there remained the squabble between the current *amir* Nasir al-Dawla and his demoted brother Sa'id. Alp Arslan wanted no problems at his back while campaigning in Syria. Here the evidence is conflicting, some indicating that Sa'id was obliged to accompany Alp Arslan's army, others claiming that Alp Arslan went on a convenient hunting trip, leaving Nizam al-Mulk to arrest Sa'id and have him taken to al-Hattakh near Sa'id's powerbase of Diyarbakr. Alp Arslan then went to the massively fortified city of Diyarbakr but instead of seizing control he camped outside its gates, feeling benevolent towards its inhabitants because his wife had just given birth to a new son, named Tutuş. Bar Hebraeus wrote that the Sultan: 'drew nigh to its wall, and he passed his hand over it and then over his face, as if to be blessed by its strength'.

Though it was winter, Alp Arslan led his army over the mountains towards Edessa. On the way he seized several significant Byzantine border fortresses. Some were taken by storm but (unidentified) Tulhum resisted so strongly that Alp Arslan began negotiations. This made the defenders relax their guard, whereupon some of Alp Arslan's troops – against his orders – suddenly overwhelmed the fortifications. According to Matthew of Edessa, 'When Alp Arslan heard of this, he was surprised and deeply regretted the slaughter of the inhabitants, for he had taken an oath [not to harm them].'

It would be Edessa's turn next and here Alp Arslan is said to have been accompanied by Abu'l-Aswar, the Shaddadid *amir* of Dvin in the eastern Caucasus. Shawar Abu'l-Aswar was one of the most renowned *ghazi* 'fighters for the Faith' but he had already been succeeded by his son Fadl Ibn Abu'l-Aswar. So it was probably this less famous Shaddadid ruler who fought beside Alp Arslan. Once again the Byzantine garrison put up such resistance that the siege stalled. Having been bombarded for 30 days (50 according to Matthew of Edessa) the defending commander, the *dux* Basil, suggested that Edessa pay 50,000 dinars on condition Alp Arslan destroyed his siege weaponry. This the Saljuq Sultan did, whereupon Basil refused to pay. Humiliated but unable to continue his siege without siege machines, the enraged Alp Arslan led his army across the Euphrates, against the much larger Muslim city of Aleppo.

The Tuteh Mosque in Aleppo is one of very few structures surviving from the 11th century. (Author's photograph)

During his unsuccessful siege of Edessa, the Saljuq Sultan had received an embassy from Emperor Romanos IV, proposing a truce. According to Bar Hebraeus the Byzantines may have thought that Alp Arslan wanted to regain recently lost Manbij (Hierapolis), so the envoy offered to hand this back in return for the Saljuqs' returning Manzikert and Archech. Alp Arslan responded favourably then set off for Aleppo, not attacking Byzantine-held Manbij on the way.

Alp Arslan's siege of Aleppo proved as futile as his attempt upon Edessa, though it was brought to an end by events farther north. Most of the small Muslim states along the Byzantine frontier had accepted Saljuq suzerainty, including the Marwanids of Mayyafariqin and Diyarbakr, and Sharaf al-Dawla the 'Uqaylid ruler of Mosul. The only significant exceptions were Mahmud Ibn Nasir the *amir* of Aleppo and the fragmented Numayrid amirate, which dominated much of the Euphrates Valley east of Aleppo.

Alp Arslan arrived outside Aleppo some time in late January or early February 1071, but before starting his siege he sent a substantial force southwards, past Hims as far as Qaryatayn on the road from Damascus to the Euphrates. This area was ravaged before the raiders returned to the main Saljuq army, which had camped between Qinisrin and al-Funaydiq. The reasons for this raid are unrecorded but it might have been to discourage Damascus from helping the potentially troublesome Numayrids.

An unusual representation of the story of David and Goliath in a late 10th-century Byzantine ivory panel portraying Goliath as an armoured cavalryman. (Cathedral Treasury, Sens)

1 Manuel Comnenus moves to Sebastea because of Türkmen raiders.
2 Yavuki Türkmen commanded by Erigsen ibn Yunus cross the Taurus to raid Cappadocia.
3 Manuel Comnenus is ordered to attack Erigsen.
4 Erigsen ibn Yunus captures Manuel Comnenus on banks of the Halys then leads his men west against Alp Arslan's orders.
5 Alp Arslan sends army under Afşin to bring back Erigsen.
6 Erigsen is persuaded by Manuel Comnenus to enter Byzantine service.
7 Erigsen and his followers go to Constantinople.
8 Afşin reaches coast near Constantinople and demands that Emperor hands over Erigsen but Romanos refuses.
9 Afşin attempts to cross the Taurus in winter but is trapped by snow.
10 Nasir al-Dawla Ibn Hamdan, the Fatimid *wazir* in dispute with the Fatimid Caliph, sends delegation encouraging Alp Arslan to overthrow Fatimids.
11 Alp Arslan invades Byzantine Armenia, taking Archech and Manzikert, summer 1070.
12 Alp Arslan sends Nizam al-Mulk to Mayyafariqin to heal quarrel between the Marwanid *amir* Nasr Ibn Ahmad and his disinherited brother Sa'id (after 9 October 1070).
13 Alp Arslan marches to Diyarbakr, where his son Tutuş is born.
14 Alp Arslan besieges Edessa; an ambassador arrives from Romanos proposing the restoration of a previous truce.
15 Governor of Tyre and Safad revolts against Fatimid authority, is attacked by governor Badr al-Jamali of Damascus, hires a Türkman chieftain to attack Badr al-Jamali.
16 Alp Arslan abandons siege of Edessa and marches towards Aleppo.
17 'Uqaylid *amir* reportedly brings army to support Saljuq siege of Aleppo.
18 Saljuqs raid as far as Hims and Qaryatayn.
19 Saljuq demonstration towards Harran is checked.
20 Embassy from Fatimid Caliph to Romanos IV urges revival of previous alliance.
21 Rival delegation is sent by Fatimid army commander, Nasir al-Dawla.
22 Romanos prepares a major campaign, winter of 1070–71; sends embassy to Alp Arslan during latter's siege of Edessa.
23 Romanos and Balkan troops cross the Bosporos; army assembles at Helenopolis.
24 Romanos sends pardoned Norman mercenary rebel Crispin and his troops to Abydos.
25 Byzantine army marches to Sangarius River, end of March.
26 Paul the *katepano* of Edessa is recalled to Romanos' camp; returning Byzantine ambassador reports Saljuqs to be weak.
27 Hervé Phrangopoulos, joins the Emperor's staff from Amasea.
28 Major clash between Byzantine army and Armenians in Sebastea.
29 Byzantine army reaches Theodosiopolis, late June.
30 Romanos sends Erigsen ibn Yunus back to Constantinople.
31 Romanos sends small force to assist Bagrat IV in Georgia.
32 Afşin returns to Azarbayjan, early 1071.
33 Second Byzantine embassy demands that Alp Arslan control Türkmen raiders; Alp Arslan learns that Emperor Romanos is already marching east so abandons his siege of Aleppo, 26 April 1071.
34 Alp Arslan dismisses bulk of his army which disperses, some as far as Central Asia.
35 Alp Arslan and his *askar* head for Khoy, recruiting Kurdish troops on way, while Alp Arslan's family and the *wazir* Nizam al-Mulk go to Hamadan.
36 Alp Arslan establishes base between Khoy and Salamas.
37 Nizam al-Mulk organizes mustering of new army; professional *ghulam* troops also mustered in Baghdad.
38 Mahmud of Aleppo occupied Baalbak, accompanied by Turkish mercenary Aytakin al-Sulaymani; Mahmud's rival 'Atiyya finds refuge in Antioch from where he attacks Ma'arat al-Numan, so Mahmud returns to Aleppo.
39 Aytakin al-Sulaymani rejoins Alp Arslan.
40 Alp Arslan advances towards Lake Van, early August 1071.

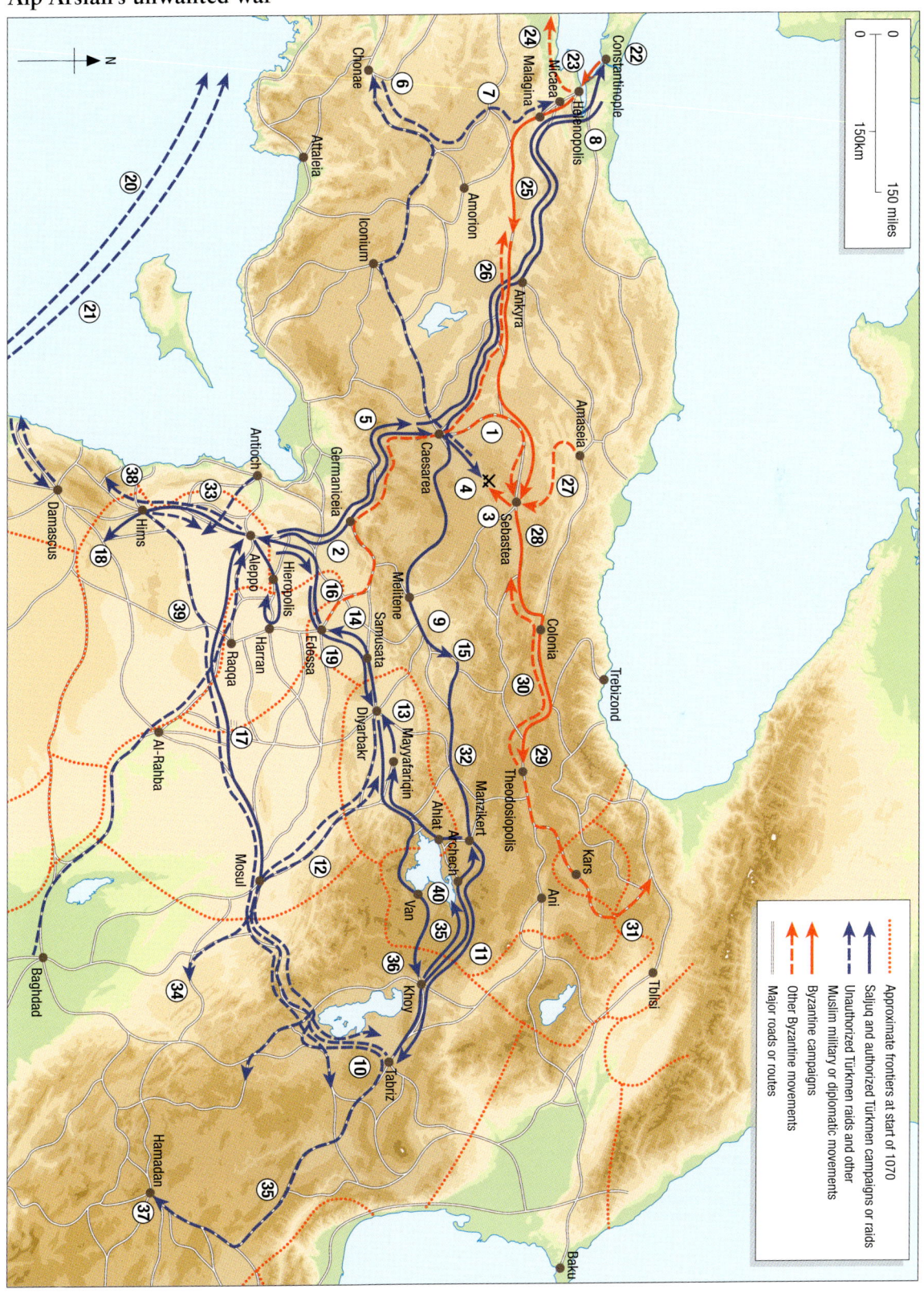

Alp Arslan's unwanted war

Little remains of the great fortress known as the Taht-i Sulayman at Ahlat, on the northern side of Lake Van but it was a strongly garrisoned Muslim outpost in 1071. The area was also known as Dhat al-Jawz or 'Rich in Nuts' under Arab rule. (Author's photograph)

Most troops in Alp Arslan's army were Turks or Kurds but the Arab vassals of the Saljuq Sultan also contributed troops like the light cavalryman shown in this early medieval Iraqi ceramic. (Keir Collection, London)

Alp Arslan raised his tent upon an ancient settlement or *tel*, thereafter known as Tal al-Sultan. Still Mahmud refused to submit and the Sultan was reluctant to make a direct assault on an Islamic city that was also a key position in Islam's resistance to a resurgent Byzantine Empire. A thrust against Numayrid-ruled Harran failed and for a while Alp Arslan seemed unsure what to do. Meanwhile a blockade continued, along with a steady bombardment of Aleppo's fortifications. It was during this that the citizens wound a huge black cloth around one of their main towers, the Burj al-Ghanam, sending their tormentors a message that the bombardment had given their tower a headache. This was more than mere defiance, as the throwing away of such quantities of expensive textile demonstrated Aleppo's great wealth. Alp Arslan felt the insult and ordered his archers to shower the civilian areas of Aleppo with arrows. In response one of the defenders' stone-throwing mangonels killed the Sultan's horse as he was riding too close to the fortifications.

It looked like stalemate. In the meantime the Fatimid Caliph and, it seems, his 'rebel' *wazir* sent rival embassies to the Byzantine capital, seeking an alliance. Neither of the competing powers in Egypt could offer much militarily and for the Fatimid Caliph it was a purely diplomatic exercise. Perhaps the Caliph wanted to encourage Romanos in his proposed campaign towards Armenia rather than coming to the support of Aleppo, which had already abandoned its Fatimid allegiance.

In fact Fatimid affairs had reached virtual anarchy. The remaining Fatimid territories in southern Syria and Palestine were wracked by civil war between Badr al-Jamali, supporters of the ousted *wazir* Nasir al-Dawla Ibn Hamdan and those seeking their own families' advantage. Nasir al-Dawla even reportedly sent 'rich presents' to the Byzantine Emperor during 1071 in a somewhat optimistic attempt to win his support, though this probably happened after the battle of Manzikert.

Manzikert sits on a hilltop (left) joined to the plateau (right) by a narrow hill. Emperor Romanos probably placed his fortified siege camp on the edge of the plateau. (Author's photograph)

ROMANOS ASSEMBLES AN ARMY AND MARCHES EAST

The Byzantine Emperor was aware of Alp Arslan's campaign when he ordered the mustering of Imperial forces. He must also have hoped that the Sultan's difficulties outside Aleppo would make a Byzantine campaign into Armenia easier, but the Armenian chronicler Aristakes Lastivertc'i's assertion that Romanos: 'decided to make war, in order not to appear unmanly and frightened, and in order not to leave to posterity a bad impression of himself', said more about Armenian prejudice than strategic reality.[5]

In fact Byzantine preparations were well advanced when the Emperor sent his embassy to Alp Arslan outside Edessa. Meanwhile Romanos and his senior officers had been successful in making large numbers of men with limited military experience into adequate soldiers during the winter of 1070–71, the troops mustering in late February and March. The Byzantine army had similarly assembled an impressive siege train, though whether this assembled near Constantinople or in Theodosiopolis is unclear.

Precisely when the Emperor attempted a peaceful accommodation with the new Norman rulers of southern Italy is unknown, but it was either during the preparations for the great expedition or shortly after it set off. Facing more serious matters in the east, Romanos apparently accepted the inevitable loss of Byzantium's final toehold in Apulia to these Norman conquerors and therefore proposed an alliance based upon the marriage of one of Romanos' sons to one of the Norman leader's daughters. The offer was rejected and Bari eventually fell anyway. Under such circumstances the Byzantine Emperor had to leave significant garrisons in the Balkans to watch the Normans and the threatening Hungarians. Some members of the Varangian Guard were similarly left in Constantinople.

---

5 Aristakes Lastivertc'i (tr. Bedrosian, R.), *Aristakes Lastivertc'i's History; Sources of the Armenian Tradition* (New York, 1985) 166–67.

Herod's soldiers pursuing Elizabeth, Zechariah and the infant John the Baptist, in an early 12th-century Christian wall painting made under Saljuq rule. (*in situ* Chapel 11, Göreme, Cappadocia. Ahmet Soğut photograph)

All sources agree that the army that Romanos mustered was large and very mixed. At its centre were elite units including the *Heteria, Scholai, Stratelatai* and some Varangians. These would serve as a firm foundation for less reliable troops. Not all the other units were clearly identified though they included Balkan troops from Bulgaria, local *tagmata* from Cappadocia, perhaps from the *themes* of Colonia, Charsianum, Anatolics, Chaldia and Armeniacs. Nevertheless some of these eastern provincial troops had low skill and morale. More reliable, perhaps, were units from Cilicia and Bithynia along with small numbers of *tagmata* from the Syrian frontier. There were also many Armenian infantry though it is not clear where they were drawn from.

More is known about the varied foreign mercenaries, most important of whom were 'Franks', largely Normans, under Roussel de Bailleul, and Germans who would however disgrace themselves early in the campaign. A substantial detachment of Oghuz and Pecheneg Turks may have been vassals or allies rather than mercenaries. Arab and Persian chroniclers added Rus probably meaning the Varangians, Khazars, Alans, Kipchaks, Persians, Georgians and Abkhazians from the Caucasus. According to al-Husayni writing in the early 13th century, 'Byzantium threw its own lifeblood at the sultan and the earth brought forth its burdens of men and equipment. To this king there flocked [those] from rabblesome elements … people by whom discords extend their forearms and by whose gathering together Christianity elevated its foundations.'[6]

Numbers given for the size of Romanos' army range from the slightly exaggerated to the simply absurd. A figure of 30,000 to 40,000 would be realistic, though there may also have been an additional 20,000 support personnel, while the figure of 30,000–40,000 may not have included infantry levies joining the army as it marched eastward. All sources agree that the siege train was huge and included impressive siege machines. Al-Turtushi, an Andalusian scholar writing in Fatimid Egypt, provided the earliest account of this campaign. He noted that the Byzantines: 'had prepared an innumerable amount of animals, weapons and mangonels and pieces of equipment made ready for conquering citadels in war'. Ibn al-'Adim added: 'With the Byzantines were three thousand carts carrying the heavy baggage and the mangonels. Amongst them was a mangonel with eight beams; it was carried by a hundred carts.'

---

[6] Hillenbrand, C., *Turkish Myth and Muslim Symbol* (Edinburgh, 2007) 53.

Others seem to have been more impressed by the wealth in the treasury, which Romanos also brought with him. According to Sibt al-Jawzi it included 'a million dinars, 100,000 silk garments and a similar number of gold saddles, belts and gold jewellery'. Greek, Armenian and Muslim chroniclers employed the wisdom of hindsight to condemn the Byzantine Emperor's presumed overconfidence, Aristakes Lastivertc'i maintaining: 'Seeing such a multitude of troops assembled in one place, he arrogantly grew proud, thinking it impossible to be vanquished.' This would be given the lie by Romanos' cautious actions during the campaign, despite the fact that his envoy, Leo Diabatenus, returned from his meeting with Alp Arslan outside Aleppo to report the Saljuq army to be weak and frightened. Before leaving Constantinople the Emperor also made the *caesar* John Dukas and his sons swear loyalty, then sent the elder Dukas 'across the Bosphoros' where this potential focus of political opposition would supposedly be less able to cause trouble.

In an age when omens and portents were taken very seriously, a number of disturbing events were recorded by subsequent chroniclers. According to Sibt al-Jawzi it was Romanos himself who told Alp Arslan, following his capture, how he had gone to the great church of Santa Sofia to pray before his campaign: 'And there was the cross which had fallen from its position in the direction of the Islamic *qibla*. I was amazed at that and I re-arranged it towards the east. The following day I came to it and there it was inclining towards the *qibla*. So I ordered it to be bound in chains. Then I entered on the third day and there it was inclined towards the *qibla*.' Even if the Emperor did give such an account, he was probably trying to placate his captor.

With the probable exception of the Emperor's guard units, the army mustered on the eastern, Anatolian side of the straits, Romanos himself crossing during the second week of March. That was when the next omen supposedly occurred: a pigeon alighting on his ship and then on his right hand, though none was sure whether this was a good or bad sign. Byzantine forces traditionally assembled at Nicomedia (İzmit) for eastern campaigns but instead Romanos ordered an initial muster at the naval base of Helenopolis (Hersek). This the soldiers unhelpfully nicknamed *Eleinopolis* or 'miserable city'. Furthermore, the central pole of the Imperial tent broke, which all agreed was bad.

It is far from clear where the Byzantines assembled the huge herds of cattle, which served as food on the hoof for the army. Units from eastern and southern garrisons would join the army along the way, at the Sangarius (Sakarya) River, or Sebastea or Theodosiopolis. Amongst them was Paul the *proedrus* who was recalled from his command as *katepan* of Edessa, who may have joined the Emperor at Helenopolis bringing up-to-date, though not necessarily correct, information about Alp Arslan's army outside Aleppo.

A lead seal of Hervé Phrangopoulos, a high-ranking Norman soldier in the Byzantine army during the second half of the 11th century. (Private collection, Paris)

While the army prepared for the first stage of its march, a detachment of Normans was sent to, or left in, Abydos on the Dardanelles under the command of the pardoned Norman rebel Robert Crispin. During the early medieval period, Malagina on the Sangarius River was the first major military staging area on the road from Constantinople. It was around here that Emperor Romanos decided to send back those generals whom he did not trust, including the highly experienced Nikephoros Botaneiates. The even more doubtful Andronikos Dukas was nevertheless kept close to the Emperor.

The army was now reorganized before heading for Sebastea. Sending most of the troops ahead, Emperor Romanos remained to supervise the construction of a new fortress but, on the march, further unfortunate things happened. Some would later be called omens as well as practical setbacks, such as a fire destroying much equipment and killing many animals. Meanwhile the Emperor became morose, separating himself and his camp from his men.

Perhaps a lack of close supervision lay behind the violence that erupted between local people and some *Nemitzoi* German mercenaries who were accused of commandeering provisions without paying. When the Germans complained that some of their comrades had been killed, Romanos did not support them but instead sent other troops to remove these *Nemitzoi* from their previous place of honour. Nor was morale helped by the presence of unburied bodies in an area recently ravaged by Türkmen raiders. It may have been around this time that Hervé Phrangopoulos, who had probably been campaigning from Amasea against these Türkmen, joined the Emperor's staff.

Further problems emerged when the Byzantine army reached Sebastea, where a substantial Armenian colony was accused by the Greek inhabitants of siding with the Türkmen. Matthew of Edessa claimed that, despite being courteously received by two local Armenian leaders, Romanos snubbed both of them, as well as ex-King Gagik and Erigsen Ibn Yunus the Türkmen chief who had come over to the Byzantines. The Emperor then ransacked part of the Armenian quarter, declaring: 'When I finish battling against the Persians, I shall do away with the Armenian faith.' Local Armenian monks reportedly cursed him, while the Emperor's officers hurriedly pointed out that many in the army were also Armenians.

The rebuilt Mausoleum of Baba Tahir in Hamadan marks the grave of a Kurdish-Persian *sufi* poet who lived at the time of the Saljuq Sultans Tughril Beg and perhaps Alp Arslan. (Author's photograph)

Romanos now summoned a military council to discuss whether to invade enemy-controlled territory or stay put and strengthen Byzantine defences. While Nikephorus Bryennios and the respected Georgian *magistros* Joseph Tarchaniotes urged caution, many younger officers urged a major strike towards Lake Van. What the Emperor needed was accurate information about Alp Arslan's actions and intentions, and this he definitely did not receive. In fact, the messages that reached the Byzantine headquarters were wholly misleading.

Romanos thus decided on an offensive and, seemingly carried away with the enthusiasm of younger commanders, proclaimed that the Saljuqs and Türkmen would be driven back to Central Asia. According to some Islamic sources the Byzantines were now so confident that they appointed governors for regions they expected to conquer, including the Jazira, Syria, Iran, Iraq, Khurasan and Egypt. However Sibt al-Jawzi noted: 'He [Romanos] made an exception of Baghdad and he said, Do not attack that upright shaykh [the Caliph], for he is our friend'.

The Byzantine army now marched to Theodosiopolis where its organizational structure was changed from a line-of-march to an offensive formation. Yet beneath this veneer of confidence Romanos remained uncertain, sending Erigsen Ibn Yunus and his Türkmen back to Constantinople for fear they might change sides again. He also sent a small force to assist in his Bagratid ally regaining control of Georgia.

Carvings on the Church of San Nicola in Bari were made about 30 years after the battle of Manzikert and show the Byzantine-influenced equipment used by Norman mercenaries from southern Italy. (Author's photograph)

Harput was another vital fortified frontier outpost between the Byzantine and Islamic worlds during the 11th century. (Author's photograph)

43

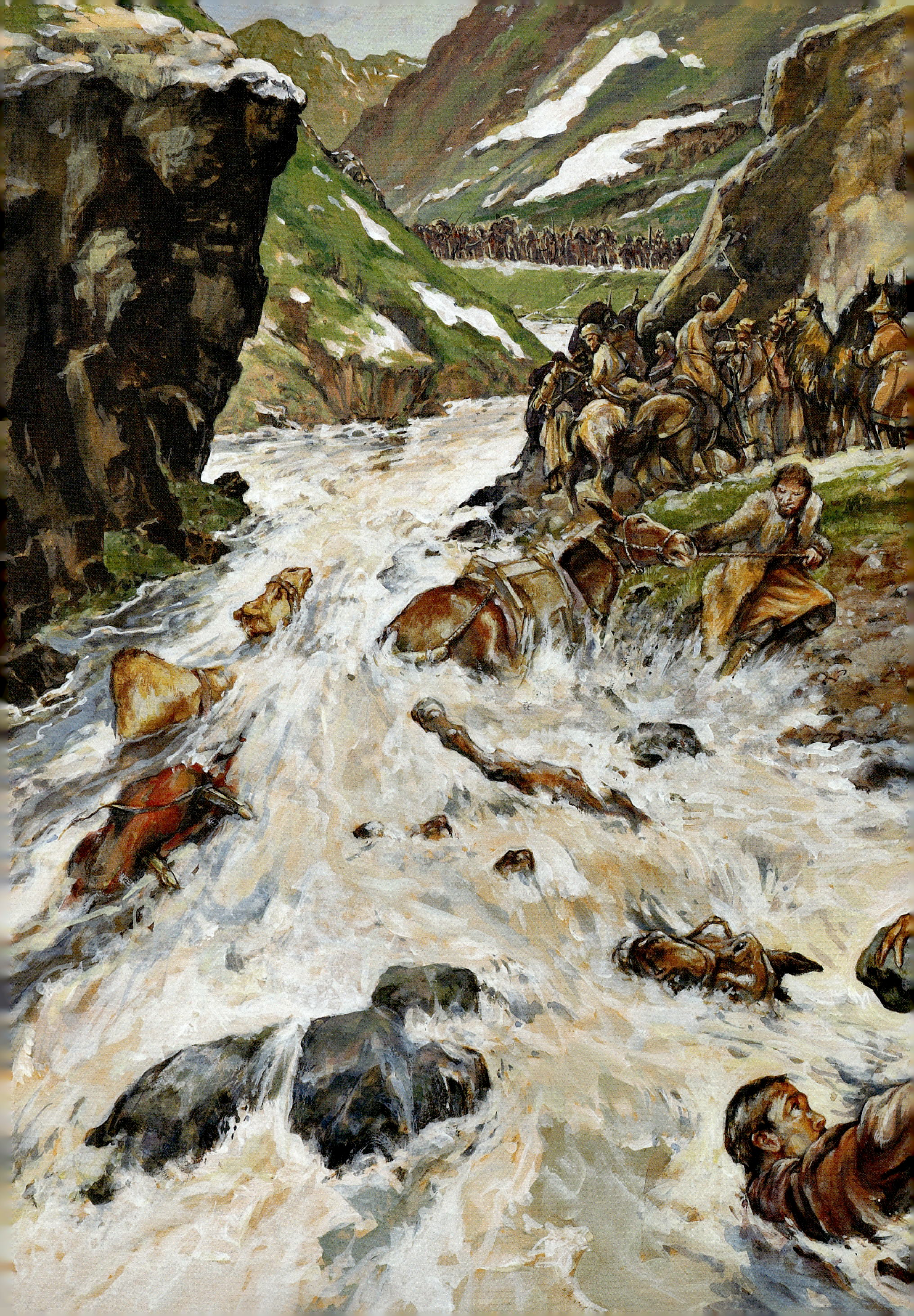

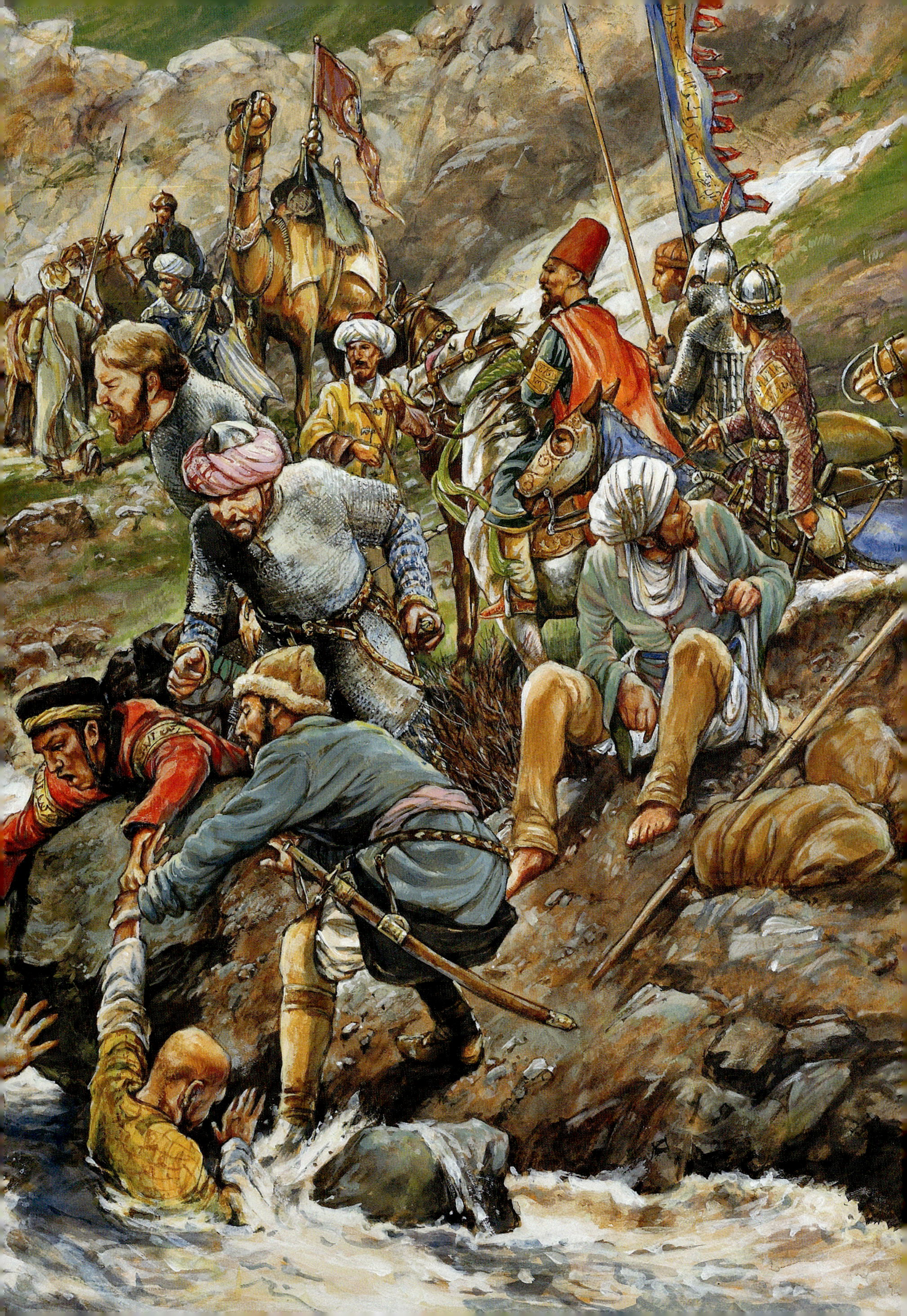

ALP ARSLAN'S ASKAR CROSSING A FLOODED RIVER IN SOUTH-EASTERN TURKEY DURING THEIR RETREAT TO AZARBAYJAN, MID-MAY 1071 (PP. 44–45)

After lifting his siege of Aleppo, the Saljuq Sultan Alp Arslan **(1)**, led his army east, across the mighty river Euphrates and north-western Mesopotamia, into the uplands of the upper reaches of the river Tigris. Here the bulk of the army was dismissed. Sultan Alp Arslan then pressed on with his 4,000-strong *askar* 'household troops' of *ghulams* (elite *mamluk* troops of supposed slave-recruited origin) **(2)**, plus their servants **(3)** and a baggage train **(4)**. With these elite units, Alp Arslan was able to push through the mountains of what is now south-eastern Turkey. They were heading for Khoy in what was the traditional military mustering area of Azarbayjan (the province in north-western Iran rather than the modern independent state of the same name) where they would be pasture for the cavalry's horses. However, the late spring which promised ideal mustering conditions in Azarbayjan also meant that the mountain snows of eastern Anatolia were melting. So the little army had to cross several rivers that were already in flood. Many of the baggage animals and even some cavalry mounts had already been swept away in the hurried crossing of the river Euphrates east of Aleppo. It now seems that others were lost in the rush to reach Khoy. On the other hand, Alp Arslan was able to recruit substantial numbers of warlike local Kurdish tribes during this difficult and dangerous journey.

An 11th-century stucco wall decoration from Rayy, northern Iran, probably portraying an early Saljuq ruler. (Archaeological Museum, Tehran. Author's photograph)

ALP ARSLAN'S SUPPOSED 'FLIGHT' FROM ALEPPO

Matthew of Edessa maintained that Saljuq siege engineers had breached Aleppo's fortifications but that Alp Arslan still could not take the city. To add to the Sultan's concerns the Emperor Romanos sent a second embassy, which supposedly arrived on the day that Alp Arslan learned of the start of the Byzantine campaign. It could not, therefore, have arrived in May as by then the Sultan had already abandoned his siege of Aleppo. This time Leo Diabatenos, the Emperor's ambassador, demanded the exchange of towns mentioned by the first embassy and insisted that the Sultan stop all further Türkmen raids, which Alp Arslan was in no position to do. Furthermore the Sultan's correct assumption that the Byzantine army was already heading towards Armenia meant that the Emperor's ultimatum should be interpreted as a declaration of war.

If Alp Arslan believed that a truce had been agreed as a result of the first Byzantine embassy back in March, he must have seen the Byzantine campaign as a betrayal. Whether he saw it as offering him a face-saving excuse to abandon his siege of Aleppo is doubtful. Mahmud, the *amir* of Aleppo, is more likely to have been offered a face-saving formula. According to some sources he offered to recognize Saljuq overlordship while leaving Aleppo with his mother. According to others, Alp Arslan left one of his sons to supervise things around Aleppo.

A lost work by the Baghdad chronicler Ghars al-Ni'ma Ibn Hilal al-Sabi', written shortly after the event, probably provided the chronicler Ibn al-Qalanisi with the information that Alp Arslan left Aleppo on 23 Rajah 463 AH (26 April 1071). The following day he and his army crossed the Euphrates 'on horseback without boats', according to al-Husayni. At that time of year the river would be in flood as snows melted in the Taurus Mountains, so it is not surprising that large numbers of animals and baggage were lost. Perhaps the Emperor Romanos had believed such a crossing was impossible.

Alp Arslan now had from 15,000 to 20,000 horsemen, including his *askar* numbering 4,000 *ghulams*. This force was strong enough to discourage the Byzantine garrison in Edessa from attacking and indeed Matthew of Edessa claimed that: 'The *dux*... provided him with horses, mules, and victuals. Taking these, the sultan passed through the confines of Edessa, unharmed, and went in an easterly direction towards the mountain called Lesun [probably the Karacadağ].' Perhaps this helpful Byzantine governor was the supposedly 'perfidious Roman' who, according to Matthew of Edessa, sent Alp Arslan a letter urging him not to flee 'for the greater part of our forces is with you'. Perhaps that was why, when he reached the security of Marwanid territory, Alp Arslan sent the bulk of his exhausted troops home while he led his tough and loyal *askar* of 4,000 across the mountains of Kurdistan to Khoy in north-western Iran.

An ivory chess knight from Iran, dating from the 11th or 12th century. (Metropolitan Museum, Rogers and Straka Gift 1974.207, New York. Author's photograph)

The routes taken by both parts of the Saljuq army are unknown, though those heading homeward are thought to have travelled via Mosul before scattering across Iran, Iraq and beyond. Alp Arslan probably travelled via Diyarbakr, through the mountains south-east of Lake Van, gathering Kurdish volunteers along the way. The fact that it took him two months highlights the immense difficulty of even a small force traversing these mountains and crossing streams swollen by melting snow.

Whether his *wazir* Nizam al-Mulk, his wife the Khatun al-Safariyya and infant son Tutuş remained with Alp Arslan or took the easier road is unknown. The Sultan's family and the army's remaining baggage then headed for Tabriz or Hamadan while Nizam al-Mulk set about raising a fresh army. Emperor Romanos, however, received the dangerously inaccurate information that Alp Arslan had fled to Iraq.

Azarbayjan's abundant spring pasture made it a traditional mustering place for armies and Khoy could serve as a forward base, close to the mountains of Armenia. The Saljuq Sultan therefore established himself and his growing army between Khoy and Dilmagan (Salmas) where further troops gradually joined him. Nizam al-Mulk was busy in Tabriz and other major cities including Hamadan, Isfahan and perhaps Baghdad, summoning troops from across the Saljuq sultanate and its vassals.

In Tabriz or Baghdad (there are two versions of the story) the *ghulam* who would later capture the Byzantine Emperor was amongst those mustered for inspection. Being described as 'puny', this man failed the tests and would have been dismissed until a senior man, sometimes identified as Nizam al-Mulk, joked: 'What can be expected of him? Will he then bring captive to us the Roman Emperor?' For whatever reason, the anonymous *ghulam* was then accepted and would later win himself a small niche in the hall of fame.

For his part, Alp Arslan declared himself a *ghazi* – a Fighter for the Faith – and in so doing proclaimed that the forthcoming struggle would be fought in the name of God, not in that of the Saljuq Sultan. He also stated that, should he be killed, his son Malik Shah was to succeed him. Ibn al-Jawzi

Manzikert (now Malazgirt) citadel seen from the location of the Byzantine siege camp in 1071. In the distance is the Upper or Eastern Euphrates River. (Author's photograph)

Byzantine lead seal, c.1070, found during archaeological digs in Winchester, southern England. (Winchester Excavations 1962, no. 1141A. Winchester Excavations Committee photograph)

wrote that this was well received by his commanders: 'They responded to him with prayers and hearing and obeying. That was by the doing, organizing and judgement of Nizam al-Mulk… Each *ghulam* had a horse to ride and a horse to go by his side.' By the time that Alp Arslan led his army against Emperor Romanos, it may have numbered up to 30,000 men, including up to 15,000 elite cavalry upon whom the outcome would ultimately depend.

Mahmud, the Mirdasid *amir* of Aleppo, did not accompany the Saljuq Sultan on this campaign. Instead, in May 1071, he took a Turkish mercenary named Aytakin al-Sulaymani and an army of Banu Kilab Arab tribesmen to seize Ba'albak in Lebanon. From there Mahmud planned to take Damascus which was currently under the control of Mu'alla Ibn Manzu, the Fatimid governor of Syria, Badr al-Jamali, having been confined to a few coastal ports. Mahmud's ambitions were nevertheless thwarted when his uncle 'Atiyya, having found refuge in Byzantine Antioch, pillaged the central Syrian city of Ma'arrat al-Nu'man. Mahmud hurriedly returned to secure his powerbase in Aleppo while Aytakin al-Sulaymani took his men to join Alp Arslan in Azarbayjan. In Syria the stage was set for the Saljuq conquest, but first Alp Arslan had to face Emperor Romanos IV.

Al-Turtushi recorded that the Byzantine advance caused concern across the Islamic countries and although that was probably an exaggeration, it was clearly a serious threat. Amongst several events which boosted Alp Arslan's confidence was the 'Abbasid Caliph's order that a specially written prayer should be read in all mosques. It was the work of a respected Islamic scholar named Abu Sa'id Ibn Mawsilaya and it asked God to: 'Grant the sultan Alp Arslan, the Proof of the Commander of the Faithful, the help by which his banners are illuminated… Cause his troops to be helped by Your angels and his decisions to be crowned with good fortune and a happy outcome.'[7]

---

7   Hillenbrand, op. cit., 53.

Looking towards Manzikert from a rocky outcrop on the plateau south of the town, perhaps where Alp Arslan studied the Byzantine fortified siege camp. (Author's photograph)

THE ARMIES APPROACH

It would seem inconceivable that Emperor Romanos did not learn that Alp Arslan was assembling an army north of Lake Urmia. However, it is generally accepted that, in June or July, the Byzantine leader was very badly informed. Convinced that Alp Arslan had 'fled' from Aleppo in apparent rout, he probably assumed that Saljuq military preparations were defensive. The chronicler Nikephoros Bryennios specifically blamed the Emperor's disastrous decision to divide his army on a letter sent by the *vestarchos* Leo Diabatenos, the man who had led the Byzantine embassy outside Aleppo. Its contents show that it was written some time later when Leo Diabatenos may have been responsible for Byzantine intelligence reports and it maintained that the sultan, being aware of Romanos' expedition and fearing its strength, had left Persia (western Iran) and fled to Babylon (Baghdad).

Other sources of information proved equally misleading, as when the Armenian officer Basilakes arrived at the head of substantial reinforcements from Syria and Armenia. Final Byzantine preparations were now being made at Theodosiopolis, where, however, the huge Byzantine army seemed to be in danger of running short of food in an area ravaged by Türkmen raids. Romanos was nevertheless confident his numerically superior troops could defeat a Turkish army in open battle and may also have been confident that he could achieve his objectives before Alp Arslan appeared – if he ever did.

So the order to advance was given. Romanos ordered his men to assemble provisions for a two-month campaign in an area where food and fodder would be scarce. Such a volume of supplies would require so many pack animals and perhaps carts that Byzantine movements would inevitably be slow. It was probable that, as the main army set off, a detachment of Pecheneg auxiliaries was sent south to the area around Ahlat. It was closely followed by a detachment of Frankish cavalry under Roussel de Bailleul. Their role, it is said, was to secure the harvest for the Imperial army and prevent it from being gathered by Saljuq garrisons.

An 11th- or 12th-century Byzantine carved ivory panel showing a man armed with spear, sword and bow. (Hermitage Museum, St Petersburg. Author's photograph)

The Emperor and his main army then moved slowly eastwards along a major route and over relatively easy ground, reportedly defeating a Türkmen force and retaking the unidentified fortress of Mempet on the way. Having reached a point (probably Kapetron) where his heavily burdened army could cross the hills, Romanos turned southwards towards Xinus (Hinis) and then towards the Murat River. Quite where the Byzantine army divided is unrecorded though the Murat would seem likely. Somewhere, however, Romanos ordered almost half of his troops, including many of the most effective cavalry, to support those already operating under Roussel around Ahlat.

Under the command of the *magistros* Joseph Tarchaniotes they were to blockade Saljuq-held Ahlat, perhaps even seizing it by a *coup de main*, though there was no mention of siege equipment with this force. It nevertheless included Varangians and Armenians from the *ducate* of Theodosiopolis. Whether they really totalled almost half the army seems doubtful. Byzantine sources are silent but some Muslim chroniclers maintained that they were commanded by the enemy's 'hardest commander' and had with them their 'greatest cross'.

The fact that Tarchaniotes had disagreed with the Emperor's offensive strategy was taken by both chroniclers and modern historians as a reason for the seemingly feeble actions of a highly rated commander. In fact the approaching defeat is not inexplicable, especially when one looks more closely at the written evidence and the terrain. Emperor Romanos was presumably confident that having much of his army almost 50 kilometres away from the main force was not a problem. He could recall it if serious danger threatened or he could hurry to its support if necessary. It would be a matter of timing and terrain, both of which the Byzantine commanders got wrong. Meanwhile Romanos headed for the fortified city of Manzikert with his massive siege train. Perhaps he then planned to march east to retake the strategic northern shore of Lake Van and perhaps even Vaspourakan, leaving the strong fortress of Ahlat to be dealt with later.

The northern fortifications of Manzikert (Malazgirt) town. (Author's photograph)

The details of Alp Arslan's movements at this point are less well known than those of the Emperor Romanos. According to Ibn al-Azraq al-Fariqi, 'A large group of the people of Ahlat and Manzikert went down after him [Alp Arslan], informing him that the king of Byzantium had come back to the country… With them was the *qadi* [senior judge] of Manzikert.' These may have been from the Saljuq garrisons or from their local militias, and it must have occurred after the Byzantine army moved out of Theodosiopolis. All the evidence points to Alp Arslan being regularly and accurately informed of Byzantine movements – perhaps even of Byzantine intentions – a stark contrast to the situation in the Byzantine camp.

The Sultan had meanwhile arranged the command structure of his army near Khoy. Rashid al-Din claimed that it numbered 15,000 cavalry (perhaps referring only to the Turks) and 5,000 'veteran' infantry, naming the tribal leaders as Artuq, Saltuq, Mengücük, Danişmand, Çavlı and Çavuldur. Several would go on to found ruling dynasties of their own, so Rashid al-Din may have drawn upon heroic tradition rather than reliable reports. The Sultan

1 Basilakes with substantial forces from Syria and southern Armenia, joins Emperor, bringing incorrect information about Saljuqs.
2 Letter from Leo Diabatenos informs Romanos that Alp Arslan fled from Persia to Iraq; Emperor reorganizes army for two a months campaign.
3 Romanos sends Pechenegs, closely followed by Roussel de Bailleul and Normans, towards Ahlat to seize control of the harvest.
4 Romanos heads for Manzikert with main force, mid-August.
5 Joseph Tarchaniotes is sent with up to half the army to help Roussel, probably taking direct road west of Manzikert.
6 Warning is probably sent by Manzikert garrison to Ahlat and Alp Arslan.
7 Alp Arslan and his army arrive from Khoy.
8 Alp Arslan is joined by Türkmen *begs* who were raiding Anatolia.
9–10 Alp Arslan is joined by a large part of garrisons and militias of Manzikert and Ahlat.
11 Route taken by Alp Arslan is unclear, but a route north of Lake Van is more likely.
12 Small Saljuq force under Sundak al-Turki hurries to strengthen Ahlat garrison.
13 Alp Arslan probably intends to strengthen garrison in Manzikert.
14 Joseph Tarchaniotes and Roussel de Bailleul are defeated outside Ahlat, Tuesday 23 August.
15 Move by Alp Arslan may have cut Joseph and Roussel off from Romanos.
16 Joseph Tarchaniotes and Roussel de Bailleul retreat to Muş, perhaps intending to rejoin the Emperor via Eastern Euphrates valley.
17 Romanos arrives outside Manzikert, probably Monday 22 August.
18 Alp Arslan makes camp at the northern edge of the Süphan Dağ.
19 Saljuq garrison in Manzikert surrenders late on Tuesday 23 August.
20 Romanos IV is defeated and captured by Sultan Alp Arslan, Friday 26 August 1071.
21 Fleeing Byzantine court heads for Trebizond.
22 Large numbers of fleeing Byzantines find refuge in Dokeia.
23 Saljuqs pursue Byzantines, perhaps as far as Doghodaph.
24 Joseph Tarchaniotes and Roussel de Bailleul pull back to Harput and Melitene.
25 Alp Arslan releases Romanos after eight days.
26 Alp Arslan returns to Azarbayjan.

Lake Van, the crucible

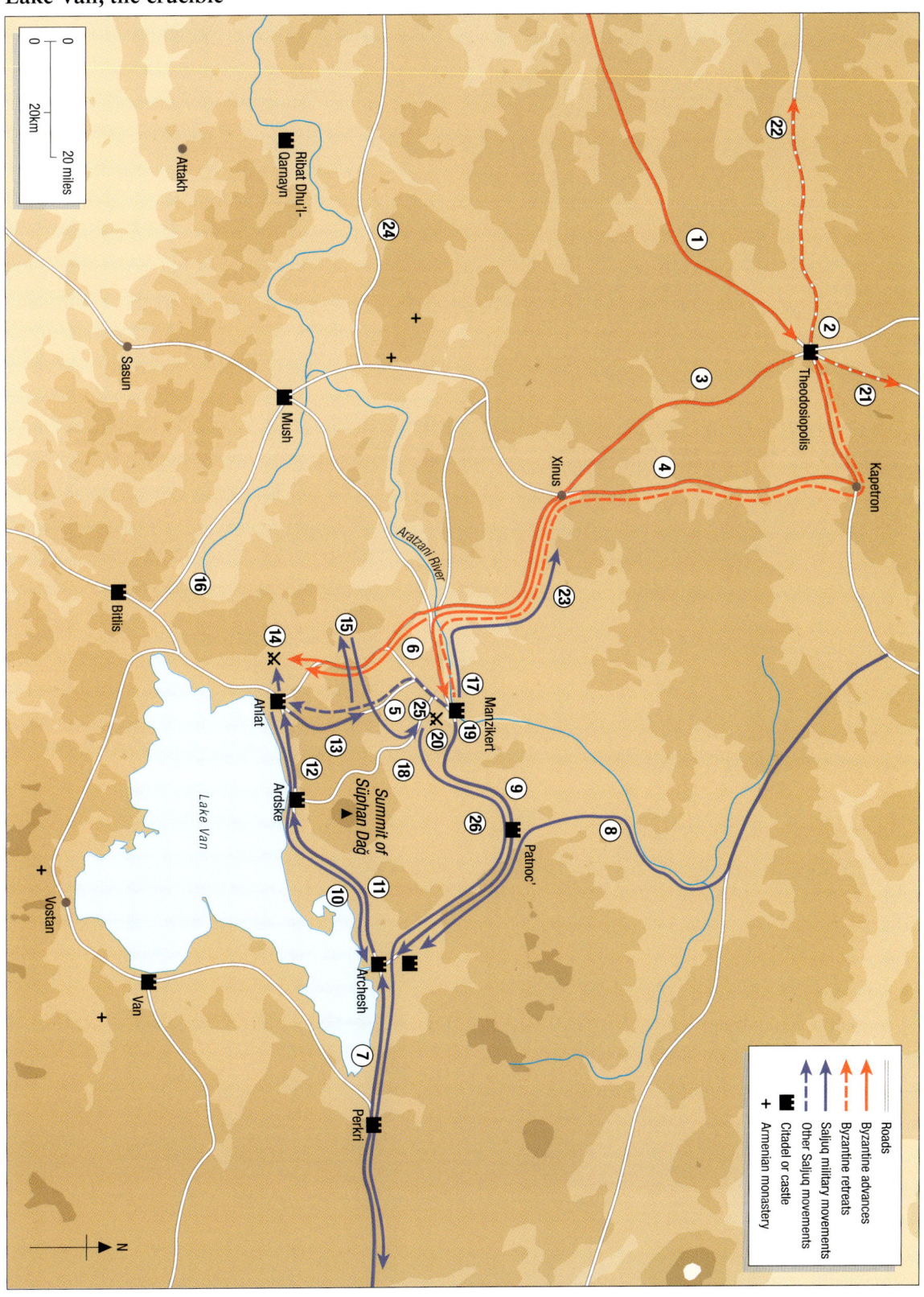

Unlike most Byzantine illustrations of the Crucifixion, the centurion shown in this Armenian Gospel of 1038 is unarmoured. (Matenadaran Library, Yerevan)

may also have been joined by Kutalmış' sons Sulayman and Mansur, along with other Türkmen *begs* who had been raiding Anatolia. The size of Alp Arslan's army before the battle of Manzikert is unknown, though it was probably half that of the Byzantine total but – more importantly – not much smaller than the force which remained with the Emperor outside Manzikert. Nishapuri naturally allows himself considerable poetic licence in his epic *Saljuqnama* but was probably not far off the mark when he wrote: 'They [the victorious Saljuq army] recited the verse: "How often a little company has overcome a numerous company by God's name."'

Alp Arslan's route from Khoy to Ahlat is unknown, and he could have gone along the southern shore of Lake Van, thus threatening Roussel and Tarchaniotes from the rear. But such a route would be longer, more difficult, slower and would have pushed the defeated Byzantine commanders towards their Emperor, whereas in fact they fled in the opposite direction. All that Sibt al-Jawzi writes in his chronicle is: 'He [Alp Arslan] set out making for the king of Byzantium. He sent one of the chamberlains who were with him with a group of *ghulams* as an advance party for him.' The latter rushed to support the exposed garrison of Ahlat so the Sultan could be expected to follow this vanguard.

The plateau seen from the Byzantine camp outside Manzikert, southward towards Süphan Dağ mountain. (Author's photograph)

BYZANTINE DEFEAT AND BYZANTINE SUCCESS

The two battlefields of the Manzikert campaign, near Ahlat and outside the town of Manzikert, were both dominated by the Süphan Dağ, which, at 4,434m, rose almost 2,800m above the level of Lake Van. Seemingly an isolated volcanic peak, the Süphan Dağ is in fact part of a range of hills lying between the lake and Manzikert. Today's roads and tracks presumably follow much the same lines, determined by the terrain, as they did in the 11th century. There were, therefore, two possible routes between the Murat River west of Manzikert and Ahlat on the north-western shore of Lake Van. It is likely that the troops Roussel led and those who followed under Tarchaniotes took the easier, westerly road passing the small Nuzik lake and reaching Lake Van just west of Ahlat. This passed close enough to Manzikert for its garrison to have sent a warning to Ahlat and, more importantly, to have informed Alp Arslan.

Perhaps this is why the Sultan sent a substantial force of some 10,000 horsemen under Sanduq al-Turki hurrying forward to strengthen Ahlat which, according to Nikephoros Bryennios, 'was defended by a fairly strong Turkish garrison'. The Taht-i Sulayman citadel of Ahlat, though ruined by earthquakes, remains impressive and, enclosing about 11 hectares, was a much stronger position than better-preserved Manzikert.

Sanduq al-Turki had already shown himself to be an effective commander in Syria and Anatolia. He was now credited with saving Ahlat, arriving at almost the same time as Roussel and Tarchaniotes, a few hours ahead of the main Saljuq army. All that is known for certain is that the two Byzantine commanders were defeated, though not necessarily as a result of a bloody clash, despite Muslim chroniclers proclaiming the capture of a senior enemy officer along with the aforementioned 'great cross'.

Byzantine and Armenian chronicles merely accuse Roussel and Tarchaniotes of fleeing down the Murat Valley without warning their Emperor of the danger he now faced. Given the reputation of the two leaders, cowardice seems impossible and outright treachery also seems unlikely. The most logical explanation lies in the location of the confrontation, the fact that the Saljuqs were also in two main formations, and the nature of the terrain. Roussel and Tarchaniotes had presumably passed the crest of the hills and their troops may have been scattered, securing the harvest as instructed, when they found themselves confronted by the

The 'Legend of Abgar' frontispiece of the *Alaverdi Gospel*, was made in Antioch in 1054 which was a significant Christian cultural centre as well as a strategic Byzantine outpost. (Georgian Institute of Manuscripts, A 484, f.316v, Tbilisi)

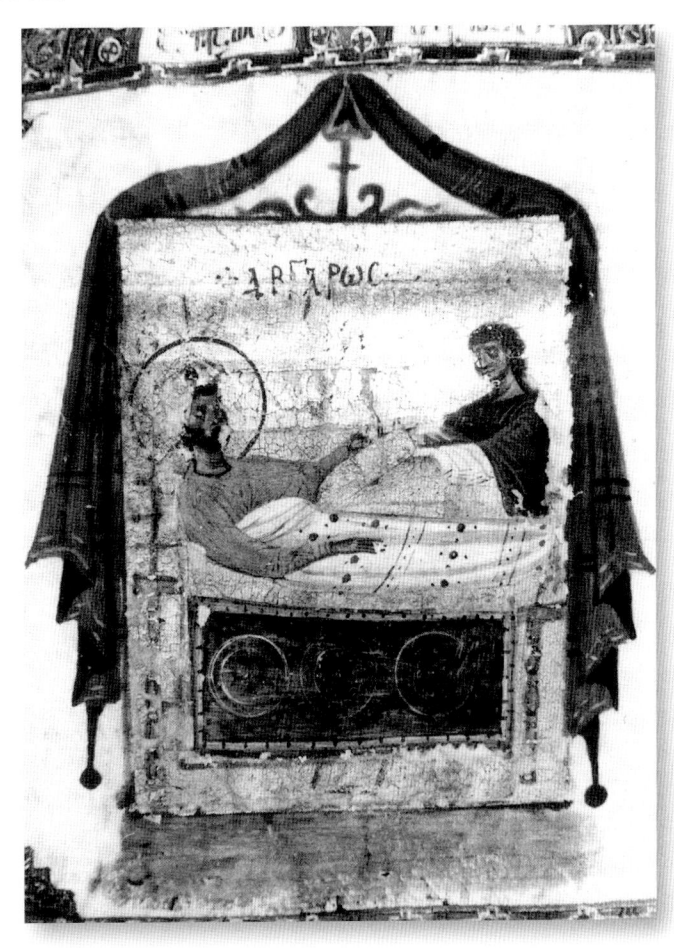

The seemingly open plain south of the fortified Byzantine camp is crossed by small but steep-sided stream beds. (Author's photograph)

A mail-clad cavalryman on a 10th- or 11th-century bowl from Nishapur. He wields a straight sword typical of the pre-Turkish Middle Eastern armies. (Museum für Islamische Kunst, inv. nr. I. 11/62, Berlin. Author's photograph)

suddenly reinforced garrison of Ahlat. Nor had they reason to know that this was part of a much larger enemy army. If Alp Arslan was not in Ahlat, perhaps he was heading into the hills to reinforce his second garrison in Manzikert, logically taking the direct road across the western flank of the Süphan Dağ. Learning of the looming confrontation outside Ahlat, it would have been within Turkish military traditions and within Saljuq cavalry capabilities to turn off the road, along the open hillsides, to isolate Roussel and Tarchaniotes from Romanos.

If this hypothetical interpretation is correct, then the Byzantine commanders' rapid retreat southward along the lake shore and then down the valley to the citadel of Muş, made military sense. It might also explain how no warning got through to Romanos, the hills between Muş, Ahlat and Manzikert probably being dominated by Turkish horsemen and unhelpful local inhabitants. From Muş, Roussel and Tarchaniotes could rejoin their Emperor, north-eastwards along the main Murat Valley. But they did not and herein lies the only convincing evidence of betrayal. A few days later, after learning of the Emperor's defeat outside Manzikert, Roussel, Tarchaniotes and their men withdrew farther west, to Melitene.

The senior Rus commander, who was reportedly captured during this ignominious affair and who is then said to have had his nose cut off, may have been commanding the Varangian unit. The captured Byzantine cross was described as being of 'wood and on it were silver and pieces of turquoise, and a gospel in a silver casket'. Alp Arslan ordered that Sanduq send it to Hamadan with instructions that Nizam al-Mulk give it to the 'Abbasid Caliph in Baghdad.

The defeat of Roussel and Tarchaniotes took place on the same day – Tuesday 4 Dhu'l-Qa'da in the year 463 AH or 23 August 1071 – that Manzikert surrendered to the Byzantine Emperor. This makes Ibn al-Azraq's assertion that Alp Arslan stayed in Ahlat 'some days' unlikely as the Sultan is known to have been close to Manzikert two days

One of the streams that cut the apparently open ground between Manzikert and the Süphan Dağ. (Author's photograph)

later. Romanos probably appeared outside Manzikert late on 22 August. The Saljuq garrison was probably smaller, and the defences undoubtedly more accessible for an attacker, than those at Ahlat. As such, Manzikert served the same purpose as it had under the Marwanids, as an outpost of the main defensive position in Ahlat. It overlooked the valley of the river Murat (Upper Euphrates) but was a few kilometres from it, lying at the northern edge of an extensive, seemingly level plateau. To the south rose the foothills and massif of Süphan Dağ.

The Byzantine chronicler Michael Attaleiates was with the Byzantine army and so the details of his account are accurate, even if his interpretation of events is less so. 'When the emperor came to Manzikert he ordered that the encampment with all its equipment be set up nearby and an entrenchment be made in the accustomed manner, while he, taking with him the elite of the army, went around the town, spying out where it was suitable to make attacks on the walls and to bring up the siege engines.'[8]

These Byzantine field fortifications were almost certainly on a hill, now partially occupied by a cemetery, facing the southern walls of the city and citadel. They gave the attackers a height advantage, security from sorties behind a steep gulley, and commanded the only piece of level ground leading to the fortifications. Furthermore, this location blocked the approach of any relief force from the south or east. To some extent the Byzantine position was also partially protected on that side by the bed of a small stream, which flowed across the plateau. Sadr al-Din al-Husayni added some colourful details: 'The Byzantine emperor set up a stately marquee (*fustat*) of red satin, a tent (*khayma*) like it and tents (*akhbiya'*) of silk brocade. He sat down on a throne of gold, above which was a golden cross set with priceless jewels, and before him was a host of monks and priests reciting the Gospel.'[9]

---

8 Hillenbrand, op. cit., 229.
9 Sadr al-Din al-Husayni (tr. Bosworth, C. E.), *The History of the Seljuq State: A translation with commentary of the Akhbar al-dawla al-saljuqiyya* (London, 2011) 38.

The subjects of medieval Islamic art tended to be less warlike than those in medieval European art, one of the most popular 'courtly' subjects being a musician as shown in this 11th-century silver plate from Iran. (Museum für Islamische Kunst, inv. Nr. I. 582, Berlin. Author's photograph)

Some sources suggest that, when faced by the Emperor's massive stone-throwing mangonels, the garrison surrendered without a fight. Others make it clear they at least made a show of resistance, 'shouting the war cry and baring their swords and using far-shooting weapons' as Romanos made his reconnaissance around their defences. Having returned to the Byzantine encampment, the Emperor ordered his Armenian foot soldiers to attack. They 'made many assaults' but nevertheless 'took it without a blow' in the late afternoon, suggesting that the confrontation was more symbolic than bloodthirsty. In all probability the town fell with ease, whereupon the garrison in the citadel sent representatives to the Emperor, asking for and receiving clemency.

Having 'honoured the ambassadors with gifts', Romanos sent an officer to take control of the citadel but this seems to have disturbed the garrison who refused to hand over so quickly 'for fear that some evil might be wrought… by night'. This in turn made Romanos think the Saljuq defenders were reneging upon their agreement. The battle trumpet was sounded and 'the entire army issued forth from the encampment, making for the walls', whereupon the terrified inhabitants promptly came out of Manzikert 'with their household effects and knelt before the emperor'. Unfortunately they still had their weapons, and Michael Attaleiates was appalled to see the unarmed Emperor Romanos 'who mingled without body armour among murderous men who pass their lives in recklessness and madness'.[10] No one ever accused Romanos Diogenes of cowardice!

The Muslim chroniclers were probably correct in maintaining that the garrison of Manzikert formally surrendered on the promise of safe conduct on Tuesday 23 August. Most of the population were Christian Armenians, plus a smaller number of Muslims, and al-Bundari stated that they spent the night of Tuesday–Wednesday on the town's 'pavement' under the Emperor's protection. Other sources indicate that they evacuated Manzikert on Wednesday. Having placed a Byzantine garrison in the citadel, Romanos returned to camp where there were big celebrations, held, of course, in ignorance of the Byzantine defeat outside Ahlat and of the nearness of Alp Arslan's army.

10 Hillenbrand, op. cit., 230.

CONFRONTATION, NEGOTIATION AND BATTLE

The sequence of events that immediately preceded the battle of Manzikert are straightforward. On Wednesday 24 August Alp Arslan heard of the fall of Manzikert and either now headed north or, if he was already marching northwards, did so with greater urgency. The distance was 46km as the crow flies, around 52km taking the most direct route, but of course Alp Arslan did not go all the way to Manzikert. Instead he established his camp somewhere in the northern foothills of the Süphan Dağ.

Michael Attaleiates reports that Emperor Romanos spent Wednesday having the defences of Manzikert repaired at the expense of its remaining inhabitants while also readying his army for the march to his next objective, Ahlat. Those of the people of Manzikert who either wanted or were obliged to leave were placed under escort, ready to march with the army. This, according to Islamic sources, coincided with the arrival of the Sultan's army, presumably at its camping place in the foothills. Byzantine sources initially focus upon affairs within the Imperial camp where Romanos imposed a degree of discipline that surprised even a supporter like Michael Attaleiates and reportedly undermined morale. One soldier had his nose cut off for stealing a donkey from a Turk but more shocking for the chronicler was that his call for mercy in the name of the Sovereign Mother of Blachernae, 'holiest of the icons carried by the Emperor', was ignored.

While this was going on, news came in that some Byzantine foragers were being attacked by Turks, but no one knew where these attackers had come from. As further reports came in, Romanos summoned Basilakes to ask his opinion. The Armenian officer was convinced the attackers came from the Saljuq garrison in Ahlat. The chronicler Nikephoros Bryennios (the Younger) somewhat unfairly blamed Basilakes for being overconfident in his assessment, which was, nevertheless, a natural one since there were, as yet, no reports of the Sultan's army being in the area.

The Byzantine Emperor's error was his failure to send reconnaissance troops to get more accurate information. Instead, as harassment of the foragers grew worse, Romanos sent the commander of the army's left wing, the *magistros* Nikephoros Bryennios (the Elder) with a relatively small force to support these foragers. He in turn found himself facing more enemies than expected. His units were lured into ambushes and were in danger of being surrounded, so General Nikephoros Bryennios withdrew while requesting reinforcements. As Michael Attaleiates made clear, the enemy fought in their traditional and very effective manner:

A soldier wearing a short-sleeved, full-length mail hauberk in a Byzantine wall painting of the Crucifixion made within a year or so of the battle of Manzikert. (*in situ* Sakli Kilise, Göreme, Cappadocia. Ahmet Soğut photograph)

THE FALL OF MANZIKERT AND THE ARRIVAL OF ALP ARSLAN, WEDNESDAY 24 TO MIDDAY THURSDAY 25 AUGUST

Following the rapid capitulation of the Turkish garrison in Manzikert, Alp Arslan acts cautiously, refusing the Byzantine Emperor's attempts to bring him to battle.

MANZIKERT

YARAM

ROMANOS

Note: Gridlines are shown at intervals of 2km (1.24 miles)

DOĞANSU

ALP ARSLAN

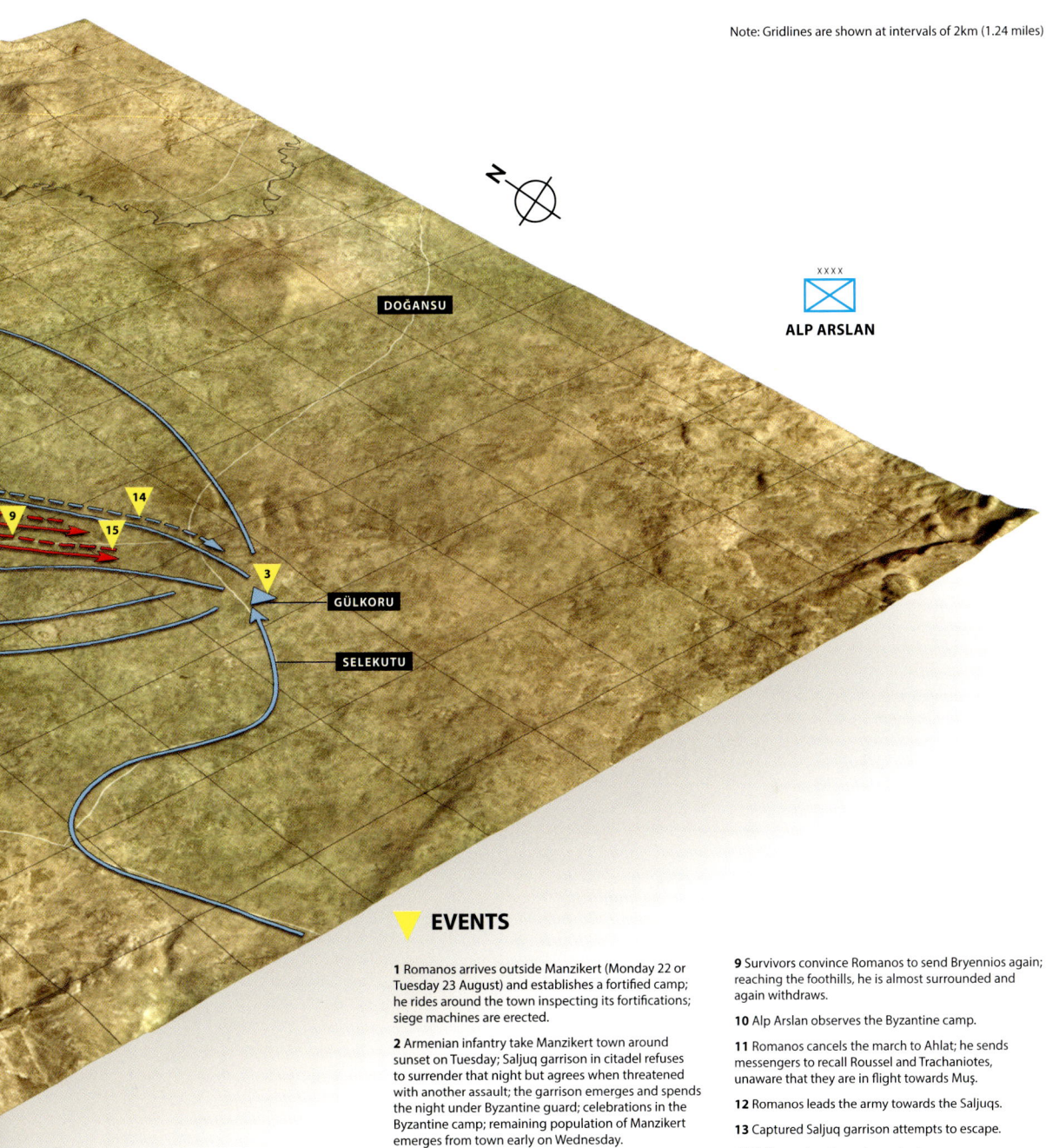

GÜLKORU

SELEKUTU

EVENTS

1 Romanos arrives outside Manzikert (Monday 22 or Tuesday 23 August) and establishes a fortified camp; he rides around the town inspecting its fortifications; siege machines are erected.

2 Armenian infantry take Manzikert town around sunset on Tuesday; Saljuq garrison in citadel refuses to surrender that night but agrees when threatened with another assault; the garrison emerges and spends the night under Byzantine guard; celebrations in the Byzantine camp; remaining population of Manzikert emerges from town early on Wednesday.

3 Hearing of attack on Manzikert, Alp Arslan moves north and makes camp north-west of Süphan Dağ, probably near Selekutu or Gülkoru.

4 Romanos prepares army for advance towards Ahlat, taking captured Saljuq garrison with them.

5 Byzantine foragers are attacked; Nikephoros Basilakes advises Romanos that the enemy are a small Turkish detachment from Ahlat.

6 Nikephoros Bryennios supports the foragers but is ambushed and retreats towards the Byzantine camp.

7 Romanos refuses to send support; meanwhile the army assembles for a religious service.

8 Romanos finally agrees to support Bryennios; he sends Nikephoros Basilakes who is captured and taken to Alp Arslan.

9 Survivors convince Romanos to send Bryennios again; reaching the foothills, he is almost surrounded and again withdraws.

10 Alp Arslan observes the Byzantine camp.

11 Romanos cancels the march to Ahlat; he sends messengers to recall Roussel and Trachaniotes, unaware that they are in flight towards Muş.

12 Romanos leads the army towards the Saljuqs.

13 Captured Saljuq garrison attempts to escape.

14 Saljuqs refuse to make contact.

15 As dusk approaches, Romanos orders the Byzantine army to withdraw.

16 Late Wednesday evening, a Saljuq detachment attacks Oghuz Turks in Byzantine service outside the camp; other attacks on the camp during the night.

17 Emperor Romanos decides to take the offensive on Friday.

18 Some Oghuz desert to the Saljuqs; Michael Attaleiates gets the remaining Oghuz to pledge loyalty.

19 Seljuk detachment unsuccessfully attempts to seize a riverbank 'opposite the Roman camp', Thursday morning.

20 Alp Arslan establishes a forward camp by a stream about a *farsakh* (5km) from the Byzantine camp.

'Standing at the front line, he [Bryennios] fought with discharges of missiles and cavalry actions which were not effective, for they fought one another a few at a time ... many of the Romans were injured, and others also fell, for they [the enemy] are braver than the other Turks of whom we have had experience, dashing more boldly and opposing their assailants in hand to hand combat.'[11] It would take the Byzantines some time to realize they were not facing Türkmen but part of a more disciplined, committed and well trained Saljuq force. According to the Andalusian chronicler al-Turtushi's *Siraj al-Muluk*, the latter were part of Alp Arslan's vanguard.

Tensions between Romanos and Bryennios may have contributed to the Emperor's initial refusal to send reinforcements, even reportedly accusing the *magistros* of cowardice. On the other hand, Romanos was busy getting the rest of the army ready for its intended march to Ahlat. After being harangued by their Emperor 'in an unaccustomed way' and with 'words of extraordinary violence', according to Attaleiates, the men attended a religious service, during which the chosen Bible reading for the day from the Gospel of John proved somewhat unfortunate. It included the lines: 'If they have persecuted me, they will also persecute you' and 'yea, the time cometh, that whosoever killeth you will think that he doeth God service'.[12] This again did nothing to improve morale.

Perhaps beginning to realize that a sizeable enemy force was nearby, Emperor Romanos sent messengers to recall his troops from around Ahlat, not knowing that they were already defeated and had fled. Romanos also decided that decisive action was needed to protect his foragers. So he sent the Armenian *dux* of Theodosiopolis, Nikephoros Basilakes, with a larger detachment of 'local soldiers' – probably Armenians – to do what the *magistros* Bryennios had failed to do. Unfortunately Basilakes then acted with what chroniclers on both sides and, in the event, Alp Arslan himself regarded as impetuous foolishness. Followed more cautiously by Bryennios, Basilakes charged in pursuit of the now retreating Turks, went too far ahead, fell into the almost inevitable ambush and was captured. His surviving troops fled pell-mell back to the Byzantine camp. Medics and the litters for injured men, which had long been a feature of Byzantine armies, were sent to collect the wounded, all bringing back news of a rout.

Sanduq al-Turki is said to have been responsible for this new Saljuq success, and Basilakes was brought before the Sultan who berated him for making such a basic tactical error. By this time the Saljuq army had properly established camp in the foothills, dominating but unseen from the plateau, which stretched south and south-east of Manzikert. This plateau was clearly the area variously known as the Zaho, Zehve, Zahva, Rahve, Rahva or Rahwa. (In Persian *Rahwah* actually means 'high ground').

On the Emperor's orders, the *magistros* Nikephoros Bryennios now hurried forward with the entire left wing but was too late to save the situation, learning the shocking truth from a dying man. After fighting off several attacks by a now formidable Saljuq force, making a number of counter-charges to avoid being surrounded, and himself having two arrows stuck in the armour on his back plus a spear thrust in his chest, Bryennios brought his troops back to the Byzantine camp. This time he found Romanos more sympathetic, being sent to the Imperial tent to have his wounds dressed.

11 Hillenbrand, op. cit., 231–232.
12 From the Gospel of John, chapter 15, verse 20 and chapter 16, verse 2; King James translation.

Within a few kilometres of Manzikert, the plateau is broken up by numerous rocky outcrops, as here alongside the road to Ahlat from Manzikert. (Author's photograph)

The Muslim chronicler al-Bundari merely wrote that, 'the gerfalcons of both armies met in the contest. The cavalry rushed, the torrent flowed, the rearguard swept along from earth to sky… They [the Byzantines] were thrown back to their perch in their camp and, by what had been achieved in the wedding feast of Islam, they were removed to their [own] funeral ceremony.' The Byzantine chronicler Nikephoros Bryennios the Younger admitted that it had been a hard fight: 'a mass of Turks perished, but the Romans also suffered huge losses'. It was probably around this time that Muslim captives from the Manzikert garrison tried to escape while the Byzantine army's attention was focused elsewhere. Some succeeded but others were killed.

Finally the Emperor Romanos accepted the seriousness of the situation and that Alp Arslan's army had arrived. Apparently abandoning his march upon Ahlat, he reorganized the army for an advance against the enemy close at hand. The Byzantine army then moved in battle array across the plateau, with the enemy equally steadily falling back before them. Frustrated by the Saljuqs' refusal to allow contact – in which the Byzantines were confident they would win – but still taking care not to lose cohesion, nor fall into significant ambushes, Romanos pressed ahead until late afternoon. By then his army had reached the first foothills and he was faced with a dilemma. Further advance would not only take the large Byzantine army into broken ground where it would be difficult to maintain a unified front, but would also mean that any withdrawal to the fortified Byzantine camp would be in the dark. Frustrated but accepting the inevitable, Romanos halted, waited a while in case the enemy accepted his challenge, then took the army back to their encampment.

According to Rashid al-Din, some time during Wednesday, Alp Arslan climbed a small hill to inspect the Byzantine camp – there being several such outcrops within a few kilometres of the Byzantine position. The Sultan was apparently worried by the size of the enemy, but one of the senior Türkmen commanders, Malik Muhammad Danişmand suggested that they should turn back and not fight until Friday, using Thursday to prepare for battle and for possible martyrdom. This would presumably have been early in the day and have resulted in the Saljuq army's cautious refusal to be drawn into a full-scale confrontation. A different impression is given by Sadr al-Din al-Husayni, who recorded that when Alp Arslan saw the enemy's strongly fortified camp, he exclaimed: 'By God, they're as good as defeated, for digging a trench round themselves, in spite of their great number, is a sign of their cowardice and weakness.'

Made in 1009, this copy of the *Book of Fixed Stars* by Umar al-Sufi shows Perseus in typical Islamic costume and wielding a characteristic straight sword. (Ms. Marsh 144, Bodleian Library, Oxford)

Another story in Rashid al-Din is unlikely to contain any truth. It maintained that Alp Arslan and a small group of companions had actually been captured while out hunting before the main battle, but, being unrecognized, were released by the Byzantines as a gesture of goodwill during negotiations. Perhaps this happened to another Saljuq commander. What is certain is that the following night was a hard one for the Byzantines, being spent 'in the greatest and most extreme agitation' according to Ibn al-'Adim. Byzantine sources agree, reporting that during the evening a number of Oghuz mercenaries were attacked by Alp Arslan's Turks while doing business with local traders and merchants outside the fortified camp. When they fled into the Byzantine camp, great confusion ensued because Oghuz and Türkmen looked so much alike to Greeks and Armenians.

As Attaleiates put it: 'All jammed together one after another, they were chased into the entrance way, which caused tremendous confusion among the troops within… For there was no moon that night, and you could not tell who was being chased and who was doing the chasing. They did not, however, retreat but the whole night they kept up a din, riding round and about the Romans' encampment, striking with arrows and vexations and buzzing around on every side and terrifying them, so that all passed the night with open and sleepless eyes.'

Next day, Thursday, the Saljuq army seems to have advanced closer to the Byzantine camp, reaching a river, according to Ibn al-'Adim. The theory that Alp Arslan took his men close to the Murat River simply does not fit other information about this battle, so perhaps the Arab chronicler's sources referred to a smaller stream, the steep-sided bed of which cuts across the plateau not far from the location of the fortified Byzantine encampment. Michael Attaleiates similarly mentioned this stream, claiming that the Turks tried to win control of both banks but were prevented from doing so by Byzantine infantry archers. There also seems to have been an attack upon the Byzantine camp, perhaps as part of a Saljuq attempt to take control of the entire plateau and deny the Byzantines access to sufficient drinking water.

Potentially just as dangerous was the desertion of some of the Byzantine army's Oghuz mercenaries to the Saljuqs. Their number is unknown and it is clear that most of their comrades remained loyal after Michael Attaleiates, the future chronicler, pursuaded them to swear oaths to that effect. Even so, doubts now hung over the reliability of these and other Turkish mercenaries. A small but interesting piece of additional information was provided by the southern Italian poet William of Apulia in his biography of the Norman ruler, Robert Guiscard. Perhaps having heard from Norman mercenaries who survived the battle of Manzikert, William reported that the Emperor Romanos distributed his wealth to the troops. But 'the silver was gathered in by the mercenaries, who fled [perhaps the Oghuz]. The Greeks were obliged to spend the night without sleep.'

Attaleiates maintained that, following these desertions and losses, the number of Byzantine troops remaining with Emperor Romanos were fewer than those who had been sent to Ahlat. If that is correct, they would probably have been around 20,000 men, perhaps excluding the Oghuz and other Turkish mercenaries, which was not many more than those who followed Alp Arslan. If the infantry and the siege train were included, the real number may have been up to 30,000, though this still excluded the substantial number of administrative staff and camp followers. Amongst these Byzantine non-combatants were senior men, such as the judge Basil Maleses who would be captured at the end of the battle but then released. Another was Eustratios Choirosphaktes who held the rank of a *protonotarios* or high-ranking imperial clerk.

The Saljuqs, of course, were convinced that they faced a far greater number. Some Muslim chroniclers gave the impossible figure of 600,000, and even Ibn al-Jawzi maintained that Romanos 'had with him 35,000 Franks and 35,000... [gap in text] with 200 generals and commanders; each of them having between 2,500 horsemen. He [also] had with him 15,000 Ghuzz [Oghuz] who were [living] beyond Constantinople; and 100,000 sappers and diggers and 100,000 siege engineers.' Ibn al-Jawzi's figures are nevertheless interesting in making clear that the proportion of second-line personnel far exceeded that of the fighting men.

The most likely number for Alp Arslan's army as it readied itself for battle outside Manzikert is 15,000 to 20,000 front-line cavalry. Yet Ibn al-Qalanisi maintains there were 40,000 'from amongst the Turks and other contingents' – this latter distinction perhaps being more significant than the figure itself. Sibt al-Jawzi was more specific, noting, 'He who mentioned that there were 4,000 *mamluks* with the sultan was more correct, because of what we have mentioned about the [other] troops having dispersed.'

During Thursday, Alp Arslan moved his army forward and, in the words of al-Bundari, 'camped by the river [probably the aforementioned stream], accompanied by 15,000 horsemen from amongst the Turkish fighters who knew nothing but killing and subjugation'. Meanwhile the Emperor Romanos found himself being given conflicting advice. Some officers urged an immediate attack while the wounded *magistros* Nikephoros Bryennios the Elder continued to urge caution, awaiting the arrival of those troops recalled from Ahlat who would, of course, never arrive.

On Thursday there was apparently an exchange of letters 'about making a peace treaty' according to al-Husayni. Ibn al-Azraq agrees, 'letters began to go back and forth between the two of them', while Bar Hebraeus stated: 'because the Turks were few in number the Sultan 'Alb 'Arslan was afraid, and he sent an envoy to [Romanos] Diogenes, a certain noble whose name was Sawtakin [the eunuch Sav-Tekin], that they might make peace and say to each other, "we will go back each to his own country"'.[13] The seriousness with which the Saljuq Sultan approached these negotiations is surely reflected in the fact that he sent an embassy to the Emperor, led by a senior judge from the 'Abbasid Caliphal court in Baghdad. His name was Ibn al-Muhallaban but it is not known how long this dignitary had been with Alp Arslan's army.

Ibn al-Muhallaban already had experience of direct negotiations with the Byzantine Emperor who, it was said, held him in high regard. Al-Muhallaban's team now arrived in the Byzantine camp late on Thursday, and were shocked

---

13 Bar Hebraeus (tr. Budge, E.A.W.), *The Chronology of Gregory Abu'l-Faraj... commonly known as Bar Hebraeus* (London, 1932) 220.

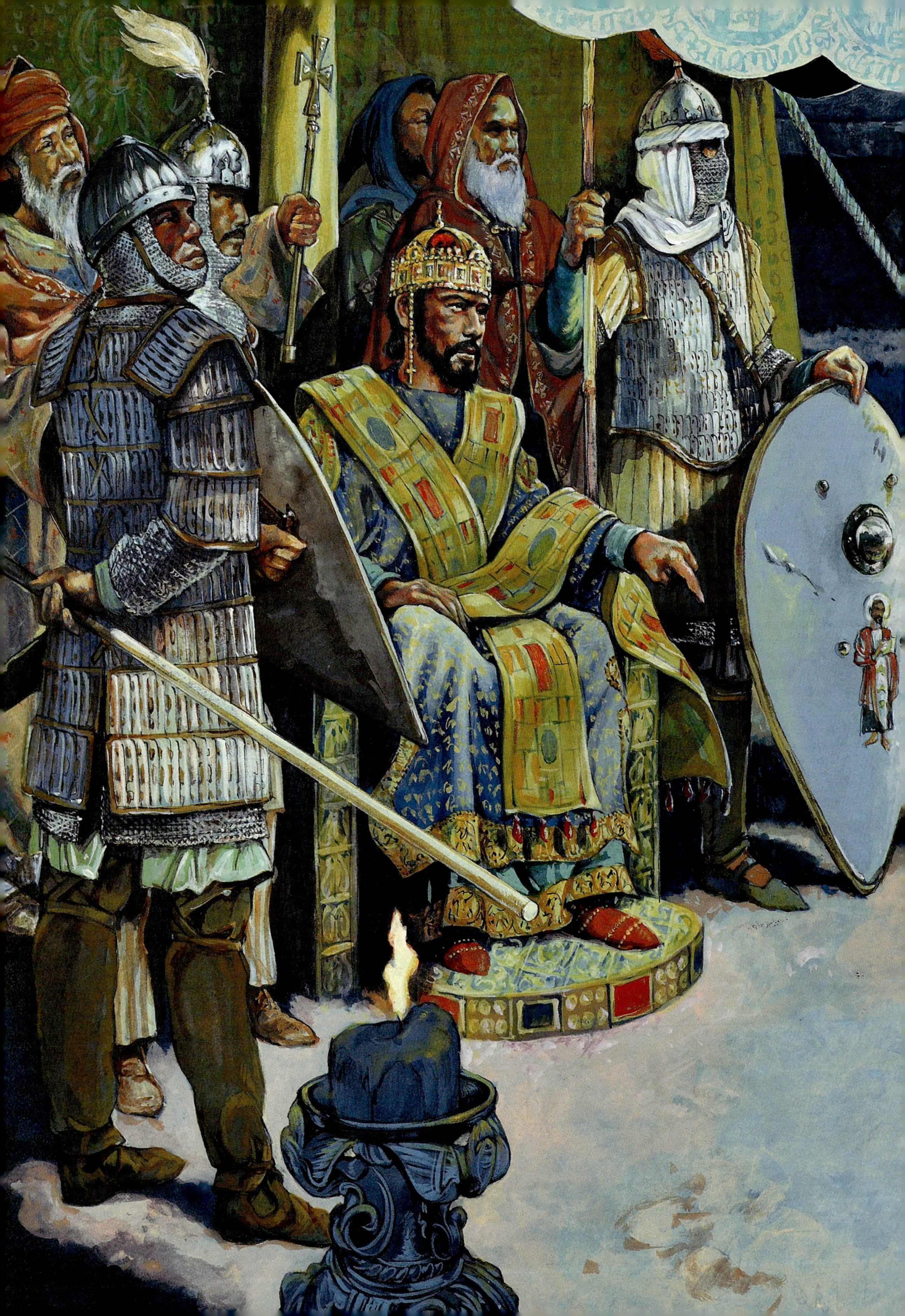

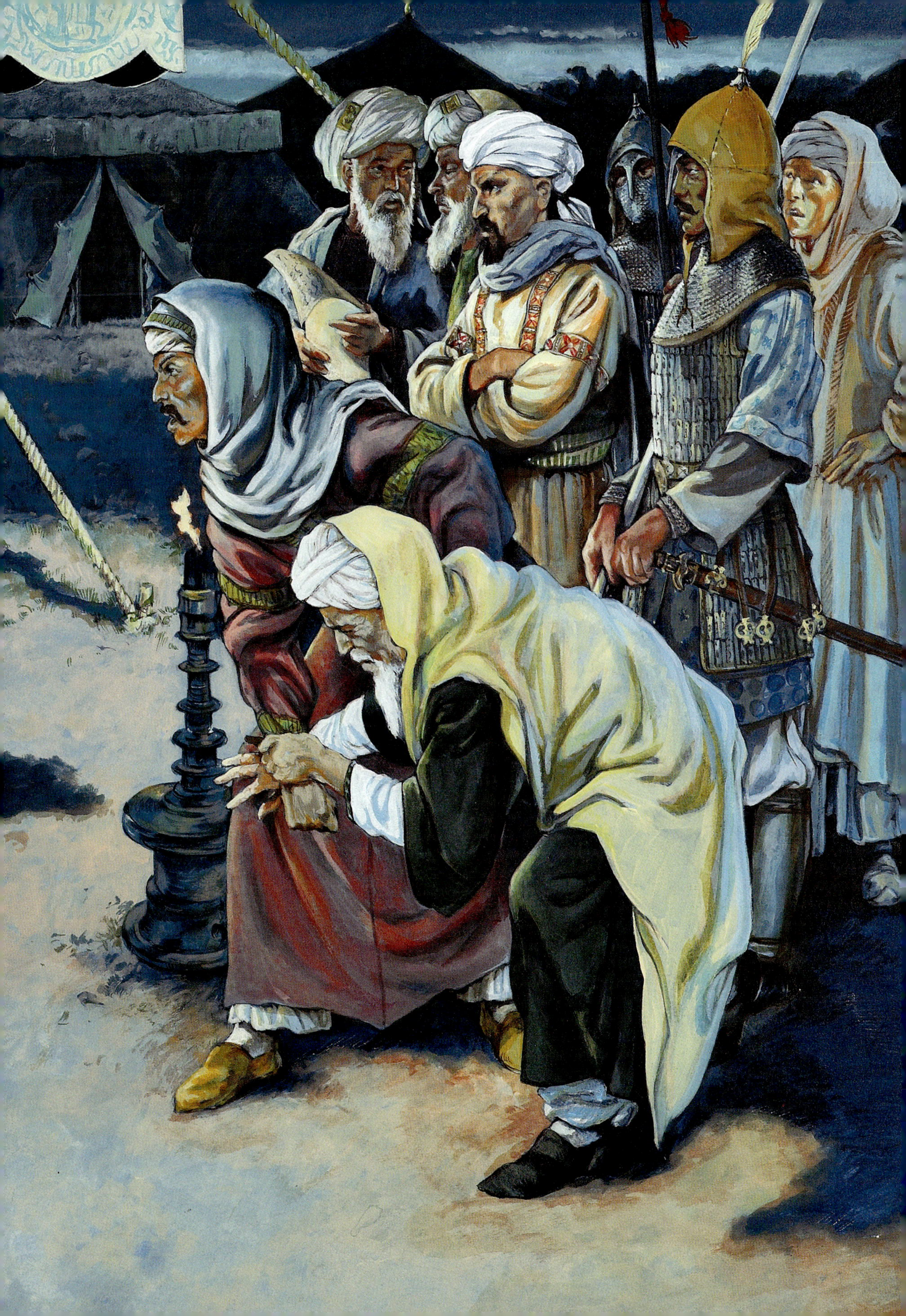

EMPEROR ROMANOS IV HUMILIATES A SALJUQ PEACE DELEGATION, LATE EVENING, THURSDAY 25 AUGUST 1071 (PP. 66–67)

Sultan Alp Arslan sent a negotiating delegation to the Byzantine Emperor Romanos IV the day after the brief Byzantine siege of the fortified town of Manzikert had come to a successful conclusion. It was led by Ibn al-Muhalban, a senior jurist or Islamic legal scholar, who had been sent by the 'Abbasid Caliph in Baghdad to support Alp Arslan, probably in anticipation of a campaign against the rival Fatimid Caliphate rather than in a campaign against the Byzantine Empire. Similarly, the Sultan still did not see the Byzantine Emperor as his most important adversary - that being the Fatimid Caliphate in Egypt and Syria. Furthermore, Alp Arslan feared that his seriously outnumbered army would be defeated in a full-scale battle. In contrast, Romanos **(1)** was supremely confident. Despite having met Ibn al-Muhalban **(2)** before and apparently treating him with respect on that occasion, the Emperor now insisted that the old man performed the full *proskynesis*. This entailed kissing the ground in front of the Emperor's throne, which was a serious humiliation for the 'Abbasid Caliph's representative. Furthermore, the Emperor also made virtually impossible conditions which would have seriously humiliated the Sultan. The splendour of Byzantine display during this meeting was later recalled by Sadr al-Din al-Husayni, writting early in the 13th century. With some exaggeration he claimed that Romanos sat a golden throne, above which was a golden cross set with priceless jewels, while before him was a host of monks and priests reciting the Gospel.

As the Byzantine army pursued the steadily withdrawing Saljuqs they entered increasingly broken, rock-strewn terrain, as here, 3km along the road to Agri. (Author's photograph)

by the churlish manner in which they were received. The aged ambassador was even forced to make the *proskynesis*, or full bow to the earth in front of the Emperor, which was a calculated humiliation for such a senior representative of the 'Abbasid Caliph. By then, according to Michael Attaleiates, the Emperor had already decided to accept those arguing for a military solution, rejecting peace proposals 'as making a mockery of the affair and a deception rather than an expedient solution'.

To add insult to injury, Romanos laid down impossible conditions, insisting that the Sultan withdraw to a greater distance, permitting Byzantine troops to take over and fortify the Saljuq camp. He similarly refused to start real peace talks, saying: 'I will agree to that opinion [in Arabic ra'y] [only when I am] in [the Iranian city of] al-Rayy.' He then asked the ambassador which was best in winter, Isfahan or Hamadan, adding that he had been informed Hamadan would be cold. According to Ibn al-Azraq, Ibn al-Muhallaban agreed that Isfahan would be more pleasant, whereupon Romanos announced; '"As for us, we will winter in Isfahan and the riding animals will be in Hamadhan." Ibn al-Muhallaban replied, "As for the riding animals, it is true that they will winter in Hamadhan. As for you, I do not know."'

According to al-Husayni:

I heard from Khwaja Imam Musharraf al-Shirazi … while we were going down to Khwarazm. He said; 'I heard from my elders that when the troops of the sultan Alp Arslan and the troops of Byzantium were fighting each other, the king of Byzantium sent a messenger to the sultan who said to him; "I have come to you accompanied by troops that you cannot resist. If you become subservient to me, I will give you from the lands that which will be sufficient for you… If you do not do that, I have with me in the way of troops three hundred thousand cavalry and infantry. I have fourteen thousand carts on which are coffers of money and weapons. Not a single one of the Muslim troops can resist me and none of their cities and citadels will remain shut in my face." When the sultan heard this message, the glory of Islam overcame him and the pride of kingship stirred in his breast. He said to the envoy: "Tell your master: It is not you who have sought me out, but it is God… Some of your troops will be killed by me; others will be my captives. All your treasures will be in my possession and [become] my property."

The die was cast. Romanos had concluded that Alp Arslan was afraid because he had too few men and was therefore trying to delay matters until reinforcements arrived. If that had been correct, then the Byzantine decision to attack as soon as they felt ready would have been correct, offering the real possibility of crushing the Saljuq army. Furthermore, the morale of the Byzantine army would probably decline with further delay. So Romanos decided to prepare for a battle the following day, Friday, having realized that the missing troops from Ahlat would not appear. Nevertheless the Byzantine chronicler Michael Attaleiates was surely wrong in stating, 'While the Turks were working out the terms of peace among themselves, the emperor, sounding the battle cry, inexplicably decided on battle.' By now both sides had probably accepted that a fight was inevitable.

The only chronicler to hint that Nizam al-Mulk was with Alp Arslan's army was Sadr al-Din al-Husayni who stated that, after these negotiations had failed, the *wazir* was sent back to Hamadan 'in order to defend Iraq [then meaning western Persia and Iraq], Khurasan and Mazandaran from malcontents and evildoers'. Meanwhile the arrogance of the Byzantine Emperor and his brutal rebuff of Alp Arslan's negotiator reportedly enraged the Saljuq army. Nevertheless, Alp Arslan was far from confident of the outcome and almost all the Islamic sources emphasize his pessimism before the battle. Al-Husayni specifically stated that the Sultan was alarmed: 'His *imam* and *faqih* [personal religious guide], Abu Nasr Muhammad Ibn 'Abd al-Malik al-Bukhari al-Hanafi, said to him: "You are fighting for God's religion. I hope that Almighty God will have written this victory in your name. Meet them [the Byzantines] on Friday at the hour when the preachers will be on the pulpits [during the main congregational service] praying for victory for the warriors of the faith against the infidels and the prayer will be answered."'

Until then, both armies spent the moonless night of Thursday–Friday readying themselves for battle. Confidence, it is generally agreed, was higher on the Christian side, as confirmed by al-Turtushi: 'So the Muslims passed the night of Friday [i.e. Thursday–Friday] whilst the Byzantines were in a number which nobody except He who had created them could enumerate, and the Muslims had nothing with them except gnawing hunger. The Muslims remained silent with fear about what had befallen them.'

On the morning of Friday 26 August 1071 both sides prayed and prepared, crosses and icons being paraded before the Byzantine troops. Although Matthew of Edessa gets several events muddled up, his description of these final preparations was probably close to the mark: 'In the morning hours the battle trumpet was sounded, and heralds went forth and proclaimed the wishes of the emperor [Romanos] Diogenes. He promised honours, high positions, and jurisdiction over the towns and districts to all those who would courageously fight against the Persian forces.' The chronicler Nikephoros Bryennios the Younger seems to be alone in maintaining that the Saljuqs were the first to move: 'The emperor, seeing that the Turks were attacking, also ordered the troops out to fight and ranged them in battle order in front of the camp. The right wing was commanded by [Theodore] Alyates, a Cappadocian and close friend of the Emperor, the left wing by Bryennios, and the centre by the Emperor himself. The rearguard had been entrusted to the son of the Caesar, the *proedrus* Andronicus [Dukas], the commander of the foreign troops and of those of the *archons* [aristocracy].'

In fact the Imperial army was arrayed ahead of its fortified camp and prepared to advance in battle formations. On the morning of Friday 26 August, it prepared to advance against the Turks. The left under the '*dux* of the west', Nikephoros Bryennios, included the western *tagmata* which he had commanded for some years. The right under Theodore Alyates consisted of the Cappadocians and probably most of the other Anatolian units. It would have been traditional for the Oghuz, Pechenegs and other Turkish auxiliaries and mercenaries to be on the flanks – perhaps with more emphasis on the traditionally 'offensive' right rather than the 'defensive' left. Others would have been with the rearguard, though no specific mention was made of these troops.

In the centre the Emperor Romanos IV commanded the *scholai* and most of the remaining palace or guard units, plus the best-equipped Armenian infantry and probably most of the remaining Byzantine heavy cavalry. Most of the Byzantine archers had either been sent on the disastrous expedition to Ahlat, or stayed back to defend the Byzantine camp. Unfortunately Matthew of Edessa's statement that the Emperor 'appointed as commanders of his troops Khatap and Vasilak, Armenian nobles who were brave and were regarded as great warriors' fails to identify these men in greater detail.

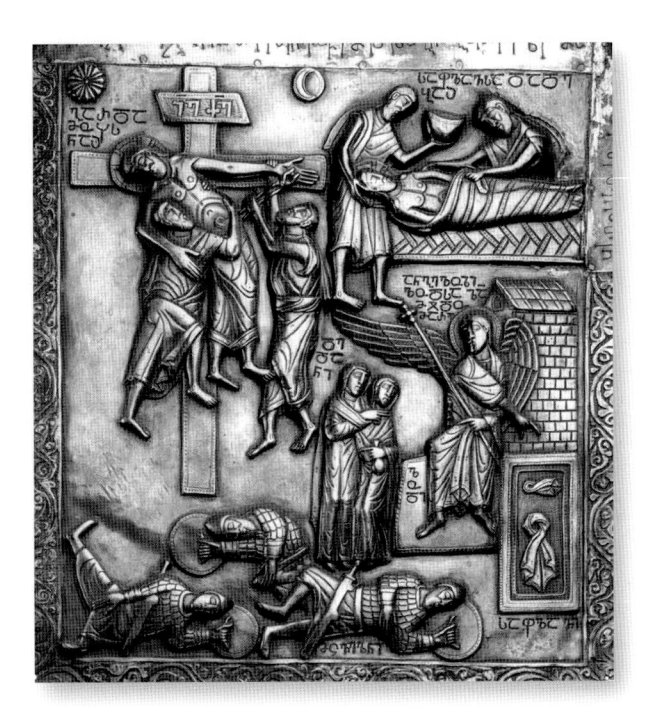

Scenes of the Passion of Christ on a silver-gilt Georgian icon, made between 1050 and 1100. (Georgian State Art Museum, V-939.G-76-A, Tblisi)

Much criticism has been directed at the Emperor's decision to place Andronikos Dukas in charge of the rearguard, which apparently included the personal or quasi-feudal military retinues of the great Byzantine landowners. Whether it is correct to believe that Andronikos Dukas could do least harm if he commanded this rearguard is doubtful. But whether or not the command structure was an error, the fact that the rearguard lagged some way behind once the Byzantine advance began was within accepted Byzantine tactics. Its role was to serve as a reserve, being able to support the other formations if needed, and to stop the enemy from attacking these formations from the rear. In this it would play its part correctly until the closing stages of the battle.

It was still normal for Byzantine emperors to make themselves distinctive and highly visible in warfare, perhaps donning armour only if they expected to enter combat personally – as Romanos would do. There is no record of what Emperor Romanos IV Diogenes wore during the battle of Manzikert, but more is known about the Emperor Romanos III Argyros in battle near Aleppo some 40 years earlier. He was captured by the Fatimids and his clothing was described in detail by a Muslim chronicler. It consisted of a felt mantle garnished with pearls on the hems, sleeves and around the neck, while on the Emperor's back and chest were crosses in gold, encrusted with rubies.

Michael Attaleiates was surely wrong in stating: 'When the report reached the enemy, it astounded them. In the meantime, however, they armed themselves and drove the useless multitude ahead of them in retreat, while in the rear they gave the appearance of battle array.' Here Muslim and Armenian chroniclers are almost certainly more reliable, indicating that the Muslim

Looking northwards from rising broken ground about 15km along the Ahlat road. (Author's photograph)

troops rose on Friday morning, readied themselves for combat and then adopted their battle array. This envisaged a prolonged withdrawal at the start of the battle, and here I can do no better than to quote John Haldon's excellent summation: 'At some distance from the Roman lines, but well in advance of this rougher land, Arslan had drawn up his own, less numerous force in a crescent formation, although he was himself not among the main body of troops, preferring to observe events from the higher ground to the rear. The Seljuk army was, in effect, divided up into a centre and two wings, but in traditional nomadic fashion these divisions in turn consisted of several smaller groupings which could, where needed, act independently.'[14]

The Andalusian chronicler al-Turtushi maintained that Alp Arslan had his troops counted that morning, finding that they included only 12,000 Turks. He then held counsel with his leaders to decide how best to face the more numerous Byzantine hosts. Then 'they made peace with each other, swore oaths to each other and showed sincere intentions towards Islam and its people. Then they made preparations for battle and they said to Alp Arslan: "We will invoke the name of God Most High and we will attack the people [the enemy]."' According to Bryennios, command in the fighting itself was given to his chief of staff, the eunuch 'Taranges' – namely the *sarhang* Sav-Tekin. 'This man divided his army into several groups, set traps and organized ambushes, and ordered his men to surround the Byzantines and to riddle them with arrows.' While most sources indicated that the Saljuq army was arrayed in three major divisions, al-Bundari insisted that there were four, 'with each division... being in an ambush'. Alp Arslan then checked to see that each ambush was firm and that hidden troops were indeed out of sight of the enemy.

Al-Turtushi's account is in his *Siraj al-Muluk*, a book of advice for rulers, which included several battles of tactical interest. Though written in Fatimid Egypt around 1122, the author had contact with scholars in Saljuq Baghdad and thus presumably drew upon the accounts of those who took part in the battle or knew men who had done so. Amongst several interesting bits of information were Alp Arslan's decision to hold back through the day, counter-attacking only at dusk, his focus on capturing the Byzantine Emperor, the role of his own elite troops and the subsequent humiliation of Emperor Romanos.

14 Haldon, J., *The Byzantine Wars*, op, cit., 122.

Muslim sources naturally emphasize Alp Arslan's pious and heroic speeches during the battle. Whether these can in any sense be taken literally is doubtful, though they reflect the attitudes of the time. They also confirm that the steady Saljuq withdrawal was part of a prepared plan that demanded considerable command and control. The fact that this succeeded while both armies moved for several kilometres across increasingly rocky and eventually rising ground, says a lot for the cohesion of both sides. The battlefield then reached rolling but still bare hills, broken up by shallow gullies and stream beds.

The biggest question concerns the location of the initial Saljuq camp in the foothills and the direction along which the Saljuqs withdrew during Friday. It might have been southwards towards Ahlat or south-eastwards towards the modern village of Gülkoru. Both directions would have offered Alp Arslan suitable locations for a commanding overview of the battlefield while providing ample cover for ambushes. Most historians have preferred the southerly route, whereas the Turkish military historian Feridun Dirimtekin prefers the south-easterly. This would also have offered an easier escape route in case the Saljuqs were defeated. The road to Ahlat would surely have resulted in the Sultan and his army being trapped in that strong citadel.

After completing their array, the Byzantines advanced, probably at mid-morning of Friday. Their tactics were those of Byzantine tradition during this period, seeking to close with the enemy to use their superiority in armoured close combat before suffering too much from enemy archery. This meant maintaining a steady pace and close cavalry formations.

One interesting feature, which is mentioned by al-Husayni, concerns the 'dusty wind ... which blinded the eyes of the Muslims, and the sultan's army almost took flight'. A northerly wind would be common at that time of year and the dust was presumably stirred up as large cavalry formations trotted over dry ground. It would also have been more of a problem for the steadily withdrawing Saljuq army. As Alp Arslan's centre fell back, the wings did so more slowly and with more frequent ambushes and wheeling around to harass the advancing Byzantines with close-range archery. As the day progressed, it was the Byzantine army that began to lose cohesion, its lines becoming ragged, its centre pushing forward while its wings were slowed by persistent enemy harassment.

Muslim chroniclers tended to revert to poetry and piety in describing this phase of the battle whereas the Byzantine sources were more factual. Nikephos Bryennios the Younger, for example, explained how: 'The Byzantines, seeing their cavalry under attack, were obliged to follow it, which they did, while the enemy pretended to flee. But, falling victim to the traps and ambuscades, they suffered great losses. While the emperor, determined to risk all, was advancing slowly, expecting to encounter the Turkish host, engage them in close combat, and thus bring matters to a head, the Turks scattered in all directions.' Of course the Saljuqs only seemed to be scattering; in reality they doggedly followed their prearranged plan.

By mid-afternoon the Byzantine centre had reached and overrun a Saljuq camp and was still pushing ahead. This camp is mentioned only by Christian sources and is likely to have been the Muslims' forward command position rather than their main camp in the foothills. Nevertheless the Byzantines soon reached broken and rising ground, which must have made the Emperor's control over his increasingly separated left and right wings more difficult. Furthermore, none of the main Byzantine formations had been able to make

Note: Gridlines are shown at intervals of 1km (0.62 mile)

XXXX
ROMANOS

MANZIKERT

▼ EVENTS

1 Initial negotiations between Romanos and Alp Arslan by letter on Thursday 25 August; embassy from Alp Arslan to the Emperor is rebuffed.

2 Alp Arslan and his commanders are not confident; the senior religious adviser suggests fighting the next day, Friday, at the time of Muslim congregational prayer.

3 Romanos arrays his army on Thursday morning: right under Theodore Attaliates, centre under Emperor Romanos, left under Nikephoros Bryennios, rear under Andronikos Dukas.

4 Byzantine army advances, trying to close with the enemy.

5 Alp Arslan arranged his forces in four or five divisions: Alp Arslan with the centre, the *sarhang* Sav-Tekin in command of a 'trap' probably consisting of the rearguard.

6 Dusty wind from north-west.

7 Saljuq centre withdraws, refusing close engagement.

8 Turkish wings retreat, attack Byzantine wings, repeating this while generally withdrawing.

9 Byzantine centre overruns Saljuq camp or command position by mid-afternoon.

10 Byzantine line grows ragged as wings are slowed by Saljuq attacks and ambushes.

11 The Emperor's division reaches rougher terrain after mid-afternoon, thus entering Alp Arslan's 'trap'.

74

NEGOTIATIONS AND THE BYZANTINE ATTACK, THURSDAY AFTERNOON TO LATE AFTERNOON FRIDAY, 25–26 AUGUST

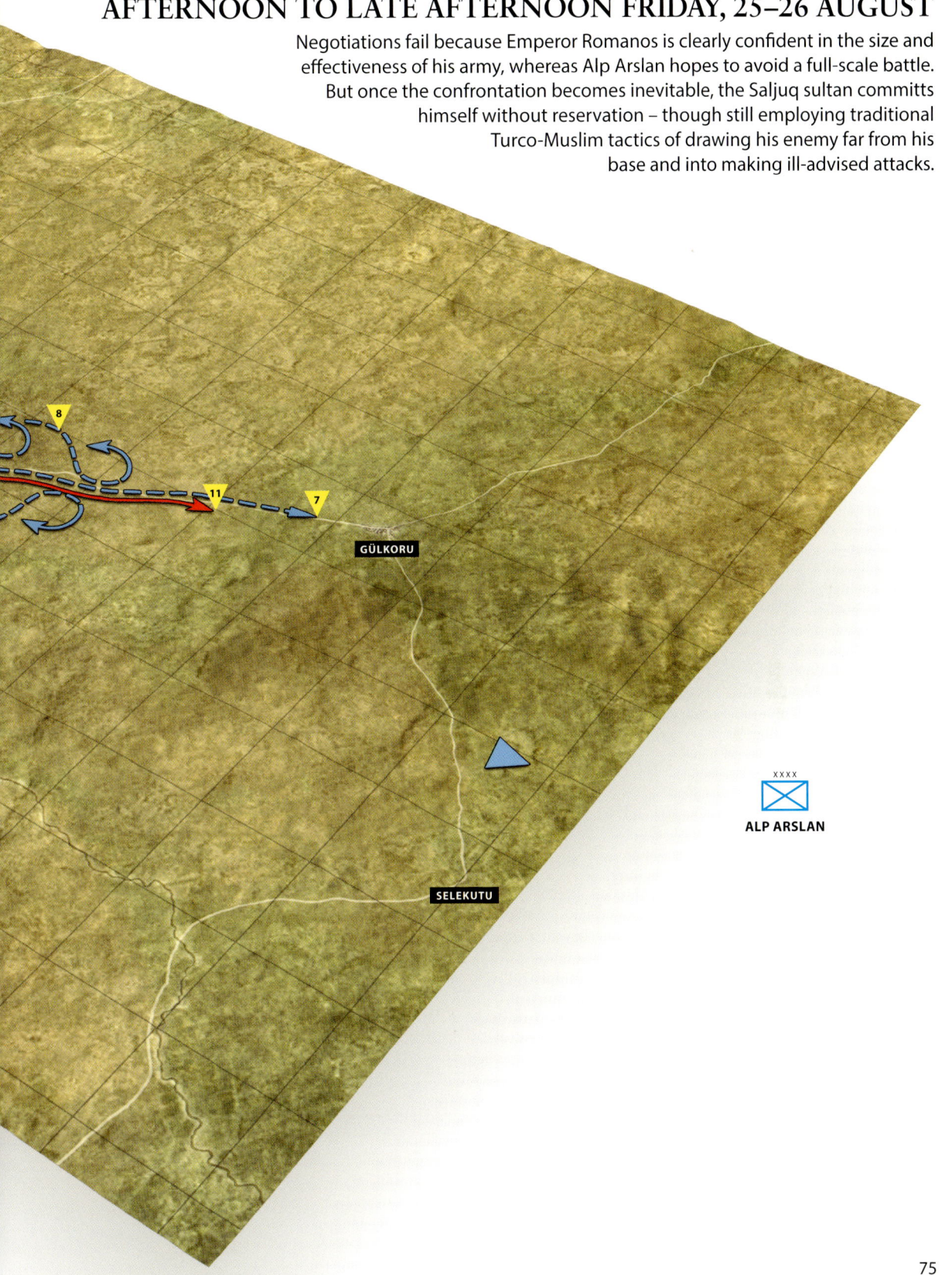

Negotiations fail because Emperor Romanos is clearly confident in the size and effectiveness of his army, whereas Alp Arslan hopes to avoid a full-scale battle. But once the confrontation becomes inevitable, the Saljuq sultan committs himself without reservation – though still employing traditional Turco-Muslim tactics of drawing his enemy far from his base and into making ill-advised attacks.

David returning with Goliath's head on a spear, in a Byzantine psalter made less than 20 years after the battle of Manzikert. (Vatopedi Monastery Library, Cod. 761, f.13v, Mount Athos)

effective contact with its enemies, yet continued to suffer from enemy archery. This must have been wounding if not killing many horses, if not so many of the armoured men. It seemed that each time they retaliated by charging the enemy, they fell into yet another ambush and occassionally some Turks were able to get behind some Byzantines.

Emperor Romanos now reached the area where Alp Arslan had reportedly planned his main counter-attack. This claim by the Muslim chroniclers might, of course, have been crediting the Sultan with more foresight than was really the case. The timing is also somewhat unclear, for Muslim accounts generally agree that Alp Arslan's counter-stroke was delivered at the time when the main congregational Friday prayers would be ending and Muslim preachers would be delivering their sermons from the *minbars* or pulpits. Christian sources indicate that, in reality, it was rather later as the afternoon drew towards a close – perhaps around four o'clock.

Before this, however, Emperor Romanos ordered a halt. As had happened two days earlier, he realized that he was far from his fortified camp, which was itself vulnerable to attack. The gaps between his centre and wings were larger than they should be, his troops were undoubtedly getting tired, thirsty and perhaps short of supplies as well as frustrated and perhaps demoralized. It seems unlikely that 'twilight took him by surprise' but evening would soon arrive – as it does quite suddenly in this part of the world. So the Emperor reluctantly ordered another withdrawal.

On the other side, according to al-Husayni, Alp Arslan was praying that the wind would change and the dust would stop. The dust did indeed stop, almost certainly because the armies had done so. Wind directions can also change in the cool of evening, but al-Husayni was probably stretching a point when he claimed that the dust now became a problem for the infidels. Nevertheless the armies did change direction as Emperor Romanos ordered a general but controlled retreat, apparently starting with the central division.

As was normal practice, this was signalled by a reversal of the Imperial standards or, in the words of Michael Attaleiates, 'He turned round the Imperial standard, ordering a return.' Unfortunately for the Byzantine army, this signal was misinterpreted by some of the divisions farthest away who apparently thought that the centre, under the Emperor, had been defeated. This not surprisingly led to confusion, especially on the right wing where many thought that Romanos himself had fallen.

It was the moment that Alp Arslan had been awaiting. There is no reason to doubt that he was dressed in white, as some Muslim accounts maintain. Meanwhile, he put aside the bow and a quiver of three arrows, which he carried as much as a traditional mark of Türkmen leadership than as weapons. By taking up a sword and mace Alp Arslan similarly indicated that he was entering close combat – and that the rest of his army should do likewise. Even the Christian chronicler included these details, though placing a shield and spear rather than a sword and mace in the Sultan's hands. By knotting his horse's tail Alp Arslan was carrying out another action, which had, for centuries, been both symbolic and practical in Turkish warfare. It again indicated that he would enter the mêlée and wanted to make it harder for opponents to disturb his horse by grabbing hold of its tail. Sibt al-Jawzi and Imad al-Din both add that the Sultan now put on his helmet and coif, thus becoming a fully armoured but otherwise ordinary cavalryman.

These symbolic actions were apparently followed by prayer and a speech, which, though recorded in several versions of flowery prose by chroniclers, was probably more pungent and direct at the time: 'We are with a depleted number of men. I want to throw myself on them [the Byzantines] at this hour when prayers are being said for us and for the Muslims on the pulpits. Either I will achieve that goal or I will go as a martyr to Paradise. He amongst you who wants to follow me, let him follow me, and he who wants to leave, let him leave my company. Here is not a sultan commanding, nor an army being commanded, for today I am only one of you and a *ghazi* with you. He who follows me and gives himself to God Most High, he will gain Paradise and booty. He who goes away, the Fire [of Hell] and ignominy are obligatory for him.' None, it is said, chose to leave.

Seeing what was happening on the Byzantine right wing and perhaps being informed by scouts that the enemy's rearguard was farther away than it should have been, and apparently withdrawing more rapidly than it should, Alp Arslan launched his counter-attack. Michael Attaleiates, who was still in the Byzantine camp at this time, reported: 'Those of the enemy who were standing on ridges saw the sudden misfortune of the Romans, reported the fact to the sultan... He returned straightway and battle all at once beat against the emperor.' The Muslim sources insist that evening was now drawing on, Sibt al-Jawzi declaring: 'They shouted with one voice at which the mountains trembled, and they pronounced the *takbir* [*Allahu Akbar*, 'God is Most Powerful']. They went into the centre of the Byzantines and fought them.'

Although Alp Arslan's centre attacked the Byzantine centre, it was the Byzantine right that crumbled first, enabling Saljuq troops to get between it and the Byzantine rearguard. According to Nikephoros Bryennios the Younger, the right was routed. As its men fled towards the safety of the camp, the rearguard, instead of coming back to assist, reportedly speeded up its own withdrawal. This was later interpreted by Michael Attaleiates, and by most modern historians, as treachery by Andronikos Dukas. For Nikephoros Bryennios the Younger, it was this that enabled the Turks to 'surround the emperor and assail him on all sides'.

Betrayal or not, the failure of the Byzantine rearguard to fulfil its proper role by protecting the withdrawal led to infectious panic in the other divisions. For Attaleiates, Romanos now became the doomed hero: 'and so the emperor, seeing the inexplicable flight from battle, stood with those around him, recalling his men from flight in the usual way. But no one obeyed him.' In fact some did. Nor were they alone in trying to prevent disaster.

Nikephoros Bryennios the Elder, in command of the left wing, attempted to support the centre but found his division being attacked from the rear, so he too was forced to retreat, eventually breaking up in flight. Some have credited Sav-Tekin with this success, maintaining that he had been in

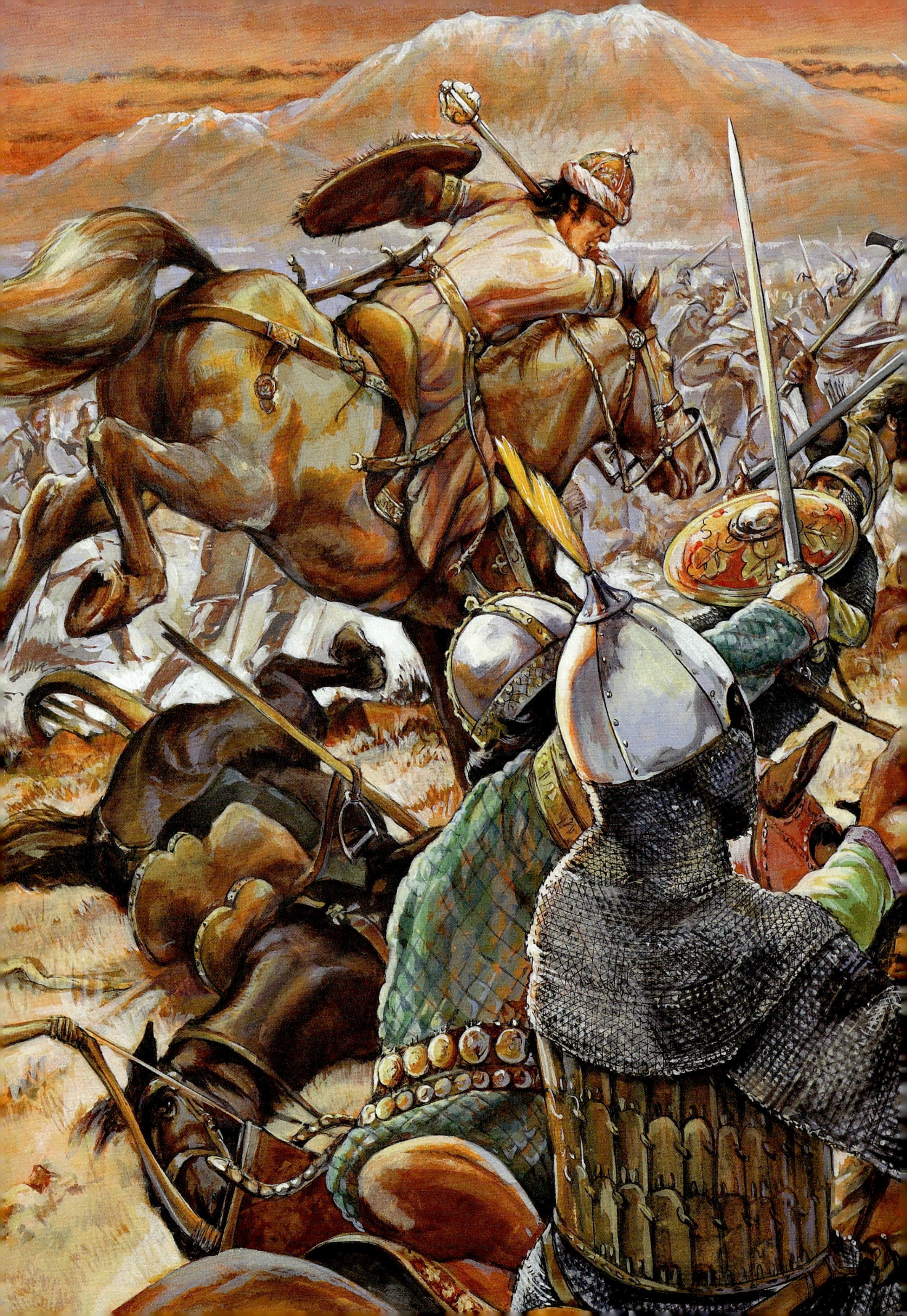

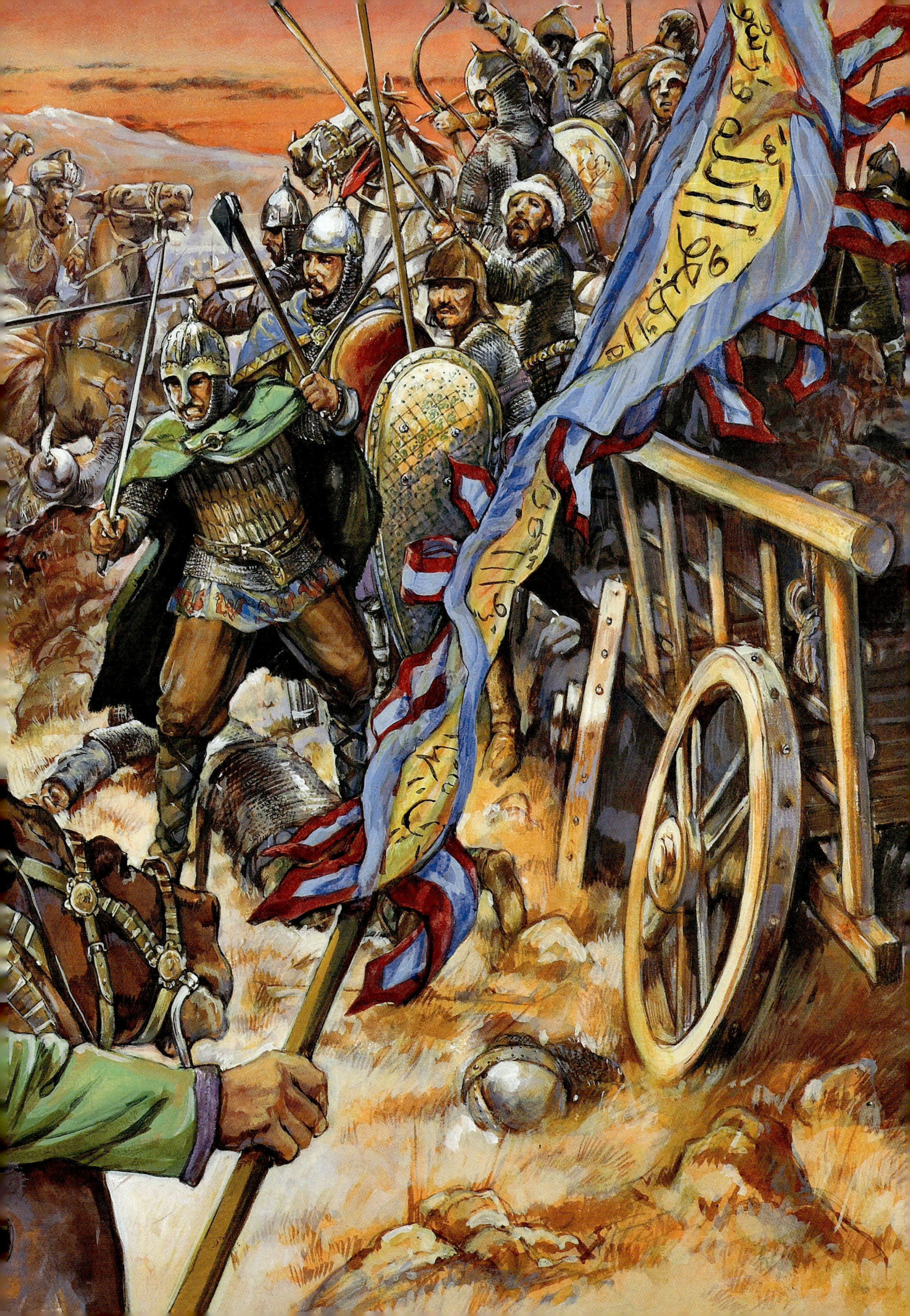

THE EMPEROR ROMANOS IV MAKES HIS FINAL STAND, SUNSET, FRIDAY 26 AUGUST 1071 (PP. 78–79)

The final stage of the battle of Manzikert saw the Byzantine army in disarray, its wings collapsing and in retreat towards its strongly fortified encampment outside the recently captured town and citadel of Manzikert. Some Byzantine units found that Saljuq forces were already between them and the hoped-for security of their camp. Worse still, the Byzantine reserve formation did not move forward to support the crumbling forward formations. This not surprisingly led to rapidly spreading panic. However, the Emperor Romanos (1) attempted the rally the Byzantine centre, which he himself commanded, hoping to launch a counter-attack and thus enable the rest of his army to reach safety. His efforts failed and so, with his remaining bodyguard (2) and those other troops who remained with him (3), Romanos made a final stand on one of the many rocky outcrops or small hillocks which dot the battlefield of Manzikert. Those who remained with the Emperor included many Armenian infantry (4), probably because, as foot soldiers, they could not escape Alp Arslan's entirely mounted army. In fact the most numerous Byzantine casualties were suffered by the Emperor's personal troops and these Armenian foot soldiers. There are several different versions of these final moments of the struggle. Most agree that Romanos IV was eventually taken captive by a low-ranking *ghulam* or supposedly 'slave soldier' (5). This unnamed man seems to have been of Byzantine origin, having probably been recruited as a prisoner of war during an earlier campaign. One version of this story maintains that the Emperor was finally found sheltering beneath a wagon (6), or that he was not identified and seized until the fighting had moved on towards Manzikert.

Foothills of the massif culminating in the Süphan Dağ. It was probably near here that Alp Arslan ordered his main counter-attack. (Author's photograph)

command of a Saljuq reserve that lay hidden behind the main army.[15] Aristakes Lastivertc'i, though far from favourable to the Byzantine cause, was at pains to highlight the loyalty of those Armenians who fought by the Emperor's side in the central division, despite Romanos' prejudice against them: 'Yet, when he saw them with dedication, when he saw the boldness of those braves who did not fear the able Persian archers, but rather were stoutly resisting and not turning tail and did not abandon the king as many had, no, instead they risked death so that after death they would leave a good name of loyal bravery, then did he display great affection for them and promised them unheard of rewards.'[16] Writing a short time after the event, Aristakes also maintained that it was only in this desperate situation that Emperor Romanos 'arose and dressed and armed himself like a warrior', perhaps basing his assertion on the recollections of surviving Armenian soldiers who had been with the Emperor at the time.

Sibt al-Jawzi agreed that Emperor Romanos had not been mounted on his horse when the crisis erupted, not believing that the Saljuqs could advance against him. Whatever the truth of the matter, Romanos Diogenes and those who remained with him now made a stand, hoping to stem the Saljuq attack and enable the army to regroup or escape. Soon surrounded, they fought on and, in the words of Nikephoros Bryennios the Younger, 'The emperor, abandoned and completely cut off from help, unsheathed his sword and charged at his enemies, killing many of them and putting others to flight.' Michael Attaleiates agreed: 'Ordering those around him not to give in or soften, he [the emperor] defended himself vigorously for a long time.' Matthew of Edessa saw matters in a different way: 'When the emperor learned of this [the retreat of the rearguard], he realized the treachery of his own Romans.' Al-Turtushi was told by his sources, 'They began shouting in the language of Byzantium: "The king has been killed! The king has been killed!"… and they scattered and were totally torn to pieces.' Al-Bundari was more detached in his account: 'One group did not stand firm for fighting and did not remain steadfast. Another group did stand firm and was killed [or] in captivity.'

15 Başan, G., *The Great Seljuqs, A History* (London, 2010) 80.
16 Aristakes Lastivertc'i, op. cit., 168–69.

A ceramic plate from Nishapur made in the 10th or early 11th century, decorated with images of cavalry and infantry. (Museum of Oriental Art, no. 2629-3558, Rome. Author's photograph)

Being present in the fortified Byzantine camp, Michael Attaleiates offered a personal account of the unfolding disaster: 'Meanwhile, as the others in their flight flooded over the entrenchment outside, there was a mixed cry from all and disorderly flight and no informed statement was made. Some said that the emperor had vigorously stood in array with the men remaining with him and had routed the barbarians; others announced his slaughter or capture... As to whether I, confronting those who fled, gave a good account of myself against many, urging the reversal of defeat, let others say... and finally the Turks surrounded us on all sides. Then each entrusted his salvation to flight with as much impetus, haste or strength as he had.'[17]

There are various versions of how the Emperor Romanos IV was eventually captured but several facts emerge clearly. Romanos was wounded in his hand – by a sword according to Michael Attaleiates – and his horse fell, wounded by an arrow, 'dragging its rider down with it' according to Nikephoros Bryennios the Younger. Romanos may either have lain amongst the wounded all night on the battlefield before being captured, or have been amongst other wounded captives who spent the night tied to his captor's tent pole. Michael Attaleiates added that the captured Romanos 'slept on the ground, dishonourably and painfully'. Bar Hebraeus shows how the best medieval chroniclers, like modern historians, tried to compare different sources: 'Now I have found this history in two manuscripts, Arabic and Persian. But the blessed Mar Michael wrote, "The son of the sister of the Sultan captured the king, and another Turk came and killed the Sultan's nephew, and took the king, so that the merit of the capture might be his."' However, he rejected this story as unbelievable.

The Islamic chroniclers focus on the fact that the Emperor was actually captured by a lowly soldier, thus demonstrating how Islam humbles the proud. The lowly status of the Emperor's captor was certainly emphasized by al-Bundari and Ibn al-'Adim: 'Amongst the amazing things that were related about the king being taken prisoner was that Sa'd al-Dawla Gawhara'in had a *mamluk* [*ghulam*] whom he gave to Nizam al-Mulk [the *wazir*] as a present. He [Nizam al-Mulk] sent him back and did not look at him.'

17 Hillenbrand, op. cit., 234–235.

There are again several versions, though they differ only in minor details and can be assembled into a reasonably cohesive whole. Seemingly a horse belonging to one of the *ghulams* in Alp Arslan's division strayed during the chaotic aftermath of the fighting. This man followed the animal and found another horse with an ornamented bridle and a saddle of gold that obviously belonged to someone senior. Next to this horse was a man with a gilded helmet and armour. When the *ghulam* attacked him, the wounded man said: 'I am Caesar of the Rum. Do not kill me for the slaying of kings is an ill omen.' Other versions maintain that ten young boys from amongst the wounded man's servants urged the *ghulam* to put down his weapon because he had captured the Byzantine Emperor. Nishapuri, in his *Saljuqnama* epic verse history of the Saljuqs, claimed that the *ghulam* was himself of Greek origin and therefore recognized his captive, while Rashid al-Din added that Romanos was found hiding under a cart. Meanwhile, most agree that Romanos was not taken before the Sultan until the following day.

Elsewhere on the battlefield the Byzantine army was in full flight but, despite laments by Byzantines and claims by Muslim chroniclers, the army's losses in killed and wounded were relatively light. The worst fighting had been concentrated in one area, though it is also likely that many Byzantine troops were cut down as they struggled to get within the temporary safety of Manzikert. Ibn al-Qalanisi's perhaps inflated claim was that, 'Many of the Byzantine troops were killed, to such an extent that a valley there where the two sides had met was filled [with corpses].'

Bryennios recorded that, 'The entire camp was seized along with the Imperial tent, the treasure and the most beautiful of the Imperial jewels, among them the famous pearl known as The Orphan.' Yet the loss of Byzantine prestige was worse, as Michael Attaleiates made clear: 'What could be more piteous than for the entire Imperial army to be driven away in flight and defeat by savage and relentless barbarians and the Emperor, helpless, to be surrounded by barbarian weapons, and for the tents of the Emperor, the commanders, and soldiers also to be possessed by men such as these and for the whole Roman state to be seen as ruined, and the empire as all but collapsing?' Bryennios concluded: 'The survivors of the battle dispersed in all directions, each one hastening to return to his own country.'

For the Saljuq army this perhaps unexpected triumph undoubtedly brought in vast booty, while the pursuit itself lasted all night. Presumably this was why Romanos was taken by a man who had seemingly lost his horse and was not presented to Alp Arslan until the Sultan had returned to camp the following day. Night also helped the fleeing Byzantines, while others found refuge inside Manzikert, which closed its gates to the victorious Saljuqs. An otherwise inexplicable statement by the Arab chronicler Kamal al-Din Ibn al-'Adim claimed that part of the battle was fought near Tolotaph; namely Doghodaph, which was a short distance east of Xinis [Hinis]. If there is any truth in this, it may indicate that the Saljuq pursuit of the fleeing Byzantines reached that point where the road north-westward from Manzikert crossed a significant tributary of the Murat River.

The number of commanders and officers captured in the battle was clearly significant and it has been suggested that as many as 20 per cent of the total troops may have been captured, though the majority were later released. The rearguard and reserve units under Andronikos Dukas escaped virtually unscathed and made their way back to the Imperial capital of Constantinople,

Note: Gridlines are shown at intervals of 1km (0.62 mile)

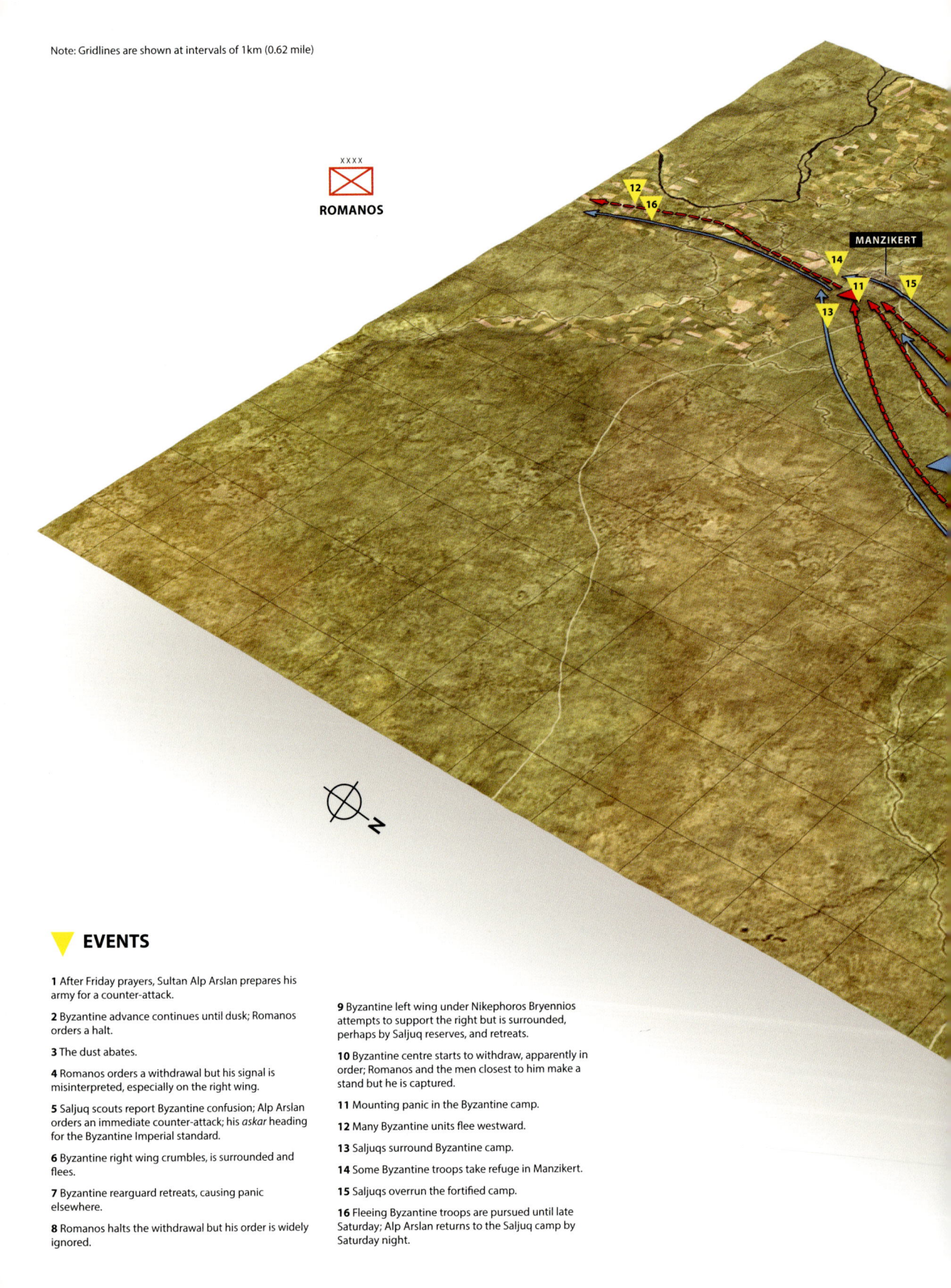

ROMANOS

MANZIKERT

▼ EVENTS

1 After Friday prayers, Sultan Alp Arslan prepares his army for a counter-attack.

2 Byzantine advance continues until dusk; Romanos orders a halt.

3 The dust abates.

4 Romanos orders a withdrawal but his signal is misinterpreted, especially on the right wing.

5 Saljuq scouts report Byzantine confusion; Alp Arslan orders an immediate counter-attack; his *askar* heading for the Byzantine Imperial standard.

6 Byzantine right wing crumbles, is surrounded and flees.

7 Byzantine rearguard retreats, causing panic elsewhere.

8 Romanos halts the withdrawal but his order is widely ignored.

9 Byzantine left wing under Nikephoros Bryennios attempts to support the right but is surrounded, perhaps by Saljuq reserves, and retreats.

10 Byzantine centre starts to withdraw, apparently in order; Romanos and the men closest to him make a stand but he is captured.

11 Mounting panic in the Byzantine camp.

12 Many Byzantine units flee westward.

13 Saljuqs surround Byzantine camp.

14 Some Byzantine troops take refuge in Manzikert.

15 Saljuqs overrun the fortified camp.

16 Fleeing Byzantine troops are pursued until late Saturday; Alp Arslan returns to the Saljuq camp by Saturday night.

THE TURKISH COUNTER-ATTACK, LATE AFTERNOON AND EVENING, 26 AUGUST

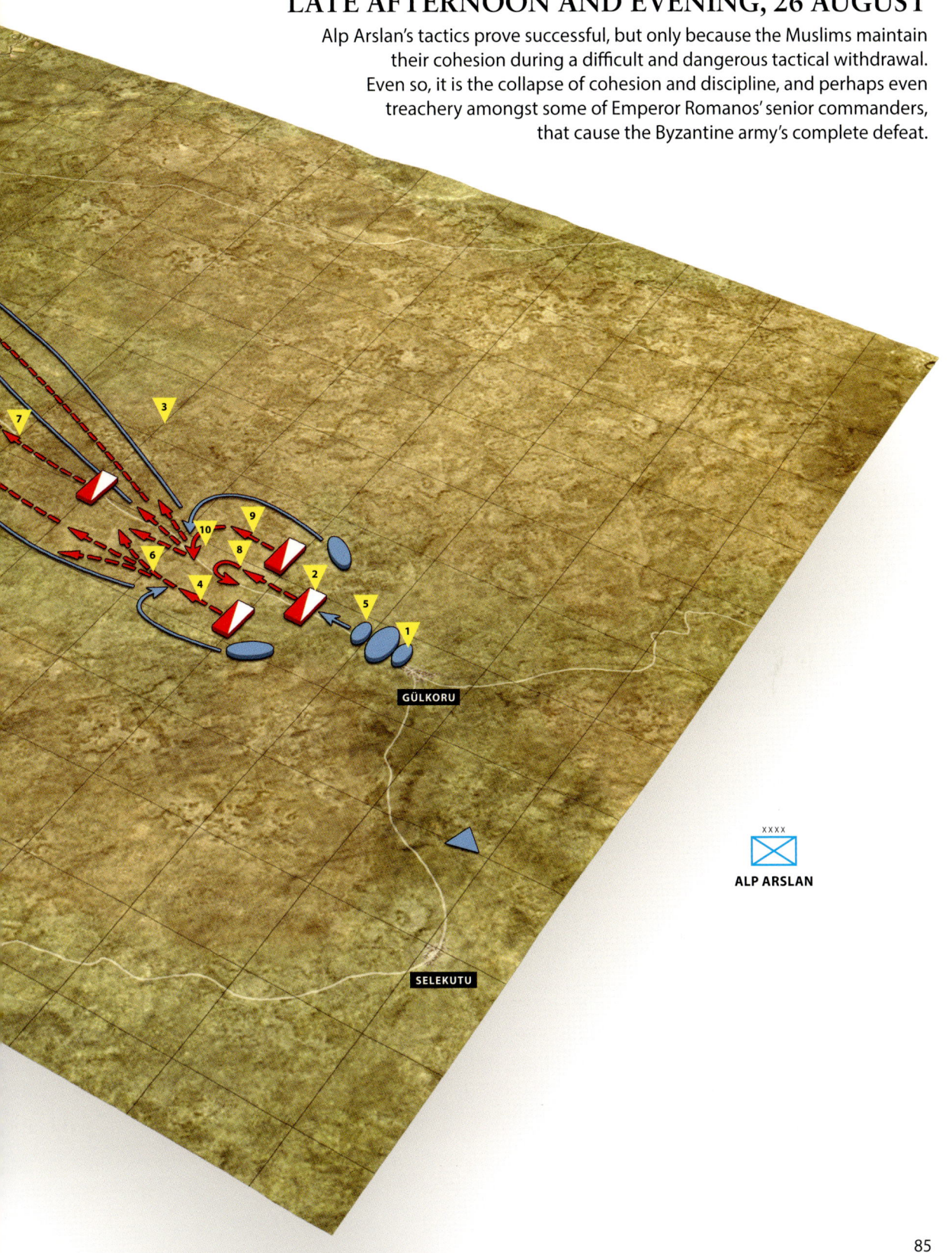

Alp Arslan's tactics prove successful, but only because the Muslims maintain their cohesion during a difficult and dangerous tactical withdrawal. Even so, it is the collapse of cohesion and discipline, and perhaps even treachery amongst some of Emperor Romanos' senior commanders, that cause the Byzantine army's complete defeat.

GÜLKORU

SELEKUTU

XXXX
ALP ARSLAN

as did most of the right wing under Nikephoros Bryennios the Elder. Several of its units were recorded campaigning against Pechenegs and Balkan Slavs the following year. Many troops from the shattered right wing also escaped, the Cappadocian *tagmata* seemingly withdrawing intact as did some elite units, which had been with the Emperor Romanos in the central division. Many subsequently gathered at the important fortress of Dokeia [Tokat].

In fact it has been calculated that between 5 to 10 per cent of those troops who took an active part in the battle of Manzikert fell, most of them having been around the Emperor, including large numbers of Armenian infantry. Even the *tagma* of the *Stratelatai*, which was not mentioned again after Manzikert, may have been disbanded rather than destroyed. Named casualties included the Armenian noblemen Khatap and Vasilak, according to Matthew of Edessa, though Khatap may simply have disappeared from the chronicles. Amongst the civilians who died was the senior bureaucrat Eustratios Choirosphaktes. Another was Leon, the *epi ton deseon* or official responsible for receiving and answering petitions to the Emperor. As nephew of the archbishop of Patras in Greece, he was also a respected man of great culture and firm supporter of Romanos Diogenes as Emperor.

The foothills south-east of Manzikert were ideal for hiding large ambush forces. (Author's photograph)

THE CAPTIVE EMPEROR

The varied accounts of Romanos' capture continue with differing accounts of his captivity. For example Sibt al-Jawzi claims that the senior Saljuq officer, Sa'd al-Dawla Gawhara'in went to Alp Arslan and said: 'One of my *ghulams* has taken the king of Byzantium prisoner', while Ibn al-Jawzi recorded that the sultan doubted this claim. So he sent a *ghulam* named Shadhi who had met the Emperor Romanos during the course of previous negotiations. Shadhi returned and announced: 'It is he', despite the fact that, according to Michael Attaleiates, Romanos was now in the 'shabby costume of an ordinary soldier'. Al-Husayni claimed that the *ghulam* who had captured Romanos tied the Emperor's hands before dragging him to the Sultan's camp and, on the way, 'Not one of the Byzantine prisoners saw him without sticking his [own] forehead in the dust.'

The Andalusian chronicler al-Turtushi added: 'The king of Byzantium was brought into the presence of Alp Arslan with a rope round his neck.' Sultan Alp Arslan was in his tent with a falcon and a hunting dog when Romanos was brought before him. According to Ibn al-'Adim, the Armenian Nikephoros Basilakes, who had been captured at the start of the battle, was also there and reportedly fell to his knees in tears. The 'Abbasid envoy Ibn al-Muhallaban similarly confirmed the prisoner's identity.

Al-Husayni further wrote: 'The chamberlain seized him [Romanos] by the hair and chest and threw him down to the ground so that he should kiss it, but he did not kiss it in the presence of the sultan because he was carried away by the pride of kingship.' Nevertheless, Alp Arslan ordered them to leave the Emperor be and, in Michael Attaleiates' words, the Sultan said:

'Do not be afraid, O emperor, but be hopeful… since you will encounter no bodily harm but will be honoured in a manner worthy of the pre-eminence of your power. For foolish is he who is not cautious before the unexpected reversal of luck.'

In the meantime, Bar Hebraeus and Ibn al-Jawzi agreed: 'The Sultan gave orders quickly, and they pitched a great royal tent for [Romanos] Diogenes and took him there. And they put iron fetters on his hands and round his neck, and set one hundred Turks to keep guard over him.' Not surprisingly, news that the Byzantine Emperor had been captured caused jubilation in the Saljuq camp but, in Michael Attaleiates' opinion, the Turks attributed their success to God 'as they had accomplished a greater victory than they could have under their own strength'.

The still unnamed *ghulam* who actually captured Romanos naturally asked for a reward, but here the reports, while agreeing factually, present an account that hardly makes sense unless the ill-regarded and 'lowly' *ghulam* was tricked by his superiors. Ibn al-Jawzi recorded that the man gave a personal account of the affair to the Sultan who gave him the traditional highly valuable 'robe of honour' and then asked what reward he wanted. The man, perhaps foolishly, is said to have asked for the governorship of Ghazna in Afghanistan. Al-Husayni maintains that it was given to him – but Ghazna was capital of the rival Ghaznawid Sultanate and was never ruled by the Saljuqs. In fact history shows that, after Ibrahim Ibn Ma'sud acceded to the throne in Ghazna in 1059, there was half a century of relative peace between Ghaznawids and Saljuqs. Might the man have asked for command of an unrecorded and unsuccessful expedition against Ghazna, or did those who reported the conversation mishear the name of the governorship requested? As far as is known, the captor of Romanos now disappeared from history.

Despite Alp Arslan's promise of good treatment, some ritual humiliation was thought necessary, so the Sultan struck him three or four blows with his hand and kicked him a similar number of times. The Sultan also criticized Romanos for having refused an offer of peace and what he regarded as the Emperor's tactical errors. Al-Jawzi wrote that Romanos replied, pointing out that he had spent a great deal of money assembling a huge army, had superior numbers and what he thought was the upper hand, so it would have been impossible for him to go home without trying to do something 'but the victory was yours. So do what you want and stop rebuking me.'

When asked what he would have done had victory been his, the Emperor judged that honesty was the best policy, answering according to some: 'Do you doubt that I would have killed you?' According to others: 'I would have put you with dogs with a lead collar [round your neck].' To which Alp Arslan replied, according to Ibn al-Jawzi: 'He has spoken truthfully, by God! If he had said otherwise, he would be lying. This is an intelligent, strong man. It is not fitting that he should be killed.'

A different version of this encounter has the Sultan saying: 'You are too trivial in my view for me to kill you. Take him and sell him to the person who pays most', after which Romanos had to endure further humiliation for a while, being offered for sale as a slave amongst the other prisoners. Al-Turtushi says that the Emperor was exchanged for a dog and that the dog and Romanos were then brought back into the Sultan's presence, Alp Arslan

A Turkish horse archer shooting rearwards towards a cavalry pursuer, on a 12th-century Byzantine silver and bronze bowl. (Hermitage Museum, St Petersburg)

A 12th-century Saljuq carved relief found in the Citadel of Ahlat during archaeological excavations led by Professor Emin Bilgiç. (Archaeological Museum, Ankara)

giving the dog back to its original owner, himself taking charge of the prisoner. These rituals completed, Emperor Romanos was released. Alp Arslan similarly sold some of the other senior Byzantine officers and gave others to his own senior followers.

Clearly Alp Arslan saw his captive as a valuable diplomatic asset. Once the symbolic punishment was over, he asked the Byzantine Emperor what he, Romanos, thought might be his fate. The Emperor replied that he might be executed, or paraded through the Sultan's domains, or he might be sent back to Constantinople as an ally though he thought the latter unlikely. Whether the speech recorded in Sibt al-Jawzi's chronicle is accurate or not, its main point was clear: 'Pardoning me, accepting money [ransom] and the treaty, dealing kindly with me, handing me back to my kingdom as a *mamluk* of yours and of some of your commanders and being your deputy in Byzantium, for your killing me will not be of any use to you. They [the Byzantines] will merely appoint somebody else.' According to Bar Hebraeus, Alp Arslan claimed that this was what he planned to do anyway.

The Saljuq Sultan's initial demand for a ransom of ten million gold coins was impossibly high according to Sibt al-Jawzi who probably had access to the official report of these negotiations that was subsequently sent to the 'Abbasid Caliph's court. A sum of half a million plus 360,000 in annual tribute was eventually agreed. Romanos now pointed out he would have to go to Constantinople in person to ensure this agreement was fulfilled, and that he was likely to be deposed if he did not reappear soon. In this the Emperor was entirely correct. Furthermore he agreed to release all Muslim prisoners in Byzantine hands and not to interfere in the lands of Islam in the future.

Romanos' treasure had of course been lost in the sacking of the Byzantine camp but, having returned to the tent provided for him, he managed to raise a loan of 10,000 dinars, which he distributed to his remaining retinue. He is also said to have 'sold a group of his generals and given others away', perhaps in reality leaving them as hostages. A final symbolic act seems to have been when Alp Arslan gave back the Emperor's cloak and hat, and put earrings on his ears, symbolizing that Romanos was now one of his servants or vassals. It is interesting to note that almost two centuries later Lu'lu, the Turkish ruler of Mosul, took his life in his hands by similarly placing rings on the ears of Genghis Khan's grandson Hülegü, the Mongol conqueror of Iraq. This he did to fulfil a boast made before the Mongols overran Mosul, and in the hope that the Mongols did not know that such rings were an ancient sign of servitude in the Middle East. Fortunately for the *atabeg* and for Mosul, he was correct.

Other terms of the eventual treaty between Alp Arslan and Romanos were the handing over to Saljuq rule of Antioch, Edessa, Hieropolis [Manbij] and Manzikert. Romanos even agreed that, if necessary, he would send troops to force the garrisons of these places to leave. In the event, civil war erupted in the Byzantine Empire before the first three places were handed over. Instead the Saljuqs had to fight for them, and where Antioch was concerned this would take a long time. Manzikert and Ahlat were then formally transferred from the Marwanid *amirate* to the Saljuq Sultanate. These were the Saljuqs' only immediate territorial gains but they ensured the Sultan's strategic domination of the region north of Lake Van at a time when Alp Arslan's main preoccupation remained the Fatimid Caliphate in Egypt and Syria.

There was even talk of a marriage alliance between their children, though of course this never happened. Yet the chroniclers do agree that, by the time Romanos was released, he and Alp Arslan were behaving like friends. The Emperor and 'as many Romans as he asked for and ambassadors drawn from his close associates', in the words of Michael Attaleiates, were released eight days after the battle of Manzikert. Alp Arslan and his entourage escorted the party for a *parasang* (a league or approximately 5km, not to be confused with the modern Iranian *parasang* of 6km). Then, refusing to allow Romanos to humble himself in front of his men, the Sultan gave him an escort of two *amirs*, one hundred *ghulams* and a banner bearing the Muslim declaration of faith, 'There is no god but God. Muhammad is the Prophet of God.' This symbolized that the Emperor was now the vassal of a Muslim ruler – not something which would make Romanos' position within the Byzantine Empire any easier.

Alp Arslan also received a letter of congratulation from the 'Abbasid Caliph, addressing him as: 'The son, the most lofty, supported, assisted, victorious lord, the most mighty Sultan, the possessor of the Arabs and the non-Arabs, the lord of the kings of nations, the light of religion, the support of the Muslims, the helper of the *imam*, the refuge of mankind, the support of the victorious state, the crown of the resplendent community, the sultan of the lands of the Muslims, the proof of the Commander of the Faithful.'

With such titles ringing in his ears, Alp Arslan led his army back to Azarbayjan. In fact Ibn al-'Adim and al-Bundari maintain that this march began while Romanos was still a prisoner. It would indeed have been unusual for a victorious army to remain on a battlefield scattered with the corpses of men and horses in the height of summer. This possibility is strengthened by the fact that the Saljuqs did not attack Manzikert, which remained a safe haven until it was handed over following the release of Emperor Romanos IV. Its contents were then added to the already vast booty, which Muslims had won when the Byzantine camp was overrun, from ransoms and from the sale of lower-ranking prisoners as slaves.

Several sources maintain that the booty from the camp was so huge that the Turks could not take it all with them. Instead the people of Ahlat and those who now returned to Manzikert seized what the Saljuq army could not carry. Some of this treasure was reportedly still seen in the two towns a century later. According to Ibn al-Azraq al-Fariqi, 'they distributed amongst themselves the gold and silver in *ratls* [units of 1.85 kilos, according to the medieval Syrian measure probably used in that area]. The inhabitants of Ahlat and Manzikert plundered from their [the Byzantines'] possessions enough to keep them rich until now [writing in the mid-12th century], for they went out, stayed with the army, fought and took most of the plunder. From that year the people of Ahlat were rich and became possessors of wealth.' Al-Bundari similarly wrote: 'The values of riding animals, beasts, weapons and commodities fell until twelve helmets were sold for a sixth of a dinar, and three coats of mail for a dinar.'

Byzantine forces that had been defeated by the Saljuqs outside Ahlat fled westward, finding refuge in the citadel of Muş. (Author's photograph)

AFTERMATH

ROMANOS RETURNS

During Emperor Romanos' brief captivity, the Byzantine authorities attempted to maintain order and assemble those who had escaped the disaster, both civilian administrators and soldiers. Most of the court had escaped and made their way to Trebizond, from where they probably took ship for Constantinople. The *proedrus* Paul, who had been recalled from his command in Edessa, took over the vital frontier fortress of Theodosiopolis whose *dux* had been captured. This he did without explicit Imperial authority while the Norman mercenary Hervé Phrangopoulos may have taken temporary command of the remaining eastern forces while Romanos and his senior commanders were held captive. More important, however, were events in Constantinople where the Empress Eudocia's son was now proclaimed Emperor as Michael Dukas VII.

Some of those then released with Romanos hurried to re-establish themselves, including the judge Basil Maleses who joined forces with Roussel de Bailleul. Perhaps those who always opposed Romanos Diogenes did not expect him to be released so soon – if at all – while many modern historians have assumed Alp Arslan's freeing of the Emperor was intended to stir up civil war in Byzantium. In reality the Saljuq Sultan cannot have known, within the eight days in which he held Romanos, that Michael Dukas would be raised up as his replacement. It is just as likely that Alp Arslan hoped to reach an accommodation with the Byzantine Emperor so that he could concentrate on his primary aim of dominating the Islamic Middle East.

The Byzantine Empire still had large numbers of troops, most of those units involved in the recent battle having escaped relatively unscathed. These were, even now, making their way to various Byzantine citadels while the substantial Byzantine forces in northern Syria had hardly contributed to the Manzikert campaign and were therefore still in place.

The 'Court of King Abenner' in a Byzantine manuscript of *Barlaam and Joasaph* made between 1075 and 1125. (Monastery of Iveron, Cod. 463, Mount Athos)

After the Saljuq Turkish conquest of the eastern part of the Byzantine Empire, some Armenian monasteries were rebuilt and even enlarged, one example being Surb Bartolomeos, close to what is now the Iranian frontier. (Author's photograph)

Romanos' first action was to pay what he had promised Alp Arslan, starting with 200,000 dinars from the citadel of Dokeia, which he gave to the Saljuq *amirs* who accompanied him. They then returned to the Sultan, leaving Romanos free to decide his next move. In Dokeia were many units that had escaped from the battle so the unseated Emperor had an army again. The *dux* of Antioch, Katchatourios, also supported Romanos.

As a deposed Emperor, Romanos knew he would be in great danger if he did not regain the throne so, in the words of a Byzantine chronicler: 'When a crowd of soldiers had flocked to him, he marched with his entire army to … Amasea.' Michael Attaleiates may have been correct in judging that Romanos made a major error in not immediately marching to Constantinople, instead building up his military strength. The resulting campaign – the first in a series that would almost bring the Byzantine Empire to its knees – did not go well for Romanos. His ally Theodore Alyates, who now led those Cappadocian troops supporting Romanos, was defeated, imprisoned and blinded. Then Romanos Diogenes was defeated at Sebastea and again at Adana where he surrendered on condition he would be allowed to live out the rest of his life as a monk. Blinded and then denied medical attention, the rest of his life as a monk proved painfully short, Romanos Diogenes dying in a monastery in July 1072.

THE DEATH OF ALP ARSLAN

Alp Arslan died less than four months later. Immediately after releasing Romanos, he appointed governors for Ahlat and Manzikert, which now passed from Marwanid to Saljuq control, then returned to Azarbayjan. Several commanders remained in Armenia to watch the Byzantine frontier and, as the Empire fell apart, some went on to carve out territories for themselves. From Azarbayjan the Sultan proceeded to Hamadan and Rayy.

The Saljuqs' unexpected victory was celebrated across the Sunni Islamic world, if not the Shi'a, being equated with early Muslim triumphs at Yarmouk and Qadisiyah during the 7th century AD. Alp Arslan, however, had pressing matters to deal with, most immediately a rebellion by one of his subordinates in Transoxania and rumbling conflict with the Western Qarakhanid Khan. Assembling a huge army, Alp Arslan crossed the Amu Darya River intending to attack Samarkand, but this never happened. Instead the Sultan was diverted to deal with Yusuf al-Harani, the reportedly Kurdish rebel commander of a minor fortress.

Perhaps over-eager to press on against his Qarakhanid enemy, Alp Arslan gained the governor's submission by promising the rebel 'perpetual ownership of his lands'. When Yusuf al-Harani was brought before him, the Sultan ordered that he be shot, but before the archers could raise their bows Yusuf seized a knife and threw himself at Alp Arslan, striking three blows before being slain. Four days later on 24 November 1072 Alp Arslan died and was buried at Marw, having designated his 18-year-old son Malik Shah as his successor. Nevertheless, the Saljuq Sultanate was plunged into civil war before Malik Shah could consolidate his position.

THE FALL OF ANATOLIA

The Byzantine or 'Roman' Empire, as it regarded itself, had for centuries been seen as a permanent factor in world affairs. But the capture of an Emperor seriously undermined Byzantine prestige throughout the Middle East and much of Europe. Even within the Empire, the self-satisfied image that the Byzantines had of themselves began to be questioned. Worse still was the resulting and prolonged Byzantine civil war. Revolt seemed to follow revolt and it was these years of chaos that really drained the military and financial capabilities of the Byzantine Empire.

While the Byzantine Empire was tearing itself apart, the Türkmen tribes took full advantage. Most military historians maintain that the Byzantines should have lost only the Armenian uplands as a result of Manzikert, there being no particular reason why the Empire should not have re-established the defensible frontier that had existed before the Byzantine conquests of the 10th century. This did not, of course, happen. Instead the Türkmen broke through that mountain frontier onto the high plateau of central Anatolia where they found a territory that was ideally suited to their own pastoral, upland way of life.

Whereas Alp Arslan had been largely unable to prevent previous Türkmen raiding, in 1072 he and his successor Malik Shah apparently urged some tribes into Anatolia where they would not only cease to be a problem for the Saljuq Sultanate but might extend it further. According to Matthew of Edessa, Alp Arslan announced: 'Henceforth all of you be like lion cubs and eagle young, racing through the countryside day and night, slaying the Christians and not sparing any mercy on the Roman nation.'

THE BATTLEFIELDS TODAY

At the time of writing Syria is off limits for tourists, though the northern regions which were involved in the Manzikert campaign used to be amongst the easiest to visit. Alp Arslan also assembled his army in north-western Iran, a country which is far more straightforward to visit than is generally realized.

Most of the Manzikert campaign was, however, fought within Turkey. Byzantine preparations were made, and its army assembled in and around Constantinople – now Istanbul – which remains one of the world's major tourist destinations. Eastern Turkey receives less tourist attention, which is a shame for this is an exceptionally interesting region, culturally, historically and scenically. It is also well provided with transport and hotels. Nevertheless, outside the main centres, eastern Turkey can seem primitive to the unadventurous traveller. For example, while Van has hotels in all categories and a large array of restaurants, one has to travel only a few kilometres to find things much more basic. A self-drive car is the best way to get around though some of the minor roads remain 'exciting'.

The Manzikert campaign focused upon the towns of Malazgirt [Manzikert] and Ahlat. The former has adequate hotels and restaurants, but the latter is poorly endowed with tourist facilities, despite its superb location on the shore of Lake Van. The battlefield of Manzikert has recently been marked by a monument called the 'Gateway to Anatolia', which, unlike some military monuments, seems to be in the correct location. The citadel and some of the fortified walls of Manzikert town were also restored to commemorate the 900th anniversary of the battle in 1971. Meanwhile the continuing tensions between Turks and Kurds, which too often result in violence, can be seen even amongst the business community of Malazgirt. Fortunately they tend to be restricted to friendly banter over numerous glasses of *raki*, the Turkish aniseed-flavoured spirit.

A modern statue of Alp Arslan dominates the road leading into Malazgirt, the medieval Manzikert. (Author's photograph)

In 1068 the Nestorian Church, which had flourished under Islamic rule for centuries, established a new bishopric at Urmiah and there is still a substantial Nestorian community in this part of north-western Iran, notably in Rezayah. (Author's photograph)

FURTHER READING

Amedroz, H. F., 'The Marwānid dynasty of Mayyāfāriqīn in the tenth and eleventh centuries A. D.', in *Journal of the Royal Asiatic Society* (1903) 123–154

Amitai, R., 'Armies and their economic basis in Iran and the surrounding lands *ca.*1000–1500', in Morgan, D. and Reid, A. (eds.), *The New Cambridge History of Islam vol. 3: The Eastern Islamic World Eleventh to Eighteenth Centuries* (Cambridge, 2010) 539–560

Angold, M. J., 'The Byzantine State on the Eve of the Battle of Manzikert', in *Byzantinische Forschungen*, 16 (1991) 9–34

Azhari, T. K. el-, *The Saljūqs of Syria during the Crusades* (Berlin, 1997)

Balivet, M., *Romanie Byzantine et Pays de Rûm Turc* (Istanbul, 1994)

Bar Hebraeus (tr. Boyle, E.W.), *The Chronology of Gregory Abu'l Farag* (London, 1932)

Başan, A., *The Great Saljuqs* (London, 2010)

Benedikz, B. S., 'The evolution of the Varangian Regiment in the Byzantine Army', in *Byzantinische Zeitschrift*, 62 (1969) 20–24

Bowlus, C. R., 'The Tactical and Strategic Weakness of Horse Archers on the Eve of the First Crusade', in Balard, M. (ed.), *Autour de la Première Croisade* (Paris, 1996) 159-166

Brand, C. M., 'The Turkish Element in Byzantium, Eleventh-Twelfth Centuries', in *Dumbarton Oaks Papers*, 43 (1989) 1–25

Brandileone, F., 'I primi Normanni d'Italia in Oriente', in *Rivista storica italiana*, 1 (1884)

Bryennios, Nicephorus (tr. Gautier, P.), *Nicéphore Bryennios Histoire* (Brussels, 1975)

Cahen, C., 'La Campagne de Mantzikert d'après les sources Musulmanes', in *Byzantion*, 9 (1934) 613–642

——, 'La Première pénétration Turque en Asie-Mineure (Seconde Moitié XI. s.)', in *Byzantion*, 18 (1948) 5–67

——, 'Une campagne du Seldjukide Alp-Arslan en Géorgie', in *Bédi Kartlisa (Revue de Kartvélologie)*, 41–42 (1962) 17–20

Canard, M., 'La Campagne Arménienne du Sultan Salguqide Alp Arslan et la prise d'Ani en 1064', in *Revue des Etudes Arméniennes*, 2 (1965), 239–259

Cheynet, J-C., 'Du stratège de thème au duc; chronologie de l'évolution au cours du XIe siècle', in *Travaux et Mémoires*, 9 (1985) 181–194

——, 'Les effectifs de l'armée byzantine aux Xe.-XIIe. s.', in *Cahiers de Civilisation Médiévale*, 38 (1995) 319–335

——, 'Mantzikert; un désastre militaire?', *Byzantion*, 50 (1980) 410–438

Ciggaar, K. and Metcalf, M. (eds.), *East and West in the Medieval Eastern Mediterranean I: Antioch from the Byzantine Reconquest until the end of the Crusader Principality* (Leuven, 2006)

Ciggaar, K., 'L'émigration anglaise à Byzance après 1066', in *Revue des Études Byzantines*, 32 (1974) 301

Dédéyan, G. 'L'immigration arménienne en Cappadoce au XIe siècle', in *Byzantion*, 40 (1975) 41–117

——, 'Les Arméniens sur la frontière sud-orientale de Byzance, fin IX-fin XIe s.', in *La Frontière, Travaux de la Maison de l'Orient*, 21 (1993) 67–85

Freely, J., *Storm on Horseback: The Seljuk Warriors of Turkey* (London, 2008)

Frenkel, Y., *Ibn Hassul and the Early Seljuqs: Studies in the history of Iran and Turkey, 3* (Curzon, 2002)

Friendly, A., *The Dreadful Day, The Battle of Manzikert 1071* (London, 1981)

Garsoïan, N., 'The Byzantine Annexation of the Armenian Kingdoms in the Eleventh Century', in Hovannisian, R.G. (ed.), *The Armenian People from Ancient to Modern Times* (New York, 1997) 187-198

Haldon, J. F., 'La logistique de Mantzikert', in Barthélemy, D. and Cheynet, J-C., *Guerre et société, Byzance – Occident (VIIIe –XIIIe siècle)* (Paris, 2010) 11–25

——, *The Byzantine Wars* (Stroud, 2001)

Hamdani, A., 'Byzantine-Fatimid Relations before the battle of Manzikert', in *Byzantine Studies – Etudes Byzantines*, 2/2 (1974) 169–179

Heidemann, S. 'Arab nomads and Seljuq military', in Schneider, I. (ed), *Militär und Staatlichkeit* (Halle, 2003) 201–219

Hillenbrand, C., *A Muslim Principality in Crusader Times* (partial trans of Ibn al-Azraq, *Tarikh Mayyafariqin*) (Leiden, 1990)

——, *Turkish Myth and Muslim Symbol: The Battle of Manzikert* (Edinburgh, 2007)

Janssens, E., 'La bataille de Mantzikert (1071) selon Michel Attaiate', in *Annuaire de l'Institut de Philologie et d'Histoire Orientales et Slaves*, 20 (1968–72) 291–304

Janssens, E., 'Le Lac de Van et la Stratégie Byzantine', in *Byzantion*, 42 (1972) 388–404

Kaegi, W. E., 'The Contribution of Archery to the Turkish Conquest of Anatolia', in *Speculum*, 39 (1964) 96–108

Kai Kā'ūs Ibn Iskandar (tr. Levy, R.), *A Mirror for Princes, The Qābūs Nāma* (London, 1951)

Kuhn, H-J., *Die byzantinische Armee im 10. und 11. Jahrhundert, Studien zur Organisation der Tagmata* (Vienna, 1991)

Lange, C., and Mecıt, S. (ed.), *The Seljuqs: Politics, Society and Culture* (Edinburgh, 2011)

Lastivertc'i, Aristakes (tr. Bedrosian, R.G.), *Aristakes Lastivertc'i's History* (New York, 1985)

Laurent, J., 'Le Duc d'Antioche Khatchatov', in *Byzantinische Zeitschrift*, 30 (1930) 405–411

——, *Byzance et les Turcs Seldjoucides dans l'Asie Occidentale jusqu'en 1081* (Nancy, 1913)

Markham, P., 'The Battle of Manzikert: Military Disaster or Political Failure?' *De Re Militari website* [http://deremilitari.org/resources] (2005)

Mathieu, M., 'Une Source Négligée de la Bataille de Mantzikert', in *Byzantion*, 20 (1950) 89–103

Matthew of Edessa (tr. Dostourian, A. E.), *Armenia and the Crusades* (New York, 1993)

Minorsky, V., *A History of Sharvan and Darband* (Cambridge, 1958)

Moayedi, H. G., 'Invasions seljoukides en Arménie byzantine', in *Tarih arastirmalari dergise*, 6 (1968) and 10–11 (1972) 127–133

Nizām al-Mulk (tr. Darke, H.), *The Book of Government or Rules for Kings: The Sīyasat Nāma* (London, 1960)

Oikonomides, N., 'L'Épopée' de Digénis et la frontière orientale de Byzance aux Xe et XIe siècles', in *Travaux et Mémoires*, 7 (1979) 375–398

——, 'L'organisation de la frontière orientale de Byzance aux Xe et XIe siècles et le Taktikon de l'Escorial', in *Actes du XIVe Congrès Internationale des Etudes Byzantines, vol. 1* (Bucharest, 1974) 285–302

Peacock, A. C. S., *Early Seljuq History: A New Interpretation* (New York, 2010)

Psellus, Michael (tr. Sewter, E. R. A.), *Fourteen Byzantine Rulers* (London, 1966)

Sadr al-Dīn al-Husaynī (tr. Bosworth, C. E.), *The History of the Seljuq State* (London, 2011)

Schlumberger, G., 'Deux Chefs Normands des Armées Byzantine au XIe siècle', in *Revue Historiques*, 16 (1881) 289–303

Seibt, W., 'Übernahm der Französische Normanne Hervé (Erbebios Phrangopolos) nach der Katastrophe von Mantzikert das Kommando über die Verbliebene Ostarmee?', in Cheynet, J-C. and Sode, C. (eds.), *Studies in Byzantine Sigillography 10* (Berlin, 2010) 89–97

Shepard, J., 'The Uses of the Franks in Eleventh-century Byzantium', *Anglo-Norman Studies*, 15 (1993) 275–305

Simpson, A., 'Three sources of military unrest in eleventh-century Asia Minor: the Norman chiefs Hervé Frankopoulos, Robert Crispin and Roussel de Bailleul,' in *Mésogeios*, 9–10 (2000) 181–205

Stephens, A., 'The battle of Manzikert: genesis of international cultural cultivation', in *Tarih arastirmalari dergisi*, 6 (1968) and 10-11 (1972) 73-84

Ter-Ghewondyan, A. (tr. Garsoïan, N. G.) *The Arab Emirates in Baghratid Armenia* (Lisbon, 1976)

Treadgold, W. T., *Byzantium and its Army, 284–1081* (Stanford, 1996)

Vryonis, S., *The Decline of Medieval Hellenism in Asia Minor* (Berkeley, 1971)

Whittow, M., 'How the east was lost; the background to the Komnenian reconquista', in Mullet, M. and Smythe, D. (eds.), *Alexios I Komnenos* (Belfast, 1996) 55–67

INDEX

Note: Page references in **bold** refer to photographs and captions.

'Abbasid Caliph 7, 8, **12**, 14, 20, 32, 49, 56, 65, **68**, 89
Abu'l-Aswar 35
Afşin 15, **16–17**, 24
Ahlat 11, 88, 93
   siege of 51, 55–56
Ahlat Gate, the **18**
Alaverdi Gospel (illustration) **55**
Aleppo, siege of 36–38, 47
Alexios, emperor 22
'Ali Ibn 'Uqail 33
alliance rejected by Normans 39
Alp Arslan, Sultan 15, 18, **22**, 23, 30, 31, 32, 41, 52–54, 56, 91–92, 93
   and battle of Manzikert 59, **60–61**, 63–64, 65, 72–73, **74–75**, 76–77
   invades Syria 32–38, **36–37**
   and peace talks **68**, 70
   retreat to Azarbayjan **44–46**, 47–49
   treatment of captured Emperor Romanos 86–88, 89, 90
Alyates, Theodore 22, 70, 71, 91
Anatolia, fall of 92
Armenian church 6, **6**
Armenian society 7, 10
askar (paid soldiers) 28, 48

Badr al-Jamali 33, 38, 49
   see also Fatimid Caliphate
Bailleul, Roussel de 22, 40, 50, 55, 56
   see also foreign mercenaries in Byzantine army
Barlaam and Joasaph (Byzantine manuscript) 90
Basilakes, Nikephoros 22, 50, **52**, 59, 62, 86
Betrayal of Christ, The (drawing) **27**
Bitlis, citadel of 33
Book of Fixed Stars (Umar al-Sufi) **64**
border security 26
Bryennios, Nikephoros, The Elder 21, 59–62, 65, 70, 71, 77, 86

Bryennios, Nikephoros, The Younger 50, 59, 63, 70, 73, 77, 81, 82, 83
Byzantine campaign against Saljuqs
   of 1068 15–18
   of 1070-71 39, 39–43, 47, 50–51
   at battle of Manzikert **16–17**, 50, 54, 56, 56–57, **60–61**, 63–65, 70–71, 73–86, **74–75**, 78–80, 84–85
   defeat at Ahlat 55–56
   secures Manzikert garrison 57–58, **60–61**
Byzantine chroniclers 10, 39, 55–56, 57
   at battle of Manzikert 59, 64–65, 71, 77, 81–82, 83, 87, 91
   see also Bryennios, Nikephoros, The Younger; Matthew of Edessa
Byzantine empire after Manzikert 90–91
Byzantine empire and other frontiers 4–5
Byzantine expansion into Armenia 8–10, 11
Byzantine foragers ambushed by Saljuqs 59–62
Byzantine infrastructure 26
Byzantine military plans and tactics 29–30, 70–71, 73–76
Byzantine rule from the tenth century 10–11

carvings 6, 11, 33, 43, 51, 88
casualties 86
cavalryman on bowl **56**
ceramics 25, 34, 38, 81
chess piece 48
Christianity 6, **6**
   Great Schism 6, 10
chronicles 25, 26, 41, 62
   see also Byzantine chroniclers; Islamic chroniclers
chronology of events 19–20
collapse of Byzantine empire 91, 92
Comnenus, Manuel 16, 18
Constantine IX, emperor 11
Crispin, Robert 15, 42
Crucifixion, the (Byzantine illustration) **54**

Dandanaqan, battle of 14
defensive structure 9, 26
desertion from Byzantine army 64–65
Diabatenos, Leo 47, 50, **52**
differences between Byzantine and Islamic chroniclers 73
Dukas, Andronikos 22, 71, 77, 83
Dukas, Caesar John 15, 41

earrings, as sign of servitude 88
Edessa (Urfa) 24, 35–36
empires and nomads in the region 5–6
engraved bronze dish 21
Erigsen Ibn Yunus 16, 18, 43
Eudocia, Empress **14**, 15, 21
events in years before Manzikert 16–17

Fatimid Caliphate 8, 31, 32, 38
   see also Badr al-Jamali
foreign mercenaries in Byzantine army 10, 15, 22, 40, 42, **43**, 64, 90
   see also Bailleul, Roussel de
frontier zone in Armenia/with Islamic world 7–8, 11, **43**

'Gateway to Anatolia' (monument) 93
Ghaznawid Sultanate 5–6, 12–13, 23, 28, 87
ghulam (slave recruits) soldiers 28, 48, 54, 80
   take Emperor Romanos prisoner 82–83, 86, 87
Great Schism between Christian churches 6, 10

Haldon, John 30
Harput 43
Herod's soldiers (painting) **40**
Hisn Kayfa (Hasankayf) 30
historical presentation of battle of Manzikert 5, 10

Ibn al-Muhallaban 65–69, **66–68**, 86
intelligence 50, 52, 59, 65, 77
intermarriage among Byzantine elites 25

95

Islam and Jesus Christ 6
Islamic chroniclers 11, 33–34, 40–41, 47, 54, 55–56, 57, 58
  at battle of Manzikert 63-4, 65, 69, 70, 71–73, 77, 81, 82–83, 86–87
Islamic expansion 12, **12–13**
Islamic schism 8
Istanbul (Constantinople) **16**
ivory panel of David and Goliath **36**

khan, Saljuq tribal leaders 27
Kurds, the 10, **46**, 92

Lake Urnia, Iran **8**
Lake Van 28, 93
  and battle of Manzikert **52–53**
  strategic importance 10, 11, 30, 51
lead seal **49**
Lu'lu, Turkish ruler of Mosul 88

Mahmud, *amir* of Aleppo 15, 36, 38, 47, 49
Malekan 31
Malik Shah 48, 92
Manicheism 12
Manzikert (Malazgirt) **34**, **39**, 50, 52, 54, 93, **93**
Manzikert, battle of 59–64, **60– 61**, **69**, 70–73, 76–86, **78–80**, **84–85**
  peace negotiations 65–69, **66–68**, **74–75**
map of the Turkish peoples **23**
Marwanid amirate 8, 10, 30, 33, 33–34, 36
Matthew of Edessa 32, 35, 47, 48, 70, 71
medieval superstition 32, 41, 42
Michael VII (Dukas), emperor 21, 22, 90
military manual 31
military structure of Byzantine army 25–26, 40
military traditions 26
Monophysites 6, 10
multi-ethnic composition of Saljuq army 28, **38**
Muslim settlement in Armenia 7–8, 10

Nasir al-Dawla 34, 35, 38
Nemtitzoi (German mercenaries) 42

Nestorian church, the 6, 12, **93**
Nizam al-Mulk 23–24, 28, 33–34, 48, 70, 81
Norman mercenaries in Byzantine army 42, **43**, 64, 90

Oghuz, the **12–13**, 12–14, 40, 64, 65, 71
origins of battle of Manzikert 6–8
Orthodox Christianity 5, 6

peace negotiations 65–9, **66–68**
Persian-Islamic forms of government 28
Phrangopoulos, Hervé 90
  seal of **41**, **52**
prayer as preparation for battle 70, 76, 77

Qarakhanids, the 12

Rahwa plateau 62, 63, **63**, 64
ransom and tribute paid by Emperor Romanos 88, 91
rearguard of Byzantine army, failure of 77–81, **78–80**, **84–85**
relations with neighbours 5–6
religious beliefs of the Turks 11–12
religious persecution 6–7
Romanos (Argyros) III, Emperor 71
Romanos (Diogenes) IV, emperor 14, 15–16, **16**, 18, 21, 24, 29, 30, 36, 59, 91
  1070–71 campaign **39**, 39–43, 47, 50–51
  and battle of Manzikert 63, 64, 65, 70, 71, **74–75**, 76, **78–80**, 81–82
  humiliates peace delegation **66–68**, 69–70
  secures Manzikert garrison **52–53**, **57–58**, **60–61**
  sends Basilakes to reinforce Bryennios 59–62, **60–61**
  taken captive 82–83, 86–88, 89, 90
roots of Byzantine civilization 5

Sa'id al-Dawla 34, 35
Saljuq army, the 11–14, 27–28, 52, 88–89
  at battle of Manzikert 59–65, **60–1**, 70, 72–73, **74–75**, 76

major battles and events **12–13**
retreat to Azarbayjan **44–46**, 47–49
Sultan sends peace delegation 65–69, **66–68**
victory at Ahlat 55–56
Saljuq military plans and tactics 30–31, 63–64, 72–73, 76
Sanduq al-Turki 55, 62
Sav-Tekin 24, 77–81
Scenes of the Passion of Christ **71**
settlement of foreign peoples 5, 6
Shaddadids 8, 35
Shi'a Islam 8
siege of Edessa 35–36
soldier in Byzantine wall painting **59**
steppe society and Turkish nomads 11
stradioti (light cavalry) 26
stucco wall decoration, 11th century **47**
Sunni Islam 8, 92
Süphan Dağ (mountain) **54**, 55, **59**, **81**
supplies for Byzantine army 50
Surb Bartolomeos (Armenian monastery) **91**
Syria, invasion of 32–38, **36–37**
Syriac church 6, 10
system of authority in Saljuq army 27–8

Taht-i Sulayman fortress **38**
Tarchaniotes, Joseph 51, 55, 56
territorial gains of Saljuqs 88–89
Theodosiopolis (Erzurum) 26
thughur (frontier provinces) 8
tourism today in battlefield region 93
training of soldiers 39
treasure and booty in Manzikert 89
treaty between Alp Arslan and Emperor Romanos IV 88
Turkish chieftain **15**
Turkish counter-attack at battle of Manzikert **84–85**
Turkish horse archer **87**
Türkmen control of Anatolia 92
Türkmen settlement in Azarbayjan 14
Tuteh Mosque, Aleppo 35

wall painting, 10–11th century **29**

The Making of GEORGE A. ROMERO'S DAY OF THE DEAD

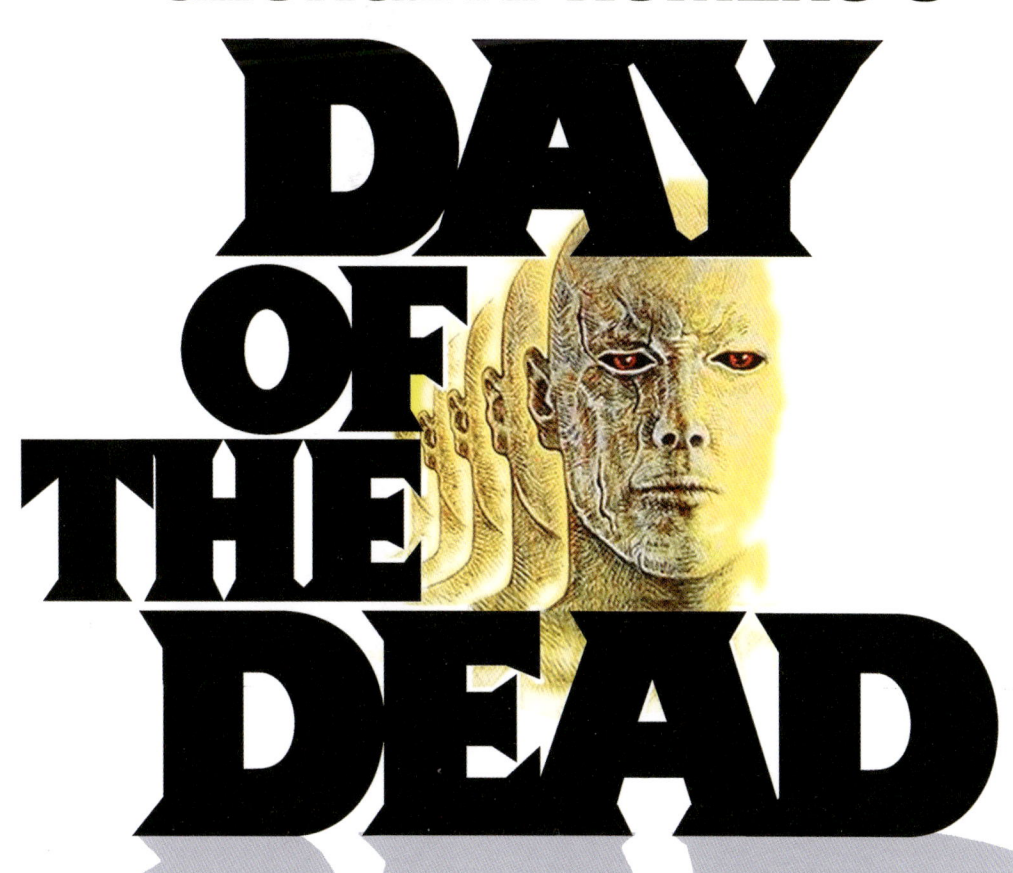

The Making of
GEORGE A. ROMERO'S
DAY
OF
THE
DEAD

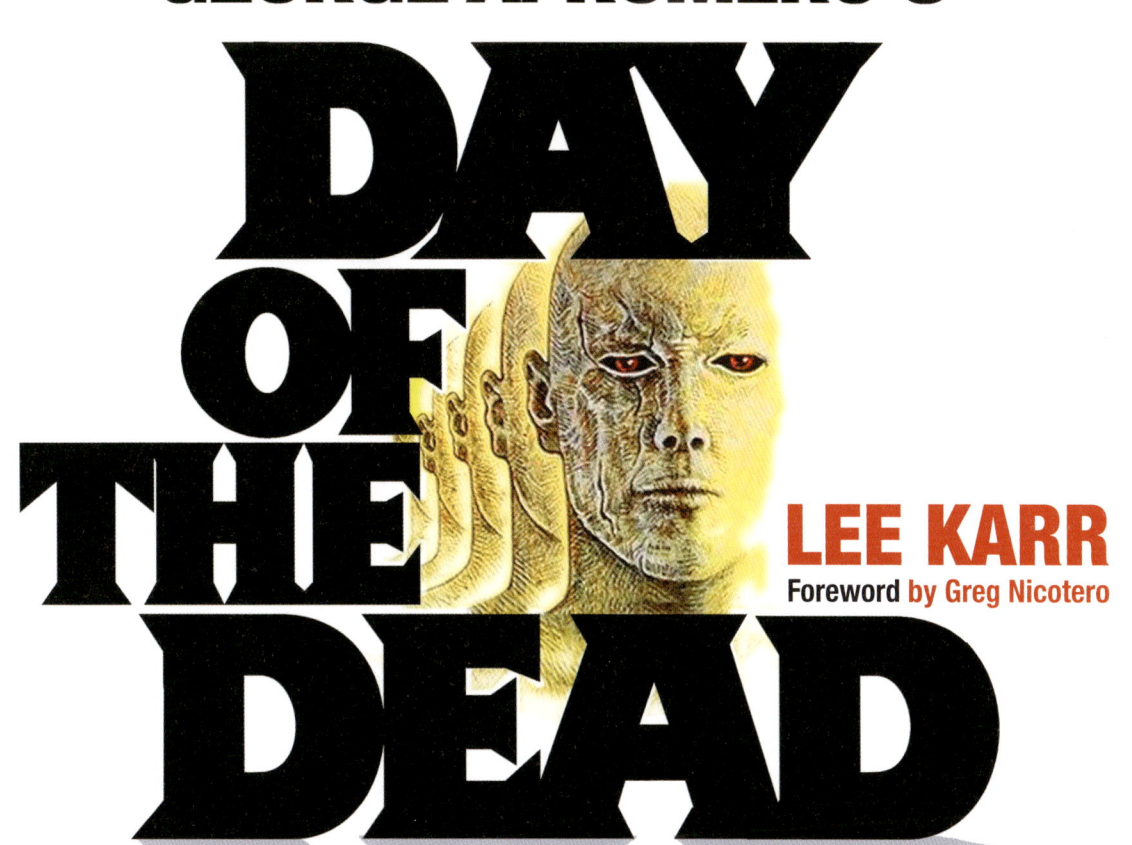

LEE KARR
Foreword by Greg Nicotero

Plexus, London

All rights reserved including the right of
reproduction in whole or in part in any form
Copyright © 2014 by Lee Karr
Published by Plexus Publishing Limited
The Studio, Hillgate Place
18-20 Balham Hill
London SW12 9ER

British Library Cataloguing in Publication Data
A catalogue record for this book is available from
the British Library

ISBN-13: 978-0-85965-518-7

Book design by Coco Wake-Porter
Cover design by Christian Stavrakis
Front and back cover: *Day of the Dead* poster,
artwork and logo title © Taurus Entertainment.
Back cover photo copyright © 1985 by Dead Films, Inc.
Printed in Great Britain by Bell & Bain Ltd, Glasgow.

This book is sold subject to the condition that it
shall not, by way of trade or otherwise, be lent,
resold, hired out or otherwise circulated without the
publisher's prior consent in any form of binding or
cover other than that in which it is published and
without a similar condition including this condition
being imposed on the subsequent purchaser.

Contents

Foreword by Greg Nicotero — 6

Preface — 8

Chapter 1 The Dawn of a New Day — 12

Chapter 2 The Day is Coming — 24

    Section A: Zombies Are Us — 24

    Section B: Laurel-Day, Inc. — 53

Chapter 3 One Day at a Time — 78

Chapter 4 At the End of the Day — 194

Chapter 5 The Light of Day — 204

Chapter 6 Reflecting on the Day — 216

Acknowledgements — 222

In Memoriam — 224

Foreword by Greg Nicotero

July 1984

I'm flying down McKnight Road in Pittsburgh hitting about 70 miles per hour. My heart is racing. I am exhilarated. The cop behind me doesn't seem as thrilled as I am, but what he doesn't know is that I just got hired on *DAY OF THE DEAD*, for fuck's sake! An hour before, I had met George and Christine Romero for lunch and these words came out: "We just got a green light on *Day of the Dead* . . . do you want a job?"

Now, we need a bit of history here. The roads between zombies and I intersected in very unique and strange ways in my youth. My uncle, Sam Nicotero, an actor, writer, and local disc jockey in the 1970s, wrote one of the first mainstream articles about George in *Cinefantastique*. He and George knew each other then – he actually had a supporting role in *The Crazies*. I grew up about twenty minutes from the Evans City Cemetery, where *Night of the Living Dead* was filmed, and I was in high school in 1977 when a friend mentioned that his dad worked at the Monroeville Mall and they were shooting a movie there. "Do you want to go visit?"

It goes on and on from there. In Pittsburgh, George's contributions to the horror genre and, more specifically, zombies were nearly as popular as Iron City Beer, Primanti's, and the Steelers. Thank God for Bill Cardille and *Chiller Theatre*: it was the one thing I anxiously awaited every Saturday, the chance to watch horror double features from 11:30pm until 3:00am. Cardille, a local weatherman, also played himself in *Night of the Living Dead* (see, I told you everywhere you looked it was zombies). It was on this program that I first saw an interview with George televised. Our worlds collided with full force in an Italian Restaurant in Rome during August of 1976. While on vacation with my family, I noticed a tall, lean, bearded man a few tables over and knew INSTANTLY that it was "*The George Romero*". What are the chances of that? Of course, my younger brother and I were in awe, and once we were done not eating ('cause we were geeking out – even though I don't think that term had been invented yet) we timed our departure with theirs.

"Hey, are you George Romero?" my brother Brian asked. He turned and smiled. "Yes!"

I stepped in, my hand outstretched. "My name is Greg Nicotero . . . I believe you know my uncle?" That was my opening line – of course, at thirteen that was pretty good.

He lit up, smiled and shook my hand. We chatted for a moment and then he said, "Come visit the office when you get back to 'the 'burgh'." Low and behold, on returning to the States I was even more enthralled with this man, and went to his office on Fort Pitt Boulevard several times to say hello, walk through the offices and get a taste of "Hollywood".

Flash forward to to 1981. I had recently graduated from high school and was about to leave for college. George was prepping *Creepshow*, and I'd gone to visit while they were building the sets for "The Crate" in a warehouse, not seven miles from the mall. At this point, George and I had been trading VHS tapes – we had quite a collection and I'd offered to make him copies of any rare films he did not have. On one of my visits, I found myself on the stage, exploring the basement set where "Fluffy" was soon to be found, when I stumbled upon Tom Savini. He and his assistant, Darryl Ferrucci, were getting ready to meet Adrienne Barbeau, who had just arrived from LA, but in the midst of his prep Tom stopped, smiled, and introduced himself. Within an instant, a barrage of people entered, including George, Adrienne and a few other crew people. I graciously bowed out, vowing to return and visit. This is where it all changed. I had loved creature stuff – *Planet of the Apes, The Exorcist*, anything Harryhausen or Jack Pierce related – but becoming friends with Tom only solidified my interest in make-up. Granted, in Pittsburgh back then, the available filmmaking opportunities were pretty much only with this group of people, but I honestly never imagined that this hobby, this interest, would ever have taken me where it has.

Cut back to July and I am getting a speeding ticket. Oh well, what do I care? I just got hired on *DAY OF THE DEAD*! By the time I got home, I called Tom and very excitedly informed him that I'd just been hired and would like to be his assistant. One thing I had learned in my dealings with George and Tom was that Tom's enthusiasm and passion for what he did was unparalleled, and to have a chance to work with him, handling the day-to-day tasks of wrangling résumés, ordering supplies and coordinating for him would allow me to get hands-on training, and leave Tom free to focus on realizing the gags at hand. This proved to be a perfect fit, and not only carved out a place for us to collaborate on many more projects, but allowed me to develop the skills that led me from Pittsburgh to New York then LA in a year's time.

Day of the Dead has always marked the most creative period of my life. The transition to filmmaking, the relationships I cultivated with people who would forever change my life, and the ability to express my creative instincts changed me to the core. I wanted

FOREWORD BY GREG NICOTERO

to remember every moment, every nuance as it happened. I photographed nearly every aspect of the production, documented the prep and shoot with Tom's video camera, and even wrote an outline immediately after wrap with the hopes of crafting a "Making of" book. Sadly, at the time the book was deemed "competition" for Paul Gagne's book about George and his films, *The Zombies That Ate Pittsburgh*. But lo and behold, so much of what I chronicled is represented here, in the dedicated hands of Lee Karr.

**Gregory Nicotero,
From the set of *The Walking Dead*,
Spring 2013**

Since beginning his career on *Day of the Dead*, Greg Nicotero has gone on to co-found one of the most successful and prolific make-up effects studios in the business: the prestigious KNB EFX Group. To date, his incredible efforts have won him four Emmy Awards, two Saturn Awards and a BAFTA award. Besides handling the makeup effects and zombies on *The Walking Dead*, Nicotero has become an executive producer and accomplished director on the popular television show.

Right: Greg Nicotero inside the "whirlybird" helicopter on Sanibel Island, December 1984. (Courtesy of Taso Stavrakis.)
Below: Greg Nicotero with zombie friend on the Georgia set of season four of *The Walking Dead*. (Courtesy of AMC Network Entertainment LLC.)

Preface

Though I didn't know it at the time, in 1985 my life changed forever. While watching one of my favorite TV shows, *Late Night with David Letterman*, I caught a demonstration by a man named Tom Savini, showcasing how gory make-up effects were created for horror films. Before this I was afraid to watch anything with blood in it, and would never watch horror films – never! I was basically a wuss. But Savini changed all of that with one television guest appearance.

That evening Savini was promoting the newest zombie film from George A. Romero, *Day of the Dead*. Somehow, I was aware of what these types of films were about. I knew that they showed explicit gore and people being eaten. How I knew that, I can't quite remember. I think I'd figured it out from perusing video-store shelves, and assumed that they were definitely not for me. I mean, I cringed when Elliott cut his finger on a saw blade in Steven Spielberg's *E.T.*! Seeing graphic scenes of blood and guts? No way.

Well, after Savini's entertaining demonstration for Letterman my tune changed completely. I went to Waldenbooks in the Oglethorpe Mall in Savannah, Georgia, my hometown, and I looked through the various magazines on the rack until I discovered the latest issue of *Fangoria* magazine. Its cover read "*Day of the Dead* – Tom Savini's Zombie FX". That was it for me. I must have read that issue a million times, over and over again. I was totally fascinated by this film. I was hooked.

Just a couple of months later, on Halloween night to be exact, I had the opportunity to see *Day of the Dead* in the theater during its initial run. That night I went with my cousin, Jacquie, to see the film at the Abercorn Cinemas and, as we were standing in the lobby, the previous screening's audience exited the auditorium. I'll never forget one young teenage girl laughing about how disgusting and gross the movie was. I looked at Jacquie and thought: This is going to be awesome! And awesome it was. It did not disappoint at all. It was everything I'd hoped it would be, and then some.

After that I returned at least twice more to watch the film. Once, I think, by myself, which is funny since the box-office attendants never asked how old I was. The film contained scenes of violence, which may be considered shocking, and no one under seventeen was supposed to be admitted – never mind that I was fourteen! But thank goodness no one cared to ask. I had my money and that's all that mattered.

The other time was with my uncle, Kinnon. As we got to the end of the film and the gore montage began,

Top: Me, with my beloved grandmother, Grace, sporting my Bub t-shirt. Christmas Day 1986. **Middle:** The evening that would lead to me writing this book: cousin Jacquie (dressed as Madonna) and I on Halloween 1985, before heading out to the cinema to see *Day of the Dead*. **Bottom:** Me with stars, and good friends, Lori Cardille and John Amplas inside the Wampum Mine. January 2011. (Photos courtesy of Kay and Lee Karr.)

Above: Me with George Romero and his puppet mini-me in 2009. I'd just interviewed him at his Toronto home for Home Page of the Dead. (Courtesy of Lee Karr.)

Kinnon looked over at me and said, "Jesus Christ, Lee! What the hell did you take me to see?" What do you mean? I thought. Isn't this awesome? This is great!

A little over half a year later, in May 1986, the film was released on home video and I rented it over and over, mainly from my favorite video store, Turtle's Records & Tapes. I believe I may have even hooked up my two VCRs and dubbed a copy. I bought the soundtrack album, got a reproduction poster of the one sheet, and wore out a t-shirt featuring Bub saluting with the film's logo at the bottom. Around the same time, Tom Savini's *Scream Greats* video was released, and it featured loads of behind-the-scenes footage from the film. Again, I devoured this repeatedly.

During this period I was in the NJROTC (Navy Junior Reserve Officers Training Corps) in high school, so, with my military enthusiasm at its zenith, I even got a pair of dog tags made – in my mind, just like the kind Captain Rhodes wore in the film. Later that year, my Mom gave me a birthday cake decorated with Bub's face and the film's logo. It was safe to say that *Day of the Dead* was one of my favorite movies.

Flash forward to the late 1990s, and I made my first ever trip to a *Day of the Dead* filming location when I visited Fort Myers, Florida. Exploring all of the downtown area, checking out sites like the Edison Theater and the First National Bank, I had a great time.

A couple of years later, I made my first trek to visit the Wampum Mine, where most of the film took place. I called ahead of time informing the manager that I wanted to check out the facility and take photos because a movie had been shot there back in the mid-1980s. When I arrived, somehow the story had morphed, and they thought I was a movie scout who wanted to take photos for a possible upcoming film. I informed the incredibly nice lady who greeted me, Therese McShea, that there was a misunderstanding: I wasn't a movie scout, and if it was a problem I would leave. Instead, she told me no problem and took me on a tour anyway! My photos of that visit ended up being featured on Robert Telleria's *Day of the Dead* website *Dr. Logan*, which at the time was a tremendous thrill.

One other interesting tidbit about that visit involves an article that appeared later that year (2000) in the *New Castle News* in New Castle, PA. It was about Lori Cardille returning to visit the mine after fifteen years, and mentions me – though not by name – as a man from Savannah, Georgia who traveled to the mine posing as a movie scout. It just goes to show that you can't believe everything you read.

Above: With surgeon zombie Greg Nicotero on the Toronto set of *Diary of the Dead* in 2006. Note how Greg stays in character for the photo! (Courtesy of Greg Nicotero.)

Later on I would make return visits to Fort Myers and Sanibel, as well as the Wampum Mine. I would also make several journeys to the former Nike Missile Site to explore the elevator bay that was used in the film. Climbing under and jumping over fences, while risking getting caught for trespassing, just seemed like a risk worth taking. You know?

In 2003 Anchor Bay Entertainment released a special edition DVD of the film and, thanks to Michael Felsher, who was producing the DVD release, I had the opportunity to contribute photographs to it from the collection of Bill and Kathy Love, who were zombie extras in the opening scenes in downtown Fort Myers. Seeing my name listed alongside someone like Greg Nicotero in the thank you section of the DVD was, once again, a tremendous thrill.

Thanks to Norman England, a close friend who works in Japan, just recently I was able to help contribute to a Japanese blu-ray release of *Day of the Dead* from Nikkatsu, by arranging for Gary Klahr to write a brief essay about working on the film.

Over the years, and mainly after moving to Pittsburgh, I was fortunate enough to form friendships and relationships with a lot of the people who worked on the film, even venturing into the horror convention guest-booking business, in a part-time capacity. Lori Cardille, Terry Alexander, John Amplas, Phillip Kellams, Joe Pilato, Gary Klahr, Tim DiLeo, Taso Stavrakis, Michael Gornick, John Vulich, Mark Tierno, Debra Gordon, Barbara Russell, Eileen Sieff, and Jeff Monahan are some of the people that I've been lucky enough to work with on the convention scene.

I've gotten to know George Romero personally, even spending time in his Toronto home and chatting with him on the sets of his newer Canadian zombie features.

Going with Tom Savini and some close friends of mine to see Hal Holbrook perform *Mark Twain Tonight* and then – thanks to Tom – getting the opportunity to meet Mr. Holbrook backstage is a wonderful memory for me.

Greg Nicotero befriended me like I was someone he had known for years. Spending time in his LA home, visiting his company KNB EFX, being able to be a zombie extra in *Land of the Dead*, hanging out with Quentin Tarantino, Robert Rodriguez, Simon

PREFACE

Above: Fan's dream-come-true: my zombie cameo in *Land of the Dead*. My bloody makeup – courtesy of Greg Nicotero – was so graphic that my face (far-right) had to be airbrushed clean for this publicity still.
(© 2005 Universal Studios.)

Pegg, Edgar Wright, and Frank Darabont – all of these things were made possible for me by Greg.

My friendship with Michael Gornick has been amazing. Getting to spend my first ever trip to the Pittsburgh Steelers training camp with Mike was a blast. Having the opportunity to drive to conventions with him, pick his brain and listen to his incredible stories about working with George Romero and Richard Rubinstein, and those years at Laurel, their production company, are priceless to me.

Being able to have dinner with Lori Cardille and her husband Jim and then going to a movie together. These things would have seemed absurd to me when I first watched the film and became fascinated by it. But you never know where life will take you, or the friendships you'll make along the way. I could write a book solely about the memories and experiences I've had knowing all of these wonderful people.

In early 2010 I got the genius idea – and I use the word *genius* in the most sarcastic way possible – to write a book about the making of this film *Day of the Dead*. After all these years, there had never been one published, and I figured that if I wanted to see it happen, then I was going to have to make it happen myself. I set off on my journey by tracking down as many people as I could from the film and interviewing them – easily over 100 interviewees. With the help of Greg Nicotero, I had at my disposal a small filing cabinet's worth of memos, files, and zombie sign-in sheets to aid me in this task.

During the journey this book has taken me on, I've dealt with a cancer diagnosis and surgery, the death of my beloved uncles Kinnon and Tollie, the death of my beloved cat, George, who earned his namesake due to my George Romero fandom, and the wrath of one my idols – Tom Savini. Despite all of this, I've kept my nose to the grindstone and attempted to write a book that I, myself, as a fan, would want to read about the making of this film. I hope that you, the reader, will enjoy this book and hopefully learn something that you didn't know about *Day of the Dead*'s creation.

Lee Karr
Pittsburgh, PA

Above: Back page of the 1978 official *Dawn of the Dead* poster book, which briefly mentions the then scheduled 1988 release date of *Day of the Dead*. (Originally published by MW Communications. © 1978 The MKR Group, Inc.)

Chapter 1 The Dawn of a New Day

In 1968, George A. Romero began a three-film trilogy tracing the growth of a "zombie" society. The first film was the now classic Night of the Living Dead. Dawn of the Dead *(in 'Living' color) is his long-awaited second film. The last film,* Day of the Dead, *should hit the screens about 1988.*

A former Pittsburgh publishing company, MW Communications, printed those words on the back page of the official *Dawn of the Dead* poster book in 1978. The grand vision Romero had for his trilogy's conclusion was just a germ of an idea back when he created the original *Night of the Living Dead* in the late 1960s. His original story, referred to as *Anubis*, was divided into three parts. The first act would introduce the oncoming of a new society, a zombie society; however, the humans would still be in control. The second act would take place at a point when the balance is equal, with no one side gaining an edge. The third act of his story, which was nothing more than a brief paragraph then, featured gun-toting zombies chasing a lone surviving human who they eventually shoot and kill. Years later, the proposed release date on the *Dawn of the Dead* poster book was just the first of many changes in store for George A. Romero and the third act of his zombie parable, *Day of the Dead*.

To fully understand the story of how *Day of the Dead* ended up becoming the film it is, you have to go back to 1978, and the deal that Romero's producer Richard P. Rubinstein entered with the Hassanein family of United Film Distribution Company (UFDC). The small distribution house was run by United Artists Theater mogul Salah Hassanein and his son, Richard Hassanein. The little distributor had made a name for itself a year earlier, in 1977, by releasing the John Landis comedy *The Kentucky Fried Movie*.

Before getting too far into the story of the Hassaneins, though, you need to backtrack just a little bit further, to the partnership that George Romero formed with Richard Rubinstein.

In 1973, Richard Rubinstein met George Romero for an article he was writing about the director for *Filmmakers' Newsletter*, which would coincide with the release of Romero's *The Crazies*. Interestingly enough, Rubinstein had turned down an opportunity to work on *The Crazies* when famed film distributor Irvin Shapiro, who also dealt with Romero, offered him a job on the production. Both men were native New Yorkers – Romero from the Parkchester neighborhood of the Bronx, Rubinstein from Brooklyn – and got along well during the interview. This meeting spawned a friendship that would eventually lead to a successful twelve-year business partnership between the two men. Rubinstein had attended Columbia University in New York, where he received his MBA, after getting his undergraduate degree from the American University in Washington, DC. Rubinstein helped form The Laurel Group with Romero, and together they would go on to produce a series of sports documentaries called *The Winners*, which led to their first feature, *Martin*, which would eventually lead to *Dawn of the Dead*. Rubinstein proved himself to be a shrewd businessman; helping to lead Romero out of a dark financial period, when going bankrupt had been a strong possibility for the filmmaker. (Romero's apparent lack of business sense will be explored later, when producer David Ball enters the story.)

Truly the embodiment of the American dream, Salah M. Hassanein came to the United States from Egypt as a young man in 1945. He served in the US military and after his service started work as an usher for the Skouras Theaters Corporation. He worked his way up the ladder to become the corporation's president by the early 1960s. Eventually he would become the executive vice president of United Artists Communications and president of United Artists Eastern Theaters. "I mean, nothing extraordinary," says the modest elder Hassanein. He made his home on Hoffstot Lane overlooking the Long Island Sound, which was featured in F. Scott Fitzgerald's classic novel *The Great Gatsby*. During this period he would form United Film Distribution Company and hand over the controls to his son, Richard Hassanein. In 1978, during a fateful trip to the MIFED (Mouvement International des Femmes Démocrates) film market in Milan, Italy, Richard Hassanein would cross paths with Rubinstein and Romero. It turned out to be a prosperous encounter for both parties.

"We acquired *Dawn of the Dead* for distribution for North America," says Richard Hassanein. "I saw that for the first time at MIFED in Milan – *Dawn of the Dead* – and that was my introduction to Romero and Rubinstein. And then after our relationship developed we entered into a three-picture deal.

"The way I remember the deal being structured," he continues, "we didn't have any designated projects except for *Day of the Dead*." The relationship with UFDC would bring great financial success for Romero and Rubinstein's company The Laurel Group – later to become a public company named Laurel Entertainment – but at the same time it would significantly alter the fate of *Day of the Dead*.

Above: The May 4, 1983 advertisement in *Variety* magazine for future Laurel Entertainment productions, including early poster art for the film.

Until that eventful meeting with Richard Hassanein in Milan, Romero and Rubinstein had struggled to find a distributor for *Dawn of the Dead*. Their biggest issue was the graphic violence and "Grand Guignol" in the film, which they refused to cut to secure an R rating with the Motion Picture Association of America (MPAA). If they were willing to cut some of the blood and guts from the picture, both Warner Bros. and Sam Arkoff's American International Pictures would be interested in distributing the film. The idea of going out with an R rating and a tamer film was, however, simply unacceptable to Romero. Eventually the film would end up with the Hassaneins at UFDC, who agreed to distribute the film without an MPAA rating. "I called New York [UFDC offices], I said, 'I want to buy a picture, but it doesn't have a rating,' and they said, 'We're going to have to discuss that a little more,'" recalls Richard Hassanein. "So I told George and Richard I needed to have a screening for my executives in New York and we would give him the decision whether we would go with the picture in the version it was in or not. If not, then he was free to go with Sam Arkoff or anyone else. When I screened it for my executives they all felt that the film that had to be released was the version that George wanted, otherwise the fans would have felt ripped off. And it was really kind of a no-brainer."

Dawn of the Dead would go on to perform extremely well at the box office in 1979, and as a result of its performance UFDC offered a three-picture deal to The Laurel Group. An important condition of the deal was that one of the films produced would have to be the final part of Romero's zombie trilogy, *Day of the Dead*, and it would also have to be completed by 1985. "The three pictures ended up being *Knightriders*, *Creepshow*, and *Day of the Dead*," recalls Richard Hassanein. "The deal was struck maybe about a year after the release of the picture, of *Dawn of the Dead*. So there were two pictures unnamed, but it was a three-picture deal and *Day of the Dead* was specified."

According to the United States Copyright Office, a copyright for a third Romero zombie film was secured when The Laurel Group registered a five-page synopsis for *Day of the Dead* on December 13, 1979. After the release of *Creepshow*, while on vacation in California, Romero would begin the process of writing the first draft of his now legendary original script for *Day of the Dead*. On December 28, 1982, a 216-page first draft of the *Day of the Dead* screenplay was registered for copyright by Laurel Entertainment under the claim of "New Matter: Screenplay Version". Just a little over two weeks later, on January 13, 1983, another copyright was registered for a 145-page screenplay entitled *Old Soldiers Never Die, Satan Sends Them Back!: Day of the Dead* by Laurel Entertainment, this time under the claim of "New Matter: Revisions & Additions". "I was looking for something like the thing in *Dawn*, you know, 'When there's no more room in hell,' so I just came up with a line," recalls Romero on the genesis of that peculiar title.

On Saturday, February 25, 1978, George Romero was a guest of *Pittsburgh Post-Gazette* film critic, George Anderson, on channel 53 WPGH-TV for a screening of *Night of the Living Dead*. It was the first time that the film had ever been shown on local Pittsburgh television and, following the feature presentation, Romero was interviewed by Anderson about the film. It was a remarkable evening. Not only did Romero get to see his classic debut film presented on Pittsburgh television for the very first time, it also provided him with an opportunity to show unedited clips from his just completed sequel, *Dawn of the Dead*. It was the first time fans laid eyes on footage from the film, most of which was very raw.

During the interview with Anderson, Romero briefly mentioned the third zombie film while discussing *Dawn of the Dead* and gave a hint as to where the series would go. "The zombies are a little more sympathetic. We see them organizing slightly now and if there's ever a third film that's what it will be about," said Romero to Anderson. "Dario Argento, who we're co-producing this film with, an Italian director, said that the third one

THE DAWN OF A NEW DAY

has to be 'Zombies in the White House'. And maybe that's what it will be, I don't know [smiles]."

Over a year later, while promoting the release of *Dawn of the Dead*, Romero was interviewed by Kevin Thomas in the Friday, June 22, 1979 edition of the *Los Angeles Times*. At one point during the interview, the topic of film offers was brought up and Romero delivered a humorous statement about the conclusion to his zombie trilogy. "Everyone wants to do the third part of the Living Dead Trilogy, but I don't want to do that right now," said Romero. "All I have is a sketch for it. I'm threatening to do a 'Zombies at Home', a kind of 'My Three Sons', non-violent and totally boring."

The original script for *Day of the Dead* ended up

Right: Tom Savini with United Film Distribution Company president, Richard Hassanein. **Below:** George Romero, unknown female guest, UFDC president Richard Hassanein, and actress Cynthia Adler at a New York City party celebrating *Knightriders* in 1981. (Photos courtesy of Richard Hassanein.)

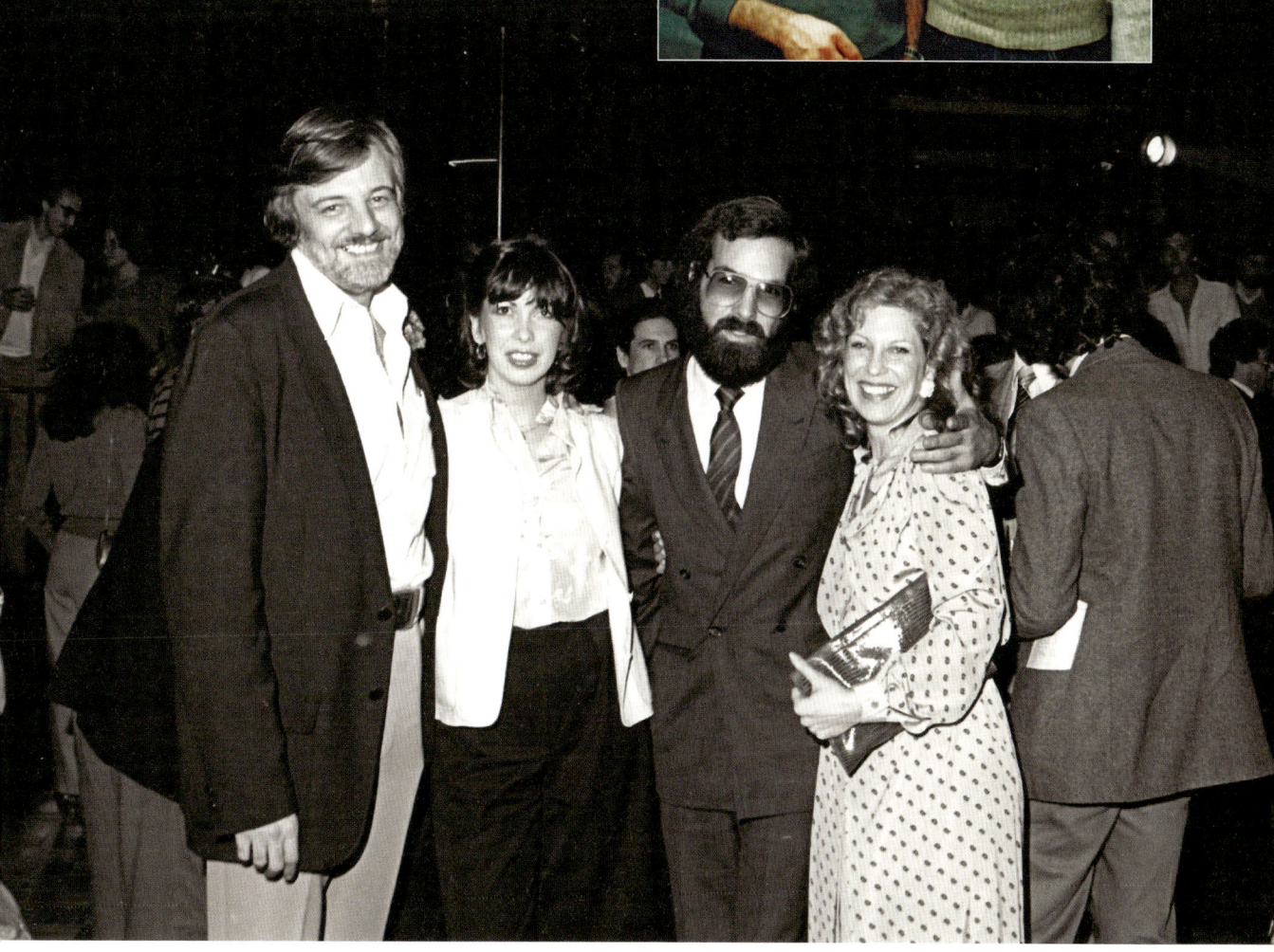

15

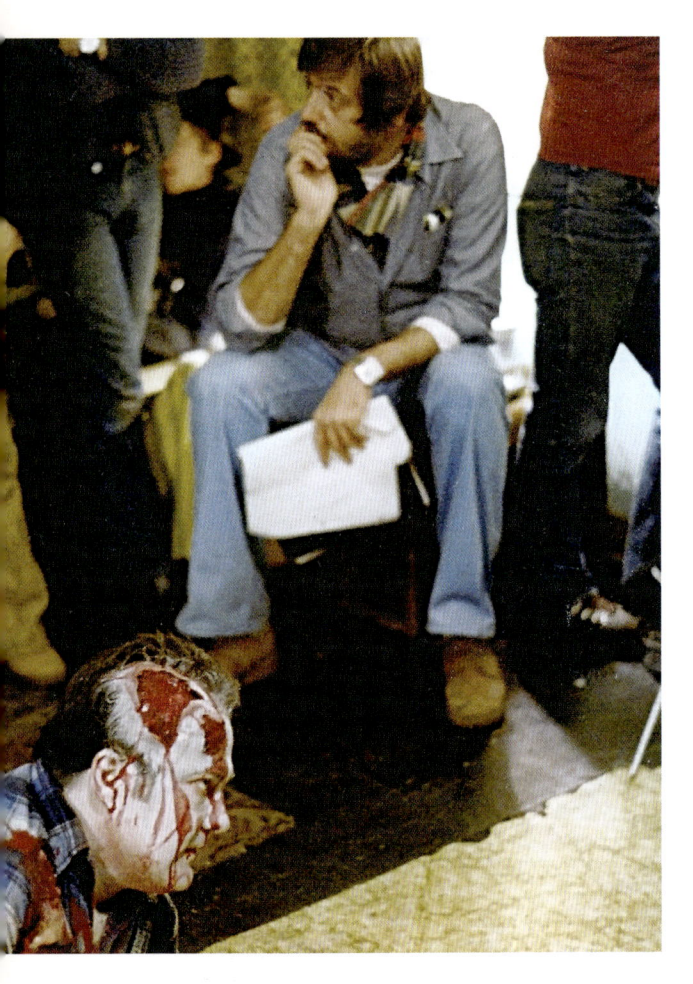

Above: George Romero directing zombie extra, Gary Peabody, on the Pittsburgh set of *Dawn of the Dead*, 1977. (Courtesy of Tony Buba.)

being anything but boring. It was a massive, sprawling, action-adventure film – with zombies! Some of the original characters would survive and end up in the revamped filmed version, while others would be combined together into one character, or discarded completely. The following plot summary is from the 155-page second version of Romero's first draft.

Romero's original unfilmed storyline opens in a similar way to the filmed version. We're presented with a desolate downtown Fort Myers, Florida, and descriptions of empty, abandoned buildings. There are many more alligators in this version of the opening. The gators scurry through the streets and alleyways in fear of the undead, who now dominate the dead city. The jawless zombie that signals the actual film's opening title is also included in this script. Romero wonderfully describes a corpse hanging from a noose on top of a tall building, with a sign on his chest that reads: "Take me, Lord. I love you." Suddenly it comes crashing down after the rope breaks, and the bones shatter on the ground below. The sign the poor suicide victim had on his chest blows away on the wind toward the harbor.

This leads us into a spectacular and harrowing action sequence filled with gun battles, explosions, and plenty of zombie carnage that spans over 20 pages of the script, involving two different groups of guerilla fighters battling on a marina boat dock. We are introduced to some familiar names during this opening, including Sarah and Miguel. Unlike the filmed version, though, Miguel is not a soldier and Sarah is not a scientist – they are rebel fighters. Most of the guerillas are killed in this opening spectacle, except for Sarah, Miguel, and another unnamed character referred to as Man #2 (later, in a more tightly-scripted version of this same storyline, he would be called Chico). During the battle Miguel is bitten by a zombie and, as she does in the filmed version, Sarah quickly amputates his arm with a machete in an attempt to save his life. Miguel, who is already on the brink of insanity, is now pushed even further over the edge.

Sarah, the unnamed man, and Miguel eventually flee in their boat to a nearby island. As they make their way across the swampy wetlands they encounter alligators and rattlesnakes. Miguel eventually succumbs to the heat and delirium and passes out, so Sarah and the other man head out to explore the nearby surroundings. As they explore they are stunned to discover a platoon of military soldiers on a giant elevator platform that rises from a large underground compound. The script offers its first glimpse of Captain Rhodes – described by Romero as a super-villain of the first order – who is busy training a group of zombies wearing red vests, nicknamed "Red Coats", who have been taught to use weapons. Eventually it becomes clear that there are different ranks of these soldier zombies, with "Blue Coats" and "White Coats" as well. A strange siren noise rings out and zombies appear from the jungle! Rhodes feeds the zombies human meat from refrigerated cartons as a way to placate them. While watching the macabre scene unfold, Sarah and the man with her are attacked by zombies coming out of the jungle and forced to open fire in order to save their lives. Rhodes hears the firing and sends his soldiers out to investigate. Another fire fight breaks out, this time between Sarah, the man, and Rhodes' soldiers.

Suddenly Miguel, who has essentially gone mad by this point, appears out of nowhere, wildly firing his weapon. He is eventually shot and killed by Captain Rhodes' group of special zombie commandos. During the fight, the unnamed man is shot and taken prisoner by Rhodes, while Sarah escapes into the jungle. He's strung up from a tree and tortured by Rhodes until a subordinate soldier, Toby Tyler, kills him out of mercy.

Moments before this happens we get a brief glimpse into the sadistic mind of Rhodes, as he amuses himself by placing a grenade inside the mouth of a zombie and watches it struggle until the grenade goes off, killing the zombie and several others nearby. The shot that kills the tortured man sends Rhodes into a rage. He already has it in for Toby, and this action infuriates the captain even further.

Meanwhile, Sarah is struggling to make her way through the jungle. She has an encounter with a zombie near a stream that is described brilliantly by Romero. The zombie is standing in the marsh, with vultures at its feet picking bloody holes into its rotten flesh. Sarah flees and runs into a man named John and his friend, Bill McDermott, two more names that will ring a bell for fans. In this first version, however, John is not a helicopter pilot, but a spiritual leader, and Bill is a repair man rather than a radio communications guy. Two more characters, a deaf mute named Spider and a young man named Mapmaker, are also with them. John and Bill inform Sarah that she is on Gasparilla's Island, named after the legendary pirate. However, it's the former Governor of Florida, Henry Dickerson, who now uses that moniker and controls the island. After a couple of harrowing encounters with zombies and alligators, in which some zombies are killed, the group takes off together through the jungle. The zombies that are killed and left behind will come back into play later on, however.

Back in the underground compound, we observe classes of zombies being "trained" by videos that instruct them who to shoot, based on what color of vest they wear (orange is a safe color for humans). Captain Rhodes then enters a special unit in the compound, which houses the elite "Red Coats": zombies named Tonto, Bluto, Fatso, Grumpy, Samson, and one very familiar name . . . Bub. Rhodes is feeding the zombies severed human heads – one of which belonged to the tortured prisoner from earlier – when he is confronted by two scientists named Mary Henried and Julie Grant. (The characters of scientist Mary Henried and rebel fighter Sarah would eventually be combined into one character, Sarah, for the revamped filmed version.) Mary is furious with Rhodes for feeding the zombies human flesh because the scientists have been trying to wean the zombies onto alligator meat. Julie is shocked to learn what Rhodes is doing and runs off upset, especially at Mary for being aware that it was being done, even though Mary did not condone these actions. During the fight we also learn that Mary and Rhodes once had a brief affair.

After her confrontation with Rhodes, Mary heads back to her living quarters, when she runs into Toby Tyler. It becomes apparent that Mary and Toby are lovers, which explains why Rhodes has it in for Toby. During their talk, Rhodes sends soldiers to arrest Toby for the shooting of the tortured prisoner. He is taken away and banished to a place known as Stalag 17.

Stalag 17 introduces the degenerated world spawned by the zombie plague, which is graphically – and at times hilariously – described by Romero. People defecating in the streets, open drug abuse, prostitution, and perverted sex. John, Bill, Mapmaker, Spider, and Sarah make their way to the hospital in Stalag 17. It's here that Dr. Logan is introduced, as he saws the head off a corpse. It transpires that John, Bill, Mapmaker and Spider are allies with Dr. Logan. Sarah is introduced to the circle of rebel friends, including some more characters, one by the name of Diesel. After their meeting, John and Bill escort Sarah to her new home in Stalag 17, nicknamed "The Ritz" – a large room filled with cots and many suffering people.

The next morning Sarah is awakened by the sound of Rhodes' voice outside in the street. He has discovered the bodies of the zombies that Sarah and John's group killed the night before. He wants to know who is responsible, and how the perpetrators were able to get outside of the complex to begin with. As proof that he means business, he executes three people in the street and promises to return the next day to do the same unless the ones responsible step forward.

The script cuts back to inside the complex and observes the scientists working with the "Red Coat" zombies some more. Bub demonstrates his skill in handling a weapon and Mary's bond with the trained zombies becomes evident.

A glimpse of Ted Fisher is then offered, as he attempts to get zombies to eat alligator meat – with forks! Mary spies Julie Grant and attempts to talk to her, but Julie storms off, wanting nothing to do with Mary.

In another section of the compound, in the council chamber room, Gasparilla is finally introduced. A kangaroo court is taking place, and the former Governor of Florida demonstrates his megalomania as he decides the fate of a prisoner on trial. A second trial follows – this time Toby Tyler is being tried for shooting the tortured prisoner, with Captain Rhodes acting as prosecutor. Tyler is eventually sentenced to live temporarily in Stalag 17 for several months. Afterwards, Gasparilla insists on Mary attending a private party in his quarters. The scene is described hysterically by Romero, as party-goers dine on *hors d'oeuvres* and drink wine, all while watching a cage fight between two zombies battling for a scrap of human meat. The decadence continues as Gasparilla orders the females to strip and work out, using his gym equipment, to satisfy his bizarre fetish. Mary is disgusted by the display, and is all but held captive for the night by the fat and boorish general.

The following day Rhodes returns to Stalag 17, this

time entering "The Ritz", and terrorizes the residents again by executing several more people. John informs Sarah that Rhodes is just looking for an excuse to kill people to feed them to the trained zombies. Overhearing this conversation, Toby introduces himself to John and tells him that he has a plan to escape the island.

Later that day, Toby meets up with John and the other rebels at the hospital in Stalag 17 to organize some of the supplies that Toby's friend, Tricks, has smuggled out to him via Red Cross crates. Dr. Logan prepares vials of nitroglycerine that will be used by the rebels in a plan to destroy the powder magazine in the compound, which would cause a catastrophic explosion, nearly destroying the island altogether. Dr. Logan has clearly gone insane. John, Sarah, Mapmaker and Toby leave to formulate a plan to do some damage inside the cave – but nothing catastrophic – and then get back to the boat that Sarah arrived on a few days before so they can all leave together. They'll get a little help in executing their plan from Datura Metel, a toxic flower that grows on the island. When they return they discover that Dr. Logan has left with some of the other rebels – including Spider, under whose skin Dr. Logan has implanted the vials of nitroglycerine. They are headed for the compound to accomplish their mission of destroying the island. Along the way, Dr. Logan is attacked by a zombie – with a metal hook for a hand! Dr. Logan's group manages to escape, however, and they make it inside the compound, while the other group of rebels (with Toby at the helm) takes off for the compound as well. Toby wants to save Mary before the compound is destroyed by the insane Dr. Logan. It's revealed that Julie Grant has partnered, along with Ted Fisher, to help Spider and Dr. Logan with their plan. However, she was unaware of the full scope of what the rebels had intended. During a gun battle with some of the guards, Fisher is killed and control panels are destroyed, which automatically opens all of the doors to the compound. In a control room the crazed Dr. Logan pulls the feeding siren, which brings the zombies out of the jungle. The zombies head toward the cave looking for their "food". Julie Grant and Dr. Logan are both devoured by zombies inside the control room.

There is total chaos as alarms blare throughout the cave and zombies roam freely – a sight "straight out of Dracula's tomb", as Romero describes it. Spider, along with Diesel, begins her journey to the powder magazine. Meanwhile, Mary is attempting to help a group of children to safety as they are pursued by Rhodes and his soldiers. They run into the area where the trained soldier zombies are kept. Mary quickly hands out weapons to Bub and the other zombies and removes her orange vest. She desperately tries to get the zombies to shoot at the orange vest, which they eventually do. Suddenly the soldiers burst inside, wearing orange vests, and Bub and his fellow "Red Coats" open fire on them, allowing Mary and her party to escape.

During all of this there is total carnage unfolding inside the complex. Gasparilla and his cohorts are trapped in his chambers, which the zombies have overrun. People are torn apart and devoured, including Gasparilla himself. By this time, Mary and the children have met up with Toby and the other rebels. They flee the compound and head into the jungle towards Sarah's boat. On their way out they come across the body of Miguel, which is still lying on the jungle floor – unrevived.

The action is fast and furious during the finale. Rhodes is bitten by a zombie, abandoned by the rest of his soldiers, and stalked by Bub, who shoots him during a showdown. By now Diesel has managed to guide Spider through the cave towards the powder magazine. They are besieged by zombies and Diesel is killed. Spider is finally able to get close to the powder magazine, but is also attacked by zombies. One zombie bites her and pulls out a vial of the nitroglycerine. He takes it out of his mouth and flings it towards the door of the powder magazine, causing a massive explosion that destroys the entire compound and everything in it.

The following morning the group of rebels starts a new day, and hopefully a new society, on another nearby island. John performs a baptism of the children and adults in a river. The script ends with John and Sarah keeping watch on the unrevived bodies of Mapmaker and Tricks, who died during the battle to escape. They keep watch, hoping that the zombie plague is finally over. Romero ends the script with a little wink to the audience: "The End (I promise)".

In the summer of 1980, on the set of *Knightriders*, Romero was interviewed by Cynthia Heimel for the July 21, 1980 issue of *New York* magazine for an article entitled "The Living Dead Ride Again". Talking about the business side of his productions, Romero made the following brief remark: "There's a way to stay true to your aesthetic and still resolve your business problems." That statement, and Romero's resolve about his aesthetic, would be greatly challenged just four years later, when the time came to produce *Day of the Dead*.

After submitting the estimated budget of nearly $7 million for his initial script to UFDC, bad news awaited Romero. Investing that much in an unrated film simply wasn't something UFDC was willing to risk. If Romero was willing to shoot an R-rated film, UFDC would front the money, however if Romero wanted to go unrated then UFDC would only put up roughly $3.5 million. "We did originally for *Dawn* [go unrated] in order to break through and show the original picture," recalls Richard Hassanein. "By *Day of the Dead* it became more and more difficult for theaters to play movies that were not rated, so we couldn't gamble our money on not getting an R rating."

As it turns out, the decision not to fund the larger budget was not a difficult one for Hassanein. "It was easy and I don't even remember George objecting to it." This led to Romero attempting to cut the script down to size, without changing the essential storyline. Romero made several passes at the original script, finally revising it down to a version that would still keep his initial vision a possibility. Even then the budget was still too high and unacceptable to UFDC. Towards the end of the summer of 1984, with the fall soon approaching – which meant production was just around the corner – Romero made the tough decision to completely change the script altogether. What once had been described by those involved with the film as *Raiders of the Lost Ark* or *Ben-Hur* with zombies would now become a drastically different script. "The most eagerly awaited day in horror film history," would end up being an entirely different *Day* than Romero had originally envisioned.

The scaled-back version, the one that hit screens during the summer of 1985, would be radically different from its original incarnation. Romero completed a third version of his second draft, dated September 21, 1984 – just one month before principal photography began – and this formed the basis of the *Day of the Dead* we know today.

The film begins inside a nightmare. The story's central character, Sarah (Lori Cardille), is sitting on the floor inside a white cinderblock room. She's staring at a calendar featuring a photo of a pumpkin patch, the month of October. She walks towards the calendar with a tranquil look on her face and, just as she lifts her hand to touch the calendar, dozens of rotted

Below: On the Pittsburgh set of *Knightriders*. From left to right: director George Romero, UFDC president Richard Hassanein, director of photography Michael Gornick and producer Richard P. Rubinstein. (© 1981 United Film Distribution Company – United Artists Corporation.)

zombie arms punch through the wall to grab her! She suddenly jolts awake, out of her vivid nightmare, and we see that she's in a helicopter. Sarah is part of a search team patrolling the gulf coast of Florida, looking for other survivors of the zombie apocalypse. Inside the helicopter we meet Sarah's lover, Miguel (Anthony "Tim" DiLeo), a soldier who is having issues of his own, much worse than nightmares. We are also introduced to helicopter pilot, John (Terry Alexander), and his radio man, Bill McDermott (Jarlath Conroy). The group lands the helicopter so that they can take a closer look at the city they've scouted. As Sarah looks on, Miguel calls out on a bullhorn to see if any survivors can hear them. The city is desolate, with debris scattered everywhere. A newspaper blows in the wind; its headline reads, "The Dead Walk!" The group soon discovers that the only things stirring in the dead city are zombies – and lots of them!

The search team returns to their base of operations, a fenced-off compound, where two soldiers, Torrez (Taso Stavrakis) and Johnson (Greg Nicotero), are awaiting the return of the group. Upon heading to a large elevator that will take them below the surface, the group discovers the fresh grave of Major Cooper, who was previously in command.

As the elevator descends into the cave/facility below, the group is met by another soldier, Miller (Phillip Kellams), who taunts them for having embarked on another wasted trip. The group exit into a large corridor, where two other soldiers – Steel (Gary Klahr) and Rickles (Ralph Marrero) – drive up to meet them in one of the facility's golf carts. They are on their way to round up a couple of zombies for a mad scientist, Dr. Logan, to experiment on, and will need the help of Miguel, who seems wary of going. Sarah notices this and volunteers to assist the soldiers in their task.

The motley crew drives off into the cave until reaching a corral area, which is used to capture zombies for Dr. Logan and his team of scientists. Steel and Miguel climb atop the corral and wait for some of the living dead to approach, which they hungrily do. The first two zombies to appear are a male zombie (Mark Tierno) and a female zombie (Debra Gordon). During the struggle to secure the "specimens", Miguel accidentally drops his pole, which is holding the female zombie – putting Rickles' life into immediate danger. Before the female zombie can attack Rickles, however, Sarah swoops in and grabs the pole, defusing the situation. Steel, however, is furious with Miguel and grabs him, hanging him over the corral inches away from the ravenous male zombie. Again, Sarah steps in and takes control of the situation by threatening to shoot Steel if he does not release Miguel. Afterwards, the two captive zombies are brought inside the main complex and chained to a wall to be used later for experimentation.

Back in their private quarters, Sarah sedates Miguel, who falls onto his bed, distraught and defeated. Meanwhile, in the facility dining hall, we are introduced to Ted Fisher (John Amplas), who is arguing with the film's arch villain, Captain Rhodes (Joe Pilato), about the working conditions in the facility. As they argue, Sarah enters the room and attempts to calm things down by asking for mutual cooperation between the scientists and military personnel. Rhodes, however, takes the opportunity to mock Sarah and her lover, Miguel. Disgusted, Sarah and Fisher leave the dining hall, but not before Rhodes tells her to return that evening for a group meeting. As she leaves, she informs Rhodes that she has sedated Miguel, which will prevent him from attending. This infuriates the Captain.

Sarah heads to the laboratory of head scientist Dr. Logan (Richard Liberty), nicknamed Dr. Frankenstein by both the military personnel and scientific team. Sarah walks in and observes Logan talking into his voice recorder, discussing the specimens he's currently experimenting on. Just then, she's startled by Logan's favorite and most promising subject, Bub (Howard Sherman), who is chained to the wall. Dr. Logan invites Sarah over to see some of his latest findings. On a medical gurney we see an eviscerated zombie (Mike Trcic) and across from it, on another gurney, a zombie (Barry Gress) who's had his entire face and head cut away to expose the brain. Logan ramblingly tells Sarah that the zombies do not need any internal organs to motivate their desire to eat humans, and that as long as the brain is left intact – the creatures will still attempt to rise up and walk. It's at this point that Sarah learns the awful truth: unbeknownst to the soldiers, the mad doctor is experimenting on the corpse of Major Cooper. Later, Logan's deceit will cost him dearly. Suddenly the eviscerated zombie breaks free from one of his bindings and attempts to get up, leaning over with his arm outstretched towards Sarah. His guts begin to slide and then fall out of his abdomen, landing on the laboratory floor with a loud, nauseating splat! Logan quickly moves in and inserts a drill into the zombie's head, killing it instantly.

Later that evening, in the dining hall, the group meeting is underway. The different factions argue amongst themselves as usual. Tired of listening to the back and forth bickering, Sarah decides to leave, but is told to sit back down by Rhodes. Sarah refuses to do so, in turn causing the megalomaniacal Rhodes to threaten her life. A brief but intense standoff occurs. Sarah eventually returns to her seat. It's then that Dr. Logan enters the dining hall, and immediately incurs the wrath of Rhodes. It's obvious that the military are frustrated and ready to leave as soon as possible. The meeting ends with Rhodes giving the scientific group more time to prove that they're making progress with their research, but he warns that if anyone disobeys his command they will pay with their lives.

Back in her personal quarters, Sarah has another nightmare, this time about Miguel. In it, Miguel is lying on the bed and, as he turns over to face her, his stomach opens up and his guts spill out – just like the eviscerated corpse in Dr. Logan's lab. She awakens to see Miguel watching her. They argue and Miguel storms out. Upset herself, Sarah also leaves and runs into the soldiers fighting amongst themselves in the hallway. As she is caught up in the brawl, McDermott appears out of nowhere and helps her out of the melee. They both head back to McDermott and John's living quarters, located further back in the mine, called "The Ritz". Sarah sits down and engages in a long discussion with John about the group's situation, and whether or not what they are doing is simply a waste of time.

The next day, Sarah notices Ted Fisher working with the male zombie that was captured earlier in the film. Fisher is attempting to wean the zombie onto something called "Beef Treats", which has been supplied to them by the Army. Dr. Logan appears at the door requesting that the two accompany him to another room so he can show them something.

Logan takes Sarah and Fisher into another experimentation room, where we once again see Bub, Logan's star zombie pupil, examining some ordinary household items, including a toothbrush and book. Rhodes and Steel appear at the door, enter the room, and walk over to observe what Logan is doing with his specimen. Logan gives Bub a telephone and encourages him to use it. After noticing Rhodes in his military uniform Bub salutes the captain, but Rhodes stubbornly refuses to return the gesture. In an attempt to impress the soldiers, Logan takes Sarah's unloaded pistol and hands it to Bub, who immediately takes to the weapon and points it directly at Rhodes, pulling the trigger.

Back at the corral the next day, Sarah, Miguel, Miller, Steel, and Johnson are busy capturing more zombie specimens for the mad doctor. All hell is about to break loose. The collar on the end of the pole that Miguel is holding breaks, releasing the zombie in that collar (Barbara Russell). The zombie quickly ambushes Miller and bites his throat out, unleashing a chain reaction of carnage that leaves Johnson and Miller dead, and Miguel with a chunk bitten out of his arm. Miguel runs through the mine screaming, with Sarah in pursuit, eventually reaching "The Ritz". John and McDermott emerge from their trailer and see Sarah knock Miguel unconscious with a rock, then

Above and below: Front and back of a promotional film market flyer by the UFDC advertising their upcoming release, *Day of the Dead*, 1983. (Courtesy of Michael Gornick.)

use a machete to amputate his arm, cauterizing the wound with a torch.

At this point Steel, Rickles, and Rhodes show up with weapons drawn. After a heated standoff with John and Bill, Rhodes backs down, telling them that Miguel is no longer allowed inside the complex and that the following day the remaining soldiers will destroy any living dead left in the cave.

After settling Miguel inside "The Ritz", Sarah decides to head back inside the complex to get painkilling medication for him, with McDermott accompanying her as protection. In the complex, inside Dr. Logan's lab, Sarah searches for morphine. As she looks around, McDermott picks up Logan's voice recorder and pushes the play button, exposing the private ramblings of the mad doctor, and then discovers the severed – and re-animated – head of Johnson! Sarah and McDermott quickly leave the laboratory and spot Logan walking down to Bub's experimentation room with a small bucket. They follow him and hide inside another room to watch what he's up to. The doctor teaches Bub how to listen to music – Beethoven's "Ode to Joy" – on a tape recorder, and rewards his pupil with the bucket, which is filled with bloody chunks of meat. As Logan starts to leave the room, he's grabbed by Rhodes. Upon opening the doctor's freezer, the soldiers discover the butchered remains of their comrades, which Logan has been feeding to Bub. Enraged by this discovery, Rhodes guns down the mad doctor.

Back at "The Ritz", John has grown concerned that it's taken so long for McDermott and Sarah to return, so he heads out to investigate. After John leaves, Miguel begins to come around, clutching the religious medallions around his neck. After concealing himself behind some piles of clutter, John aims his gun at the soldiers, but Rhodes turns the tables by threatening to kill Fisher, McDermott, and Sarah unless John surrenders, which he does.

With a gun to Fisher's head, Rhodes tells John that they are leaving on the helicopter without Sarah, McDermott, and Fisher. John refuses the order, so Rhodes executes Fisher

Above: Page 100 of George Romero's original, more expensive script. In this version, Gasparilla is the main villain, whilst Mary would eventually be melded with another character to create Sarah – played by Lori Cardille. (Courtesy of Tim DiLeo.) **Below:** Page 36 of Taso Stavrakis' shooting script, highlighting part of scene 35 – complete with Stavrakis' notes for his character, Torrez. (Courtesy of Christian & Taso Stavrakis.)

and then orders Steel and Rickles to shove Sarah and McDermott into the zombie-infested corral. John retaliates by punching Torrez, but Rhodes orders Steel to pummel John, hoping that it will "knock some sense" into him and convince him to pilot them to safety.

A siren echoes through the cave. Miguel, completely insane now, has taken the elevator up to ground level. Inside the facility, Bub has managed to free himself from his chain. Besieged by zombies, Sarah and McDermott navigate the pitch-black mine as they look for a way out, narrowly escaping with their lives.

Back at the corral, Rhodes waits for Steel and Rickles to return from investigating the cause of the elevator siren when John suddenly ambushes Rhodes, leaving him unconscious and disarmed. At the elevator bay, Steel and Rickles discover that Miguel has torn the control-box wiring out. Rhodes and Torrez come around to discover that John is gone and has taken their weapons.

Back inside the mine, John searches for Sarah and McDermott as they travel through the darkness, surrounded by zombies. Above-ground, Miguel unlocks the fenced gate entrance to the facility, and swarms of living dead waiting just outside flood in. Miguel runs back to the elevator and lies down as the zombies engulf him. As he's being devoured by the zombies, he finishes his suicidal mission by pressing the button on the elevator, which descends back down into the complex. As the elevator lowers, revealing hundreds of zombies, Rhodes panics and takes off in one of the facility's golf carts, abandoning his men.

The action now cuts back to Bub, who discovers the dead body of Logan. It slowly dawns on the pathetic creature that the doctor is no longer alive, and the zombie lets out a painful cry for his fallen friend. He then sees pistols lying on the floor.

The living dead swarm inside the facility as the soldiers each go their separate ways, trying to escape. Among the first casualties are Torrez and Rickles, both torn apart by zombies, their agonized screams echoing through the cave. Steel makes it back inside the complex, with hundreds of zombies in pursuit. He runs into Bub, who is now armed and fires his gun at Steel. After ducking into the experimentation room to dodge Bub's gunfire, Steel is accosted by a zombie who bites a chunk out of his neck. His fate is sealed.

Back in the mine, John has caught up with Sarah and McDermott. He gives them each a weapon and they lay waste to any zombies in their path as they make their way to an emergency escape located in a silo.

Meanwhile, Rhodes has grabbed another weapon from the arsenal room and is making his way back through the complex when he runs into Bub. Stunned, Rhodes quickly attempts to load his machine gun as Bub takes aim. Bub opens fire on the captain, knocking him to the floor. Rhodes manages to get back up, and staggers down to the door that leads to Logan's laboratory. Slowly, agonizingly, Rhodes finally makes it to the door, screaming for Bub to follow him, and is horrified to find more zombies waiting on the other side. Rhodes turns to see Bub aiming once again right at him. Bub fires his pistol one last time, hitting Rhodes in the stomach, and makes a mocking salute to the fallen captain. The zombies tear Rhodes in half, in one of the most spectacularly gory deaths ever put on celluloid. As the zombies make off with his legs, Rhodes screams, "choke on 'em". We are then treated to the patented Romero gore montage, as zombies feast on the entrails and limbs of the soldiers.

Aboveground, we find Sarah, John, and McDermott racing to the helicopter. Sarah opens the helicopter door and is grabbed by a zombie! She screams and then suddenly wakes up – she's had another bad dream. But this time she awakens in paradise rather than a nightmarish reality. She's on a beach. She sits up and sees a beautiful blue sky and ocean, as John fishes and McDermott feeds seagulls. She reaches into her duffle bag and pulls out a handmade calendar. She takes her marker and crosses out November 4 – another day alive . . . but for how much longer?

In the May 4, 1983 26th International Film Annual edition of *Variety* magazine, Laurel Entertainment took out a nine-page spread advertising their upcoming projects, including *The Stand*, *Creepshow 2*, *George A. Romero's Frankenstein* and several other titles that would ultimately never be produced. Each ad featured preliminary artwork with some basic credits. One of the titles featured was *Day of the Dead*. The art featured part of the moon on the top with the words, "First there was *Night of the Living Dead*." Just below that was a depiction of the sun rising with the words, "Then *Dawn of the Dead*," and at the bottom, taking up the majority of the layout, was a painting of the sun with a zombie face in it, numerous other zombie faces trailing behind it, and the words, "And now *George A. Romero's Day of the Dead*." This artwork, created by Bill Spewak, would end up being the US poster art for the film and was eventually turned into crew sweat shirts and t-shirts. It also advertised, among its credits, David E. Vogel as the film's co-producer: yet another change that was on the way before all would be said and done for the Laurel production.

A little over a year later, pre-production began on *Day of the Dead*, with the production team beginning their odyssey with the original, grander version of Romero's tale. However, no one was aware of the upheaval in store for the director's epic vision.

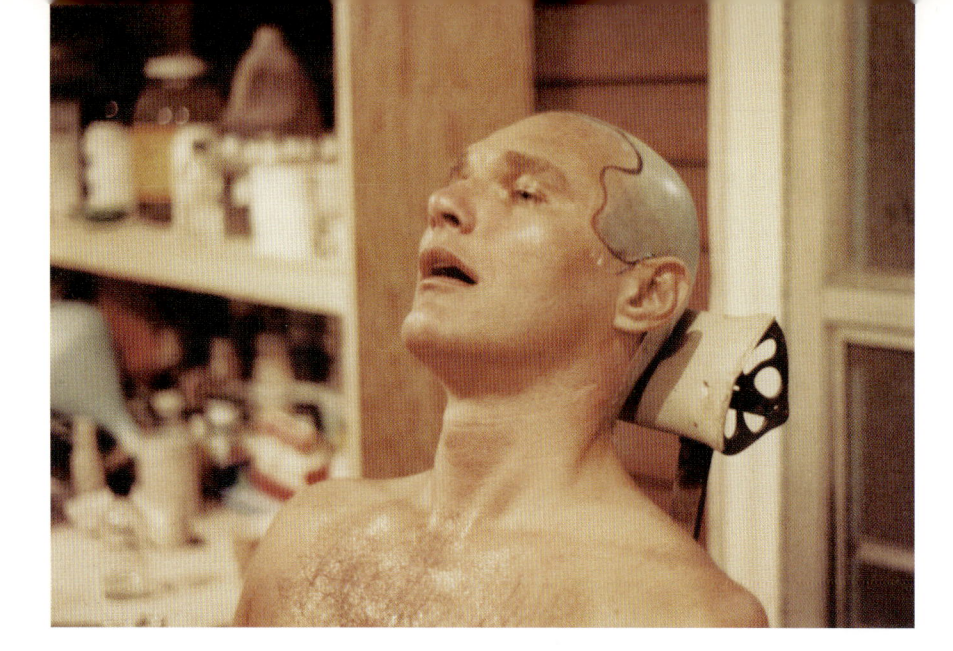

Top: Actor Howard Sherman, aka Bub, preparing to have his face cast at Tom Savini's house in Pittsburgh. August 1984. **Middle:** Tom Savini casts Howard Sherman's face as Greg Nicotero assists. **Bottom:** Howard Sherman waiting for the casting process to be completed, with graffiti provided by the effects crew. (Photos courtesy of Dave Kindlon.)

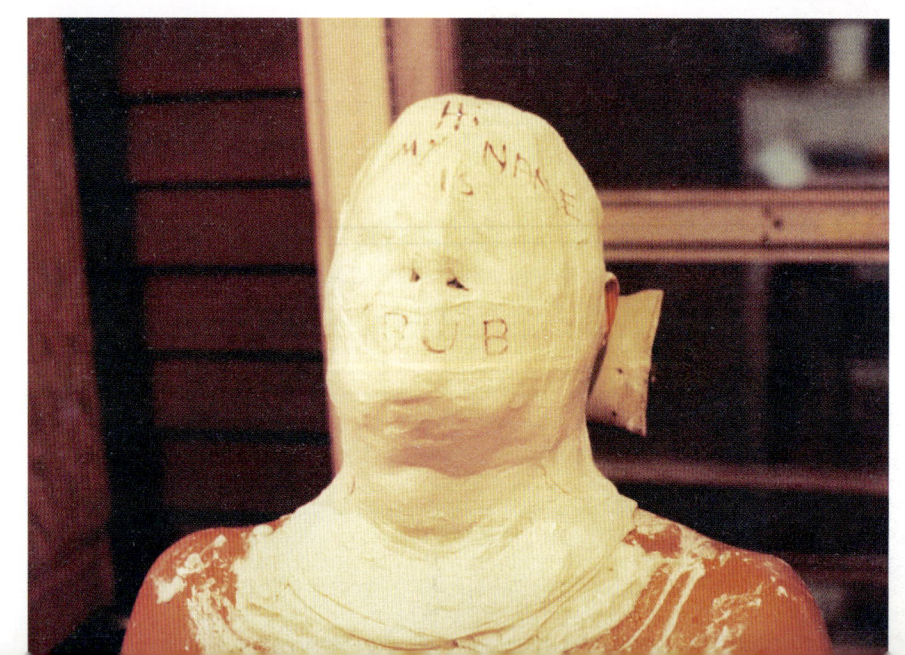

24

Chapter 2   The Day is Coming

Section A: Zombies Are Us

By early July 1984, pre-production work on *Day of the Dead* had kicked off. A large chunk of the prep work was being tackled by Tom Savini and his initial make-up effects crew at his home in Pittsburgh. While *Day of the Dead* would allow Savini to demonstrate how far his make-up effects skills had come, it was his acting that Savini really wanted to showcase. Having played smaller roles in previous Romero films like *Dawn of the Dead* and *Creepshow*, and more significant parts in *Martin* and *Knightriders*, Savini was interested in the role of *Day of the Dead*'s main villain, Captain Rhodes. Unfortunately for him, Romero had other ideas. "Yes, I really wanted to play Rhodes," recalls Savini. "He didn't think I could do the make-up effects and play Rhodes. He thought that was a big chunk." Looking back it's something that Savini still wishes he had pursued with Romero. "He didn't say no right off the bat. When he first gave me the script I said I wanted to play Rhodes. But his first script was so monumental, it was so big. It was like *Indiana Jones* with zombies, I mean it was a huge adventure. He had to cut back and back and back on that thing every time they lowered the budget. But back then maybe because it was so big that he thought . . . and there was so much going on effects wise that maybe that's why he thought [that I couldn't do both] . . . maybe I should have just kept badgering him about being Rhodes. I don't know."

The talented crew assembled by Savini was basically a team of young "prospects" who would eventually become "all-stars" in the make-up effects industry years later. The first hire on Savini's gang was a young and eager fan named Greg Nicotero. In fact, Savini didn't actually hire Nicotero – it was George and Christine Romero who offered him the opportunity to be a part of the film.

Greg Nicotero grew up a horror and sci-fi fan in Pittsburgh, and had a special affinity for George

Below: John Vulich sculpting the amazing face that would become Bub's. September 1984. (Courtesy of Dave Kindlon.)

Romero's films – *Dawn of the Dead* in particular. Nicotero first met Romero when he was in his early teens in the mid- to late 1970s, while on vacation in Rome, Italy with his family. Romero would remember the young and confident fan after returning to Pittsburgh. During the production of *Creepshow*, Nicotero was able to visit the set, and became even chummier with Romero by appealing to his love of video collecting. "This is the funniest thing," recalls Nicotero. "I took a list . . . my dad's a big video collector and I knew George was as well. So when I went to visit I had taken the list and when I went to see George I said, 'Oh, here's a list of all the movies that my dad has on video and if you ever want any copies . . .', and he went, 'Wow!' He went through and he circled about twenty movies that he was interested in, so that weekend I stayed up the entire weekend and copied all twenty movies. And on Monday morning I drove back out there and handed him a box. He's like, 'Did you stay up all weekend?' I'm going, 'Nah! It was no big deal.'"

Flash forward to 1984. It was just another ordinary day when an opportunity presented itself to Nicotero – an opportunity that would change his life forever. "When *Day of the Dead* came up, I had driven downtown to have lunch with George and Chris [Romero] and they said, 'Hey, we just got a green light on *Day of the Dead*. Do you want a job?' They had offered me a job on *Creepshow*, but I had to turn it down, and I thought, 'You know what, I'm not going to make the same mistake twice.'" During this time, Nicotero was going to college to become a doctor, but that didn't matter now. Having the opportunity to work on the sequel to his favorite horror film of all time? There was no way he could say no! During the years in between *Creepshow* and *Day of the Dead*, Greg had also become good friends with Tom Savini. "I instantly called Tom and said, 'I just got hired on *Day of the Dead*, I want to work as your apprentice.' That's how it fell into place. It was just me going to visit them one day and they said, 'Oh yeah, we're getting ready to do *Day of the Dead*,' and that's it. It was literally as simple as just, 'Are you interested?'"

Having Nicotero on board would provide a sort of comfort blanket, if you will, for Savini and Romero. "It was a very exciting premise for George," explains Nicotero. "Because they felt to have somebody sort of keep Tom on track and sort of manage the department, like order the supplies, get the résumés together, and sort of organize purchasing, as well as breaking down the shooting schedule – all the stuff that Tom never really needed to do before, because he never had a big show like this. This was a really big, complicated movie and they wanted to make sure that Tom was free to concentrate on the gags."

One of Nicotero's first duties was to read Romero's script – the second version of the first draft – and break down the number of effects shots that would be in the film. He compiled 99 special effects sequences from that original version, 24 of which were considered essential and would not be cut during any possible script revisions. After putting together the effects list, he turned his attention to assembling candidates for Savini's crew. He went through Savini's mail and files for names, some of which included Howard Berger, Everett Burrell, John Vulich, Dean Gates, Mike Maddi, Steve Fiorilla, and Rich Alonzo. Four of those names would eventually end up working on the production, and all would end up working in the effects industry in some capacity or another.

An effects budget was completed and Nicotero began ordering supplies and materials for the production. With the years passing and his skills sharpening, *Day of the Dead* would provide Tom Savini the opportunity to charge Laurel a premium for his efforts this time around. "I only made $15,000 for *Dawn of the Dead* and that was including paying for materials and for helpers, but I wanted to make up for that on *Day of the Dead*," says Savini. "So I think it was about $85,000 . . . $80,000 or $85,000." In a July 19, 1985 interview titled "Dead Man Tells Tales", with Al Walentis of the *Reading Eagle*, Savini estimated that $33,000 was spent on materials and supplies for the production's make-up effects.

Having finished putting together a selection of candidates for Savini to consider, Nicotero then turned his attention to contacting other make-up artists with regard to purchasing any leftover prosthetic body parts they might have around their shops. Artists such as Dick Smith, Tom Burman, Carl Fullerton, Steve Johnson, and Ed French were all contacted and eventually deals would be struck with three of them.

$1,000 was spent on two latex and polyfoam emaciated corpses from Steve Johnson – plus a surprise severed head thrown in as well. Ed French sold the production some burned hands and arms, some severed legs, a few gelatin heads, and a box of miscellaneous gory parts for $200. Finally, a deal was struck with Carl Fullerton that would allow Savini to rent three body molds from the film *Gorky Park*, which he could use to fabricate his own bodies. Nicotero would later make a trek to Rye, New York to work on this task (more on that later).

The next artist to join Savini's crew – on July 18 – was mechanical expert Dave Kindlon. Kindlon was from Rochester, New York and had met Savini prior to *Day of the Dead*, when Savini came to his hometown for a convention. Kindlon's friend, Pat Tantalo, who would also work on the film's pre-production, took Savini to check out Kindlon's small studio and see his friend's work. Savini was so impressed with Kindlon's talent

Above: Dave Kindlon at his work bench creating one of several mechanized heads used in the film. Summer 1984. (Courtesy of Dave Kindlon.)

that he promised to hire him on his next project. That next project ended up being the *Tales from the Darkside* episode "Inside the Closet", for which Kindlon worked on the "Lizzie" creature. Kindlon accepted the offer, even though he had been working for several months on *The Muppets* in New York City. After completing work on *Tales from the Darkside*, Kindlon returned home to Rochester unsure if he had made the right decision. Not long after that, however, Savini again contacted him with an offer to work on *Day of the Dead*. Kindlon remembers the production fondly. "It was one of the best work experiences I've ever had. It was one of the best films I've ever worked on; I've worked on a bunch over the years. Probably the most fun I've ever had on a movie."

Meanwhile, prep continued at Savini's abode. A cast of Nicotero's head was taken on July 20 to be used as one of the soldiers, who is killed and decapitated early in the script. The eventual script overhaul would lead to Nicotero having a larger part in the final version, due to the fact that they had already cast his head and started work on the head's fabrication.

On July 23, another member of the crew was added when sculptor Derek Devoe was hired. Devoe would handle a lot of the sculpting duties on the generic zombie appliances that were used extensively on the film. He also designed an early make-up effects crew t-shirt featuring a skeletal zombie figure wearing a large belt buckle, with the initials SMUD on it, which was an acronym for "Suck My Un-dead Dick". Devoe only lasted on the crew until August 12, when he returned home to Rochester, New York. If you ask the other effects guys who were there, you'll get different stories as to why Devoe was let go from the crew, and none are 100 percent sure – even Savini couldn't remember exactly why Devoe was let go. "Well, it's hard to say. I know Derek's work was great," says Mike Trcic, soon to join the crew. "I don't know if there were personality conflicts or it just turned out that Tom [Savini] had to take a cut in the crew at that time. I thought, [with] me being low man on the totem pole, I thought, well I'm out, and Tom said, 'Nah, you're not making enough money for me to fire you.' So, I guess Derek got axed."

"You know, that's an interesting question, 'cause I was right there for all of that, and for some reason right now, I'm like, I can't say exactly what happened," laughs Dave Kindlon. "I know he was on very early on the project – very, very early – and I think they just didn't mesh."

Above: John Amplas preparing to get his head cast at Tom Savini's house. (Courtesy of Dave Kindlon.) **Below:** Dave Kindlon, Mike Trcic, and Derek Devoe working on molds at Tom Savini's house, summer 1984. (Courtesy of Greg Nicotero.)

"It could have been because by the time we were done sculpting stuff, it was time to then turn around and start going to set and applying things, and I don't think that was Derek's deal," says Greg Nicotero. "I don't think Derek was an application guy, I think he was a sculptor."

What is known for sure is that when Devoe left Pittsburgh, another make-up artist, John Vulich, flew in that same day. (Unfortunately, Devoe could not be reached for an interview for this book.)

As previously mentioned, Pat Tantalo was also around for the pre-production work. Like Derek Devoe, he wasn't brought onto the production in the mine and afterwards wrote, along with Devoe, a scathing mini-comic entitled *Tommy, Dearest* about working on the film's prep for Tom Savini. Some of the jabs contained in the comic included dealing with Savini's ineptitude during the prep, his monstrous ego, and how he would refer to himself as "The Fucking President". "He relished in torturing us and he tortured us a lot," says Greg Nicotero about Savini. "Especially, I remember one specific time when we were in his basement cleaning stuff out and there was

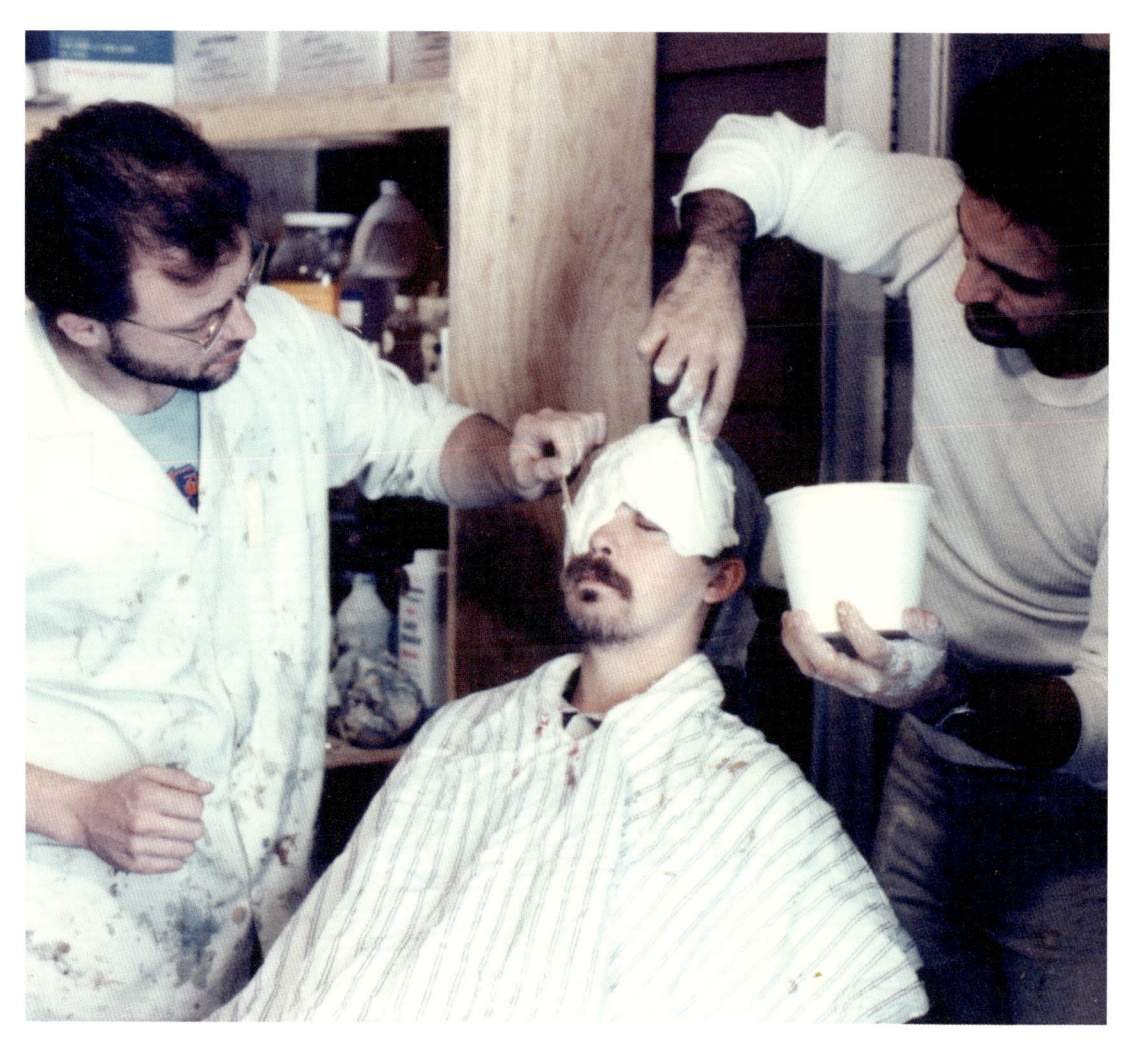

Above: At Savini's house, Tom Savini and Dave Kindlon begin casting John Amplas' head for the actor's upcoming death scene. This effect would eventually be handled without the use of a prosthetic. (Courtesy of Dave Kindlon.)

a plaster mold that was wounds from *Dawn of the Dead*, like a tray mold that he had sculpted wounds, done from this mold. And we were like bowing down to, 'Oohh, *Dawn of the Dead*!' And he was like, 'Oh you like that?', 'Oh my god yeah, it's so great! We should run it!' And he literally took a hammer and smashed it in front of all of us, just to sort of prove that he's Tom Savini and he can do whatever he wanted. And that's where the 'I'm the fucking President' came from. 'Cause every once in a while, if anybody ever disagreed with him or had anything to say that was contrary to him, he would just say, 'You guys don't know anything. I'm Tom Savini. Go fuck yourself,' and would pull out *Fangoria* magazine and read – that was back when they had the free subscriber ads. There was one ad that was like – I remember it 'cause Tom read it over and over again – it said, 'I would disembowel my sister for you, Eric the Demon Dog,' that was it. And then Tom would be like, 'See, look, my name's in the free subscriber ads.' He would just do that to prove to us that he was the man."

Tommy, Dearest also contained some not so flattering illustrations of the other crew members on the team, such as Dave Kindlon drawn with a bunch of marijuana joints in his mouth and Nicotero literally kissing Savini's rear end. "I don't want to say anything bad, but I don't think Pat's skills at the time were up to snuff," says Nicotero. "And that's why he plays me up like a big kiss ass in that comic book, because he was just pissed." At the time the comic didn't sit well with Savini either, but the intervening years have softened his take on it just a bit. "We didn't like it at all, we hated it. But now I think it's hilarious," says Savini. "It's like *Mad* magazine. *Mad* magazine goes to *Day of the Dead*."

Despite being dropped before filming began, Tantalo remembers working on the prep as a fun time. "Actually, we stayed in the house behind Tom's house. Tom's father owned a bunch of houses there and he stayed in the house behind Tom's. So, we'd just roll out of bed and go down into the basement – at the time it was before he had his shop or anything," says Tantalo. "We set everything up on *Tales from the Darkside* to do *Day of the Dead*. We set his basement up as a shop, his back porch we closed in and put a big oven in; everything was done in this little space. We just kept making pieces and loading and packing them in boxes and putting them away. It was fun. We'd just watch movies constantly or listen to movie soundtracks, whatever. Actually while we were working, the guys down the street from Tom's – the movie theater – they would come by at night and drop us off all the leftover popcorn from the movie theater [*laughs*]. So, we'd sit up all night eating popcorn and watching movies while we were working on stuff." He also remembers what a prankster Savini could be. Savini, his brand-new wife at the time, Nancy, and the guys would put the "Lizzie" creature from *Tales from the Darkside* in a baby stroller and parade the little monster around Savini's Bloomfield neighborhood to see the reactions on people's faces.

On July 25, two days after bringing Devoe aboard, another member of the crew was hired, Mike Trcic. Trcic was attending Point Park College and studying at the Pittsburgh Filmmakers at the time. He was also working part-time for Rick Catizone at Anivision, an animation company that had previously worked on *Creepshow*. Like Nicotero, Trcic was a native of Pittsburgh and a fan of Savini's. "Tom had just released his book *Grande Illusions* and he was doing a book signing at Eide's Comics in downtown Pittsburgh. I went to see him and took him photos of some of my work and he said, 'Oh yeah, why don't you come over to see me?' So, I went over to his house and interviewed with him and, as it turns out, I ended up staying and helped him make a mold for 'Lizzie', the creature from his *Darkside* episode. So, I got to know Tom that way and I guess he liked my work and told me to keep in touch – that he was going to be hiring guys soon for *Day of the Dead*." Just a year earlier, Trcic had been working at the Showcase Cinemas in Monroeville, right down the street from the famed Monroeville Mall, because he was willing to wear a Darth Vader costume for the opening of *Return of the Jedi*. And just like Nicotero, his life was about to change completely.

Trcic's first day of film prep at Savini's would be a memorable day, for him and the other effects guys. "We all sat around chatting for a little bit and then Tom said, 'Okay, now we're going to Kennywood,'" recalls Trcic. "My first day of work was spent riding amusement rides at Kennywood and I just remember coming home that night and thinking what a great job!" Such occurrences were not rare for Savini during the film prep. Another time Savini had the crew stop working on what they were doing because they were all going to go to a church picnic in Bloomfield that had lots of wonderful Italian food. And yet another time the group went to Greg Nicotero's family home and watched Savini shoot arrows into a dummy with a bow and arrow and small crossbow.

Being on the *Day of the Dead* crew was definitely a source of pride for Trcic and his fellow crew members. "Oh gosh, all of us were just beaming. We knew that we were kind of the epicenter of what was going on in the film industry at that point," says Trcic. "There were guys from LA that were calling Tom and wanted to come and work on the film. So, we felt very privileged to have nailed the positions."

One of the first cast members to land a role in the film was Anthony "Tim" DiLeo, who played Miguel. His arm, wrist, and neck were cast at Savini's house on July 25 in anticipation of his death very early in the original script.

During this period, the idea for the deep background pullover zombie masks was developed. The masks were designed by Terry Prince and then created by David Smith. Smith was a young, fledgling make-up artist out of Salinas, California who had posted ads in *Fangoria* magazine's classified section. "I got a letter from Savini's people and I talked to, not him, but one of his assistants on the phone," recalls Smith. "They sent drawings of three different zombie faces, these kind of generic background zombies. And they sent three colors, color swatches, and basically they wanted like 50 of each of the designs, and then among those they'd be equally divided up with these three colors. The three colors were like a yellow tan, sort of sallow flesh color, a grey green, and a grey blue." Smith would get started on designs created by Terry Prince, which Smith says Prince told him were altered. "What they had done is they had taken his drawings and xeroxed them and took white out and changed them with a marker or whatever, redesigned them basically," says Smith. "More generic, I think, than the kind of stuff he was doing, which was a little more flashy and comic book sort of, over the top." This story makes sense, as Pat Tantalo claims the designs were done by his co-author of *Tommy, Dearest*. "Derek [Devoe] did all the designs for the masks that David Smith made," says Tantalo. On one of the drawings, underneath Terry Prince's signature, are the words "w/ a little help from Derek Devoe".

"I picked the simplest one, which had the mouth closed, and no ears, right away," says Smith. "Then the other two, they had different style mouths and different style ears. So what I did was I sculpted the most basic one, it was a full head sculpture and I decided to make masters, basically, for making other

Above: Tom Savini and Mike Trcic casting Joe Pilato's body for his demise as Captain Rhodes. Summer 1984. (Courtesy of Greg Nicotero.) **Below:** Joe Pilato having his body cast at Tom Savini's home. (Courtesy of Dave Kindlon.)

molds off of this one. So what I did was, I had the original sculpture and I snatched, with alginate, I took little molds of the ear areas and the mouth, and some other parts of the head and made little plaster copies and sculpted ears, another mouth, that sort of thing, all as appliances that would go onto the original head. I would cast the original head and use these add-ons to modify it into the other designs. So, in other words, basically I had a head that had been modified with these appliances and I would remold that, make another plaster mold with that and then use that to make the actual mask out of. Out of that I managed to manufacture the three different styles." Smith also mixed in, for free, about twenty other masks from a couple of alternate designs based on a mask he already had in his portfolio. "I also had an old man mask that was sort of inspired by the Dick Smith make-ups for *The Hunger*," says Smith. "I took some copies of that, and modified it with some appliances and things. I also did a thing where I took one of those and chopped the nose off, sort of modified the whole thing, and made new molds off that. So, I really had about five different zombies, but there were the

THE MAKING OF GEORGE A. ROMERO'S DAY OF THE DEAD

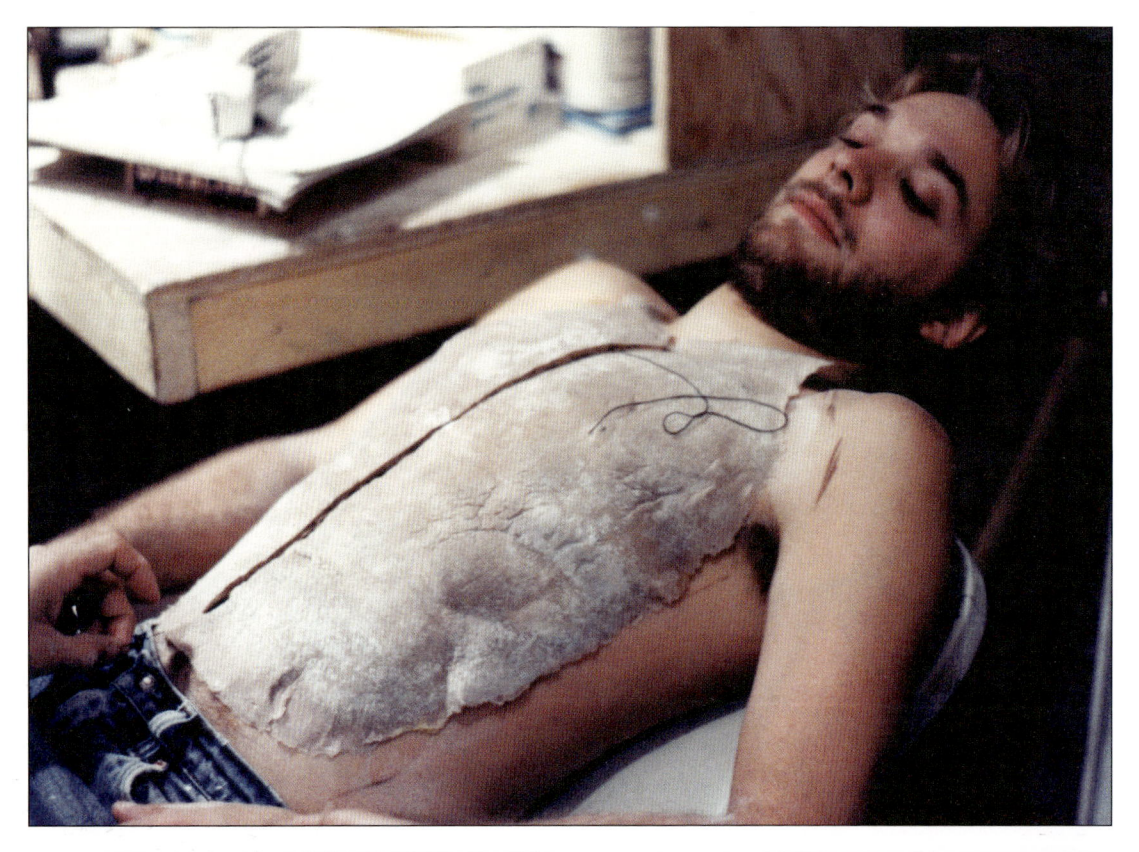

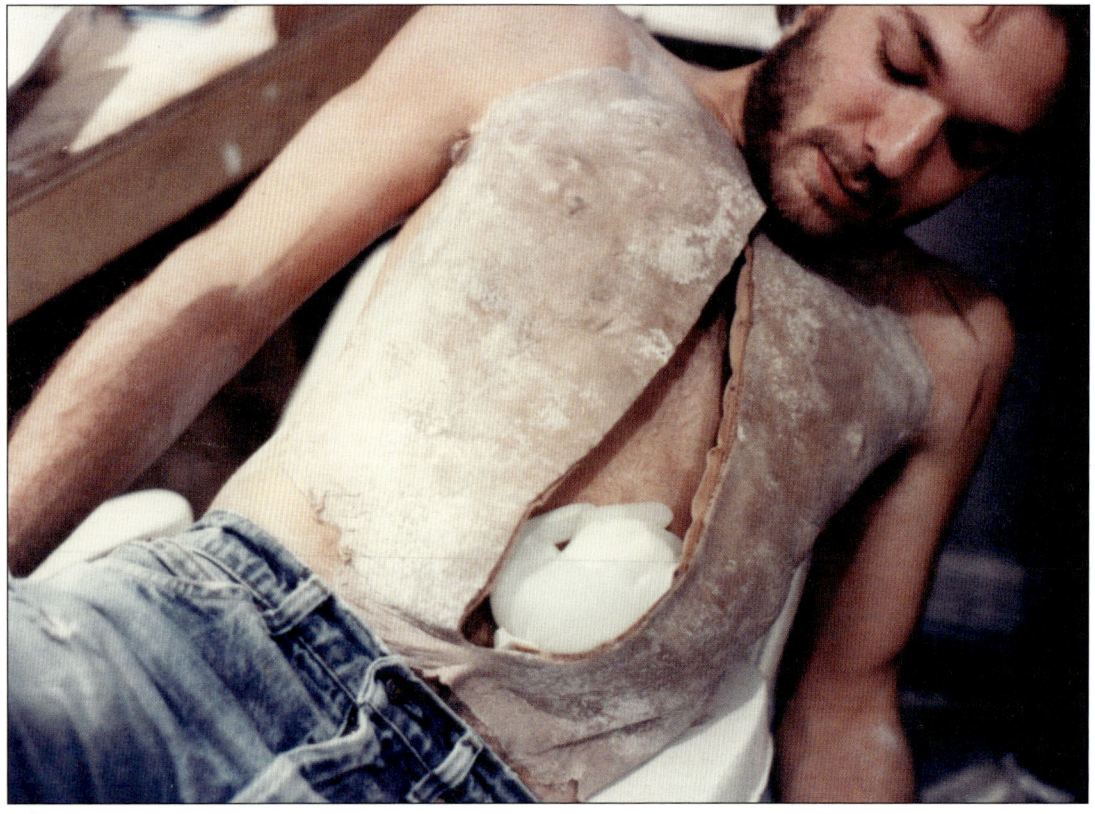

three basic ones that they wanted. And I just started pouring, I poured them all and painted them all myself. Mainly they were painted with Pax and then also with a paint formula that I was using at the time, which was like enamel paint, like you'd buy in a model store, and you would just thin it out and then add, like, a drop of castor oil to it. I'd heard this was a Don Post formula from years back. It worked pretty well and it was cheap. I'd paint the whole thing dark brown and then dry brush whatever the base color was going to be, whether it was going to be one of the yellow ones, the blue ones, the green ones. And then I would use these enamels with castor oil as a kind of shading over the top of that. And then I'd go back in and paint the teeth and kind of age them, stain them. And I put crepe hair on some of them too."

Using medical and criminal reference books as a guide, work on the generic zombie appliances also began. The idea was to create small, medium, and large prosthetic appliances that could be used on zombie extras, based on the size of their face, when they arrived on set. Casts were taken of Tom and Nancy Savini, Dave Kindlon, and Leon McBryde (aka "Buttons the Clown") to be used for sculpting. "We tried to make everything sort of mix and match, where it would be like some of them were full-face pieces, and then some of them were just foreheads and lower parts of the faces," explains Greg Nicotero. "We had this book that Tom called *The Medicolegal Investigation of Death*. It was a forensic text book and we used that book as reference."

A few days later, on July 28, Savini began sculpting the zombie that would bite Miguel, played by Dave Kindlon. This too would carry over from the original script into the filmed version. Not long after that, a cast was taken of Savini to be used as the first zombie seen in the film, the "Jaw zombie", later to be known as "Dr. Tongue". For Tom Savini there was a feeling of excitement at having such an honor. "Dave Kindlon was gonna play a featured zombie and then Savini wanted to be the first zombie in the movie," says Greg Nicotero. "He was really, really excited about it, 'I gotta be the first zombie that anybody ever sees in *Day of the Dead*.'" On August 4 a cast was taken of Savini's chest to be used for the "Dr. Tongue" puppet. On August 10 molds were made from the hands of Tom and Nancy Savini, and Dave Kindlon, to be used for sculpting zombie hand appliances.

The next crew member to be added was one of the guys that Mike Trcic had mentioned before calling from southern California, John Vulich. Vulich flew in on August 12 – the same day as Derek Devoe's departure. He had previously worked with Savini on *Friday the 13th*: *The Final Chapter*, and his hiring would prove to be pivotal. He became the unofficial leader of the young effects crew and contributed some truly mind-blowing work to the finished film. And, just like the other guys on the crew, he had grown up an enormous fan of Romero and Savini. "Initially it was like a dream of mine to work on *Day of the Dead*," says Vulich. "I'd known, I guess probably through magazines like *Fangoria*, that they'd been talking about doing it at some point and I was a huge fan of *Dawn of the Dead*. When I was younger, living in Fresno, I was corresponding and calling Savini on the phone a lot to basically ask him for advice on doing make-up effects. So, I had somewhat of a relationship with him and, based upon that, he had told me that if he ever did a film in Los Angeles – which is near where I lived in Fresno – that he would make sure to hire me on the project. And sure enough he did when we did *Friday the 13th Part 4*, which was the first film I worked on with him and the first professional film that I worked on. So, I kind of already had made some inroads towards working on *Day of the Dead* just from having a relationship with him. So, when I worked with him on *Friday the 13th* I definitely made it clear that [it] was kind of a dream of mine to work on it, and I'd be very excited to be a part of it. So, I think he kind of tucked that away in the back of his head, but didn't really make any firm commitments on it; kind of like [a] 'let's see what happens', kind of thing.

"So, one day – after I'd worked on *Friday the 13th* – a year later or something, I get a phone call from him and they'd, I guess, already been in production. He had somewhat of a crew put together, I think either some guys locally in Pittsburgh or people that were close, like east coast guys from New York. And apparently he was having a personality conflict with one of the guys he hired from New York, so he was looking to replace this person and asked if I would be interested. So, of course, I was extremely excited about the prospect. I got together . . . actually did some very quick little make-up demos of some zombie and wound type make-ups I thought would be appropriate to further attract his interest. I don't quite remember at this point . . . I don't quite remember if he'd asked for it or if I just kind of did it just to further cinch my deal, you know? I went ahead and did some photos and actually . . . I know Howard Berger was one of my victims. [*laughs*] I've got the photos I did, I still have a box of them somewhere here – and [of] a couple of other friends that let me do zombie make-ups on [them] – and sent them off to Tom, which got him more excited. I was definitely then a part of the crew and they flew me out. I replaced the person that they had, and started to work right away on it."

During all of this effects prep work, the script's

Above and below: An early test of Miguel's autopsy chest effect is carried out on Greg Nicotero at Tom Savini's house. (Courtesy of Dave Kindlon.)

budget was becoming a major issue. Romero attempted to trim down his story, taking out sections that would still leave his original vision intact onscreen.

In the meantime, Savini's crew continued their work. During a crew meeting, the effects team attempted to conjure up some grisly zombie deaths. Romero usually tended to work this way, allowing Savini the freedom to decide exactly how the gore effects would play out in the film. Some very interesting and wild ideas came out of the meeting, some of which, unfortunately, did not make it into the film. One of the ideas thrown out involved a zombie struggling with one of the heroes, and its eyeball falling out of its head – into the mouth of the struggling hero! Strangely enough, a couple of years later, a similar gag would show up in *Evil Dead 2*. Another idea involved one of the heroes punching a zombie and its face crumpling around the hero's hand. One idea from this meeting that *would* make it into the film was suggested by John Vulich, who also ended up playing the zombie when it was filmed. "A lot of the deaths in the script weren't particularly thought out, like, in detail," remembers Vulich. "It was just 'a zombie gets killed' and there were very brief mentions in the script of what the methods of dispatching them were. So Tom would have us kind of sit around his kitchen table – he used to do things like make, I don't know, pepperoni bread for us, I think it's a recipe that

Above: The *Spookies* mansion in Rye, New York – where Nicotero and Kindlon traveled to create background bodies in rented molds, originally used by Carl Fullerton on *Gorky Park*. *Spookies* crew members Gabe Bartalos and Al Magliochetti would assist with the job. (Courtesy of Greg Nicotero.)

he inherited from his dad. So we were probably sitting there eating pepperoni bread just chit chatting and he's saying, 'Let's brainstorm some ideas for how to kill zombies and we can plug them into the film. Does anybody have any ideas?' And the 'chop top' thing was one of the ideas I came up with. I think entirely kind of predicated on the idea that, if you shoot them in the head, the brain dies and that's what stops them. So, I just thought that the irony of a zombie that just had the least amount possible of his head left [and] could still survive. I mean, he doesn't even have a jaw, he just has the top of his head, and he would just be stuck in that cave for probably all eternity just not being able to do anything. I thought that was kinda like a horrific and bizarre idea. So, I threw that out and he seemed to respond well to it, and then somehow it turned into, 'Why don't you play it? We'll all get to play cameos,' and this and that. That was one of the fun things about working with Tom and the Romeros, 'cause it was not really like this compartmentalized Hollywood method of doing films. It was really like a family making something together. So, you had these relationships where Tom would just say, 'Hey, do you mind if my guys play some zombies?' and like, 'Yeah, sure. Why not?' You know? It's like all one big happy family. So, he offered me up to play it or asked if I was interested, so I said, 'Of course I am.'"

Now, getting back to the trek to Rye, New York for the *Gorky Park* bodies: Tom Savini had a struck a deal with make-up artist Carl Fullerton to rent time with some body molds he'd created for the film *Gorky Park* a couple of years previously. Greg Nicotero and Dave Kindlon were dispatched by Savini to handle the task. When they got there they enlisted the help of fellow effects artists Gabe Bartalos and Al Magliochetti, who assisted with the fabrication of the bodies. "We were shooting a movie in New York state called *Spookies* and Tom Savini had called us up to ask if we had any space," recalls Magliochetti. "Basically what was going on is, they needed to make a bunch of bodies and they were borrowing Carl Fullerton's full body molds for the dead bodies from *Gorky Park*. They were pretty sizable though, and Carl didn't have a whole lot of work room at his house. We happened to be working kind of just up the road from there, and our location was a 27-acre estate. So, Tom called up and asked if he could send Greg Nicotero and David Kindlon over just to basically use our space. And we cleared with the production and everything was fine, so they came over and we all made bodies." The process was a method of saving money for the production, as well as having access to already completed, quality work.

"They arranged to get pulls out of the molds; it's a thing that's done fairly common if somebody has a really kick-ass mold, you rent time with the mold and you pull your parts out of it," says Bartalos. "It saves you the cost of going through the entire casting, molding procedure – which can be significantly expensive if you don't need to have those molds or just need a pull; exactly like the case of *Day of the Dead's* background stuff. It was a good way to go if someone's willing to rent it. They made a deal and they needed a place to do it. I had a full running effects facility in this basement of this mansion; I had already been there two months. So, we were fully up and running and they said, 'Hey, we're just on the other side of the bridge – can we bring these over and run them? We'll bring our own materials.' I said, 'Absolutely, sounds great!' Just another excuse to hang out, you know? So they brought the molds over." The assistance Magliochetti and Bartalos

Below: Prosthetic bodies cast from Carl Fullerton's molds lay on the *Spookies* property, Rye, New York. (Courtesy of Al Magliochetti.)

THE MAKING OF GEORGE A. ROMERO'S DAY OF THE DEAD

ZOMBIES ARE US

Above: "Zombies Are Us" sign that hung on the door of the make-up effects room during filming. (Courtesy of Greg Nicotero.) **Below:** August 1, 1984 memo from Tom Savini regarding the casting of roles in the film's original, larger script. (Courtesy of Greg Nicotero.)

provided eventually led to an opportunity for both to be zombie extras in the film.

As previously mentioned, Tom Savini had a new wife during the prep for the film, Nancy, and the bachelor party would apparently be a memorable one for those who attended. "Tom got married to Nancy while we were in pre-production on that, right, and there was the weirdest bachelor party I have ever been to in my entire life," recalls Dave Kindlon. "I haven't been to that many, but this one, this one was better than strippers, hookers, and midgets. Later on it was one of those, 'Gentlemen, of this we shall not speak.' [*laughs*] It was just a weird night with Tom." *Fangoria* editor, Robert "Uncle Bob" Martin, who covered the film for the horror periodical and would also have a cameo as a zombie, shared some interesting tidbits he heard second-hand about that "weird night with Tom". "At Tom's bachelor party the entertainment was tapes of him fucking various women," recalls Martin. "I'm just glad I wasn't invited. God, I don't wanna see Tom Savini fucking women." Martin recalls another funny bit about Savini and his fascination with members of the opposite sex: "I remember on the *Friday the 13th* stuff he sent me negatives of some stuff that he had shot of Jason and stuff – totally exclusive shots that we had. But on the same roll there were naked chicks." [*laughs*]

Everett Burrell, along with Howard Berger, would join the make-up effects crew after principal photography began in late October (more of which later). I discovered that Burrell could also be very blunt about Savini's interest in the opposite sex. "If you're gonna really do a 'tell all' book, you gotta tell the truth about Tom. I love Tom like a father – don't get me wrong – I have great respect for him, but he's, you know, as dysfunctional as they come," says Burrell. "Tom and his penis, I think is a great story right there. Tom just likes getting laid, no matter what. I swear to

God that guy worships vagina more than he does Dick Smith . . . and he worships Dick. Isn't that funny? He worships Dick and vagina. [laughs] God yeah, Tom, he had this weird knack about sex and girls, he just was so fascinated and he couldn't stop fucking. He just had to fuck everything that moved." Burrell continues, "It got kind of silly after a while. We had to keep covering for him, 'Where's Tom?' 'Well, he's fucking some extra in a trailer somewhere.'"

Savini's appetite for women is the stuff of legend, and it's a topic that Savini himself is not shy at all to discuss. "I definitely used my position, let's say, to score with a number of zombie women actually. I can safely say it now," says Savini. "We had mine fever; they were coming to the hotel and seeking us out. I challenge any guy to resist temptation like that. There were nights in the motel room with one in the shower, one on the bed, it was like an orgy. But in the whole schedule, like of the show, most of the time it was lonely. The instances I'm talking about were few and far between, maybe once or twice in a couple of months. The rest of the time you're doing your job and basically lonely."

"Years later I'd be talking to Greg [Nicotero] about something, duh da duh da duh," says Dave Kindlon. "And Greg would go, 'Oh, you know every day when Tom would disappear for twenty minutes?' and I'm like, 'Yeah,' and it's like, 'Oh, well he was doing this,' you know, whatever, and I'm not going to say, [laughs] but I'm like, 'You've gotta be fucking shitting me!'"

Working on a film with Tom Savini could be thrilling, at times sordid, and definitely very memorable. Sometimes it could even be dangerous, as Greg Nicotero found out first hand. An incident involving a blank gun occurred during the prep on *Day of the Dead*. Born out of horseplay between Savini and his young crew, it was truly a close call for Nicotero. "There were constant jokes and constant fucking with each other and he had a gun in his house that had blanks in it," recalls Nicotero. "We would be sculpting in the basement, and he would come to the top of the stairs and open the door and pull the trigger and shoot into the basement while we were all down there. It was so loud and I remember [John] Vulich getting pissed and Dave Kindlon getting pissed, people were getting angry because he kept doing it." In an attempt to get even with Savini, Nicotero snuck up to Savini's bedroom to get the blank gun and turn the tables on the practical joke master. Nicotero flung the basement door open and fired the blank gun down the steps repeatedly, hoping to scare Savini. With the joke now over, he and the other effects guys headed back down into the basement to see Savini's reaction. Savini took the gun from Nicotero's hand, checked it, pointed it back at Nicotero, and fired – at close range – with the ejected wad hitting Nicotero directly in the head.

"That kind of grew in intensity," remembers Savini. "Like, I remember I splashed water on him or something, and then he splashed blood on me, and I would like throw latex on him and he would throw something else on me. It just escalated to the point where he went upstairs and got my blank gun and came down and I think he like fired a shot at me or something. I first took the gun away from him and I opened it and I looked at the rounds and I saw that every round was spent – there was a dent in the back of every round. But I said, 'Hey, there's one left in here!' and I pointed it at his head to scare him, after I said there's one left in here, and I pulled the trigger – this is point blank range. And the gun went off. A blank fired right at his face, he got mini little burns on his face. But what made it bad was me saying there's one left, but I was just joking because I saw that they were all spent. I don't think he believes me to this day."

Mike Trcic witnessed the entire event as it happened, "I was standing about six feet away and it was like watching an assassination," remembers Trcic. "It's like, oh my God! He's lucky he didn't lose an eye, really. He had powder burns all over the side of his head and a nice big mark from where the wad hit him. It's just a good thing he wasn't closer."

For Nicotero, the close call was something that he preferred to keep as quiet as possible. "I couldn't go home that night because I didn't want my dad to see the powder burns on my face and wonder what the fuck was going on," says Nicotero. "And then, I think, that weekend I went up to Westminster College where I used to go to school and saw some of my friends and they were like, 'Dude, what the fuck?'"

John Vulich humorously summarized how dangerous working with Savini could be. "We had a joke that working with Tom Savini was like the Bugs Bunny routine, like 'Shoot me now.' 'No, no, no. I'll shoot you later.' 'No, I insist. Shoot me now!' 'No, I'll shoot you later.' That kind of sums up working with Savini," says Vulich.

Another bizarre story from the prep involved the idea of using actual cadavers from the morgue. "They wanted to have some full bodies of dead corpses," recalls John Vulich. "I guess they wanted, like, maybe a desiccated body or a body that was like shriveled up or slightly mummified or something, like a cadaver, not like a regular healthy person. And Greg Nicotero's father was a doctor and I remember one evening, probably late at night, we're just sitting in Tom's basement and they're talking about, 'You know, if we could just get in there and get a real body to mold, like in silicon and just pull polyfoam bodies out of it. Wouldn't that be cool?' and they're talking about this for like a half hour. [laughs] So, Nicotero's like, 'Well, my dad's a doctor. Maybe he can get us in to get a cadaver,' and I'm like, 'Wait, wait, wait, wait . . . time

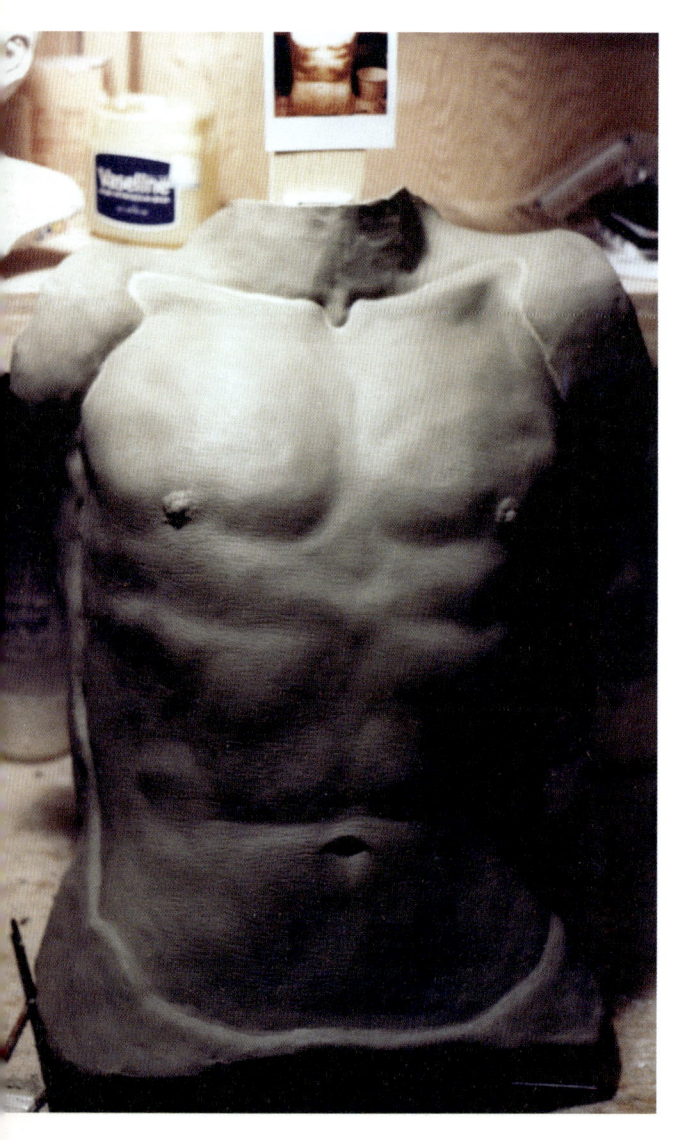

Above: The sculpture used to create a prosthetic chest for actor Tim DiLeo, enabling him to spill his guts in Sarah's nightmare sequence. (Courtesy of Dave Kindlon.)

out. What are you guys talking about? [*laughs*] We're not going to mold a real body, that's just morbid. I mean, you can't do that. It's disrespectful, it's morbid. We're supposed to be artists here, let's just make it from scratch or something.'"

"I vaguely remember that discussion," says Nicotero.

Meanwhile, the issues regarding the script's budget had reached a crossroads. It was now obvious that the scale of Romero's script was simply too much for the budget parameters that the financiers were willing to risk. (See Section B.) On August 22, a conference call was held between Romero and Savini in which the news was delivered that the original script was now being completely overhauled. The large-scale action sequence that opened the film was now gone, along with the "Red Coat" zombies, and the majority of the Florida locations and characters. The Dr. Logan character was now changed from a rebel doctor to a mad scientist, and the Miguel arm amputation scene was switched from the beginning of the film to closer to the end. Also, instead of just a background soldier, Nicotero would now be an actual character in the film, rather than just a severed head. "What happened was the script got pared down and a bunch of gags got cut out and then all of a sudden the little severed zombie head soldier that I was supposed to play became a character in the movie!" says Nicotero. "We had already started building this and there were maybe eight characters in the entire film. So all of a sudden it wasn't just sort of a throwaway gag, it was like I had dialogue and I had to do stuff! I wasn't an actor, I mean . . . I was nervous about it because I had no idea. I just thought it was exciting, it was fun, but I'm not an actor. I didn't know what to do." Initially, the nose was to be removed from his severed head, which Logan would refer to when talking on the tape recorder. But those details would slightly change by the time the script was finished.

Even things such as the color of zombie blood were thought out: fresher zombies would have red blood, semi-rotted zombies would have brownish blood, and severely decayed zombies would have black blood. The autopsy zombies were also introduced, as was the idea of using a rod puppet for the headless Major Cooper zombie. Another key change in the script was that Bub was now the only "intelligent" zombie and would play more of a role in the story. Howard Sherman was cast as the sympathetic zombie, and on August 28 he flew into Pittsburgh to have his face, teeth, and hands cast for the role.

On September 5, a new draft of the final screenplay was received and, as he had done before, Nicotero would work out another breakdown of the film's effects sequences. A fortunate break for the make-up effects team was that a lot of the prep work they had already begun would carry over into the new script. The next day, September 6, work continued on the mechanical heads and generic zombie appliance sculptures. Wound trays were sculpted by Vulich, Trcic, and Nicotero as well. Trcic also would begin sculpting ribs over a life cast of Anthony DiLeo's chest for the dream sequence in which his character spills his guts.

A week later, September 14, a major department head meeting took place to discuss the production start date and preliminary shooting schedule. Production would begin on October 22 and would call for a proposed eight-week shoot. There was also a discussion of the crossover between the art department and the make-up effects department.

THE DAY IS COMING

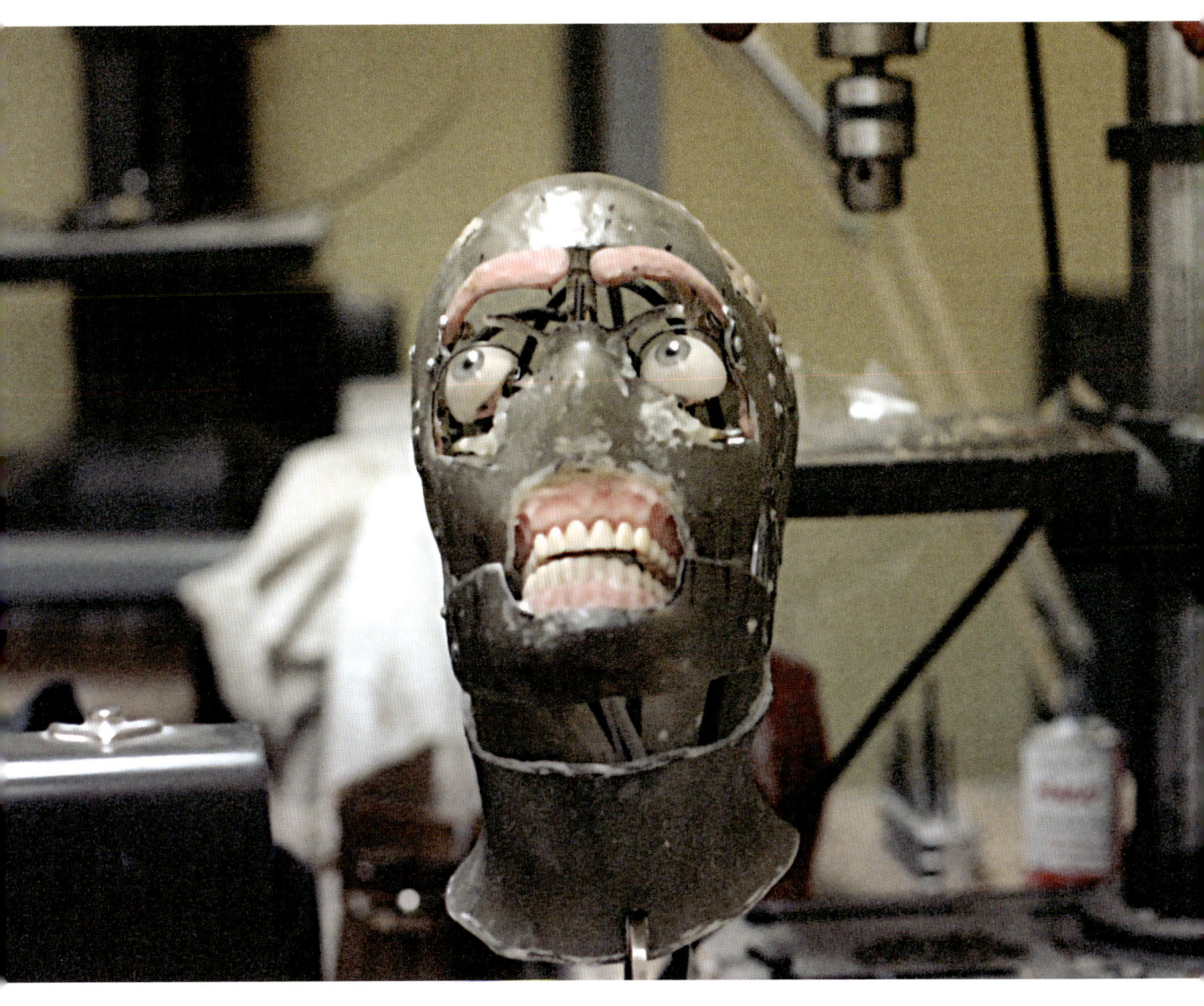

Above: The inner mechanics of Greg Nicotero's severed head. (Courtesy of Al Magliochetti.)

While the art department would create such things as the wall of arms, the make-up effects team would take care of the trick shovel for the shovel "pop-top" effect with John Vulich. More topics – such as the creation of the autopsy table with the hole in it for Mike Trcic to lay in, the retractable scalpel that Dr. Logan uses to dispatch the Trcic zombie, and the zombie extra assembly line – were all discussed. Another point of focus was how to achieve the death of Captain Rhodes. Ideas including having the actor in a standing position, utilizing a fake wall, or having him lying down inside a fake floor were brainstormed. Also discussed was the way it would end up being shot.

On September 18, John Vulich would begin creating one of the most iconic zombies in film history: Bub. The inspiration for Bub's look came from two different films. "Approaching Bub . . . there was a make-up that Tom [Savini] had done in *Dawn of the Dead*, I think, on Scott Reiniger, where he turns into a zombie, where he kind of did what looks like a stretch and stipple make-up on his face, where it's all wrinkly and cracked," says Vulich. "I was just thinking of doing a more elaborate prosthetic version of that same style of make-up. Because it seemed to me that was already a part of the style of the show, or the tone that he had already set design-wise for it. I just wanted to do an extension of that. I don't really remember us talking too much about the approach. I don't remember if Tom gave me any notes on what his vision of it was or anything. I'm not sure if I had free rein to go ahead and try something out and have him look at it and review it, I don't really remember the process.

Above: Derek Devoe at work on a zombie-face sculpture at Tom Savini's house in Pittsburgh. Devoe would leave midway through the pre-production. (Courtesy of Mike Trcic.)

"The other thing is: I wanted to look at the photos at the time of some of the make-ups that I think Alan Ormsby had done for *Shockwaves*. I was asking Tom if he had any books with that make-up in it, if he'd want me to look at it, or if he would mind if I looked at it or not. And he got somewhat incensed about it, and then later on I found out that, I think, him and Ormsby kind of had a little bit of a rivalry or something and I think he just didn't want me being inspired by a rival's make-up. Actually, he virtually forbid me to use that as a reference. But it was the same kind of thing, like stretch and stipple make-ups. I just thought they were a very nice design. But that was in my head: the make-ups in *Shockwaves* and the make-up that he did on Scott Reiniger were the two inspirations, mostly, for Bub."

Not only was the make-up design done flawlessly by Vulich, but it was done rather quickly as well. "I don't think it took more than two or three days to do Bub, if I remember correctly, probably a couple of days. I think I found, with prosthetics, when you're trying to sculpt something that's organic and natural-looking, I just found for my methodology of working that, for me, it's better if I do it quicker, because it tends to be a little more haphazard and it looks more organic that way. If I take too long and start thinking about it too much, then it starts to look sculpted. I think it was more [that] it just seemed to suit my work flow better to operate in that manner."

A few days later, September 21, another department head meeting took place to further discuss some of the important details on the upcoming shoot. Some of the previously covered topics were elaborated upon, including the specifics of accomplishing the death of Captain Rhodes, the zombie assembly line, and Vulich's zombie "pop-top" effect. A minor change was made regarding the scene where Dr. Logan kills the Trcic autopsy zombie with a scalpel to the head. Instead of a scalpel, the doctor would use some type of drill to accomplish this feat. Another juicy new decision was that the zombie eating scenes would be presented in montage form, linking together the deaths of the soldiers at the film's conclusion.

With October looming, the cast was falling into place. Most of them would make a trip to Savini's home to have casts made of different body parts for their eventual demise onscreen. John Amplas, who won the role of Fisher, was brought in for a cast of his forehead for a bullet hit effect. Ralph Marrero, who was cast as Rickles, was brought in for a cast of his forehead and hand. Phillip Kellams was brought in for a cast of his head for a bullet hit effect. Fortunately for Kellams, a neck cast that had been previously taken from Anthony "Tim" DiLeo fit him perfectly, making a cast of his neck unnecessary. Not long after this, a

Above: Derek Devoe, Greg Nicotero and Tom Savini in the basement of Savini's Pittsburgh home during the film's prep. (Courtesy of Mike Trcic.)

decision was made to swap the roles of Torrez and Miller, with Taso Stavrakis being cast in the role of Torrez. Basically, many of their scenes would now simply flip flop. Finally, Joe Pilato, who was cast as Rhodes, came to visit Savini and company for a cast of his chest, hips, and legs for the spectacular death that awaited him on location.

Having already secured the film's primary location, the make-up effects prep would move from Savini's house in Pittsburgh to the location site in Wampum. "We prepped until the beginning of October," recalls Greg Nicotero. "Most of it we prepped at Tom's house, and then probably two weeks before we started shooting we moved to the Wampum Mines and set up our lab there and everything was on site. Even though I lived in Pittsburgh and Mike Trcic lived in Pittsburgh we actually moved. I moved from my parents' house, where I was living, because I was twenty, and stayed at the Beaver Falls Holiday Inn. We all stayed there."

One of the choice jobs for Nicotero on the production was the handling of guts and entrails, which would inspire his nickname on the film: "Gut Boy". After the prep moved to Wampum, Nicotero had to call around to different meat-packing companies in search of animal entrails to use during filming. After several attempts, he located a nearby packing company that sold the production 44 pounds of pig entrails. They were cleaned and stored in a refrigerator in the make-up effects shop inside the Wampum Mine.

By this point day players were being cast for some of the featured zombie rolls, and the generic zombie appliances were being used to fit their faces. Mark Tierno was cast as the "Beef Treats" zombie, Debra Gordon was cast as the female captive zombie who gets corralled with the "Beef Treats" zombie, Barbara Russell was cast as the zombie who bites out Miller's throat, and Don Brockett was cast as the "Splatterhead" zombie who gets shot by Terry Alexander's character late in the film.

One of the last things Savini's crew did during prep was cast Mike Trcic for the autopsy zombie who spills his guts. Trcic was cast with his back recessed into a platform to achieve the illusion. During this time Savini's friend, Barry Gress, was also cast for the Major Cooper headless corpse. Gress was cast with his head recessed into a platform so that his real body could be used in the scene.

The film's prep had been a whirlwind of non-stop excitement for the young crew, but it was also filled with long days. Greg Nicotero recalls it fondly. "When we were prepping we worked July to October, six-day weeks, ten o'clock in the morning to ten o'clock at night, and I made $200 a week – and I didn't care. It was funny because the girl I was dating at the time, she was like, 'I never see you anymore.' I said, 'I'm working, what do you want me to say? I'm working.' And then Tom was on *Pittsburgh Today* and said to the interviewer, 'Oh yeah, I have a crew that's at my house and they're there six days a week from ten in the morning to ten at night.' I said, 'See, I'm not making this up.' That's literally what we did, but we didn't care. We just had a great time."

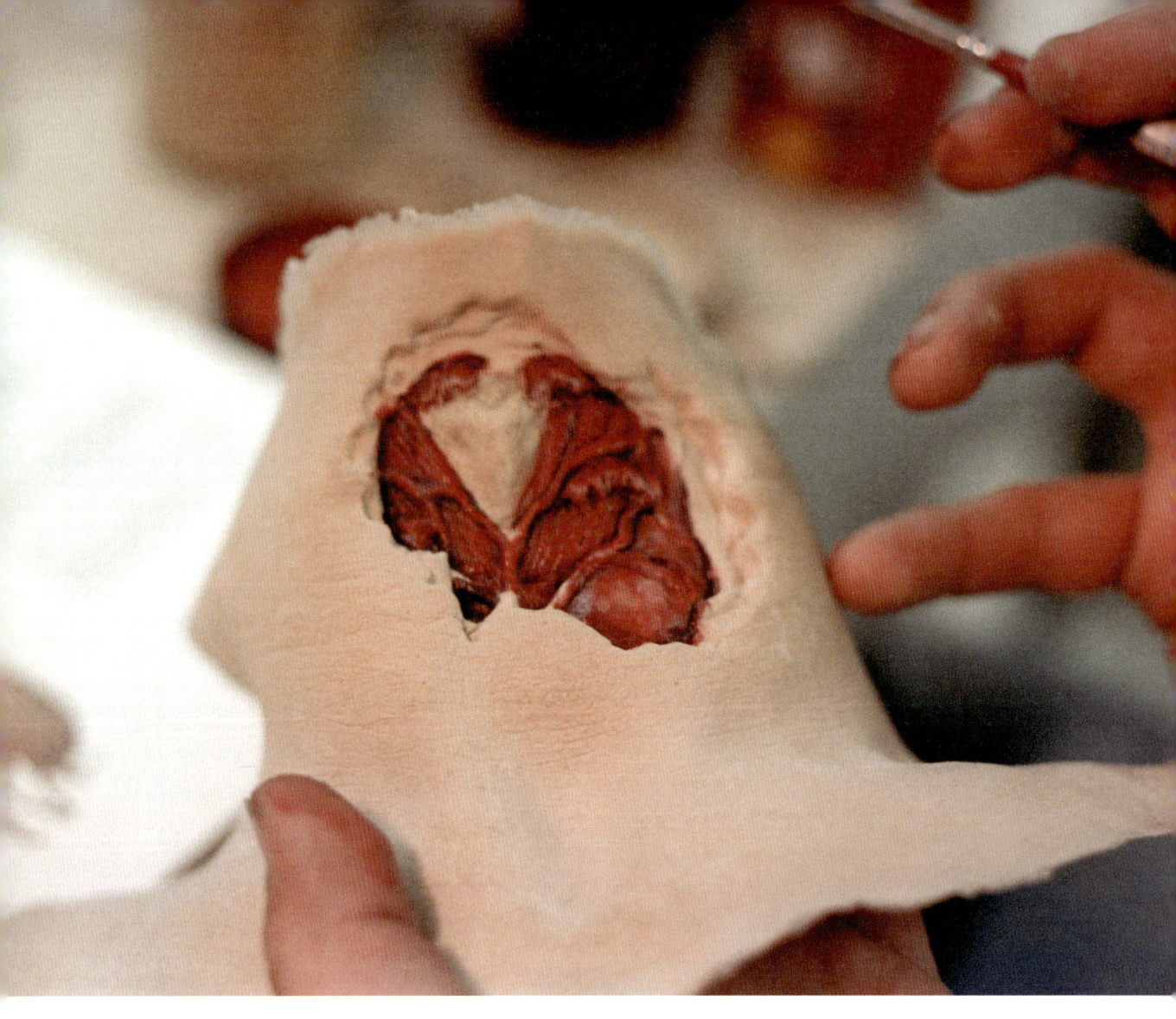

For Nicotero especially it was an incredible learning experience that would serve him well in the years to come. "For me it was a crash course, because I hadn't studied make-up effects," says Nicotero. "I was a fan of make-up effects, but I had never studied it. But it was the ultimate apprenticeship, because I learned everything that I needed to learn. I learned how to read scripts, I learned how to do breakdowns, I learned how to manage the entire department . . . and I just taught myself. I mean, no one taught me." And despite the long hours, the low pay, and the near-death experiences, it was more than worth it for the novice artist. "It was kind of funny, we didn't care,"

Above: Close-up of the throat appliance used for Phil Kellams' death scene at the corral – originally cast from Tim DiLeo for his death scene on the elevator platform. Luckily for Kellams the appliance was a perfect fit, saving him the trouble of having his own neck cast. (Courtesy of Al Magliochetti.)

says Nicotero. "At that point we didn't care how much money we were making, it's just we were getting a chance to work on *Day of the Dead*. As far as we were concerned that was it, it didn't matter how much money we made, we didn't care. Mike Trcic actually thought he was going to have to pay us to work on it."

With principal photography on the horizon, the crew that would proudly proclaim "Zombies Are Us", with a sign on their effects-shop door, was now shifting into high gear and felt very confident about what lay ahead. "Everything seemed to go pretty smoothly, we seemed to have forever to get everything ready," remembers Mike Trcic. "By the time we got to the mine we were as prepped as anybody. We were ready for them to throw anything at us."

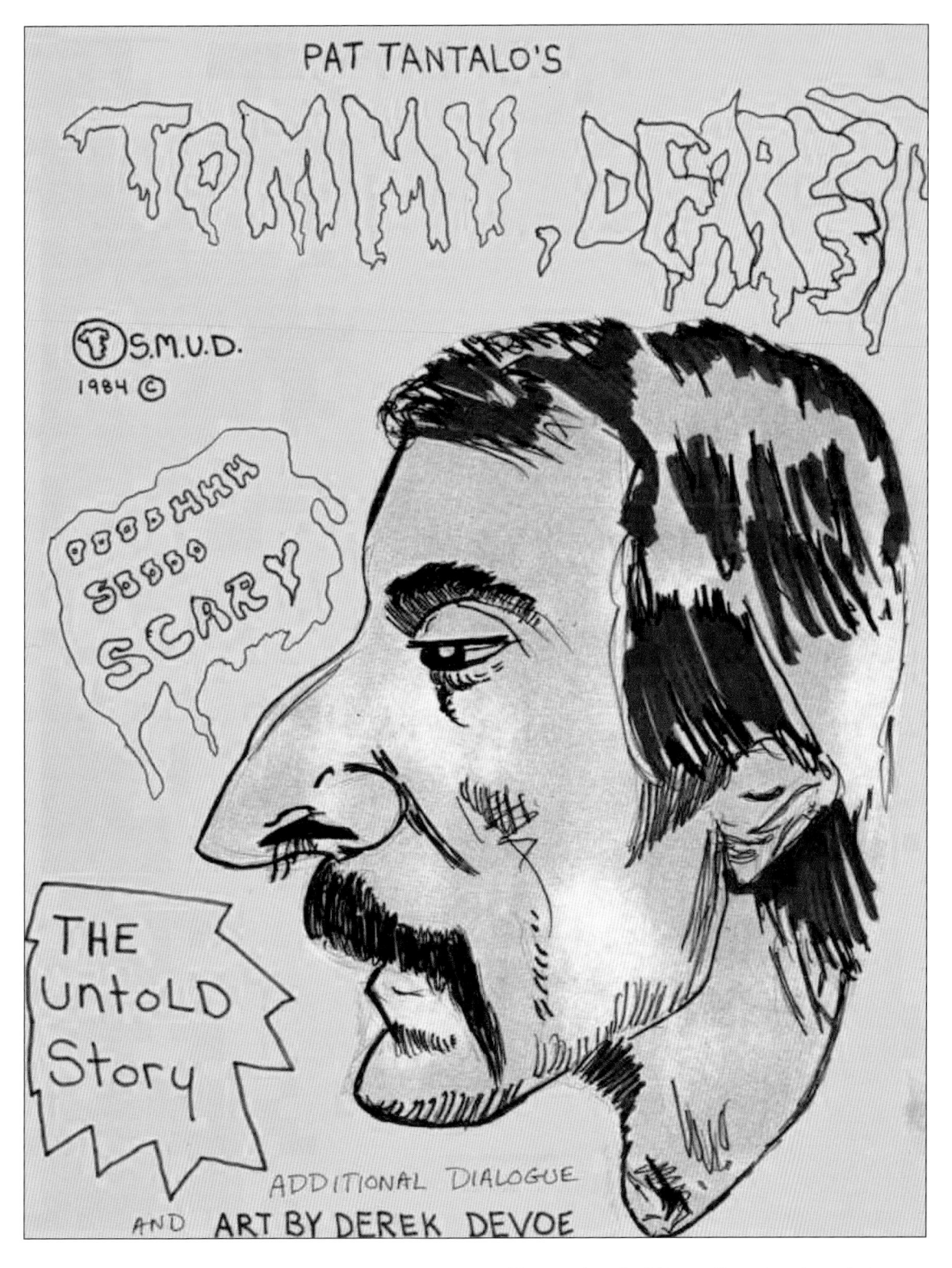

Above and overleaf: *Tommy, Dearest* comic created by Pat Tantalo and Derek Devoe, about the pre-production make-up effects process under Tom Savini. (Courtesy of Pat Tantalo.)

WHEN I FIRST MET TOM...
CHAPTER 1 - ANY RESEMBLANCLE OF THESE CHARACTERS TO ANYONE ELSE IS PURELY INTENSIONAL.
CREATION CONVENTION, '77
GEE - I WONDER WHY NOBODY WANTS TO BUY ANY OF MY GREAT STUFF???
WOULD YOU TAKE A POST-DATED CHECK? FER 1997 OR 98 PERHAPS.
HEY - I THOUGHT MAYBE I CUDDA SOLD SOME OF DIS SHIT AT TH' STORE - BUTT FUK MAN - EVEN TH' KING OF SLEAZE HAS HIS LIMOTATIONS !!!!!!!!!!?
CAUSE FANGORIA MAGAZINE HASN'T COME OUT YET. SHIT HEAD HAS JUZ GOTTA CHANGE HIS NAME... SOUNDS LIKE SOME DISH MAMA THE WOP WOULD SERV
DAWN OF DICK
DARRYL F.
PFFT
MOVIE SADASS
DAWN O' DEAD (WORK PRINT) DAWN O' DEAD (WORK PRINT) (DOESN'T WORK) (LIVE LONG) (AND SHUD)
VHS
FUCKER WANT SCARY ME.
D.K.
HEY BILLY! DIS LOOKS LIKE YOU AFTER KISSIN TEACHERS ASS!
SCUZ ME... BUT IZ DIS A FOAM RUBBAH HEAD? O.K THANKS!
ARE WE NOT MEN? WE ARE DEVOS
NOW SHOWING FEAR NO... BEAVER

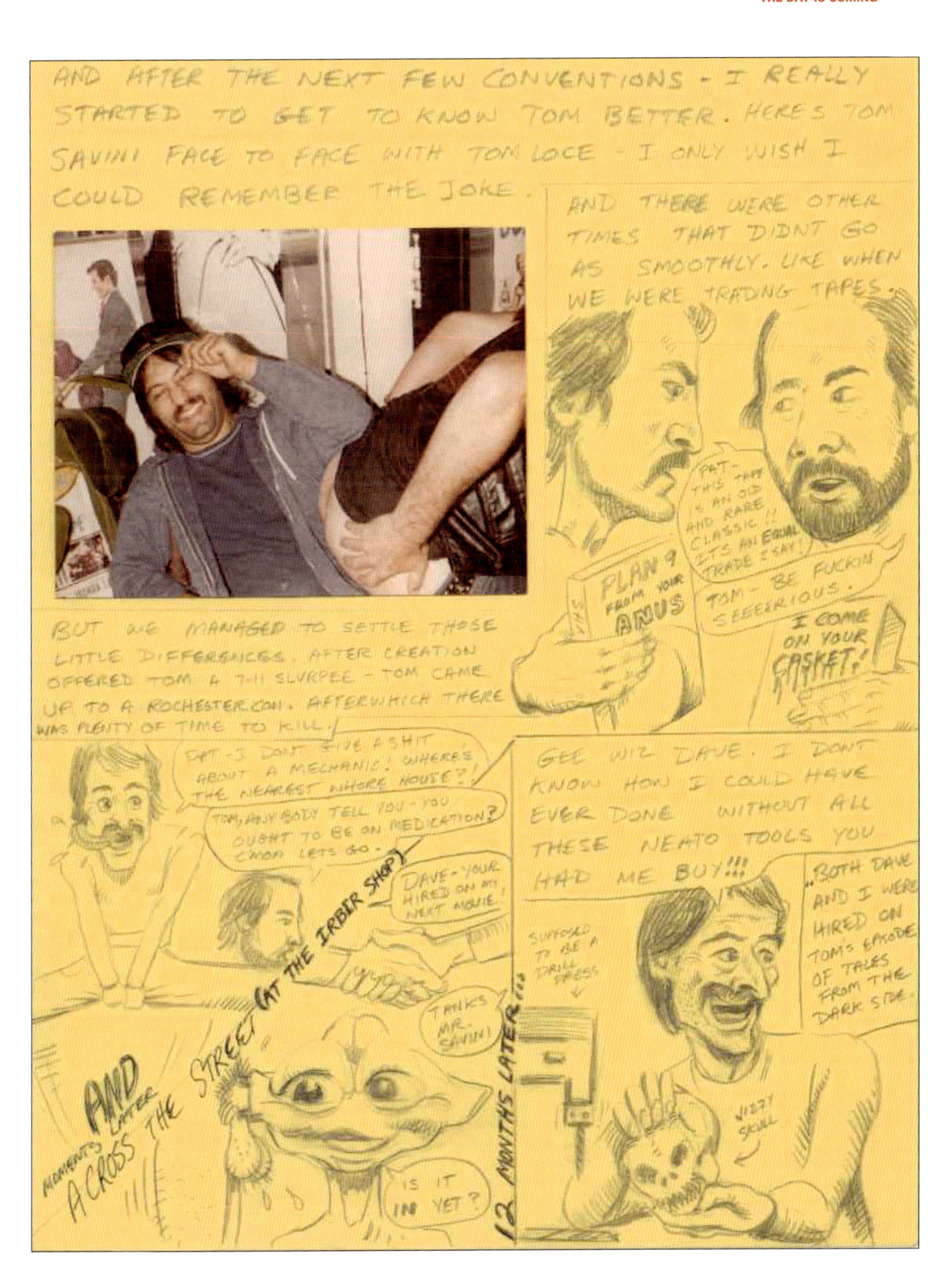

AND AFTER THE NEXT FEW CONVENTIONS - I REALLY STARTED TO GET TO KNOW TOM BETTER. HERE'S TOM SAVINI FACE TO FACE WITH TOM LOCE - I ONLY WISH I COULD REMEMBER THE JOKE.

AND THERE WERE OTHER TIMES THAT DIDN'T GO AS SMOOTHLY. LIKE WHEN WE WERE TRADING TAPES -

PAT - THIS TAPE IS AN OLD AND RARE CLASSIC!! IT'S AN EQUAL TRADE I SAY!

PLAN 9 FROM YOUR ANUS

TOM - BE FUCKIN SEEERIOUS.

I COME ON YOUR CASKET!

BUT WE MANAGED TO SETTLE THOSE LITTLE DIFFERENCES. AFTER CREATION OFFERED TOM A 7-11 SLURPEE - TOM CAME UP TO A ROCHESTER CON. AFTER WHICH THERE WAS PLENTY OF TIME TO KILL.

PAT - I DON'T GIVE A SHIT ABOUT A MECHANIC! WHERE'S THE NEAREST WHORE HOUSE?!

TOM, ANYBODY TELL YOU - YOU OUGHT TO BE ON MEDICATION? C'MON LETS GO.

DAVE - YOUR HIRED ON MY NEXT MOVIE!

AND MOMENTS LATER ACROSS THE STREET (AT THE BARBER SHOP)

TANKS MR. SAVINI

IS IT IN YET?

GEE WIZ DAVE. I DON'T KNOW HOW I COULD HAVE EVER DONE WITHOUT ALL THESE NEATO TOOLS YOU HAD ME BUY!!!

SUPPOSED TO BE A DRILL PRESS

...BOTH DAVE AND I WERE HIRED ON TOM'S EPISODE OF TALES FROM THE DARK SIDE.

12 MONTHS LATER...

VIZZY SKULL

THE DAY IS COMING

45

THE MAKING OF GEORGE A. ROMERO'S DAY OF THE DEAD

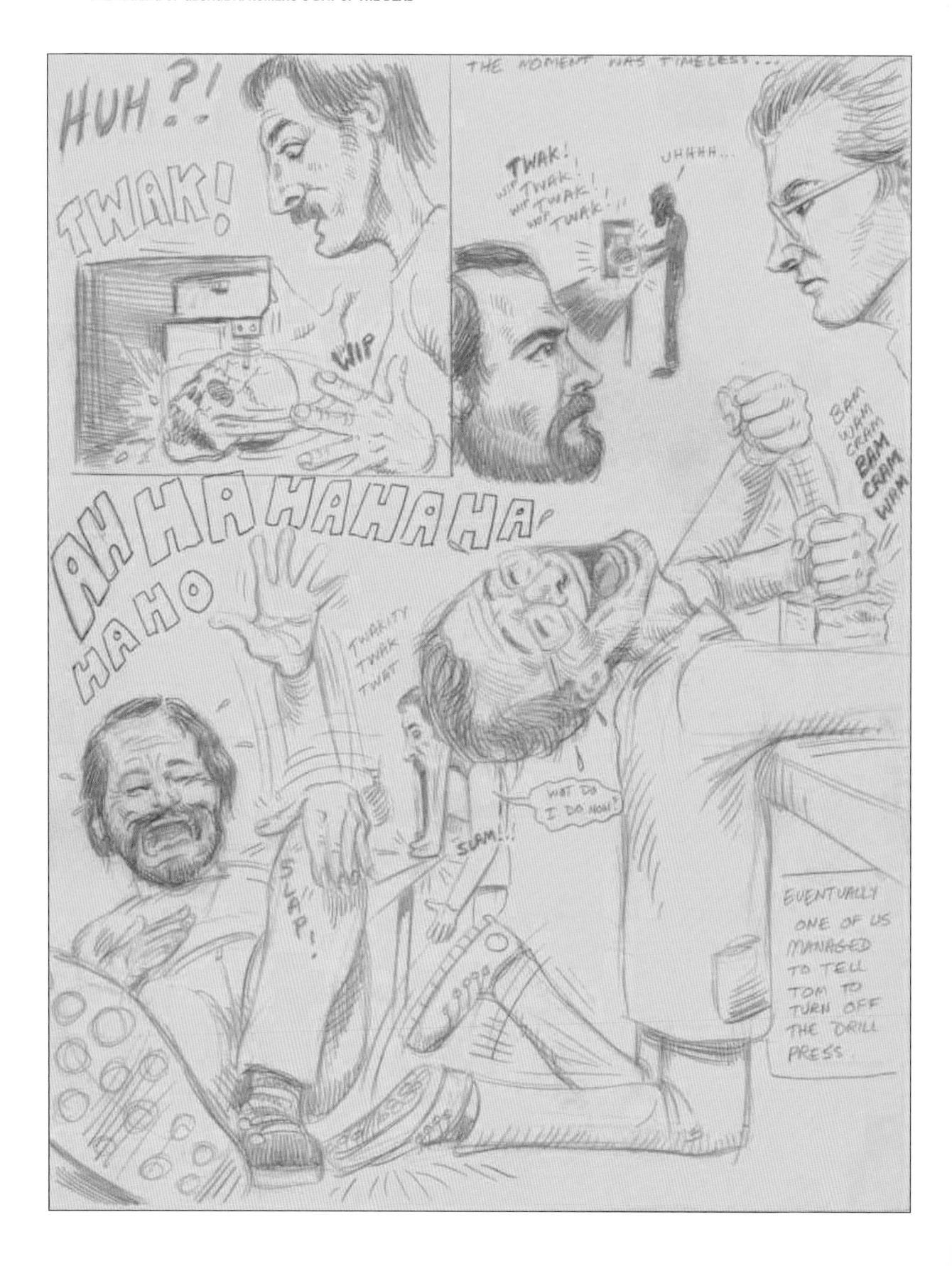

THE DAY IS COMING

THE MAKING OF GEORGE A. ROMERO'S DAY OF THE DEAD

THE DAY IS COMING

WHO SAID THAT TOM SAVINI ISNT A CRUDE PERSON? YES - HERE IN THIS ARTISTS SO CALLED RENDERING IS TOM SUCCESSFULLY IMITATING ONE OF HIS MOST FAITHFULL EMPLOYEES.

"HEY DAVE! GUESS WHO I IS?"

"TOM - YOURE A FUKIN SCREAM!"

AND WITHOUT TOMS PERMISSION, I WAS ABLE TO TAKE THIS PHOTO OF THE LOCAL STRAY DOGS AND CATS TOM CAUGHT DURING MATING SEASON. - YOU SHOULD SEE WHAT HE DOES WITH HIS OWN PETS!

49

OF COURSE - I CAN ONLY REMEMBER THE HIGHLIGHTS OR THE OUTSTANDING BAD TIMES I HAD WITH TOM.
BROWNERS
ONE OF THE MOST TERRIFYING TIMES WAS WHEN DAVE AND I LEFT TOMS TO GO TO OUR "SO CALLED" LIVING QUARTERS!
PAT! WE NEED RE-ENFORCEMENTS! RETREAT!
SPLAT!
THE PREVIOUS TENANTS I RECKON
TAKE THIS YOU COCK SUCKIN' BASTARDS!
SWAK
RATTATTATATAT
FORTUNATELY I HAD TIME TO GRAB OUR NAPSACKS AND SLEEPING BAGS. BUT UNFORTUNATELY 4 HOURS LATER...
JEE-ZUZ GUYS! I PAY YOU TO FUKIN SUNBATHE? BACK TO WORK!
AH, BUT ONLY IF LOOKS COULD KILL.
MUTHA FUKAZ
WEEKS LATER...
HEY TOM - CAUGHT YOU AT LAST! WHEN DO I START WORK ON DAY OF THE DEAD?
WELL PATRICK - ITS LIKE THIS, THE BUDGET IS SUPER-LOW. BUT I DO HAVE YOU ON LIST OF THE PEOPLE THAT I WANT! TRUST ME.
RED FOXX
SHEMP HOWA
SCAT MAN CROT
DON POST JR
DAVID SMITH
ELVIS PRESLEY
MOE
RICK BAKER
JOHN BEECLER
ARNOLD GORGINZOLA
PAT TANTALO

THE DAY IS COMING

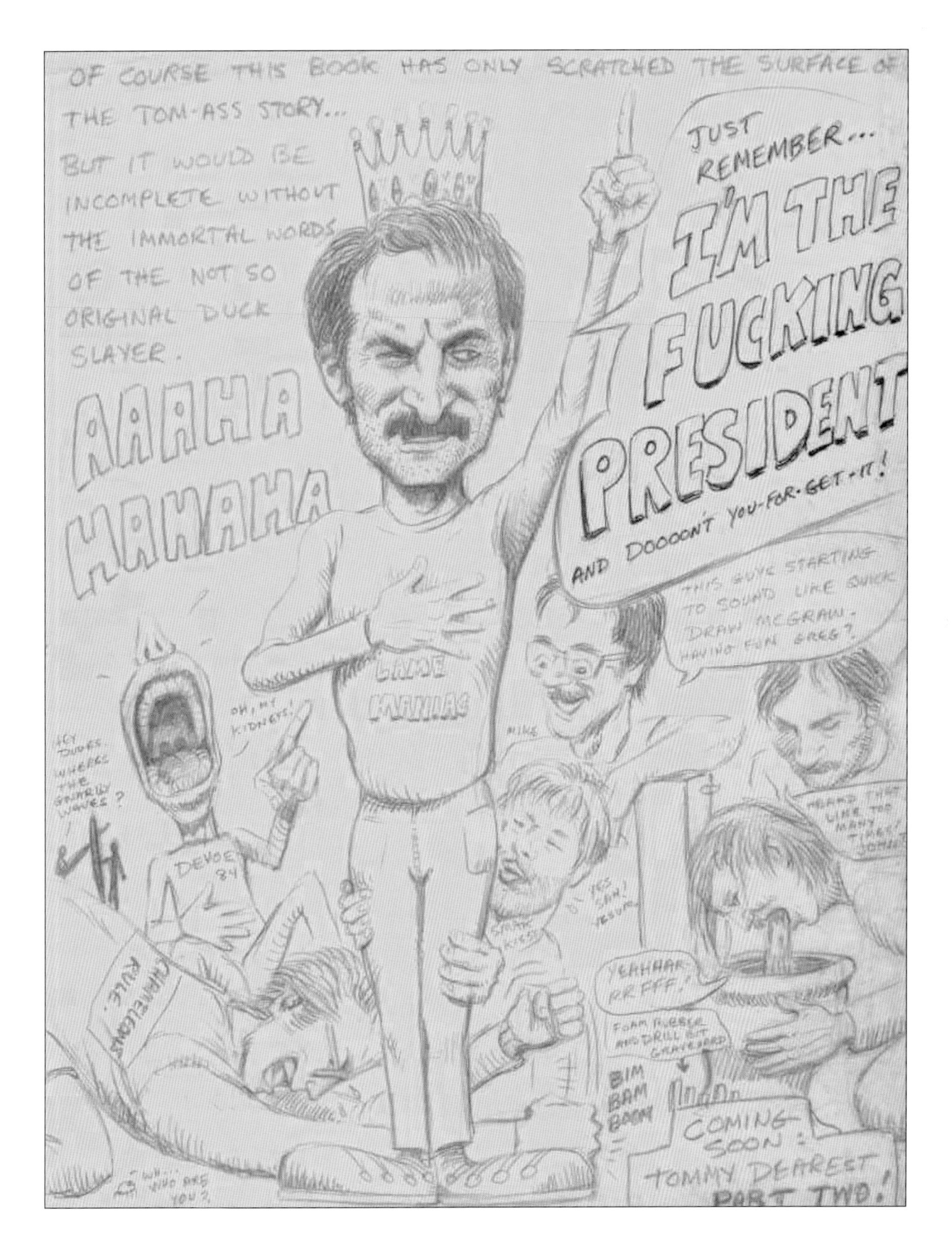

Pat Tantalo's

S.M.U.D.
1984 © Presents

TOMMY DEAREST

Co-written + Art by Derek Devise

Section B: Laurel-Day, Inc.

While Team Savini was busy handling the enormous make-up effects preparation, the rest of the production team was just as busy. The Romero "family" of filmmakers – including some new additions to the group – had begun work in earnest on the larger-scale version of Romero's script. "When I wrote the first script I was hoping that we'd be able to pull it off," says George Romero. "But then when I got together with Cletus [Anderson] and everybody else, and we worked out the budget, it just became, you know . . . it was impossible."

Cletus Anderson was the production designer on *Day of the Dead*, and had served in that capacity on Romero's films since first teaming up with the director on *Knightriders* in 1980. Cletus Anderson grew up in Cleveland, Ohio. Raised by his grandparents, he learned from them the traits that would make him such a successful designer and beloved teacher – art, craftsmanship, humanity, and respect for others. While attending Yale University he met his future wife of over 40 years, Barbara. They would both move to Pittsburgh and become fine arts professors at Carnegie Mellon University, and eventually professional colleagues of George Romero. Sadly, in March 2007 Cletus lost his battle with cancer. As a key member of the production, his fingerprints are all over the film that was envisioned and the film that eventually came to be.

"Cletus did sets for the whole movie, he did sketches for all the stuff that was supposed to be above-ground in Florida," recalls costume designer Barbara Anderson. "So, we worked a lot on that one. We used to talk over the scripts with George regularly and try to figure out how to do what we needed to do with the amount of money that he had. Because he always over-wrote the scripts, they were always much more than could ever be built for the money he had. And a lot of times they were ingeniously done, a lot more than you would think we could get done with that. But Cletus did design that whole town and everything that was supposed to be built down there [in Florida]. And then it got completely changed when we went to the mine."

While Cletus worked on the design of the film's sets, Barbara was busy working on the look of the characters' costumes. "I did sketches for all the main characters. We had to have duplicates a lot because of what they had to go through," she recalls. "I did sketches, I would talk them over with George, I would find what we wanted. We didn't build a lot for that one, but I always did sketches for all the films and then went and found what I wanted that was going to be along the lines. But usually it wasn't a question of building as much as it was finding and distressing."

Working with a budget of around $10,000, Anderson would go to department stores to look for costumes for the lead actors. "When I'm shopping a show, I'm shopping everywhere. So, I'm just going around and finding what I think is right for the character," says Anderson. "I used to love shopping at Syms, I was really upset when they left town because it was a great place to get men's stuff."

While the leads would have new brand-name clothing, the look of the zombies would require a trip to the thrift store instead. "The majority of the zombie costumes were bought at the Red White and Blue," says Anderson. "So my theory was that wearing polyester makes you a zombie because they were all bad, polyester clothes that we would just get and then distress up like crazy." Anderson recalls how a typical trip to the thrift shop would go: "I'd go in and get a giant basket full of old clothes and we'd take it out there [to the mine] and distress it up and spray it down." Though destroying all of those clothes would occasionally gnaw at her conscience. "Sometimes I felt guilty because I'd get clothes real people could have enjoyed wearing."

One of Barbara Anderson's trusted assistants on the film was Eileen Sieff, who had previously worked with her on *Creepshow*. Among her many duties during the prep, Sieff would carry out the "distressing" of zombie extra wardrobe with fellow assistant Howard Kaplan, in the costume shop in the Margaret Morrison building at Carnegie Mellon University. "On *Day* we dyed, shredded, torched, wrinkled and then painted the costumes to get them to be 'zombiefied'," says Sieff. "Howard [Kaplan] came up with lots of materials that could be attached to the paint that looked like mold and dried blood. One of our best discoveries was perma-dirt."

Another person helping out with this task was Kevin Ritter, who would eventually move from working in wardrobe to working in the prop department. One of the key items needed for the zombie costumes were the neck collars used to hook them. "We literally took load after load after load of clothes from the Goodwill and put them in dyes first. And then we all sat around tables with all kinds of crap and latex and oatmeal and paint and just 'zombiefied' all of these clothes," says Ritter. "And one of the things we were doing was making the collars. I remember using the machinery in the shoe room at Carnegie Mellon and actually distressing the leather and making those collars."

While the Andersons were busy designing the look of the film and its characters, the production unit had their hands full with the financial side of things. Producer Richard Rubinstein decided to bring in a new associate producer for the film, Ed Lammi. Born in Pittsburgh and raised in the same Bloomfield neighborhood as Tom Savini, Lammi attended Penn

State and had spent time working on the production crew at WQED Television in Pittsburgh. By the time the opportunity to work on *Day of the Dead* rolled around, he was living in Los Angeles doing freelance work.

"Well, a good friend of mine, John Harrison, who actually wound up being the first Assistant Director and did the music on the film, who had known George [Romero] for many years and had known Richard Rubinstein, recommended me to Richard the summer of – and I'm not sure I have this year right – but I think it was, like, June of 1984," recalls Lammi. "Richard and I met here in Los Angeles and then he asked me to come to New York and basically hired me as . . . in those days the title was associate producer, but effectively it was what's known these days as a line producer. And what Richard kind of said to me is, when he's in town he's the producer, when he's not in town I'm the producer. And he basically came in and out about a day a week or an afternoon a week, because he was in New York and we were in Pittsburgh. And so, if I have that year correct, the summer of 1984 was when I began to work on the picture, and George and I and the production manager, Zilla Clinton, spent the summer – George spent it writing and rewriting and I spent it budgeting and re-boarding – until we got to the place where Salah and Richard said, 'That's a budget we can work with.'"

The summer of 1984 would be a hectic one for Lammi, as he dealt with the issues surrounding the script's budget and the ramifications of having it continuously cut down by Salah Hassanein. "I was in the Pittsburgh office all summer, and at various times we started bringing in the departments; I couldn't remember exactly when people came on board," says Lammi. "But, it was an interesting story because when Richard first contacted me I thought, 'Geez, it's awfully early Richard, to prep this long,' and then when I read the first draft of the script on the flight from Los Angeles to New York I realized [*laughs*] why he wanted me in early, because the script was gonna be way too expensive for the kind of money that they could get. So that's when I realized that my summer was going to be spent working with George, and he was rewriting and I was scheduling and boarding and budgeting, and that's how we were gonna get to the place where we had an acceptable budget that Salah Hassanein could sign off on. So Zilla [Clinton] and I were there . . . Michael Gornick – because he was part of their company – he was there all summer. And then we started location scouting and so forth, but I would say hard prep probably started more like late August or September for an October production start."

As it became increasingly clear that the film's script was too ambitious for the dollars allocated, and that Salah Hassanein was entrenched in the belief that going unrated simply was too much of a risk for the investment, Romero decided to plead his case directly to the man himself. "When we went down to meet with Salah, down in Florida, we had a budget that was still kinda high and I think George, with Richard's [Rubinstein] sort of acknowledgment, said, 'Let's go see if Salah will step up a little bit more money,'" says Lammi. "And we sat down at the dinner table and Salah said to George, 'Can you give me an R-rated movie?','cause George's [zombie] movies were always unrated, and he said, 'I can't, 'cause if I do that my fans will just abandon me.' So Salah said, 'Then this is done with what I have.' So we kind of got our answer and we went back and worked to that budget number. Anyway, George understood that. I think, like any creative person, he would have loved to do exactly what he wanted to do and, at the end of the day, he had to tailor it a bit towards something that we could afford to do as a feature."

That news would force Romero to totally rework his script to accommodate the budget limitations, something he did fairly quickly while in Florida. "We hadn't even bought our place down there yet when we made that film," says Romero. "Because I remember I stayed in a motel when I was writing it. We went down and scouted it, we had a location scout, and we went down and scouted the locations for the original film and then found that it was going to be too expensive and couldn't do it. I stayed, I literally stayed there, and checked myself into a little motel. I think I wrote the abbreviated script in, I don't know, four or five days or something. So yeah, now that I recall, we hadn't even bought our place down there yet. We had rented a place – Pat Buba's wife, Zilla [Pat Buba was *Day of the Dead*'s editor], her parents had a place down there and we would rent their place. That's how we got introduced to Sanibel [Island], renting their place. We went down to scout and then the word came down, 'Well, this is going to be too expensive,' and I just literally stuck around and said, 'I'm just gonna sit here and do this goddamn thing!' I would go out and drive around the island and look for locations and then I'd come home, and I sat in the motel and wrote the script."

It should be noted that Romero's memory of this long-ago period is shaky at best. Everyone that I spoke to for this book that mentioned Romero's house on Sanibel Island always referred to it as George's home. I asked Zilla Clinton about this over the phone, and she told me that Romero was already living on Sanibel in his own place by the time production began on *Day of the Dead*. She also said that Romero had a tendency to go off on his own to write sometimes. So his recollection of being in a motel could very well be accurate. Unfortunately, neither Zilla Clinton nor Christine Romero was interested in doing an official interview for this book – for reasons that I understand and respect.

THE DAY IS COMING

For Ed Lammi, adhering to a stricter budget, while still trying to help Romero make a film he could be proud of, would require some creative thinking. "Our job at that point was to just keep the budget intact, but try to get him all the tools that he needed to do his work," says Lammi. "To me, that's the fun of the other side of line producing, to come up with the continuity zombie ideas and the mask ideas – just stuff to give him what he wants and still be able to afford to make the movie."

Lammi would assume the role of associate producer from David E. Vogel, who had served previously in that capacity on *Knightriders* and *Creepshow*. Originally Vogel was to serve as the film's co-producer, but that title was given instead to David Ball (more of which later). The story of Vogel's departure from Laurel Entertainment is an intriguing one, very much like the case of Derek Devoe leaving the make-up effects crew. Depending on who you ask, you'll get a different story regarding Vogel's departure. As stated in the previous chapter, the advance artwork that appeared in the 1983 *Variety* film annual listed David E. Vogel as the film's co-producer. A promotional flyer, featuring the same artwork, was given out by UFDC, and also advertised Vogel as the film's co-producer. When asked about it, Lammi was a little hesitant to disclose the exact story of Vogel's departure, citing "some sensitivity and some political stuff" being involved.

Michael Gornick, who was Romero's longtime cinematographer and the unsung hero of Laurel Entertainment, was a little more candid regarding Vogel's departure. "I think [there were] incredible disagreements between George [Romero] and David Vogel," says Gornick. "I think in some fashion George imagined that David, on a corporate level, was subverting all of his efforts in terms of maintaining the original script and then there was incredible animosity at some point in time. Richard [Rubinstein] had no choice except to have David fall back into the background and totally remove himself." John Harrison, another Romero veteran, who was the film's first AD as well as the composer of its score, had a different view. "He worked with Richard, and he and Richard and George got *Tales from the Darkside*, the TV show, off the ground and then he left to go work for Spielberg, for Spielberg's NBC show called *Amazing Stories*, and that's why he left," says Harrison. "It had nothing to do with *Day of the Dead*."

Harrison was one of the earliest people to join the production. After having appeared in bit parts in Romero's *Dawn of the Dead* and *Knightriders*, Harrison graduated to performing first AD duties on *Creepshow* after the original AD was let go due to a personality conflict. He also ended up writing a large portion of the *Creepshow* score. "I will always love the *Creepshow* score," says Harrison. "I tried things in that, that I thought really worked and it was just a

Top: Co-producer David Ball in his office at the Wampum Mine. Fall/winter 1984. (Courtesy of David Ball.)
Middle: Outside the Laurel-Day offices at the Wampum Mine. Fall/winter 1984. (Courtesy of George Demick.)
Bottom: October 8, 1984 Laurel memo from John Harrison regarding the roles of Miller (Phillip Kellams) and Torrez (Taso Stavrakis) being swapped. (Courtesy of Taso Stavrakis.)

55

Above: Costume designer Barbara Anderson assists a zombie extra on Sanibel Island. (Courtesy of Greg Nicotero.)

wonderful . . . it was a lark, you know? It happened so accidentally and it just turned out to be so much fun."

Romero was so impressed by Harrison's musical skills that he insisted on him writing the entire score for *Day of the Dead*. Harrison would be heavily influenced by Romero's original large-scale script for his score. "When George started talking about it he said, 'I want you to do the score for *Day*.' So I just started noodling some ideas. I sent George little tapes of things that I screwed around with, with my gear. Because of that script, the tone of that music had the kind of Caribbean feel that ended up in the final score," says Harrison. "Now we get to the point where Richard [Rubinstein] has the money, we're going to go do the movie and George wants me to do the score. But Richard wants me to come back and also be George's AD, like I did on *Creepshow*. I said, 'Okay. I'll definitely do it, but I want to know that I'm definitely doing the score as well, that I'm doing both these things.' And to his credit Richard said, 'Yeah, that's fine. That's what we want.'" And when it came to the budget fiasco, even Harrison, someone very closely connected to the production, was left in the dark regarding the inner workings of the situation. "They had determined, for whatever reasons, reasons I wasn't privy to, that the *Day of the Dead* movie as a business model, as a business proposition, couldn't sustain the bigger budget," says Harrison. "And I don't know what that was, by the way. Nobody ever told me what the bigger script would come out at."

Interestingly, in the lead up to pre-production, the idea of using 3-D was discussed. In the early 1980s, several horror and sci-fi films were released using 3-D: *Friday the 13th Part 3*, *Amityville 3*, *Jaws 3*, and *Spacehunter: Adventures in the Forbidden Zone* all used the 3-D sales gimmick. However, considering the additional money it would have added to the cost of the production and exhibiting the film, the idea never really built up any steam behind it. "George [Romero] has always been kind of fascinated with the possibilities of 3-D," says John Harrison. "At one point he and Richard [Rubinstein], I believe, came out to Los Angeles. There was a company that wanted to promote their process but it's nothing like it is today – very cumbersome, cumbersome product. It was not gonna work, it was never a serious consideration."

As previously mentioned, David Ball would join the production team, taking on the role of co-producer. Ball is a no-nonsense man, brutally honest at all times. Ball had a long history with Salah Hassanein and would basically serve as UFDC's representative on set, ensuring that things were coming in on budget – even though there was already an on-set producer on board in Ed Lammi.

"This story originates from the making of *Creepshow* in 1981 in Pittsburgh," recalls Ball. "David Vogel was a Laurel employee working with Rubinstein;

basically they were over-budget and they were over-schedule because George [Romero] had never had to work to a certain discipline. I had worked for the financiers on three or four movies, mostly in Mexico actually. The principal financier was a man called Salah Hassanein. Now, Salah and I had a working relationship which went back to 1977, 1978 where I did three, four, five pictures straight off for him, which he was financing with CBS. He was worried that this bunch of amateur filmmakers, if you like, because they were, he was worried that his $7.1 million was gonna be exceeded. So he called me up and he said, 'Hey, David. I need you in Pittsburgh.' So I said. 'All right, what's happening?' He said, 'Well, we're doing a film called *Creepshow* and they're at least a week behind schedule and I don't know why, there's no reason for it and I'm not getting my numbers. And I want you to go and take over the production.' So I said. 'Alright, fine'. Well, you know that you're going to be met with hostility because you've got an in-house scenario with Vogel and Rubinstein and George [Romero] and Gornick and Savini and John Harrison. These guys have all worked together. These guys have learned together, they've grown up together. And along comes this sort of cockney-sounding Londoner that says, 'Okay, guys. I've got to lift you into shape.' Well, they're not going to like it. [*laughs*] I was a young guy, I was only 30. I was a young guy then, I was a really young guy. But I had a mad passion for movie making and an even madder passion for tidy accounting and tidy production. So I went in there, I went to Pittsburgh, and was treated like I had leprosy." [*laughs*]

Ball eventually broke through to the Laurel team, though, proving that it was strictly business on his part. "Finally Vogel and Rubinstein decided that I wasn't the enemy. And I think they understood that I had a certain passion for doing this sort of thing – the business and not the art form, and it couldn't be the other way," says Ball. "So ultimately what happens is that I leave Pittsburgh, I leave the 'Burgh, with a lot more friends than I joined it with."

Ball's addition to the production could very well have been seen as a slap to the associate producer who was already in place, Ed Lammi. "I think Lammi was a bit upset that I was brought in. I think Lammi thought he could handle it. I think Lammi thought that I wasn't necessary. But then Lammi didn't have to raise the money and wasn't responsible for it – was he?" says Ball. "What actually happened was that, when I explained why I was there to Lammi, and also explained how I could, if necessary, eat him for breakfast and how I was satisfying the financiers' insecurity, and I would not fail them, the investors, because that's what I did for a living – when I explained that to Ed . . . we went and had a couple of beers, and he needed to understand how

Above: Director of Photography Michael Gornick – seen here during the filming of *Knightriders* – was one of the most important, loyal members of the Romero film family. Yet, working on *Day of the Dead* would turn out to be a less than desirable experience for the trusted veteran. (Courtesy of Mike Gornick.)

things were. When I explained why I was there – and I was there, not because I was somebody's son or somebody's brother or uncle or cousin, I was there because I knew what I was doing and Hassanein put me there because I'd proven [myself] to him for five years . . . We were working with him and Hemdale [Film Corporation], we were doing pictures in Mexico with Farrah Fawcett and that sort of thing. We were doing difficult stuff, but on a tight budget, and it needed tight control. So I did three or four of those and Hassanein . . . of course, I became his favorite

Above: Actor Tim DiLeo in a 1972 modeling shot. (Courtesy of Tim DiLeo.)

boy, because I knew how to get quality on film, but not go over budget. It's only because I was trained in film production. When I explained that to Lammi, when he understood that I wasn't going to learn anything off of him, he was going learn something from me, we became good friends, actually. And we never had any run-ins on the production because he was . . . it wasn't his decision. I had to make the decisions. I'd say, 'Okay, do me a new schedule, Ed, please and let's go through it. I don't want to do it in here in this fucking horrible limestone mine. I want you and me to go have a couple of beers and kick the schedule around.' So that's what we'd do and that's what we did. I think it's a question of, if I line produce my producer is called sir, and if I produce then my line producer calls me sir. That's sort of how it is."

Lammi proved himself to Ball by demonstrating how professional and dedicated to his job he was. "He was a young, very good – let me say very, very good – production manager. I'm sure he has gone onto better things, I'm sure he's done very well for himself because he had a level of commitment in his head, which was refreshing because there's a certain tendency to be doing it for the money in some cases. But Ed was very, very committed and I liked Ed and we got on quite well. And I did fancy Felice [Lammi – Ed's wife] at the time, I tell you. She had a great pair of tits, that girl." Felice Lammi would handle the casting of zombie extras, along with Holly Wagner (more of which later). These days Ed Lammi isn't doing too badly for himself: he's the executive vice president of production for Sony Pictures television. Nice work if you can get it.

As Ed Lammi previously explained, the meeting with Salah Hassanein failed to rescue Romero's plans for his original script, and it was now up to David Ball to keep things afloat, in particular with Romero himself, who was apparently upset about having his request denied by Hassanein. Ball met individually with the various department heads and discussed ways to stretch their thin budgets even further to help Romero when it came time to shoot. "I mean George, he wanted 100,000 zombies, and this was long before those letters CGI had ever been invented," says Ball. "So you couldn't have 100,000 and you couldn't create 100,000, it couldn't be like that. And Hassanein was not convinced that big budget was the way to go. I don't know, perhaps because there had been too much time between *Dawn* and *Day*. You know what I mean? It's like the bubble may have burst, because it had been some years between the movies and so he was erring on the side of caution, was Hassanein. So what happened was, George became angry and he said, 'Ahh, fuck him, man! I don't do this, fuck you! Fuck it, I don't want to do it if I ain't gonna get the right money!' So it sort of became my job to say, 'Well, what we've done George is we've worked out a scenario where whatever we get will look like double on the screen. Because Cletus [Anderson] is gonna cheat, Savini's gonna cheat, Gornick's gonna cheat, and I'm gonna cheat. So we're all gonna cheat and give you a look that is far bigger than the budget. That's what we're gonna do. We'll just tailor the script to one or two big effects, or big sequences, that will give you the type of movie you want or as close as we can for the money.' And so that's how we set about making the movie and that's how we set about making the movie for a price. And that was something George had never done, because he had never had a budget anyway. He never had any money for his movies. So for him to be tied down to a budget figure, it was upsetting him. But I don't know why it was upsetting him because he didn't have the first idea of what a dollar would buy you in movie terms. George will admit to you that he was absolutely fucking clueless. He didn't do schedules, he didn't understand schedules, didn't understand budgets. He wanted two cameras, he wanted ten shots for every set-up . . . George is the most – at that time – was one of the most undisciplined people I've ever met in my life."

To Ball's way of thinking, Romero was completely ignorant of the business side of filmmaking, which makes sense considering that Romero nearly went bankrupt before Richard Rubinstein appeared on the scene. "He wouldn't know how much a trolley full of supermarket shopping would cost," says Ball. "He wouldn't because that's not where his head's at." And sometimes this could lead to heated disagreements between the two men. "But it was me, Mr. Asshole, from London . . . Mr. Asshole would say, 'You can't have that George, can't afford it.' 'Oh, fucking hell, man! It's my fucking movie, man! You're saying I can't fucking have it, man?'" says Ball. "He'd swear at me in every sentence. He used, 'Fuck this, fuck it, I can't fucking believe this fucking . . .' you know, every sentence."

In the end, Romero would let go of the original script and grudgingly accept the decision to revamp the story. "He wanted the shock factor to continue with *Day of the Dead* . . . and fair enough for him to want that," says Ball. "Fair enough, but the money said no it's not gonna work that way. We're not doing that. We're not giving you an unrated movie because we want to make sure we're gonna get our money back."

Director of photography Michael Gornick had been joined at the hip with Romero since the early 1970s, when they worked together on *The Crazies*. Gornick grew up in Pittsburgh and had just returned home from serving in the US Air Force when he was hired by The Latent Image, Romero's former company. Gornick would go on to become an invaluable member of the Laurel team, serving as cinematographer on *Martin*, *Dawn of the Dead*, *Knightriders*, and *Creepshow*. But his duties went far beyond just shooting the features. He would also serve as post-production supervisor on those films, handling duties such as assisting with the editing, Foley work (when everyday sound effects are added during post-production), and answer prints (the first prints of the film). He did voice work in *Martin* as Barry the talk-show host, and in both *Dawn of the Dead* and *Creepshow* he can be heard as a radio news person. On *Dawn of the Dead* he also helped to pick out a good deal of the DeWolfe library music that fills the movie, and contributed a lot of the zombie moaning sound effects that are heard throughout the film. He was, as stated earlier, truly an unsung hero in Romero and Rubinstein's company, Laurel.

By the time *Day of the Dead* came around, however, the relationship between Gornick and Romero was changing. It was a painful time for Gornick. "Honestly, I must tell you – at that point in time – given the option I wouldn't have worked on that film," says Gornick. "Because George and I – there was so much water

Above: Taso Stavrakis as "Sir Ewain" from *Knightriders*. Stavrakis was a longtime veteran of working with both George Romero and Tom Savini before being cast as Torrez in *Day*. (Courtesy of Taso Stavrakis.)

over the dam at that point in our relationship; it wasn't anger, but it was a discomfort that I had. Literally at one point in time, prior to making that film, George left the Pittsburgh office without saying goodbye to Vince [Survinski, Laurel's bookkeeper and an original investor in *Night of the Living Dead*] and I, and we were deeply disturbed. Both Vince and I had supported him for a number of years and so, with his departure one afternoon, realizing that he wasn't coming back, it was an emotional moment."

Romero had decided that *Day of the Dead* would be the last film he'd direct as an "employee" of Laurel, thus creating an awkward situation for Gornick. On one hand, he felt a certain loyalty to Romero, having worked alongside him for so many years. But on the other hand he was married with two young children, and had to consider his family in the decisions he would now make. Gornick decided to stay with Laurel and Rubinstein, a decision that Gornick believes upset Romero. Work had begun on the *Tales from the Darkside* TV pilot episode, and Gornick made the decision to go to New York to start work on that project. "I think in the next step in our relationship, what happened is that George took offense because I actually went to New York at that point to help produce the pilot and worked in the post-production," says Gornick. "He never voiced any complaints to me or offered any cautions, but I knew when I went out and did that, I knew that the silence on his end from Sanibel was there and he was dissatisfied. We had one final conversation, and again this is prior to the making of *Day of the Dead*, where I was – I think I called him, actually, to tell him that the pilot looked decent, we missed him, it was obviously his script, I'd hoped he would be proud of it. Lots of silence on the other end and I said, 'You know, I sense you are unhappy with me going off to work on the project, but from a filmmaker's standpoint, from a father of two children I needed to work.' I remember that conversation and he said, 'Man, if you haven't made the money over these years, I can't imagine why you need it now.' I was aghast." Gornick continues: "Subsequently, the situation became, in later conversations, pretty business-like, where I would call him or we would set up a conference call and we'd discuss proposed changes. Nothing was coming from his end. Richard [Rubinstein] put me in a situation where he said, 'I want you to look at the script. I want you to see where you can make some cuts, make budgetary savings.' I would meet subsequently with David Vogel and say, 'Here are my thoughts. These don't feel good, but these could make savings.' So I would then, born out of those kind of strategy sessions, contact George and try to persuade him to do some rewrites or at least acknowledge his acceptance of those changes. Gosh, it was painful. It was ugly. We're talking about hour-long conversations where I did all the talking!"

From John Harrison's point of view, Gornick and Romero's working relationship was almost like that of a longtime married couple. "Michael and George had a long, long relationship. It's like a marriage, you know? And then after a while you get to the point where, 'Well, we've kind of explored everything we can here. What now . . . ?', and that becomes a creative frustration for both sides. And I think that there was frustration on both their parts," says Harrison. "It's like any work, man. We all kind of create these romantic notions about what filmmaking is like, and what it's like to be involved in making iconic movies like George's movies. But at the end of the day it's a job! You know? And you gotta go to work and sometimes you're not having a great time with the people you're working with. That's just the way it is, you know? I love the Steelers, man, but I know in the locker room some shit goes down! Know what I mean?"

Nick Mastandrea, Romero's longtime key grip, who had worked under Romero since before *Martin*, was also aware of the issues between Gornick and Romero. "I was a little closer to it because I had known them so long – much longer – and had worked with them when it was just the three of us, or four of us [including Vince Survinksi]," says Mastandrea. "Yeah, I mean I definitely noticed it . . . It almost seemed like Mike was siding with Richard [Rubinstein]. I guess he felt like that was where his job was, because he was not a freelance guy like the rest of us were, he was still an employee of the company. But I think Mike had other issues too, it was all very strange." I asked Mastandrea exactly what he meant when referring to Gornick's "other issues". "He had a couple of different personalities, Mike. You just never knew who was gonna show up," says Mastandrea. "I don't know if anybody else has talked to you about that, but it's just . . . he just had those two different sides to him. One was super nice and would do anything, and then the other one was just a completely other . . ."

David Ball has a very different view of Gornick though, and a poignant one at that. "Mike's a great person; he is a very great person. And he raised some children and he's a God-fearing man and he took the path of regular employment with Laurel Entertainment because he had a family to raise," says Ball. "I honestly like to think that Mike Gornick could have gone so much further. He could have gone so much further. He was a very, very honest guy; a very, very creative guy. But his creative juices were not required because we were all dealing with the George Romero ego. That's what we were dealing with."

Nevertheless, for Gornick it was no longer a joy to deal with Romero and, with *Day of the Dead* looming on the horizon, it wasn't something he was particularly looking forward to. "At that point in time, *Tales from the Darkside* was in full swing. We were producing a lot of shows, I was directing a few of those, and I was hoping against hope that maybe I could just stay with *Tales from the Darkside* in Long Island and they could do their thing in Pennsylvania. But at that point I was in Richard's [Rubinstein] employ and he wanted me on set, he wanted me shooting," says Gornick. "Was it painful? Absolutely; given my druthers, I never would have done it."

Gornick's position within Laurel also gave him a unique perspective on Richard Rubinstein's view of the situation with UFDC, and just how hard he may – or may not – have actually fought for Romero's original vision. "I think [he made no effort] whatsoever," says Gornick. "I think at that point in time Richard [Rubinstein] was taking a more corporate stance, he was being wooed by the [Aaron] Spellings of the world." In 1988 Laurel

Left: A glimpse into the process and preparation of an actor. On his copy of Romero's original script, DiLeo chose to scribble a prayer to St Michael the Archangel. **Right:** Also pasted into DiLeo's copy of the script: a tranquil seascape and an iconic shot from *Psycho*. The juxtaposition was part of DiLeo's attempt to get into the same mental state as his character, Miguel. (Photos courtesy of Tim DiLeo.)

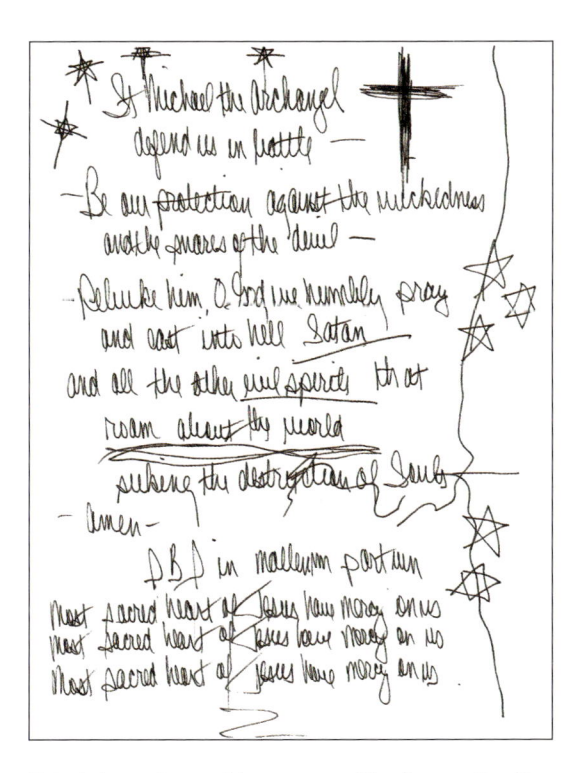

Entertainment would merge with Aaron Spelling Productions, and by the mid-1990s Laurel was under the umbrella of Viacom. Rubinstein would step down and go off to start another production company called New Amsterdam Entertainment. "Richard [Rubinstein] – being a so-called, I guess, CEO – was looking to the future and realizing, okay this is one point in the history of this company and I've got bigger and better things," says Gornick. "And I'm sure he realized George is going away and I have access to certain properties, that I've got to start developing new scripts, finding new avenues of revenue, and is it worth me fighting this battle, you know?"

Needless to say, pre-production on *Day of the Dead* was starting out a little on the rocky side. But even though there were multiple fires to put out and plenty of drama, things were being accomplished. Locations were scouted all over Pittsburgh and the western Pennsylvania region; at old military facilities, the airport, and at both the University of Pittsburgh and Carnegie Mellon University. In the end, the search for the mine location wound up being solved by a very unlikely source. "The Wampum Mine, in particular, came about just through an exhaustive search," says Mike Gornick. "At some point in time, I think through a neighbor, I heard about an underground storage facility in the western part of the state, and that led to some phone calls to this storage facility, what was then the Wampum Mines – it became a kind of storage facility for RVs. So, it was somewhat through my find, through a neighbor, that we discovered this location."

From 1870 to the mid-1940s, the Crescent Stone Company mined limestone from the Wampum caves for cement manufacturing. By the early 1960s, aviation service company, Page Avjet, joined with the Medusa Cement Company to develop the mines into the Wampum Mine Storage Company. The first tenant of the facility stored medical supplies and equipment for Civil Defense hospitals in Pennsylvania and New Jersey. Shortly afterwards, the Medusa Cement Company opened a technical center inside the mine. Years later, those abandoned offices and rooms would be used as sets for *Day of the Dead*.

Mike Butera was an employee of the mine during filming, acted as a liaison between the mine and the production company, and would end up working on the film as a production assistant. "Medusa Cement Company, who basically mined out the facility in the first place, had set those up when they used to do all their testing for the different types of cement, lots of chemical processes, testing all the strengths, whatnot of all the cement," says Butera. "They had probably, oh, I'm going to guess twelve, fifteen rooms in there – different sizes, shapes. They did all kinds of things in there and it went abandoned, pretty much, until then."

THE MAKING OF GEORGE A. ROMERO'S DAY OF THE DEAD

After Medusa opened their technical center, American Optical Company started work on an optical lab, complete with a shaft to the surface, used for measuring purposes. The shaft would also be utilized during the conclusion of *Day of the Dead*, when the heroes are attempting to escape. In 1980 Page Avjet would become the sole owner of the facility, renaming it the Wampum Industrial Facility. The facility was used for various functions, from vehicle storage, to record filing, to storage of film negatives – including the original *Star Wars* films. With a constant temperature of 50 to 55 degrees, the mine contained well over two million square feet of subsurface space, including a lake in the middle of it. In a deal that typified Laurel's resourcefulness, the production was able to rent the mine for a bargain price. "It wasn't a whole lot actually," remembers Mike Butera. "They did it get it fairly cheap at the time, I know they did." Butera estimated that the production spent around $25,000 to $35,000 for the use of the mine during production.

Another Pittsburgh location for the film was found at the old Manor Nike Missile Site, about twelve miles east of the Monroeville Mall, which would be used for the scenes where the elevator is shown descending into the ground. "The Nike Missile Site had been decommissioned and abandoned," says R.C. Staab, who worked for the Pennsylvania Film Bureau. "There was a minor bit of red tape, but, all told, relatively easy."

Nike sites were a staple of the Cold War era in the United States. In the early 1950s, the US Army began constructing installations all across the country that would house twenty-foot-long, 1200-pound guided missiles – the first of their kind, in fact – that were designed to shoot down enemy bombers, in particular Soviet ones. The Nike missiles were named after the Greek goddess of victory, the first being called the Ajax, and its successor the Hercules. The Pittsburgh region contained a dozen such installations, but by 1974 all Nike bases had been shut down.

While location scouting was being carried out in Pennsylvania, there was additional scouting going on in Florida. While visting Sanibel Island and Fort Myers on vacations, George Romero fell in love with the area and was inspired to set the storyline there. Southwest Florida would give the series a totally new flavor and distinguish *Day of the Dead* from its predecessors. For Romero, it was too interesting an idea to pass up, even though it wasn't very sound logically. "Yeah, and I know it didn't quite make sense," says Romero. "I mean**,** if you live in Florida or you know anything about Florida**,** there's no way that there is anything underground in Florida! You dig four-feet down [and]

Left: Associate producer Ed Lammi prepares to be turned into a zombie on the set of *Day*. (Courtesy of Al Magliochetti.)

you're in water. It's a bit forced. It's one thing that I always felt was wrong about the film, but nobody ever questioned it. I don't know, maybe there are some places in Florida where you actually can – where there actually are caves or where you can actually dig underground. But yeah, I mean, I just wanted to do it there because I thought it would be pretty. I thought it would be more impactful to have one of these little Florida towns that's devastated in those opening scenes. I knew that I could get the cooperation of the city there, Fort Myers, so I just went with that." Co-producer David Ball, however, perceived this decision as being about something else entirely. "They chose Sanibel, because George lived there," says Ball. "It wasn't about the best location or the cheapest location, it's because it's ten minutes from where George lived."

Location scout, Bill Dickhaut, was sent to Fort Myers to search for appropriate locales to bring Romero's exotic vision to life. In the original script there are several scenes that involve characters traveling through open expanses of swamp land, which would take Dickhaut to some very interesting and unusual places in the hope of finding just the right look for the film. "One of the places that we looked at was actually a cattle ranch," recalls Dickhaut. "And I remember going out with this guy who owned the ranch. I think it was because we called a real estate agent or something like that, and the agent said, 'Yeah, here's the guy. This is who you need to talk to.' And so I went out there and we drove out and the cattle were actually walking around in about a foot-deep, maybe two-feet-deep, water and there was a lot of vegetation growing up from the water. And I remember this guy driving his pickup truck, his four-wheel drive pickup truck, out into this standing water. He jumped out and I jumped out and I was up to my knees in water and it occurred to me, at that moment, that I'd been in Florida enough [to know] that whenever you find water like that there's almost inevitably alligators! So I said to this guy, 'Are you not concerned that there might be alligators here?' He said, 'Not a bit,' and I said, 'Well, why is that?' and he said, 'Alligators don't want to be in a cow pasture.' And I said 'I don't get it?' and he said, 'Well, they're afraid of being stepped on by cows.' So my fear of walking around in this standing water in Florida was kind of unfounded, because this guy said the alligators are more afraid of being crushed by cows than they are interested in biting a human on the leg."

Another adventure for the location scout would prove to be not only strange, but also a little unnerving. "Because we'd sort of announced to the press, through the newspapers, that we were there and we were looking for locations, I was constantly getting all these people who were, 'Oh yeah, you gotta come to my house. My house will be perfect. You're gonna love this,'" says Dickhaut. "And so I sort of had to weed through a lot of those things during the summer, and I think got to the point where, after a while, I was not taking unsolicited phone calls anymore, because most of them were bad. But I remember early on I got a call from this one young woman and she said, 'I've got the greatest location. You've gotta see it. I've got lots of swamp land and there's a boat dock.' The Orange River kind of goes into the inland of Florida from the coast there, and she said, 'It's back on the Orange River, but it's kind of secluded. I think you're gonna like it.' So I said, 'Okay, well this is worth a meeting.'"

After meeting up with the woman in downtown Fort Myers, Dickhaut rode along with her and a friend out to the house. It was literally in the middle of nowhere, off of the main road, and it was exactly as she had described. It was also obviously a very expensive home. "It struck me that it was just incredibly isolated," recalls Dickhaut. "And there seemed to be an infinite amount of all-terrain vehicles, four-wheelers and three-wheelers and motorcycles and dirt bikes, and things like that. And there was also an air strip that they had sort of cut into the jungle back there."

Upon arriving, Dickhaut decided to ask the woman about her husband's line of work. "I said, 'Well, what does your husband do for a living?' 'Well, he's in importing.' 'Well, what kind of importing?' 'Well, I don't really know.' 'Where is he right now?' 'I'm not really sure.' 'When's he coming back?' 'I don't know.'" says Dickhaut. "You know, all these little indicators that well, okay, this is probably not a good place for me to be."

After staying for an unusually long period of time, and checking out the property, the woman and her friend had disappeared for a bit when a housekeeper approached. "This housekeeper comes up to me and he says, 'Well, the man of the house is not here and he's not going to let you do anything without his okay, and he's not going to okay it,'" says Dickhaut. "And I said, 'I get it. I'm leaving as soon as I can get these people to take me back to town.' [laughs] So whatever it was that this woman thought . . . her husband was in some kind of business that required an air strip and all these vehicles and all this other stuff and had this huge house in the jungle." Luckily for Dickhaut, he was able to make it back into town without encountering "Tony 'Scarface' Montana" himself.

Casting sessions for the film would take place in New York and Romero's home base of Pittsburgh. Preliminary sessions in New York were conducted by Bill McNulty and Romero veteran Gaylen Ross, from *Dawn of the Dead* and *Creepshow*. McNulty, who was not a casting agent, but simply an actor, had gone to school with Romero's wife, Christine, and was originally offered a part in the film by Romero. With both McNulty and Ross having close ties to the Romeros, they were inspired to make sure they got it right. "I think we were better than a lot of professional casting directors," laughs McNulty. "I mean, we very carefully sifted through hundreds of submissions from agents all over the city, and picked out anybody who looked even close to what we thought might be appropriate for the role, and then we started seeing people. We gave them time to read the script in advance and then they would come in and one of us, either Gaylen or I, would read with them. We allowed them a great deal of time to work on the roles and the scenes, and went through the usual process of initial auditions and then call-backs."

One of the more interesting auditions for McNulty came from a young, up-and-coming actress named Diane Venora. Venora had already appeared in Francis Ford Coppola's *The Cotton Club* and starred onstage as Hamlet – a female Hamlet – for producer/director Joseph Papp. "I don't remember the text of the scene too well, but I know that it was confrontational – that I was playing a kind of tough male chauvinist character and I think the female character was pretty aggressive too," says McNulty. "So it was a confrontation between these two people, and at one point I think I probably said something really offensive or kind of very macho, she stepped up to me and grabbed my crotch really hard. [laughs] It's a moment that I can't really get out of my mind. It wasn't really painful, it was just firm and it certainly put her really high on my list of people." [laughs] Years later, Venora would go on to appear in films such as Clint Eastwood's *Bird* and Michael Mann's *Heat*.

Another actor considered for a role in the film was Jack Wallace. Wallace would go on to have a successful career as a character actor in film and television, appearing in *Above the Law*, *Boogie Nights*, *Law and Order*, and *Six Feet Under*. In the February 3, 1985 edition of the *Chicago Tribune*, Wallace was interviewed by writer John Blades, who incorrectly described Romero's films as containing necrophilia, and discussed turning down a role for "that dead producer". "He wanted me because I look like death warmed over," said Wallace, who does a Lugosi-like impersonation of Romero making his pitch: "'Your skin is fish-belly white. Hmmmmm. Why has it lost its color?' 'Because,' I told him, 'I just tried to cross a New York street.' Anyway, the guy tells me I got the part. I told him, 'Look, on two conditions I'll take it. One is that I'm the last one to die and the other is that I don't have to eat no human flesh.' He went along with it. I got the part. But even though my greatest wish is always to do film, I didn't take it because he offered me less money than I'm makin' now." I contacted Wallace and he initially agreed to do an interview, telling me over the phone that he turned down the role because he was offered a stage play that promised to keep him working much longer than the film would have done. However, he abruptly changed his mind about the interview, sending me an email through his wife, saying that he was "not absolutely sure about being offered that movie". The part that I believe Wallace would have been offered, the one that makes the most sense at least, was the role of McDermott, who would eventually be played by Jarlath Conroy.

Frustratingly for casting agent Bill McNulty, most of the submissions that he and Gaylen Ross made were not used by Romero, with the exception of one very memorable part. "I think we got one major actor, one major role cast from all the work that we did, and that was a guy named Howard Sherman, who played the lead zombie," says McNulty. "As far as the other lead roles are concerned, I can't tell you that we can take any credit for that."

McNulty and Howard Sherman had known each other since the mid-1970s, when they met at the Actors Theatre of Louisville and remained friends after both moving to New York. Not long after arriving in the city and doing a play together, McNulty contacted Sherman to let him know about the role of the zombie, Bub. "I had seen *Night of the Living Dead* and I knew that zombies were basically just extras with make-up and I was not interested," says Sherman. "I'm not going to do a movie unless I have a role, and he said, 'Well, this one sort of is a role. He actually has . . .' Now, you have to understand that in the script Bub didn't really figure very much. I mean, obviously he doesn't have any lines and, I don't know, he only showed up in two or three or four paragraphs of stage directions, and then at the end of the movie he shot Rhodes and that was it. So it's not like it was all that much of a presence on the page, but I said, 'What the hell,' you know, so I went to the audition. And, I don't know, I think I pulled the gun and saluted and shot the gun. I mean, I did a few things and I certainly didn't do them the way I did them in the movie. I hadn't really thought about it, I mean it was just kind of pulling it out of my ass, you know?"

At his audition, Sherman decided to bring a "prop" with him, which probably gave him the upper hand in getting the role. "The only distinctive thing is, I remember that part of the audition was gonna be eating 'cause there is the scene where Bub – they give him a bucket of meat," says Sherman. "And I brought a turkey leg with me and all this was going on tape. It was just Bill with a camera and me; George was not in the room. So I brought my turkey leg out and ate with great gusto and was probably slobbering on my chin and everything. I've always kind of secretly thought that was the thing that clinched the deal; the way that I took the trouble to actually bring a turkey leg, then ate it like a shark. But at some point I got a call saying that I got the job."

A role cast early on was the character of Sarah, played by Lori Cardille. Growing up in Pittsburgh, actress Lori Cardille was the daughter of Bill "Chilly Billy" Cardille, the host of *Chiller Theatre*, a Saturday late-night television show that aired old monster movies. Bill Cardille also had a small role in Romero's original *Night of the Living Dead*, appearing as himself. "Contrary to what a lot of people think, because my dad is Chilly Billy and he was in the first movie . . . I often hear, 'Oh, yeah of course she's going to be in it, duh!'" says Lori Cardille. "I remember even Tom Savini, he said, 'Yeah, she got it that way,' and I said, 'Tom, what the hell? I did not.' You know, I mean I'm sure that didn't hurt. But, I had been a working actor in New York and at that point done a lot of plays and Broadway and all that, I had a career." At the time Cardille was in New York starring in a play called *Reckless*, written by Craig Lucas. George Romero and Richard Rubinstein attended a performance of

Below: 1984 head shot of Jarlath Conroy. Before landing the role of McDermott, the Irish-born actor had appeared on stage in London, New York and Chicago. (Courtesy of Jarlath Conroy.)

the play and were very impressed by her. "They came to the play, I'm not even sure how they heard about it," says Cardille. "I hadn't seen George since the opening night of *Night of the Living Dead*; I was in, like, the eighth grade when I went to see it. So I guess because of old times' sake, he knew my dad, etcetera. And after they saw it he realized that I could sustain and do a large role."

Romero would actually write the role of Sarah with Cardille in mind, even during the larger, more exotic version of the script. For Cardille, though, the thought of traipsing through Florida swamplands was a bit unnerving. "I remember saying to George, 'Oh my god.' I said, 'I hate snakes, George,' because he had put this character of Sarah wading through the Everglades or something," remembers Cardille. "I said, 'Oh my god.' I was like freaked out about it. [*laughs*] 'Can you get a double? Hey, could I wear really high boots? Is there going to be somebody with a gun if there's, like, big boas in there or something?' That was my concern; I was so freaked out about that."

When the time came for the original script to be cut down, it didn't much bother Cardille, who felt that the tighter version gave more weight to the characters than the originally planned spectacle would have. "It was probably the film George wanted to make for the fans and for himself; it was a lot more money, it was a lot more explosions, and a lot of effects. It's just very different and not as character-driven," says Cardille. "*Day of the Dead* as it became, which was pared down a lot, was made for a lot less money and then it was more character-driven. So, Sarah became even more fleshed out as a character then."

For the role of Ted Fisher, Romero turned to an actor that he knew all too well, John Amplas. Having originally discovered Amplas in a play at the Pittsburgh Playhouse in the mid-1970s, Romero would go on to work with him in *Martin*, *Dawn of the Dead*, *Knightriders*, and *Creepshow*. Knowing the abilities that Amplas possessed, as well as having a comfort level with him, Romero simply offered the role to the actor. "You know what, I think it was he just called me and then I was scheduled and I went to the shoot," remembers Amplas. "Yeah, it was pretty simple." One issue that Amplas had with his character was whether or not he could sell himself as a scientist. "I thought I was a little too young for it. I grew a goatee that was kind of overly long and it looked almost like it was pasted on, you know?" jokes Amplas. "I thought perhaps I wouldn't carry the weight of somebody who had been working in the scientific field for that long and have the stature . . . but perhaps that was just in my head."

Another actor brought on board who Romero was familiar with was Anthony DiLeo – known as Tim to family and friends – who was cast as Miguel. DiLeo was from the Pittsburgh area, growing up in Penn Hills. As a youth he had gotten involved with plays in church and school, eventually going on to study acting at West Virginia University, then later attending graduate school at Southern Methodist University. He gained work as an extra on *The Deer Hunter* and says he was given an opportunity to read for the role that Christopher Walken would end up playing. Later, he had a small role in Romero's *Knightriders*, sharing his scene with Ed Harris and Joe Pilato. When he landed the role of Miguel in *Day of the Dead*, it took him completely by surprise. "He [George Romero] gave me the script and I thought he just wanted me to read it and then, I guess, just see what I thought of it. I really didn't know," remembers DiLeo. "And then Christine [Romero] said, 'Well, you know you can play Miguel if you want to.' And I went crazy in my kitchen,

Left: A young Lori Cardille in the mid-1970s. Before being cast as Sarah in *Day of the Dead*, she'd appeared on stage in NYC, as well as in TV soap operas like *The Edge of Night* and *Ryan's Hope*. (Courtesy of Lori Cardille.)

Above: Lori Cardille relaxes between shots. **Below:** Actor Jarlath Conroy as McDermott. (Photos courtesy of George Demick.)

smacking my dad over his bald head." DiLeo's casting would be more than just a paid job for the actor, though. It resonated deeper. "It meant the world to me when I got the role," says DiLeo. "It meant more than I can say, because there was acknowledgement that George and the people at Laurel had faith in me."

While not all the main cast had been selected, some of the featured zombie roles were being taken care of. For the "Beef Treats" zombie another Romero veteran, Mark Tierno, was brought on board. Tierno had previously worked on *Knightriders* as an extra, and on *Creepshow* as a production assistant, as well as performing the voice of Carl Reynolds, who is berated over the telephone by E.G. Marshall in the segment "They're Creeping Up On You".

Debra Gordon was cast as one of the female zombies who appear near the beginning of the film with Tierno's "Beef Treats" zombie. Gordon had previously worked on the film *Effects* with Tom Savini and John Harrison, and had been in the running to be Adrienne Barbeau's stand-in on *Creepshow*, until it was discovered that she was not the correct height or size. A year prior to being cast in *Day of the Dead*, she had a small role in the box-office hit *Flashdance*.

Some of the other featured zombies being cast included Don Brockett, of *Mister Rogers' Neighborhood* fame, who would play the "Splatterhead" zombie that Terry Alexander shoots in the cave. Brockett's comedy partner, Barbara Russell, was cast as the zombie who bites out Miller's throat at the corral. "I told George [Romero] that if he ever needed an extra zombie sometime to call and he did," remembers Russell. Barbara Homziuk (aka Barbara Holmes), who was a production secretary on the film, was cast as the second female zombie in the scene where Mark Tierno and Debra Gordon are wrangled at the corral.

Another of the featured zombies cast had also worked with Romero before. William Laczko had briefly appeared in *Dawn of the Dead* as a posse member during the "Cause I'm a Man" sequence. "There's a bunch of hunters standing around, it looks like they're talking. I'm standing there, I think I had a beard back then, and my head is bandaged like I got beat in the head with a baseball bat or something. I'm standing there with a can of beer, talking. And then you actually get a quick glimpse of me sitting on the back of the ambulance with the guy wrapping my head," remembers Laczko. "That was a fun thing, because when George Romero wanted the hunters to look like they were talking he didn't want, I guess, just people pretending they were talking. So he said, 'What I want you to do is basically sing a song to each other.' So basically, if you watch me when I'm talking I'm singing some song, I'm not really talking. I'm mouthing the words of 'Love Me Tender' or whatever the hell song came to my mind. And that's how George got the effect of people talking instead of just pretending they were talking."

When *Day of the Dead* came around, Laczko auditioned for a role as one of the soldiers. The audition would end up being a good news/bad news scenario for the actor. "I got an audition for a part in the movie. So I went down to the place down in Pittsburgh, had the audition . . . didn't get the part," says Laczko. "So when they called me up to tell me I didn't have the part they asked me, 'Would you want to be a zombie?' and I said, 'You know what . . . anything, anything, but a zombie. A cop, a policeman, a soldier, doesn't matter.' Well, then they proceeded to tell me it was going to be a 'Featured Zombie' and I said, 'What's that?' They said, 'Well, you'll either kill somebody or get killed onscreen, you'll have a name in the credits, and we'll pay you Screen Actors wages, plus you'll go to Florida with us for two weeks.' So, at that point I said yes. So, that's how I got the part of being a zombie in the movie."

It's a good thing that Laczko eventually got the featured zombie gig, because audition day turned out to be a little expensive for him. "I took a day off of work for one thing. I live out near Donegal, PA, I had a little place with horses and stuff. So I went out . . . I relaxed in the morning, I think the audition was early afternoon. I put a suit on; I was as serious as a heart attack about doing this thing. I was really, really excited about it," remembers Laczko. "So what happened is I walked out – there was a problem with one of the horses out in the field – I walked out there, the most gentle horse in the world, everything was fine, I turned around to walk away, walked behind the horse, the horse kicked me and knocked me down. So now I had to go change clothes. So now I'm running a little bit behind. So I jump on the Pennsylvania Turnpike, I go to get off at Monroeville, only to realize when I got on at New Stanton I never got a ticket. So now I have to pay the whole price of the turnpike to get off at Monroeville."

For the villainous role of Captain Rhodes, Romero once again turned to a local Pittsburgh actor who he'd worked with before, Joe Pilato. In the late 1970s, Joseph Francis Pilato moved from his hometown of Boston to Pittsburgh, to participate in a project at the University of Pittsburgh with famous acting director, Jerzy Grotowski. He fell in love with the city's charm and decided to stay. "Especially after 25 cent Iron City draft beers at the Squirrel Hill Café," says Pilato. "I knew it was my kind of town."

While working for a company called the City Players out of the Pittsburgh Public Theater, Pilato had the opportunity to work on the Vietnam War film *The Deer Hunter*, starring Robert DeNiro, which was shooting in the area. "I volunteered as an extra out in Weirton [West Virginia] because I just wanted to be around it," recalls Pilato. "And it was funny, it was a winter scene when he was coming back from 'Nam and they had the main street of the city . . . all these awnings were down and I pointed out to the assistant director, Charlie Okun, I said, 'Listen, if it's winter time the awnings wouldn't be down, they'd be up,' and he just kind of looked at me and then, 20 minutes later, all the awnings got rolled up. He came back to me and he said, 'What do you do, kid?' and I said, 'I'm an actor. I'm here . . . I just want to be around the experience.' He said, 'How'd you like to be a PA?' and I said, 'Sure.' So the next thing I knew I was doing crowd control and I worked my way up to wrangling talent to the set, and then I worked my way up to becoming DeNiro's stand-in, which is a glorified piece of scenery. But I was fortunate enough to watch John Cazale – who actually grew up twenty minutes from my house in Boston – Meryl Streep, John Savage, DeNiro, [and Michael] Cimino rehearse the scenes, because I had to watch rehearsals so that I could stand in for the cameraman. And then I was there to watch the shot."

After the experience of working on *The Deer Hunter*, Pilato starred in *Effects* with John Harrison, Tom Savini, and Debra Gordon. In the film, Pilato plays a cameraman and effects artist on a horror film, who begins to realize that the director of the film, played by John Harrison, is actually killing the people in it.

Pilato also had a small role in Romero's *Dawn of the Dead* at the boat dock, but only after being turned down for one of the lead roles. "I did *Dawn* . . . actually auditioned for David Emge's role in *Dawn of the Dead*," says Pilato. "I flew to New York, but there was too much similarity in stature between me and Scotty [Reiniger], both little, kind of short, wiry guys. So they made me the loading dock captain." A couple of years later, Pilato also appeared in Romero's *Knightriders*, in a memorable scene as a disgruntled troupe worker who argues with star Ed Harris.

When 1984 rolled around and Romero started casting for *Day of the Dead*, Pilato once again thought that perhaps he could get some kind of role on the production, even if it was just as a zombie. But this

THE DAY IS COMING

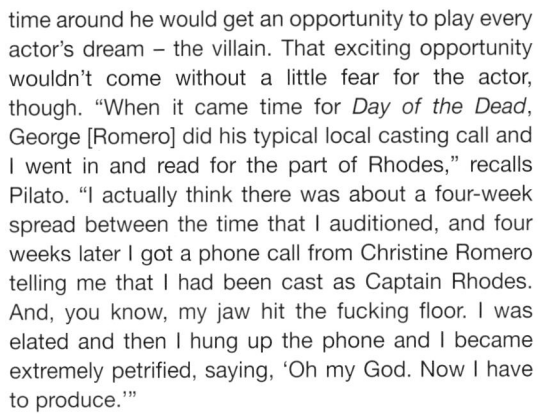

time around he would get an opportunity to play every actor's dream – the villain. That exciting opportunity wouldn't come without a little fear for the actor, though. "When it came time for *Day of the Dead*, George [Romero] did his typical local casting call and I went in and read for the part of Rhodes," recalls Pilato. "I actually think there was about a four-week spread between the time that I auditioned, and four weeks later I got a phone call from Christine Romero telling me that I had been cast as Captain Rhodes. And, you know, my jaw hit the fucking floor. I was elated and then I hung up the phone and I became extremely petrified, saying, 'Oh my God. Now I have to produce.'"

Rhodes and his world outlook is completely different from Pilato's, but the actor dove headfirst into the psyche of the character and attempted to faithfully present his side. "I was pretty left of center politically. I had been gassed, and maced, and chased by the police in Washington, DC and in Boston with anti-Vietnam War demonstrations," says Pilato. "So this guy, he in my mind represented everything that I hated about the military mentality. So, in my mind, he was an arch villain and arch villains are notoriously very enjoyable. Imagine being able to play Adolf Hitler, you have an opportunity to eat the scenery, as it were. And so my approach then wasn't to make him look negative. My approach to him was to embrace, sincerely, his militaristic, maniacal, dictatorial point of view and try to . . . because fundamentally Rhodes was right and I get that from so many fans; shoot 'em in the fucking head, they're dead, shoot 'em in

Left: Versatile actor Joe Pilato (aka Captain Rhodes) on stage with the City Players in Pittsburgh, 1979. The play in question was written by Charlie Peters, who would go on to be a respected playwright and screenwriter. **Right:** Joe Pilato showcasing his comedic talents in *The Taming of the Shrew* for the 1983 Pittsburgh Shakespeare Festival. (Photos courtesy of Joe Pilato and Joe Venegas.)

the head. This isn't a field-trip people; we're fucking around with all this bullshit. And to a certain degree I can understand that it was the military – you kill the enemy. You don't do experiments with the enemy. You don't try to domesticate the enemy. Your job is to eliminate the enemy. So, it just kind of fell into a lot of places I was coming from politically and the take was pretty easy."

The part of Rhodes' henchman, Private Steel, would be assumed by former football player turned actor Gary Klahr, whose story is an amazing and complex one. He was one of thirteen children, nine of whom were given away for adoption, all within ten miles of each other. Klahr would end up, unknowingly, dating one of his sisters for a brief time, and discovering that his best friend for more than half of his life was actually his brother. He attended college in Arizona and was eventually drafted in the NFL by the New Orleans Saints in 1970. However, his promising professional football career was cut short by a torn Achilles tendon and, after spending a few years doing different lines of work, he decided that acting was something he would love to pursue. Interestingly enough, in the late 1970s Klahr appeared in a catalogue for the Gilla Roos Talent Agency, along with Lori Cardille. He would eventually gain success in acting, landing small roles in films such as *Gloria* and *Trading Places*, before winning his signature role of Private Steel in *Day of the Dead*. Klahr learned about the casting for the film in New York through Nancy Hopwood, a mutual friend of George and Christine Romero, who had a cameo in *Knightriders*.

"Initially, as I tell the story, I read for Rhodes," recalls Klahr. "It was interesting because in the end when it all got cast . . . I guess the thing I've always kind of been amazed by is George [Romero] and his ability to see Joe [Pilato] as Rhodes and me as Steel. I've always felt it works really well because Joe is such a slight man, wonderful actor, but a slight man. And you put those bandoliers of ammunition across his chest, they literally cover his body because he's so slight and frail-looking. And the guns he has are very, very big. You can take it any way you want . . . phallic symbols, the Napoleonic complex of the little man with power, and then you got big Steel. And George, somehow . . . I read for Rhodes, I don't even recall ever reading for Steel. Then next thing we know we cast it and I'm Steel and Joe is Rhodes."

While Klahr's character, Steel, was just a private, he decided to play him a bit stronger, with a unique take. "He's Private Steel, but the way I justify it is, I played him as a sergeant," says Klahr. "Because a sergeant in the military has got a little more . . . well, obviously a greater rank and a little more say so than a private. But I looked at Steel as a guy who'd probably been busted down a couple of times for infractions, and that's why he was a lowly private, probably been in the army at that time a good fifteen years, didn't move up the chain of command because he was a bit of a . . . what's the right word? More than irreverent, I mean I think there's a certain controlled insanity about Steel, that's kind of how I approached him."

After becoming an actor, Klahr decided to remove the H from his last name professionally, so that people would then pronounce his name correctly. For most of his career he was billed as Gary Klar, but on *Day of the Dead* he was credited as G. Howard Klar. "Actually, you know what . . . truthfully? It was kind of a lark. My name is Gary Howard Klahr. I wasn't trying to . . . I kind of did it as a lark," says Klahr. "You think about it this way too . . . a horror movie, right? Not a big-budget thing, not a major big-budget Hollywood production. It's a George Romero film, we're having fun; it's a great time . . . G. Howard Klar. Why not, you know?"

Klahr's cast mate, the late Ralph Marrero, was also cast out of New York for the role of one of the other soldiers, Rickles, and the two would form a close friendship. "I loved him from the moment I met him," says Klahr. "We bonded right away. He was just a great kid from New York. Then he showed me this play he had written . . . *Cell Mates*. He said, 'Gary,

Above: Before becoming Private Steel, Gary Klahr was once a starting defensive end for the University of Arizona Wildcats. Here he is in the late 1960s. (Courtesy of Gary and Carolyn Klahr.)

wanna read this?' I read it and it was about cancer cells, because Ralph had beaten cancer. So he was a cancer survivor, and he was a writer and playwright, and a wonderful one." To Klahr, the character of Rickles admires Steel, and that shows in the film as a carryover from their behind-the-scenes friendship. "I think what we were able to do – I don't think – I know it because I think you see it in the film," says Klahr. "The friendship that we made, very quickly in Pennsylvania, carries over into the film and I think you see that. I think that is onscreen. Rickles looks up to Steel, he knows that Steel is really a real soldier and there's not much that he can't do."

During the auditions for some of the soldier roles, many actors would throw their hats in the ring, including other familiar Romero names such as Randy Kovitz, from *Dawn of the Dead* and *Knightriders*. In the end it would be the advice of Christine Romero that helped Kovitz to make a tough call regarding his career. "I was working on a production of *Henry IV, Part One* at the Yale Repertory Theater. I was the fight director and the actor playing Douglas, a major fight role, dropped out to do a film job. I was asked to do the role and agreed," recalls Kovitz. "Just after that, Chris Romero called to ask if I would play one of the soldiers in *Day of the Dead*. I told her I had just been offered the role at Yale Rep and she said I should I take it because it was a better credit than *Day*. I was torn and still wish I could have done both."

With the roles of Rhodes, Steel, Rickles, Johnson, and Miguel now filled, only two soldiers remained to be cast, Miller and Torrez.

It was first assistant director John Harrison who influenced Romero's casting of Phillip Kellams in the part of Miller. The decision to do so, however, would nearly blow up in Harrison's face during filming. "I had talked George into hiring an actor that I knew out here in LA, because I was trying to give the guy a break," remembers Harrison. "He was married to a girl that I had known in high school who was living out here [Los Angeles], and I kind of knew what they were going through. But he had a bit of a drinking problem, [*laughs*] and George being George was good enough to hire the guy." This issue would surface immediately during filming, when Harrison's good friend, Terry "Sloopy" Basilone, who worked in hair and make-up on the shoot, came to Harrison with a slight problem. "Well, the first day he's supposed to shoot, Terry, 'Sloopy', comes out to me and says, 'Listen, man, he's curled up under the make-up table and we can't get him out.' It's like, 'Oh, shit.' How can I go to George and say, 'Look, this guy you hired for me is now . . . he won't come out!'" laughs Harrison. "And so we had to go and do a little psychological work on this guy to get him out from under this table." After some persuasion, and with a little luck, Harrison and Basilone were able to get Kellams out from under that table and to the set. "Oh yeah, I got him to the set on time," says Harrison. "I kind of organized a few shots, [*laughs*] 'Why don't we do this now, George?', then we'd do those shots and then, 'All right, where is he? Where is he? Is he coming or what's going on?' 'Well, uh, listen, let's move on to this next one. How about this one, George? We'll move on to this set-up over here.' 'Okay, where is he? Where the hell is he?'"

Indeed, Kellams was an addict. When I spoke with him for this book he openly discussed his struggles and didn't deny the story. "I don't remember it," says Kellams. "But yeah I can believe that, yeah."

While Harrison and company were dealing with Kellams' drinking issues, one of his fellow actors actually took to Kellams and found him to be a good friend. "I hung out with him quite a bit in Beaver Falls," says Jarlath Conroy. "I enjoyed Phil because he had a nice, easygoing personality, non-judgmental. And he was also . . . he also had his own view of the world. He was his own man in other words. What a nice fellow."

Phillip Gene Kellams grew up in southern Indiana and as a youth had dreams of being a race car driver. He drove in his first race at age seventeen – illegally! After graduating high school he attended Indiana University, dropping out after two years. He came back home and entered the military, where he would end up serving in Guam. "We were not very good people; we were not very good guys. And some of the stuff I did over there haunts me today, to be honest with you," says Kellams. "We weren't weathermen. They just wanted everybody to think we were." After the military, he went back to school at Purdue University, where he first got involved with the creative arts. After leaving Purdue, he moved to Chicago and began working in the theater. Later he moved to Colorado, and would eventually end up in Venice, California when the opportunity to work on *Day of the Dead* came about through John Harrison. "John called and he said, 'Look, if you come down and read for this, you got it.' Oh, all right," remembers Kellams.

The role of the pot-smoking Torrez would be taken on by yet another Romero veteran, Taso Stavrakis. Appearing in Romero's *Dawn of the Dead* as one of the bike raiders (Sledge), and in *Knightriders* as one of the knights (Ewain), Stavrakis was well versed in working for the legendary director. He had also assisted Tom Savini with the make-up effects and stunts for the original *Friday the 13th*. Not long after that, just a few years prior to the start of *Day of the Dead*, Stavrakis was offered the opportunity to play a role that would go on to become iconic in the horror genre, Jason Voorhees, in the sequel to *Friday the 13th*. Unfortunately, he turned it down. "Oh, it's one of the worst decisions of my entire life. One of the dumbest things I ever did," says Stavrakis. "I was actually visiting Tom [Savini], I was back at Tom's house and he was on the phone with Steve Miner. Steve produced the original *Friday the 13th* and he was going to direct the sequel. At the time there weren't any sequels . . . there was *Jaws*, or there were one or two sequels and they were bad. It seemed like such a cheesy thing to make a sequel. Okay, you got one good movie – let's just leave it at that. So that was the feeling. He was talking to Steve and Steve said, 'Let me talk to Taso,' and I took the phone and he said, 'We want Jason, he's going to be a little older; we want him to be really physical. And I want you to play Jason in the next movie, in the sequel.' And I said, 'No, I don't think so.' [*laughs*] He said, 'Why don't you think about it?' and I said, 'No, I just said no.' And it's the dumbest thing I ever did. It would have been, even as an actor, if I would have had any brains I could have . . . it's like Karloff playing *Frankenstein*, you know what I mean? It has great acting potential and obviously it struck a chord with the audiences, because how many sequels have there been?"

One of the factors that played into Stavrakis making the decision not to take on the role of Jason was his relationship with then girlfriend, Patty Tallman – the same Patty Tallman from *Knightriders* and the 1990 remake of *Night of the Living Dead*. "Patty is an actress and she's a firm believer in you gotta do one thing – you can't do this and that. You gotta do this *or* that!" says Stavrakis. "And so I was actually trying to give up a stunt and special effects career to be an actor, because that was what I went to college for and that's what I was good at . . . it's stupid, you don't really have to. But I believed her because I was in love with her. What are you gonna do?"

Originally in the *Day of the Dead* script, Torrez was to die at the corral when the zombie breaks free from the collar attached to Miguel's pole, but just a couple of weeks prior to filming getting underway a change was made, swapping the roles of Miller and Torrez, beginning with that particular scene. So now, Stavrakis' character, Torrez, would die in the ending gore montage instead, and Phil Kellams' character, Miller, would die at the corral. Stavrakis would also handle the stunts in the film, as well as playing several zombies. His company, the New York City Stunt League, consisted of him and him alone.

Around the time that the military villains were being cast, Romero was looking for actors to fill the roles of the chopper pilot, John, and his radio man, Bill McDermott. Detroit native Terry Alexander would land the key role of John. Alexander caught the acting bug when he appeared in a Christmas play while in grade school. Later, he became part of a government grant program for the performing arts in ethnic communities, starting out in a musical. It was there that he discovered that his talents were not as a singer, so he shifted his attention towards studying acting at the University of Detroit. Afterwards he moved to New York to pursue his dream of acting. One day in the summer of 1984, Alexander was contacted by his agent concerning a role that required a Caribbean accent, which Alexander excelled at. "I read the side and it called for kind of a very big man, very huge guy, like 6' 3" or 6' 4". So, I felt maybe I'm auditioning for nothing – I'm not the type they were looking for," recalls Alexander. "I went in to see George [Romero] at my audition, and I got the monologue from him that's in the middle of *Day of the Dead*, and I just loved it, I just truly loved the words he had created. So, I went in there to see him and I said, 'Hey, George Romero. Please, I think this is wonderful, wonderful material that if you can just give me overnight to study it and make it live, I think I can bring you back something that's interesting,' and he said, 'Okay' – that's what he did. I went home and studied it, and slept on it, and played with it, and came back, auditioned the next day and he gave me the job." Alexander was intrigued by the character of John, and whatever connection was there, he believes that helped him nail the audition. "Sometimes you read scripts and you can't connect with what's on the page, and you know you're just auditioning because you have to audition," says Alexander. "But then other times you feel a very special something when you read it, and you just know. There's a knowing that you can do this role and that's what happened to me. And once in a while that will get you the role."

Alexander was familiar with Romero's original *Night of the Living Dead*, but had not seen any of the director's other films. After being cast, he decided to go back and watch other Romero films to get an idea of the director's style. He had no reservations at all about starring in a gory zombie movie. In fact, it was an opportunity to explore a character in a film from a director known for his political takes. "I felt it was a wonderful script. I thought it had wonderful social commentary, symbols were in place. I had no reservations at all about that," says Alexander. "This is a great role, man. I'm gonna do this, see if I can bring some life to this character, man. We'll worry about the gore later, because sometimes that can be edited or be played with or whatever, but I had to do that role."

The role of Alexander's "wing man", Bill McDermott, would go to Irish-born actor Jarlath Conroy. Having appeared several years earlier in Michael Cimino's *Heaven's Gate*, Conroy was a perfect complement to the laidback feel of Alexander's Jamaican character. "I played him fairly close to myself, as people do in movies," says Conroy. "I knew he had to be an individual, an individual in the sense that they both – he and Terry's character – were survivors."

Conroy actually landed the role in part due to the generosity of another actor, who recommended him for the role of the "drunken" Irishman. "What I remember about the casting was there was an actor by the name of Ken Ryan, who I met subsequently, but Ken had been auditioning and he recommended me to Gaylen [Ross], who was the casting director. And I came in on an audition for that then to meet George [Romero] and that's how I got it."

One of the most pivotal roles for Romero to cast was the part of Dr. Logan, the mad scientist. Romero decided to turn to yet another actor he was familiar with, the late Richard Liberty, who played Artie in Romero's 1973 film *The Crazies*. Liberty, whose birth name was actually Liberatoscioli, meaning "Shoulder of Liberty", came to Boca Raton, Florida in the early 1950s to work as an assistant to professional golfer, Sam Snead. Liberty had actually majored in business-hotel management in college, and gotten involved with acting as a way to keep his mind off the marital issues he was experiencing at the time. Years later, after divorcing, he would move to New York and take bit parts on soap operas such as *As the World Turns*, *Search for Tomorrow*, and *The Edge of Night*. He also did television commercials and dinner theater, until deciding that living in the Big Apple was no longer for him. In the late 1970s, he moved back to south Florida, not far from his parents in Fort Lauderdale, where he would continue working on the dinner-theater circuit and doing television commercials. Along the way, he landed small roles in films such as *The Final Countdown* and *Porky's II*, and on the hit TV show *Miami Vice*.

His signature role of Dr. Logan, aka Frankenstein, came his way late in the summer of 1984. Christine Romero contacted Liberty about his possible interest in the role and, after reading the script, he was in. By this time Liberty had remarried, and together Liberty and his wife, Kim, and their two cats, made the trek to Pittsburgh from south Florida for the production. "I just remember it was an exciting time when this all came together," says Kim Liberty. "I do remember packing the silver Datsun and making sure there was plenty of room for the cats and they'd have their cat food and

Above: Gary Klahr (far right) in the 1983 Broadway production of *Brothers*, starring alongside such respected names as Carroll O'Connor, Paul Gleason, Dennis Christopher and Frank Converse. (Courtesy of Gary and Carolyn Klahr.)

cat litter. We had a grand time. I just remember it as a very positive experience."

Richard Liberty's take on his role of Dr. Logan was pretty detailed and introspective, as he discussed with Stephen V. D'Emidio in the summer 1985 issue of *The New Dawn*, a fan club newsletter about George Romero's films. "I think his parents, of course, were wealthy. I think he resented his father. That's probably one reason he got into biology. Probably as a kid he was always dissecting things, and I think his father probably didn't like that. I think he also resented not being able to do what he wanted to do. There was the reference to his father at the country club, where they called him the great surgeon Bub. I think it was sort of a putdown of his father when he named the creature Bub." Liberty also thought about the research and experimentation that Dr. Logan was working on. "What we have to understand is that the doctor was probably hired by the President of the United States to do this work; that he was the foremost in his field at the time and he's getting very close to succeeding. I think probably the strain of working so hard makes him a little flippy, but I think basically he's of sound reasoning and everything he believes in is going to come about."

With the cast now taking shape, Laurel Productions was busy moving into its home base of operations for the next several months of filming – the Wampum Industrial Facility. One of the many people busy during that time was Simon Manses, who could be described as a jack of all trades. His history with Romero dates all the way back to the early 1970s, when he worked as a grip on a short film directed by Romero called *The Amusement Park*. Years later, he would cross paths with Romero once again, when Laurel Entertainment purchased bikes for *Knightriders* from the Honda dealership where Manses worked, which led to him being hired by the production as the motorcycle coordinator. After *Knightriders*, Manses left to run a music store, and when *Creepshow* came around he rented out a Prophet 5 keyboard and amps to John Harrison, which Harrison used to score the film. That would lead to Manses once again being hired on that film, this time as a slate, as well as assisting Mike Gornick with the post-production.

On *Day of the Dead,* Manses served as the slate/film loader, basically the second assistant cameraman, and while moving camera equipment into the Wampum Facility, along with the first assistant cameraman, Frank Perl, he had a brief scare. "We started moving in the camera room: 'We'll put the cameras here and cameras here and now we'll put the film over here and film over here,' and we're going through this door and I look at this door and it has this sticker that says 'WARNING: RADIOACTIVE MATERIAL', and I said 'Ahhhh!' and I started screaming – not literally screaming – but I knew it was a potential disaster in the making," remembers Manses. "So we immediately took all the film out of the room and put it in another room that was further removed from there, and had Pittsburgh Testing Laboratory come in – I think they were still called Pittsburgh Testing Laboratory – with the Geiger counters and stuff, to see if there was maybe some latent radiation in that room." Fortunately for Manses and the rest of the crew, everything checked out all right, the equipment was moved back into the designated camera room, and a potential calamity was avoided.

Besides moving the production into the Wampum Industrial Facility, the cast and crew were settling in at the production hotel, the Beaver Falls Holiday Inn, located about four miles down the road from the mine. "We'd be up in the morning, be driven to the mine in the dark, stay in the mine all day, and then come back to this extraordinary kind of hotel called the Holidome, which was like some sort of moon base," says Joe Pilato. "I mean everything was . . . you did not have to leave the facility for anything. So, there was a sense of claustrophobia around the whole shoot."

Production manager, Zilla Clinton, prepared information packets of well over twenty pages for all cast and crew members, greeting them with: "Welcome to the Beaver Falls Holiday Inn and/or the Wampum Industrial Facility . . . your home away from home for the next few months." The packets contained a wealth of information on pay-day schedules, per diems, call sheets, laundry services, maps of the mine itself, and a hotel room listing. It also featured directions for nearby restaurants, movie theaters, and malls. Emergency information was included as well, for the local hospital, dentist, and production physician. As it turned out, the doctor was often used during the shoot as many cast and crew became sick from working in the mine. (In a bizarre twist, the doctor who served the production, Jeffrey Nanns, would die of a morphine overdose at the age of 28, just two months after principal photography wrapped.) Anything and everything that would be of interest was listed inside the packet, to make life a little bit easier for cast and crew – most of whom were far away from home, some for the first time – while they were in the Wampum/Beaver Falls area. One of those was a young make-up effects artist named Howard Berger who, along with Everett Burrell, was brought in right after principal photography began (more of which later).

"It's one of my most favorite memories, tell you the truth," remembers Berger. "I think maybe I was nineteen years old. I'd never ever gone on location. I'd never really worked on anything of any value; I was so new in the industry. But it was really quite amazing to go – all of us living there together – it was just really amazing. We worked so hard – got paid nothing! Of course then you think you're getting paid a fortune. I think we all got paid $300 a week and then $350 per diem – so $650 for the whole week. And we were happy as clams, you know? It couldn't have been any better as far as we were concerned, it was wonderful. We lived at the Beaver Valley Holiday Inn and we all had rooms and we'd run around and be crazy. It was great; it was like *Animal House* on location."

And while the majority of the cast and crew were staying at the Holiday Inn, the production assistants were staying in what might be described as less "posh" accommodations. In fact, initially they were going to be forced to commute from Pittsburgh each day to work on the film, until a deal was made for them at the Beaver Valley Motel, a much smaller, locally owned motel nearby. John "Flash" Williams, the first PA hired for the film, was one of the "lucky" few to stay at the Beaver Valley Motel. "The hotel wasn't that bad, but it was something from the fifties era, it was clean enough," remembers Williams. "What else that was kind of cool was Zilla [Clinton] and Leslie [Chapman] actually came over, I guess they went over the day before, and went to all the rooms and put flowers in the rooms for us, and made sure they had brand-new clean sheets, that they actually had the production buy, because the place was ratty. They fixed it up all real nice for us and it was just a real nice family gesture."

Williams was hired very early by production coordinator Leslie Chapman, with an assist from *Night of the Living Dead* veteran, Russell Streiner. "He said, 'Well, George Romero's getting ready to do *Day of the Dead*' and I'm like, 'Awesome!' I just thought I was going to be a zombie blown up or something, and that would be kind of cool, and he was like, 'No, they're looking for production assistants. Why don't you do this?' So he got me the interview and I guess my 'charm' took me the rest of the way," remembers Williams. "I was the only PA for a long time until . . . probably about two days before we started shooting they [brought] in all the rest of the PAs, just because they were saving money." During pre-production, Williams spent most of his time at Laurel's Pittsburgh offices at 247 Fort Pitt Boulevard in downtown Pittsburgh, doing things like fetching coffee, making copies, picking up people from the airport, driving cast members to costume fittings and to Tom Savini's home for prosthetic make-up work – a typical gofer job. "You were making lots of copies of the script and every time George [Romero] had a revision or a change you would go and run and make more copies of the script," says Williams. "We really didn't use a Kinko's or anything like that because they were trying to save money. So you'd be standing at a copy machine for . . . I remember standing at a copy machine for, like, three hours at a time just making script copies and boxing up and shipping them out to the actors."

One particularly fond memory from the film prep was riding the trolley into Pittsburgh each day with the late Vince Survinski. "I used to ride in with him every day and hear all these cool stories about *Night of the Living Dead* and *Dawn of the Dead* and the different productions he had been on and stuff," says Williams.

Another important facet of the production going on during this time was the construction of sets inside the mine. While the mine and empty mine offices themselves pretty much provided a ready-made set for the production, there were still many things that needed to be built to bring Romero's story to life. A key member of the crew that would facilitate this was head carpenter, Norman Beck. Having worked in the past at the Pittsburgh Public Theater with production designer Cletus Anderson and art director Bruce Miller, Beck was someone Miller knew he could trust. "I think

Above: Long before he was the "whirlybird" pilot, John, Terry Alexander played Johnny Williams in Charles Gordone's Pulitzer Prize-winning play, *No Place to be Somebody* in the early 1970s. (Courtesy of Terry Alexander.)

they were having some trouble finding carpenters," remembers Beck. "And he called me up and I said, 'Well, Bruce, I haven't done movie carpentry, I'm not really an experienced carpenter,' and he said, 'Yeah, I know, but you're the kind of guy who can solve problems, you think about things and you come up with solutions and that's what I need here.' And I said, 'Okay, great. When do I start?'"

However, Beck wasn't originally hired as head carpenter. That job first went to Louis Taylor, who had done carpentry work on *Creepshow*. Just a couple of weeks into the job, though, Taylor left the production to pursue a full-time gig. This left the production in need of a head carpenter, and it came down to either Beck or a gentleman named Gary Kosko. Kosko later went on to become an accomplished art director, working on such films as *The Silence of the Lambs*, *Philadelphia*, *Deep Impact*, *Wonder Boys*, and *Mission: Impossible III*. "He actually had a great deal more experience than I did, he was far better equipped to be a head carpenter, but didn't really want the job," says Beck. "And so I took the job and he more or less trained me, because he didn't want the responsibility and he didn't want to put in the extra hours. So he more or less showed me the ropes and I learned an awful lot from Gary, who should have had my job."

One of the key set pieces that Beck and his crew built in the mine was the zombie corral, which actually didn't take long to build. "Oh, not long at all. It was really a simple construction; it was just two by four. Basically, it was something that they would have built out of what they found in the mine," says Beck. "That was one of the first things we built." The corral was designed by Cletus Anderson and Bruce Miller in Anderson's home basement – a not unfamiliar location when it came to working with the respected production designer. "We often did pre-production in his basement, we'd get things designed, we'd get models built," remembers Bruce Miller. "And then we would go out to the location, wherever it was going to be, and then start staying there when construction actually got started."

Another key job for Beck's crew was working on the outside of John and McDermott's trailer, "The Ritz". "We built the porch on the end of that trailer, and we built the billboard that was kind of like a view of a sunny vacation in Florida that was sort of the background," says Beck. "They had it set up next to their trailer so that they could look off the porch and see as if they were on the surface. It was like a Florida scene."

Besides handling the construction of the zombie corral and "The Ritz", Beck and his crew would stay busy on many other set pieces. "In the cave there were three other units that we built. One was Miguel's bedroom, his sort of quarters. That was just a piece of scenery, it was just another office space that was entirely made out of lumber so that the walls could be 'wilded'," says Beck. ("Wilding" or "Wild Walls" is an industry term for removable individual walls that can be taken out of a room on a set. The camera can sit where a wall is, making it easy for the production to shoot.) "So, that entire structure was 'wild' and then we built a unit that doubled as one of those walls," continues Beck. "There was one for him and one for Lori [Cardille]. She had a quarters, a room set too, and then another wall was built that doubled for the wall where she looks at the calendar and all the zombie arms crash through the wall. That wall was built in a separate area. In fact, I think it was just left in the shop and they came in and actually shot that shot in the shop because the thing was too heavy to move.

Above: Co-producer David Ball (in Members Only jacket) with key grip, Nick Mastandrea – whom Ball describes as "my doppelganger". "Nick and I are brothers," he says. (Courtesy of Greg Nicotero.)

Because what it was was a wall that was attached to a set of benches, and we built these benches kind of like bleachers, so that there could be three rows of people scrunched in around each other, so that they all could get their arms through in one little area. So, that was a kind of special effect that we built.

"We modified a bunch of gurneys so that they could do some of the zombie stuff in the lab, where zombies were laying on gurneys and their guts were spilling out. That was all done with gurneys that had been cut open, so that the person who was playing the zombie could be half in and half out of the gurney. So their head could be above the table and their body below it, and then the rest of the body was built by Savini and melded with the neck of the actor so that the guts could spill out the body of the zombie.

"And then we built a special platform that was installed at the end of the hallway when Joe Pilato's legs were ripped off, and that platform was actually installed in the hallway and it replicated the floor of the hallway, so that when they cut to that shot he was actually under the platform with his . . . from the chest up he was above the platform, and Tom Savini built the removable legs, and all the guts and gore and gooey stuff that disconnected from him. So that entire shot was actually done like a foot above the normal level, and they just moved the camera up that one foot and moved the floor up on our platform, and we cut a hole for him to stick out of at the end of the hall."

With Beck being new to the ways of motion picture production, he didn't understand that a lot of the time you are simply on call in case your services are needed, which meant a lot of downtime. This didn't sit too well with Beck, who was always anxious for his next project, and in turn he drove Cletus Anderson up the wall with his impatience. "Cletus and I had an interesting relationship . . . [laughs] that went on for years and years later. I can't really describe it. He always felt that I was impetuous, and impulsive, and difficult to deal with," says Beck. "He had a schedule to keep to, and he was getting things done so that they would be ready at the appropriate times for the shooting schedule. And I did nothing but irritate him. He and I got along better years later, but at the time I was so young and so impulsive that he really was frustrated by me. I remember one time when I had begged him for what we were going to be doing next, and he more or less threw the sketch together of that bleacher unit that didn't need to be ready for a long time – the thing with the zombie arms coming through the wall. He just like sat down and sketched it out, put some dimensions on it and he said, 'Here, go build this!' And he was just trying to get rid of me. So, that was the nature of our relationship at that time."

With principal photography now looming, one of the production's last and most important jobs was still up in the air – who would edit the movie? The man who eventually handled the chore of editing the film was Pat Buba, who had previously worked as an editor for Romero on *Knightriders* and *Creepshow*. Not only had Buba handled editing for Romero previously, he'd also had small acting roles in both *Martin* and *Dawn of the Dead*. While Buba was Romero's first choice, he was not the first choice for producer Richard Rubinstein. Tom Dubensky was a longtime veteran of Romero's films, having served as the assistant cameraman for Michael Gornick on *Martin*, *Dawn of the Dead*, *Knightriders*, and *Creepshow*. Dubensky would not be as involved with *Day of the Dead* as he was with those films, but he did work on the production for a day or two, and assisted Gornick with the post-production of the film. "I don't know if it was when it was on the big scale or the small scale [meaning which script], but at one point Richard Rubinstein said he wanted a New York editor to edit *Day of the Dead*," remembers Dubensky. "And, of course, George wanted to use Pat Buba, but Richard [Rubinstein] was like, 'No, I want a New York editor,'

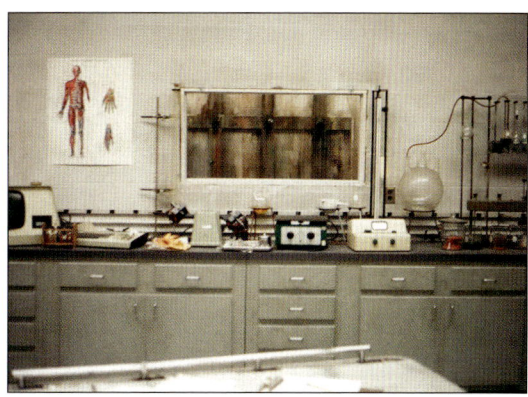

Above and below: Testing rooms and offices that once belonged to Medusa Cement were converted to laboratory sets by Laurel Productions. (Courtesy of George Demick.)

and they started talking to New York editors." Some big-name, New York-based editors were discussed during this time, including Alan Heim, who had won an Oscar for his work on *All That Jazz*. Eventually they would enter into talks with Jerry Greenberg, who had won an Academy Award for *The French Connection*, as well as handling editing duties on *Kramer vs. Kramer* and *Scarface*. "Big gun, big-name editor; he was available, wasn't working on anything," says Dubensky. "They said, 'Well, you're gonna have to come to Pittsburgh to work for a few months,' and he was okay with that. And then he said, 'Well, here's my fee,' and then after Laurel saw the fee they said, 'Well, maybe we should see if Pat Buba is available.'"

Meanwhile, Buba – ironically enough – was working on a film in New York, and jumped at the chance to work for his mentor, Romero, once again. "I was working on a film in New York . . . and they hadn't made the decision yet about editor," says Buba. "I got a call from George when I was in New York. So I had to leave, I had to find somebody for the film in New York, and I went right to Pittsburgh."

Chapter 3 One Day at a Time

This chapter focuses on the film's principal photography, which would begin on Monday, October 22, 1984 and last until Wednesday, January 16, 1985 – an "official" 56-day shoot (though an extra half-day of filming did take place, so the actual total was 57 days). The production was a six-day work week, with Sundays being the lone day off (the exception being one Sunday shoot in the Fort Myers/Sanibel Island area).

This chapter provides a diary of each day of shooting for the production. Along with the day and date of shooting, there is also a brief quote attached to each daily header. The quotes – most of which came from various cast and crew members – are taken from the daily call sheets that were handed out to the cast and crew during filming. They were usually of a humorous nature, meant to elicit a laugh and start the day out on a good note. The information contained in this chapter comes directly from those daily call sheets for the production. You might notice the word "scheduled" used quite a bit during this chapter. This is because on some days scenes *were* scheduled to be shot, but ended up being shot the following day, or perhaps even several days later. Sometimes scenes would begin on one day and lapse over into the following day of production. It's impossible to know every detail of each day's filming for certain, due to the fact that people's memories just aren't that good, and no one I could find kept a daily log during the shoot. As Eileen Sieff told me, "the call sheets were often wishful thinking", so it's possible that some errors regarding what was shot on a specific day are contained in this chapter, and I have attempted to make notations regarding this when I could. The following though is as close you will find to a daily diary from the production. And one last thing: be ready for one long chapter!

Monday 10/22/1984 – Day 1

"Remember, we never close." – D. Ball

The first day of filming would kick off with five scheduled scenes, plus two optional shots. Due to

Below: Corral zombie Barbara Homziuk (aka Barbara Holmes) in make-up as Tom Savini laughs in the background. (Courtesy of Mark Tierno.)

the low-budget nature of the production, there was no time for rehearsals for the actors, except for perhaps an hour or so on the day of filming, between set-ups. One of the first scenes on tap was scene 46, where Sarah (Lori Cardille) stops to take pain medication from a first-aid cabinet, after she leaves her work station. For Cardille, this being her first major film, there were things for her to get acclimated to during filming. "I'd done a lot of television film, but I'd never done a major motion picture and especially a large character like that," says Cardille. "I had to work on things being shot out of sequence and that was a whole new experience for me." Her desire to deliver a strong performance for Romero would also affect her in a way she wasn't used to. "I was so determined and pretty uptight in some ways, you know, working on the character," admits Cardille. "I took it very seriously, maybe too seriously." [*laughs*]

Also scheduled the first day was scene 47, where Fisher (John Amplas) is observed in a lab room attempting to feed the "Beef Treats" zombie (Mark Tierno) his US Army supplied rations.

Another scene scheduled was scene 48, where Sarah and Fisher discuss what they are hoping to

Above: John Amplas as Dr. Ted Fisher. (Courtesy of John Amplas.) **Below:** Director George Romero, with his infant daughter Tina, and Howard Sherman as Bub. (Courtesy of Hollywood Book & Poster Company.)

Above: John Vulich having fun with Howard Sherman as Bub. (Courtesy of John Vulich.)

accomplish with their work before Dr. Logan (Richard Liberty) appears in the room and gives his speech about tricking the zombies like good little boys and girls, culminating with him turning the lights off on the "Beef Treats" zombie after he turns a table over in anger. "I got sort of small," says Tierno, of his reaction when the room went dark. "Like, as if I was sort of afraid."

Other shots scheduled for the day were scenes 29 and 30, where Steel (Gary Klahr) and Rickles (Ralph Marrero) chain the "Beef Treats" zombie and the female captive zombie (Debra Gordon) to the wall and then exit the room. Gordon got into her zombie character's predicament so much that she actually frightened herself a bit during the scene. "It was scary," recalls Gordon. "I remember being into this mindset where I was playing the part so realistically that it was frightening to be chained up like that and not being able to move, and feel like you are an animal herded up. I think that came out."

Finally two optional scenes, 39 and 40, were also scheduled for Lori Cardille. Her character, Sarah, takes more pain medication from the first-aid cabinet after her fight with Miguel, and then observes the "Beef Treats" zombie in his experimentation room, enraged and pulling at his chain on the wall.

Tuesday 10/23/1984 – Day 2

**"Let's get a shot, then we'll know what to do."
– Nick Mastandrea**

The second day of filming finished up work on scene 48, with Lori Cardille, John Amplas, and Richard Liberty.

Work on scene 31 was also started, where Sarah and Miguel (Tim DiLeo) argue in their room before she finally sedates him with a needle. During the shot Romero was unsatisfied with how Cardille was giving DiLeo the sedative, so he grabbed the stand-in, Jim Wetzel, and demonstrated how he wanted her to plunge the needle into DiLeo – literally stabbing Wetzel with the needle in the process! "Yeah, I was all right," says Wetzel. "But in hindsight it wasn't cool." [*laughs*]

Jim Wetzel's life is a fascinating one. He comes from

a family entrenched in the martial arts. Wetzel, his father Willy, and his brother Roy were all trained and well versed in Pencak Silat, an Indonesian form of martial art. For many years, Wetzel suffered at the hands of his abusive father. "Because of the way I was raised and the torture my father put me through, he created my dyslexia," says Wetzel. "He broke me in a couple of different ways, but he enhanced me in others."

In March 1975 Wetzel's brother, Roy, killed their father with a pair of nunchucks during a bloody fight in his apartment, over an argument involving their father's tax returns. Reports claimed that the elder Wetzel was a Satanist, and that voodoo dolls of Jim and Roy with pins stuck in them were found in his home. (Roy ended up following his brother onto the production, appearing as a zombie in the scene where Joe Pilato is torn in half at the end of the film.)

Wetzel got involved with the production, working as the male stand-in, thanks to his good friend, Rick Granati. Granati, a native of Beaver Falls, is one of four brothers who at the time had a band called G-Force. All four brothers would end up playing zombies in the film, but Rick played a more valuable role in the beginning of the production as well. Granati's uncle had married the sister of Jessica Abrams, who was working as the assistant auditor on the film. Abrams had mentioned to Granati that the production was coming to the area, and that they would be in need of extras to play zombies. Granati provided a list of people who were willing to be zombies, as well as the names of nearby restaurants and building supply stores, which would help immensely. Eventually he provided them with the stand-in performers as well. "One of the things I did was: Jessica [Abrams] said that they needed a stand-in for Joe Pilato and a stand-in for Lori Cardille, the two main characters," recalls Granati. "So I found my best friend and my martial arts instructor, Jim Wetzel. I knew that he had aspirations of doing some martial arts films and was pursuing that. So, I immediately went to him, asked him if he wanted to consider being a stand-in for Joe Pilato, and [told him] he would probably be on the set for maybe the next couple of months, two or three months – he jumped at it. Then a girl in my neighborhood was about the same height as Lori Cardille – they were looking for someone similar to her height – a girl named Theresa Bedekovich. I went to her house, she lived about a block away from where I grew up, and banged on the door and asked her if she was interested and she jumped at it. [I] just started really bringing them a lot of key people."

"Yes, he was my neighbor and I was discovered walking the dog, like some famous actress," says Bedekovich. "I was just walking my dog and he came running over, we went to high school together, and he said, 'They're looking for somebody tall to be a stand-in,' and I wasn't working, I was right out of college,

and I said, 'All right, I'll check it out.' So that's how I got the job. And when I went down they said I was the right height."

During this time, Granati was also making connections with the production team, which led to his band being booked to perform for the cast and crew. He made fast friends with Joe Pilato, inviting him over to his family's house for old-fashioned spaghetti dinners with his brothers. "They were incredible . . . they were like The Ramones, they all looked alike," says Pilato. "I can still taste the food at their table. They were just so fucking generous." This would pay off for Granati and the brothers later in the production, when Pilato would ask them to help with the death of his character, Captain Rhodes, at the end of the film.

Work was also scheduled to begin on the first scene from the film, Sarah's nightmare. Coverage of Cardille sitting on the floor and approaching the calendar on the wall was scheduled to be shot on this day. The shots of the zombie arms coming through the wall, however, were scheduled for later in the week.

Below: Greg Nicotero with Howard Sherman as Bub. (Courtesy of Greg Nicotero.)

Wednesday 10/24/1984 – Day 3

"Keep those 'One Longs' coming." – Ed Lammi

The third day of shooting would continue work on scene 31, where Sarah gives Miguel a sedative, as well as scene 1, which was listed as optional this time, and was again only the lead-up to the zombie arms crashing through the wall. Scene 45 was also listed as optional. In it, Sarah is working in her lab, looking through a microscope, but exhaustion and pain stop her from her completing her work.

Lori Cardille had envisioned Sarah very differently from George Romero's conception of the character. She saw it as a true end-of-the-world scenario, where people are filthy and unkempt. "I said. 'George, I think we should do this character where her hair's not nice and maybe she has a couple of missing teeth.' I mean that's how I saw it, like post-apocalyptic. Really, to me that would have been the film I would have liked to have done as an actor, you know? Really real, and he just laughed, he said, 'Uh, Lori, that's just a different kind of movie,'" says Cardille. "And that was certainly not the way I would have liked to have played it, the way I played it, but it was the way I kind of had to play it."

A first attempt of scene 37 was also filmed on this day, where Miguel spills his guts in Sarah's dream. The effect didn't work exactly to everyone's expectations, however, so the scene was eventually re-shot after the Christmas break, nearly two and a half months later.

For Tim DiLeo, working with make-up effects and prosthetics took up a large amount of time during the shoot, and for him it was all about surrender when dealing with this side of things. "You learn to make latex your friend," says DiLeo. "Yeah, you have to learn to make those things your friend. I'm not kidding. It takes a real long time . . . just like you have to surrender into a role or surrender into a deity or a religion; you have to surrender into the god of latex. And then it becomes easy and not unbearable." This approach also made Tom Savini's job much easier when he came to apply said latex to DiLeo. "To me, he was just a cooperative method actor, always in deep thought and deep pain; mentally, emotionally anguished at all times," says Savini. "But all I needed him to do was stand still for a few minutes so I could strap something on him or glue an appliance on or something."

Work for scene 38 – where Sarah and Miguel argue after she awakes from her nightmare of him spilling his guts – began on this day as well. One deviation from the script that didn't make it into the film took place after Miguel storms out of the room, and involved Sarah walking over to the calendar and marking an X on the date.

Above: A glimpse behind the "wall of arms" from Sarah's (Lori Cardille) nightmare, which opens the film. (Courtesy of Greg Nicotero.)

And while Cardille may have been feeling slightly uptight as she got acclimated to film work, Romero was definitely impressed with his female lead. "She was great and really contributed and really cared about the work," says Romero. "And I just thought she was fabulous."

Thursday 10/25/1984 – Day 4

"Just tell me when it's done." – Zilla Clinton

The first part of the fourth day of filming was spent wrapping up work on scenes 31 and 38, with Lori Cardille and Tim DiLeo.

Filming for scenes 49, 51, 53, and 55 was scheduled to begin this day as well. These scenes covered the interaction between Dr. Logan, Fisher, and Sarah while they observe Bub (Howard Sherman) in his experimentation room, utilizing the book and razor. Scene 57 was also shot, where Rhodes (Joe Pilato) and Steel enter the observation room as Logan first presents Bub with the telephone.

The wall that Bub was chained to, as well as the wall that the "Beef Treats" and female captive zombie were chained to, was pretty vile and gross-looking. The person responsible for making the walls – and the wood bolted to the walls – look so disgusting was head scenic artist, Eileen Garrigan. "That was one of my big jobs on that movie, was what we would call 'zombie snot'. We mixed up copious amounts of all different kinds of recipes and concoctions and everything was getting whipped around and smeared around," says Garrigan. "There was rubber cement and dry pigment, corn starch; I would cook up corn starch and make it be thick and then put green . . . we were making things pretty much a raw umbery, green kind of snotty color."

For Gary Klahr, watching fellow actor Richard Liberty, as Dr. Logan, work with his star pupil, Bub,

Above: Lori Cardille's "wall of arms" nightmare from the film's first scene. (© 1985 Dead Films, Inc.)

was a joy. "I think his work is actually brilliant in the film," says Klahr. "I mean, I think you really get that he's off his rocker; that he's almost fallen in love with the zombie and the zombie culture, whatever is the right word there. That he kind of falls in love with his . . . Bub is his protégé, and he's more concerned with them than he is with the human element in the film. I think you get that." Klahr also says that Liberty reminded him of a kosher butcher from his childhood neighborhood. "These guys were covered in blood," says Klahr. "And Richard looked to me like a guy that worked in this kosher butcher shop, because he would come in with that bloody coat."

The man that worked closest with Liberty in the film was Howard Sherman, playing Dr. Logan's pet zombie, Bub. According to Sherman, Liberty's zest for his role was actually a part of his own personality, which meshed perfectly with his character. "Richard, it's funny, his energy as a human being just lined up perfectly with the sort of mad scientist aspect of the character he was playing," says Sherman. "I remember him just being kind of jovial and good natured, sort of chattery, and just very much like his character is in the movie. He had real quick energy, really bright, and his mind worked quickly, which translated very nicely to his character." That energy, though, would cause a bit of a snag further down the line, when they improvised one of the most memorable scenes in the film (more of which later).

Unlike a lot of the actors on set, who shared a close camaraderie, Howard Sherman kept to himself and was a bit more reserved during filming. "I think the most removed person and reserved person of the cast was Howard Sherman," says Joe Pilato. "And that's quite understandable, because [having] both his make-up put on and make-up put off took so many hours that he had very little time to socialize." Pilato is correct about the make-up being a factor of Sherman's reclusiveness during filming. "On the set I was functioning, to a degree, under duress," says Sherman. "Because wearing all of this make-up for long periods of time and any use of . . . the difficult thing was the mask, literally. The lip came over my lip and right at the threshold of when your dry lip reaches the inside, where it's wet, was right at the point where they had to put this latex and make it one skin and paint it over. And every twenty minutes it would come loose or the corners of my mouth would come loose and then they'd be in there fixing the damage. So I just had to as much as possible not talk, not drink, not eat – not do anything unless I was on camera. So part of my stoicism was essentially not stressing my mouth in any way, because if I started having a conversation there would be damage done."

When discussing Sherman's "stand-offish" behavior, one actor would not officially go on the record, but did tell me that Sherman felt he was above the material, had no true desire to participate, and simply took the role as a gig. During my interview with Sherman, he seemed to genuinely enjoy reminiscing about working on the film and his approach to his character. But, when I asked his opinion of the film, he requested that I turn my recorder off while he gave his response. Needless to say, his views of the finished product are not very positive.

Around this time, there was a memorable and unexpected phone call on set from a famous author, who just happened to be a good friend of Romero. Jim Wetzel, the male stand-in on the film, was on set every day in Wampum and remembers it vividly. "I was doing the stand-in thing for Bub, when he was in the laboratory and chained to the wall and all that stuff," recalls Wetzel. "That's when Stephen King called, and we had to stop everything while George talked to Stephen King on the phone. [*laughs*] It was the coolest thing, everything stopped dead." Wetzel eventually had the opportunity to play some zombie cameos as well, most notably as the zombie who flips after being hit with a shovel by McDermott (Jarlath Conroy).

Also scheduled for the day was scene 78, a scene that would eventually be covered weeks later and is not even in the finished film, where Bub can be heard growling in the darkness of his experimentation room after Logan is killed (more of which later).

Above: Captain Rhodes (Joe Pilato) with make-up artist Bonnie Priore. (Courtesy of Taso Stavrakis.)

Friday 10/26/1984 – Day 5

"Make it look intentional." – G. Romero

Day five would continue work on the previous day's shooting schedule, concentrating once again on scenes 49 through 58, in which Bub plays with his "toys" from Dr. Logan as Sarah, Fisher, Rhodes and Steel look on.

While Howard Sherman was busy being made up as Bub, the rest of the cast had a rare opportunity to rehearse some of their upcoming scenes for the day, in particular scene 58, where Rhodes tells Logan that he refuses to return Bub's salute, and Sarah hands over her pistol to Logan so that he can present it to Bub.

The scenes with Bub examining Logan's "presents" allowed Howard Sherman's improvisational skills to come to the fore. "The thing is, all of that stuff essentially is improvised," says Sherman. "In that it's not like . . . everything I did in the movie, essentially you know the chunks – you're gonna pick up a book and look and try to read it, or try to remember what reading is or something. But as far as the actual how it all occurs, what my fingers do, what I do – it's not planned. It's an improvisation between me and the book and my really lousy eye-hand coordination. You know? It's sort of that's what happens."

Interestingly enough, in the shooting script, when Romero describes scene 56 – when Bub first notices the copy of *Salem's Lot* – the director includes a humorous note to Tom Savini. "His eyes fall on the book (not literally, Tom . . . this is not an effect . . . I mean to say, 'He looks down at the book')."

As for his character, Bub, Sherman had a quirky interpretation of who he might have been in his "living years". "I thought that maybe he was a defrocked priest who then became a Beat poet and that he probably died in a motorcycle crash. That was kind of my picture of him," laughs Sherman. "I also thought maybe he was a very, very troubled Vietnam vet with post-traumatic stress syndrome, leading to various substance abuse issues. But I always saw him on a motorcycle and I always thought of him as a working man's intellectual. Kind of a Beat poet, a guy who thought about the big picture and was not . . . he wasn't just a regular Joe. I thought that he was sort of an outcast."

A memorable moment from the film, when Bub cuts himself shaving – which is also part of scene 56 – was shot on this day. While the task of creating Bub's shaving wound was handled first hand by Tom Savini, the design work on Bub, and many other memorable make-ups in the film, was mainly handled by John Vulich. "I don't know if you know this, but a pivotal creative force on that film was John Vulich," says Everett Burrell, soon to join Savini's crew. "Johnny was the main pivotal force on that, and so was Tom in a lot of ways, but really it was John's imagination that really brought those characters to life. I mean, through Bub and a lot of the gags. I mean, Tom's a smart, clever guy, but it was Johnny's vision, I think that kind of brought those zombies to the next level.

"And I love Greg [Nicotero] to death, I do, and he's my brother. But, you know, Greg was a PA on the show. He was truly just our PA – he was nothing more. He wasn't creative at all. Greg did nothing, he didn't

Top: Zombie extras rehearsing their shot on the elevator at the Manor Nike Missile Site. (Courtesy of Mike Gornick.)
Middle: Wide angle shot of zombie extras unmasked and taking a break at the Manor Nike Missile Site. (Courtesy of Al Magliochetti.) **Bottom:** Associate producer Ed Lammi (with his arm in a sling) and production manager Zilla Clinton (in the bridal dress) as zombies at the Manor Nike Missile Site. (Courtesy of Ed Lammi.)

THE MAKING OF GEORGE A. ROMERO'S DAY OF THE DEAD

Left: A Manor Nike zombie extra dressed up as a graduate. Zombie wardrobe would be recycled several times during filming, leading to the occasional continuity error. (Courtesy of Al Magliochetti.) **Above:** Publicity photo showing the same graduate outfit, this time worn by a zombie extra with make-up rather than a background mask. (Hollywood Book & Poster Company)

sculpt anything. Greg was never creative on that show. I think Greg became more of a creative force as he became older and wiser, but on that show we called him 'Gut Boy' and he would wrangle the pig guts. But he didn't sculpt or design anything on that show."

Lastly, scene 78 was once again scheduled but never actually filmed.

Saturday 10/27/1984 – Day 6

"I look this good 'cause I get more sleep than anyone." – Bomba

The sixth day of the shoot would continue work on one of the most iconic scenes in the film, scene 1 – Sarah's nightmare at the beginning of the film, when the zombie arms burst through the wall. This scene would turn out to be more difficult than expected and was eventually re-shot on a subsequent day due to issues with the original take. "I think what happened was the wall wasn't anchored adequately, so the first take, when everybody pushed through it, it pushed the entire wall," recalls Greg Nicotero. "When everyone went, 'Ready, and push!' the whole wall went crrsshh!" According to the call sheet, 39 extras were scheduled to have their arms made up to appear rotted and decayed when they punch through the wall to grab at Lori Cardille, including her husband, Jim Rogal, who served another purpose during the scene, as Lori's protector from "frisky" zombie hands. "You can see this one pair of arms that's keeping all the other zombie arms from touching any of her personal places," says Nicotero, referring to a behind-the-scenes video taken during the filming of the shot.

The wall-of-arms scene would also be a mild source of consternation for Tom Savini, as he sensed doubt from his fellow crew members regarding his abilities. In issue number 46, August 1985, of *Fangoria* magazine, Savini spoke with Robert Martin about that particular feeling he was getting early on in the shoot. "There was a while when *Day* was first starting when I felt like there had been a major change in the way the Romero 'family' works . . . It's hard to express exactly, but I felt that I was being picked on in some little ways; it was almost like I was working with total strangers. But, the more footage that was shot, the more we were able to get the things into the can, the more that feeling went away. I felt, in a way, that on this picture I had to regain the confidence of these people." When I asked Savini about this remark, he was open and candid about

Above: Peter Iasillo, Al Magliochetti, and Gabe Bartalos as masked zombie extras at the Manor Nike Missile Site. (Courtesy of Al Magliochetti.) **Below:** Zombie extra Gabe Bartalos lends a hand to the effects crew by helping make up fellow extras. Bartalos and colleague Al Magliochetti were invited to be extras after helping Tom Savini out during the effects prep. (Courtesy of Al Magliochetti.)

it. "I don't remember saying that, but now that you mention it, yeah, I felt like I was being bombarded with criticism," says Savini. "Not from George [Romero] especially, but from . . . like John Harrison, he was the first AD. We'd just come from *Dawn of the Dead* where I made all the zombies look the same, they were all grey. Or they were supposed to be all grey, but the lighting in the mall, the lighting that they were using on them, sometimes they were blue, sometimes they were green; I think rarely they were grey. But I think they expected, in *Day of the Dead,* for them all to look the same. I won the Saturn Award for *Day of the Dead*, for the make-up effects. That's kind of like my splatter masterpiece, because the zombies were the most realistic zombies that I've ever done. If you die in the basement or you die in the attic, you know, a cold wet basement compared to a hot attic with no air flow, you're going to be bloated in the attic and you're going to be shriveled in the basement. People die differently and decay differently – ethnic groups, you know, they just don't look the same. And that's what I tried to do. And the first thing we did was the arms coming through the wall and they were all different! And Harrison complained, 'Well, why don't they look the same?' Whether he got that note from George, I don't know. But they accepted it when I explained that people just don't look alike after they die. It depends on the situation, the ethnic group, and how long they've been dead. That was my attempt to do very realistic zombies. So because of that coming down on me . . . that was one of the biggest films that George had to do, so it wasn't as personal as *Creepshow* – even though *Creepshow* was five movies – *Creepshow* or *Martin*, where you had a very intimate relationship with George. He was almost unreachable, untouchable on *Day*. Almost, but not . . . I mean, he was still there but not there personally as he was before. Maybe that's why I said that, I don't know."

The rest of the shooting day would be taken up completing work, once more, on scenes 49 through 58, in which Logan takes Sarah and Fisher into Bub's observation room and shows him the tooth brush, shaving razor, book, and telephone – ending with Bub aiming the gun at Rhodes.

A funny aside from this day's particular call sheet was part of the advance schedule at the bottom of the page. Each daily call sheet featured a preview of what was on tap for the following shooting day. The next day was obviously the production's first Sunday off, so a special note said "A Day Off For The Dead" for Sunday, October 28, 1984.

Monday 10/29/1984 – Day 7

"Life's a bitch and then you die." – Anonymous 14th century poet

Day seven of the shoot would concentrate on just one scene in particular, number 22. It's the sequence at the corral in which Sarah argues with Rickles about not keeping track of the specimens on the clipboard,

Above and below: Tom Savini making up Taso Stavrakis at the Manor Nike Missile Site, for his continuity zombie role as the motorcycle helmet-wearing zombie who stumbles off the elevator platform. (Courtesy of Al Magliochetti.)

Steel bragging about having the "biggest piece o' meat in the cave", and Sarah telling Steel he's nothing more than a caveman to her. Work on this section of the film would take place for the next several days.

While the first week of shooting had gone relatively smoothly, there were some issues that began to bubble to the surface. One of these issues involved Lori Cardille and her make-up person, Bonnie Priore, and unfortunately lasted for quite a while during production. "There was a woman that was doing my make-up and, God bless her, she had a real problem. I kept complaining because half my face would be made up, you know? 'Oh my God,' I kept complaining, 'you

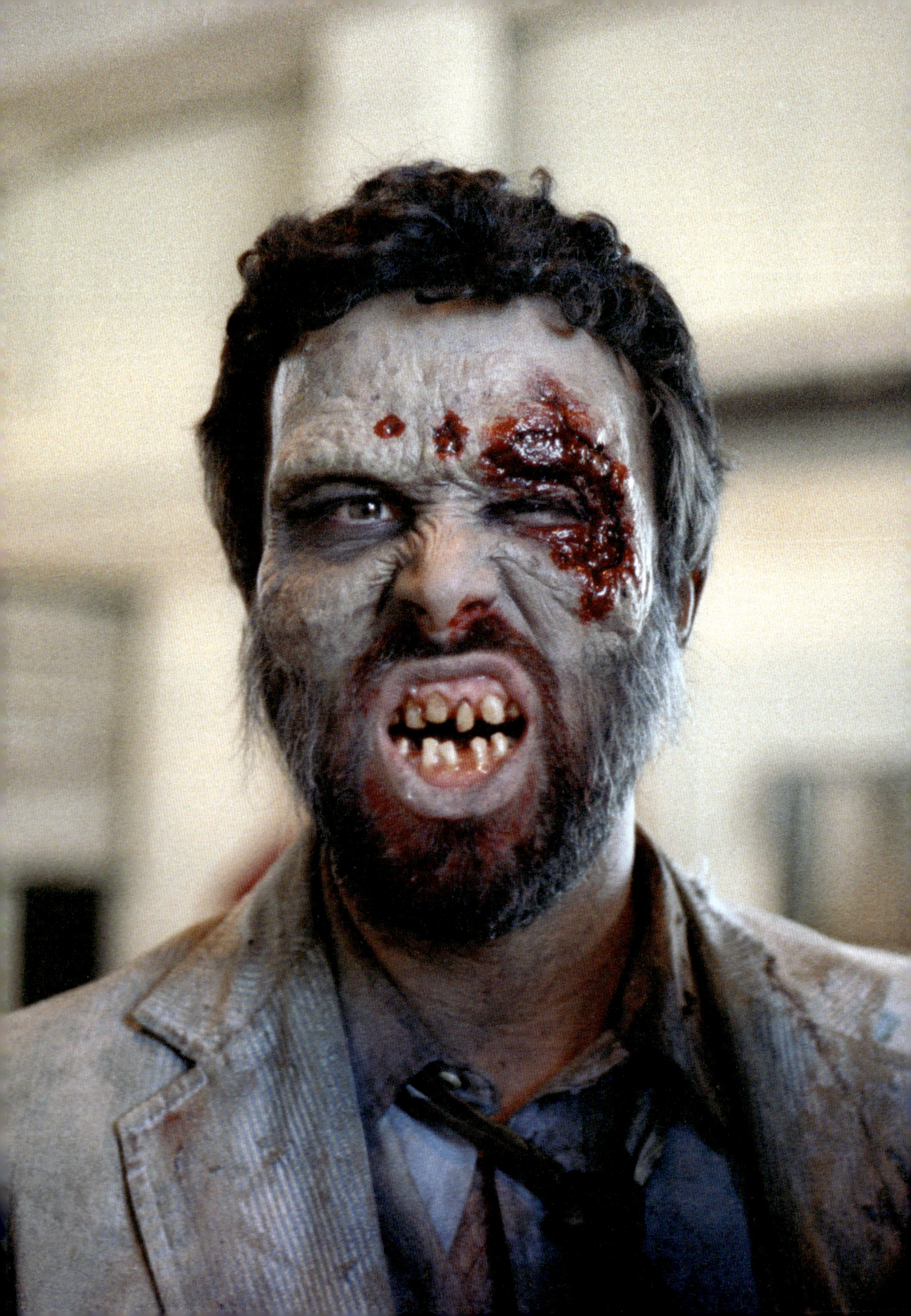

ONE DAY AT A TIME

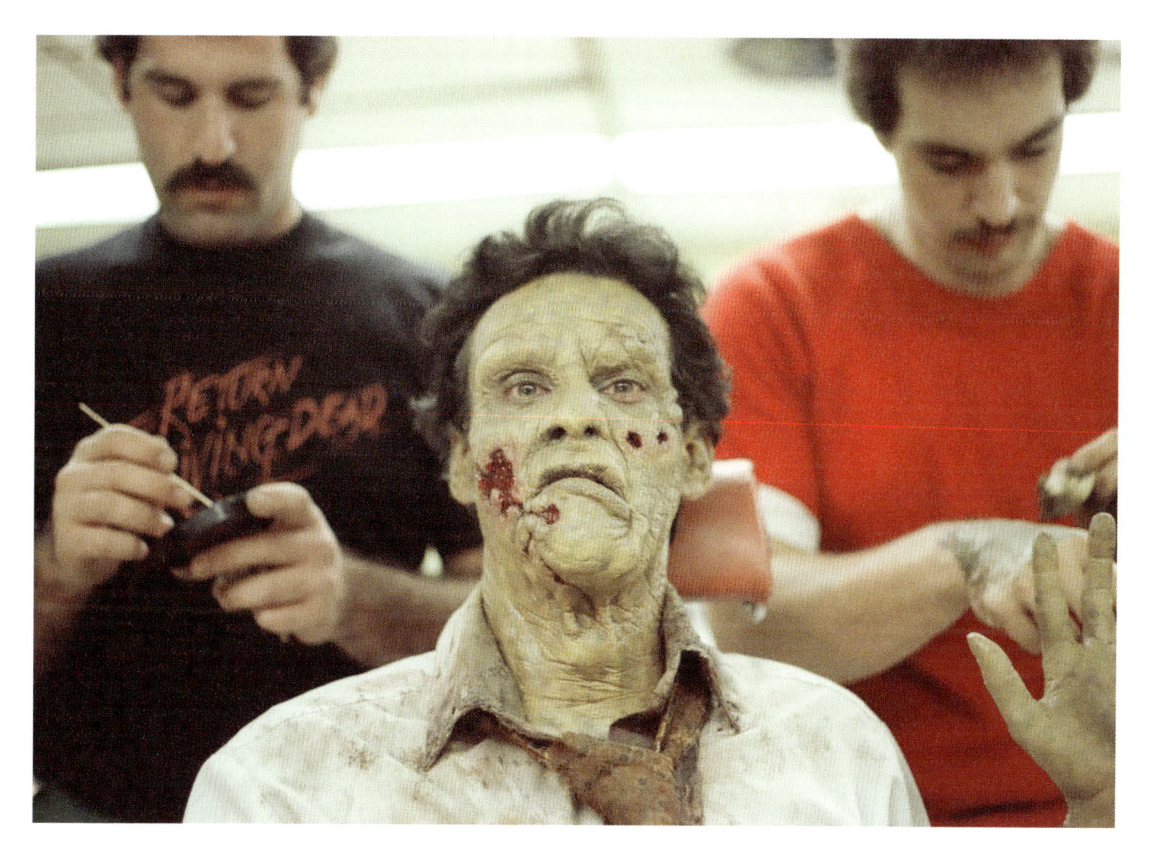

Left: Continuity zombie, William Laczko, in full make-up at the Manor Nike Missile Site. Laczko also had a cameo in Romero's *Dawn of the Dead*, as the redneck getting his head bandaged during the posse montage. (Courtesy of Al Magliochetti.) **Above:** Mark Tierno being made up as the "Beef Treats" zombie by Howard Berger and Mike Trcic. Note the *Return of the Living Dead* t-shirt that Berger is sporting, a film that would compete head-to-head with *Day* the following summer. (Courtesy of Mark Tierno.)

have to do something I can't go on camera like this'," says Cardille. "I just thought it was unprofessional, you know? Trying to fight for that specific thing – everybody wanted to turn a blind eye and you can't. You can't because it's important stuff. But this is all dish dirt shit stuff that I'm telling you . . . and I'll probably burn a lot of bridges, but I really don't care."

Eventually – very late in the production – Priore would be replaced by Jeannee Josefczyk, who had originally been offered the position. "A friend of mine, Bonnie Priore, had done George's [Romero] work before. She kept calling me every day saying, 'Hey, do you want to be my assistant?'" recalls Josefczyk. "In the meantime, Zilla [Clinton], who was the UPM [unit production manager] for George, was calling me every day to see if I wanted to do the film. I was torn between my friend and the company and finally I turned to Zilla and I said, 'Bonnie really needs this job and she thinks she has it,' and I said, 'Go back to George and talk to him about it.' She called me back, she said, 'You know you slit your own throat,' and I said, 'That's fine. I feel better that I did something the right way instead of being underhanded and taking a job when it really was supposed to be for my friend.' So that's how it came about. Then Bonnie had problems on the job and they called me to come in and take over. They originally had wanted me to go to Florida, and I said I couldn't go then. So when they came back here they called me up to do the job. I was looking at the dailies and I said, 'Which ones do you want me to match?', because all the looks were all over the place. So I basically went in and took over and did the stuff and got Lori Cardille looking the way they wanted her and that's how it went." (Sadly, Bonnie Priore would pass away just five years later, due to congestive heart failure.)

The strained relationship between George Romero and Michael Gornick would also raise its head at times during filming. It was particularly apparent to those who had known the two men for many years. "It was bad," says key grip Nick Mastandrea. "Because Mike was shooting it and Mike really was not . . . I didn't think [he] was really . . . whatever was going on was certainly affecting his work as well, in their communication between each other." First assistant director John Harrison could also sense a change between the two men. "As far as Michael's thing with Laurel and George leaving Laurel, you know, maybe

Above: Debra Gordon being transformed into a zombie by John Vulich. (Courtesy of Greg Nicotero.)

there was some tension there about that," says Harrison. "But it was hard work, in that mine, it was a very tough shoot. And there were times when Michael and George weren't communicating as effectively as they had in the past. It was not fun for them, for their relationship. Now, I don't know whether that was because Michael . . . I never really heard or thought that it was because he was staying with Laurel and George was not. That may be true, that may be Michael's impression of it."

Some crew members would talk openly and glowingly about the respect they have for Romero's longtime director of photography. "Michael Gornick is one of the – I used to say I can count them on one hand and I still can. I can only think of three people – not even five – three people that I would truly call geniuses, and Mike Gornick is a genius in terms of he doesn't forget anything," says slate/loader Simon Manses. "He never overlooks a detail, he's always thinking about additional angles and elements that might be hidden from view. He's a very strong personality. He can be a wonderful, wonderful human being, and to me he was never anything but an absolutely wonderful human being and a perfect mentor. But it's often the case with individuals like that, sometimes they have a little bit of a temper, and he did a little bit. Where he would go ahead and express his concern or disagreement, [and] there would be other people that would maybe veil their thoughts a little bit more and internalize them."

"Let me tell you, Mike Gornick is probably, singularly, the most honest person you will ever meet in your life. That's my take on Mike," says co-producer David Ball. "George [Romero], all he wanted to do was shoot, 'I just want to shoot.' So Gornick was trying to make it look nice and effective, as he would have been. Then there would have been the odd bit of friction here and there between them, and I did witness that."

For Gornick personally, it was a very painful time and his mind was elsewhere, even though he did his best not to show it. "Were there individual light moments, probably within the filming? Sure. But just the struggle – I wanted to be somewhere else," admits Gornick. "At that point in time I was directing and I thought, well that's a wonderful direction that I want to take now with my life, and I think I'd rather be doing that. There were upcoming projects. There was some promise of a theatrical, which then became *Creepshow 2*, and I thought this is probably what I need to do at this point, I *want* to do at this point, because the old relationship was gone with George." Gornick relieved some of that anxiety and pain by driving home each day, rather than staying at the hotel with the crew. "I did a lot of traveling. I didn't want to stay at the hotel at that point," says Gornick. "I had young children and so I was trying to commute back and forth, all the way from Wampum back to, in essence I lived then in Trafford, which is near Monroeville. So it was quite a commute. I made this ridiculous commute, but it was kind of therapeutic because I could get away from the set in a way, and some of the things that troubled me in my mind about shooting *Day of the Dead*."

One actor, who requested not to go on the record, said that there were open disagreements between Romero and Gornick regarding the best way to shoot some of the corral scenes, ending with Romero putting his foot down and telling Gornick that he, Romero, was the director, and that was the end of it.

Tuesday 10/30/1984 – Day 8

"Life is a bitch and then you die. Except in India, where life is a bitch and then you die then life is a bitch and then you die then life is a bitch . . ."

The eighth day of shooting would concentrate on scenes 22 through 27, in which Sarah, Miguel, Steel and Rickles first reach the corral area in an attempt to wrangle zombies, up until the point when Miguel first drops his noose pole while climbing up the ladder.

The corral set-up would be of special interest to one of the cast members – for strange reasons, to say the least. "I remember one of the actors, I can't remember who it was, one of the actors was really into, like, this mysticism stuff," says art director Bruce Miller. "And he was convinced that the corral, the line of the corral, was put between some kind of vortex between good and evil on the planet, and he believed that that's where Cletus [Anderson] had placed this, to protect the good from the evil. And he really believed that." [*laughs*] The cast member that Miller speaks of was Tim DiLeo. "Yeah, it was Tim," laughs Barbara Anderson. "Absolutely."

"Well, I was really out there back then and I wouldn't put it past me to have said something like that. I think people, even in my 'cuckooness', took me a little too [seriously] . . . yeah, probably I did," says DiLeo. "I can tell you this, that when we were doing the shots of seeing people though the corral, that was not playing around, I was 'seeing' things back there in the dark." With my curiosity now piqued, I asked DiLeo to explain in a little more detail just what he might have seen in the dark. "Sometimes I see things, and what I was seeing was not anything that made me comfortable, let's put it that way," says DiLeo. "You can sense energies, or even see energies, and I definitely was seeing energies that day. Plus the camera smelled to high heaven. It smelled like shit!" As for what might have caused that horrible stench around the camera? "I know what was causing it," says DiLeo. "It was the subject matter, the calling on dead things, the whole energy of the place and what we were filming."

On a funny side note, when I mentioned these quotes to Michael Gornick, he told me that what Tim was probably seeing on the other side of the corral was him and the camera. It's a remark that gives you an idea of the dry humor and wit that Gornick possesses. "People like Tim DiLeo – actually, and Joe Pilato – had such an intensity . . . they felt dangerous," says Gornick. "There were times when you didn't know if there indeed was going to be an actual cut to the scene."

For co-star Lori Cardille, however, DiLeo didn't feel dangerous at all. In fact, he was her closest friend on the production. "My buddy on the film was Tim DiLeo, Anthony, and I just have a lot of memories of us being so silly together, you know?" says Cardille. "I mean, oh my God, we just were like two old ladies in a way. That's what I felt like we were, two old ladies. Sorry, Tim." [*laughs*] Her feelings for another co-star, Gary Klahr, were a little different, though. "I had a crush on Gary," says Cardille. "I thought he was cute, I just thought he was nice. He was gregarious and out there, I loved him. He was the life of the party."

After they'd been on set for a few days, it became apparent that Tom Savini's effects crew was too small and needed some extra helping hands. This day would see the arrival of two new members of Savini's crew, Howard Berger and Everett Burrell, thanks to an

Top: Phillip Kellams having his false throat appliance tended to by Tom Savini. (Courtesy of Chad Ball.)
Botom: John Vulich painting detail onto the neck appliance for Phil Kellams' throat-biting scene. The throat appliance was actually cast from Tim DiLeo's neck, and would be used for his death scene in Florida. (Courtesy of Al Magliochetti.)

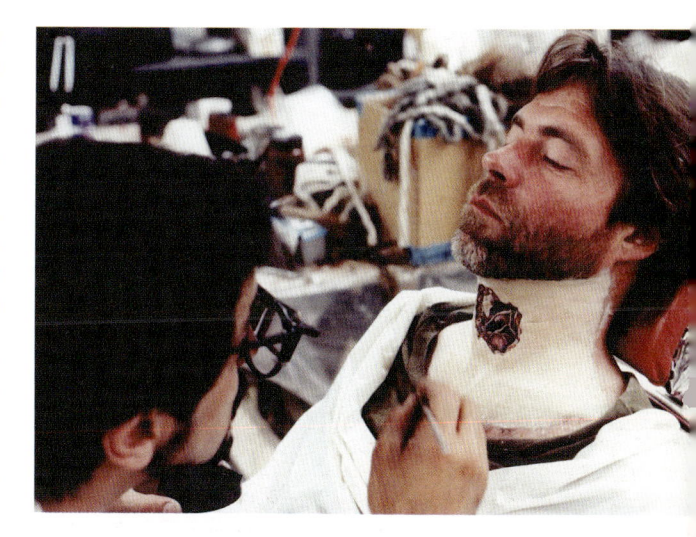

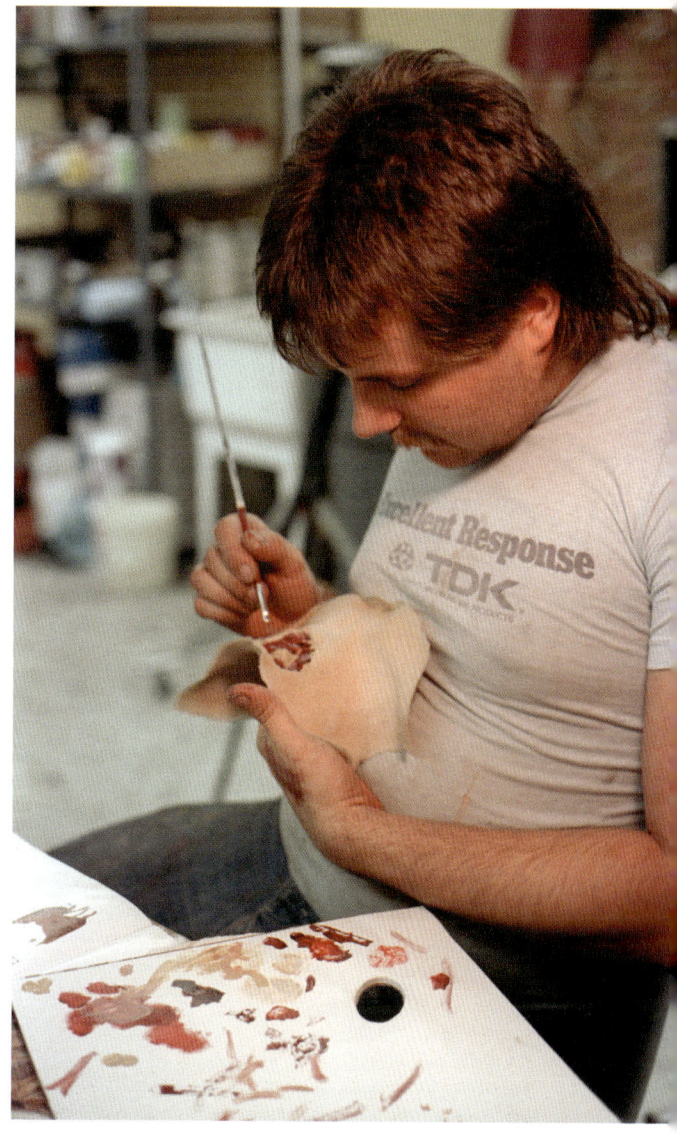

Top: Tom Savini goes to work on Dave Kindlon – soon to be transformed into the "priest" zombie that bites Tim DiLeo. **Middle:** Tom Savini and Howard Berger work on making Dave Kindlon up as the "priest" or "Don King" zombie, as he was also referred to. **Bottom:** Greg Nicotero as Johnson and Dave Kindlon as the "priest" zombie. (Photos courtesy of Al Magliochetti.)

assist from John Vulich. "I'm assuming in some ways that I probably had a big hand in the formation of KNB [Kurtzman/Nicotero/Berger Effects Group] pretty much," laughs Vulich. "Because it became apparent, when we were gonna go out to location, that we were just going to need some extra help, there weren't really enough of us. There was, like, maybe four or five of us on the crew, there wasn't really enough of us to handle the workload and the application. And so I think they'd asked me if there's anybody that I knew to bring out, that I thought would be good, and people that were talented."

"I was living in this apartment complex with Everett Burrell – we were roommates – and down below John Vulich and Mitch Devane had an apartment," recalls Howard Berger. "So, we were all friends and we all worked at John Buechler's together at the time. He [John] had gotten hired to go work on *Day of the Dead* and, during the prep, Tom [Savini] had released two of the people that he had hired, and so they needed the replacements, so Johnny had recommended Everett and myself. So, we got a call from John and he said, 'Hey, you guys want to come to Pittsburgh and work on *Day of the Dead*?' And, of course, we leaped at the chance to do that! So we packed up all of our stuff as fast as we could, hopped on a plane, and zipped right off to Pittsburgh."

"Tom had hired Johnny through correspondence that John had done over the years, and Johnny and Tom had made a friendship based on *Friday the 13th Part 4*," recalls Everett Burrell. "So, Johnny went to Pittsburgh, and Johnny called me and asked me if Steve Johnson was available. I said, 'Well, Steve's a little bit beyond working for Tom' – at the time. [*laughs*] And so he goes, 'Well, what are you and Howard doing?' I said, 'Well, we'd love to come,' so Howard and I flew out there – I think October of '84? October of '84 we flew out and we stayed there until the bitter end."

Upon arriving, Berger and Burrell's introduction to "Savini Land" would be a harbinger of things to come for them. "I remember we landed in Pittsburgh and then we had somebody pick us up, and we drove all the way to Beaver Falls and went right to the place we shot at, the mine, and walked in, and all this crazy hustle and bustle is going on," remembers Berger. "First person I meet is Greg Nicotero; it's like, 'Hey, I'm Greg Nicotero and I'll find Tom for you,' and then [he] ran away. The next thing I saw was Tom Savini running down the hall, and Everett and I went, 'Hi, we're Everett and Howard,' and he's like, 'Hi! I gotta do a practical joke, I'll be right back!', and Tom disappeared. That was our initiation into the first day of working on *Day of the Dead*."

Berger and Burrell weren't the only new arrivals to the set. But the other one was of the four-legged variety. "There was this kitten who showed up on the set and got adopted, and he kind of lived with us in the prop area for a while, and people bought him toys and he got named 'Zombie'," says properties assistant Eliza Townsend. "But he got to be a problem and they decided that they needed him to go, and so I took him. And I had that cat for fourteen years."

Wednesday 10/31/1984, Halloween – Day 9

"If it feels good . . . give it back!"

The ninth day of filming would continue work on scenes 22 through 27 at the corral, as well as starting on scene 28, which was more than three pages long. Scene 28 included the sequence at the corral in which the zombies are hooked onto their poles, Miguel dropping his pole, allowing his female zombie captive to roam free and nearly attack Rickles, and finally, Steel angrily dangling Miguel over the corral containing the male zombie captive, which in turn forces Sarah to threaten to shoot Steel.

For actress Debra Gordon, her training with Jerzy Grotowski – the same acting teacher that Joe Pilato studied under – would help bring her zombie character to life, so to speak. "I had just finished a graduate school of acting and I had done all this Grotowski work, which is a type of theater that was popular in the seventies," says Gordon. "This Polish man, Grotowski, he was rooted in the physicality of acting, and he had these poses based on animals, like tiger and lion. It was like a warm-up that you would do, where you would start with a small movement in your body, it would just build, and then you'd end up with these animal-type sounds, you know? [*laughs*] I know it sounds funny, but I think that was the root of what I did. I hadn't seen that many other zombies, I wasn't copying anything. I threw myself into it like I was an animal, and I think that it was hunger in trying to focus on something that I wanted, and that just kind of created the character. And if you do it right, it's exhausting! Because you're really emoting 100 percent, but it's in an animal-type way. So my image was always of myself as the tiger. [*growls*] The sound would really come from inside, I didn't create the sound from the outside – whatever guttural sounds came out."

Gordon would also suffer for her art, developing a periodontal infection from the zombie dentures she wore during the filming. "They were filthy because we were in that mine and you couldn't really talk too well with them on," remembers Gordon. "So if I had them on I would take them off in between shots so that I could talk, and drink, and breathe. And my hands had make-up on them – they must have gotten dirty – kept putting them on, taking them off, putting them on, taking them off. So, months later I was suffering from that."

Having the extensive make-up on also gave her an insight into how lonely the world could be when you didn't look like everyone else in it. "Whenever I had the make-up on it was like I was the most unpopular person – no one would come over and talk to me," says Gordon. "I realized because I was so ugly . . . first of all people didn't recognize me. Second of all, no one's really that interested in talking to somebody that looks like that. [*laughs*] It really gave me a different perspective on how lonely it could be to be a freak."

Gordon's feelings about being shunned while wearing the make-up weren't just paranoia on her part, as members of the crew would attest. "When we're having lunch in the huge mess hall, all the zombies would be there in their costumes and their make-up, with half a head cut off or a limb missing," says soundman Rolf Pardula. "So they'd have us sitting next to them having lunch or dinner. [*laughs*] And initially it was, 'Oh God. I can't stand this.'"

That make-up would also give Gordon an idea for Halloween night. She had a two-year-old son at home, so she thought it might be fun to come home in the make-up as a way to surprise him, but during her journey home on the Pennsylvania Turnpike she ended up giving someone else a big surprise. "I decided to go home with my make-up on since it was Halloween, so I could show my son the make-up, you know, kind of funny," recalls Gordon. "So I'm driving on the turnpike with this professional zombie make-up, and in those days they had real people that took the tolls. I rolled down my window to pay my toll and the woman in the booth was so scared I thought she was going to have a heart attack! I forgot that I had the zombie make-up on."

Thursday 11/1/1984 – Day 10

**"That which does not kill me makes me stronger."
– Hurricane Carter**

The tenth day of filming continued with work at the corral set on scenes 22 through 28. One of the scenes shot on this day was the close-up of Steel dangling Miguel over the open area of the corral containing the "Beef Treats" zombie. "I really got into that," says Mark Tierno. "I wanted it to be realistic and I thought it really came out well." Taso Stavrakis was also on set this day, to perform the stunt where Miguel is thrown off the corral catwalk by Steel.

This day of shooting was like many on the production, with the crew trying to complete what they had started the day before – or sometimes several days before. And each one of those days would begin very early for first assistant director, John Harrison. "When we were working in the mine, for the period of time that we were in the mine, it was essentially a regular work day – in early, out late," says Harrison. "I always got there early. I wanted to be there ahead of the crew because oftentimes – and George [Romero] is like this and I've been like this as a director – I like to get on the set before anybody else, just so I have some time to kind of think about the day. A lot of stuff has been scheduled, you know what you're going to try to do, you know what you didn't get done before and you have to pick it up, blah, blah, blah. So I always liked to get to the set ahead of time, and George was like that too. So I would get there and he and I would just talk over what we were going to do. Crew shows up, we start setting up for the first . . . whatever the first set-ups are, we start getting that going. And then there are the contingencies of the day, which in that case had a lot to do with the make-up effects, because there were always zombies. So you had to factor that in. How long was it going to take to get them ready? Which ones would be ready first? And that would help you dictate which scenes you were shooting. However many takes George felt he needed to get what he needed, working with the actors, leaving some wiggle room for what George used to call the 'happy accidents', things you discover while you were shooting, being able to sit with the actors and try different things and so forth. And depending on the day, whether you had small scenes with just a few actors and some zombies, or whether you had big, huge crowd scenes. So you do that until seven o'clock at night with, obviously, a lunch break. And you were in the mine the whole time, you never left. So you're always underground and it was a constant, approximately, 55 degrees all the time, no matter what was going on outside. It was damp, it was dark, there was mine dust in the air constantly; you'd blow your nose [and] it would all come out black. But having said all that, we had a great time."

The working day, however, would not end at the mine. It continued back at the hotel, in the small makeshift screening room that had been set up for the production. "Then we would go back to the hotel and watch dailies and that would take a couple of hours," recalls Harrison. "And we'd watch dailies from the previous couple of days, talk about what we'd done. Did we get it all? Did we miss something? So forth and so on and then head to the bar; however long you could stay at the bar knowing you had to get up at 5:30, 6:00 the next morning and go out and do it all over again."

The room that would serve as the dailies screening room was one of two editing rooms set up at the Holiday Inn. "They got two rooms there for the editing room," says editor Pat Buba. "George [Romero] owned the flatbeds, the two Moviola flatbeds, which they moved up to the editing rooms. And then they set up a projector in one part of the room – one room for dailies and then I had the Moviola set up in the other room." Watching dailies created something of a party atmosphere for the crew and everyone was invited, even though it wasn't the most ideal setting for the job itself. "I just remember dailies always being in a packed little room, because the editing room wasn't big enough for dailies," says Buba. "And George liked to have people at dailies, so everybody who would

Above: Barbara Russell, the zombie who attacks Miller (Phillip Kellams) at the corral, has an explosive blood squib rigged to her head. (Courtesy of Al Magliochetti.) **Below:** With a little help from Greg Nicotero, Tom Savini attaches an explosive blood squib to the head of Phillip Kellams. This would play a crucial part in the actor's upcoming death scene. (Courtesy of Al Magliochetti.)

ONE DAY AT A TIME

97

THE MAKING OF GEORGE A. ROMERO'S DAY OF THE DEAD

Dawn of the Dead, Knightriders, and *Creepshow,* Dubensky was a trusted Romero veteran who was busy with prior commitments, but willing to help out when he had time. "When they started production there was no post-production staff at all. Pat [Buba] was busy working [on another project] and there were no assistants – nothing. And so they would shoot film and send it to Technicolor in New York for processing. Tony Buba would transfer the sound in the evenings, downtown at the shop on Fort Pitt Boulevard," recalls Dubensky. "Someone decided, 'Well, we need someone to come in and put an editing room together at the Holiday Inn,' where everyone was staying. They had disassembled all the editing tables from downtown and moved them to the Holiday Inn, as well as the two Moviola flatbeds. They said, 'We need someone to go in, put the tables together and synch up all the material, send it to WRS [a Pittsburgh film lab] for edge coding and log the materials, so when Pat comes to Pittsburgh he can walk in and just start cutting right away.' There would be material there, he'd be ready to go and he could just dive in and start working on it. So, they got a hold of me and they said, 'Can you come for a week? If you had a week, could you put it all together?' and I was working on other things, but I had a week free, so I said, 'Okay.'"

Friday 11/2/1984 – Day 11

"People say I'm sick . . . I'm demented."
– Tom Savini

For the next two days, filming would move from the Wampum Mine, about an hour's drive southeast down the Pennsylvania turnpike, for scenes at the Manor Nike Missile Site. Much like a traveling circus, the production moved in a large fleet of cars and vans to the former Cold War base, which was nestled in the western Pennsylvania countryside. "That was the coolest thing," remembers production assistant, John "Flash" Williams. "That was the coolest facility to work in. That was really neat."

The first scene on the eleventh day's schedule was scene 76, where Tim DiLeo rides the elevator platform up to the top to finish his character's suicide mission. In the shooting script, Romero describes Miguel as looking like "Quasimodo in one of the towers of Notre Dame".

Also scheduled was scene 82, featuring Steel and Rickles' discovery of the control box destroyed by Miguel. A little extra dialogue between Klahr and Marrero was apparently improvised on set, because it's not in the shooting script. Steel's lines of, "Rickles, we can't get out of here" and "He tore the fucking guts out of it, Rickles! I can't fix it!" are examples of

Above: Lori Cardille with her husband, Jim Rogal, on set at the Wampum Mine. **Below:** Assistant camera, slate operator and "ne'er-do-well", Simon Manses. (Photos courtesy of Barbara Boyle.)

care to join in some cold pizza and sit on the floor would sit in there and watch dailies. It was just a regular hotel room without any beds in it. There was a sheet hanging on the wall that we would kind of screen against. But every time somebody would open the door or close the door the screen would shake back and forth, so you could never really judge focus or anything."

The editing room itself had been set up early on at the hotel by Tom Dubensky. Having worked as Mike Gornick's first assistant cameraman on *Martin,*

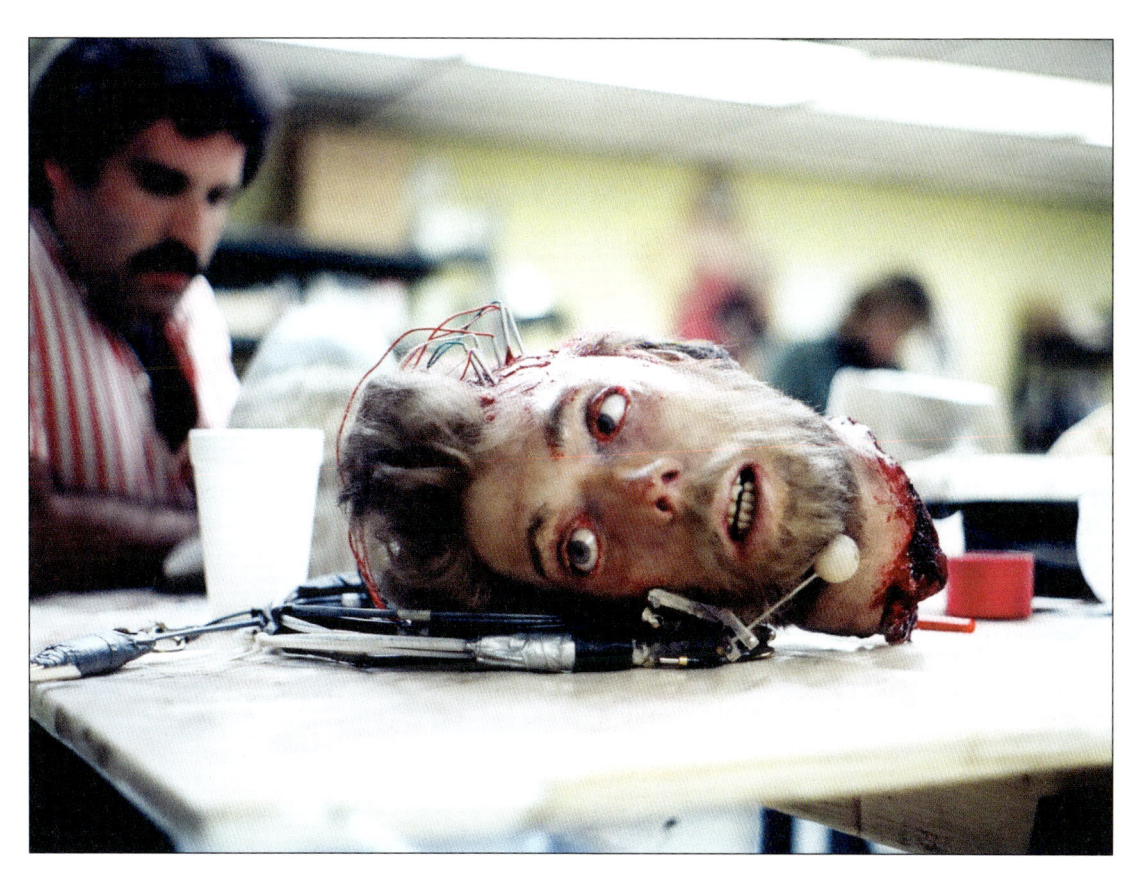

Above: Close-up shot of Greg Nicotero's fake severed head as Howard Berger studies something in the background. (Courtesy of George Demick.)

dialogue not contained in the final screenplay. If it wasn't improvised by the actors, another possibility is that it was written at the last minute by Romero himself. "George Romero does work a lot off the cuff, you know, making stuff up as he goes along," laughs stand-in, Jim Wetzel. "I used to go there in the morning and he would be there waiting for everybody else, sitting at the typewriter, banging away. I'd ask him, 'What are you doing?' and he goes, 'Oh, I'm just writing this scene.'" [*laughs*]

Scene 87 is another scene on the schedule, and would play slightly differently in the film than it did on the page. In the shooting script, while Steel and Rickles were attempting to hot-wire the control box, the screams of the dying Miguel coming from above could be heard by the soldiers below. Rhodes' dialogue about Miguel being a "little shit" and claim that "he tried to make a run for it" was a little longer; he also talks about the gates probably being open and "dumb fucks" now being inside the compound.

The remaining scene scheduled for the day was scene 89, where the elevator starts to descend and the panicked reaction of the soldiers was shot. Another interesting difference between the page and the screen is that, in the script, Romero describes a stream of blood spilling off the edge of the elevator as it descends, something that doesn't appear in the film.

Saturday 11/3/1984 – Day 12

"Zombies always take a lot of shit." – G. Romero

The second and last day of filming at the Manor Nike Missile Site would end up being quite memorable, especially for one zombie extra (more on that shortly).

The first of two scenes shot this day was scene 20, where Sarah, Miguel, John (Terry Alexander), and McDermott (Jarlath Conroy) ride the elevator down and are greeted by Miller (Phillip Kellams). The brief exchange of dialogue, where Miller says "Another waste of time, right?" and John replies, "Got that right, mon" is yet another example of lines not included in the actual shooting script.

This was the first day of shooting for both Terry Alexander and Jarlath Conroy. Being a new member of the Romero family and a late arrival to the set, Alexander found that he kept to himself a bit. "I was always a loner," admits Alexander. "I didn't really speak to Jarlath that much. We worked together, but I came in . . . they were shooting about a week and a half before I got there. And by that time all the

Above: Howard Berger examines the life cast of actor Ralph Marrero (Rickles). (Courtesy of George Demick.)

relationships on the movie had cemented themselves, who was gonna do this and that, who was friends by about after a week and a half. I came in, I was a little late – so I didn't really make any friends. I didn't really . . . I wasn't chummy with anybody really, truth be told."

This day would also be the completion of scene 89 – scene A89, to be exact – where the elevator descends with the giant horde of zombies! Over 160 extras were scheduled for this massive scene, the vast majority of whom would wear pullover masks created by David Smith. The masks had originally been conceived to be used for deep background extras, not really intended to be seen up close at all. But in fact they would end up being seen up close at times in the film, and feature prominently in a famous set photograph of George Romero surrounded by zombie extras, taken at the Nike site on this very day. "We had 150 of those made," recalls Greg Nicotero. "So they did three different sculptures and then ran the masks and painted them, haired them, and sent them out to us. I think our original idea was [that] we were going to modify some of them because, of course, once they got there they were so dramatically different than anything we were doing on the show that, continuity-wise, they never really, really worked that well. That's probably one of the reasons why we ended up working with the art department and the costume department to do all those background zombies, because we needed . . . the masks were just not quite what conceptually Tom [Savini] had anticipated."

"That was going to be done because there were so many zombies," says Tom Savini. "We made up hundreds of zombies, me and my guys, with prosthetics. But we thought for the background we could just throw masks on them, you know? And I guess that was a big mistake."

Effects artist John Vulich was disappointed in the masks too, but not for the reason you might think. "One of the ways that I used to subsidize my hobby when I was a kid is I used to make Halloween masks," says Vulich. "Not like in a mass production, but it'd be like four or five out of a mold, then I'd take them down to local costume shops and I'd sell them in order to get more money to make other masks – basically get my hobby to pay for itself. So, I kind of considered myself a mask maker and I heard that he'd gotten in contact with David [Smith] and was subcontracting the work for him. I was kind of disappointed because I thought we could have done it in-house." Vulich's mask-making skills are what got him hired by Savini to begin with – on *Friday the 13th: The Final Chapter.* The masks used to populate Corey Feldman's bedroom in that film were the work of young Vulich.

The story of how the background masks were created is an interesting one. Tom Savini contacted a gentleman named Al Taylor in the hope of finding an artist who could design and create the deep background masks. Taylor's company, THS Incorporated, licensed characters to a mask company called Distortions Unlimited, which advertised in magazines like *Fangoria*. Terry Prince was hired to draw the zombie concepts and then submitted them to Savini for approval. After that, Taylor followed Terry Prince's suggestion and contacted David Smith, who created 150 masks for $1,500. "Basically, I'd been paid half of the money up front. Al Taylor sent me a check for $750 to get started," recalls Smith. "I'd read this article by Dick Smith about being a professional and working in the industry and doing things for films. He talked about not delivering until you get all of your money because, basically, once they've got your product, if they haven't paid you they can take forever. You know, they've got what they want and you don't have your money. It's the only thing you have as far as leverage. So, Al Taylor was supposed to pay me the other half of this money when the masks were all done and I'd ship them. I contacted him and I said, 'These masks are all ready, I just need you to give me the rest of the money,' and he said, 'Okay, well I'll send you a check. It'll be there. Go ahead and send the masks off.' So I said, 'Okay, well I'll send them off as soon as I get the check.' So no check would come and the deadline was getting closer and I called him back and I said, 'You know the deadline is coming up, I need you to send the money so I can mail these masks off.' And he said 'Okay, I'm going to send you an overnight check. You send those masks off; the check will be there to you tomorrow. Overnight I'm sending it to you.' So I waited for the check next day and no check came and the day after that . . . so I call him and tell him and he's kind of getting agitated like, 'Oh, why don't you send those things off and I'll pay

Above: The "autopsy" zombie, Mike Trcic, doesn't appreciate having his picture taken. (Courtesy of George Demick.)

you.' So finally I called Savini, I called the production, and I said, 'Look, I've got all these things done' – and I sent them pictures of the things – 'I'd send them to you, but I can't because this guy won't give me the rest of my money.' So within half an hour I got a really aggravated call from Al Taylor and he's yelling at me about going over his head and blah, blah, blah, and he's 'not making any goddamn money on this thing anyway' and he'll send me a check. So finally he did send me a check overnight. But I think if I'd just sent the masks off I might not have ever gotten paid."

For Smith it was an introduction into how shady the business side of movie productions can be. "I found out later that he got $1,500 also, just for making the phone call to me," says Smith. "The whole budget for the masks was $3,000 and he basically just shopped it around until he could find somebody that would do it for half that price so he could keep the other money. I'm not sure what Terry Prince got paid."

Another cost-cutting method that the production implemented was the concept of continuity zombies, an idea born out of the budget upheaval during pre-production. "The scene where the zombies come in, from what is effectively Florida, and they go down that big elevator shaft and they come into the mine – those scenes were shot in three different places," says associate producer Ed Lammi. "So again, it's a very low-budget picture, we didn't have a lot of money. How do we tie – we weren't going to take extras to all those different places – how are we going to tie that together? So we all kind of came up with the idea that we would have what we called 'continuity zombies'. So I was one, the production manager Zilla [Clinton] was another – she was the bride and I was the guy with my arm in a sling. The idea was that, since we would be in all three places, we would be sort of foreground in the camera and we would walk by enough that when you saw us walk onto that pad in Florida, and then you saw us walk off of the elevator in Monroeville [the Manor Nike Site], and then walk into the mine in Wampum, you would feel that whole group of zombies had come on. So that was kind of a fun production thing we came up with."

Besides Ed Lammi and Zilla Clinton's continuity zombies, there was also Taso Stavrakis, as a motorcycle helmet-wearing zombie – the one who falls off the elevator platform. Longtime Romero veteran Vince Survinski portrayed one as well. Production assistant and Romero babysitter Barbara Frazzini played the zombie wearing the red bonnet, thanks to Christine Romero. "She was going to do the part, she was going to play the zombie," recalls Frazzini. "She just was like the kindest person in the world and so she gave it to me. She said, 'Oh, let Barbara fill in, Barbara could do it,' and I was an eager twenty-year-old that was like, 'Oh sure, I'd love to do it,' and they just kinda taught me how to grumble and how to walk and how to put your arms and to make yourself look. So I filled in for Christine."

Another of those continuity zombies was William Laczko, playing the bearded zombie in the grey suit who eventually bites Steel. "As the elevator is coming . . . now there are at least 100, 150 zombies on there," says Laczko. "And me being the ham that I am, I wanted to see myself. So the next time you watch the film, every zombie on that elevator as it's coming down is looking at the camera. My back is to the camera, so that when it hits I can see myself turn and come at the camera."

Some of the zombie extras that worked at the Manor Nike Site would eventually make their way to Wampum to film scenes in the mine as well. Thomas Brown, who years later went on to create a fantastic documentary for the twenty-fifth anniversary of Romero's original *Night of the Living Dead*, was one of them. Mike Metoff, of The Cramps fame, was also someone who pulled multiple days as a zombie extra.

Yet another extra who did this was Kevin Rolly, who'd heard about the filming from an advisor at the Pittsburgh Filmmakers, David Early, who had appeared in Romero's *Dawn of the Dead, Knightriders,* and *Creepshow*. Rolly was seventeen at the time, but lied about his age to get onto the film. "They just stuck me in a mask in the back and we literally waited around for like eight, nine hours for that shot to get off," remembers Rolly. "They had us in back; they had the intermediate zombies in the middle, and obviously the camera zombies in front. So what happened? Something happened . . . oh yeah! What ended up happening was, we were rehearsing the shot and a C-stand, like, blew off the top of the edge of the platform and hit an extra in the head, like totally took him out. And in all the confusion I sort of, like, shambled to the front so when the cameras rolled I was one of the first people to step off the platform, which totally pissed Savini off, like years later. He was at Penn State or something like that, he's like, 'Yeah, we spent all this time putting all these zombies in special make-up and some idiot in the back in a rubber mask walks in front of camera and makes us look like jerks.' I never admitted to it, but that was me."

The extra who was struck in the head by the falling C-stand was Al Magliochetti, who'd assisted Greg Nicotero and Dave Kindlon in Rye, New York with the fabrication of bodies from Carl Fullerton's *Gorky Park* body molds. The experience was quite a close call for Magliochetti – and a bloody one at that. "Basically, what happened was we got all costumed up, we had full over-the-head masks to wear since we were just background zombies, which were pretty thick rubber," recalls Magliochetti. "They assembled us all on this gigantic missile elevator out in the parking lot. They dropped the elevator just to see what it would look

Top: Mike Trcic sketching a picture of himself as the "autopsy" zombie. (Courtesy of Greg Nicotero.)
Middle: Richard Liberty, as Dr. Logan, on his laboratory set.
Bottom: George Romero directing on the set of Dr. Logan's lab. (Photos courtesy of George Demick.)

like from the camera's point of view, and it was just a rehearsal, the camera was set up down at the base of the shaft. And as we got down there I saw Michael Gornick and I saw George Romero, which was the first time I'd seen him that day. And next thing I knew everything went black! And I opened my eyes and I could hear this echo of like metal connecting or whatever, and all I was seeing was diamond plate with little drops of blood hitting it. [laughs] The next thing I know, I feel two guys grab me and apparently some blood was gushing out of the mouth of the mask, and my girlfriend was with me and was screaming, 'He's bleeding! He's bleeding!' I pulled the mask off, which was really tight, and this spray of blood went flying everywhere, and the next thing I do is look over at Tom Savini, who's got this look on his face of utter horror, which can tell you this can't be good. [laughs] So the two guys – whoever they were, with me – grabbed me, dragged me out of there, [and] took me to a Winnebago. At which point Zilla Clinton, who's dressed as a zombie bride, I see her hovering over me saying, 'Go get Greg! He knows CPR!' I see Nicotero's face come over mine, upside down, going 'What's wrong? . . . Oh shit!' I still have no idea what's going on. And it wasn't till I got to the hospital that I saw the skin of my forehead had been pushed down like an accordion. It was about, I think ten, twelve stitches; it wasn't a huge area. But you were seeing way more bone than you should have been seeing. [laughs] There's some story that somebody said they saw me look up, and saw this [the C-stand] coming down for my girlfriend and I got under it and blocked her. If this is true, I'd love to believe it, but I have absolutely no memory of that whatsoever."

At the hospital, Magliochetti received some concerned visitors. "The door kicked open later that afternoon and in walked George [Romero], Michael Gornick, and Tom Savini, still holding my bloody mask, which he crumpled up like a softball and threw at me and said, 'Don't ever wash that!' I have it, it's still here," says Magliochetti. "George was great. He came to the hospital and apologized really profusely for what happened. Mike Gornick actually took care of my girlfriend while I was in the hospital and was driving her around back and forth to the hotel because we were strangers in a strange land."

At the end of the day, all of the extras would return their masks and costumes, receiving their own clothes back in return. For their day's work they were paid a dollar bill, which was signed by Tom Savini. Some extras were not aware that Savini had signed the dollar and actually spent it. Glenn Charbonneau was one of those extras – he spent his at a local Wendy's restaurant! Even Lori Cardille's brother, Billy, would come out for a fun day as a zombie extra.

Along with their dollar bill, the extras received a

Above: Lori Cardille's stand-in, Theresa Bedekovich, flanked by Mike Trcic (left) and Howard Berger (right). **Below:** Theresa Bedekovich, flanked by actors Ralph Marrero (Rickles) and Gary Klahr (Steel). (Photos courtesy of Barbara Boyle.)

painter's cap that said "I Was a Zombie in *Day of the Dead*" (later on in the production some extras would receive copies of "The Dead Walk" newspaper prop, signed by George Romero). The idea for the hat came from location scout, Bill Dickhaut, while working in the Wampum Mine. "I sort of became a little concerned about the fact that there were bats flying around in that cave all the time. You would literally duck to avoid – or at least that was my perception – you would duck to avoid a bat flying at you in the middle of this mine," says Dickhaut. "And so I came up with the idea, I'll give myself credit for this . . . I said to one of the PAs, 'Go to some paint store and get a bunch of painter hats, because I'm not going in there without something on my head.' Because I'd heard stories of bats that fly into your hair and get stuck in your hair. So I was the one that sort of said, 'Can we authorize

Above: A cut on Terry Alexander's cheek is freshened up by Everett Burrell. (Courtesy of George Demick.)

a hundred dollars or something to do . . .' and from that evolved not only the crew wearing these painter hats, but we had the zombies coming in, the extras, and people would volunteer to drive from Wyoming to be a zombie in this movie. They would drive 5,000 miles to go to Wampum, PA to be a zombie in a wide shot. And so we thought it would be a good idea to give them something to sort of commemorate their trip. And so that's what we did, we printed up hats – in fact I still have one – these little painter hats that say 'I Was a Zombie in *Day of the Dead*'. I will take credit for that one."

This day also saw the return of Mike Gornick's former first assistant cameraman, Tom Dubensky, for one day of work. The production's regular first AC, Frank Perl, had to go to New York for a prior commitment.

An interesting note on the call sheet, for the make-up effects crew, read "spare parts of Miguel". Those spare parts, whatever they were, would not be seen on camera.

Monday 11/5/1984 – Day 13

"Shut up or sweep the mine." – Location

The third week of the production began with the crucial scene 60, where Miller and Johnson are killed at the corral and Miguel is bitten. It would take three days to complete this sequence.

This scene featured the death of Greg Nicotero's character, Johnson, when he is sprayed with bullets from Miller's machine gun after Miller has his throat bitten out by a zombie. It was Nicotero's first day in front of the camera and he was slightly "green" in terms of acting experience. "So they rig me up with all these squibs, I don't know what the hell is going on. I mean it was before we even ever shot any of my character stuff," remembers Nicotero. "And ten seconds before they start rolling Nick Mastandrea, the key grip, says, 'Hey Greg, just whatever you do don't fuck it up, 'cause it will take us like 45 minutes to reset the whole thing,' and I was like, 'What? What?' and as soon as I said, 'What?' George yells, 'Action!' and all I felt was 'bum bum bum bum bum boom'. I mean, I wasn't even paying attention. I just turned and the next thing I knew the take was over, and I was laying on the ground. And what I didn't realize is, once I was dead I had to lay on the ground for like two days of shooting, because I had to be dead on the ground in the background."

Interestingly enough, as a consolation to Al Magliochetti, who had been injured on Saturday at the Nike site, the production allowed him to visit the set in Wampum and play a zombie again, this time with prosthetic make-up on. "When I got out of the hospital a couple of days later they had me . . . I actually never shot the elevator scene. I was out of there before they actually rolled any film, because that did happen just on a rehearsal," says Magliochetti. "So when they brought me back I still had the bandage on my head and the stitches were in place, and Howard Berger did a make-up on me and I'm in the zombie corral directly behind the hair-dryer zombie, the one who breaks loose and bites the throat out of one of the soldiers."

Magliochetti remembers seeing Nicotero walking around with squibs on him for his death scene. "He was wired up with a bunch of bullet hits and it was like he had eggs in his pockets," says Magliochetti. "He felt like he was walking around with nitroglycerine."

Nicotero's fellow effects team member, Dave Kindlon, was also in the scene as the "priest" zombie, or the "Don King" zombie – as he was jokingly referred to due to his wild hair. In the scene, Johnson is handling Kindlon's zombie when he is shot and killed, in turn freeing the creature, who then bites Miguel on the arm. Kindlon was thrilled to be playing the part and still enjoys looking back on it. "It was great on the day. I got to thrash around like a zombie. I got to bite somebody in the arm. I got riddled with machine gun fire and I got shot in the head," says Kindlon. "You know, I'm sorry, check please! [*laughs*] Thank you very much, folks. So it was just awesome, it was just great." Years later, while flipping through some bubblegum cards called Fright Flicks, featuring images from horror movies, Kindlon came across an unexpected and very interesting image – of himself. "Just going through them and, like, 'These are kind of cool,' you know? Heck, if I was twelve I'd be collecting these like crazy," says Kindlon. "And all of a sudden, I flip to a card and I'm like, 'Oh my God, I'm a Topps bubblegum card.' It was just this weird moment, [*laughs*] like standing around, looking around, like okay, well here's another one of those moments of, 'Okay, that's it. Check please, I'm done,' you know?"

Tuesday 11/6/1984 – Day 14

"So, when are we going to rock this?"

The fourteenth day of filming would continue work on scene 60. Barbara Russell, or "Miller Chomp", as she was referred to on the call sheet, played the zombie who attacks Miller and rips out his throat during this pivotal sequence.

Russell, an actress and comedienne, worked for 35 years with her comedy partner, Don Brockett (aka Chef Brockett from *Mister Rogers' Neighborhood*), who would also appear as a zombie towards the end of the film. While Russell had a long career in theater, her background was actually in education, where she taught for years in public schools. She also appeared on *Mister Rogers' Neighborhood* as several different characters.

"Because they didn't want to mess with my hair, I was the zombie who had one of those drying hoods with the hose still attached; I looked like someone had taken a baseball bat and hit me across the eyes," recalls Russell. "When I was called to film, George said I had to go back and get my arms done since the dress I was wearing didn't have long sleeves. So I had to have my arms painted with acetate, which wrinkled the skin. It was dreadful to get off. As a side bar: I am very sensitive to pictures and accounts of injuries or operations. I do not visit people in the hospital if they have tubes attached, they are the color grey or they moan – because I faint. Well, as I was being made up I looked like an accident victim and started to get faint watching myself in the mirror. I said it was the acetate and was able to control it by not looking in the mirror."

Russell's victim in the sequence, Phillip Kellams, recalls how easily Russell was able to pull off the gag without actually biting him! "She was, as I remember correctly, she was pretty much a free spirit," says Kellams. "I mean, if you wanted her to do something in a particular way, she'd try her best to do it. I don't think she came that close to me, though, I really don't."

Kellams also remembers the direction given by Romero during this violent and over-the-top sequence. "George talked to us about that, I do remember him telling us about that . . . 'Look, I understand that there's

Above: Director George Romero ponders as assistant director John Harrison stands by at the corral set. (Courtesy of George Demick.)

going to be a lot of things [that] take place here that you may not feel comfortable with, but don't worry about that, because that's the way it's supposed to be shot and that's the way it's supposed to look.' Oh, okay," recalls Kellams. "If you would do something that he didn't like, then you would do it a number of times with a number of shots. He just had a way about him of coming up to you and kind of laughing, as he'd come up to you and say, 'Look, you're gonna have to calm down with this. You're going too far with this' 'Well, what am I doing?' 'Well, theoretically, you're dead.' 'Oh, that's right. I am.' 'Yeah, you're dead,' so he said, 'Try not to be too . . . just calm down a bit.'"

The amazing and extremely detailed make-up that made it possible for Kellams' throat to be graphically torn open can be credited to the hard work of John Vulich, whose primary goal was to make the make-up and sculpture look as accurate as possible. "I told Tom [Savini] that I wanted to come up with a very simple little . . . sort of like an Adam's apple mechanism, so when his throat gets ripped out, I wanted to see his little Adam's apple kind of bobbing in there going up and down; 'cause I just thought that would be extremely grisly and trying to push the envelope on this kind of stuff," says Vulich. "And Tom said, 'Nah, nah. Don't waste your time on it. Don't do it.' And I kept on saying, 'Tom, it'd be cool! Let me do it!' He and I argued for, like, months about this Adam's apple thing, and he kept on shooting me down and shooting me down. And then, the day we did that make-up,

Above: Make-up artist Natalka Voslakov. (Courtesy of George Demick.)

he said, 'Where's that Adam's apple?' 'What are you talking about? You told me not to do it!' He goes, 'No, I didn't.' 'Yes, you did! You absolutely told me . . .' then he starts messing around with me on that." Even though he couldn't fully realize the gag the way he envisioned it, Vulich was still able to design the Adam's apple into the sculpture. "You can see his Adam's apple in there, it's in there," says Vulich. "It's just that I wanted it moving and wiggling around, trying to swallow. So it's there in the sculpture."

Wednesday 11/7/1984 – Day 15

"Don't walk too fast – the wind might detonate it." – Mike Trcic

Day fifteen would begin by finishing up the corral carnage of scene 60. From there, filming moved on to scene 32, where Sarah argues with Rhodes about the condition of Miguel in the dining hall, and is taunted by Rhodes and Steel before finally leaving the hall with Fisher.

Scene 32 allowed the actors to simply concentrate on acting and not worry about make-up effects, zombies, or gun shots. For director of photography, Michael Gornick, the actors were one of the main reasons he was able to focus on his job, despite the personal turmoil he was going through. "The actors were genuinely – talking about the Lori Cardilles, and Gary Klahrs, and Tim DiLeos, and Joe Pilatos – part of what kept my concentration and my interest was their desire to make an honest effort in portraying the script, delivering every day," says Gornick. "And I gotta tell you, honestly, I don't think George [Romero] was always necessarily attentive to their desires, but they maintained a kind of professional interest in what they were doing on a daily basis that was a thrill for me to watch." I asked him to elaborate on his remark about Romero's lack of attentiveness to the actors. "I used to joke to Tom Dubensky about this, that I oftentimes spent more time with the actors than George," says Gornick. "That might have been just through proximity and association with, obviously, the camera, actor, you know? But it was true. I often spent a lot of times listening, getting feedback from the actors – not necessarily offering advice – but giving them a critique. That happened often on *Day*, even prior to *Day* though – talking about *Creepshow* and *Martin*."

And while it wasn't lost on anyone involved with the cast that they were working on the third entry in Romero's seminal zombie franchise, they still had no idea of how the film would fit into the series. "We had no idea what we were making," admits Joe Pilato. "We knew that *Dawn* had reached a certain amount of success, written up in *Newsweek* and the concept of the shopping mall and all the sociological implications, so we knew we had a film behind us. But nobody ever really thought we have to supersede it or go above it."

"I was fortunate enough to probably work in two dozen films and I think it's one of my top two or three experiences. Working with George and the whole cast and crew . . . no complaints. None, none whatsoever," says Gary Klahr. "We really gave our all, I think, to make that movie the best George Romero film possible. I think we basically succeeded."

Sometimes working on a film production can form new friendships and new relationships, and *Day of the Dead* would be no different. "With any film shoot like that, especially when you're on location, you're all living in the same hotel, and you're working all day together, it becomes a very close-knit kind of situation and you find ways to amuse yourself and have fun," says John Harrison. "There are the usual love affairs and other things going on in the background, friendships and stuff."

One of those love affairs was between production accountant, Charles Carroll, and second assistant director, Katarina "Kato" Wittich – and it was a bit on the scandalous side. "We had met working on a Crest toothpaste commercial a year earlier," says Carroll. "I was married to someone and Kato was actually going out with someone who happened to be one of my wife's best friends. I was in the lobby of the hotel and crew were coming in, starting to check in, and I just noticed Kato and I was like, 'Oh my God!' And we met that night at the bar and the rest is kind of history; typical location romance."

Carroll was married to Martha Pinson at the time, a successful script supervisor, who today regularly works for Martin Scorsese. "That was just, like . . . I don't think anybody could believe that was going on," says script supervisor Joanne Small. "Because it was just not nice, you know what I mean?"

"When Charles [Carroll] was 'porking' Katarina Wittich, I said, 'Charlie, you can't do this. You've got the most wonderful wife,' and he said, 'Oh yeah, this ain't gonna go anywhere. Don't worry, man. We're doing this thing, you know. We're just attracted to each other, we're doing this thing,'" says David Ball.

Another production romance was between script supervisor, Joanne Small, and Savini's assistant, Greg Nicotero. And while Small was a little older than Nicotero, it was certainly much less of a scandal. "Oh, he fell in love with me and I told him he was crazy," says Small. "There was a ten-year age difference at the time and he just pestered me and pestered me and pestered me until I finally gave up and said, 'Okay, you can be my boyfriend.' It was basically like that.

Below: One of the many themed days for the "grips from hell", this particular one being "old man day". Top row, left to right: Fred Roth ("Derf"), Kurt Rimmel ("Pinky"), Peter Beal ("The Inspector"), and John Janusek ("Beef"). Bottom row, left to right: Barry Kessler ("Wrango"), Richard Sieg ("Mr. French"), Nick Mastandrea, and Nick Tallo ("Bomba"). (Courtesy of Nancy Bennett.)

And we had a very good time; he was delightful in every way. He took me snowmobile riding behind his house and I met his whole family. He was a great guy, just a great guy."

Thursday 11/8/1984 – Day 16

"Does this look easy to you, pal!" – M. Conners

The sixteenth day of filming would continue with work on scene 32 in the dining hall. Filming for scene 59 – where Rhodes screams at Logan about teaching the zombies tricks, and Logan tells Rhodes that it's the beginnings of civilized behavior – was also scheduled to begin on this day.

One more scene, number 35, began filming on this day as well. It's a huge scene, over ten pages long in the shooting script, where the soldiers and civilian staff meet in the dining hall. The sequence is filled with tension throughout, as Rhodes makes it abundantly clear that he's the villain of the film when he threatens the life of Sarah. "My favorite scene to shoot was the whole dining hall scene, where I call out Frankenstein and have the standup with Sarah," says Joe Pilato.

"I think it's just got the right mixture of silliness

and tongue-in-cheek and over-the-top, very arched performances, and I just think it's exactly the right tone," says George Romero. "I think it's much more *me* than any of the other ones. *Dawn*, eh, maybe? But this one, there's a certain droll kind of humor in it that I really like. And I love the exaggerated over-the-top portrayals – like Joe's portrayal. I'm sure at the time Joe thought it was maybe too much and I kept saying, 'No, no, no, man. Just go for it!' That's what this kind of film is about. It has to be arch, comic book, stylistic, you know, rather than naturalistic."

"I actually believe that Joe Pilato is at the thinnest end of the wedge," says co-producer David Ball. "Joseph Pilato is a very, very good actor. And if you're not sure, just go and look at scene 35 of *Day of the Dead* where he lays it on 'em. I couldn't tell you . . . Joe was so worried about that big scene." Ball made a point of working on this scene with Pilato days before it was shot, to ensure Pilato's performance was appreciated – not just by Romero and his fellow actors, but by Pilato himself. "He was worried that he couldn't deliver. This is the actor insecurity. I mean, my wife is an actress; I have to read all the parts against her, because there is a natural insecurity that goes with it, because they don't know whether the director is going to like their interpretation. And so it does lead to insecurity," says Ball. "I can tell you that for the three nights before we shot scene 35, Joe Pilato was in my hotel room and I was playing every other part to Captain Rhodes. This is, like, an eight-page monologue, it's a massive scene, where he's strutting around with the two silver guns and the bullet belts across his chest. I can tell you that for three nights before that was shot, we were shooting it in my hotel room until midnight, one o'clock in the morning." According to Ball, Pilato is a bit of a passive personality, so the assistance he received from Ball helped to bring the edge out during the scene. "He wouldn't be capable of robbing your grandmother. He's not that type of guy, he has no aggression in him," says Ball. "And so for him to play this aggressive scene, where it's him against everybody else, was towering. I told him, 'Don't listen to Romero. This is how it's going to be,' to force him to have the balls to play that in a very tense scenario, as it was, with those grey walls and those silly desks."

While scene 35 is a tense one, and was taken very seriously by Pilato, one of the cast members found the situation a little humorous. "Joe was funny, he made me laugh," admits Lori Cardille. The reason for Cardille's amusement was the pair of army boots Pilato wore – fitted with lifts inside to boost his height. But there weren't just one or two lifts inside the boots – Pilato would use six, count 'em, six to reach his desired height! "I'm really tall, I'm 5' 9", and Joe's really short, not that short, but he's shorter. So he had to wear these shoes. [*laughs*] They made these boots that were like big platform 1970s . . . he looked like a rock star in them," laughs Cardille. "That would always strike me as hysterical. I'm trying to, like, [not to laugh] . . . thinking oh my God almighty – this is the weirdest film ever."

And, as funny as the lifts in Joe Pilato's boots were to Lori Cardille, they were a costuming choice permitted by George Romero. However, another idea of Pilato's – possibly inspired by his time on *The Deer Hunter* and watching Robert DeNiro – was shot down very early on by the writer/director. After arriving on location on day three of production, Pilato would pay a visit to the wardrobe department. "I had to go to costuming first and so costuming gave me some leniency and I said, 'I want a beret' and they gave me a beret," recalls Pilato.

"There was this underlying motif that George wanted these guys to all be National Guard. Now I don't know how you would portray that – military is military – but that was his insight. So I walk on the set with my lifts and my boots and my dog tags and my olive-green attire and a beret on my head. I walk on the set and I have to stop because they're shooting Tim [DiLeo] getting up and his guts falling out [*laughs*]. I stop, you know, you watch the shot and 'Cut!' And then I walk up to George and he looks at me and he goes, 'No'."

Friday 11/9/1984 – Day 17

"I don't do zombies." – Eileen Sieff

Day seventeen picked up where the previous day left off, with work scheduled in the dining hall on scenes 32, 59, and 35 once again.

One of the more memorable lines of dialogue in the film comes from Gary Klahr's character, Steel, during scene 35, when he is ordered to shoot Lori Cardille's character, Sarah. And it's another line that wasn't originally scripted by Romero. "I don't know, it seemed to me the only way you could do it is, '*Bang! Yer dead!*' It works. It does work because you can't do it any other way," says Klahr. "And I mimed the gun with my finger, because otherwise if I'd pulled the gun . . . and you can see if you watch my face, Steel doesn't want to pull the gun, he doesn't want to shoot her."

"I love Gary Klahr, I love him to pieces," says David Ball. "He was superb in *Day of the Dead*."

Another memorable moment from scene 35 is the little smile that Terry Alexander gives after Pilato makes his second death threat, this time to the entire group. "That was all George [Romero], that was *all* George," says Alexander. "I just sat back down and chilled – that was my instinct, to just sit down and say, 'It's okay.' And George suggested that, 'When you sit back down just give him a little smile.' And I said, 'Hmm, what kind of smile? What kind of smile should I give? Hmm?' Because you have to think of why I'm doing this as an actor, and I came out with a nice little evil glint in my eye – that kind of smile. He fell out laughing and he said, 'No, no, no, that's good, but take the little glint out, take the evil out. Just, you know, like, "I know you can't do this to me and I'm the only one that can fly the chopper."' So, I did it again and he liked that take and we went on from there. He would do things like that all the time with suggestions."

"Terry and I are very similar, I think, come from similar theatrical backgrounds – same kind of study, classically trained," says Lori Cardille. "So, on that level I had tremendous respect for Terry as an actor and I loved working with him. He was a serious actor. He took his work seriously, very professional."

Greg Nicotero, despite having no acting experience at all, still attempted to approach his role in a serious way by concocting a back-story for his character, Johnson. "It was like him and Taso [Torrez] were, like, best friends and sort of balanced each other out," says Nicotero. "He was the pot head and then got me smoking pot, all this weird, weird stuff."

Nicotero's cast mate, Taso Stavrakis, made notes to himself in his copy of the shooting script during scene 35. And a lot of the notes pertained to – you guessed it – pot! "Puff old joint / Look at joint – needs light / Look at Johnson – wave joint, receive matches, tear one out / Light joint / Pass joint to Johnson" were just some of his notes for this scene. "I had some oregano or some kind of herbal, I don't know what it was, but it stunk – it smelled like pot," says Stavrakis. "And so everyone on the set thought it was pot. Of course, it's not – it wasn't pot."

Another interesting point is the haircuts of the soldiers. No one in the film has a military-style haircut, which was definitely appreciated by Joe Pilato. "My Jack Lord hair," says Pilato. "I was always very concerned, and I was happy that George let me get away with it, because as a military guy I should have some sort of really militaristic haircut."

As for the soldier's uniforms: they were cobbled together from Ralph's Army Surplus in Monroeville, Pennsylvania and Colonel Bubbie's in Galveston, Texas.

From top to bottom: Gary Klahr (Steel) getting ready to punch Terry Alexander (John) during the showdown at the corral; Director of photography, Michael Gornick, with Joe Pilato (Captain Rhodes); Gary Klahr resting on a golf cart between shot set-ups; Director of photography, Michael Gornick, at the corral set. (Photos courtesy of George Demick.)

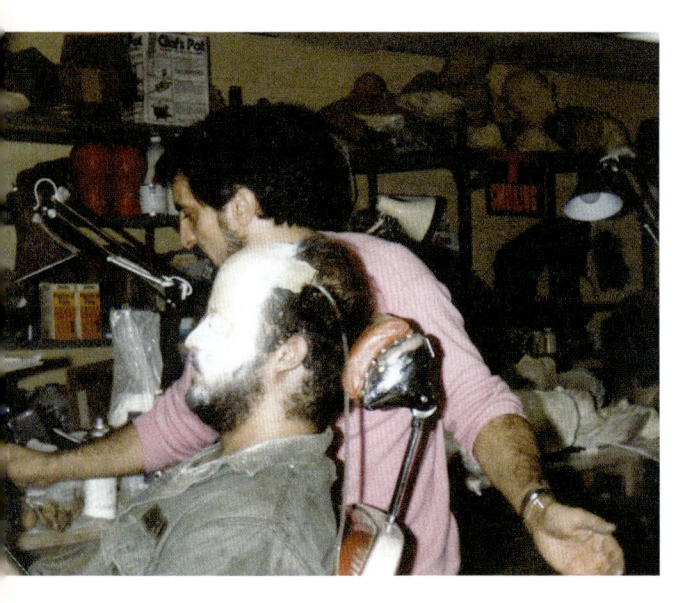

Above: Tom Savini preparing Ralph Marrero with a prosthetic forehead and eyeball for his death scene. (Courtesy of Barbara Boyle.)

Saturday 11/10/1984 – Day 18

"If the CIA had me working for them – they wouldn't be such a ____ed up organization" – Peter Levy

The eighteenth day of shooting commenced with an insert shot for scene 58 – of Sarah and Fisher reacting to Bub aiming the pistol at Captain Rhodes. Lori Cardille and John Amplas were the only actors on set for the shot.

Also on tap for the day was scene 42, where McDermott talks Sarah into drinking some brandy from his flask, after being caught up in the soldiers' brawl in the hallway.

Work on scene C97 would be done on this day, in which Steel runs for his life through the open cave as zombies flood in. The shot that would be memorable for both Gary Klahr and Taso Stavrakis was of Steel running through the mine and knocking the zombie to the ground. Memorable because of how painful it was for both men! "I literally pulled my left hamstring, and I pulled it so bad, if you watch very carefully you'll really see me start to stumble and [I] probably should have gone down on my face, which was not in the script," says Klahr. "Had it happened I would have made it work, it would have been easy to work in, because I'm not a guy that goes, 'Stop! Can we do the take over?' You try to use those things, they can be very helpful because they're not really planned and sometimes they can actually make a scene. But I blew my hamstring out to the point where, the next day, from the back of my knee to my left buttock was totally black. It means that I was bleeding internally, because I tore the muscle that badly. Never said anything to anybody; never complained. I just had this giant hematoma, it healed up and it was fine, didn't need any surgery or anything like that. But I'd never pulled a hamstring like that."

"Gary Klahr knocked me out of the way; he gave me a forearm to the chest. That was the scariest stunt I did for the entire movie," says Stavrakis. "Gary used to play for the New Orleans Saints, he's an NFL football player, he's a big guy, and he was running full blast. He said, 'Just pad up your chest and I'm just gonna hit you,' and I said, 'Okay.' And he sent me flying through the air and I hit the ground, and there was about a half minute before I could catch my breath after that. He hit my sternum and, of course, the blow was so . . . it was like getting hit by a tree or something. And you look at it in the movie, it's like he shoves me out of the way, it doesn't look like anything. But him coming at you and hitting you with a forearm, it was so painful." [*laughs*]

The abuse inflicted on Stavrakis by Klahr wasn't the only pain that he was scheduled to endure on this day. A late addition to the day's filming was scene 92, where Joe Pilato runs over a zombie – played by Stavrakis – in his golf cart. (Interestingly, Tom Savini was supposed to double Pilato driving the golf cart.) However, the scene would be pushed back three weeks, and was eventually shot on day 34.

Monday 11/12/1984 – Day 19

No quote of the day.

On the nineteenth day of filming, work continued on scenes 59 and 35 in the dining hall.

Filming a huge scene such as number 35, a scene that took several days to complete, requires an extreme eye for detail and continuity – and that job would fall on the shoulders of the script supervisor. "Joanne Small was the script supervisor. Those pages had so many lines on them, in terms of the amount of coverage, that you can no longer see the text underneath it," says editor, Pat Buba. "It was the most coverage of any scene I've ever worked on. She ran out of room on the page to draw lines because of the amount of coverage George [Romero] did."

"I essentially align the script for the editor and provide all the director's comments and notes – they need that to kind of organize and work while they're cutting," says Small. "I provide a daily report for the production that gives the first shot of the day, and what time we break for lunch, and what's been shot during the day – all that sort of information for the production team, so that they can send that to executives or whoever else needs it. And I do breakdowns, like a time plot of the script, so that everybody's on the same page – we know what day it is in the script so that wardrobe, and make-up, and the props department, all the art departments, know that its day two and I give them the time of day."

And as much as that is to handle, her job doesn't stop there. "I have to be on top of the directors to make sure that they have all the shots that they need for the editing. Because they'll walk away without the close-up and I have turn around and say, 'Excuse me, I think we need a close-up here.' Basically a script supervisor is . . . I approach the job as kind of 'Set Mom', because I kind of figure that anybody can come to me for any question that they have."

One of the duties that Small mentioned is writing

Below: John Vulich working on Howard Sherman as Bub. (Courtesy of Dave Kindlon.)

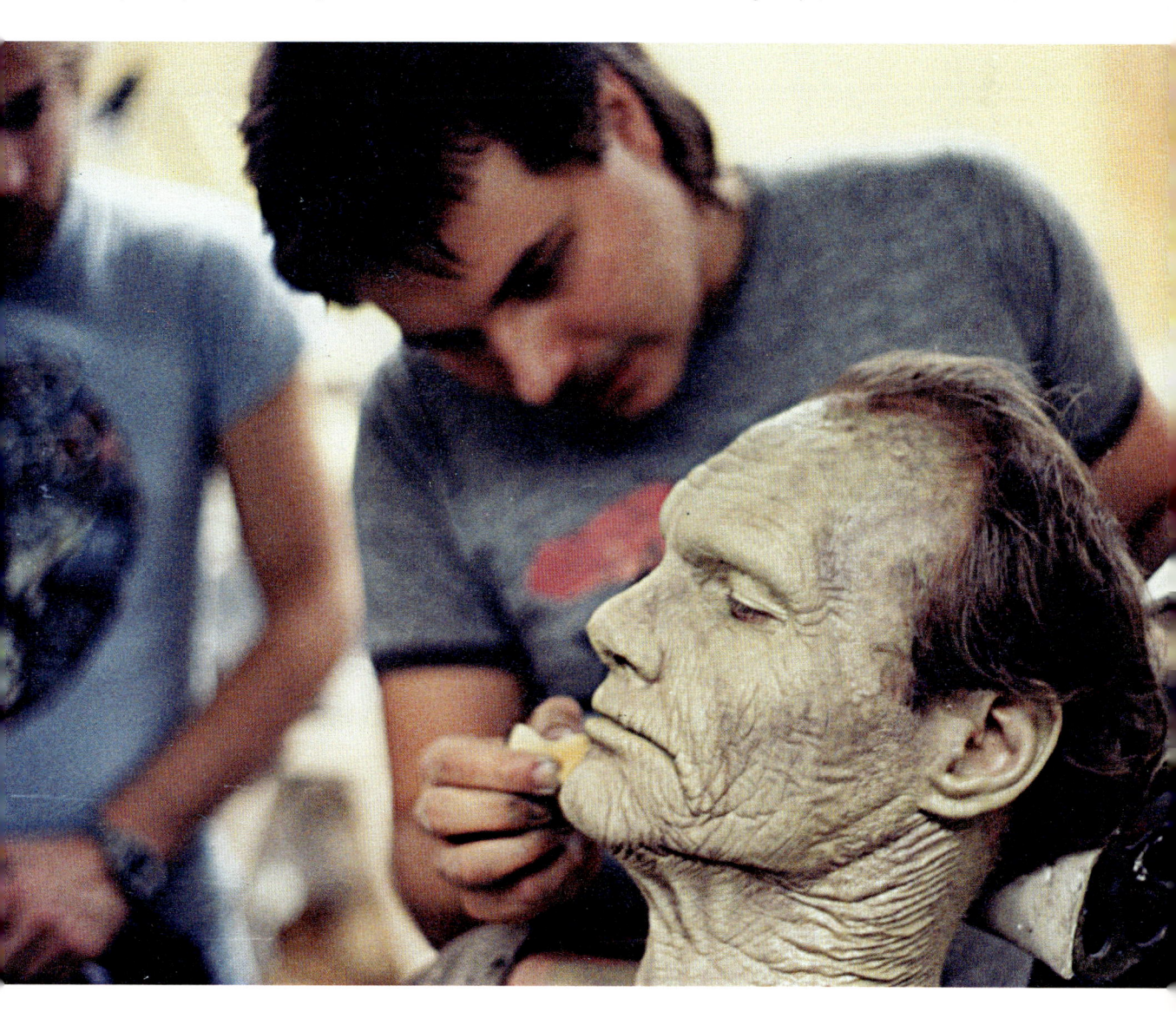

a time plot of the script. On *Day of the Dead*, Small would compile a three-page time plot detailing each scene number, which "screen day" it was, what time of day it was, etc. According to Small's time plot, *Day of the Dead* contained 104 scenes, 42 different time periods, and four screen days (with a special note at the end alerting people to a possible fifth screen day). Of particular interest is the number of scenes, listed as 104. The shooting script itself contains 103 scenes, but in the time plot introduction, Small explains that scene A21 is an additional, unscripted scene that follows scene 21. This would explain the 104 listed scenes, instead of 103. Another important distinction in the time plot introduction is that the fourth screen day begins at scene 63, where Miguel is placed inside "The Ritz" after having his arm amputated. This differs from the shooting script, in which the fourth screen day begins at scene 83, where Miguel opens the compound gates to allow the zombies in.

Pat Buba faced a challenge when editing scene 35 – and lots of other scenes, for that matter – due to the issue of voices echoing in the cave. "We had a dialogue issue because of the amount of echo reverb in the cave, because of the amount of yelling," says Buba. "It was really hard to work around the dialogue sometimes, because of the overlaps of the echo return. You know, somebody would yell and it would go on for twenty seconds. So it was hard to keep some of the dialogue cut tight for that reason."

While Buba would have to worry about the reverb during the edit, soundman Rolf Pardula had to deal with it while filming was taking place. "There was so much reverb, so we had to put radio mics on the actors," says Pardula. "And then boom it as well, to give it a little presence."

At the bottom of this day's call sheet is a funny tease regarding the weather in the southern part of the country . . . "Ft. Myers weather report – 85 degrees + sunny!"

Tuesday 11/13/1984 – Day 20

"If it's disgusting – I like it." – P. Levy

Day twenty of principal photography would be spent working on scene 66. In the scene, Sarah and McDermott search through Logan's lab for pain-killing medicine for Miguel, find the tape recorder containing Logan's mad ramblings, and eventually discover the severed head of Johnson.

The duty of creating the mechanics for the severed head of Nicotero's character, Johnson, would be handled by Dave Kindlon. "There was a lot of experimentation," says Kindlon. "A lot of it was being too stupid to know I couldn't do something, and just figuring out how to do it anyways." Kindlon also handled the mechanical work for the Dr. Tongue puppet, Taso Stavrakis' severed head, the shovel pop-top zombie head, and the drill that Logan uses to kill the autopsy zombie with. Years later, after moving out to southern California, Kindlon discovered just how much his time spent working on the film meant. "Coming out here and just walking in for an interview on something and saying, 'Yeah, I was the mechanic on *Day of the Dead*,' strangely enough had a huge amount of cachet out here. So it was really nice."

Dr. Logan's bizarre lab – or "operating theater", as it's called in Romero's script – owes a great deal to the hard work of set decorator, Jan Pascale.

Jan Pascale started out working for the children's show *Mister Rogers' Neighborhood* at WQED Television in Pittsburgh. She was hired thanks to the help of her then boyfriend and longtime Romero veteran, Nick Tallo. Her first experience working for George Romero would be on *Dawn of the Dead*, when she played a zombie extra at the Monroeville Mall during the film's climax, when the bike raiders break into the mall. "It was when I was living with Nicky [Tallo], and I went out there because he was doing one of his motorcycle scenes that night and they needed a few people," recalls Pascale. "I guess they didn't have enough zombies show up, so they 'greened' me up. I was bumping into the wall, the glass doors, before the bikes broke through."

Pascale later worked on *Creepshow* as a painter, working under production designer Cletus Anderson. "For my very first day we were woodgraining on Masonite, which is a challenge on a good day, and I was absolutely terrified," admits Pascale. "I was terrified of Cletus when I first started, because I thought, 'Oh my god. Here's the head of the drama department [of CMU] and he is so brilliant and here I am, I don't know what the hell I'm doing.' [*laughs*] I was trying to draw a straight line and my hand was just trembling, [*laughs*] it was unbelievable. So, I always was a little bit intimidated, I guess, by Cletus, just because I didn't have formal training."

For *Day of the* Dead, when it came time to populate Logan's lab with lots of crazy equipment, she turned to the full-time employer of her boss Cletus Anderson, Carnegie Mellon University. "We had to rent these trucks and drive into the city and we got all kinds of stuff from Carnegie Mellon; I'm sure Cletus had arranged it. But they loaned us all this equipment and we ended up putting it all in the one laboratory," says Pascale. "I just remember conning this guy, and like, 'Oh yeah! Well, could we have this? Could we have that? Oh, this would be great!' I'm sure they left scratching their heads, like, 'What did we just do? These crazy kids, we gave them all this equipment.'" [*laughs*] And, since Pascale had little to no money to work with, that's exactly what she paid them. "I think I paid them, like, you know, a couple hundred bucks or some ridiculous amount of money," says Pascale.

Along with Kevin Ritter, Pascale would also be in charge of all the jars filled with strange specimens in Dr. Logan's lab. "I was the co-prop master and the co-decorator," laughs Pascale. "I don't think they were completely convinced that I could do the whole thing by myself. There was a guy named Kevin Ritter. He and I kind of were supposed to be co-decorators, but he was actually a costume design student, so we sort of put our skills together, you know, and cobbled it together."

Pascale and Ritter, encouraged by the freedom given on a Romero production, sought to really push the envelope and bring Logan's lab to life. "I remember sitting with a catalog from Carolina Biological and

Kevin and I going, 'Wow, that would look creepy in a jar,'" says Pascale. "We ordered, like, brains and spines and, you know, anything that looked creepy. We literally would just go through the catalog and we'd place this huge order, and unbeknownst to us, it all arrived in coffee cans! Kevin and I looked at each other, like, 'What do we do now?' [*laughs*] So, we had to buy all this formaldehyde and, literally, I remember Kevin volunteered to do the dirty work. We were working in that mine . . . and we went out in the back and set up this little crazy shop. Kevin got respirators and gloves and he opened the cans and took out the body parts and the brains and whatever and put them in these jars. It was completely insane, you know?"

Pascale's then boyfriend, Nick Tallo – or "Bomba", as the crew referred to him – was also on board as part of the grip crew for *Day of the Dead*. Tallo had earned the nickname of "Bomba" one day during *Knightriders*, when he was caught reading a copy of *Bomba, the Jungle Boy* in the lobby of the hotel where the cast and crew were staying.

Right: George Demick in zombie make-up for the scene where Rhodes first opens the door to discover a horde of the living dead. **Below:** Joe Pilato with the Granati brothers, who would help rip him in half during his spectacular death scene. (Photos courtesy of George Demick.)

THE MAKING OF GEORGE A. ROMERO'S DAY OF THE DEAD

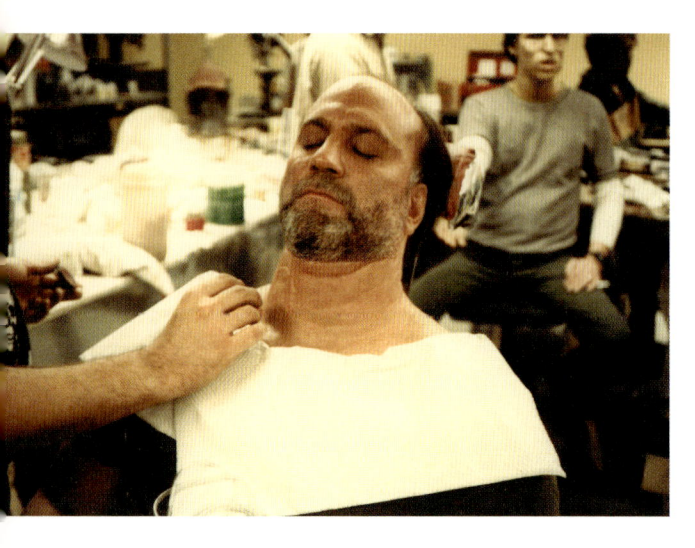

Above: Gary Klahr having a prosthetic neck applied for his death scene. In the background associate producer, Ed Lammi, is being made up as a zombie. (Courtesy of Greg Nicotero.)

Tallo's history with Romero dated all the way back to Mister Rogers' Neighborhood, when the two met while working on a segment of "Picture, Picture", about a light bulb factory for Fred Rogers. "He never did anything bad, which was weird," says Tallo of Mr. Rogers. "I mean, there were days when he'd be, like, sort of bummed out because he was tired and stuff, and I would think of the absolute filthiest joke I could think of and I would tell him. And most of the time he got it, but sometimes he didn't even get it, you know, because he was so fucking straight. But if he thought it was funny, he'd want other people to hear the joke, but he wouldn't tell them. He'd call them over and make me tell them because he wouldn't repeat it."

Other nicknames were given out by key grip Nick Mastandrea. The genesis of these came from the first day of shooting on Knightriders, when some of the crew were playing scrabble, under a tent in the rain, because a large storm had destroyed the film's sets. Rich Dwyer, one of that film's grips, spelled the word "zoot", for zoot suit. An argument ensued about whether or not that was a real word, so from that point on he was called "Zoot". And after that, everyone started getting nicknames. Tom Savini was called "Sir Sleaze", which would later become just "Sleaze". "Sleaze – those were just, like, little things you'd say in conversations, you never really used that name for him [Savini]," says Mastandrea. "We just felt it was sort of a behind-the-scenes name for him, but he certainly lived up to it." Script supervisor Joanne Small got the moniker of "Shoe". "There was a phrase we used to say, 'shoehorn', and that was just a shortened version of it," says Mastandrea. "She was short and little – she'd always stand underneath the camera and she just sort of slid in there like a shoehorn. So we just called her Shoe."

Second assistant cameraman Simon Manses earned the dubious nickname of "Slime". "He was a cad . . . a ne'er-do-well," says Mastandrea. "He was always trying to get laid." Jim Bruwelheide was called "Rawhide", which was simply a play on his name. First assistant cameraman, Frank Perl, was called "Motown" because he was from Detroit. And Peter Bennett Beal received the name of "The Inspector" due to his expertise as an electrician. "He used to go, and he'd put on his glasses, and he would go check . . . he sort of did a lot of the electrical work," says Mastandrea. "So he sort of checked the boxes and made sure we were not gonna get fried. Most of us were not very good electricians."

This day on set would be a particularly memorable one, thanks to a special visit from executive producer Salah Hassanein. "I think Richard [Rubinstein] brought him to the set and it was sort of a sales pitch scenario of, 'Look! Here's a cool special effects make-up and there's a puppet head and that's the guy it's supposed to be,'" says Greg Nicotero. "So there was a little bit of that razzle dazzle scenario, you know?"

Hassanein's visit to the set was simply to see how things were progressing, as his faith in Romero never truly wavered. "I thought he was a great person, myself. Very, very capable . . . always came in on budget . . . I think he was a pro," says Hassanein. "I was always very satisfied because he stayed on budget and he delivered a piece of merchandise that was accepted as quality. The risk we took was lessened by his product."

A stunt rehearsal was also scheduled for scene 41, where the soldiers brawl in the hallway corridor.

Wednesday 11/14/1984 – Day 21

"I'll hang just about anything from my ears." – Eileen Sieff

The twenty-first day of filming would showcase some of the best work done for the film by Tom Savini and his young make-up effects crew. The shoot concentrated on scene 34, in Dr. Logan's lab, when Sarah sees the eviscerated autopsy zombie and the headless corpse of Major Cooper.

The role of the eviscerated autopsy zombie that Logan is working on when Lori Cardille's character, Sarah, walks into the room was played by effects team member, Mike Trcic. To achieve the effect, Trcic was placed inside a medical gurney with an area cut away by the head carpenter, Norman Beck, and his crew. A false chest, complete with exposed rib cage sculpted by Trcic himself, was placed on top of him, so it appeared that his whole abdomen had been cut wide open. Pig intestines were placed in the stomach area, so that when he attempted to rise up and reach towards Sarah they would fall to the floor and splatter.

For Trcic, filming the scene was like having a free pass for the day. "Oh gosh, it was fun. I guess as much fun as that could be, having all this stuff glued to you," says Trcic. "Tom [Savini] took great care to use an excessive amount of glue where you shouldn't use glue at all, so that was fun, removing that at the end of the day. It was almost like a day off, you know? It's like, woo-hoo! Just being in the make-up was bizarre." In the scene, Trcic's zombie is dispatched by Dr. Logan with a drill to the forehead. But with Savini at the helm, that too became an adventure. "I do remember Tom – when he was talking to George [Romero] about the Dremel tool that Logan would use to kill me – George came up and he says, 'Okay, Tom. How does this work?'" says Trcic. "And Tom said, 'Well, okay. It's a fake Dremel, it's got a retractable fake bit, it's spring-loaded,' and he says, 'You can do this anywhere! You can do it in the ear or the eye!' He had dropped it that morning and so the tip wasn't retracting as easily as it should and I said, 'Tom, you're not doing that in the eye.' [laughs] So, we settled on the forehead, you know, 'Okay, we can go on the forehead.' So yeah, I kind of talked him out of the softer parts of the body."

The other amazing effect shot this day was the headless corpse of Major Cooper, with just the brain left intact. The part of the headless corpse would be played by the late Barry Gress, a good friend of Savini's at the time. "He was the guy that was always, 'Tom, you gotta put me in a movie! Tom, put me in a movie!'" says Savini. "So when I thought of the guy on the slab with his head gone, which meant that an actor would have to lie there with his head back as far it could physically go for hours, okay . . . I gave that to Barry." [laughs]

The responsibility of creating this intricate sculpture, which would be affectionately nicknamed "Moose Clit" by the effects crew, was handled by John Vulich. Using detailed anatomy books that Tom Savini had on hand, Vulich created mind-blowing accuracy in the design. "I was really fascinated by trying to do this really anatomically correct gore, with all the detail and tendons and esophagus and all that," says Vulich. "It seems to be, oftentimes, in a lot of these kind of films you just see shredded meat that doesn't really look like anything but shredded-up latex. And you know if it's a bomb blast or something like that, it probably should look like that, probably shouldn't be too detailed. But this was an instance where it just seemed to apply to the scenario, where you have a doctor cutting away with scalpels and carefully cutting these parts out, so it seemed like an ideal situation to show. I mean, there's a tremendous amount of detail in these things where you're seeing the bone's layers, the fascia; the different strata all through the sculpture on that, with the little pores on the bone. I remember . . . I think I probably exaggerated, like, the thickness of a lot of things just so they would show up on film, from the medical books. I think even at that point I kind of understood that you're seeing these things onscreen just for fleeting moments, so sometimes you want to make them a little broader than they would be in real life. But other than that, I mean, it's fairly detailed." The latex and polyfoam brain, sitting atop Vulich's intricate sculpture, was actually cast from a plastic brain.

Mike Gornick's former assistant cameraman, Tom Dubensky, made it out to the mine on this day to shoot extra coverage of the Trcic autopsy zombie effect with a second camera. Though according to second assistant cameraman, Simon Manses, the deployment of two cameras during filming was not very frequent. "The use of two cameras was sort of limited, it was sort of limited," says Manses. "I don't think we did tons and tons of two camera stuff. I think maybe some of the effects things that we did." Dubensky's replacement as first assistant cameraman, Frank Perl – or "Motown" as he was nicknamed – proved himself to be invaluable to director of photography, Mike Gornick, who was dealing with personal issues with George Romero that could, at times, distract him from the task at hand. "Frank Perl was my Tom Dubensky replacement, and he was a wonderful replacement – technically well versed, very supportive," says Gornick. "Honestly, on set, if I didn't have Frank, you know, didn't have his attention, didn't have his energy – the product wouldn't be there, it wouldn't be as good. He was marvelous, he was marvelous." Besides his AC, Frank Perl, Gornick also relied on the team of grips that had been around for prior Romero productions. "We all grew as a team – people like Nick Mastandrea and his crews, who were with us," says Gornick. "So we all experienced and got better with time. Honestly, I'm one member of a collective team that provides the visual look and, as we all got better, we all could be proud of what we produced on the screen."

"We basically were all self-taught, we were sort of learning on the job, and Mike [Gornick] knew more than any of us about lighting and all of that, and the technical sides of things," says George Romero. "I mean, I knew how to stick up a light and read a light meter, but I could never have shot that film myself in that cave. I mean, even though I'd done a lot of the shooting myself on earlier stuff, I wouldn't have known how to do that. Mike was great – he was also a jack of all trades. I mean, when we had that little company we all did everything, man. We all knew a little bit about everything – how to record sound, how to edit, how to run the dubbers . . . we were just sort of all around filmmakers and any of us could do anybody else's job, to some extent. But Mike was the techno-guy, he was the guy that knew the most about all of it."

Romero, in a fairly candid moment, revealed how important Gornick was to him, due to his own lack of expertise. "I was never disciplined enough to, you know, really sit down and learn all of the technical stuff. I used to just fly by the seat of my pants," admits Romero. "So, Mike made tremendous contributions, not just [on] that film, but all the films that we worked on together. He held it all together and made it happen."

Those words would ring true for Simon Manses who, like Romero, also observed Gornick's invaluable contributions while filming. "When you're dealing with lots of money and lots of responsibility between Salah Hassanein, and George, and Richard Rubinstein, and Michael who was really, I mean, did a yeoman's job – he was involved in everything," says Manses. "And it's not that he was a busybody, it's just there were certain things . . . I have a feeling that if he didn't address them they might not get addressed. He was so very, very capable."

Thursday 11/15/1984 – Day 22

No quote of the day

Day 22 would continue work on scene 34, in Dr. Logan's operating room. Due to problems with Trcic's autopsy zombie gut spill the day before, the scene was re-shot. Once again, Trcic was put through the paces of becoming the autopsy zombie and, in a behind-the-scenes video filmed by Tom Savini, you can hear Trcic, while being made up as the zombie, joking about a TV commercial for an eviscerated doll for kids, after Savini cracks a remark about merchandising. "I want the first eviscerated corpse doll that comes out," joked Trcic. "'Just press the button and it comes up and spills its guts! And then you can reload them to do it again and again! Thrill your friends!'"

Later in that same video, Savini follows with his camera when Trcic needs to go to the restroom. Unfortunately for Savini, and fortunately for Trcic, he ran out of video cable! "You never wanna do that with Tom around," says Trcic. "Because when you're trying to wash the damn thing off he's going to sneak around with the camera and try and get a nude shot of you."

Lori Cardille and Howard Sherman would also be on set this day, to shoot the scene of Bub lunging out of the darkness at Sarah, startling her. These two days of filming would be memorable for Lori Cardille – not because of the blood and gore, but because of her co-star Richard Liberty's performance as Dr. Logan. "He had trouble remembering his lines," laughs Cardille. "Especially that one scene, where he's dissecting that guy, and he's just laying on the table with just that brain."

Friday 11/16/1984 – Day 23

"Do zombies blush?" – Kevin Ritter

Day 23 would revisit familiar territory with scenes 35 and 59, once again in the dining hall.

Working on a film production is usually a tedious and slow process. Some might even say it's dull waiting around between set-ups and takes. "I have to tell you, working on a film – doing still photography, where you're not busy all the time – you have to have something to do," admits unit still photographer, Susan Golomb. "I mean, it can be boring. I brought knitting."

While Golomb brought her knitting to pass the time, the make-up effects crew found more adventurous things to do when they experienced a lull during filming. And usually it was at the behest of their leader, Tom Savini. "Tom was the first to, like . . . any downtime was play time," says Howard Berger. "On the film, each department had a golf cart that we would use to get around the mine. But while they were shooting, while other departments were filming and we weren't, Tom would instigate us into taking everybody's golf carts and driving through the mine. So what we would do is, we would grab everybody's golf carts because they weren't using them, but they didn't need to know we took them. We had a big boom box and we'd play the *Raiders of the Lost Ark* music, and we would drive through the mine playing Indiana Jones or playing *Raiders of the Lost Ark*, leaping on each other's carts like we were Indiana Jones and fighting Nazis, throwing people off and all this."

Sometimes the shenanigans and horseplay would lead to accidents, though, such as damage to some of the stored property located within the mine. "Because it was winter time, people would store their cars, boats, RVs in this mine so that there wasn't any weather damage – but little did they know there would be make-up effects damage. So, I remember driving through there, I think I was with Trcic – it was pitch black – and Trcic hit something. We turned the flashlight on and he ran into a boat and made this giant hole in the boat," laughs Berger. "It was so stupid and so dangerous, but it was also so highly encouraged by Tom Savini that we just couldn't resist."

The playing around, once again encouraged by Savini, would lead to John Vulich donning a full gorilla suit and running on set through a scene rehearsal. The gag barely fazed the crew, however, since they were getting used to such things from the make-up effects crew.

Above: Zombie extra Jeff Monahan (aka Broccoli Man zombie) and Howard Berger. (Courtesy of Jeff Monahan.)
Below: Zombie extras and good friends Geoff Burkman (left) and Steven Watkins (right). And a bloody stump. (Courtesy of Steven Watkins.)

117

Above: Casting assistant, Gaylen Ross, and United Film Distribution Company president, Richard Hassanein, visit the Wampum set. (Courtesy of Taso Stavrakis.)

One particular series of practical jokes would develop into a mini "war" between the make-up effects crew and production accountant, Charles Carroll. And, like most things of this nature, it started out very small. "What they did, they, like, blackened my phone. So, I would talk on the phone, without knowing it, and get this black stuff all over my ears. That was the start of hostilities," says Carroll. "So then I dummied up these tax forms or something, and sent them all these tax forms and got them all freaked out – and then they found out that was me."

Another high point during the war – or low point, depending on your perspective – for one particular effects member was very memorable for all of "Savini Land". One day, while Charles Carroll was getting a haircut in an adjacent room, Greg Nicotero thought it would be funny to surprise Carroll from above – but in the end it would be Nicotero who received the surprise. "Oh God, that was great! That was funny as hell," says Howard Berger. "Yeah, it was yet another . . . see, Tom is an instigator. Tom Savini instigates us into getting into trouble. And it's one of these things that we love about Tom and that attracts people to Tom, because he's so much fun. Normal people wouldn't have the boss, where the boss would be causing all the trouble and making his employees do dangerous things, but Tom's not that way. [laughs] So, I'm the first guy to go,

"Hey let's light a fire!' you know? So what happened is that – and I want to say this is the ongoing; this was part of the ongoing torture of Charles Carroll. Greg climbed up into the rafters in our room, and it was like one of those cruddy little drop ceilings, and I remember Tom was sitting in the make-up chair and I was facing Tom talking to him, and Tom's back was to what was happening. Greg was already up in the roof, and I heard him walking around and I just kept talking to Tom and Tom was talking to me. And then all of a sudden the roof gave in. And I kid you not, in slow motion, Greg fell out of the roof, the whole roof came tumbling down. Greg hit a table, his Betacam flew off, smashed on the floor, and Greg rolled off. And Tom sat there, and said afterwards that he'd watched the whole thing happen on my face and my eyes, because I just saw this thing happening. What Greg was trying to do was climb into the ceiling and over, and like drop something on Charles on the other side of the wall, but apparently the ceiling gave out and Greg came tumbling through."

"I climbed up on the table and moved the ceiling tile and started climbing up the wall. The way the mine was built, the cinder blocks didn't go all the way up, so you could actually go up over the cinder block and go down into the next room," remembers Nicotero. "I'm like, 'Oh my God, this is going to be great,' so I jump up and I grab the top cinder block and, as I'm pulling myself up, the cinder block just comes loose. Everett [Burrell], Howard [Berger], everybody's in the shop working and all of a sudden you just hear this

'Crash!' and I came flying through the ceiling tiles, bounced off the table, and hit the ground."

"He almost killed me when he did that," laughs Dave Kindlon. "That was pretty funny."

Undeterred, however, the make-up effects crew decided to raise the stakes a little higher – and in a very "explosive" way. "We got the accountant, Charles, we got him really bad one day," says Mike Trcic. "He walked into our studio, unsuspecting, and we had set up a charge by the door and it just scared the bejesus out of him."

"We knew that Charles was coming over and Tom [Savini] had set, like, a pile, a fistful of gun powder on the floor, probably on a piece of wood or something like that, hooked up to some wires," says John Vulich. "When he saw Charles come through the door, he lit this off and Charles went into, like, a standing fetal position, kind of like a stork or something; grabbed his head, lifted his leg up, and hunkered down while still standing on one leg. I think, if I remember correctly, we heard shortly after that explosion – which was very loud, by the way, [*laughs*] it was an enormous amount of gun powder – apparently they heard it where they were shooting somewhere in the mine. I don't know how far, like probably a quarter mile away shooting somewhere in the mine, they had heard the explosion and asked what it was on the walkie-talkie. [*laughs*] It was so loud!"

Carroll's revenge on the make-up effects team for this prank would be legendary, but required the assistance of other production members to pull it off. To help him get his revenge, Carroll enlisted the services of Steve Kirshoff and Mark Mann, who handled special effects duties such as squibs and gunfire blasts. "So I went to them and said, 'Look, I really need some help. I really want to get these guys,' and they were like, 'All right,'" says Carroll. "We talked about how to do it, and we decided that since they had this habit, they would come out at night from the mine, jump in their car – it was kind of like a hill, and they would just send the car rolling and then turn their lights on and start the car up. It was a little game they played every day, Tom Savini and, I guess, his three or four helpers. It was an old station wagon, so we rigged it; we put these smoke bombs in the car. They were rigged to the headlights so they wouldn't ignite till the headlights went on."

"We're driving along and all of a sudden a little bit of smoke starts wafting out from underneath the dashboard. And Tom [Savini] was driving, I believe, and he's like, 'There's . . . there's . . . there's smoke! It's on fire! The car's on fire!' He stopped, everybody went running out of the vehicle," remembers John Vulich. "I got trampled by, I think, Mike Trcic on his way out – I was in the back part of the station wagon and I think he trampled over me to run out."

Above: Funny illustration by a member of the make-up effects crew – most likely Everett Burrell – poking fun at Greg Nicotero's plunge through the ceiling. (Courtesy of Greg Nicotero.)

"We get out and walk about ten feet, run literally about ten feet, away from the car and turn around, and there's Charles and the rest of the crew," says Trcic. "Their sides are splitting."

"And Tom Savini, their fearless leader, who is driving, pulled the car over, panicked, jumped out of the car and ran away," says Carroll. "Leaving some of his young colleagues stuck in the back of the station wagon as the car filled with smoke."

The make-up legend learned a valuable lesson: "We never fucked with him [Carroll] anymore after that," admits Savini.

The make-up effects team didn't just feud with the production accountant, though. They became involved in a squabble with Bruce Miller's art department as well. "I just remember the art department being annoyed with us," says Greg Nicotero. "Because Tom [Savini] told us, 'Don't ever clean up any blood.' He's like, 'You don't have to clean up the blood.' I'm like, 'What do you mean we don't have to clean up the blood?' He said, 'No, no, no. It's not your job.' So we would go in and we would do the gags and there would be blood everywhere, and then we would just leave. And at the wrap party, Bruce Miller came up to me and said, 'You know, we fucking hated you guys because not once did you ever clean up blood. You literally left set and

Above: Bryan Gregory of punk rock group, The Cramps, seen here holding a guitar, came out to be a zombie during filming. Interestingly enough, The Cramps would contribute a song, "Surfin' Dead", to the soundtrack of *Return of the Living Dead*, released just one month after *Day* during the summer of 1985. (Courtesy of Tim Irr.)

made us clean up your shit every day.' And I said, 'Bruce, that's what we were told to do.' I didn't know; none of us knew any better. None of us knew, like, 'Oh, we're supposed to clean up after ourselves.'"

"We called it the 'blood wars' because they would come in and they would do these fabulous effects, and it would look great, and then they would walk away. And we were like, 'Uh, excuse me? There's another part,'" laughs Jan Pascale. "I remember we were so mad one day, we wrote this letter to them. Kevin [Ritter] typed it all up and we splattered it with blood and snuck it under their door. [*laughs*] It was like, 'Who are we, the flunkies? We have our own job to do; we're not here to mop up your crap.' But we ended up mopping up their blood all the time. So it was pretty dreadful."

Saturday 11/17/1984 – Day 24

"Health is a state of mind." – Joe Pilato

On day 24, filming was completed for scene 59, in the dining hall with Pilato and Liberty.

Work on scene 67 – where Sarah and McDermott hide behind a corner, watching Logan walk into Bub's room with his bucket of flesh – was also filmed, as was scene 69. In it, Sarah and McDermott observe Logan feeding Bub in the observation room, and are then startled by Rhodes and his men.

Also scheduled for the day were scenes 78, where Bub is heard growling from the experimentation room, and scene 79, where he breaks loose from his chain – a scene that played very differently from how it was originally scripted.

The most memorable thing about this particular day of the production wasn't the shoot itself, however, but the party that was held that night at the Holiday Inn – or "Sodom and Gomorrah" as it was described by key grip, Nick Mastandrea. "That's what the hotel was like. I mean, we just . . . you know . . . yeah, we were having a little too much fun I think," says Mastandrea.

"I just remember on weekends everybody would go nuts getting drunk and partying," says John Vulich.

An all-night "Fear and Loathing" party was held on this evening, in the main hallway of the third-floor annex at the Holiday Inn. The party was of such note that an official production memo was sent out to all cast and crew members, detailing the location and planned festivities for the evening. Beer, soft drinks, and a "fear and loathing punch" were provided, along with cold cuts and tuna for sandwiches, potato chips, pretzels, and macaroni salad. Music was provided courtesy of dolly grip Richard Sieg's cassette "blaster" and people were encouraged to bring their cassette tapes. "I remember dancing in the hallways and stairways, we just took the hotel over," says Nick Mastandrea. "It was nuts."

The following week, a playful memo entitled *The Laurel Enquirer* was circulated, dated Monday, November 19, 1984. The headline read "Fear and Loathing Party Rocks Holiday Inn" complete with "scandalous" photos of various crew members and a description of the evening's activities.

While a lot of the cast and crew were doing some serious partying during the production, others were having some family time instead. "My husband had a sabbatical, so he was able to be there with Katie, our daughter, some of the time, and I had her on the set a lot. Just having her, watching her – she learned how to walk there," recalls Lori Cardille. "It was just funny to see these little babies, because George Romero's baby, Christina, was there, and so Katie and Chris would play amongst these monsters in Tom Savini's shop where they would put the make-up on."

For Cardille's father-in-law, the late Alvin Rogal, who handled the insurance for Laurel Entertainment productions, having the opportunity to visit the set was really more of a chance to spend time with his new granddaughter. "I went up there a lot and she had, at the time, my second grandchild and they used

Top: Tom Savini with United Film Distribution Company employee Terry Powers. **Middle:** Media Day: Tom Savini transforms *Fangoria* magazine editor Robert "Uncle Bob" Martin into a zombie, while in the background Everett Burrell works on Paul Gagne of *Cinefantastique* magazine. Gagne would go on to write the fantastic book, *The Zombies That Ate Pittsburgh*, about the films of George Romero. (Photos Courtesy of Terry Powers.) **Bottom:** Howard Berger, Robert "Uncle Bob" Martin, Tom Savini, and Everett Burrell. (Courtesy of Everett Burrell.)

to have a little . . . George [Romero] prepared a little room, for a couple of the staff that had to bring their children," said Rogal. "So I used to love to go to that set because I would play with my grandchild and her little friends around her, because Lori used to take her every day."

The privilege of family visits wasn't just limited to the film's stars and hierarchy, however. Romero fostered a welcoming atmosphere for all of the crew members involved. "There was always like one day, or two days if I remember, in the course of the shoot that would be 'family day', where your family could come and kind of watch what we're doing, and kind of be a part of it and all that," says grip Barry Kessler. "People would take pictures with the zombies, and all that sort of thing."

As previously mentioned, the production was a six-day work week, with Sunday being the sole day off. Going into the mine each day before sunrise and

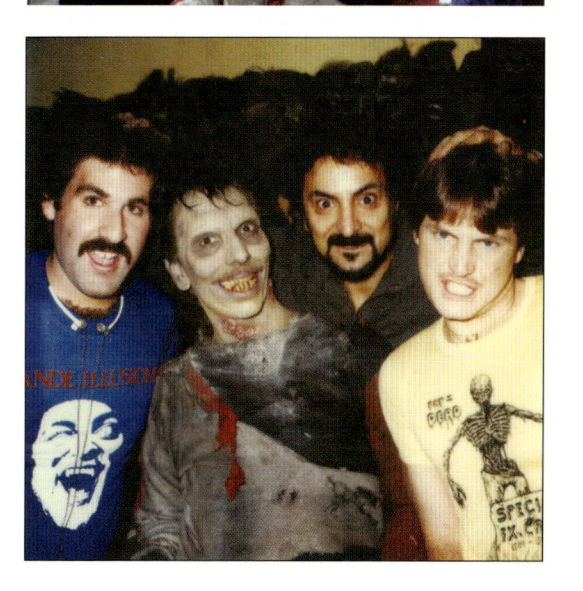

121

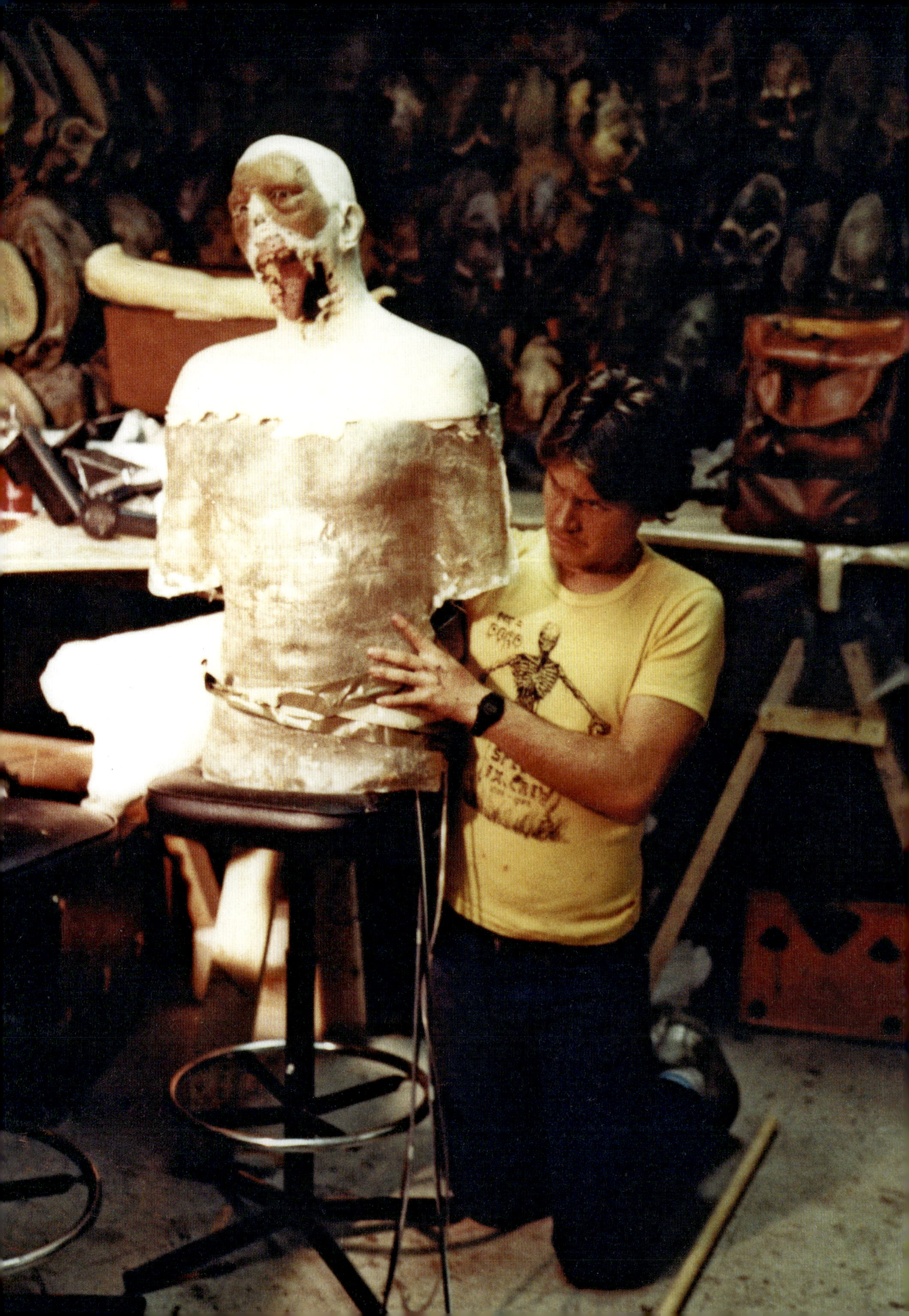

ONE DAY AT A TIME

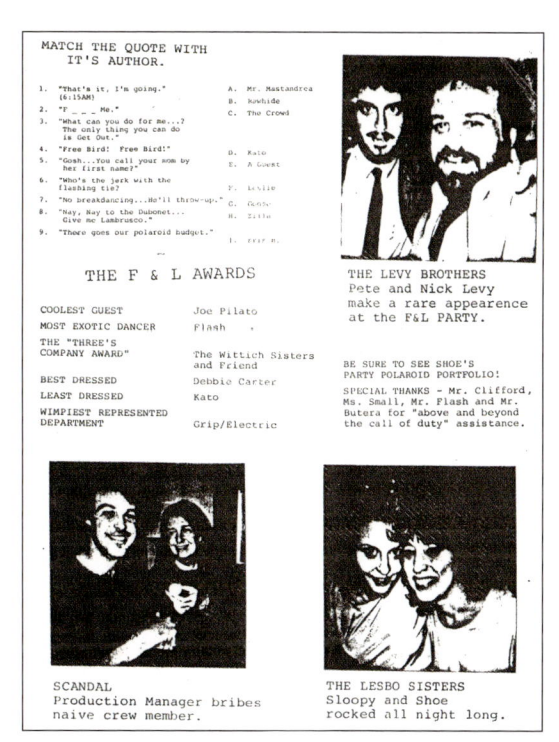

Above left and right: *The Laurel Enquirer* was a light-hearted memo circulated amongst the crew detailing the scandalous activities of a "Fear and Loathing" party held at the cast and crew's hotel, the Holiday Inn, on Saturday, November 17, 1984. (Courtesy of Greg Nicotero.)

leaving the mine after sunset created cabin fever amongst the cast and crew. "It was crazy! We'd get up and see the sun on Sunday mornings and we, like, lost our minds," remembers Dave Kindlon. "I remember we'd grab the station wagon and head off to a mall, and just act crazy and do donuts in snow-covered parking lots just to burn off some energy. I don't know, it was weird; none of us at the time, you know, didn't quite catch it right away. But later on it's like, 'We didn't see the sun for six days a week.' So I think we were going a little stir crazy or something."

"Sunday was our only day off and there was always a nice spread for brunch," remembers Gary Klahr. "Joe's [Pilato] classic line to me would be, 'Ehh, the Steelers are on in an hour. Grab a plate and let's do some brunch and get a couple, buddy, and we'll watch the Steelers play,' which we would do. But usually Sunday being the only day off, I would do my laundry."

"I know I just slept," says Joanne Small. "I don't know what anybody else did, but I slept."

"It was shot during the winter, so then when you did have your Sunday off it was basically sleeping, doing laundry, throwing some meat into the old lady and having her do your laundry or whatever, recuperating and blowing grey stuff out of your nose," says Simon Manses. "And then going back Monday morning and starting it all over again."

Left: Everett Burrell practices with the unfinished Dr. Tongue puppet. (Courtesy of Taso Stavrakis.)

Monday 11/19/1984 – Day 25

Quote correction: "Health is a state of mine." – Joe Pilato

Day 25 started it all over again with work on one of the film's more crucial scenes: scene 75, where Rhodes executes Fisher and throws Sarah and McDermott into the corral.

The execution of John Amplas' character, Fisher, was one of the effects in the film that slightly annoyed Tom Savini. "I wish they'd thrown some light on the effect," says Savini. "'Cause you couldn't see it!"

As noted on the call sheet, the quote of the day was a correction from the previous production day. Joe Pilato's remark "Health is a state of mind" was supposed to be "Health is a state of mine", referring to the sickness that was taking over the cast and crew inside the mine. "We all got deathly ill because there was so much dust; we all had upper bronchial infections," says Joe Pilato. "We had a guy we called 'Dr. Death', who actually ended up dying of a drug overdose. Yeah, we would come in and, I mean, B12 shots were flying all over the place because people were falling like flies. I actually missed three days of shooting."

breathing in. So, it was a rough environment to work in. It was not that pleasant."

"It was awful, just a depressing environment," recalls Everett Burrell. "It's cold and there's dead bats frozen to the wall."

The limestone mine was a truly spooky environment to work in. Many parts of the mine had no lighting and, on a production map of the facility, a large chunk of the space was simply labeled "Darkness". "It's so extensive. There are signs to help so you don't get lost, because you can easily lose your way underground," remembers Taso Stavrakis. "And we would hop in these golf carts and just go for miles, not try to get lost, but we would go off on these side trails and turn the lights off just to see how dark it was. [*laughs*] And we found an underground lake that seemed to go on indefinitely into the dark, which made me think of Gollum [from J.R.R. Tolkien's *The Hobbit*]. That was really cool." That lake, which is no longer there, was created when the mine was first pumped out and the ground water settled at a low point. A fog or cloud hung over the lake and, like Taso Stavrakis, Dave Kindlon described it as something out of "Middle-earth" from *The Lord of the Rings*. Huge earth berms were put in place to prevent it from flooding into the rest of the mine even further. On the other side of the lake, which could only be crossed by boat, there were even further miles of the mine that were rarely explored. Huge fluorescent stripes were painted on the columns to prevent you from getting lost, but in the middle of the lake, the columns were covered up completely by bats, which hid the fluorescent stripes.

But even the safer areas of the mine could still offer bizarre experiences. "You'd go down one passageway and you'd look over to the side, and you'd shine your light into an area and there would be like 50 ice-cream trucks parked there," recalls Nick Tallo. "And then you'd go a little further, and you'd shine your light on the other side, and there would be like a hundred golf carts parked there. So that was always very strange. And then we found, like, containers – big ass containers that were rusty and looked like they were corroded and leaking shit. It would say, like, United States Government – we were all like, 'I don't even want to know what's in these tanks.' Look, they're keeping it inside a mountain, so that might not be so good." [*laughs*]

Above: Rock group NRBQ as zombies. (Courtesy of Terry Powers.) **Below:** Prop man Kevin Ritter as a zombie. (Courtesy of Kevin Ritter.)

"Well, the cave . . . I mean, it was a nightmare," laughs George Romero. "Everybody came out with a mild case of black lung."

"This doctor came to the mine after shooting one night, and he attended 39 members of the crew, [*laughs*] who had bad throats or bad ears or a bad nose or whatever – all pretty much ear, nose, and throat because of the limestone dust that would continue to drop in this place," recalls David Ball. "I'd put my work in the drawer at lunchtime because when I got back there would be another half inch of dust."

"We'd set a light and when you turned on a light, you didn't see it with just your eye," says Barry Kessler. "But when the beam of light shone, you could see all the dust particles in the air that you were obviously

Tuesday 11/20/1984 – Day 26

"My God!! The car's on fire!! THE CAR'S ON FIRE!!!"
– Tom Savini

The twenty-sixth day continued filming of scene 75, where Rhodes and John have their standoff and Sarah and McDermott are thrown into the corral.

A major presence felt on the set, but not seen very often, was that of producer Richard Rubinstein. The reason for that was two-fold. Firstly, David Ball and Ed Lammi were on set daily, to ensure that the production was staying on schedule and budget. Secondly, Rubinstein was concentrating on expanding Laurel Entertainment, especially via television, with *Tales from the Darkside*. "I think wisely he stayed away. In flashing back I rarely have memory of Richard on set," says Mike Gornick. "I think he realized at that point in time that his relationship was ending with George, and he was protecting his own little firm, his business firm, which was Laurel Entertainment. Best to finish the film, get it produced, and get it exhibited. What else was left?"

"He would come in usually once a week to check in, see how things were doing, sign the checks, and generally headed back to New York," says Ed Lammi.

"Richard was great in one way. I mean, he really would let me make the movies and he would try to make as much out of the money as he could," says George Romero. "I know a lot of people dislike him for that. I don't have any complaints about Richard's behavior or the way he did things at all. I mean, I think he actually did us all a big service by being strict and stingy, and all that. A lot of people object to that but I don't object to that at all."

"I think that a lot of times there's a lack of respect for actors," says Lori Cardille. "I think that [Rubinstein's] attitude was, 'Well, you haven't done anything on film, so you're lucky to have this part.' I don't know if that was his attitude or what? But I don't think he realized

Above: Another of the many themed days for the "grips from hell", this particular one being "Arab day". From left to right: Barry Kessler ("Wrango"), Nick Mastandrea, John Janusek ("Beef"), Nick Tallo ("Bomba"), Kurt Rimmel ("Pinky"), Richard Sieg ("Mr. French"), Peter Beal ("The Inspector"), and Fred Roth ("Derf"). (Courtesy of Nancy Bennett.) **Below:** Head carpenter, Norman Beck, and head scenic artist, Eileen Garrigan, dressed as their mentor, Cletus Anderson, who can be seen walking out the door. (Courtesy of Norman Beck.)

where a lot of the actors came from, or the level of respect that other people in the field had given them. I'm not talking about bowing down or ingratiating themselves or being ridiculous. I'm talking just mainly about adhering to SAG rules . . . I don't think he was very . . . look, I guess he was a businessman, the bottom line and all that. But I don't think that the actors were much respected on the set. That's not by George or anybody that was on the set at the time,

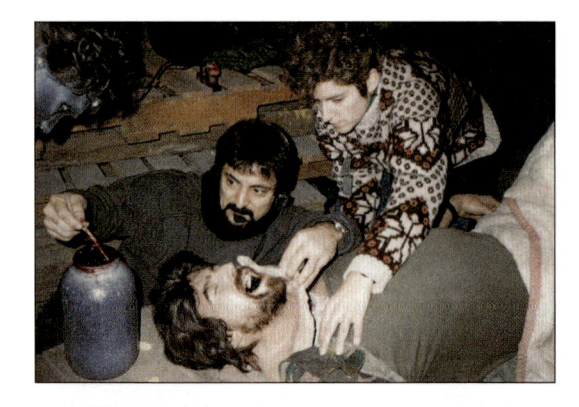

Above: Tom Savini adds gel blood inside the neck area of Taso Stavrakis' fake head, as assistant costume designer Eileen Sieff helps out. (Courtesy of Greg Nicotero.)
Below: Zombie extra Tim Irr sharing "lunch" with college roommate and fellow extra Brett Hudak. Irr was picked to help tear off Taso Stavrakis' head due to the length of his arms. (Courtesy of Tim Irr.)

Richard Rubinstein," says Cardille. "And that made it tough, because I would talk to my father-in-law about, 'You know, he may be a really nice guy to you, but he wasn't very nice to the actors or he wasn't very respectful.' You know, you would think that somebody that was a friend of my father-in-law – 'supposed' friend . . . it was a real bone of contention for me."

When Cardille talks about a lack of respect for actors, one of the things she's referring to is an addendum to the actors' contracts, which basically signed away their rights to future residual profits, in exchange for a one-time lump sum payment. Depending on which cast members you ask, you'll get varied responses regarding that subject. "God bless Tim DiLeo, who was very, very upset, that literally right . . . within an hour before we started the first day of shooting in the mine in Wampum, they added this little codicil to the contract," says Gary Klahr. "Tim said, 'No, we shouldn't sign it,' and then we all kind of got together and said, 'Nah, let's sign it, 'cause we'll deal with it later. We're ready to go to work.' And everybody was hungry to work, we liked the script. But, you know, I've never been a businessman and nobody's going to accuse me of being a good businessman. Tim's gut instinct – I remember and I give him credit for [it] – [was] 'We shouldn't sign this. You know, what are they gonna do, stop production right here? We're ready to go, the crew is here.' But we signed this little thing and I think they kinda hung onto it. Although, in talking to numerous people within SAG over the years, you cannot sign your rights away universally. It was kind of worded like that."

"I had absolutely no idea about that. I think . . . I believe I had an agent at the time, so they would have looked at the contract and I wouldn't have questioned it. So if that clause was in there, I don't know. I do know there was a one-time payment and that was it. We never saw any more residuals from it," remembers Jarlath Conroy. "This was not up front. This was sometime after the movie came out and it was a one-time payment after the deal was made, but I was not consulted on any kind of deal like that. And I don't know how they got around the union with it."

"They owe me literally, probably $80,000 to $100,000 [from] over the years, in residuals and penalty fees," says Joe Pilato.

"At the end we signed something that bought us out of our residuals for the movie. We got, like, maybe three grand or 3,500 hundred dollars for the whole package," says Terry Alexander. "I thought, 'Well, three thousand dollars is, you know, better than nothing,' because residuals in movies don't pay that much unless you've got a special deal or contract."

"Well, I probably signed it and probably paid no attention to it," says John Amplas. "So, no, I don't really remember any of the particulars of the contract.

working on the set. I'm just saying that I think that . . . I think that if I would have not felt so beholden or whatever – maybe I was young, I don't know – I think that it could have been a little bit different, and should have been different."

Cardille's disdain for Rubinstein was complicated even further by the fact that her father-in-law, Alvin Rogal, handled the insurance for Rubinstein and Laurel Entertainment. "That was another complicated thing – my relationship with Richard. My father-in-law always had a very professional, good relationship with

I was working on a weekly principal contract and so whatever it brought, it brought and I was probably satisfied to have it."

Wednesday 11/21/1984 – Day 27

"RE: 'The wimpiest represented department' . . . Next time we'll all just come naked and take it from there!" – Barry Wrango Kessler

Day 27 would continue scheduled work on scene 75 at the corral. Featured zombies Bruce Kirkpatrick and Kimet Maxwell would be on set this day, even though they weren't featured much at all in the finished cut of the film.

Scene 77, where Steel and Rickles leave the corral to investigate the sound of the elevator alarm, and scene 81, where John overpowers Rhodes at the corral, were also scheduled on this day.

Following this day of shooting, the production took two days off for the Thanksgiving holiday. For some of the local Pittsburgh crew, that meant an opportunity to spend time at home with family and enjoy the holiday. Greg Nicotero, who was one of those lucky crew members, also opened his family's home to those who were far from their own. "I had Thanksgiving at Greg's with Greg's family in 1984," says David Ball. "They took me in, being that I was living a long way away, and I had Thanksgiving with them. It was wonderful."

Nicotero also used the opportunity to play a practical joke on his Mom, by placing his severed head in his bedroom and then calling her into the room to discover the grisly surprise. Needless to say, his mother wasn't too happy with him for the rest of Thanksgiving Day!

Saturday 11/24/1984 – Day 28

"Based on years of experience, I would say I have no idea." – Tom Savini

After the two-day break for Thanksgiving, the production resumed for its twenty-eighth day of filming. Two scenes would be covered on this day: scene B97, where Rickles is chased down, grabbed by a horde of zombies, and torn apart; and scene A100, where zombies eat the remains of Rickles (which would be edited together with shots of zombies feasting on the other soldiers' remains).

Early on, Ralph Marrero had decided to add a bit of texture to his character, Rickles, and his co-star Gary Klahr helped facilitate this. "I don't wear jewelry, but I had my wedding ring with me and Ralph said, 'Gary,

Above: Wampum Mine employee Debbie Sudano sits on the lap of mine manager, and zombie extra, Overton Bernard Capps III. (Courtesy of Debbie Sudano.)

can I borrow your wedding ring?' and I said, 'Sure,'" remembers Klahr. "It's a small thing, but it helped him. Because he wanted to be a guy – that even though we were down there with the only woman being Lori – that he was a married guy, that he had a wife and family somewhere within his 'movie' life that weren't there. And that was his way. Matter of fact, when he's getting torn apart you'll notice [that], when he gets his finger bit, you can see my ring."

Marrero also added a memorable touch to his death scene. "Ralph had an idea for his character, which I liked, too, because Ralph laughs his way to death," says Klahr. "That was a conscious choice by Ralph. And I remember him thinking it through. I thought it was great, it was totally insane."

Marrero's grisly onscreen death required a prosthetic piece that covered his entire forehead and left eye, with a fake eyeball protruding from the eye socket. In the scene, one of the zombies, played by Tom Savini, rips his eye socket open, tearing his forehead open in the process. In addition, his fingers would be bitten off. The task of sculpting Marrero's fingers fell on Mike Trcic. Greg Funk, an aspiring young make-up effects artist attending Point Park College, was brought in with the crew as an additional helping hand on big zombie extra days, and remembers the incredible sculpture that Trcic turned in. "That's actually an interesting story, maybe somebody would back this up or not, but Mike Trcic sculpted fake fingers that were then applied as an appliance," says Funk. "And all the LA guys that were in town were kind of treating Mike, maybe, a little 'lesser than', as the local guy – which you get, that's what happens. They assigned him to sculpt these fingers, so he sculpted these fingers and presented them and they all went, 'Oh, uh . . . wow.' So he got instant respect, if he didn't already have it, from them. That's the way I

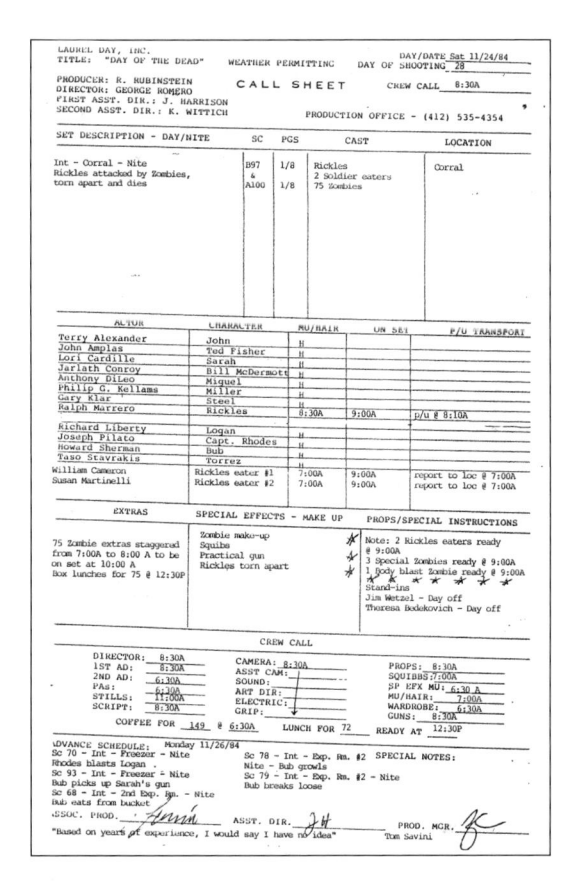

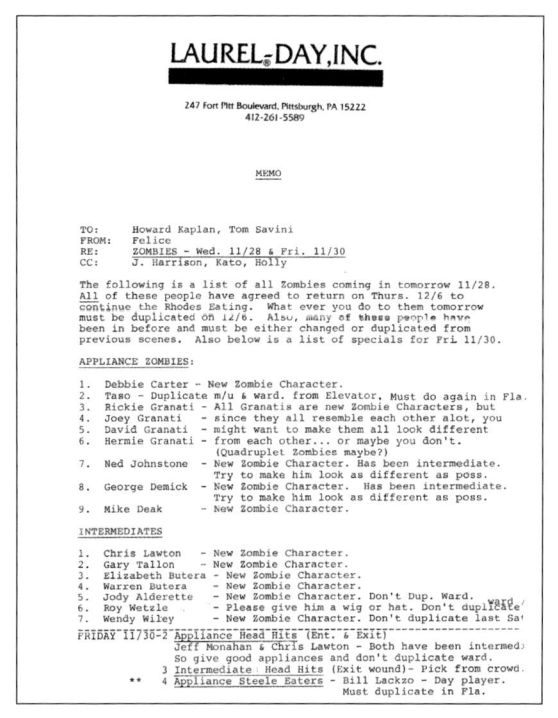

Left: Saturday, November 24, 1984 call sheet for Ralph Marrero's (Rickles) death scene. **Right:** Memo from Felice Lammi regarding zombie extras required for the death of Captain Rhodes. (Photos courtesy of Taso Stavrakis.)

understand it, and the way it was told to me years and years ago from some of the guys."

One of the LA-based artists Funk is referring to was Howard Berger, who backed up Funk's story. "At that time, Mike Trcic was really coming into his own. Prior to some of the stuff he had done on this show some of his sculptures were a bit rough, you know?" says Berger. "But man, all of a sudden he did this one sculpture for Ralph Marrero, I think it was his fingers getting bit off, and God they were spot on! I mean they looked like a life cast, you know? All Mike's work just altered and was so bloody amazing."

"Yeah, I guess those fingers were the turning point in my acceptance by the LA effects guys on *Day of the Dead*," says Trcic. "Howie [Berger] did do an excellent job of applying the finger appliance to Ralph, they really looked great."

The zombie extra who would get the honor of biting off Marrero's fingers was Joe "Jefferson Street" Abeln, nicknamed after the former Pittsburgh Steelers backup quarterback, Joe Gilliam (whose nickname was "Jefferson Street Joe"). Abeln was another veteran of Romero's films, having served as a grip on *Creepshow* and *Knightriders*. He also had a cameo in *Dawn of the Dead* as one of the redneck posse hunters who, while shooting zombies on a hillside, says, "Ahh, got him. Aww, missed."

Abeln wasn't aware of a reason why he was picked for the dubious job of biting the fingers off. "I don't know why I personally got picked just for that shot. I guess I was in the right place at the right time," he says. "I was actually sitting down on the ground – we shot that kind of in a sitting position. Some of the special effects guys had some tubes running up the actor's arm or something, so that when I bit the fingers off, some blood would come out – you know, it was like one of those deals. Well anyway, somehow a bunch of this fake blood that they were pumping in there, I guess it was like Karo syrup and food coloring or something, it ended up, like, down on the ground and I ended up sitting in it. So when the scene was all done my pants were soaked with fake blood, it was like this big mess. And, of course, I had all that make-up and a latex appliance on my face and the fake teeth and everything. So it was kind of uncomfortable to be soaked through to the bone in your seat area with sticky red Karo syrup. But, you know, you have to suffer for your art, your moment of glory."

For Abeln, the most exciting thing about having done the scene was that a still of him biting Marrero's fingers off appeared in the September 1985 issue of *Playboy* magazine, featuring Madonna on the cover!

Abeln was one of about 75 extras used on this day of shooting. Two "featured zombies" were on set:

Top: Unlike their onscreen personas, Joe Pilato and Lori Cardille share a friendly moment on set. **Middle:** Joe Pilato and Jarlath Conroy take a break inside the Wampum Mine. **Bottom:** Ralph Marrero, Joe Pilato and Gary Klahr having fun on the set in Wampum. (Photos courtesy of Joe Pilato and Rusty Nails.)

William Cameron and Susan Martinelli. However, their zombies weren't featured in the final cut of the film.

An extra who was featured briefly onscreen was school teacher Ralph Langer, who had previously worked as a zombie extra on *Dawn of the Dead*, thanks to forming a relationship with George and Christine Romero after discovering that a former student of his – Cliff Forrest, Christine's brother – was a grip on the film. After that, every time the Romeros made a film, they would invite Langer and his students out to the sets for field trips.

When *Day of the Dead* rolled around, Langer was once again invited to be a zombie. Langer can be spotted munching on the arm of the dead body of Ted Fisher, along with several other extras, and is then shot repeatedly by Rickles.

"They brought us into the room and they put us on our knees," recalls Langer. "There's me, and this teacher that's next to me, and there's another guy that's a principal, and a lawyer and the four of us are on our knees and they gave me an arm and they gave

Above: Everett Burrell having fun with the false body of Joe Pilato before filming the spectacular death of Captain Rhodes. Note the pelvic bone sticking out from inside the false torso. (Courtesy of Everett Burrell.)

somebody some stuff, like, different body parts, and at the end of them they put chicken meat with barbeque sauce so it looked red. They said, 'okay whenever it's time to film you start growling and you start eating the meat off the . . .' you know, 'cause it was chicken you could eat it. So anyway, the woman next to me, halfway through the shot, started laughing because to her it was just so absurd, four grown people on their knees like this eating chicken out of fake arms. The thing is the guy next to her all [of a] sudden started laughing, and for some reason it struck me as funny. So we're trying to mix the growling in with the laughing so that we wouldn't mess up the shot. The four of us are, like, [*makes growling/eating sounds*] sort of laughing and growling at the same time, but they put the shot in the movie, so we pulled it off I guess."

While waiting for his scene to be filmed, Langer had, of course, been prepped by the make-up and wardrobe departments. He was fitted with some type of suit coat that had been lined with blood squibs, which he wore for the entire day while waiting for his shot. At the end of the day, he was given proper respect by George Romero for having done such a thing. "George Romero said, 'It's not everybody that would walk around all day wearing explosives,'" says Langer. "He was joking around about it, 'cause I was spending the whole day, [when] they should have done this shot first, I guess."

When the scene was shot and the squibs were detonated, Langer did receive powder burns. "I have an arm with the chicken meat in it and I get three bullet holes in front and three in the back; so that shot is in the movie," says Langer. "But I put my hand forward and I got powder burns on my arm from the wrist to the elbow. Nobody said anything and I wasn't thinking, but you know, it wasn't bad. But it took about a week to heal I'd say, it was all red and speckled-looking, I guess from the gun powder flying out. So I did get powder burns, so that was my war wound from that movie."

Another extra on set this day was Vini Bancalari, whose journey to becoming a zombie extra was a unique one. Bancalari worked for a Manhattan company that sold industrial video equipment to broadcast and cable channels, and one day was assigned to write a column for the company newsletter. He decided to write a piece about filmmakers, and one of the people he wanted to interview was George Romero. In the early summer of 1984 he called the Laurel offices in Pittsburgh looking for George, but could never reach him. Each time he called, he kept getting the same person on the phone, someone named Mike. Months went by and he never did get George on the phone, but by this time, after numerous phone calls, he had formed a friendship with Mike. One fortuitous call ended up with Mike offering Bancalari an opportunity to come and be a zombie in *Day of the Dead*. Bancalari, thinking perhaps he had been talking to the office janitor all this time, asked just who Mike was and discovered it was none other than Mike Gornick. Bancalari gladly accepted the offer and asked if he could also bring a friend, which Mike said was fine.

Bancalari and his friend showed up at the mine on the day of shooting and were put through the usual paces of becoming a zombie, getting make-up and being fitted with ratty clothes. Afterwards they were seated with the other extras in the holding area. "We had our little box lunch with the sandwich and the apple," recalls Bancalari. "After a while they started hitting so many delays, people just started getting real anxious and uncomfortable because we were all sitting around for so many hours in the freezing mines with all this make-up on. So they wheeled out a TV cart with a monitor and an old VCR and they just started showing us episodes of *Tales from the Darkside* [*laughs*] to keep us entertained. At one point somebody, one of the zombies, actually just got up and started dancing the Michael Jackson *Thriller* dance, so of course everybody else jumped in."

ONE DAY AT A TIME

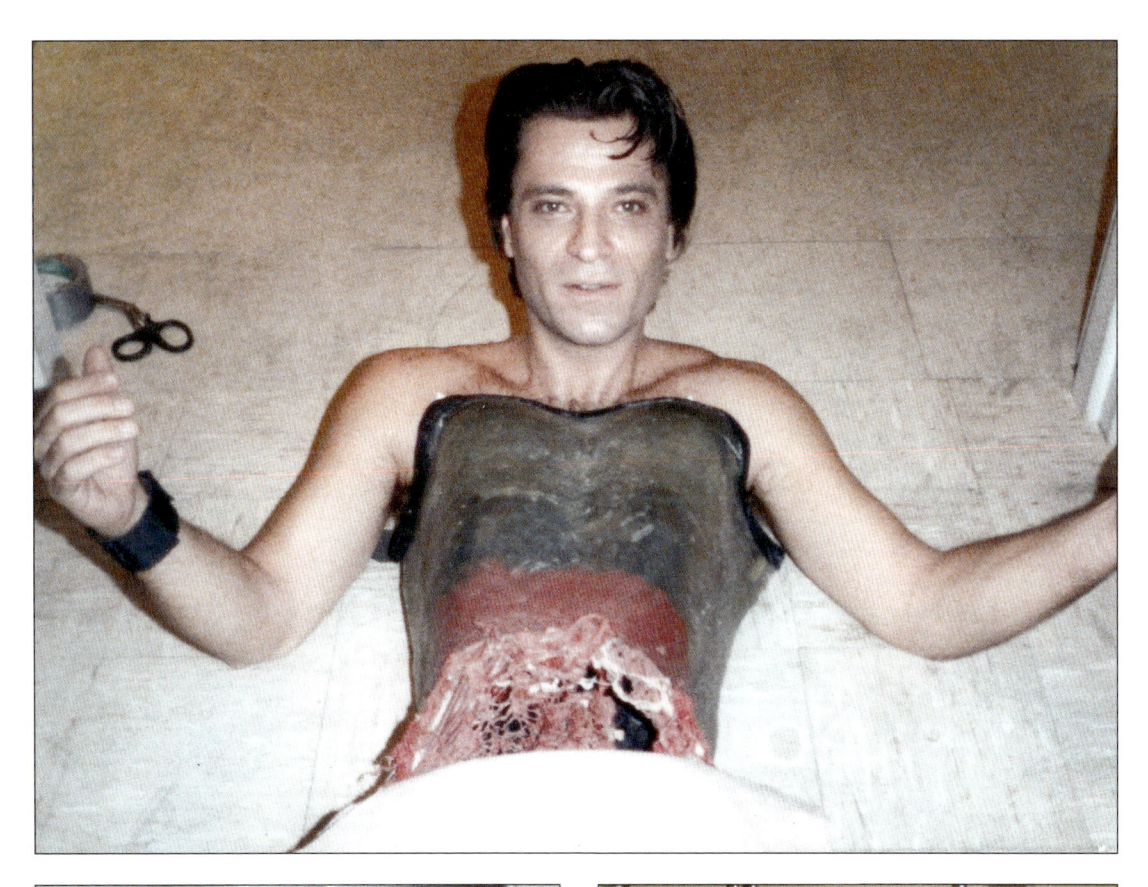

Clockwise from top: A great day to die: Joe Pilato inside the false floor with a prosthetic abdomen attached to him. Pilato's endurance would be tested to its very limits once the rotten pig intestines were brought in; Howard Berger plays with a prosthetic intestine. This same item was glued inside Joe Pilato's false abdomen for his spectacular on-screen death; With Greg Nicotero watching in the background, Joe Pilato jokes around with a toilet seat around his neck. Upon arriving on set the morning of his death scene Pilato discovered the crew had left a toilet seat over the hole in the false floor that said "Pilato's Potty". (Photos courtesy of Joe Pilato and Rusty Nails.)

When he was finally called on set, Bancalari discovered he would be part of a group of extras, which included Ralph Langer, called the "Fisher Eaters" because they would be munching on the remains of John Amplas' character, Ted Fisher. It was then that he finally got to meet the gentleman who made it possible for him to be there, Mike Gornick. "Got to meet Mike Gornick face to face finally," says Bancalari. "And as soon as he realized who I was, 'Oh, we're gonna put you over here Vini. We're gonna make sure we get you on camera,' he was like my buddy."

Interestingly – and this happens quite often with people's memories – his recollection of what happened with the zombie extras during the scene differs from Ralph Langer's. "We got our take done after about four or five takes," remembers Bancalari. "Because during the scene there was a bunch of zombies munching on people, and I remember the first take one of the zombies must have just gotten disgusted by what he was doing and started to gag and that set off a chain reaction. So you had about, I'd say, eight to ten zombies all gagging like they were going to vomit. [*laughs*] George [Romero] had to keep yelling 'Cut!', but after about a half dozen takes or so he got what he wanted."

Years later, Bancalari, along with Don May, Jr., would form Elite Entertainment and go on to release *Night of the Living Dead, Dawn of the Dead*, and *Day of the Dead* on LaserDisc.

The unfortunate crew member who had to be on the ground during this scene, doubling for John Amplas, was prop man Kevin Ritter. He won the unenviable assignment because he was the crew member that most closely resembled Amplas and was a similar size. "I remember getting into clothes and stuffing turkey meat dipped in barbeque sauce under the watch band of the character's watch that was around my wrist, and then having to lie on that 52-degree ground for so long I was actually shaking uncontrollably," recalls Ritter. "And I remember George [Romero] coming in and getting really upset that it wasn't getting done. I remember him, 'Just shoot it. Just shoot it!' I was supposed to be dead but I'm shaking because I was so cold and I didn't have any control over it. He was just like, 'Get it. Cut!' He was aggravated at the fact that it was taking so long."

Zombie extra Kevin Rolly, who had previously worked at the Manor Nike Missile Site, was also on hand for this day's filming. This time around he would graduate from being a masked zombie to getting sprayed down with Streaks 'N Tips as an intermediate zombie. "That one I was all over the place; basically just kind of painted your face and greased your hair down, put you in . . . everyone had the same sort of outfit, the whole zombie typical ruined outfits. And I was all over the place in that," says Rolly. "You saw my hand in shots, I was walking in the background when people got shot, which I thought was the awesome thing. Basically it was a big thing on the set – if you could get shot, that was the preeminent thing that you could possibly get as a zombie. You wanted to have squibs and things blowing up."

Production accountant Charles Carroll also appeared as a zombie on this day. He's shot by Ralph Marrero and then later, in the gore montage, can be spotted having a snack. "I'm also seen in front of a fence, I think, chewing on a human thigh bone or something like that," says Carroll.

Monday 11/26/1984 – Day 29

No quote of the day

Day 29 of filming began with scene 70, in which Rhodes discovers the contents of Logan's freezer, kills the mad doctor and then disarms Sarah, McDermott, and Fisher.

In the November 1, 1985 edition of the *Fort Lauderdale News and Sun-Sentinel*, Richard Liberty told writer Candice Russell all about his demise onscreen. "They take a lead rectangle, put a charge of powder in it and run a wire down your leg to a control box," Liberty said. "When it's exploded, so are blood squibs. I was told not to put down my head or arms. This is a shot they can't retake. It was a two-hour set-up for the eighteen charges, since I was shot eighteen times." Indeed, there were only two lab coats rigged with squibs; the front one for Liberty, the second for Taso Stavrakis, who doubled for Liberty for the reverse angle of his back.

Also on tap for the day was scene 93, where Bub discovers the guns left on the floor outside the freezer containing Logan's dead body. For Liberty, shooting the scene provided a brief scare, as he had to lie on the floor surrounded by dry ice. The carbon dioxide from the dry ice caused his heart to beat much faster, which in turn disrupted his performance of lying dead and motionless on the floor. So, quite a bit of time was taken to get the scene completed.

In Romero's shooting script, scene 93 is very brief and makes no mention of Bub discovering Logan dead on the floor. In fact, Romero simply describes the

Clockwise from top left: Joe Pilato inside the false floor and ready to be torn in half; Joe Pilato surrounded by zombies moments before his onscreen demise; The aftermath: After being torn in half, Joe Pilato is assisted with a respirator by extra Roy Wetzel, to help with the smell coming from the rancid pig intestines; Greg Nicotero stuffs guts into the lower half of Joe Pilato's body as zombie extra George Demick holds on to one of the legs. (Photos courtesy of George Demick and Greg Nicotero.)

ONE DAY AT A TIME

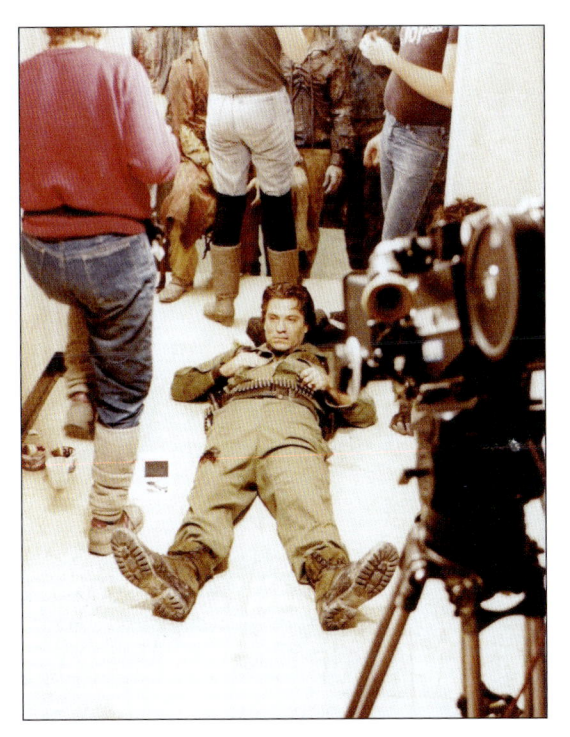

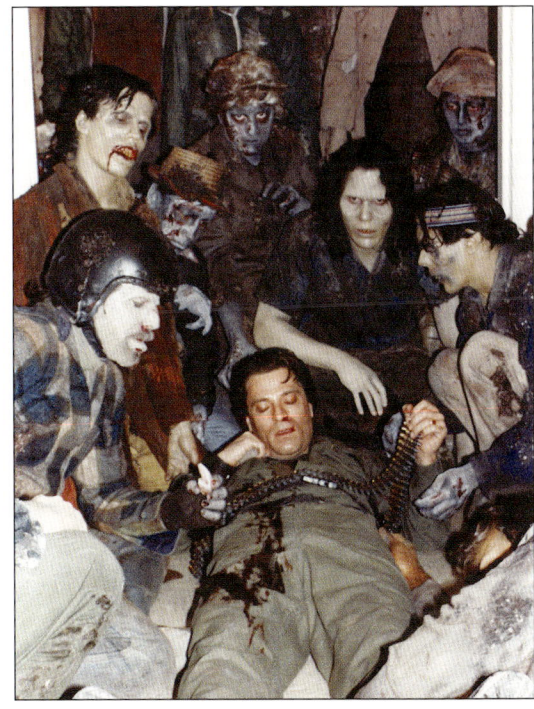

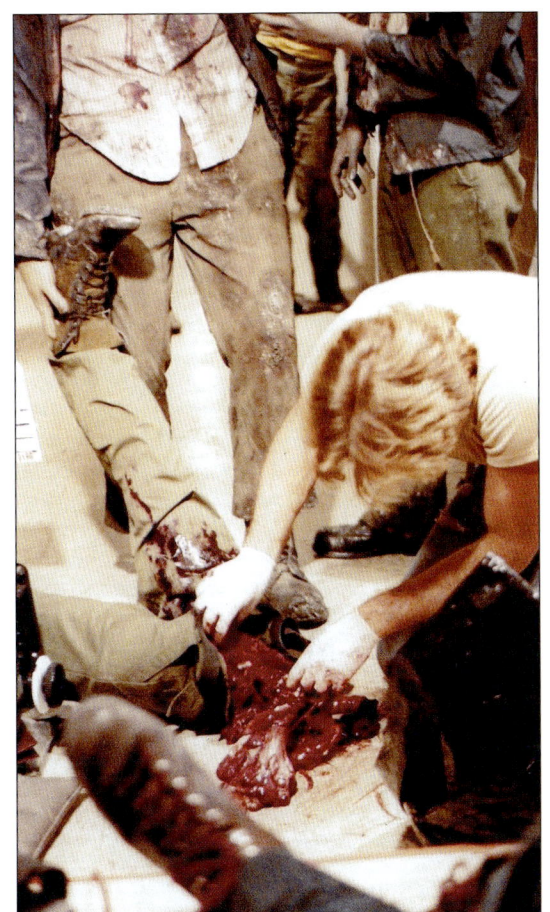

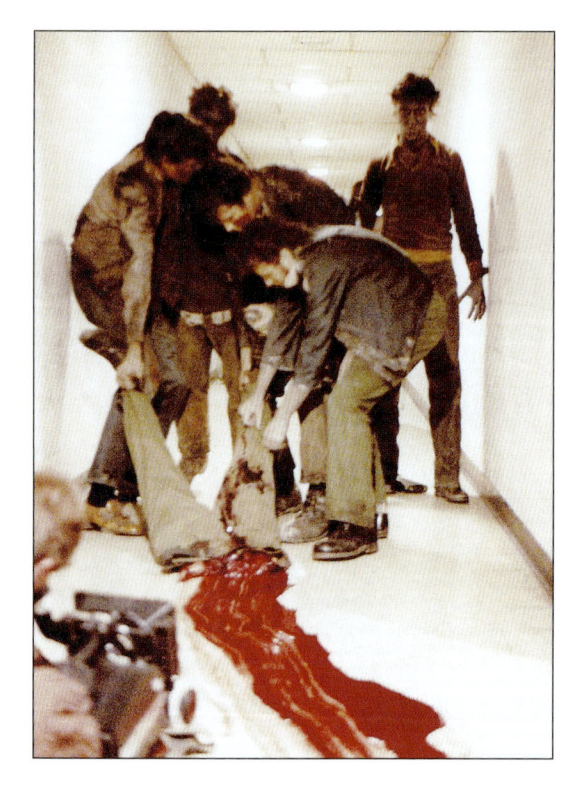

Left and right: Filming the zombie extras dragging Rhodes' legs down the hall with a long smear of blood. (Courtesy of George Demick.)

guns lying on the floor and then writes, "Bub, noticing the weapons, seems to smile. Strange but true. You saw it here first, folks." And that was it. When it came time to put the scene on film, Romero, having become very fond of Sherman's impressive improvisational work as Bub, decided that there should be more to it than what was described on the page. "Well, I don't remember how that came about. I think it was more of a . . . I don't remember who thought of that. It might have been one of those things on the set where you suddenly realize this doesn't make sense. Why am I gonna . . . I mean, he's laying there. I wouldn't be indifferent to that," says Sherman. "You know, now that I think of it, because I remember, that was the one scene in the whole shoot that I really had . . . we had to do several takes before I found it; couldn't quite figure out what it was. Does Bub cry? Does Bub, you know, what's the reaction? But my recollection is that it was George [Romero] [who] made the connection. George, before we approached shooting the scene, he realized that Logan's death needed to motivate the gun moment. To just have it be about guns rather than be about the death of my friend, which then leads to the gun which will lead to revenge, is a much more satisfying and logical progression. I think George figured that out on the day that we got there, and then it was up to us to figure out, well, what is that emotional reaction? How does it manifest? What's the level of behavior? Is it soft and subtle? Is it big? So we tried a few things."

To find the right feeling for Bub's discovery of Logan's body, Sherman attempted several different takes, but nothing was working. Nothing he was coming up with felt genuine, and the clock was ticking. "My recollection is that I was doing what felt like was going to be the last take, or one of the last takes. I knew that time was running out, they had to move on," says Sherman. "The behavior that ended up being in the movie just kind of came out of me, and part of it was the frustration of not being able to . . . I think I had been going for being sad. Somehow we thought that he'd be heartbroken. And I think that what came out was this rage, you know? But again, it was an improvisation, it's like it occurred to me in the moment. They said, 'Action!' and I looked at him and this thing just came out of me. It wasn't like I had the idea of, 'I know what I'll do. I'll flail about.' I looked and that's what came up. And then as soon as it was happening I knew okay, I knew I got it. I knew, okay, this is real."

The evolution of Dr. Tongue. Clockwise from top-left: before the application of its hair and tongue; being worked upon by Tom Savini; inching closer to completion at the Wampum Mine; having finishing touches of blood and gore added by Savini; and filming in downtown Fort Myers. (Photos courtesy of George Demick, Greg Nicotero, Everett Burrell and Hollywood Book & Poster Company.)

ONE DAY AT A TIME

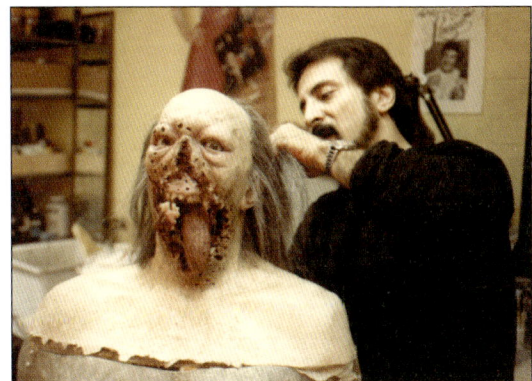

A key addition that Sherman brought to the scene was Bub's excitement to show Logan that he had broken free of his chain. "Very often there's a kind of practicality, it's discovering the way the brain works, discovering the way perception unfolds from one micro event to the next to the next to the next. Which normal human beings, in real life, are doing it all the time, but they don't know that they're doing it, it just occurs," says Sherman. "But actors study this nano second to nano second kind of process of unfolding realizations; that's how you create authentic behavior. Ideally you're so much in the life of the character that it just unfolds all by itself, but sometimes you actually have to tinker with things and realize that I look, I see . . . a human would instantly know he's dead on the ground. I can't know that right away, because that would be fake zombie reality. Zombies work slow, their minds perceive slowly, so my first reaction should be, I see my friend, but then objectively I think that would look weird from the outside to an audience, because people don't think about how a zombie thinks. It would just look odd that I look at him and I don't see that he's dead. However, if I add the beat of, 'Look what I did,' and then I discover that he's dead a beat later, that will look realistic and it will honor the zombie reality that I'm trying to . . . the slow thought process. Just having that little beat that will interfere with

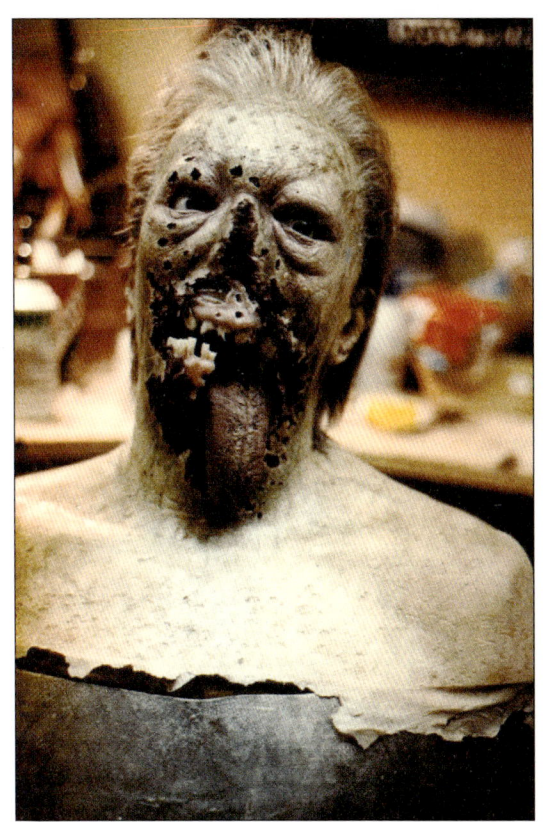

135

my moment of discovering that he's actually dead, rather than just seeing it and spontaneously I already have my own agenda. 'Look what I did,' and then I see makes it real in a way that just looking and not reacting and then reacting late would just seem . . . you know? But you don't know that in advance, you discover it while the camera is running. You discover it by doing a take where I just look and then I see he's dead and it doesn't feel right and I know it's not gonna look right. So the next take, 'Oh, it's the chain!' It's all an unfolding improvisation, and ideally a good director will take the best takes and sew them together."

Sherman's performance hadn't just made an impression on Romero; the entire crew was noticing his incredible work. "You would sit and you'd practically weep sometimes," says second assistant director Katarina Wittich. "He was very, very moving to watch."

"He is like the everyman zombie," says Eileen Sieff. "With a touch of George's [Romero] fashion sense thrown in."

"I'd just been golden. Everything I did was golden. And it was kind of the buzz all over the set," remembers Sherman. "And it was great because every time I'd do a scene after the first couple of days, more and more people would be standing behind the camera. When you can interest the guys who move the wires and move the lights; they're notoriously . . . they just don't give a shit. They're just there to get their money – when those guys stop what they're doing and pay attention. Whenever I was acting in front of the camera all of those guys were there watching. They'd come up to me afterwards at the craft services table and say, 'Hey man, I really like what you're doing.' So, there was a kind of a sense on the set that Bub was an *event*! And that's cool when you're an actor."

Also on the day's schedule, once again, were scenes 78 and 79, where Bub breaks free of his chain. One last scene, scene 68, in which Logan rewards Bub with his bucket of flesh, was scheduled for this day as well.

Tuesday 11/27/1984 – Day 30

"It's all mine over matter." – D. Ball

Day 30 of filming featured a scheduled scene that didn't end up in the finished cut of the film. Scene 65 would've taken place between Sarah and McDermott leaving "The Ritz" and then searching through Logan's laboratory for pain medicine for Miguel. In the scene, Sarah and McDermott are wandering through one of the corridors when they overhear Rhodes, Steel, Rickles, and Torrez arguing about whether to leave the facility. However, for the real hardcore, nerdy fans

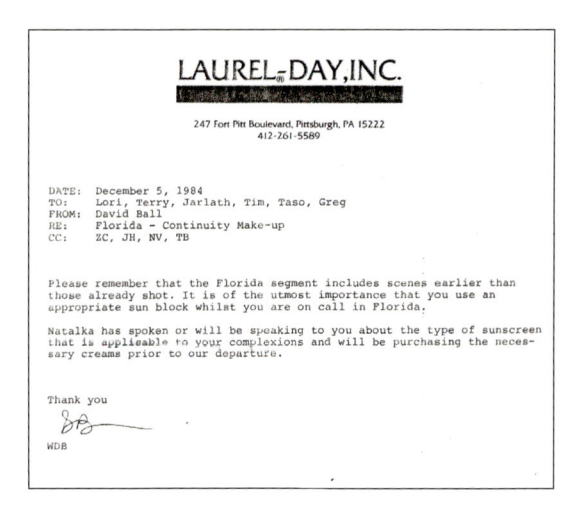

Above: December 5, 1984 memo from co-producer David Ball advising the cast members traveling to Fort Myers, Florida to use sun screen for continuity reasons. (Courtesy of Greg Nicotero.)

out there – like myself – if you listen very carefully you can hear part of Rhodes' dialogue from this scene layered into the soundtrack during scene 62. Right after Sarah cauterizes Miguel's stump, you can hear the voice of Rhodes saying, "Goddamn, Rickles" and "bury my ass down here waiting to die". It's layered in along with the voices of Steel and Rickles, as if they were yelling to one another as they made their way through the cave to "The Ritz". Check it out next time you watch the film.

Scene 41, where the soldiers brawl in the hallway, was also on the docket for this day; oddly enough it came two weeks after a stunt rehearsal had been performed on day twenty. Another scene, number 94, would also be shot. In the script, Romero describes Rhodes looking for a weapon, but unable to find one. However, in the film he does find a gun but is unable to load the clip when he runs into Bub.

Scene number 96 was also shot. Again, it's a case of the script being slightly different from the film. In the script, Rhodes is described as staggering though the meeting room, the large dining hall area, pulling himself along the side of a table. In the film he simply staggers through the corridors.

Also scheduled for the day – yet again – were scenes 78 and 79, involving Bub inside the observation room, then freeing himself. Scenes 95 and A95, where Bub shoots Rhodes in the corridor, were scheduled as well.

The final scene scheduled for the day was scene 68, where Logan tells Bub how proud he is of him and rewards him with his bucket of flesh. In the script the preceding scene, 67, shows Sarah and McDermott following Logan into Bub's experimentation room as they watch him from the observation room. What

Above: Terry Alexander enjoying a laugh next to the "whirlybird" on Sanibel Island. (Courtesy of Terry Alexander.)

isn't described in either scene is Logan putting the headphones on Bub and teaching him how to listen to the music on the tape recorder. That's because it was an idea that Howard Sherman thought of during the production. "I was out running one day and, as I was coming back to the hotel, I suddenly thought, 'What would Bub think of music? Oh, wouldn't that be interesting!' That would be interesting, I don't know, whatever I was listening to at the moment, what would Bub think of it? That would be kind of fun," laughs Sherman. "Anyway, I talked to George [Romero] and George liked that idea. Somehow, I don't remember, how we evolved the beginning, middle, and the end of that actual scene where the music plays and then I think once we're on the set, then certain things become, 'Well he's gotta put the headphones on. Well, there's a problem – he's a zombie. Will he bite me?' You know? And then there was the moment where I grabbed his arm, which I believe was an improvised moment. I think we said, 'Well he'll put the headphones on,' and he went to put the headphones on and I just got a zombie impulse [*laughs*] to attack him. I think that was a surprise. He stiffened and I looked at him and realized that I liked him more than I wanted to eat him. [*laughs*] And it was a nice little moment of humanity, and then he did the headphones and he turned on the music. Anyway, I think we sort of evolved what the steps of that scene were pretty much on the set, I think."

Sherman had previously discussed his co-star in the scene, Richard Liberty, and how energetic he was. However, that energy caused a minor problem for Sherman when they worked together on the tape recorder scene. Liberty moved so fast when he turned the recorder off and on that it was like a blur for Sherman, who was staying in character as Bub. "I said I can't learn that fast – I'm a very, very, very dumb creature. So if you just show me or do the thing I'm not gonna get it," says Sherman. "He said, 'Oh, yeah, yeah, yeah.' So he would go [*mimes turning on and off the recorder quickly*]. 'Richard,' I said, 'that's way too fast.' I remember we had to take several . . . and finally after several attempts he just didn't seem to . . . his energy was just too fast. I don't remember whether we did this on camera or whether we were still rehearsing before we started but I just decided . . . I was in odd terrain already, because there is a very, very longstanding and sort of holy protocol – one actor does not direct another actor. The director does the directing. And I thought it was sort of my idea and we were sort of experimenting to discover, but I'd already said, 'You need to slow down,' two or three times and he wasn't getting it, and so if I then took the next step to say, 'Well, what if you do this and then do this and then do this' – well, then I'm clearly

Above: George Romero, Michael Gornick, and Terry Alexander walking along Bowman's Beach on Sanibel Island. **Below:** Everett Burrell sword-fighting with Tom Savini on Bowman's Beach, Sanibel Island. (Photos courtesy of Taso Stavrakis.)

directing, I've really overstepped my boundaries. So what I did was I just retreated to just being Bub. So he'd show me something and if he did it too fast I'd just look at him and not do anything. And I, that way, forced him to slow it down and show me. And that's what he did, to his credit. He figured it out, but he didn't figure it by Howard telling Richard, you gotta slow down so Bub can see it. It was Bub looking at his friend, [*laughs*] and my own stupidity [that] forced him to show me his finger and then slowly work its way down to the thing. And again, the scene ended up working that way."

Another thing worthy of note in this scene is that Sherman almost has Bub talk when Logan turns off the tape recorder. It was, again, an improvisation on Sherman's part that just slipped out. "You know, you're the first one that's ever asked me that," says Sherman. "Because it's an improvisation the thought kind of starts to go to speech and right in the moment I realized, 'Oh, fuck. I can't talk!' [*laughs*] But what comes out is this sort of, [*moans like Bub, then laughs*] where it's sort of like the rhythm of the sentence is there with hardly any articulation. You know? And there are two or three places . . . I mean, you know, the 'Hello, Aunt Alicia' is like there's just the *least, least, least* brush with an actual consonant and a vowel of Alicia, just *barely*. But the rhythm of the sentence is sort of there, and that was my version of the muscles of the tongue and the brain and all of the stuff that a normal human engages when they attempt to speak just don't work very well, and that's how it would come out, I discovered in the moment of improvisation. That's essentially how that worked. But I did have exactly that thought, 'I'm not trying to . . .' but it just happened in the moment. It was just like as soon as the sound went off, I mean as soon as he hit the thing it was, [*roars like Bub, then laughs*] I was having fun, you know?"

For the record, I'd like to point out that I'm a little unsure whether or not this scene with Howard Sherman and Richard Liberty was shot on this day. It's unclear whether it was considered to be part of scene 67 or scene 68, since it was the brainchild of Howard Sherman and was thought up during filming. I've done my best to figure it out and asked the people involved, but memories can be fleeting.

Wednesday 11/28/1984 – Day 31

No quote of the day

Day 31 of filming began with scene H97, where Steel is chased into an experimentation room because Bub is shooting at him.

Scene A67, where Sarah and McDermott are in the corridor and see Logan walking with the bucket, was scheduled. Scene 64 was also scheduled, where Sarah and McDermott sneak through the corridors and then hear the soldiers arguing about whether they should leave. Like scene 65, which this scene leads into, it would not be in the final cut of the film.

Scenes 95 and A95 – in which Bub shoots Rhodes as he attempts to flee in the corridor – were rescheduled for this day. During this sequence, Joe Pilato added one of two very memorable lines of dialogue to the film when he refers to Bub as a "pus fuck", much to the amusement of his director. "The sound guy . . . George goes, 'Is everything okay?'" remembers Pilato. "And the sound guy goes, 'Wait a minute,' and he listens to it and he goes, 'Uh, did he say pus fuck?' and George [Romero] goes, 'Yeah, I like it. Let's keep it.'"

Also on the schedule for this day were scenes 99 and A99, where Rhodes heads down the last stretch of the corridor to reach the door at the end of the hallway, only to discover zombies waiting on the other side of it. The start of the scene where Rhodes is shot, falls to the ground, and begins to crawl along the wall, was a painful moment for Joe Pilato. "When Bub is chasing me down the hallway, if you watch, he shoots me in the leg and I'm kind of sliding along the wall and I fall down and I'm crawling military style," says Pilato. "I really whacked my head against the concrete wall, I mean really whacked it hard. I almost busted the shot."

Also included in this sequence was Pilato opening the door at the end of the hallway and being engulfed by zombies. Sixteen zombie extras were scheduled for this shot; nine "special" or "appliance" zombies and seven "intermediates".

One of those appliance extras was Mike Deak, a close friend of John Vulich's from Fresno, California. Deak and Vulich used to make Super 8 movies together and, while hanging out one night, the two had quite an interesting and prophetic conversation. "Vulich and I were talking one night and he says, 'George Romero ever makes another zombie movie, I want to work on it,'" remembers Deak. "And I said, 'Well John, if you would end up working on that zombie movie I'd sure as hell want to be a zombie in it,' and that was, like, years before *Day of the Dead*."

Flash forward a couple of years, and Vulich was hired by Savini to work on *Friday the 13th: The Final Chapter*. A requirement of him being hired was that he had to be local to Los Angeles. Deak was living in

Above: George Romero directs Tim DiLeo and Lori Cardille in downtown Fort Myers. **Below:** Tom Savini and crew work to set up the Dr. Tongue puppet. (Photos courtesy of Barbara Boyle.)

Los Angeles at that time, and allowed Vulich to crash at his place so that he could work on the film. A year later, when Vulich was hired by Savini to work on *Day of the Dead*, he called Deak and offered to repay him the favor. Vulich told Deak that if he could make his way to Pittsburgh he could crash with him in his hotel room, and they would do their best to get him hired on the film in some capacity. Deak visited family in New Jersey for the Thanksgiving holiday and then made his way to Pittsburgh, arriving in Wampum the day of Richard Liberty's death scene. "The day I arrived on set they were machine-gunning Richard Liberty, Dr. Frankenstein," says Deak. "Literally the minute I walked on set everybody was, like, 'Okay, fire in the hole,' and then they just had all the squibs blown off on him. I went, 'This is nice, I'm glad I'm here.'"

While hanging out with the effects guys, Deak was offered the opportunity to be a zombie, which he of course jumped at, even at the expense of being offered a paid job on the production! "I remember we started shooting that scene . . . 'cause it was over the course of a couple of days and we established myself as a zombie," recalls Deak. "That's when the production said to me, 'Listen, we have a job for you where we can actually pay you' – because I was kind of living on good graces at this point – 'We'll hire you to drive one of the trucks down to Florida for the Fort Myers shoot.' And I went. 'Well, that's great!' and they said, 'Well, you have to leave . . .' whatever day it was, and I said, 'Well crap, I can't now because I've been established as a zombie in this scene, for the Joe Pilato scene,' so I missed the opportunity for that job, so they had to give it to somebody else. So I opted to be in the film as opposed to take the paying job to get down to Florida." Deak is referring to the fact that, while the shot of Pilato being engulfed by zombies was shot on this day, the actual ripping in half of Rhodes wasn't shot until over a week later, by which point part of the production was already leaving for Fort Myers. In the end it would all work out for Deak, who still managed to find his way down to Florida.

In the scene, Rhodes makes it to the door that he thinks will be his escape route, only to find a horde of zombies waiting on the other side. To make sure that he could easily spot himself onscreen, Deak did something similar to what zombie extra William Laczko did during the elevator scene at the Manor Nike Site. "I remember when we were getting ready to shoot that thing everybody, all the zombies that were there, all those guys that were behind the door, were all facing forward, like, ready for Joe to open the door so that they could just like come out," says Deak. "I said, 'You know what? I'm gonna do one thing different.' I turned, like, sideways so that when the door busted open I could actually, since I was the tallest one back there, because I'm 6' 6", I could actually turn and then face the door and I'd be the only one, so I could pick myself out of the crowd."

The final scene scheduled for this day was scene A101, where Bub salutes Rhodes after shooting him one last time.

Thursday 11/29/1984 – Day 32

"It's okay, I just fell off my lifts." – Joe Pilato

Day 32 kicked off with Richard Liberty recording his wild track for scene 66, in which Sarah and McDermott listen to Logan's bizarre ramblings on

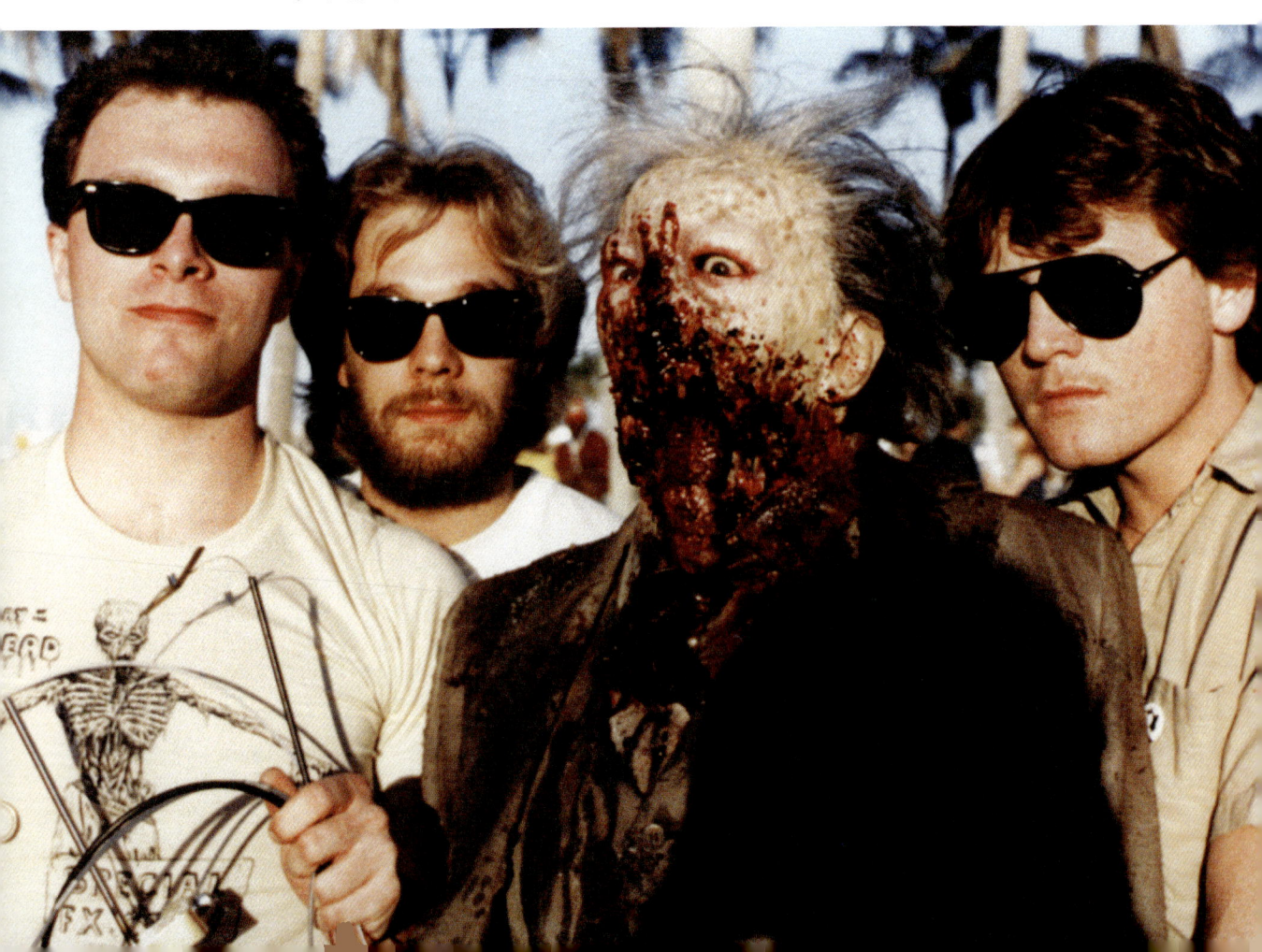

Below: Dave Kindlon, Greg Nicotero, and Everett Burrell with the incredible Dr. Tongue puppet. (Courtesy of Greg Nicotero.)

Above: George Romero flanked by Taso Stavrakis and Greg Nicotero on Sanibel Island. (Courtesy of Taso Stavrakis.)

the tape recorder in his lab. From there, work would continue with scene 33, where Sarah and Fisher walk down the hallway and Fisher laments that Cooper "was a sweetheart next to Rhodes".

Following completion of scene 33, filming of scene 36 took place, where John talks with Sarah in the hallway, after Rhodes has threatened to kill her in the dining hall, and warns her and Fisher that their lives could be expendable in Rhodes' eyes.

Following scenes 33 and 36, a brief re-shoot was done for scene 32, the first appearance of Rhodes in the film, which was an insert shot of Rhodes. Scene 79 was finally completed on this day as well, where Bub frees himself from his chain.

Also scheduled later in the day were re-shoots of scenes 29 and 30, where Steel and Rickles chain the "Beef Treats" zombie and female captive zombie to the wall. "It became a bigger part than I really thought," says Debra Gordon. "Because they kept featuring me in these parts where I was tied up in chains, and they were filming close-ups of us reacting as humans, as real emotional people."

Working on this film and having to endure the unpleasantness of being in the mine – which was dirty, cold, damp, and filled with bats – was trying for some people. But what made the effort worthwhile for the cast and crew was the fact that they were doing it for George Romero. With one big exception, each and every person I spoke with had nothing but high praise for Romero and the atmosphere he fostered on set.

"I didn't know a whole lot about the plot or whatever of the movie, but I knew it was zombies and it was George so that's all that mattered to me," says Nick Tallo. "For me personally, I never felt like I worked for George. I always felt like I worked with George. And I think a lot of people sort of had that attitude too. If it had been any other director, he just would have been some jag-off, but because it was George people were willing to go the extra mile and work hard. We put up with a lot of weirdness, but nobody really complained about it."

"What I remember is there was always respect for George Romero. *Always*," says Jan Pascale. "He was such a nice person and a supportive person. I think there always was, 'We're gonna do the best we can do for George' – I feel like that really permeated everything, that's what drove us all."

"George Romero – a gentle giant, I call him. For a man who created those films he was absolutely opposite of the person that you'd think would create those films, I believe," says Kevin Ritter. "He thanked his crew every day at the end of the day for their work for the day. I've done a lot of pictures and projects since then and I have to tell you, that is a rare quality, it doesn't sound like a lot, but it is a lot. In retrospect it might mean even more today than it did then."

"For weeks I was just there kind of like hanging out and, you know, no one said anything," says Mike Deak. "And one day I was walking through the mine and I ran into George Romero, who was just walking there. I reintroduced myself, I said, 'George, I'm Mike Deak. I appreciate the fact that no one's thrown me off the set,' and he says, 'Oh no Mike, I know who you are and I thank you very much for helping.' I thought that was the coolest thing in the world, that he actually acknowledged that I was there and doing that. So, it was a really good thing."

"It says something about George and the way he made his movies, I think, that we all felt like a family," says Joanne Small. "It comes from the top and we wouldn't have felt that way if it hadn't been for George."

"You can't do better than George. He's just the sweetest guy and he's very talented and he knows what he wants," says Ed Lammi. "And he's very funny to work with."

"He's absolutely, the sweetest, most considerate man I've ever met. He's just a great human being and I really enjoy him, he takes time for friends," says Alvin Rogal. "I know my wife hated horror films, and George went to the trouble of lecturing her about how this was just a comic book, it shouldn't be taken too seriously from a standpoint of real horror."

"George Romero was such a nice man and he seemed to set the tone for the whole movie," says stand-in Theresa Bedekovich. "Everyone was friendly, everybody was happy – nobody held grudges about going home late or coming in early."

"It was very easy to work with him. He just says what he wants. He's very low-key, which is nice," says Jarlath Conroy. "He's very easy to work with . . . he has a good instinct for actors. He just would tell you what he wanted and when you hit it he'd go on."

"The best thing about the shoot is that I had just an extraordinary kinship with George," says Terry Alexander. "As far as [him] enjoying the character come to life and watching him enjoying that."

"Everybody knows George Romero," says Gary Klahr. "I was very familiar with George and his work and I thought, what a great opportunity."

"I think one of my fondest memories is waking up at 5:30am, getting ready to go down and have breakfast, and knowing my teamster was coming to pick me up and lighting up a cigarette looking out the window on this chilly, frosty, freezing Pittsburgh winter day," recalls Joe Pilato. "And I see this huge guy in the parking lot scraping frost off his windshield and it was fucking George! I was going, 'Jesus fucking Christ!' I mean, if anybody needs a teamster and should have the opportunity to sleep in late it should certainly be the director, but here was George up early and scraping off his own car and driving to the set."

As mentioned, there was one exception among the cast and crew members eager to heap praise on Romero: co-producer David Ball. "You'll go into this horrible limestone mine every day, you never go anywhere else, you go to the same place for four months. And you wait for George Romero to like it," says Ball. "The fact that Gornick might have liked it – if George didn't – then we wouldn't shoot. And there were times when we wouldn't shoot, and there were times when the heads of departments would have used the old expletive under their breath. You were dealing with an ego and the ego was George Romero; simple as that. It's as simple as that. I speak with conviction on it because, for me, it's as though it were yesterday, and because I come across this [kind of] ego as part of my routine in my daily life now. I worked with directors; I've worked with some wonderful directors. But George Romero hates producers. You ask him, 'Do you like producers, George?' You know what answer you're going to get, don't you? You don't need me to tell you, you know what you're going to get. 'I fucking hate producers. They're all assholes and wankers.'"

Dolly Grip, Richard Sieg, remembers Romero as being the type of guy who would get in line behind you at lunch, but it was for more self-serving reasons. "It was like, 'Well, you need to do some paperwork or talk to the producer,'" says Sieg, meaning perhaps Romero should take priority in line. "George would say, 'I know, that's why I'm waiting in line.'" [laughs]

Friday 11/30/1984 – Day 33

"I give good memo." – J.H.

Day 33 concentrated on scenes D97, listed as G97 on the call sheet, and B100 – the death of Steel. "When you work with George [Romero], he's a wonderful director. He's an actor's director; he gives you freedom to explore your character. He's not high bound to certain things," says Gary Klahr. "I believe an actor's job is always to serve the writing; it should be about the writing. But if you want to try something, George would say, 'Let's do it. Show me what you mean.' If he liked it, you know . . . like my death scene, which was not really written that way initially."

Indeed, Steel's death in the shooting script briefly mentions him being bitten on the neck, and then Romero moves onto describing the gore montage. Klahr decided that his character would approach his death in a very particular way. "I said, 'George,

Top: George Romero directing Tim DiLeo. (Courtesy of Michael Gornick.) **Middle:** George Romero lying down on the false elevator platform, instructing Tim DiLeo. **Bottom:** George Romero on Sanibel Island, directing zombie extras for their entrance into the fenced compound. (Photos courtesy of Dave Kindlon.)

nobody hates zombies more than Steel. You see it, you hear it. I can't die meekly.' I wanted him in a way to be redeemable. So he saves the last bullet . . . once Steel gets bit in the neck; he's taken out as many zombies as he can, but once Steel gets bit in the neck he knows that what? He's gonna become what he hates most! Unless you do what?" says Klahr. "I talked it through with George and he loved it. But nobody gets the subtleness of, okay, I put the gun in my mouth, I blow my own brains out and therefore I cannot become what I hate the most. But I cross myself; I make the sign of the cross with the gun, so I made him a Catholic. Now here's the dilemma – in the Catholic Church suicide is a mortal sin." Klahr continues: "I figured, okay Steel made peace within himself, with his God, by saying, 'I'm taking myself out because I do not want to become what I hate the most, and I will trust that my creator will understand that what I am doing is my redemption.'"

The continuity zombie that bites Klahr's character, Steel, causing him to kill himself, was played by William Laczko. In a funny little twist of fate Laczko,

Above: Michael Gornick and Tom Savini confer on the best way to shoot Tim DiLeo's death scene as George Romero looks on. (Courtesy of Taso Stavrakis.)

who had auditioned for one of the soldiers, ended up playing the zombie that helps bring about the downfall of the soldier he'd originally auditioned to portray. "So, as he goes to shoot Bub and says the line, 'You want to learn how to shoot, you pus brain bag of shit?', blah, blah, blah, he points the gun and goes to pull the trigger," says Laczko. "I come from behind him, I bite him on the neck, rip out his jugular vein, he throws me down, blows my head off, and then eventually commits suicide. Well, the irony to the whole thing is the part of Steel is the part I auditioned for. So I got to kill the bastard that got my part."

Filming the scene was interesting for Laczko, as he had to attack someone considerably larger than himself. "We did that scene with me and Gary more than once, maybe three or four times. And by the end of it we were covered with red food dye," remembers Laczko. "I'm not a big guy, but I'm not a small guy – I go about six foot and, at that time, about 180 pounds. And all I can remember is [that] jumping on Gary was like climbing up the side of a mountain. He was a big man!"

In the scene, Laczko is thrown to the ground and Klahr shoots him in the head. For a brief time, the effects crew flirted with the idea of using a "synthetic" part of Laczko to enhance his onscreen death. "I wear a hair piece," admits Laczko. "I forget what they were doing one time, and the subject came up about the hair piece and Tom Savini was talking about maybe blowing it off my head. I said, 'I got no problem with that,' you know, 'cause I figured the more exposure the better." [*laughs*]

Besides featured extra William Laczko, 24 other zombie extras were scheduled for this day. One of those was continuity zombie and associate producer, Ed Lammi, who played the zombie with his arm in a sling. Lammi was amazed at the turnout by fans who were so excited to be a zombie extra for George Romero. "It was just amazing, the fan base," says Lammi. "We literally had college kids from four states away that would drive all night long to come and be a zombie in George Romero's *Day of the Dead*. It was fascinating."

Jeff Monahan, who years later went on to appear in Romero's *The Dark Half* and *Bruiser*, was an extra on this day. Monahan portrayed the "Broccoli Man" zombie, nicknamed by Christine Romero, due to his incredibly gross make-up by Howard Berger. In the scene, Monahan suddenly appears out of a doorway and grabs Gary Klahr's hat off of his head. Interestingly enough, Monahan was shoved out of the doorway by George Romero himself. Seconds later he is shot in the head by Klahr. Preparing for his demise, Monahan was the victim of a playful joke by Berger and crew. "One thing I remember is that Howard was doing my make-up, and there was someone assisting him and he put an explosive device on my forehead to blow out," recalls Monahan. "They attach a condom to the back of your head that's filled with blood that explodes for the exit wound and it was an appliance on my face. And after the appliance was on and glued down and they were applying the make-up, they started having a conversation about if the explosive was pointed in the right direction. They weren't sure because it could have been the wrong way. And I'm lying there pretty worried after awhile until I realized they were only kidding." [*laughs*]

Even though it was a tiny part, seen only briefly, it inspired Monahan to pursue his dream of being involved in movies. "It was a great experience in terms of me at the time just being a huge fan. I've always been a big fan of horror films, grew up and watched *Chiller Theatre* every Saturday night in Pittsburgh. So it was a great experience doing that," says Monahan. "But it also – when you're seeing it done for real it gives you hope and faith that you can be a part of it and do those sort of things yourself."

Besides Monahan and Laczko suffering gun shots to the head, extras Matt Bartlett, Sally Hart, and Nancy Ross would also have explosive squibs attached to their heads. With all of these squibs exploding

Above: The crew sets up Tim DiLeo's death scene on the elevator platform. (Courtesy of Michael Gornick.)

blood everywhere, in fairly tight quarters, a small, but significant problem would arise for the boom operator, Stuart Deutsch. "Probably trying to keep the fake blood out of the microphones," recalls Deutsch. "I one time didn't have a windscreen on one of my Schoeps microphones, and it got splattered with blood when someone's head got drilled in the laboratory. I remember that, but from then on I remembered to make sure to put something on the mics so that the elements didn't get covered with blood."

Kevin Rolly, by now a veteran zombie extra on the film, was also on set this day, and ended up getting significant screen time. "The first people get kind of shot and you're trying to get your . . . what you'll see is you'll see a lot of hands going up in the air. When people are going, zombies are going . . . because that's all you're going to get to see. It's like, 'Well, if I can't be seen at least I can get my hand in the shot.' So, that was the first shot," remembers Rolly. "Then came the shot of him . . . he shoots himself. I think they shot that a little bit later, maybe, or they took us away and they shot that. Then they brought us back and it was the big eating scene. And I guess that was my close-up, as it were. Greg [Nicotero] said, 'Hey, I know, put Kevin in front of the camera,' and they handed me this arm with a wristwatch on it. George [Romero] gave me the direction to eat up the arm then bite the wristwatch and have this sort of 'Yuk' look. I'm not quite sure if that played or not. But what they really liked was, I grabbed the end of the arm and just started pulling it, just stretching the skin out, the rubber skin. And everyone thought that was awesome. I remember someone taking pictures of it and that shot ended up in [the book] *The Zombies That Ate Pittsburgh*."

Rolly's friend, Steve Godlewski, can also be seen in this scene viciously chewing on one of Steel's severed legs. The night before filming, Godlewski had been to an all-night party and was extremely hungover the next morning – so hungover, in fact, that during the trip to Wampum he vomited in the car! Upon arriving, and with no time to clean the mess up, they simply left the car in that condition. At the end of the day's filming, they were offered a choice by the make-up crew regarding their prosthetic make-up. "It's like, 'Well look, we can take your make-up off or you can wear it home and you can take it off using these materials,'" remembers Rolly. "We're, like, 'Hell, you know, look we got a zombie make-up. Hell, we're gonna trot this pony out.' So, basically Steve and I got back in a vomit-smelling car and drove through just about every drive-thru that we could find watching people recoil in horror."

Long-time colleague and friend of George Romero, Vince Survinski takes a break from filming on Sanibel Island. Survinski, who played a continuity zombie in *Day*, was one of the original investors in the classic that started it all, *Night of the Living Dead*, back in the late 1960s. (Courtesy of Taso Stavrakis.)

The "big eating scene" mentioned by Rolly was indeed partially shot this evening, concentrating only on the remains of Steel. Listed on the daily call sheet under props/special instructions was the word "guts". And guts, edible ones, were certainly used on this night. The job of making sure there were plenty of delicious and tasty entrails for the extras to dine on fell on the shoulders of Jan Pascale. "I sort of inherited the job of what John Harrison used to call 'eatage' – the food that the zombies would actually chew on," remembers Pascale. "I'm thinking, okay how are we gonna do this? So we came up with – I don't remember whoever came up with this idea – but I remember going down to this local little butcher shop and looking around going, what looks right? And so we came up with turkey legs. And I remember coming in with turkey legs and showing it to Bruce [Miller], and Cletus [Anderson], and Kevin [Ritter], and Marty [Garrigan], and going, you know, if we hammer the elbows maybe it would look jagged, like they ripped it off. So, it was determined that we would use turkey legs, and then I had them make up special sausages for us that were, you know, they were like six-feet long with no pinching in between, so it was just one long thing, so that would look like the intestines. And then liver was good, too, because that looked kinda like our liver."

The turkey legs were shoved into the prosthetic severed legs to make it look like the bone had been ripped away. Pascale created a special edible blood formula as well, made up of ketchup, barbeque sauce, and food coloring.

"It was interesting how involved the art department was with crossing over with our department," says Greg Nicotero. "I think maybe it was because – past history with Tom [Savini] – they knew that they needed to pick up the slack and let Tom concentrate on the hero stuff. But it was just funny, like, 'Oh yeah, we got edible guts.' 'Oh, okay. Great!'"

On many occasions during the shoot, Tom Savini was the victim of some good-natured ribbing, sometimes on video. This night, for example, Nick Mastandrea and Mike Gornick would showcase how they could pull off squib effects for shooting a zombie in the head – with a pair of cigarette lighters. "We would do those little sort of gag effects that were, like, really stupid, and video them just to make fun of Tom," says Mastandrea.

"Nick and I loved to rile up Tom," remembers Gornick. "He was the maestro in special effects, but we tried to bring him back to earth all the time, you know, and prove to him that we could do effects also."

"You know, back then Tom was making 'bank', he was making a lot of money back in the eighties. I think he was making $1,000 a day kind of thing – back in the eighties that was a fucking fortune," says Everett Burrell. "So yeah, he was getting picked on because he was making a ton of fucking money. And if he didn't perform a first take he was the first guy to get 'shit'."

Saturday 12/1/1984 – Day 34

"Can zombies and humans mate?" – Felice Lammi
"I don't know, but we can try." – Ed Lammi

Day 34 of production was press day, as members of various media outlets would be on hand to cover filming for the day . . . as zombies! Scenes E97 and F97 featured these hordes of zombies swarming through the cave complex.

The person responsible for arranging this massive media invasion was Barbara Pflughaupt, who worked for the public relations agency England & Company, owned by Elise England, who was married to Salah Hassanein at the time. "I brought about seventeen journalists to Beaver Falls to be made up as zombies to participate in the film so that they could then write articles and do television pieces," says Pflughaupt. "We had Cynthia Kayan from *Entertainment Tonight*

Right: Miguel (Tim DiLeo) is devoured by zombies on the elevator platform. (Courtesy of Taso Stavrakis.)

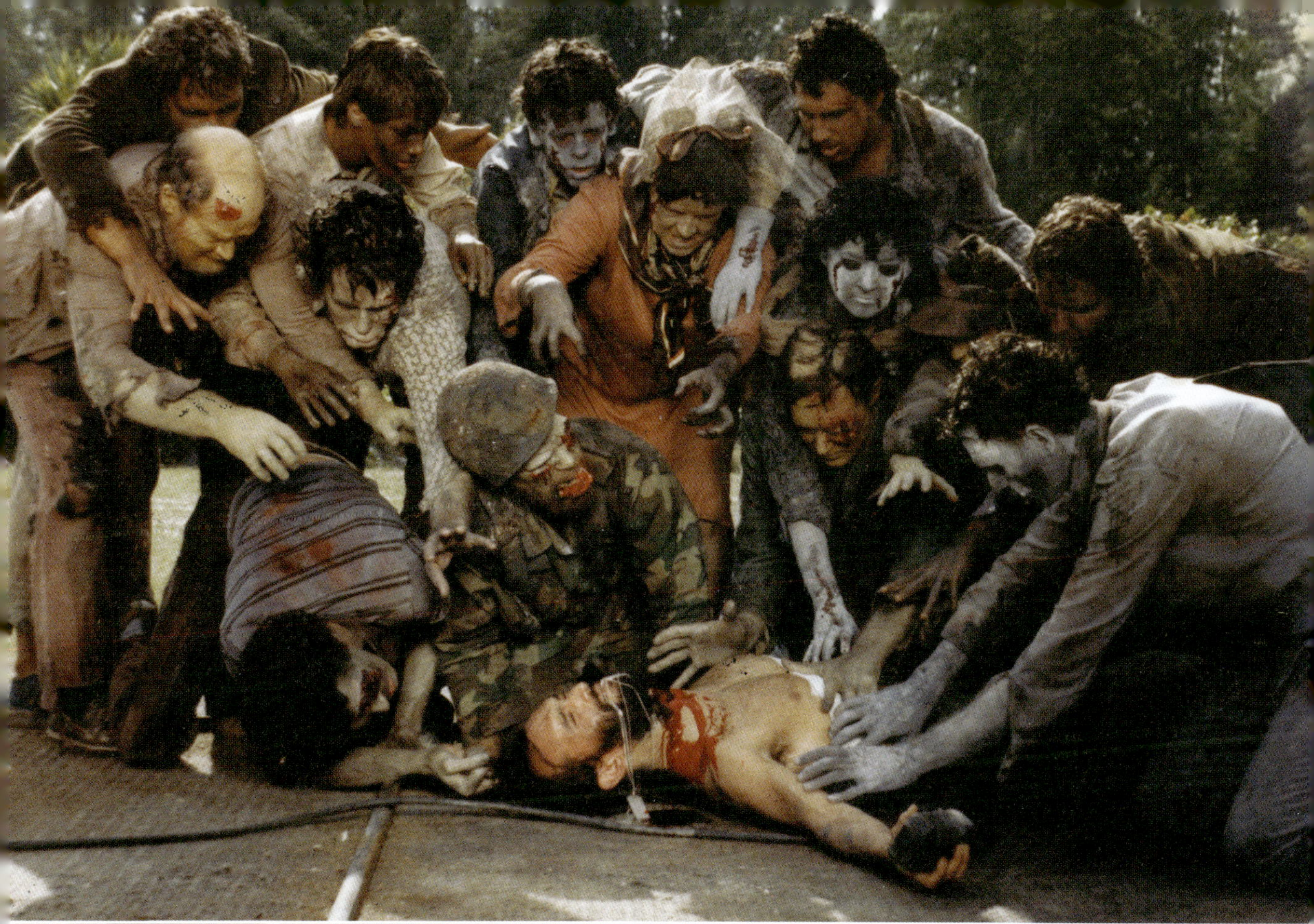

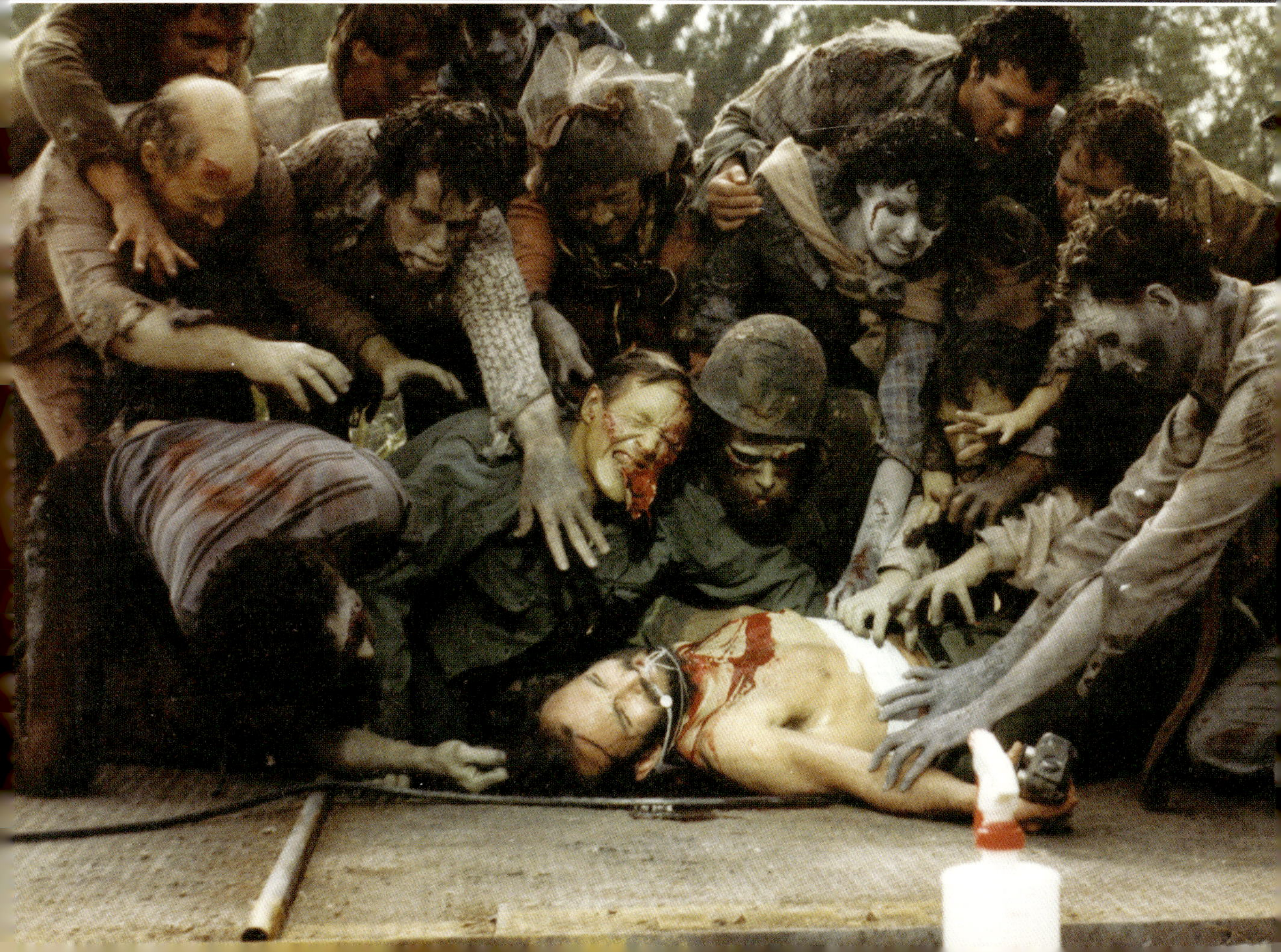

and Michael Musto from the *Village Voice*. There were a number of people, wonderful people, that were zombies that year and then they did stories about it so that it coincided with the release of the film."

Pflughaupt's job was all-encompassing and kept her busy every second that weekend. "I had to work with the location director and the film set itself to arrange everything I needed to do there: airline tickets, meet them at the airport, get them to the set, arrange hotel rooms, make sure we were feeding everybody, and making sure that I was with them throughout the filming process so that nobody was just wondering around," laughs Pflughaupt. "I had to make sure that I was arranging time between set-ups for George [Romero] to speak with them and do interviews, for the actors too; in addition to arranging with costume and make-up to get them where they needed to be at the right time to be made up and to be used in the film – and to get them home safely. And then it was mostly follow-up to make sure they were getting everything they needed from us to create the stories that would then help sell the film."

One of the press members that Pflughaupt mentioned was Michael Musto, whose article would end up in *Us* magazine. Musto, openly homosexual, attempted to bring a new and unique take to being a zombie. "George Romero told us not to be the stereotypical zombies – don't do the arms outstretched, bulging eyes kind of thing," remembers Musto. "I overdid it and went in the other direction, flailing my arms up in the air, like I was Diana Ross or something. He singled me out as having done too much and I went right back to doing the stereotypical zombie thing."

Also on hand this day was Robert "Uncle Bob" Martin, co-editor of *Fangoria* magazine. Martin and *Fangoria* had a long history with George Romero, having covered his films and acted as a booster of his work over the years. "I always had a warm spot in my heart for George," says Martin. "So whenever anything George-oriented came along, I would wanna deal with it myself."

For Martin, being on the set of the third Romero zombie film, and being able to get in front of the camera as a zombie extra, wasn't the standout memory in his mind. What he remembers most is of a much more personal nature, and involved one of his fellow journalists. "I feel badly about it now, but I'll tell you. Maybe it will count brownie points for me in that I freely talk about it and I admit my shame over it," says Martin. "But Michael Musto was one of the people there, also in make-up, and a make-up freshener came around and was hitting people with a brush to freshen their make-up, and he freshened Michael Musto's lips, then came straight over to me and offered me a freshen and I said, 'No, thank you.' So it

Top: One of the film's alligator wranglers, Bill Love, being made up by Tom Savini for the scene where he comes out of the bank with the gator on its steps. **Middle:** Bank zombie Bill Love being tended to by make-up assistant, Mike Deak, in downtown Fort Myers. **Bottom:** Bill Love and his fellow extra, dressed as prisoner zombies, exit the First National Bank in downtown Fort Myers. (Photos courtesy of Bill and Kathy Love.)

didn't happen, but I just felt very weird at that moment and I basically had to confront my own attitudes at that point, because I didn't think that was the type of thing I would react to. But Michael being so out, so completely out and gay, and in those days AIDS hysteria being at a peak – I didn't think I was subject to it, but there I was subject to it. So it taught me something about myself and it's the most memorable moment of that day for me really, me confronting that aspect of myself."

Another journalist on set this day was Paul Gagne of *Cinefantastique* magazine. Gagne would go on to write arguably the best book ever published about George Romero's work, *The Zombies That Ate Pittsburgh*. In a 2008 interview I conducted with Gagne for the website homepageofthedead.com, he briefly spoke about the experience of being a zombie extra on the film. "For anyone who loves George's movies, it's a dream come true to be a zombie extra!" said Gagne. "I was very impressed with how well-organized it was, going through a wardrobe area first to find clothing, then getting the basic make-up done – blackened hair gel, etcetera. As a member of the horror fanzine press, I was lucky enough to be an 'appliance' zombie, spending several hours in a make-up chair having latex glued to my face by Everett Burrell, who was one of the make-up artists on Tom Savini's crew. I still have the photos!"

Writer Mark Steensland was also on set, and remembers the specific orders he received from his editor. "My editor Jim Steranko, I was writing for *Prevue* magazine at the time, he said, 'Listen, don't try to talk to Savini. Don't try to talk to George [Romero] while you're there. We can make those arrangements later.' He said, 'What I want you to do is, I want you to get all of the lower guys on the make-up crew. I want you to invite them to your room at night and talk to them because they're going to give you the real stories,'" says Steensland. "I said, 'Guys, I'm the reporter from *Prevue*. You guys want to talk to me about this article I'm working on?' Well, of course, being as young as I was at the time, they were all excited about talking to a reporter because they saw everybody else was trying to talk to Tom and all that. Well, when Uncle Bob and Don Farmer got wind that this is what I was doing, they said, 'Could we come too?'" [*laughs*]

Some of the other media reporters present included the aforementioned Donald Farmer from *Fantastic Films*, Diana Maychick from the *New York Post*, and freelance writer Alan Petrucelli.

Another zombie on set this day, who was not just another ordinary extra, was Terry Powers of United Film Distribution Company. "My title was associate director of national advertising," says Powers. "So, I worked for the head of advertising, and I was there [at UFDC] with Richard [Hassanein] and Salah [Hassanein] in setting the advertising campaign for the US." Powers would get the "intermediate" zombie treatment, along with a couple of small wounds. "I was in the movie for a quick nano second. I'd probably have to super slow-mo the DVD to see myself today," says Powers. "I do remember flying back to New York and still having eye make-up that was just incredibly difficult to get off."

Probably the most exciting thing for Powers was that Terry Adams, Tom Ardolino, Al Anderson, Joey Spampinato, Donn Adams, and Keith Spring – also known as NRBQ and the Whole Wheat Horns – were also on set as zombies. The well-known rock band had driven all night from a gig in Massachusetts to Wampum to be extras in the film.

Judith Conte was a zombie extra on this day, too, and stood out as quite an unusual one. Conte was a member of the faculty for the school of drama at Carnegie Mellon University, teaching dance, and was friends with Cletus and Barbara Anderson when she got the opportunity to be an extra for George Romero. "Barbara [Anderson] said to me, 'George is needing people to be zombies. You need to be a zombie!'" says Conte. "And I would go, 'Oh, I don't know if I have the time.' 'Yes, you have the time!' and I said, 'Well, do you think George would let me be a ballerina zombie?' and she said, 'I bet he will. We'll ask him.' And he was absolutely fine and thrilled."

The make-up effects crew loved creating the look of the zombies, and genuinely considers the work to hold up very well. But, looking back, they concede that perhaps they could have been much more. "The zombies to me look kind of silly. I wish we'd used more contact lenses," says Everett Burrell. "I just think the designs were all over the place. I think Tom [Savini] didn't really trust his instincts on *Day* and just stuff's kind of all over the place."

"The zombies – we were all kind of disappointed," says Mike Trcic. "We wanted to use a lot of scleral lenses but there just wasn't the budget for it. That really could have enhanced the zombies. I don't know, I guess we were kind of thinking of Rick Baker's *Thriller* at the time and we were going for a *Thriller* look. So, that was playing pretty loudly in our minds – you know, how are these going to compare to Rick's zombies?"

With the background zombie masks now being used sparingly on the really big zombie days – like this one, for example – the make-up guys worked in tandem with the wardrobe department to process the long assembly line of zombie extras. "The funny thing that a lot of people don't realize is that Cletus and Barbara Anderson had all these students at CMU," says Greg Nicotero. "So when it came time to do the hero zombies and then the background zombies, we did all the hero zombies, and then a bunch of CMU students helped do all the background zombies.

So, all the blue-faced people with oatmeal, those weren't done by us, those were done by Barbara and her people."

One of the biggest tools used in this process was Streaks 'N Tips, a temporary color highlight spray for hair, which was sprayed all over the skin and costumes of the zombie extras. "Every time I smell Streaks 'N Tips that's all I can think about, *Day of the Dead*. Every time," says Nicotero. "It's really weird."

"You'd walk onto the set or into the mine, and they used cases of that stuff a day and the air just permanently smelled liked Streaks 'N Tips," says Barry Kessler. "I think I still smell it."

"I'll never forget the smell of Streaks 'N Tips, to make them distressed," says wardrobe assistant, Karin Wagner. "We'd spray Streaks 'N Tips on their costumes to get them more distressed." For Wagner, working on the film was a bit of a "family affair". Her sister, Holly, worked with Felice Lammi in extras casting to bring in the hordes of zombies for filming. Karin Wagner's duties in wardrobe were mainly to handle the throngs of zombie extras who constantly came in. "I think everything was on racks and then they would come and we would get their clothes, sort of like a coat check system," remembers Wagner. "And they would come in and we would hand them zombie outfits, then they would gather it all back up."

One unexpected problem for the wardrobe and costume department was the size of some of the extras being brought in. "It seemed that some really fat people kept volunteering," says Barbara Anderson. "And we kept telling the people who were acquiring the zombies, 'C'mon, we can't costume that many great big guys!'" [*laughs*]

Day of the Dead was also a "family affair" for Anderson. As well as her husband Cletus, who was, of course, the production designer, their daughter Cathy worked as a wardrobe assistant on the film.

You could also never predict who you might see as a zombie extra on set. "We had big, big zombie days, where one day the dean of the fine arts college of Carnegie Mellon wanted to be a zombie," says John Harrison. "And I hadn't known this because that was all part of the casting; the big group things were taken care of by other people. But he was the dean when I was there, [*laughs*] at Carnegie Mellon. And I'm walking out and here's this guy that was essentially my boss at the university when I was taking my masters degree! Akram Midani, he comes out and he's in zombie make-up – him and his wife!"

"It was really funny, the people who wanted to come in and be a zombie for that movie was interesting," says Dave Kindlon. "In fact, at one point Cyndi Lauper was trying to come down and be a zombie, and at the last minute something happened with her schedule and she couldn't."

"I had no idea about the fans. I mean, the fans are amazing. That was one thing that impressed me," says Felice Lammi. "People are so dedicated to George's [Romero] movies. I mean, I had people coming from all over the country to be in this and they were not getting paid. [*laughs*] They traveled and they put up with a lot of – I don't want to say hardships – but long, long days sitting around wearing uncomfortable make-up. They just really wanted to be there."

This was also a theme day for a couple of different factions of the crew. Usually the theme days belonged exclusively to Nick Mastandrea and his grip and electrician crew, such as "old man day", when they would spray their hair and beards grey, or "skirt day", when all of the guys would wear skirts on set all day. "Of course, there was always one – Nick Tallo, Bomba – who never wore underwear when he wore a skirt and always climbed a ladder to fix a bulb," remembers Barry Kessler.

"The grip crew was always a source of high amusement," laughs John Harrison.

Today's theme would be "suit day" for the grips and electricians. "We all went out to the Goodwill store and bought suits," says Nick Tallo. "You know, buy a suit for seven bucks, you wear it to work and then you throw it away."

But it wasn't just the grips who dressed up on this day. Cletus Anderson's art department participated in their own version of theme day when they all showed up dressed like him! "He always looked so elegant, no matter what he was doing, even if he was painting, he always looked elegant," says Jan Pascale. "He would often wear his sweater tied over his shoulder, draped over his shoulder and tied in the front. I think one day we all showed up on that set . . . all dressed like Cletus, we all wore khakis and shirts."

The other parts of scene E97, involving Steel's attempts to escape, were also shot on this day. The shot of Steel blasting the door with his machine gun and then escaping through the doorway was filmed.

Scenes A92, B92, and C92 – of Rhodes fleeing on the golf cart and hitting the zombie, played by Taso Stavrakis, then opening the complex door and locking it behind him – were also shot on this day. Another shot involving Joe Pilato, on which work originally began on Tuesday November 27, was picked up on this day. It was for scene 95, where Rhodes is shot in the shoulder by Bub as he's trying to round the corner.

Monday 12/3/1984 – Day 35

"Fuck the quote of the day." – Kato

Day number 35 began with work on scene 21, where Sarah, John, McDermott, and Miguel return to the underground facility after exploring the abandoned city and are greeted by Steel and Rickles, who inform the group that Miguel needs to accompany them to capture two more specimens – or "dumb fucks", as they are referred to in the script.

Also shot on this day was scene 90, where Rhodes frantically jumps in the golf cart and flees after the zombies descend on the giant elevator platform, leaving behind Steel, Rickles, and Torrez to fend for themselves.

The last scene scheduled for the day was another pick-up shot of Rhodes for scene 32 in the dining hall.

As this day's quote of the day suggests, the word "fuck" makes its presence known often in the film, being used well over 50 times in the screenplay in one form or another. "If you took the F word out of that movie it would be about ten minutes long," says Mike Trcic. "Uh, geez, they really could have used some more creative dialogue in this movie. It was probably my major criticism of it."

The liberal use of profanity in Romero's shooting script caused some concern for UFDC head Salah Hassanein, and rather late in the game. "Hassanein said to me . . . he phoned me up in the limestone mine and he said, 'You know, David, somebody told me there are 108 expletives in this script. How can we remove some of them?'" remembers David Ball. "And I said to him, 'Salah, we're in week seven of shooting and we've already filmed 107 of the 108. You told me you're making a movie. You told me you were funding it. You told me to get on a plane. And now you're telling me you don't like the bad language in this movie? It's too late. You can't do anything about that now, my lovely boy.'"

David Ball's role in the production was always a little mysterious to many of the cast and crew. "David was brought in, I believe, as part of the financing plan. Which is not to say like someone who comes in on a completion bond-type situation, but sort of in that range, was my recollection," says Ed Lammi. "And beyond that, I really couldn't . . . whatever the back-story as to how that actually came about, I really wasn't privileged to know the rest of it, but that was the sense that we sort of had in the production office."

"I do remember that there was a lot of insinuation that he was sort of like – he's the corporate spy, that he was there to sort of keep his eye on everybody and make sure we didn't go over budget," recalls Greg Nicotero of Ball. "I really liked David because I thought David was a straight shooter. But I do remember that there was a little bit of, like, 'Oh, well David Ball's here,' like he's the 'suit'. And you know George is kind of a hippie guy to begin with, so you get the authority guy in there and all of a sudden George is like, 'Uuhh.'"

"He worked for the entity that made the film," says Salah Hassanein. "He made sure the production was stable in budget."

Top: Assistant director, John Harrison (in the leather jacket), confers with alligator wrangler, Tom Crutchfield, about the upcoming shot on the bank steps. **Bottom:** Second unit cameraman, Ernest Dickerson (in the camouflage pants), outside the First National Bank. Dickerson has gone on to a very successful career as a director in film and television, including his role as one of the top directors on AMC's hit show *The Walking Dead*. (Photos courtesy of Bill and Kathy Love.)

"My daily duties were purely to ensure that we made the film's schedule," says Ball. "All I really had to do was to keep the crew sleek, keep the cast happy, and make sure that we adhered to the schedule."

Ball's taskmaster approach to filmmaking could wear thin on some of the crew and, according to Ball, none more so than George Romero. "He'd say, 'I can't do this, man.' I'd say, 'You can't do what, George?' 'I can't do this fucking schedule, man.' And I said, 'Why can't you do it, George?' 'Because I have just too much brain ache, man; there's no value, the

Above: Production designer Cletus Anderson talks with David Garber, of Garber/Green, about the matte shot of the deserted city street. (Courtesy of Mitchell Lipsiner.)

schedule's short, everything's too tight,'" says Ball of Romero. "He came to me and said he couldn't do it. He came to me, I think, lunchtime on Friday or Saturday of week two. And he just stood there and put his hands on his head and said, 'You know, man, I just can't fucking do this,' and I said, 'What are you talking about, George? What are you talking about? You are, as I can see it, a day ahead of schedule.'"

According to Ball, Romero's frustration with him and the tightly adhered to schedule led to some heated discussions between the director and producer at times. "We would have a few words together behind closed doors, because he was insecure and I wasn't," says Ball. And Romero's insecurities had Ball boiling over inside at times. "'I'm here to help you. If I was your enemy, do you think I'd be sitting in this fucking shithole limestone mine with you? Get out of my face! I'm a movie maker. You give me 100 sheets of paper I'll give you ten rolls of celluloid. That's what I do. You're the director, I'm your friend. I'm here to help you. Don't fucking shout at me and don't fucking swear at me, asshole! Or I'll fucking swear back at you, asshole! And you can fuck off George Romero, because you don't mean diddly fucking squat in London, where I live!' You know?" laughs Ball. "I almost felt like saying, 'Well, fuck off and we'll do it without you.'"

According to Ball, however, and surprisingly enough, by the time the production ended things were slightly different from Romero's perspective. "Let me tell you, George and I got on so well at the end of *Day of the Dead*, he said, 'Thank you, man. Thank you for giving me my movie.' And I said, 'George, that's what I get paid to do, man. That's what I do.' I'm very good at what I do because people like George Romero give me experience in handling the next George Romero that comes along."

"I found him very patronizing," says Lori Cardille of Ball. "There was a lot of crap going on behind the scenes." Unfortunately, Cardille would not elaborate any further on what she meant.

Tuesday 12/4/1984 – Day 36

"I jump to conclusions all day . . . That's all the exercise I need." – Howard Kaplan

Day 36 concentrated on scene A97, the death of Torrez. As previously mentioned in chapter 2, the role of Miller and Torrez would be swapped, beginning with scene 60 at the corral. Instead of Torrez dying at the corral, Miller would now be the victim and Torrez would buy it at the end of the film. Originally, the death was described by Romero in the shooting script as the character losing his leg, but instead it would now be his head that was removed!

In the film Torrez, played by Taso Stavrakis, is running over stacks of pallets attempting to escape when he is cornered by a horde of zombies, thrown down on top of one of the pallets, and has his head completely torn off. To achieve the effect, Stavrakis was positioned on a pallet with his head tilted back into a pre-cut hole. A prosthetic head of him, complete with cable controls for facial expressions, was then attached to his shoulders. On cue the zombies would rip into the neck area, tearing at it until the head was totally removed. All the while Stavrakis' real body would kick and flail. It was a fabulous effect, but – much like Barry Gress when he was involved in creating the Major Cooper corpse effect – Stavrakis would have to be incredibly calm and willing to deal with some claustrophobia. "Yeah that took a lot, that took a lot," says Stavrakis. "Of course, I do scuba and I train myself to be pretty calm about it. It wasn't just claustrophobic, but I was upside down. My head was completely cut off, it was dark, and I was upside down. And so, the blood was rushing to my head and it was . . . I knew what was going on, so I just kind of relaxed into it. It took about two hours maybe; maybe more, maybe three? The worst part was that during the effect the blood was running up my nose. All the blood that was shooting out was running down my real neck and down my face and up my nose and into my eyes upside down. But by then I was supposed to be kicking and screaming anyway."

A very young and very green make-up artist, Greg Funk, participated in pulling this grand illusion off. Funk, who'd been on set previously, still had to contain his excitement about being involved. "It was just a wonderful experience and I was star-struck, man. I was like, 'Oh my God, there's Romero! Oh my God, there's Tom. Don't act like an idiot!' You know?" says Funk. "I was in heaven. I was in school at the time, I was in college, but when I realized I was gonna get a few days' work, I mean, it didn't matter. [*laughs*] It's bad, but it didn't matter what I was doing. I didn't care if I had a mid-term, I didn't care what I had to do, or anything going on with school – if they called me for work, that's where I was. That's how important it was to me."

The opportunity to contribute during this scene was a bit nerve-wracking for the young artist. "They actually let me puppeteer part of the head for that," says Funk. "Yeah, so I was a little bit nervous about that. Anything they asked me or wanted me to do I was nervous about, you know? Trying to learn . . . I didn't know anything at that point. [*laughs*] I hardly knew a thing."

Another big fan who didn't know very much about make-up effects was zombie extra, Tim Irr. Growing up in Pittsburgh, Irr was a neighbor of "Chilly Billy" Cardille, and became an enormous fan of George Romero. While attending Duquesne University in Pittsburgh, Irr and his roommate, who was an even bigger fan of Romero, learned about the shoot and volunteered to be extras.

Upon arriving, Irr, his roommate, and the other 150 scheduled extras were handed a bag lunch and a dollar bill. After being put through make-up and wardrobe and sitting around for hours, Irr was picked to be part of a fairly large group of extras, which Savini himself would then whittle down even further. "So they pull about 30 of us over and Savini walks down the row and he says, 'Put your arms out' and everybody puts their arms straight out in front of them, zombie style," says Irr. "And he's walking down and he's picking one out, two out . . . and I stuck my arms out and he picked me!" And what was the reasoning for Savini's choice? Irr was picked as a finalist because he had very long arms, which would be of great help in the scene. "Savini just took about four of us and said, 'Come with me,' and we went with him," says Irr. "I guess he said maybe my arms were the longest, and I just got really lucky. He said, 'You're going to be the first zombie to open up this guy's throat.'" Initially very excited to be chosen, Irr quickly realized that Savini was placing a lot of responsibility on his shoulders. "He said, 'There's only one take and this head is worth $10,000 dollars, so if you blow it then your head's going on there. I'll cut your head off and put it on there,'" recalls Irr. "I started to laugh, but I was like, 'You know what, I've seen what Savini does, I don't know. Maybe he's being serious!' So I thought, 'I've got to get this right!'" Savini quickly gave Irr a lesson on what to do. "He showed me right where to do it. And then he touched the spot on the appliance, on where that needed to be. And he said, 'Use two fingers and poke it and then tear, but when you poke you have to poke hard enough to break the latex,'" says Irr. "He said, 'You have to use your fingers to break that latex,' and it did, it just popped right away and it did exactly as he said it was going to."

Another lucky and fairly memorable zombie extra featured in this sequence was stand-up comedian

Billy Elmer. "I was the cigar-chomping zombie," says Elmer. "I had a cigar with me because I brought it. So I put the cigar in my mouth and I had, like, sort of an old suit coat and stuff. So, I considered myself a dead agent or manager."

Elmer brought the cigar to set in case he got bored and needed something to occupy his time. When the time came to film, Elmer didn't want to walk back to put the cigar back with his belongings, so he ad-libbed by putting it in his mouth. "One of the minions, underlings were going, 'No, no. No cigar,' and I said, 'Well, it's not lit,' and they said, 'No, no,' and then Romero came over at one point and he goes, 'No, no. Keep the cigar. I like that. I like that look. Move him over into the middle now.' So now I went from the way back area, kind of in the middle thing. I thought, 'Well, at least it worked.'

During our talk I asked Elmer if he recalled who was responsible for applying his make-up, a standard question that I asked a lot of the zombie extras I interviewed. "Hey, you know what, do I remember that first chick that I had sex with? I think her name was Tina. Why the fuck would I remember that?" yells Elmer. "Are you really doing a book, or does some chick want to get even with me on a reality show?"

Wednesday 12/5/1984 – Day 37

"Go for the sausage! Go for the sausage!" – Mike Gornick

Day 37 would begin work on scene 62, where Miguel arrives at "The Ritz" after being bitten and has his arm chopped off by Sarah, then the soldiers arrive and have their showdown with John and McDermott. The filming of Miguel's arm being chopped off wouldn't take place until after the crew returned from the Florida part of the shoot and, in fact, Tim DiLeo wasn't scheduled on set for this day at all.

This was the last day of filming for both Gary Klahr and Ralph Marrero, with all of their scheduled scenes having been completed. The following day would be Joe Pilato's last, and it was the stuff that legends are made of.

Thursday 12/6/1984 – Day 38

"Boy, am I glad I'm dead." – Dead zombie extra watching eatage

Day 38 would end up being the entire production's most infamous day of shooting. Scenes B99 and 101 were scheduled – the spectacular death of Captain Rhodes. The corridor by the production wardrobe room was where Joe Pilato stamped his place in the annals of horror film history.

As most fans know, the pig entrails used in this scene were stored in a bucket in the refrigerator located inside the make-up effects room and, somehow, that refrigerator was unplugged during a break in the production. For years the story that's been told is that the refrigerator in the effects shop was unplugged over the Christmas break, which was after the crew returned from the Florida part of the shoot, which would have been well over three weeks. I'm not sure how this story came to be so muddled over the years. Greg Nicotero even mentions it in the classic *Scream Greats* video about Tom Savini, and a lot of the people I interviewed for this project all remembered it being after the filming in Florida which, again, would have been after the Christmas break. Joe Pilato, Taso Stavrakis, Greg Nicotero, Mike Gornick, etc – each one remembered it being *after* Florida. But thankfully, two key extras in the scene, one of whom was also a member of the effects crew, would help set the record straight. The one part of the story that I'm still unsure of is when and how the refrigerator was unplugged. Who unplugged the refrigerator and for what reason? Also, is it likely that it was unplugged over the two-day break for Thanksgiving? Most of the people I spoke with remember it being after the Christmas break, but are they perhaps confusing that with the much shorter Thanksgiving break? Those answers I don't have, but two people who were there that day and in the scene itself are positive of when the scene was shot, which I'll explain in further detail a bit later.

Upon arriving on set this day, Joe Pilato was greeted by script supervisor Joanne Small. "She said, 'Good morning, Joe. It's a great day to die.' And I said. 'Yes, it is. I need to speak to George,' and she said, 'Well, he's very busy,' and I said, 'Well, I really need to speak to him,'" remembers Pilato. "So George came in and said, 'What's up, Joe?' and I said, 'George, listen I really, really, sincerely believe that Rhodes is not gonna die without saying something.' And he said, 'Well, let's think this through. Your legs are being torn apart from your torso, your torso's being ripped apart, probably your wind pipe's being ripped out . . . how in the name of hell would you say anything?' And I said, 'I don't really care,' and I said, 'It's bad you're thinking about that. We're in trouble,' and he said, 'Hmm. Well, what do you think he would say?' and I felt a little bit embarrassed, because there were other people in the room. So I said, 'Let me whisper it in your ear, I don't want to kind of give it away,' and this big 6' 4" guy leans over to me, a 5' 8" guy, and I whispered in his ear, 'Choke on 'em,' and he kind of pulled his head back and looked at me and he said, 'Well, if you can pull it off, go for it.'"

Above: Matte photography unit members David Garber, Mitchell Lipsiner, and John Green pose with a zombie extra in front of the Fort Myers Exhibition Hall. (Courtesy of Mitchell Lipsiner.)

The carpentry team had prepared a false floor with a section removed for Pilato to lie down in, exposing only his head, shoulders, and arms. After getting into position, a false body would be attached to Pilato, cast from his own body, even complete with part of a skeleton inside! It was then filled with pig intestines, liver, long pieces of sausage, and finally dressed in his military uniform. Before getting in though Pilato was given a warning. "I was informed to not eat or drink anything," says Pilato. "And I asked why and they said, 'Because you're going to be in a hole in the ground for anywhere from four to six hours,' and I said, 'Well, that's good motivation not to drink or eat anything,' because they said, 'Once you're in, you're not going to be able to get out.'"

When Pilato arrived to climb into his hole for the day he found the crew welcomed him with a humorous amenity. "So I actually walked over to the false floor and there was a hole . . . they actually had a toilet seat," says Pilato. "They put a toilet seat over the hole. So I picked up the toilet seat and put it around my neck like some sort of astronaut and slid into this fucking hole and they put a pillow behind my back and that's when the madness started."

The madness that Pilato's referring to, of course, is enduring the godawful smell of the rancid intestines that were used to fill the inside of the fake body. Unfortunately for Pilato, he was locked into a position where he couldn't move at all, and was forced to put up with the smell. "And this smell just enveloped the entire set. I mean, it was horrendous! I can smell it to this day!" says Pilato. "That prep took about two hours; that stuff in my torso, with these putrefied guts. They put a respirator on me; people were walking around with bottles of Aramis and Jade East at that time, just trying to kill the smell. It was just horrendous, horrible. Then they kind of flapped over and closed up the torso, the thing subsided a little bit, but not that much."

When it came time to actually film the scene, right before the cameras rolled, Romero and Pilato shared one last conversation about how Pilato would attempt to reach down with his left hand and protect himself from literally being separated by the zombies, even grabbing an organ if he could. By the time the scene was over, though, Pilato was spent emotionally and physically. "They called action and they started, they ripped me open and I did that big inhale thing, and, 'Choke on 'em,' screaming it out – 'Choke on 'em' – and they're dragging the legs down the hall and you're seeing the whole separation," says Pilato. "They yell 'Cut' and I immediately started dry heaving, and when you're dry heaving in a hole where you can't get out it's pretty scary and dangerous, because you could hyperventilate or aspirate. So, all these PAs came over and just whipped me out of that hole."

"The smell was *unearthly*! I don't know how Joe did it," says Mike Trcic. "He should get a special Oscar for being the closest person to have bad guts touch you . . . and the winner is Joe Pilato! It just permeated the mine."

Taso Stavrakis, who played the motorcycle helmet-wearing zombie that reaches into Pilato's abdomen cavity and pulls out a large handful of guts, was prepared for the smell. "I took the earplugs that we were all using for the gunshots and I stuffed them up my nose. 'Cause I was stuck right there with Joe, neither of us could move for hours with these rotting intestines," says Stavrakis. "So yeah, I stuffed the earplugs up my nose so I wouldn't gag."

Some of the zombie extras who participated in Pilato's onscreen demise were the Granati brothers, who had a local band called G-Force, out of Beaver Falls. The brothers struck up a friendship with Pilato earlier during the production, and that friendship led to their opportunity to help kill his character at the end of the film. All four of the brothers grew up huge fans of the original *Night of the Living Dead*, so much so that in their teenage years they would go out to the Evans City Cemetery, where the film was shot, and hang out in the graveyard getting drunk or stoned, thinking that they might actually run into zombies! The experience of being in *Day of the Dead*, safe to say, is one that none of them will ever forget.

"It had a realism to it . . . it was like an out-of-body experience," says Herm Granati. "It felt like you were pulling the guy's guts open! It was really weird. I had, like, a fear of it almost, kind of like I was afraid to do it."

"We had to make it look like we were really hungry and excited," says David Granti. "And it was like, 'Oh, God!', all you wanted to do was back away from it and run out of the room."

"It was hideous because the smell was so bad everybody was fighting to keep from bringing up their breakfast or lunch, whatever. It went on, it seemed, like a short eternity and then finally they said, 'Cut!'" remembers Rick Granati. "Then they told us later, they said, 'Look, we have to admit that stuff spoiled. Somebody unplugged the refrigerator, but we had to go with it.' You didn't know it until the body was pulled apart."

"At the time we kind of looked at it as a rite of passage, because my brothers and I were very popular. We were like, 'Yeah they should ask us to be in the movie,' you know, because when you're young and cocky that's how you think," admits Joey Granati. "Looking back on it now, when I tell people that I was in that, they freak out because that's become some super pop culture. There's a real pop culture thing to Romero's films. So it's more of a pride thing now. At the time I was cocky enough to think I belonged there. [*laughs*] You're fooling yourself – rock'n'roll does that to people anyway, makes people think that they're bigger and better than they are. And I will admit to having that addictive personality back then, I thought that I deserved to be in that movie. I mean, I thought it was cool even then, but I even kind of laughed at it, saying, 'Ahh, who gives a shit? It's just a stupid zombie movie.' Looking back on it, I feel very fortunate that we did it, and it's bragging rights on a really cool level now."

Now, back to the confusion of when exactly this scene was shot. As mentioned before, for years the story was that it was shot after the crew returned from Florida, because the refrigerator was unplugged while the crew was away. Thankfully, two people who were in the scene, and whose memories are very reliable, helped to solve this mystery.

Mike Deak, John Vulich's friend, who came to hang out on set and worked assisting the make-up crew, remembers very well when it was shot. "As for Joe Pilato's death scene, it was before going to Florida," recalls Deak. "I had been working as an unpaid assistant up to that point, but they had decided to use me as one of the zombies to rip off Joe's legs. We shot part of the lead-up scenes revealing the zombies, and then were down for a day or two to put in the fake floor for the gag. At that point production offered me a paying job of driving one of the equipment trucks to Fort Myers and hire me there as a local, but I would have to leave before the end of the week, before the leg-ripping scene was shot. I chose to stay."

The other individual who vividly remembers when the scene was filmed is George Demick. Growing up a fan of *Night of the Living Dead*, Demick met George Romero at a convention in Pittsburgh when he was a teenager and became pen pals with the legendary director. Romero would often invite Demick down to

Right: Fort Myers zombie extra with cane. (Courtesy of Mitchell Lipsiner.)

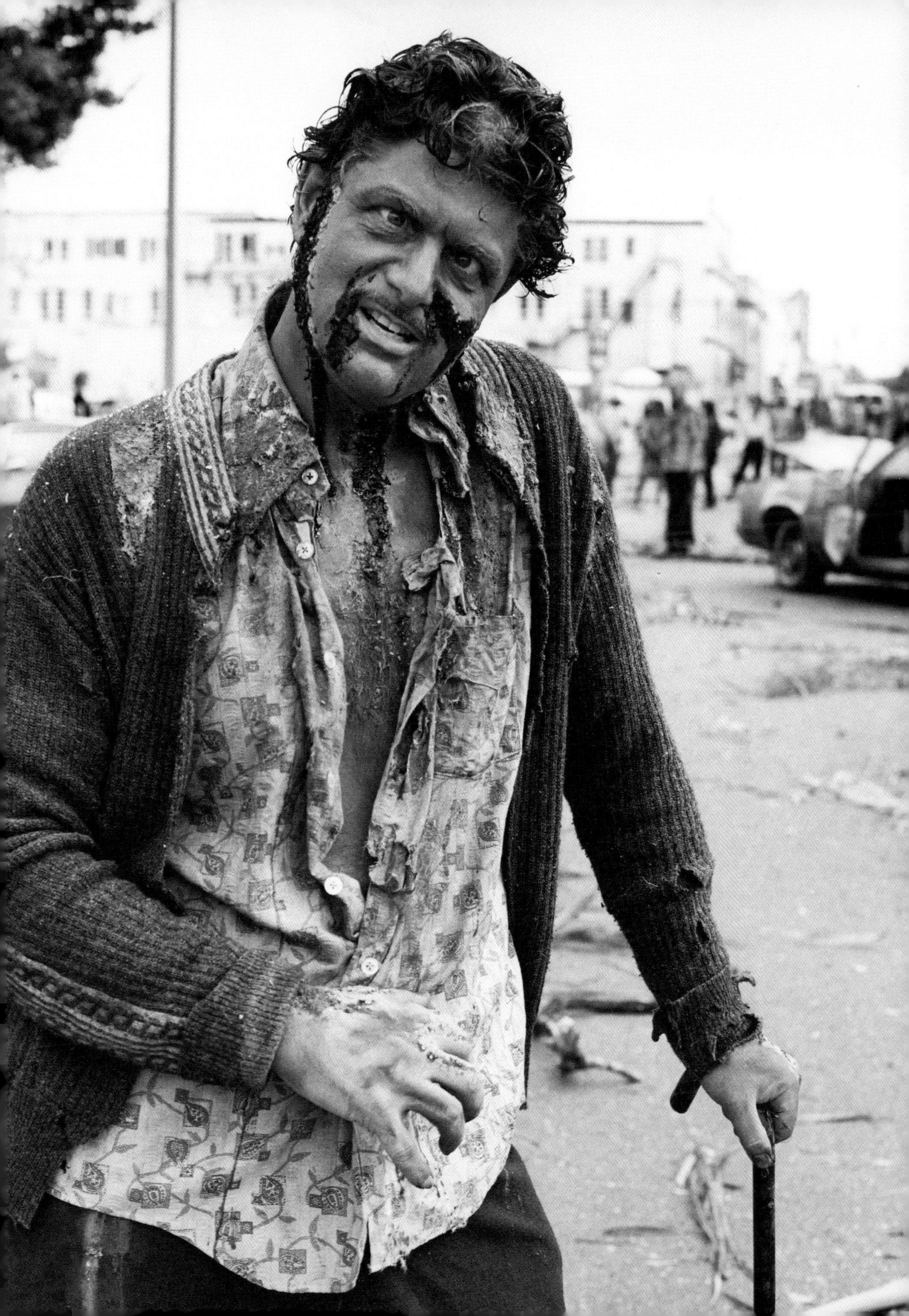

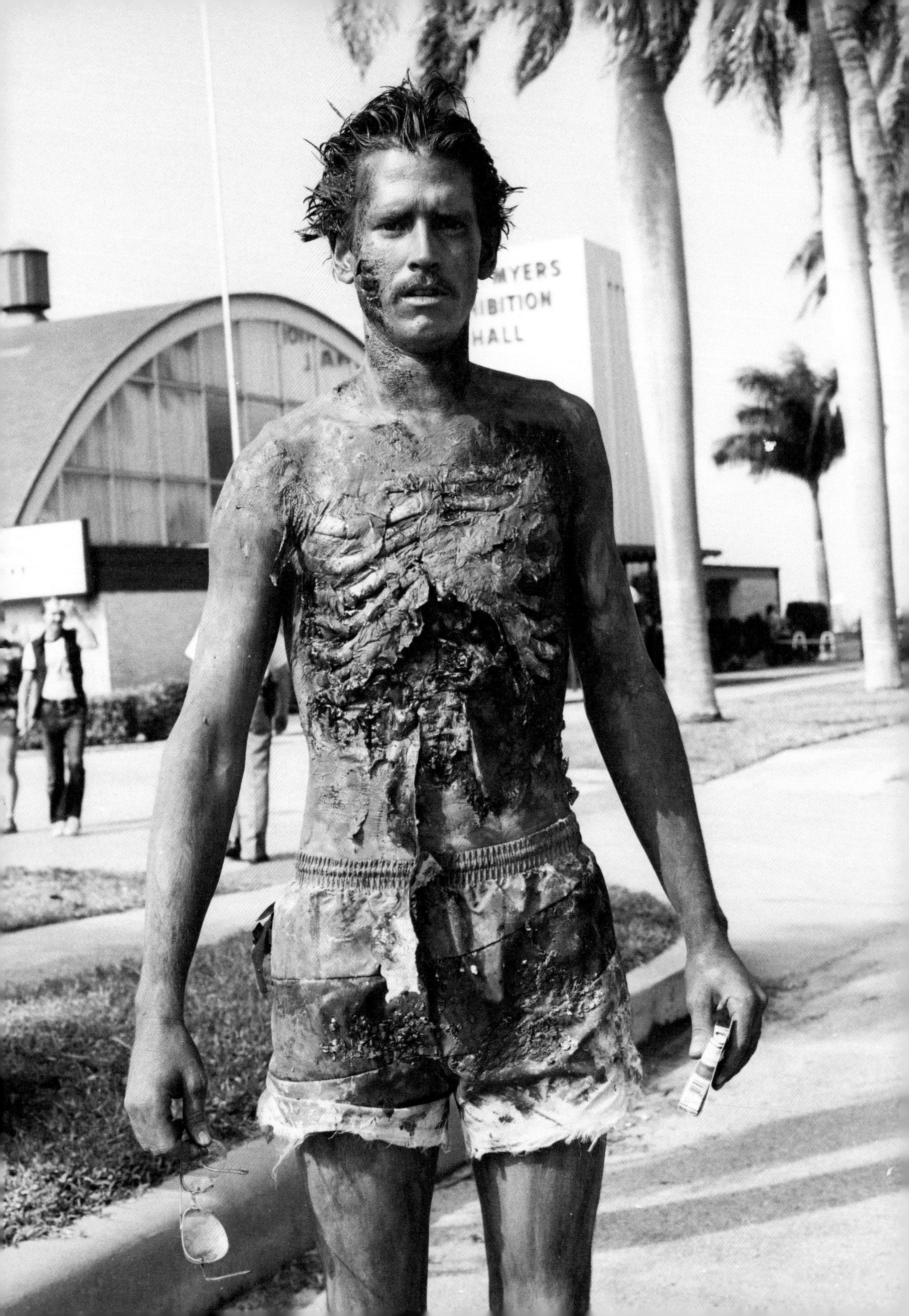
MYERS
IBITION
HALL

his Laurel offices in Pittsburgh and eventually to the set of his movies, including *Knightriders*. Demick was also invited out a couple of times for *Day of the Dead*, but this was a very special day for him and that's why he remembers the date so well. "When we pulled apart Rhodes, that was actually my twenty-first birthday. And I remember at one point I was passing George [Romero] in the hallway and I'm going, 'This is my twenty-first birthday,' he goes 'What are you doing here?' and I'm going, 'Where the hell else would I be? This is the greatest birthday . . . this is what I love!'" Demick's birthday is on December 6.

In the scene, Deak and Demick were two of the three zombies pulling Rhodes' legs down the hallway. "While they were cleaning up Joe, that's when they turned the camera around and then they had the three of us dragging the legs down the hallway," says Deak. "The two guys on the right of the frame, one of them had a Hudson sprayer strapped to his back, and the other guy was actually controlling the blood flow and then I was just pulling the legs on the left-hand side, so that we'd have the nice smear of blood going down the hallway when we walked off with it."

Before pulling the legs down the hallway, though, both Deak and Demick would help tug on the legs, just at the bottom of the frame when Pilato is torn in half. "Savini says, 'All right, you need to grab this here,'" recalls Deak. "And then Savini was literally behind me pulling my legs and pulling me back so that I was sliding underneath the camera pulling the legs off."

"When I was doing it, I was more concerned about being a zombie and being true to what I was supposed to be doing. You know, 'Okay, I gotta pull this leg. I gotta make sure this comes apart,'" laughs Demick. "Greg Nicotero had my camera and was shooting pictures of us dragging the body down the hallway. He's like, 'This should be the poster.'" [*laughs*]

Deak's memory has spared him the smell that engulfed the hallway when Pilato was pulled apart. "Everybody talks about the stench of the guts and everything like that, and I know people were retching and it was pretty disgusting," says Deak. "For me personally, I never really smelled it – one because I was being pulled away from it. And two is that you were inside that lime mine for days on end, with all the dust and dirt in there and, I don't know, it just seemed, like, naturally you lost all sense of smell while I was down in the thing. Even though I was there and I could see the reaction of everybody, I never really got a full-on whiff or the full-on horror of that stench because everything I was involved in was taking the legs way from Joe."

Left: A Fort Myers zombie extra in swim trunks, featuring amazing make-up that wasn't even featured in the finished film. (Courtesy of Mitchell Lipsiner.)

Not that it particularly mattered to Pilato by this point, but it wasn't just rancid guts that he was covered in during the scene. The appliances used to create Pilato's false body might have had a secret ingredient in them, supplied by one of Savini's assistants. "I really probably shouldn't tell this story but I'm going to go ahead and do it anyway," says John Vulich. "Apparently, I think, the chest appliances that Pilato was wearing, I think the foam latex batch – Everett [Burrell] ran that – I think he actually, as a test, like pissed in one of the batches of foam latex that he was doing for those chest appliances." Why would someone piss in it, you might ask? Because at the time, there was a rumor going around effects shops that R&D foam latex was so stable and so easy to work with that you could urinate in it, and it would turn out fine. According to Vulich it did just that.

Up until this point, with the Florida shoot looming on the horizon, Pilato had been attempting to persuade Romero to let him come to Florida with the other cast and crew. Unfortunately for Pilato, there was no chance of that happening. "I begged, I tried . . . I said, 'George, I think you should have Rhodes digging Cooper's grave,' and he said 'You're not going to Florida.' And I said, 'Well, let me come up with this . . .' and he said, 'Joe, you're not going to Florida. We can't afford it,'" recalls Pilato. "I was begging to get out of fucking Pittsburgh, because I knew these people were going to spend the week on the fucking coast of Sanibel and the warmth, beautiful . . . although they weren't allowed to hang out in the sun much because they had to match, make-up-wise, what it was like to be pale and underground for so much time. But I tried my hardest."

Indeed, the six principal actors who were going to Florida were sent a memo from David Ball during this week, stating the following: "Please remember that the Florida segment includes scenes earlier than those already shot. It is of the utmost importance that you use an appropriate sun-block whilst you are on call in Florida. Natalka [Voslakov, make-up artist] has spoken or will be speaking to you about the type of sunscreen that is applicable to your complexions and will be purchasing the necessary creams prior to our departure."

While Thursday, December 6 was the last day of filming before leaving for the Florida portion of the shoot, a lot of the crew had already been making their way down to Fort Myers. As early as Monday, December 3, crew members were arriving in Fort Myers, in preparation for filming. The crew member arrivals were staggered during the week, with some flying down and others driving crew trucks.

A four-page memo from Zilla Clinton was sent out to cast and crew, detailing their flight information for Florida, housing situation while in Florida, and information about how much luggage to bring. A funny, yet stern, note regarding airline tickets was included in the memo: "Leslie [Chapman] will hand them out [plane tickets] to you sometime next week. DON'T BUG HER . . . You go when you go and that's that. Trying to travel some 60 people is no box of chocolates . . ."

A note about the weather down in Florida was also included. "It does rain – and at this time of year, the rain is not usually a quick tropical shower, but more than likely a three-day, grey, poopy, downpour. If we know that a weather front is settling in before we leave, there is a chance that we will not go. We would continue shooting in the mine and deal with Florida in January." That, of course, would not be the case.

The last order of business for the cast before heading to Fort Myers was a scheduled photography session with unit still photographers, Susan and Richard Golomb, on Friday, December 7. The memo sent to the actors humorously reminded them to dress themselves, because the wardrobe crew would be on an airplane heading to Florida. Lori Cardille, Joe Pilato, Terry Alexander, Jarlath Conroy, Tim DiLeo, Gary Klahr, and Ralph Marrero would each participate in the session with the Golomb team. "The most interesting people on a film for me are the people in the background, the grips, the people that actually work on the film," says Susan Golomb. "I found the actors the least interesting people on the film."

Tuesday 12/11/1984 – Day 39

No quote of the day

December 11 saw the thirty-ninth day of filming get underway in beautiful Fort Myers, Florida. Leaving the harsh conditions of working inside the mine in Wampum and suddenly finding themselves in tropical, sunny southwest Florida was a welcome gift for the cast and crew of the film.

"Oh my God, it was wonderful to get out of that cave," says Terry Alexander. "It was quite special to go down and get some respite from that dank place."

"We went from terrible conditions to wonderful conditions," remembers Barry Kessler. "So we all went kind of crazy."

"It was like a mole coming out of a cave and seeing light for the first time," says Karin Wagner.

"Here were all these twenty-year-olds who had been working really hard in a mine, on a plane to Florida," remembers Eileen Sieff. "I remember wearing winter clothes over some tropical get-up. We flew from Pittsburgh to Atlanta and changed planes. Many of us had a few too many cocktails on the plane and had to be herded onto the connecting flight. I can't remember who was doing the herding, but when we got to Florida we were ready to get undressed and enjoy the sun! Nothing too scandalous, but it was the closest to spring break that I ever got."

"Going to Florida I remember being a lot of fun. We were out of control," recalls Nick Mastandrea. "We got on the plane and hadn't seen the sun and we were actually getting stoned on the plane, and we got off and we were so high, and we saw a Chrysler Fifth Avenue sitting in the airport, and we immediately went and rented one. We all jumped in this huge Chrysler Fifth Avenue and started driving around, getting even more stoned, and went to the hotel. I don't even remember what we all shot down there."

While Mastandrea and other crew people were getting stoned or high, not all members of the production were particularly enthused about this apparent drug use. "There were some things that were going on that were just so unprofessional. It was really, really bad stuff on the set," says Lori Cardille. "I don't know; there were a lot of drugs on the set." Cardille did not want to name anyone, but another member of the production confirms her assertion. "There's stuff I could say, but I don't know if I should say it, 'cause it's like kind of incriminating," says John Vulich. "I do know when we were in Florida that they borrowed our scale." [laughs] Vulich could not remember – or didn't want to name – the crew members in question, but admitted that he wasn't exposed to drugs very much during the filming.

As previously mentioned, one person who was glad to be in the warm weather of Florida was Terry Alexander. Unfortunately for Alexander, he encountered a rather rude greeting upon arriving. "We were staying in condos, like townhouse condos, that are connected on both sides – I had just got there. I put my luggage in the upstairs part with the bedroom and I was unpacking, and I left the front door open because there was nobody really there," says Alexander. "And the next thing I know there's a cop standing at the door. I said, 'Oh my, what's going on?' and he says, 'The people next door reported you, saying they don't know who you are,' and blah, blah, blah. Luckily the cop was black. [laughs] So, he said, 'Well, you know, let me see your ID,' and I gave him my ID and told him what I was doing. He said, 'I'm sorry man, you know how people get paranoid,' and so on and so on. And that was the encounter. So, I guess he went back to the neighbors and told them, 'Listen, the brother's over here, get over it!' or something . . . I don't know." [laughs]

The condominiums that Alexander refers to were the South Point West Condominiums located in Fort Myers, which were located about eight miles from the

Right: A zombie extra stands in the middle of Hendry Street in downtown Fort Myers. Looking behind her gives you a glimpse of the view she and her fellow extras had as they marched towards camera. (Courtesy of Mitchell Lipsiner.)

ONE DAY AT A TIME

filming locations in downtown Fort Myers, and twenty miles from the shooting locations on Sanibel Island. Most of the crew shared a unit with another crew member, while a few lucky ones – the lead actors, for example – had a unit all to themselves.

As when the cast and crew first arrived in Wampum, a welcome packet was distributed to everyone, containing maps of the Fort Myers and Sanibel areas, recommended bars and restaurants, fishing and shelling information, shopping, etc. Also included in the packet was a letter from the Louis S. Wegryn, MD Medical Center, with warnings about the natural wildlife found on Sanibel, such as alligators, snakes, and sting rays.

The filming scheduled for this first day of shooting would basically bookend the film, and concentrated on Sanibel Island – Bowman's Beach, to be exact. Scene 2, where Sarah awakens from her nightmare, realizes she is in the helicopter, and then instructs John to land so the group can search the city, would be shot on this day.

Spending a lot of time inside the closed quarters of the helicopter created plenty of time to gossip. "Jarlath [Conroy], and Terry [Alexander], and myself, and Lori [Cardille] were in the helicopter – we had a lot of laughs about all the dramas that were going on during shooting," remembers Tim DiLeo. "Just with one look we would go and say, 'Oh yeah, we saw that. Did you hear that? Oh yeah!' It wasn't mean or ill-spirited, but it was something that we could laugh about."

Another scene shot on this day was scene 14, where the helicopter is flying over wetlands heading back to the compound. The very last scene in the film, scene 103, where Sarah awakens from her last nightmare and discovers that she is safe on the beach, with John fishing in the surf and McDermott feeding the seagulls, was also shot. The idea of these characters surviving and making it to "an island someplace" was a very intriguing notion for some of the actors involved.

"I think George [Romero] should do a movie about them," says Lori Cardille. "I always thought let's do a real movie about where they ended up. I mean a real, raw kind of film. Playing those characters, those three characters, as they were; how they may have ended up in reality. I mean, that would be fun."

Terry Alexander so enjoyed the experience and the characters' relationships with each other that he took the time to write Romero, pitching him an idea for a way to continue the storyline. "I wrote him a letter and I said, 'Why don't we write something around the characters?', blah, blah, blah," says Alexander. "He sent me a letter back. He said, 'No, we can't do that. The characters belong to Richard Rubinstein, not to me.' So, that was a disappointment because I thought we could have fashioned another film called 'George Romero's The Island of Life', or something, around there – that's the title I thought of. It would have been interesting to see what happened."

Even though he enjoyed the ending, at least one member of the cast thought the future for those surviving characters might still be a tough road to travel. "I like it because they're not in paradise, you know? It's not gonna last forever, trouble is brewing," says Taso Stavrakis. "That's what it makes you feel like, you know? It will reach them sooner or later."

Wednesday 12/12/1984 – Day 40

No quote of the day

Day 40 saw the production move from Sanibel into Fort Myers for shooting downtown, near the Fort Myers harbor and Exhibition Hall.

Up first was scene 13, where John and McDermott sit in the chopper and call out on the radio for survivors as John realizes that the city is a "dead place". This scene would be cut into two parts. One half would fit in right after scene 4, of Sarah and Miguel exiting the helicopter.

Also shot was scene 3, where the helicopter is seen flying over the city, and scene 4, where the helicopter lands and Sarah and Miguel exit to go and scout for survivors.

The logistics of filming these types of scenes are always slightly more complicated than you might think. Behind the scenes, there are a lot of folks coordinating and making sure that everything runs smoothly, to pull off the illusion that this is an abandoned and lifeless city. And inevitably there are always issues to deal with. One of those people was location scout Bill Dickhaut, who handled part of that coordination. "It involved clearing the port of Fort Myers of recreational craft so we could convey the look of an empty city," says Dickhaut. "When the helicopter lands in the beginning of the film, I believe there [are] boat docks in the background. It required me coordinating with the harbor master to say, 'Please move all those boats out of there on Tuesday-the-whatever, because that's the day that we're gonna try to shoot that scene and make it look like it's an abandoned city,' And that reality doesn't come across if you've got a bunch of people in pleasure boats docking their boats at that moment."

"It was a big scene; it was really quite a big scene. I think it was heard from miles around, the helicopter landing downtown," remembers Florida production coordinator, Melanie Muroff. "He [George Romero] wanted to land it downtown, and they have these, like, 100-year-old Sabal palm trees that are 50 feet tall. So there was something where we had to redesign the location."

Above: Sister and brother Eileen and Marty Garrigan work on dirtying up an old car for the abandoned city sequence in downtown Fort Myers, Florida. **Below:** Head scenic artist, Eileen Garrigan, with "window dressing" wrapped around her waist during the Fort Myers shoot. (Photos courtesy of Eileen Garrigan.)

Romero coming to Fort Myers with a feature film was quite a moment for the film community in Florida. "Fort Myers was in the middle of nowhere," says Muroff. "The fact that he decided to shoot there is such a huge milestone in the history of Florida film production. To actually shoot a feature there and to hire people locally was such an opportunity, and it was very exciting."

The overhead view of the abandoned city from inside the helicopter was also shot, which contains a huge blooper of a car driving down First Street! An unexpected member of the production, featured extra William Laczko, helped make sure that the shot happened on schedule. Laczko had lots of spare time on his hands while in Florida, so he decided to put himself to work as a glorified production assistant. "On one particular day they were doing aerial shots, I think Mike Gornick and one or two other people were going up in the helicopter," remembers Laczko. "They called the production office, they needed some filters for the camera, so they could shoot it the way

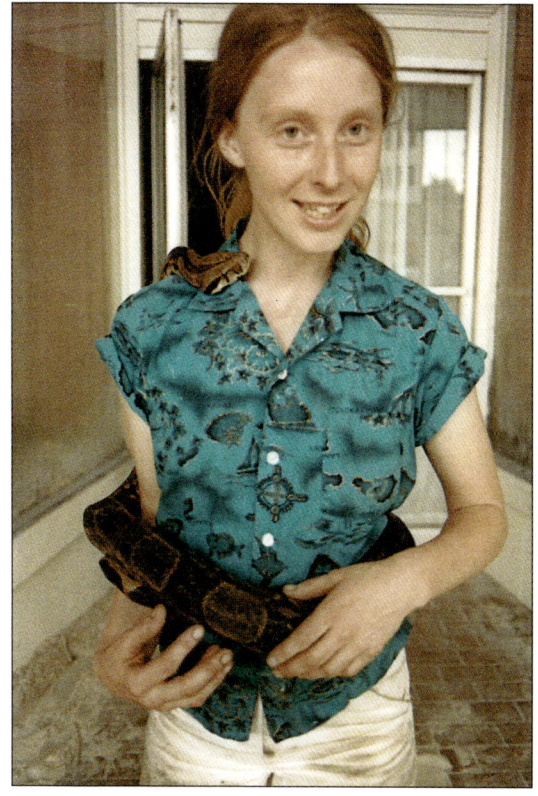

Above: Florida wrap party at George Romero's house: Romero (left) talking with production assistant Michael Johnson; costume designer Barbara Anderson (center) chatting with Tim DiLeo; production assistant Barbara Frazzini (center right) watches as Jarlath Conroy snaps photos; Terry Alexander (far right) looking sharp. (Courtesy of Barbara Boyle.)

they want it. Zilla [Clinton] was there and she had the filters, and basically turned to me and said, 'Can you get these out to the airport?' I said, 'If you can get me something to drive, I can get them anywhere you want them to go.'"

Also lined up for this day were scenes 6 and 7, where Miguel calls out on the bullhorn as Sarah stands by. Scene 11, where Miguel runs away in a panic at the sight of the horde of living dead in the city, as Sarah stoically looks on, was also shot.

Two other scenes were scheduled for this day, scenes 8 and 9. These scenes would feature the Dr. Tongue zombie puppet (or the "jaw" zombie, as it's referred to on the call sheet). There's a little uncertainty about whether or not this scene was shot on this day, however.

"The last thing we shot was the zombie at the beginning, Dr. Tongue," remembers Tom Savini. "And the sun was going down and his face was almost completely in black, dark shadow. And I was yelling for somebody, 'Get a reflector! Let's get some light on this thing!' So there's a light on it only briefly, but that was around 4:30 in the afternoon. And we were all chomping at the bit for that shot to be over so that we could all rush to Disney World." Indeed, a lot of the effects guys drove to Orlando to visit Disney World after the production wrapped in Florida. Savini's memory is that it was the very last thing shot before going to Orlando, but the call sheets for the rest of the week never list the scene again. Savini's memory could very well be accurate, but there's still a slight bit of uncertainty. Photographs supplied for this book by Barbara Frazzini show George Romero, and other crew members, wearing the same exact outfits for the scene with Dr. Tongue and the scene of Miguel and Sarah with the bullhorn. Savini also mentions the fact that a lot of Dr. Tongue's face is obscured. This was written into the script deliberately by Romero to pay homage to a scene from a classic David Lean film. "He [Romero] always had the image of *The Bridge on the River Kwai*," says editor Pat Buba. "There's a shot that's very similar in that, in which you can't see the person's face until they move and then the sun blocks it down so you see the exposure on their face."

The Dr. Tongue puppet would go on to have quite an adventurous life, so to speak. It would be featured on *Late Night with David Letterman* when Savini was promoting the release of the film, and today is part of the personal collection of Metallica guitarist, and horror aficionado, Kirk Hammett.

Thursday 12/13/1984 – Day 41

No quote of the day

Day 41 would see the production return to Bowman's Beach on Sanibel Island. This time filming would take place at the Bowman's Beach helistop, which was used by the Lee County Mosquito Control District. The area would be used as the outside entrance to the underground compound, and was literally right next door to the beach seen at the end of the film.

After being turned down by the Ding Darling National Wildlife Refuge, location scout Bill Dickhaut, acting on a tip from production manager Zilla Clinton, was able to convince the higher-ups within the Lee County government to let them use the Mosquito Control helistop for filming. In the end, the location would turn out to be serendipitous for Romero's production.

"This is something that we thought, 'Ah well, why in the world wouldn't they want us down here?' and I got the cold shoulder from a couple of places," recalls Dickhaut. "But the Mosquito Control and Bowman's Beach were literally . . . I mean, they were literally one-eighth of a mile from each other. You literally went from the Mosquito Control area through some wooded area out on to the beach and you were there. I think that was part of George kind of rewriting the script, once he saw what he had in terms of locations. He said, 'Okay, well this is the way we're gonna have to do it.' That may not have been his original vision, but that's the way it worked out."

Work would begin on scene 17, where Sarah argues with John about whether or not to refuel the helicopter, then attempts to assist Miguel, who isn't interested in her help. It ends with Sarah noticing the new grave belonging to Major Cooper. The vast majority of this scene would be shot over the next two days, however.

Work on scene 15, where the helicopter lands at the compound, was also scheduled for this day. In the scene, as the helicopter lands, Taso Stavrakis' character, Torrez, is seen watering and tending to a marijuana plant, which would end up causing unexpected troubles for the production. "Barbara and Cletus Anderson, from the costumes and art departments, had bought some plant at Wal-Mart or one of the plant stores or whatever that looks a lot like marijuana. Of course it wasn't, but it looked just like it," remembers Stavrakis. "We were in the middle of shooting and a helicopter dropped out of the sky, and these federal marshals came over and said, 'What are you doing? You can't have this illegal plant here.' I think we were actually shooting on federal property and that was their problem. [*laughs*] Barbara and Cletus had to produce the receipt and explain it to them at length that it's not really marijuana, it's this plant that looks like it, we just bought it and we're not really using pot! Nobody's using pot." [*laughs*]

Also on the agenda for this day's filming schedule were scenes 16 and 18, where zombies are seen at the compound fence and gate clawing and moaning at the sight of the humans inside the compound's fenced-in area; and scenes 83 and 86, where Miguel opens the gate and draws the zombies to the elevator.

Extra Rob Coscia was one of the living dead in these scenes and recalls how a good friend of his, Tim Smith, a fellow zombie extra, caused a break in filming due to some very un-zombie-like behavior. "I remember they stopped the camera at one point, because I guess when they were recording the sound, one of the zombies was making a motorcycle sound . . . I guess he didn't realize they were also recording our voice versus our actions," says Coscia. "And I think it was Tim Smith that was going like, 'Vroom, vroom, vroom, vroom,' 'cause he had his hands out there and was kinda, like, making motorcycle noises and whatever. So, they corrected him." [*laughs*]

Goofy behavior like that did not go unnoticed by editor, Pat Buba. "At the fence there were a couple of extras that just drove me up a wall, because they were so over – well, I don't know how you overact as a zombie – but they were doing something that really pissed me off, being cute," says Buba. "And they were in a bunch of shots and I did everything that I could as an editor to get them out of the movie, because they kept driving me nuts."

During scene 86, when Miguel is drawing the zombies to the elevator, just before making the sign of the cross – as written in the script – Tim DiLeo would also throw in a dash of mysticism, as he clutches his medallions. "It meant a lot to me, let's put it that way.

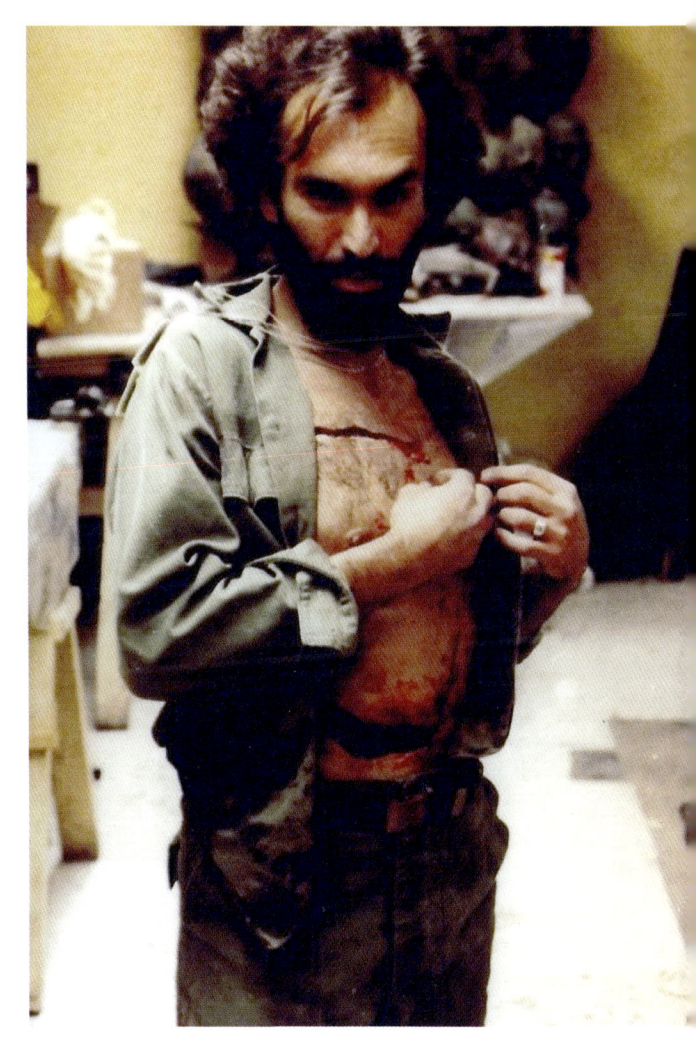

Above: Tim DiLeo in the make-up effects room posing with his prosthetic chest for his gut spill scene. (Courtesy of Tim DiLeo.)

And that's why I'm holding them at the end, that's why I do what I do at the end before I cross myself and banish the air," says DiLeo. "You can do things with your mind, in your mind, or you can do them physically or you can do them both. I did most of it in my mind and then physically I did that, banishing negative spirits away. It's Magick." As we all know, though, the negative spirits would not be banished away.

One of the people playing a negative spirit on set this day was Deborah Sharp, who was assigned to cover the filming for the *Fort Myers News-Press*. Sharp's background was in more serious news journalism, so the opportunity to tackle the assignment – and play a zombie – was was a big thrill. "We had been aware that they were going to be doing filming in the area, so this is something we were following right along," says Sharp. "We knew and I definitely knew because I loved George Romero – even then I knew who he was,

I was aware of the films and I was like, 'Oh, this would be a great assignment!' And when they gave me the assignment and said I could write it in the first person, I mean that was, like, unheard of for me because I was coming out of a pretty straight news background. So it was a lot of fun."

Indeed, Sharp knew all about the production as she'd covered it in the *Fort Myers News-Press*, dating back to the summer, when it was uncertain how much – if any – filming would be done in the southwest Florida region. In August, Sharp had written a story concerning a vacant terminal building at Page Field Airport, which was one of the original locations being considered by the production, just before the drastic script overhaul. Suffice to say, even if the script had not been changed, the finances would definitely not have worked for either Laurel-Day or Lee County regarding that particular location. Laurel Entertainment's offer to rent the terminal for $15,000 for five months was turned down by the county airports director, Gary LeTellier, who said in Sharp's article, "I can't even turn on the air conditioning for $15,000."

While covering the progress of the film's production, Sharp dealt with a competitor when it came to breaking news about it. And that competitor was in her own home – her husband! "This was like one of the very few fights that my husband and I ever had, because he worked for the television station and I worked for the *News-Press*," says Sharp. "And, of course, both of us, the TV station and the *News-Press*, were angling to do what we could to break the story that they were coming. And my husband overheard me talking to my editor about knowing something – the details are a little fuzzy now about exactly what I knew, and really how big of the story it was – but I knew a little something about when they were starting filming, or where they were going to film or something. My husband overheard me and immediately called his desk and spills all the beans that he's just overheard me talking to my editor about. So, I was furious. It's kind of like something out of [1974 film] *Front Page*."

Sharp's husband is Kerry Sanders who would go on to notoriety as a reporter for NBC News, while Sharp would become a reporter for *USA Today* and these days writes mystery novels. She looks back on the assignment with a great deal of fondness. "A real high point of my life and my career, honestly. Because I've never done anything else like that. I mean, that's probably the only time I'll ever be in a movie, and just to be involved with it and part of it was kind of a blast," says Sharp. "It was just so different and so fun. It was a real lark and I just really enjoyed it. I still look back on it with a lot of fondness and still think about that every time I pass by that part of the beach area between Sanibel and Fort Myers. I still think about that."

The last shot of the day would be part of scene 102, where Sarah, John, and McDermott are running to get to the helicopter. The large crowd shots, of the zombies roaming around inside the compound, heading towards the helicopter, were completed on this day.

After a long day of being members of the living dead, and spending lots of time waiting around to film, the extras there that day would have to endure one final long period of waiting before leaving. "Apparently there was a bus full of zombies outside of the Mosquito Control headquarters and they had just wrapped for the day," says Bill Dickhaut. "It was like four o'clock, and the bus that went out there got itself mired in the sand in the parking lot. And so they had to hire a tow truck to pull the bus full of zombies out of the sand." [*laughs*]

Friday 12/14/1984 – Day 42

"Don't put the hand down the pants yet."
– Kato to Eileen

Day 42 would pick up work from the previous day with scenes 15, 17, and 102 at the Mosquito Control site on Sanibel. The big scene on the day's schedule was scene 88, where Miguel is devoured on the elevator platform. Tim DiLeo would have a long day in prosthetics, culminating with a claustrophobic death scene in which he is bitten on the left breast and his throat. "I got a little spooky during the death scene in Florida, people were way too into it," says DiLeo. "Through the prosthetic and other things I definitely got bit. We took it off and there were teeth marks on my breast."

One of the extras in the scene was the supervisor of elections for Lee County, Enid Earle, who is wearing an orange-reddish dress with a veil on her head. Contrary to DiLeo's recollection, Earle remembers it being a different part of the body that he suffered a bite mark on. "We were supposed to tear his throat out," recalls Earle. "Well, right in front of me was this soldier fellow who was a zombie and, boy, when the director said to go . . . first of all every time we'd get into the mood to kill him the sun would go under a cloud and then we had to stop. They said, 'Stay where you are. Don't move! We've got to get this perfect now!' So everybody stopped, we were just like statues. Then the cloud went by and the sun came out and he said we should go for it. So this soldier reaches down – we were all trying to get at him – and he pulls the guy's throat out and the blood starts popping all over and he was screaming! Oh my God he was screaming! I never heard such screams in my life as this guy we're killing. When the director yelled cut, the guy got up and he ran like crazy, and we didn't know why he

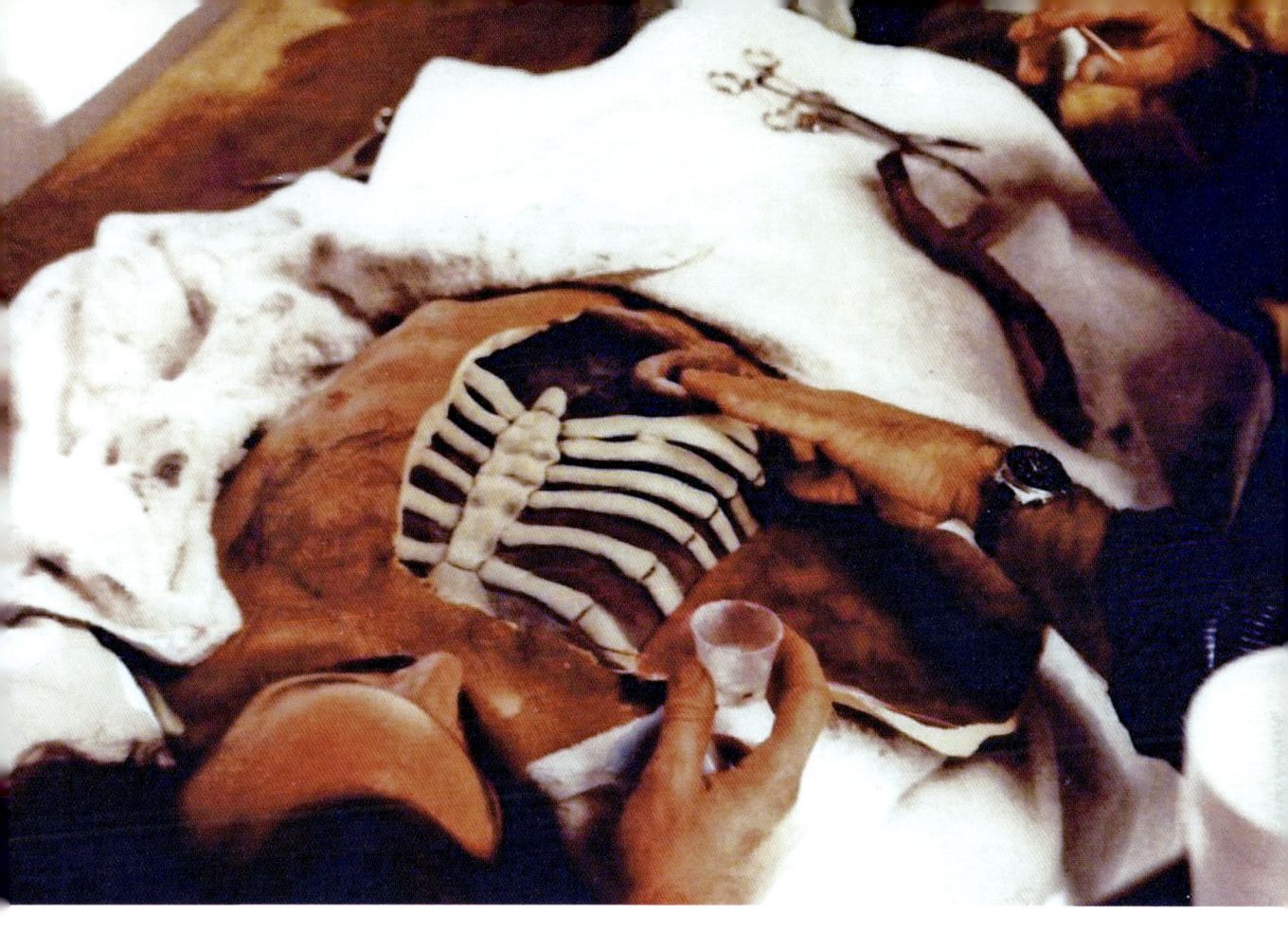

Above: Close-up view of Tim DiLeo's prosthetic chest appliance. (Courtesy of Tim DiLeo.)

was running. Heck, the scene was over. We found later that the soldier bit so deep, he bit into the guy's throat! [*laughs*] He really did, he left prints in his throat. That's why he was screaming so much. I thought, 'Oh, what an actor! Oh gosh he's good.' He screamed so realistically it gave us goose pimples and here he had his own throat being torn out. Oh, that was awful."

As Earle states, DiLeo got up and immediately left in quite a hurry. Depending on whom you ask, you'll get varying accounts of just how big a hurry DiLeo was in. "It was really hot and I was really mentally fried and it had been coming since five o'clock or four o'clock in the AM, starting, and all these people hovering over you and biting you it kind of became actual," says DiLeo. "And I think I went from a lying position to a straight up standing position, walking away with squib hoses and shit coming out of my body all over the place, and I kind of went running to Tom [Savini]."

"They had everything rigged up and so on, and then, of course, the zombies came and they started attacking and chewing at him," says Florida unit make-up effects artist Barry Anderson. "After Romero said, 'Cut,' he just started screaming, got up, and started running down the field and everybody just sort of stood there with their jaws open."

"I don't think he ran, I don't remember that part," says John Vulich. "But I do remember like a little, just like a huff, where he kind of turned and abruptly . . . like, as soon as it was done, he just jumped off the set. I don't know that he ran away, but he was actually very upset by the event."

"Some of these zombies, they get pretty enthusiastic, and they were, like, really grabbing and pushing down on him. I know when they finally did the scene the one guy bit out the throat really good and that was cool. Unfortunately when the other gentleman who bit out a chunk of his chest, he was a little too enthusiastic and actually bit into him just a little bit, which was like, 'Okay, that's going to leave a mark,'" says Florida unit make-up effects artist Rick Gonzales. "He was trying to dig in there and get the thing and sometimes it's not easy to do when you're wearing those dentures. You know, he felt a little discomfort. And then when the scene called cut, he jumped up and was walking away and he was pulling everything off. Some of the other people ran over there, 'Okay, it's fine. Calm down, don't worry. No big deal.' He was like, 'Get these people off me. I've had enough.'"

DiLeo's death scene provided an extra challenge to the make-up crew, in particular John Vulich, since it was being shot in open sunlight. The prosthetics on his chest and throat would need to match his skin tone perfectly, but as extra Enid Earle had mentioned

Above: Terry Alexander (John) and Jarlath Conroy (McDermott) outside "The Ritz". (Courtesy of Terry Alexander.)

before, clouds played a role on this day. "Back then, if you were using grease paint make-ups, lots of times you would have to do the grease paint part that's on the prosthetic a little redder than the rest of the face. Let's say you just do a forehead, the forehead actually needs to be a little redder than the rest of the face, because the light doesn't reflect properly and some of the color gets washed out," says Vulich. "So, I kind of kept this in mind in working on that, and there's some things on Tim DiLeo when he gets attacked, he's outside of this compound they're in and I think they were having problems with the lighting that day. I think there were clouds coming in and out of the sunlight and so at some point they just brought in a bunch of lights to try to mimic the look of the sun, just to be able to shoot while the clouds were covering, and I'd set up his make-up to look right for the sunlight, but then when the clouds came in all of a sudden the make-up went green. I thought it was 'cause when the lights came in, because they were colored differently, for some reason the make-up turned green, and I didn't have an opportunity to go in and change it, and that's how it went on film. So, I noticed his prosthetics have a bit of a green cast to them." For Vulich, it's most noticeable in the tight closeup of DiLeo grimacing in pain with his chains in his mouth. "You'll notice that his face gets redder than his neck, because I made up his neck to look like his normal color when he's in a normal state," says Vulich. "But since the actor was getting all amped up for the scene, he's being killed so he's freaking out and screaming, his face starts flushing red at a certain point in the scene and the prosthetic doesn't follow along with it." [*laughs*]

Both Rick Gonzales and Barry Anderson were part of the Florida make-up effects unit, a group of extra hands that Tom Savini brought on board through make-up artist Dean Gates. The crew Gates put together consisted of Gates himself, Gonzales and Anderson, Linda Arrigoni, Mary Lefore, and Brian Burgstaller – not Barry Burghstaller, as incorrectly listed in the credits.

The opportunity to work on a major motion picture was a thrill for the group, but having it turn out to be a George Romero zombie movie was something that some of them couldn't believe.

Barry Anderson had attended the Art Institute of Pittsburgh and was a huge fan of *Dawn of the Dead*, even going to the Monroeville Mall to look for fake bloodstains. While working for a costume shop in south Florida, he discovered that the owner also owned a costume shop in Pittsburgh and knew Tom Savini. The owner sent Anderson to Pittsburgh to handle some business for her, and also gave him Savini's home number. Anderson called Savini when he was in Pittsburgh, hoping that he might be able to meet the legend, but unfortunately it didn't happen for the young artist.

Some time after returning to Florida, though, Anderson would get a phone call that changed his life. "So, not long after that, I got back to Florida and Dean [Gates] called me and just said, 'I'm gathering up some people to work on a film. Are you interested?', and of course I was like, 'I'm always interested. What is it?' and he said, 'Well, it's going to be a zombie movie, working with George Romero and Tom Savini.' Of course, I thought he was joking with me. You know? I probably did some kind of crazy happy dance; I think I was probably in shock. I was like, 'What!'" recalls Anderson. "He actually explained it nice and calm, 'Well, I need to get a couple of people together. We're gonna go over to the other side of the state and they're gonna pay you money to work on this.' I was like, 'You're gonna pay me money? Hold on here, this is too crazy.'"

Prior to *Day of the Dead*, Anderson had done some acting, having a bit part on the hit TV show *Miami Vice*. Working on the Romero zombie film, however, would completely change Anderson's career. "Honestly, when I went to work on *Day of the Dead* it made me

Above: Director George Romero, star Lori Cardille, and producer Richard Rubinstein on location in the Wampum Mine. (Courtesy of Hollywood Book & Poster Company.)

decide that what I really wanted to do was that, not acting," says Anderson. "I was invited to go back to the second season of *Miami Vice*, I never did. I just decided, 'No, I like being behind the scenes, I like doing this stuff.'"

Linda Arrigoni, another member of the Florida effects team, also recalls how exciting the opportunity was. "George Romero? *Night of the Living Dead*? Big time stuff here. It's like, oh my God, how fortunate," remembers Arrigoni. "George came on set one morning and it's like, oh my gosh, this is an icon. We really didn't know what to do, you know, stand to attention or whatever. And he came over and he was just so laidback and . . . just so Floridian. [*laughs*] He just complimented us and thanked us and [said] how much he appreciated our work. I remember talking to him, but I was probably babbling." [*laughs*]

Arrigoni also remembers the fear she felt when Tom Savini made a point of drawing the rest of the team's attention to her first bit of work. "My first zombie was a female and I did her make-up and stuff," says Arrigoni. "Tom came up and he told my zombie to stand up and, oh my God, I'm looking for a hole to crawl into because, oh my God, maybe he hates it. And he said, 'Guys, you see this? You see this! This is what I want my zombies to look like.' Oh my God, it was like, 'Whew!'"

Rick Gonzales would have the chance to create one of the most memorable and iconic zombies seen in the film, the soldier zombie who bites out Miguel's throat. Gonzales' make-up was applied to one of several extras picked out from the previous day's large group of zombies to come back to film Miguel's death scene. "This guy was a one-day zombie, so do whatever you want," recalls Gonzales. "They had all these appliances that they used through the whole movie, and part of the rule was don't make him look blue, and just try and make him look as unique as possible, especially if they're a one day. So I did and everybody seemed to like it. I was a little unnerved because everyone was, 'Hey! You gotta come see this!' When one person starts getting attention out of the group you always wonder, it's like, 'Uh-oh.'" Romero and Savini were so impressed with the look of Gonzales' zombie that they picked him to be the one that would tear out Miguel's throat. Both Gonzales and the extra were ecstatic, but it would actually prove to be an even bigger challenge for Gonzales the second time around. "I couldn't find another prosthetic like that one exactly, because I had torn it all up to make it unique, and added my own little touches," says Gonzales. "So I spent part of the night finding another one and kind of putting it back together quickly, so we had the same sort of look. So I was very proud that each day they both looked the same. And then, of course, he had a great time biting out the guy's throat."

For these big zombie days on Sanibel, the set-up would start very early in the morning. The man who got the "harrowing" task of making sure the make-up tables were up and ready to go was Mike Deak, who had hitched a ride down to Florida – unbeknownst to the higher-ups – with one of the very last production trucks that left Wampum. For the two days it took to drive to Fort Myers, Deak sat on a cooler chest in the production truck and was then dropped off once in town. "As soon as we arrived to where the crew was staying, they dropped me off, like, about a couple of blocks away with my suitcase, and I said, 'Thanks, guys,' and they drove in and then I just came walking down the road and said, 'Hi, guys! I finally got down here,'" laughs Deak. "And they hired me, so I got two weeks' worth of work on that, which was actually great at that point."

Deak remembers his jaunt into the brush during those early morning hours on Sanibel. "Where we were filming, there was this big tall grassy field and then, if you walked a little bit, there was this bridge that went across the river to another, like, sandbar and then the ocean was on the other side," recalls Deak. "But as you're walking across this bridge, literally, this river was filled with gators in there, and you could see them swimming up and down the river, and they were all on the banks of the shore, literally just feet from where we were filming. So the morning came where I had to do a bunch of extras and they said, 'All right Mike, we want you to set up over there' – well, the electricians hadn't come yet and there was no light. I'm walking around in pitch blackness setting up tables in, like, waist-high grass, knowing that there's alligators everywhere within feet of where I'm at. I'm kind of sitting there going, 'I can't say no. If I say no they'll fire me and I'll never work in Hollywood again,' you know? I was horrified."

But it wasn't just alligators that Deak and his fellow effects guys had to worry about – it was the voice talents of Rick Gonzales. "I do this yell, we call it the pterodactyl scream, where I make this loud screeching noise," says Gonzales. "And I just thought, hey, for fun, we're walking in the woods, some of the guys were also heading back; I just gave this loud screech in the woods." That screech would freak out the out-of-town effects guys, who were unfamiliar with the local terrain and its inhabitants.

Someone who was learning about some of the local inhabitants of southwest Florida was Tom Savini, who was up to his old "tricks" again. "There would be, like, some neat zombie that was, like, showing me, disrobing in the woods, that sort of thing," recalls Savini. "I disappeared from there one day and left those guys in charge because there was a female zombie that lived close by."

One very important aspect of this day's filming was the false elevator platform that Tim DiLeo lies down on during his death scene. The responsibility for creating that platform fell on the shoulders of head carpenter, Norman Beck, and head scenic artist, Eileen Garrigan. For Beck and Garrigan, it turned out to be one of the most challenging yet rewarding creations they fabricated for the production.

"We built the Nike site out of lumber. We built it in Pittsburgh out of four-by-eight standard theatrical platform pieces and it was covered with a big overlay of vinyl. They make a product that looks like boilerplate steel, but it's vinyl. That was laid on top of it and then Eileen Garrigan, who was the head scenic, spent a long time researching and developing techniques to paint this vinyl so that it looked like steel," recalls Beck. "Quite honestly, we were convinced that the United States government was going to get satellite footage of that, or that the Russian government was going to get satellite footage of that thing, and wonder how a Nike site appeared overnight."

"It was difficult making it stick and making it match. It was a fun project and I was happy, I just had the feeling I was happy with how it turned out," says Garrigan. "I think it was called diamond plate. It's something you see, like, on a truck, it's an industrial metal that's got little bumps, little herringbone kind of bumps all over it. When it's painted, the paint peels and breaks and they scrape it off and paint it again. So, I wanted it to have that layered look of broken, chipped paint that reveals back down to the rusty steel. It was black with, I think, a big yellow band on either side. So you want it to be all textured and gritty, but you kind of have to be careful, actors are going to be using it, you don't want anybody to get injured. So I did use sand, I made a gritty paint of sand and Japan paint, so that it would dry and stick well and just have a flat . . . I didn't want it to be shiny. The rusty parts of it you don't want to be shiny, but then the yellow paint does have a little bit of shine."

Saturday 12/15/1984 – Day 43

1st unit – No quote of the day
2nd unit – "Oh, my god."

Day 43 saw the production split off into two filming units. The first unit would continue work on Sanibel Island, completing scenes 15 and 17. They would also film scene 19, where Sarah and John walk to the elevator platform and argue about whether there is a better alternative to what they're currently doing.

And while the rest of his fellow effects colleagues would travel back into Fort Myers for the downtown shots of zombies roaming the streets, Greg Nicotero stayed on Sanibel to continue filming his role as

Johnson. "Unfortunately that part of the shoot is really blurry for me and I don't know why," admits Nicotero. One thing not blurry for Nicotero was the *Playboy* magazine he's reading when the helicopter lands at the compound. The issue was actually his, and he was so infatuated with the playmate in the issue, he even wrote her a letter!

As for the second unit in Fort Myers, that group was headed up by first AD, John Harrison. This unit would film scenes 5, 10, and 12, where you see the devastation of the city as the hordes of living dead march through the streets. The tight scheduling in Florida, due to the limited amount of time allocated by the production, necessitated the use of Harrison's second unit. "We couldn't do that all in the schedule that was allowed," says Harrison. "So I went off and I directed those with Ernie Dickerson, a cinematographer that we brought down, who's emerged in his own right as a good TV director."

One of the highlights of this day's filming would be the scene featuring the large alligator on the bank steps. The job of securing that prehistoric creature for the film belonged to herpetologist Bill Love. "Well, there must have been a call for the scene with a big alligator that went to a friend of ours," remembers Love. "A reptile dealer named Tom Crutchfield had a business called Herpetofauna Incorporated, and it was probably the biggest, most well-known reptile supplier in the United States during those years, and they asked if he could supply an alligator for the scene. I worked for Tom at the time, and he called all his other friends and said, 'Well, why don't you borrow one from our little nature park in town, it's over at the Shell Factory in North Fort Myers.' And he said, 'We've got a pretty good-sized one in the pond here who hasn't been out of the pond in years, you'll have to get in there and catch it. No problem, just go in and pick it up the day before.' And that turned into, like, a seven-hour task, trying to rope this animal out of this pond. The pond was probably the size of our living room, probably 40 feet across. So, I mean, this alligator could just sink in the water and you could have no idea where in the pond it was, and we were wading in there trying to get a noose around its neck. And we finally dragged it up and taped its jaws shut and it was much bigger than we expected to use. It was a humongous, fat, old alligator and it probably ran somewhere like twelve feet."

To ensure that there were minimal problems with the alligator, Love was recruited to play one of the zombies who appear in the scene with the large beast. "And then, I guess, later they wanted somebody in the scene with the alligator, and thought it would be better to have somebody that was at least a little familiar with the animal," says Love. "So Tom [Crutchfield] said, 'Wanna be in it?' and I said, 'Yeah, sure. Why

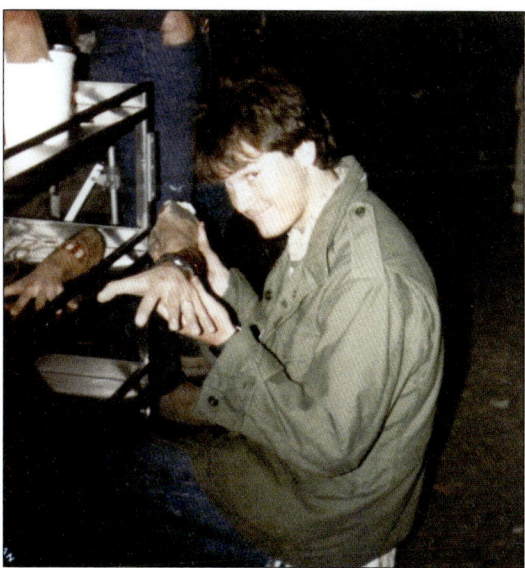

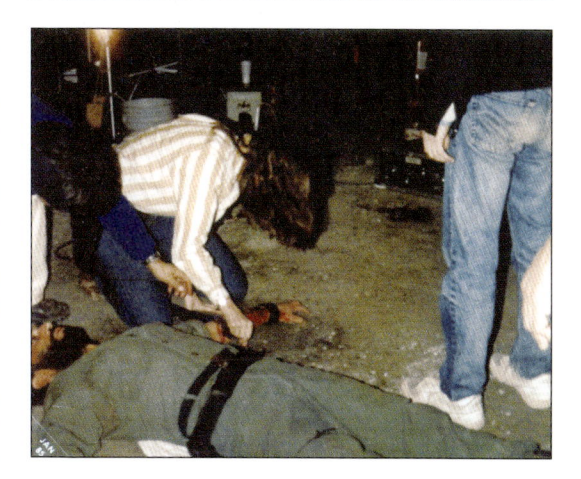

Top: George Romero stands above Lori Cardille's stand-in, Theresa Bedekovich, outside "The Ritz". **Middle:** Everett Burrell with Tim DiLeo's severed arm. **Bottom:** Lori Cardille rehearsing cutting off Tim DiLeo's arm. (Photos courtesy of Barbara Boyle.)

THE MAKING OF GEORGE A. ROMERO'S DAY OF THE DEAD

not, sounds great.' So I ended up being one of the two zombies, the well-fed zombie that steps out first."

Love's wife, Kathy, was also an extra this day. Both Kathy and Bill shared a love of photography, so while Bill was filming his scene with the alligator, Kathy was busy trying to capture some photos for them to enjoy later. "It was kind of neat during the shoot, when he was up there on the bank steps, and I was standing up on one of the wooden benches on the sidewalk that are there all the time, and a bunch of people were there, there were lots and lots of people there," remembers Kathy Love. "And every time that alligator would move a muscle the local cops that were watching things would go, 'Get back! Get back! It's dangerous!' and they're trying to push everybody back."

One person on the crew who experienced a fright with the alligator was Mike Deak, even though the

Top and middle: Filming the p.o.v. shot of the heroes shooting the zombie in the silo. (Courtesy of Barbara Boyle and Al Magliochetti.) **Below:** George Romero directing zombie extra Gene Saraceni – the worst zombie extra director of photography Michael Gornick had ever seen! (Courtesy of Al Magliochetti.)

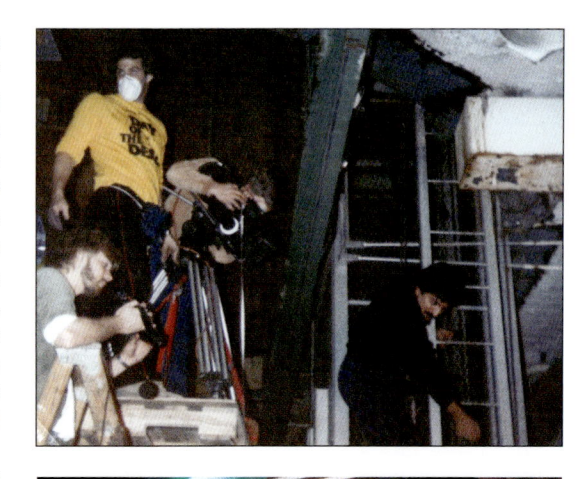

Above: Extra Winnie Flynn as the zombie who Terry Alexander shoots in the silo during the film's climax. (Courtesy of George Demick.)

alligator wasn't aware of it. "I got on the set a little late for the alligator, for that alligator scene," says Deak. "And [John] Vulich says, 'Yeah, you should go look inside . . .' They had a panel truck or something like that. 'You should go look inside there, the alligator's in there,' and I'm like, 'Really?' and he's, like, 'Yeah, he's all tied up,' and I was like 'Well, all right. I'll go take a look.' I go in and I stick my head into the door and, yeah, the alligator was tied up, he was duct-taped, the snout and over the eyes. But when I stick my head in the door I was six inches away from the face of the alligator!"

Deak's encounter with the alligator wasn't his only harrowing experience that day. On set his duties were to spray down extras with Streaks 'N Tips to give them a decayed look and color, so Deak was handed a brown paper bag filled with various colors of Streaks 'N Tips. And that's when the fun began. "There was also a guy with us that was the animal wrangler, because he was putting spiders and snakes on the zombies when they were sitting in their place and stuff," recalls Deak. "And I remember I sat the bag down and they were doing something, and then John [Harrison] said, 'Uh, we need a snake around this one here,' and the snake wrangler guy came over and he picked up my bag with the make-up in it, and he looked and he goes, 'Oops, that's the wrong one' and he grabbed the bag next to it and it was filled with snakes. I was like, 'Holy crap! You mean to tell me I could have grabbed the wrong . . .' 'cause I'm terrified of snakes! I was like, 'I'm very glad I'm not the one that made that mistake,' that he opened up a bag full of make-up as opposed to me opening up a bag full of snakes, 'cause I would have shit myself."

While Deak was dealing with reptilian horrors, the other effects members were busy preparing the throngs of extras who turned out. One group of extras, who were apparently very enthusiastic about becoming zombies, took Rick Gonzales a bit by surprise. "We had a lot of senior citizens!" says Gonzales. "Oh my God, I made up a lot of senior citizens and they just wanted to be the goriest, bloodiest thing ever! 'Oh yeah, cut my throat. Hey, could you have part of me hanging off here?', you know, they loved it! I had a couple there – they took their teeth out – anything to make them look creepier."

And while Gonzales handled the senior crowd, who were into being disgusting and horrific-looking, Barry Anderson found some younger, differently inclined extras to work on. "There was a girl, she came and she had put her own make-up on, and she wanted to be a pretty zombie. And I was like, 'Oh, well I don't know if I can do that,'" laughs Anderson. "So I was trying to . . . it's like, 'Well, do you try to do what the pretty girl wants?' So I was like, 'Well, let me just . . .' and I remember Tom [Savini] looked and goes, 'Who did her make-up?' I was like, 'Uh . . .', he's like, 'You gotta make her uglier than that.'"

Even though there were some enthusiastic extras in Fort Myers, who were excited to be zombies for George Romero, there were also some who just didn't understand what it was all about, which was noticeable to the crew. "You had a few lazy zombies, you know?" says Linda Arrigoni. "It sounded like a good idea until somebody glued all that stuff all over your face."

"The first thing I noticed was that Florida zombies are nothing compared to Pittsburgh zombies," says grip Nick Tallo. "Pittsburgh zombies have the real – the walk, the look – they look like zombies. Florida zombies look like people trying to be zombies, and you could just tell."

During this weekend, there was actually a third unit working in Fort Myers. This unit, headed up by David Garber and John Green, of Garber/Green, took care of the matte photography shots. Garber was a Pittsburgh native and graduate of the Carnegie Mellon School of Architecture, and had previously worked on *Creepshow* for Romero. "We took a small crew, a matte painter crew, a matte painter DP, [Director of Photography] an assistant, a couple of cameras – a pretty small crew, three or four people," remembers Garber. "And we went back and worked with them for about a week, I think, and did the shots and then brought them back to LA, painted them out, enhanced them, and extended the set."

The set Garber is referring to is a long view of Hendry Street in downtown Fort Myers, designed to create the feeling of a desolate, dead city, which was later painted by artist Jim Danforth (more on that in the next chapter).

The task of creating a deserted city in southwest Florida would fall upon Cletus Anderson's crew. Martin Garrigan was set dresser on the film and he remembers the fun of being able to transform downtown Fort Myers from a beautiful small gulf coast town into a city of the dead. "We had some scenes down there where we had to dress up the town, the ghost town, that the zombies are roaming around in. That was a lot of fun," remembers Garrigan. "We had a scene where they walk by these different store fronts and they have wedding dresses . . . we put cobwebs on everything because it's been deserted for so long. So you got all these mannequin brides, with cobwebs on them and snakes, pythons, like, crawling around. So we got to hold the pythons, stuff like that you don't get to do every day."

Garrigan and Anderson's crew would scatter pieces of palm trees and bags of sand all over the roads. Old cars were brought in to help convey the idea that people had just panicked and abandoned their vehicles in the streets. "They tried to find some older beat-up cars," says Bill Love. "But if they weren't beat-up enough, they kind of put this, I guess, this kind of temporary spray paint and they laid palm fronds and stuff on them to make them look kind of bedraggled and forgotten."

"Everybody was working on the palm fronds distribution," says Martin Garrigan's sister, Eileen Garrigan, head scenic artist on the film. "It was all hands on deck for that, because there were truckloads and truckloads of dried-out palm leaves that we were distributing."

Large airboat motors were brought in to blow debris and trash down the streets, especially for one of the film's signature shots. "The Dead Walk" newspaper was designed by Cletus Anderson's art department, but trying to find someone who can remember the details of its creation is a little challenging. Unfortunately Cletus Anderson is no longer with us, and art director Bruce Miller could not recall anything about it. One person with a vague recollection was set decorator Jan Pascale, who seems to remember Bruce Miller working on its creation. "In my mind I can see him cutting things out and pasting – we might have done the paste-up. It might have actually been a group project," says Pascale. "I think we all sort of pieced it together."

Interestingly enough, the production was able to save a lot of money filming these downtown scenes, due to the cooperation of the city of Fort Myers. "I think that, in terms of paying fees, we basically relied on the goodness of their hearts," admits location scout Bill Dickhaut. "I don't think we paid anything for the downtown scenes except to the extent that there was collateral damage. We had to replace the windows we broke and things like that, we had to clean up. I know the set decorator's crew, Cletus Anderson's people, spent a lot of time going back and cleaning up."

Unfortunately, a lot of great zombie make-ups and zombie scenes from this Fort Myers shoot would get left out of the final cut. A shot of a zombie inside the bridal window, with a boa constrictor around her neck, can be seen very quickly in a long shot. However, the close-up shot was the victim of a technical glitch involving the camera. The zombie extra in the scene, Kat Kelley, a friend of Bill and Kathy Love, was a Florida Fish and Wildlife officer. A surfer zombie with his abdomen opened and exposed was another great make-up that never made it into the film. And a suicide victim that came back to life after hanging himself would be another editing-room casualty. "John Harrison and I had been trying to figure this out. We got into a long philosophical discussion about

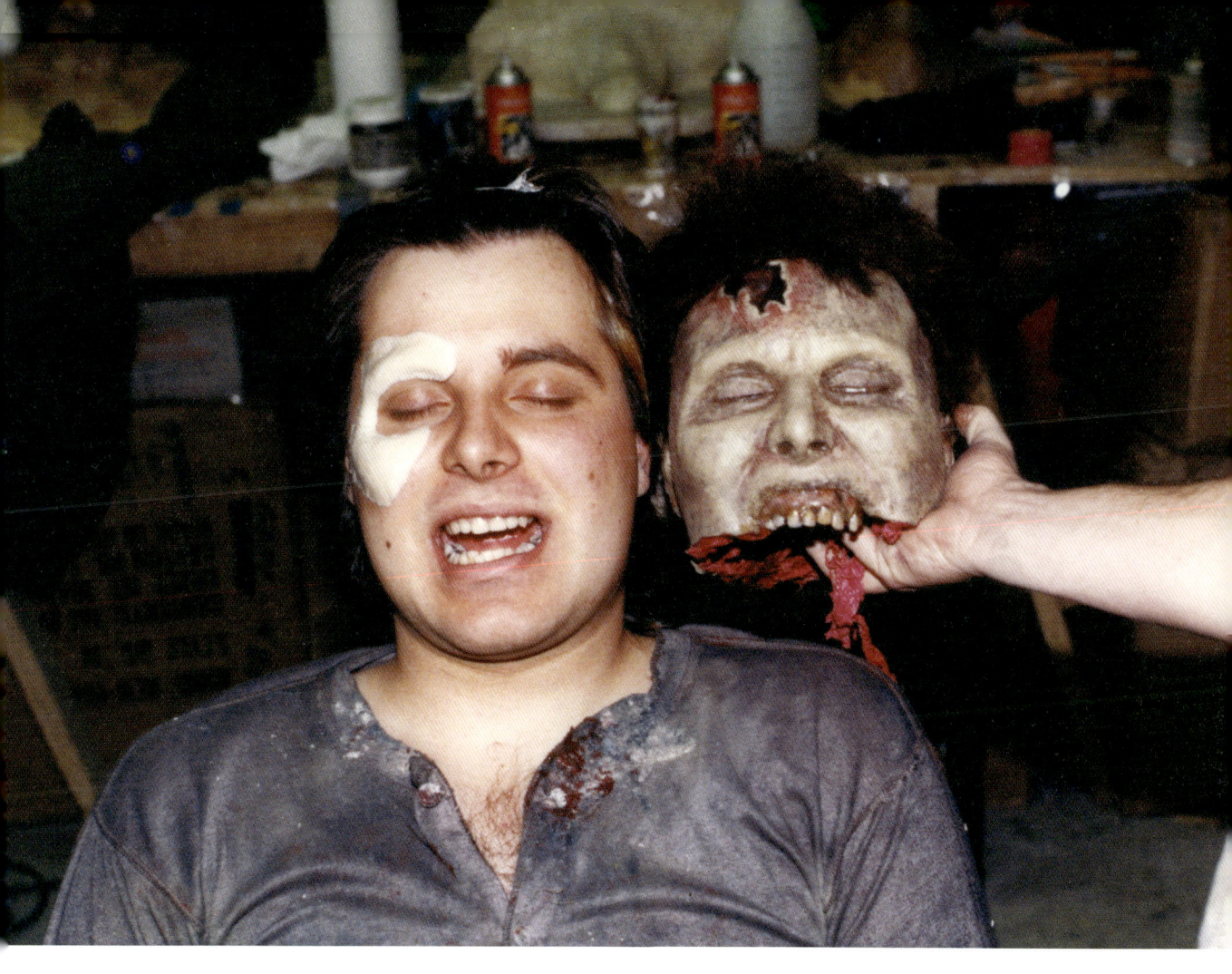

Above: John Vulich and the "pop-top" head, being prepped for the scene where he attacks Lori Cardille in the cave. (Courtesy of Richard Alvarez.)

zombies committing suicide," recalls editor, Pat Buba. "We had this really detailed philosophical discussion. I don't know if it interrupted the flow as much as the fact that we could never resolve the problem that we had with the philosophy of whether or not the zombie would be twitching or not. I think that was the case."

Sunday 12/16/1984 – Day 44

**"Without you guys, Wampum has given a new meaning to 'Stick it where the sun don't shine'."
– Jessica & Rawhide**

Day 44 would be spent re-shooting part of scene 17 at the Mosquito Control site, due to a damaged negative in the lab. While this day would wrap up filming in Florida, it didn't wrap up the cast and crew's time in Florida. The next day they celebrated at the Romeros' home on Sanibel with an evening cocktail party. Slate and film loader Simon Manses remembers the evening well, because he surprised George Romero with one of his many talents. "When we were down in Florida I met George Romero's father, who's from Cuba," says Manses. "And I was speaking Spanish with him and George is like, 'I didn't know you spoke Spanish. I didn't know you spoke Spanish – very good Spanish!' George speaks a little bit, a few words, but not much. But he understands it a bit. And I said, 'Oh yeah, I speak Spanish. I also speak German and a little bit of French.' And then he looked at, I think, Mike Gornick and said, 'Man, that cat must be a thousand years old,' because of all the different things I have done. But again, when you're a freelancer you do a lot of different things because you gotta eat."

The production's time in Florida went by very fast, and failed to exploit all of the beautiful scenery and landscapes of the gulf coast area, much to the chagrin of certain crew members. "I witnessed this a lot throughout the whole production, that George [Romero] was kind of clean and efficient about his shooting, but didn't put his soul into all the material," says Mike Gornick. "He just wanted to get there and get out. I don't know what that was all about."

While some cast and crew headed back to Pennsylvania, others, such as members of the make-

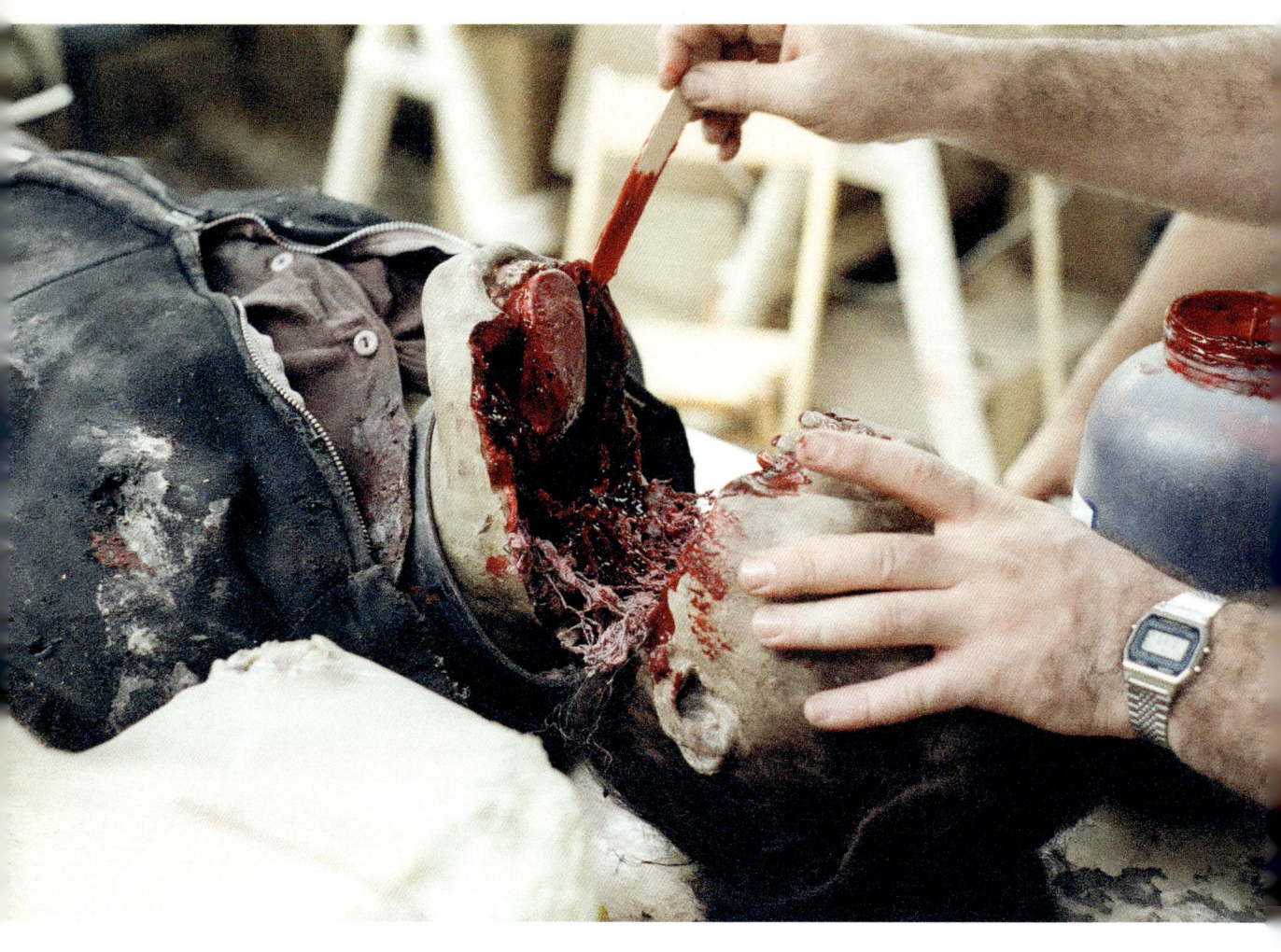

Above: The shovel-head gag, aka "pop-top", being prepped with gel blood in the effects shop. (Courtesy of George Demick.)

up effects crew, took a day trip to Orlando to visit Disney World. And some simply stayed a few extra days in Fort Myers because they were forgotten about by the production! William Laczko had taken vacation time and drove down to Fort Myers in his own vehicle. So while the cast and crew had cleared out of the condos they were staying in, Laczko stayed behind and enjoyed the area. "I actually stayed there, like, three or four days longer than I was supposed to because they forgot that I was in the damn place! And I just kind of toured around Sanibel Island and all that area for a while, and had a good time," says Laczko. "When I got tired of bumming around, I walked into the production office and gave them the keys and they said, 'Oh, we forgot about you.'"

After this, the production would take the next two and a half weeks off to enjoy the Christmas and New Year's holidays. The brief trip to paradise was now over, and it was time to return to the cave. Production would officially start back up on January 3, 1985 in Wampum, but was actually preceded by an early bonus day of shooting on January 2.

Wednesday 1/2/1985

Call sheet unavailable

This is an interesting one – the bonus day mentioned previously. On the preliminary shooting schedule, dated 11/26/1984, this day was earmarked for the re-shooting of Miguel's gut spill during Sarah's nightmare. Whether or not there was a call sheet produced for this day I don't know. According to the shooting schedule, the company would reconvene in Wampum by morning, with shooting starting in the afternoon. It was originally supposed to be day 44, but with the production re-shooting on Sunday 12/16/1984, that obviously changed things. Why then wouldn't they consider it day 45? Who knows?

Regardless, the re-shooting of Miguel spilling his guts was done today. This day offers yet another piece of evidence relating to the rotten intestines story involving Joe Pilato. As explained previously, the question of whether Pilato filmed his death scene before or after the holiday break has been cleared up by Mike Deak and George Demick – it was before. But interestingly, there have never been stories of a horrid smell plaguing Tim DiLeo during filming of his second gut-spill scene. It's likely, then, that some new, "fresher" intestines were purchased from the butcher shop, or perhaps they used some of the sausage and turkey from the props department? No one recalls now.

One of the key people on set this day was John Vulich, who remembers Savini pulling off his magic when it appeared there were more elaborate ways of accomplishing the effect. "There's a lot of instances where I just thought, kinda, Tom was crazy about setting an effect up and I thought it wasn't gonna work, and then it just kind of came off flawlessly," admits Vulich. "That was right after Christmas vacation, I think Tom made me come like a day or two earlier than everybody else, 'cause he wanted me to help him with it, to do the prosthetics and glue it down. When he was putting all that together I just [thought], 'This isn't gonna work.' I was probably over-thinking, like, 'We need cables or wires to pull it and make sure of this, this, or that,' and he was just relying on the weight of the . . . they look kinda like forceps, that clamp on, he was relying on the weight of those when he flips over, to carry and flap the piece over, and I was just convinced it wasn't gonna work and it worked flawlessly."

Thursday 1/3/1985 – Day 45

"My mind's a blank." – Nick Mastandrea

Day 45 would be the production's first "official" day back at work after a two and a half week hiatus, and once again the cast and crew found themselves in the hostile conditions of the Wampum Mine.

"We did go back and we had to spend another week or two weeks in the cave," says Rolf Pardula. "I would rather have died, I think. I was miserable. Nobody was a happy person there when we came back. We really didn't want to come back into that cave again. "

"There was something about that cave, man, that just like sucked the energy, the life force out of you," says Simon Manses. "And being dark and cold and shooting in the winter and always being in a moist, cool environment, you know? You'd go back to the hotel and the first thing you wanted to do was jump in the sauna."

"There were parts that were muddy and drippy – there was water dripping out of the ceilings and shit like that," says Nick Tallo. "The mine people, they had

Above: Tom Savini and John Vulich setting up the "pop-top" gag before filming. **Below:** Filming the "pop-top" gag. (Photos courtesy of George Demick.)

guys driving around in trucks with big long poles, and they would drive along and smack part of the ceiling to see if there was any loose shit falling off the ceilings."

Nick Tallo was a member of the grip department, a department that had acquired a special nickname. "If I remember [correctly], the grip community in Pittsburgh, which was pretty small at the time, was known as the 'Grips from Hell'," says grip Barry Kessler. "And I think one of the reasons is because of everyone working down in that mine."

The leader of this band of misfits was key grip Nick Mastandrea, and under his guidance no one on the production was safe from mayhem. "The grip department, they were a bunch of practical jokers," says location manager Jim Bruwelheide. "They knew that I had to be at the mine much earlier than anybody else, and we were all staying at a hotel in Wampum, Pennsylvania. They ended up in the middle of the night, somehow, someway without me knowing it, 'pennying' me in my room. And what that means is you push on a door from the outside and you insert coins between the door and the door jamb, and it gets so tight to the point that you can't even turn the door knob to open the door. It was probably six o'clock in the morning, and I'm ready to head to the mine before everybody else is there to get everything opened up . . . I couldn't open my door! And for the life of me I had no idea what was going on. I started to just literally bang into the door until it finally opened up; I guess I dislodged the coins. When I opened the door there were a couple of the grips standing in the hallway just laughing like hell. I wasn't very happy about the situation because I probably had about five minutes to get to this mine."

"The moon shots, I'm sure you heard about," recalls Nick Mastandrea. "We'd steal people's cameras and take pictures of Bomba's ass, and then I'd put the camera back and then people would get their film back and there'd be his ass. We did that to everybody's camera."

"When we did *Knightriders*, he [Mastandrea] and I started theme days," says Nick Tallo. "We did a couple of little things, like we had neck tie day and stupid hat day and ladies' underpants day – everybody wore ladies underwear on their heads. But when we did *Day* . . . we didn't have as many theme days, but we had like Streaks 'N Tips day, where everybody sprayed their hair and their beards silver, so we all look like old men."

"To Nick's [Mastandrea] credit, the morale was always pretty high and that was kind of his doing," says Barry Kessler. "And part of it was this kind of stuff, the theme days, little competitions and things like that. That kind of stuff really helped."

And while the grip crew was an endless source of hijinks, they didn't exactly have a monopoly on crazy antics or "tomfoolery", so to speak. Tom Savini's effects crew played just as hard, and sometimes dangerously so. One incident involving Tom Savini, Everett Burrell, handcuffs, and a fire extinguisher would end with a trip to the hospital for one of them.

"Tom had handcuffed Everett to the make-up chair, which was bolted to the ground," says Howard Berger. "Tom was spraying Everett with Streaks 'N Tips, which is a spray, like a color you spray into your hair or whatever, and just kept spraying Everett with this stuff until Everett would say, 'Tom Savini is the greatest make-up artist alive.' And Everett would say, 'F you, Tom!' and then Tom would spray him and he's like, 'Okay, okay, okay.' And then Tom's like, 'Okay, you gonna say it?' and Everett said, 'Yes, I will say it,' and so, just as he unlocked his handcuffs to remove the handcuffs, Everett just went, 'F you, Tom!' and then Tom locked the handcuffs. Everett got out of the handcuffs, they were running around and Everett ran into the make-up room and grabbed a fire extinguisher. Tom walked in, and I'm telling you, this is all in slow motion, I'm standing right there with everybody. Tom walked in and then Tom took a deep breath, went, 'Huhhhhh,' and his eyes opened wide. Everett shot the fire extinguisher off and blasted Tom in the face with the powdered fire extinguisher stuff. Tom took a whole lung fill into his lungs, scratched his eyes, and soon as the dust cleared Tom was on the floor gagging and tears pouring out of his eyes. And I just looked at Everett and I said, 'You killed Tom Savini.' Everett was devastated. I think Greg [Nicotero] took Tom to the emergency hospital. Tom's corneas were all scratched and they had to evacuate his lungs or something, or I don't know. But we felt so bad – well, Everett felt so bad."

"They had to take me to the hospital and I had to wear bandages over my eyes, one eye," recalls Tom Savini. "The whole crew for the whole time that I wore the bandage, they wore a bandage over their eye as well."

As for this day's work, it concentrated completely on scenes inside "The Ritz" set. Scene A44, where Sarah and McDermott walk through the interior hallway of the trailer towards the back end, was shot. Another scene, A71, where John stands in the doorway before heading out to check on Sarah and McDermott, was also filmed. As was scene 63, in which Sarah and McDermott decide they will go back into the complex to look for morphine for Miguel, while John offers up one of his shirts for Sarah to wear.

Later in the day, scenes 72 and 74 – where Miguel is lying down inside the trailer, just before he makes his fateful decision to ride the elevator up top – were shot as well. Lastly, three other scenes were listed, if time permitted: scene 61, where Sarah chases a crazed Miguel through the cave after he has been bitten (this would end up on the following day's schedule); scene 43, where Sarah and Bill walk through the mine heading towards "The Ritz"; and finally scene 73, in which John leaves the trailer (this was basically just the same shot as A71).

Friday 1/4/1985 – Day 46

"Can I pull his stump off now?" – Eileen Sieff

Day 46 began with work on scene 61, where Sarah chases Miguel through the mine after he's been bitten, and continued with scene A62, when she chops his arm off in an attempt to deal with the bite.

The actual cutting off of the arm proved to be a little bit trickier than originally anticipated, when Lori Cardille swung the machete into the arm and it literally bounced off it. The fix required the replacement of the arm, so that the machete would properly cut into it

ONE DAY AT A TIME

upon action. "I supervised, I think, Miguel's arm chop," says Everett Burrell. "We did it a couple of times – the Tom [Savini] way, and then we did it the right way. [*laughs*] There's a Tom way and there's the right way."

A very important part of scene 62 would be an unscripted moment that was mainly contributed by Lori Cardille. After cutting off her lover's arm and then being confronted by the soldiers at gun point, Sarah breaks down and shows emotion that she's been holding back throughout the film. It was at this pivotal moment that Cardille felt a little more texture to her character would be appropriate. "George [Romero] always gave his actors freedom to explore," says Cardille. "I do remember talking to George about what I think Sarah's state of mind would be at that moment. I also felt that this was her moment to show her vulnerability and humanness. It was very organic as an actress to know this is the way it had to be. George was very respectful of my choice and let me do it."

"George [Romero] was in touch with all his characters in *Day*. That makes for good, perhaps even great acting in a film," says Terry Alexander. "Less focus on special effects made George refocus on emotional interactions. It was direction; the scene was intense enough as written. Great directors always, always enhance their talent . . . sensing with them within the characters, working with each differently, causing them to give their best. Remember . . . back in the day, the director was sitting or standing very close to you, feeling you. Now they're sitting in a truck somewhere, watching what the camera is picking up and giving direction and notes to the first assistant director, who relays them to you."

Cardille's motivation for adding this moment was really born out of a desire to play the role a bit differently than scripted. "As I look back, I think that the character was . . . not as many dimensions as I wish I would have brought to it. Because it was the first major film I did and it was okay, but I would like to have done it differently," admits Cardille. "The character had the arc of holding it together, holding it together, holding it together until she breaks down after she cuts off the arm, which worked at that time. But I would liked to have explored other aspects with her relationships, maybe more sexual innuendo and tension with Terry Alexander, that character."

Saturday 1/5/1985 – Day 47

No quote of the day

Day 47 would continue work on scene A62, where Miguel has his arm amputated by Sarah. Before filming could commence each day, the set had to be prepared by the grip department. And working in the

Above: Production assistant Deborah Carter, as the hippie zombie who attacks Jarlath Conroy in the cave. In the background is extras casting agent Felice Lammi. (Courtesy of Barbara Boyle.)

mine added extra challenges for the crew not usually associated with film production.

"We'd have lights all through the mine and at night when we were done shooting, we'd have to turn the lights off and let them cool, and then we'd have to cover them up with plastic so that water dripping and stuff wouldn't mess them up," says Nick Tallo. "And then in the morning, first thing we'd do when we went in is we'd have to go in the mine and uncover all the lights before we could turn them on. So when you did that it was real dark. *It was real, real dark!* Because the only thing you saw was what your flashlight saw."

"The first thing that we had to do was get the equipment to the set, to the site – we'd do that mostly with golf carts," says Barry Kessler. "I can't remember if we actually were able to drive vehicles down . . . parts of the mine we could, but most of the places where we were shooting, I don't remember us taking vehicles, but it's possible we did. We'd load up pickup trucks and things, certainly no big grip trucks or anything like that, like you'd have on a regular feature outside. And we'd have to run cable for the electric. There was power in there, but we couldn't obviously run generators down there, so we had to run huge cable lines to where the electricity was coming into the mine. So we would set up, get ready to go – that could be an hour, two hours. Then they would rehearse the scenes with the actors, obviously. Now once that got set up, we'd look at the call sheet and, if another location was after lunch, then some of us would split off and start lighting and rigging the next

179

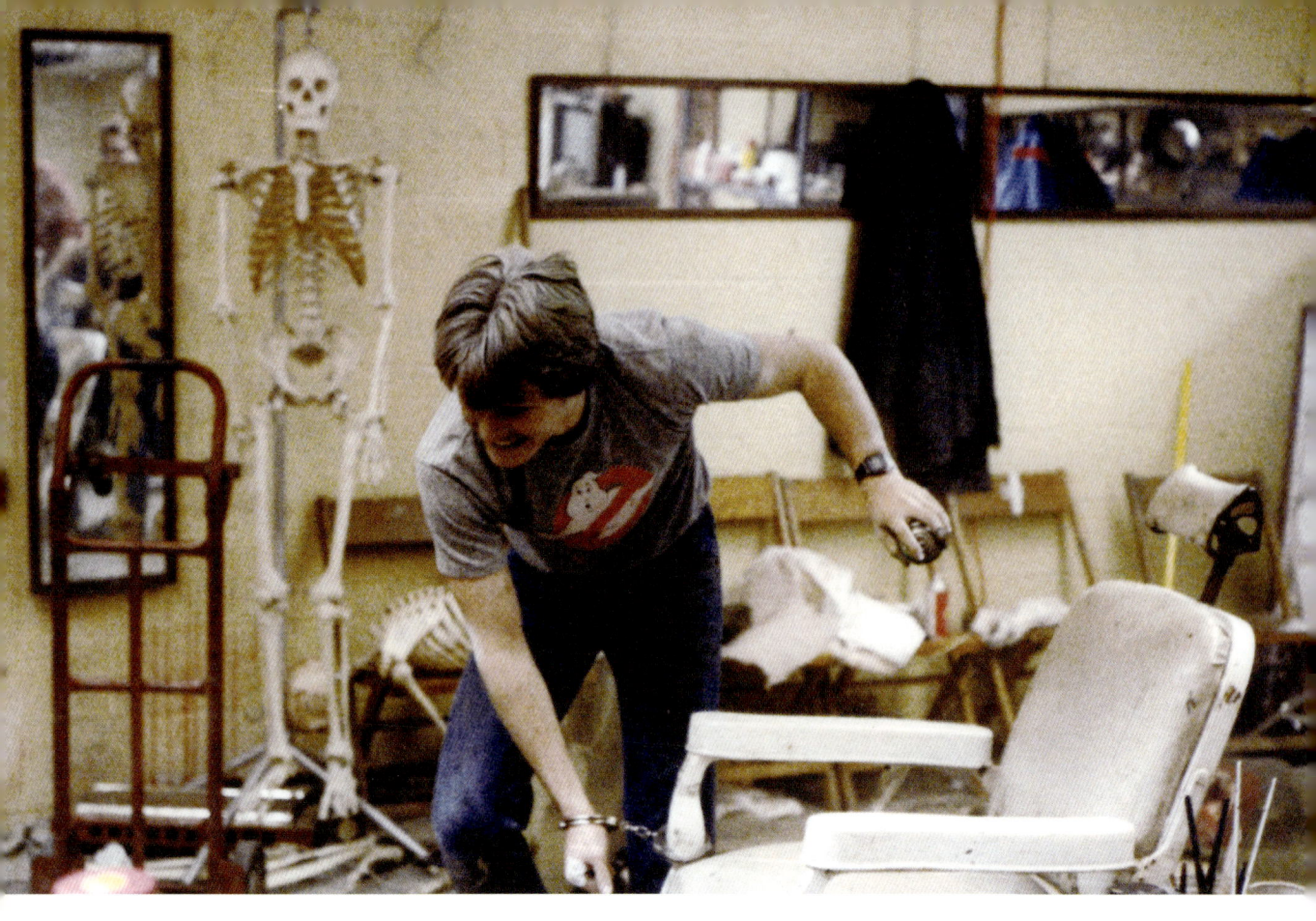

Above: Everett Burrell handcuffed to the make-up chair, by Tom Savini, in the effects shop. (Courtesy of Everett Burrell.)

location while they were shooting the first location, to give us a jump on that. So we'd split the crew like that. Some guys would be working with what was shooting at the time and then others would break off and start getting ready for the next scene, which might be somewhere else in the mine. And then when we'd go to the next location, people would split off and start tearing down the first location. So we were constantly always moving."

Another factor inside the mine was the natural inhabitants – bats. But as scary as bats can be, some people weren't bothered at all. "Every once in a while we'd find a little bat laying on the ground," says Nick Tallo. "They were little, but when people hear bats they think of these like four-foot-long things that are, like, carrying small children away. They were like mice with wings." [*laughs*]

Besides bats, the crew had to deal with the dust floating around in the cave, and one member of the crew was especially allergic to the mine dust. "Fred Roth whose nickname, once again given by Nick Mastandrea, was 'Derf' – which is Fred spelled backwards," says Simon Manses. "For some reason he seemed more susceptible to that dust, he was like our canary in the cave. He would be the first one that would be miserable with the dust. So, he took some gaffer's tape or some rope or something, I think some rope, and put around his neck a box of Kleenex and someone put on there: 'Derf Rags'."

Monday 1/7/1985 – Day 48

"It's back and forth, back and forth, around around and chop." – Lori Cardille

Day 48 finally saw the completion of scene A62, Miguel's arm amputation. This day would also see a luncheon meeting attended by, amongst others, George Romero, Tom Savini, Michael Gornick, Bruce Miller, and John Harrison, to discuss the upcoming shooting for scenes 80, 84, 85, and 91 – or the "Laff in the Dark" sequence, as it was referred to.

Scene 44, where Sarah lounges at "The Ritz" and has a long philosophical discussion with John, was scheduled to begin filming on this day as well. This scene was a special one for Terry Alexander, who won the role of John based on his interpretation of it in his audition. And, much like he did in scene 35, where he gave Rhodes a big smile, Alexander was able to collaborate with Romero to bring a little extra something to the scene. "In the speech, when I say, 'Great big fourteen-mile tombstone,' I go way high," says Alexander. "I said, 'Hey, George – hey man, I think I can go way high in volume in that and we can put an echo in there.' He said, 'Oh, that's a great idea! Let's try that.'"

Above: Tom Savini and John Vulich relax on a stunt mattress during filming. (Courtesy of George Demick.)

Scene 44 also provided a bit of a challenge to editor Pat Buba during post production, when he was having trouble getting it nailed down just right. "We spent – actually, because we cared about that scene and because it was a nice scene, it's really well written and the performances were good – we spent a lot of time working on the balance of that scene," says Buba. "It was never really clicking, something was off about it, and we would go back to it every once in a while. I remember George [Romero] was, he wasn't even there . . . he was just away. And he called me and he said, 'I know what's wrong.' He says, 'There's one reaction shot that's not working because it should respond this way,' and I went in and changed it and then the rhythms of the scene kinda fell in place after that."

Part of what helped "The Ritz" and its scenic backyard come to life was the work of set decorator Jan Pascale. After working hard on the set, it was production designer Cletus Anderson's reaction that stuck out in her memory the most afterwards. "You know, I think my favorite thing was I think I made Cletus laugh," recalls Pascale. "I can't remember the character's name now, but it was a little trailer, and we set up this little kind of patio area with pink flamingos in their little yard, a patio with beach chairs and pink flamingos – and it made Cletus laugh. And that to me was like, 'Oh my God, I actually made Cletus laugh.' [*laughs*] I felt like I graduated." Pascale's admiration for Anderson is genuine and heartfelt, and it shows. He made a significant impression on her, which would affect the rest of her career.

But Pascale wasn't alone in her admiration of the man. "He was a wonderful designer and really a mentor to the whole group of painters and designers that were working at the time," says Eileen Garrigan. "He was a very fastidious . . . it's kind of funny, you would think that, with movies like *Day of the Dead* or *Creepshow* that the scenery was, oh, I don't know, for *Day of the Dead* it's all kind of dirty and dank and dark, but he was very detail conscious, there was no slap-dash about it really. He really would cruise through the set with me, and we'd inspect everything that could possibly show up as a close up, and he didn't want to see any revealing staples or screw heads. He really had us do our best to get everything as good as we could have time to do."

The atmosphere on the set, with the Romero family as it was, really fostered creativity – the kind of creativity showcased by people like Garrigan and Pascale. "It was the best, most wonderful place to learn your craft. Because you felt nurtured, you felt like, well, if I make a mistake people won't yell at me, they'll help me. You know what I mean? It's that kind of, literally, that kind of environment," recalls Pascale,

Above: Tom Savini wrestles with the background zombie masks on the make-up effects room floor. (Courtesy of George Demick.)

fondly. "People were there to lean on and to help you see the way, they were so generous. It was just the most generous family-oriented group of people. I mean family in a wide sense, they really made you feel like family, and you felt like you were part of a team."

Pascale is certainly not alone in her feelings about the production's family atmosphere. "There was this really homey kind of feeling on the set," says Lori Cardille.

"It was a zombie movie," says Pascale. "But every single thing mattered to us and we really all put our hearts into it, you know?"

Tuesday 1/8/1985 – Day 49

"It's obviously a live head." – Mike Gornick

Day 49 would continue work on scene 44, where Sarah and John "get acquainted", as it read on the daily call sheet. This scene would be the section of the film where Alexander and Cardille worked closest with one another. "A very giving actress, a sweetheart really," says Alexander of his co-star. "I had a good time working with her, we didn't have that many scenes together, but we connected pretty well."

The other scene shot on this day was scene 98, where Sarah, John, and McDermott escape into the silo, only to be beset by two zombies. The two zombies in the scene were played by Winnie Flynn, the female zombie that John shoots, and Gene Saraceni, the male zombie that McDermott shoots.

Gene Saraceni taught acting at a local college in western Pennsylvania, and his wife, Iva, had previously worked for Romero on *Knightriders*, in which she played the abused mother of Patricia Tallman, and in *Creepshow*, where she was the little boy's mother in the wraparound segment of the film. The experience, described by Saraceni as a "hoot", was great fun for the professor, but certainly very different from what he was used to. "They had rigged my forehead with a prosthetic piece that would be pulled away to reveal what would look like a gunshot wound. But it had to be synchronized with the explosion of blood against a white wall behind my head," remembers Saraceni. "There was a condom filled with stage blood and an explosive – I was really quite frightened of that. I'd never worn one of those before." [*laughs*]

"Gene was teaching acting/theater at Seton Hill College, so we assumed he had some sort of prowess," confesses Mike Gornick. "In any event, from my perspective, watching him on set – not only the worst zombie I had ever seen in my life, [*laughs*] but I was troubled by his lack of acting, you know? We did take after take after take."

Indeed, the shots of Saraceni – for whatever reason – were deemed unsatisfactory, so four days later his scene would be re-shot. The interesting thing is, having watched Tom Savini's behind-the-scenes home video footage of both takes, it looks to me like they may have used the original take!

The other zombie, Winnie Flynn, was a veteran performance artist specializing in musical productions. Her zombie would also be dispatched with a shot to the head, but her effect required a large spout of blood to shoot from her forehead. Preparing the effect required testing the tubing line with water, simulating the blood spout. This was a habit that Tom Savini had taught his crew to practice – always put the effect through its paces ahead of time. "He would always kinda test things out in the shop until he felt it was . . . he'd run it through four or five times and make sure he'd practiced it," says John Vulich of Savini. "He was really well prepared about stuff, so by the time you got to set there [were] very little hiccups that would generally happen." In this particular instance, though, there was a slight hiccup, as when the effect was executed, a large spout of water shot out of Flynn's forehead before the blood came out. Subsequently, the effect garnered a humorous nickname from the young effects crew: brain fluid. "Everett [Burrell] never cleared all the water out of the tube," says Greg Nicotero. "I just remember thinking, 'Fuck, there's this big spray of water,' and we're like, 'Oh, its brain fluid.' We just made that up."

Savini's crew learned a lot under his tutelage. Not just about the technical side of the business, but also the purely fun and carefree aspects of life behind the scenes, not sweating about things too much. "I think Tom really ruined me for the film industry, because I had so much fun working with him," remembers Mike Trcic. "He had such a great attitude about films; it should be fun, you know? If it's too much like work, there's got to be something else that's better to do. He always kept it really light, there was always fun stuff going on."

"I just gotta say, later on, looking back in life, I feel like I was blessed to have been working with Tom at that point in my career," says Dave Kindlon. "'Cause I couldn't think of a better thing to do at that time."

"I remember Gaylen Ross coming to visit one day and we were all freaking out," says Greg Nicotero, referring to the *Dawn of the Dead* star. "Tom brought her into the make-up room because Everett and I were like, 'Oh my God, Gaylen Ross! Gaylen Ross! Gaylen Ross!' Tom goes, 'See those two guys over there? They have a crush on you,' and we're like, 'Ahhhhh, Tom!' So we were all embarrassed."

Above: Mechanical make-up effects technician Dave Kindlon. (Courtesy of George Demick.)

"I mean, God, I got *Grande Illusions* in the mail signed by him in high school," remembers Everett Burrell. "So, it was like working for my idol. And he still is my idol, I just think he's kind of a fucked-up idol." [*laughs*]

"Tom continually did these things to us and put us through the ringer, and tortured us, and hurt us," says Howard Berger. "People got darts shot into their legs with air guns."

"There were a couple of things that Tom had," recalls Nicotero. "One of them would be, 'In twenty years it won't matter.' And the other one was, 'If you were in the middle of the desert and you didn't have super glue, what were you gonna do?' Because he just kind of instilled in us, like, 'Don't worry about it, it doesn't fucking matter.'"

"Greg Nicotero looked like he just fell out of a cherub advertisement. You know, all pink cheeks and golden curls and absolutely sweet and angelic," says second AD Katarina Wittich. "They were just very young and very, very angelic-looking, and then they had this devil of a boss [Savini]."

"Those guys, they worked their asses off for him [Savini] and they learned a lot," says grip Nick Tallo. "It's so funny because I used to call them his love slaves – Tom's love slaves. He'd think up an idea, and those fuckers, he'd have them doing it."

"You'd walk into their special effects room and they'd all be, like, having a great time around a monitor," remembers Wittich. "And you'd go over and look and they'd be watching over and over again that famous Vietnamese shot of the Viet Cong guy being executed, so that they could get exactly what it looks like when somebody's head is blown off. It was just surreal because they were lovely and their job was to make these absolutely horrifying images."

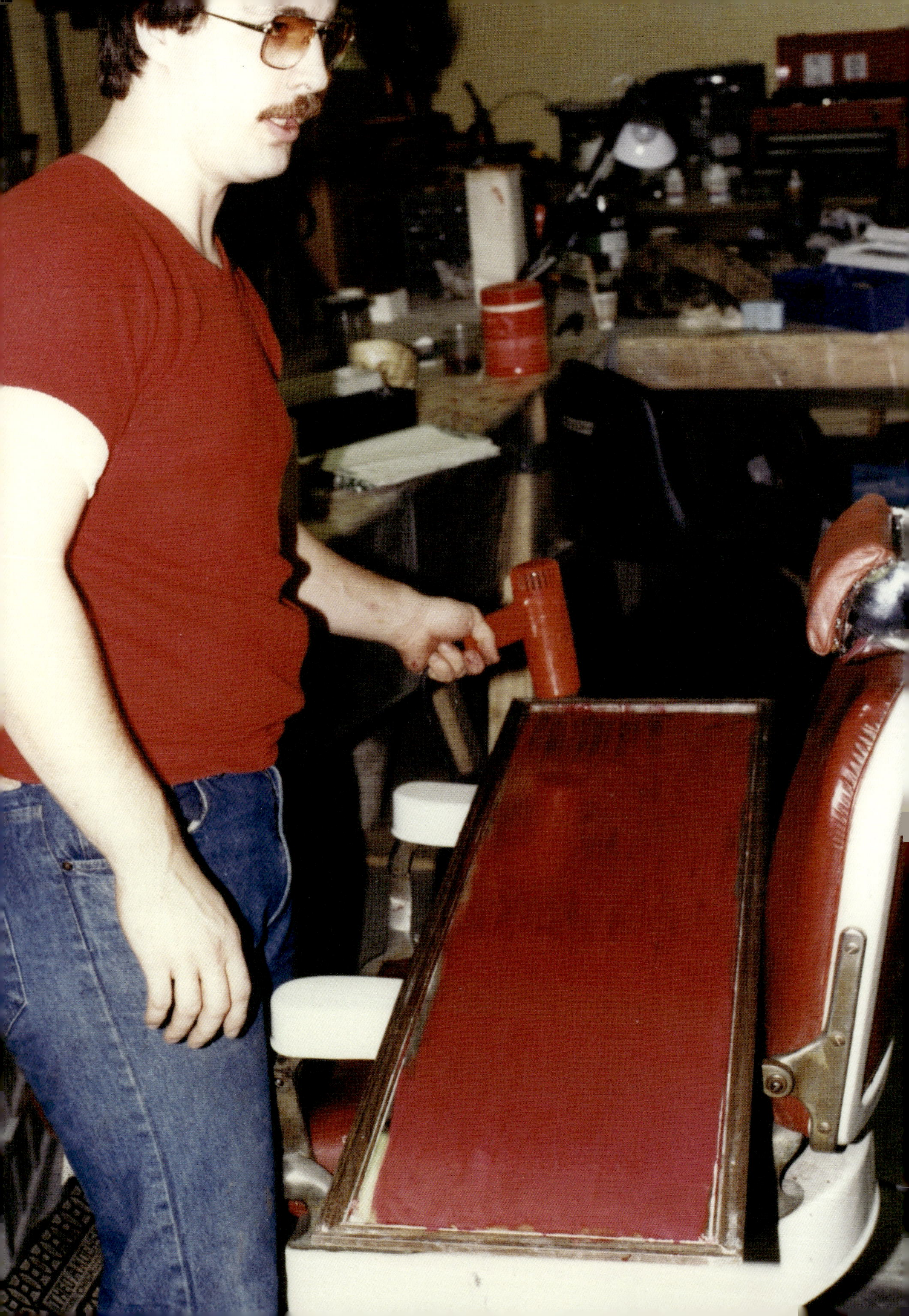

ONE DAY AT A TIME

Above: John Vulich and Mike Deak work on turning their colleague Everett Burrell into a zombie. Mine employee and film PA Mike Butera can be seen to the left being transformed by Mike Trcic. (Courtesy of Al Magliochetti.)

Interestingly, Taso Stavrakis came up with an idea to add a little extra excitement to scene 98. "Taso was hoping to shoot a high fall," recalls Richard Alvarez, a close friend of Stavrakis' who was visiting the set during this time. "I know there was a scene in the movie, they're all escaping up the silo and they're being pursued by zombies. And Taso had talked to, I think, Tom [Savini] and to George [Romero] and said, 'It would be great if somebody kicked or shot a zombie and he fell back down the silo and did a high fall.' He [Romero] said, 'Well, it's not really in the script but if we can get it we'll shoot it.' So the idea was he [Taso] was going to set it up and be ready to shoot it, sort of as a pick-up shot if they could do it." Unfortunately the restraints of time and budget would kill the idea. "They just never got around to it, just couldn't fit it into the schedule," says Alvarez. "But we did practice it several times. I've got photos of me and Taso practicing the fall."

Wednesday 1/9/1985 – Day 50

"We're starting to gel as a unit." – George Romero

As the production moved into its fiftieth day of shooting, work resumed on scene 98. I'm not sure if this was supposed to be a scheduled re-shoot of Saraceni's scene or not, because, as mentioned, it

Left: Mike Trcic drying red-colored latex, aka "chunks of flesh", on a mirror in the effects shop. (Courtesy of Richard Alvarez.)

would officially be re-shot just a few days later on January 12. Saraceni is listed on the call sheet, so it's uncertain what was going on here. A newspaper writer from the *Pittsburgh Press*, Jim Davidson, was on set for the filming of Saraceni's sequence, and in the article he penned for the newspaper he mentions it being the fiftieth day of the production. However, there is the matter of the extra day of re-shooting on January 2, for Tim DiLeo's gut-spill scene. Could that extra day be the answer to this? Or did Saraceni take three passes at getting it right? Mike Gornick did say that they did "take after take after take". It's a little unclear.

Also scheduled to begin filming this day was scene 80, the beginning of the "Laff in the Dark" sequence, where Sarah and McDermott are besieged by zombies in the cave. The process of bringing this wild sequence to life would take up the following five days of production.

Thursday 1/10/1985 – Day 51

"I don't do grovel." – Eileen Sieff

Day 51 concentrated on scene 80, the "Laff in the Dark" sequence, where the heroes fight for their lives making their way through the darkness of the

Above: In one of his many zombie cameos Taso Stavrakis sneaks up on his good friend Richard Alvarez, who was visiting the set. (Courtesy of Richard Alvarez.)

cave. "Laff in the Dark" was the name of a ride at Kennywood Amusement Park in Pittsburgh, or more specifically a dark ride, designed to scare riders, similar to a funhouse or haunted house.

The big effect for the day was the first part of the the shovel gag, where Lori Cardille's character, Sarah, is struggling to fight off a zombie when Jarlath Conroy's character, McDermott, saves the day with a shovel by cutting the zombie's head in half. John Vulich would have the honor of playing the unfortunate zombie, "Poptop", as he was referred to on the call sheet. To achieve the illusion he would have to suffer for his art – sort of. "Tom had rigged up one of these classic kind of Tom Savini effects with the shovel, where the shovel's cut out and it gets put around your mouth and you put tubing on there," recalls Vulich. "Tom was probably one of the best guys in the business I've ever worked with that knows how to rig blood tubing, and he knows exactly where to glue it and where to cut the holes, how to cut the holes in such a way to get these interesting . . . you're always trying to get these interesting splashes of blood that look creepy and he was like the master of that. So, he set the shovel up and got the tubes all glued in place. I do remember we used several different types of blood . . . the main blood is this blood made from corn syrup and food coloring and, in order to get the blood not to bead up, we used, like, a photographic wash liquid called Photo-Flo, which keeps the blood from beading up and makes it run properly, and it's generally considered toxic. So, that blood we don't use for your mouth. And then we had a special blood without that, that's made for using in your mouth. Then we had bloods that have Cavisil mixed in to them, so that they're more like a paste, for dried blood. So, what I didn't know is he had hooked up the tubing to use the regular Photo-Flo blood, which was pouring into my mouth, [*laughs*] this toxic liquid, which I remember getting kind of upset about. I think there's this video Tom took of me just sitting there gargling and spitting out all this Photo-Flo blood, which I think I found later really isn't all that toxic – it's kind of like a soap more than anything."

Another zombie extra working on this day was production assistant Deborah Carter, who would play the hippie-looking zombie with long hair that attacks McDermott and is eventually dispatched with a two-by-four, which was what she was listed as on the call sheet, "2x4 #2". Carter had managed to earn herself an amusing nickname during production, and for good reason. "We had golf carts to get around in the mine, and every department had a series of golf carts that they would use for different purposes," says location manager Jim Bruwelheide. "We'd built different boxes to fit on these things for, say, craft services, so we had a box on the back of a golf cart that would hold coffee and doughnuts, or whatever. But we'd also made one that had a really nice bench on the back of it, and that was used for transporting talent from basically the make-up/wardrobe areas within an office complex in the mine, to take the talent or the actor out to the area where the shooting was occurring within the mine. And there was a production assistant by the name of Debbie Carter that was responsible for driving this golf cart with the talent on the back. I don't recall who she had, but there were two actors sitting on this bench, and it faced backwards and she was driving the golf cart, and it was through a tight little segment of the mine where it was narrow, and for some unknown reason she caught the edge of this bench that was on the back on the side wall, and it just knocked it right off the back of the golf cart, with the two actors, [*laughs*] and everybody was just standing there looking at her and she just looked up and said, 'I didn't do that.' From then on she was known as Debbie 'Crash' Carter."

Also listed for the day was the shot of the zombie hand punching up from below the rock slide. Again, it would be a member of the crew, production assistant

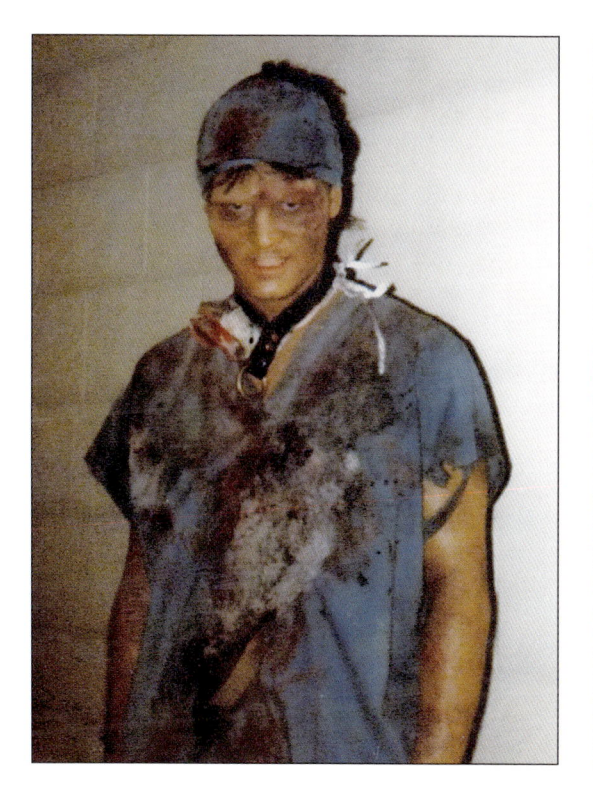

John "Flash" Williams, who would do the honors. For Williams it felt like a day off, being able to have his arm made up in Savini's workshop and then relaxing until it was time to shoot. "It took three days to build that special effect," recalls Williams. "What they did was, they built a box that was much like a coffin, and they had it hooked up to an air pump that pumped in fresh air at my feet and then up by the left side of my body, and they even had a portable tank in there with an oxygen mask if all went wrong. I would have 30 minutes of air until they could dig me out. So inside that thing I had a light, I had a pillow, something soft for my feet, they had put some sodas in there for me and water. When they closed me in there, I was in there probably, maybe four or five hours before they actually filmed that scene. Because they had to put all the rock on it, they had to run rehearsals."

Friday 1/11/1985 – Day 52

"Rockslide – we're fucked." – Lori Cardille

Day 52 would continue work on scene 80. One of the highlights of today's filming would be the shot of the other zombie dispatched with the two-by-four, Taso Stavrakis, humorously referred to as "Leon Spinks" on the call sheet. Executing the onscreen demise, though, would turn out to be much more difficult than anyone had anticipated. "Well, what seemed to give

Left: Everett Burrell as the surgeon zombie seen towards the end of the film. (Courtesy of Barbara Boyle.)
Right: Male stand-in, Jim Wetzel, as the zombie who flips after being hit with a shovel by Jarlath Conroy. Everett Burrell can be seen "photo bombing" behind Wetzel. (Courtesy of Greg Nicotero.)

us the most trouble was the thing with Taso Stavrakis, where we built a dummy of him and he has his head hit with a wooden board, a two-by-four, and the head would not crush; it just always looked like rubber. I remember it made Tom [Savini] so angry too," laughs Howard Berger. "There was an issue earlier on, when we would chop Miguel's arm off, and the arm was made a little too tough and the knife wouldn't go into it, it just kept boinging off and someone said, 'Hey Tom, maybe you should sharpen that,' and Tom was really upset because it was [one] of the very few gags that didn't work. So anyhow, when it came time to do the Taso thing and they hit the dummy it just looked ridiculous, and I think Michael Gornick said, 'Hey Tom, why don't you sharpen that piece of wood.' [laughs] We ended up doing it the right way, which was put a blood bag on a fake board and hitting Taso with it in the head and that looked much, much better, and that's what they used in the movie."

Another scene covered was scene 85, where McDermott hits the zombie with the shovel and it flips in the air, two parts of which would be improvised on set. Stand-in Jim Wetzel played the zombie and, using his martial arts skills, he would flip himself in the

THE MAKING OF GEORGE A. ROMERO'S DAY OF THE DEAD

Above: Howard Berger begins transforming Al Magliochetti into a zombie for the scene where Lori Cardille, Terry Alexander, and Jarlath Conroy machine gun a group of zombies in the cave towards the film's climax. Magliochetti was injured two months prior at the Manor Nike site when a C-stand fell onto his head and sent him to the hospital. (Courtesy of Al Magliochetti.)

air after being struck with the shovel, and afterwards Jarlath Conroy would let out an "Arfff" noise to the fallen zombie. Both were improvised contributions by Wetzel and Conroy.

Working in these sections of the cave, where there was essentially no light, would be quite a challenge for the crew. "I think it was really hard for the cameraman on *Day of the Dead* to light it because there isn't any light in a cave," says boom man Stuart Deutsch. "What's the motivation of light, you know? Sometimes you put a miner's headlamp on some people or something like that, but there isn't any moon, so what's the light? So it was hard to motivate the lighting, I think, in a cave. That's a hard thing to do."

"Well obviously the biggest challenge of them all was to work at ground zero, inside the mine, in terms of application of light values and dimension to a dramatic scene," says Mike Gornick. "I mean, you're talking about a zero situation, nothing available to us. That was the true challenge."

One way around this challenge was to put up colored lights, as if they were part of the cave lighting system. Red lamps were used, along with blue gels, to create that red/blue hue in the "Laff in the Dark" sequence.

Right: Greg Nicotero with zombie Howard Berger. (Courtesy of Greg Nicotero.)

188

ONE DAY AT A TIME

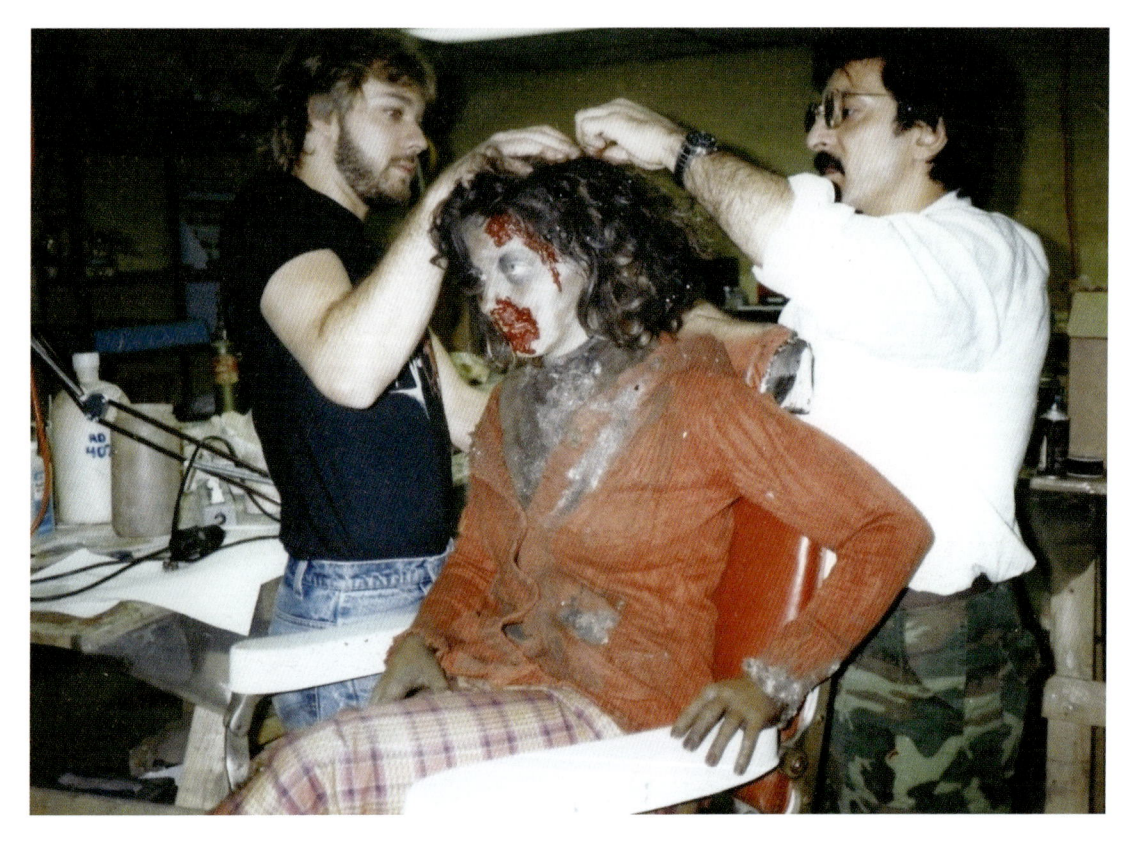

Above: Production assistant, Nancy Suzich, as the zombie who creeps along the cave wall and is shot by Terry Alexander. (Courtesy of Nancy Bennett.)

Another challenge of working in these dark portions of the mine was making sure not to hurt yourself when walking around in the dark – as dolly grip, Richard Sieg, discovered the hard way. "Because we were in the wrong part of the mine with dirt and all that, we had tools," recalls Sieg. "Sometimes we needed to put the camera down low and we had shovels, we had rakes, we had this and that. Well, it was easy to keep the equipment close because you would put it to the side and it was dark, you wouldn't see it, you could hide the stuff. Well, one day I was walking, I needed to get something like a C-stand and a flag or something, and I walked in there and I didn't have my flashlight, and I kind of knew where it was and I was walking in there, someone had left a rake with the tines up and I literally stepped on the rake and the handle hit me square in the forehead. It was out of a cartoon and it really hurt and I staggered. Finally I realized what it was, someone came over and they said, 'Are you all right?' 'Yeah, who put this here and why would you?' So I did whatever I had to do . . . later in the day I did the same thing. I walked straight into it again, it was somewhere else and all that . . . bang, right in the head again! Well now, there's a whelp! I had to just say, 'I gotta get some ice on my head.'"

Interestingly enough, Sieg himself had a history of smacking people in the head accidentally. On *Knightriders*, while working the boom, Sieg hit producer Richard Rubinstein in the head with the boom pole and then, not knowing it was the producer, told Rubinstein not to stand so close!

Finally, scene 84 – or 84K to be precise – was scheduled, where Terry Alexander shoots the "splatterhead" zombie, played by Don Brockett. However, this particular shot would be pushed back to Monday, January 14.

Saturday 1/12/1985 – Day 53

"The man who fell to earth – Greg Nicotero." – Mike Trcic

Day 53 would see work on scene 91 get underway, where Sarah, McDermott, and John team up to blast through a group of zombies as they make their way out of the cave. Of interest regarding this scene is a line of dialogue, not in the shooting script, spoken by Terry Alexander in the film's work print. When Alexander's character, John, arrives to save the day, he hands over weapons to Sarah and McDermott and says, "All the ammo we got is in these guns." Had this been

Above: John Vulich and Mike Deak in zombie make-up. (Courtesy of Nancy Bennett.)

included, his subsequent actions – when he disposes of the gun while climbing up the ladder, after running out of bullets – would've made sense. However, the dialogue didn't make it into the final cut of the film.

One of the zombies in the group that gets blasted by the heroes was played by Al Magliochetti, who had decided to visit during the final weekend to catch up with everyone before the film wrapped. The visit ended up allowing him to once again become a member of the living dead. "It was sometime in early January of '85 – I think it was their last week of shooting – and they were going to have the wrap party," recalls Magliochetti. "So Gabe Bartalos and I flew out again to Pittsburgh, just to kind of hang out with all of our buddies and go to the wrap party with them. This was back when you could fly People Express from New Jersey to Pittsburgh for 40 bucks. And when we got out there they stuck me in another scene, because I matched Taso Stavrakis' build somewhat. So they already shot him facially a lot of times, they didn't want to do that again, because they felt it was like the same person over and over. So they realized they hadn't seen me, so they stuck me in zombie make-up again. I'm in the scene where they're running through the cave . . . it's the scene where Everett Burrell is dressed in hospital greens. I'm directly next to him wearing sunglasses."

More zombies would be scheduled to be killed in portions of scene 84, including Howard Berger, as a memorable and scary-looking zombie who gets shot by Terry Alexander, spins around to face the camera and is then shot in the head.

Production assistant Nancy Suzich got an opportunity to portray a zombie as well, but the experience would be a slightly scary one for her. "I was crawling along the cave wall as a zombie and Terry Alexander shot me at close range, [*laughs*] and I fell onto a mattress. It was really neat, just being in make-up with someone like Savini. I mean, it was just such a great experience," says Suzich. "But, I tell you, it was such a scary feeling to have someone aiming a gun at my head. Of course, I know the gun wasn't loaded, but it was scary. [*laughs*] It was really scary."

(For the record, it should be noted that I am slightly unsure whether Howard and Nancy's zombie deaths were shot this day or Monday January 14. There is a possibility that it could have been either day.) Finally scene 98, featuring Gene Saraceni's zombie getting killed in the silo, would be re-shot (much to the joy of Mike Gornick).

Later this evening, the cast and crew would enjoy the wrap party held at the Victory Café in Wampum. Live music was provided by the Granati brothers and their band G-Force. For those who weren't finished partying just yet, a second party, a post-wrap-party party, was put together by Rick Granati at an after-hours club in Beaver Falls.

Monday 1/14/1985 – Day 54

Call sheet unavailable

Day 54 would finally take care of scene 84K, when John shoots the "splatterhead" zombie, Don Brockett. For years, Don Brockett was the comedy partner of fellow zombie, Barbara Russell. The two formed a musical comedy act called "Brockett and Barbara" in 1960 and performed together well into the 1990s, until Brockett's death in 1995. He was best known for his role as Chef Brockett from *Mister Rogers' Neighborhood*. "Chef Brockett: that was just like one of the craziest things in the world," recalls Dave Kindlon. "Sitting in a room and just going, 'Dude, you have no idea how much I stared at you when I was a little kid,' because he was on *Mister Rogers' Neighborhood* and it was just, like, 'God, this is awesome!'"

Brockett's "splatterhead" effect would not go as planned the first time around, as blood began spurting from his forehead just before the squib detonated on the back of his head. A second take sealed the deal, though.

A close-up shot of John Vulich's zombie dummy getting blasted by machine gun fire, one of the four zombies that the heroes gun down as they are fleeing the cave, was shot as well. "They took the head, I think, from my head cast for the 'chop top' one and just recycled it for this," says Vulich. "I think they did this kind of Colonel Sanders kind of looking make-up on me to disguise me, so you didn't notice me as the same zombie."

As noted, the call sheet for this day of filming was unfortunately unavailable to me. (Locating the call sheets was without a doubt the toughest aspect of writing this book – tracking them down was akin to an *Indiana Jones* adventure!) The advance schedule from the previous day's call sheet officially lists these scenes, but those changed quite often. I also did a lot of looking through photos, attempting to match up the clothes that people were wearing, and spent time looking at Tom Savini's home videos, as well looking at the date on the slate if it was viewable in this footage.

Tuesday 1/15/1985 – Day 55

"Okay, get in your crawl position." – Mike to Nancy

With the production nearing the finish line, day 55 focused on completing a couple of scenes left on the schedule.

First up was the completion of scene 44, where Sarah and John have their philosophical talk outside of "The Ritz". For Terry Alexander, his experience on the production would literally bookend perfectly. "The first thing I did with George [Romero] was the monologue when I auditioned, and [that was] the very last thing I did in the movie," says Terry Alexander. "After we came back from Florida, because we had two weeks off for Christmas after Florida, we came back and I did the monologue with George."

Work was then finished on scene 80, where the "pop-top" zombie's head is separated from his body and then rolls away. For the shot where the severed top half of the zombie's head rolls into frame, Tom Savini stood off camera and literally tossed the head, rolling it into the picture as if he were bowling. Of course, this led to a lot of laughter and joking amongst the crew. "We had some really funny times in that mine. I can remember Katarina, she was the second AD, and she was fierce about her job. She was wild, wild about her job. When you turn the camera over the second AD says, 'We're rolling,' and that was what she would say every time, 'We're rolling,' and I found it singularly boring. And there was a sequence where we had to roll a zombie head off camera, we had to roll into camera," remembers David Ball. "So they turn the camera over and she says . . . I couldn't let her say the words, 'We're rolling.' So as she's about to say, 'We're rolling,' I jumped in front of her radio and said, 'We are bowling!' [*laughs*] She looked at me like I had three heads. And they rolled this fucking head into camera." [*laughs*]

Wednesday 1/16/1985 – Day 56

Call sheet unavailable

Day 56, the final day of principal photography, had finally arrived for the crew of *Day of the Dead*. As with the bonus day of re-shooting Tim DiLeo's gut spill scene, and day 54, this was the third day of shooting that – regardless of my efforts – I couldn't locate a call sheet for. However, thanks to the advance schedule on the previous day's call sheet, I do know what was scheduled for shooting on this day.

A lot of today's filming would be centered around "eatage" – aka shots of zombies eating what zombies eat! Scenes scattered around the facility – including in the experimentation room, the corridors, and around the corral – would feature zombies dining on the remains of fallen humans. One of the standout zombies from this montage was assistant costume designer Eileen Sieff, who can be spotted gnawing on a large, bloody bone. "We were shooting the 'eating close-up', where the zombies had overrun the

Above: Tom Savini's make-up crew sporting their "I Survived Tom Savini" signs. Top row, left to right: Mike Deak, Everett Burrell, John Vulich, Howard Berger, Dave Kindlon, Mike Trcic. Bottom row, left to right: Greg Funk and Greg Nicotero. (Courtesy of Greg Nicotero.)

compound and were eating the remaining humans," remembers Sieff. "The day we were to shoot, there was a terrible snow storm and the extras could not make it to the set. George [Romero] looked around at the crew and stopped at me, 'Eileen hasn't been a zombie yet!' With that I was off to the make-up chair for four hours of make-up. The other assistant costume designer, Howard Kaplan, had a great time making me look like Edith Head, a famous designer of the costumes for films in the mid-20th century."

One shot that was most likely attempted on this day was of Bub's feet – listed on the call sheet's advance schedule. According to second assistant director Katarina Wittich and set decorator Jan Pascale, there was an insert shot that Romero wanted badly, which both women found to be unbelievably disturbing and gross. "I don't know if you can use this or not, but I remember having a fight with George because he wanted a zombie to kick a brain down the hall," says Pascale. "And I remember I just fought with [George] . . . and I adored him, I absolutely adored him. And I was just like, 'No, I can't. I can't allow this.'" [*laughs*]

Wittich lists it as one of her "favorite weird days" during production. "It was such an upsetting, weird . . . like, when I say favorite it's just favorite in the sense that it just stands out as the epitome of that movie," says Wittich. "Because there's sort of gentle, sweet, odd George Romero directing this scene and he's insisted on having an actual human brain for this guy to kick down the hallway. So, I'm organizing getting the human brain to set so that we can kick it, and then it's, like, too soft to really kick well, so it's sort of coming apart."

Hearing stories like this one gives you an idea of just how crazy and strange the set of *Day of the Dead* could be at times.

One anecdote that, for me, really sums up the weirdness of working on the film was shared by one of the members of the make-up effects crew, Mike Deak. And it wasn't even an actual event, but rather a dream he had one day. "I remember being really tired one day and they had a green room there with, like, an old couch inside the mine," says Deak. "I took a nap and I just fell asleep for, like, twenty minutes, and I had this dream that I was literally at a house somewhere in suburbia. I just got done cutting the lawn and everything was all warm and breezy, it was all nice. And I wake up and I'm inside a mine surrounded by zombies and stuff like that. I went, 'Wow, that's fucked up!'"

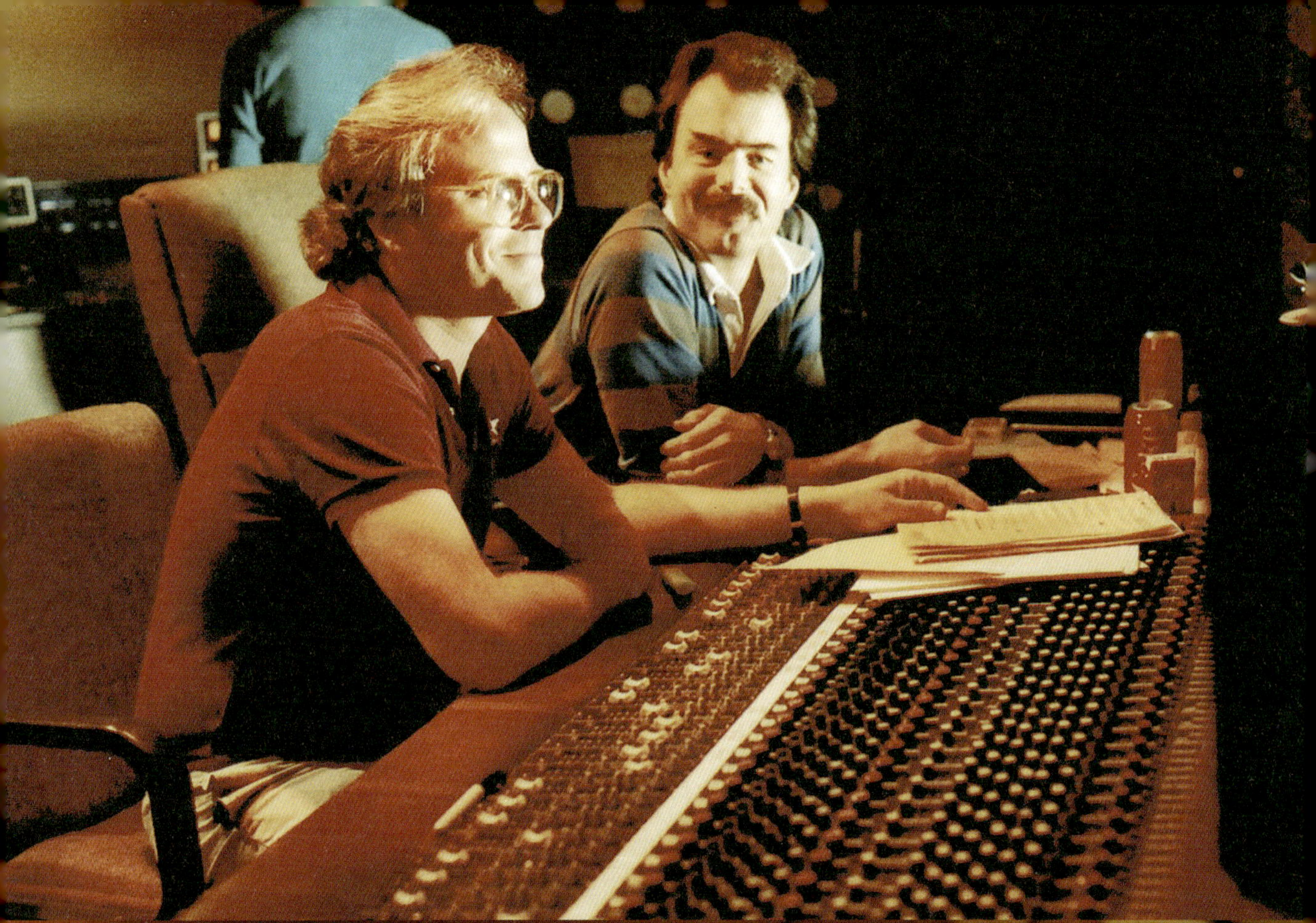

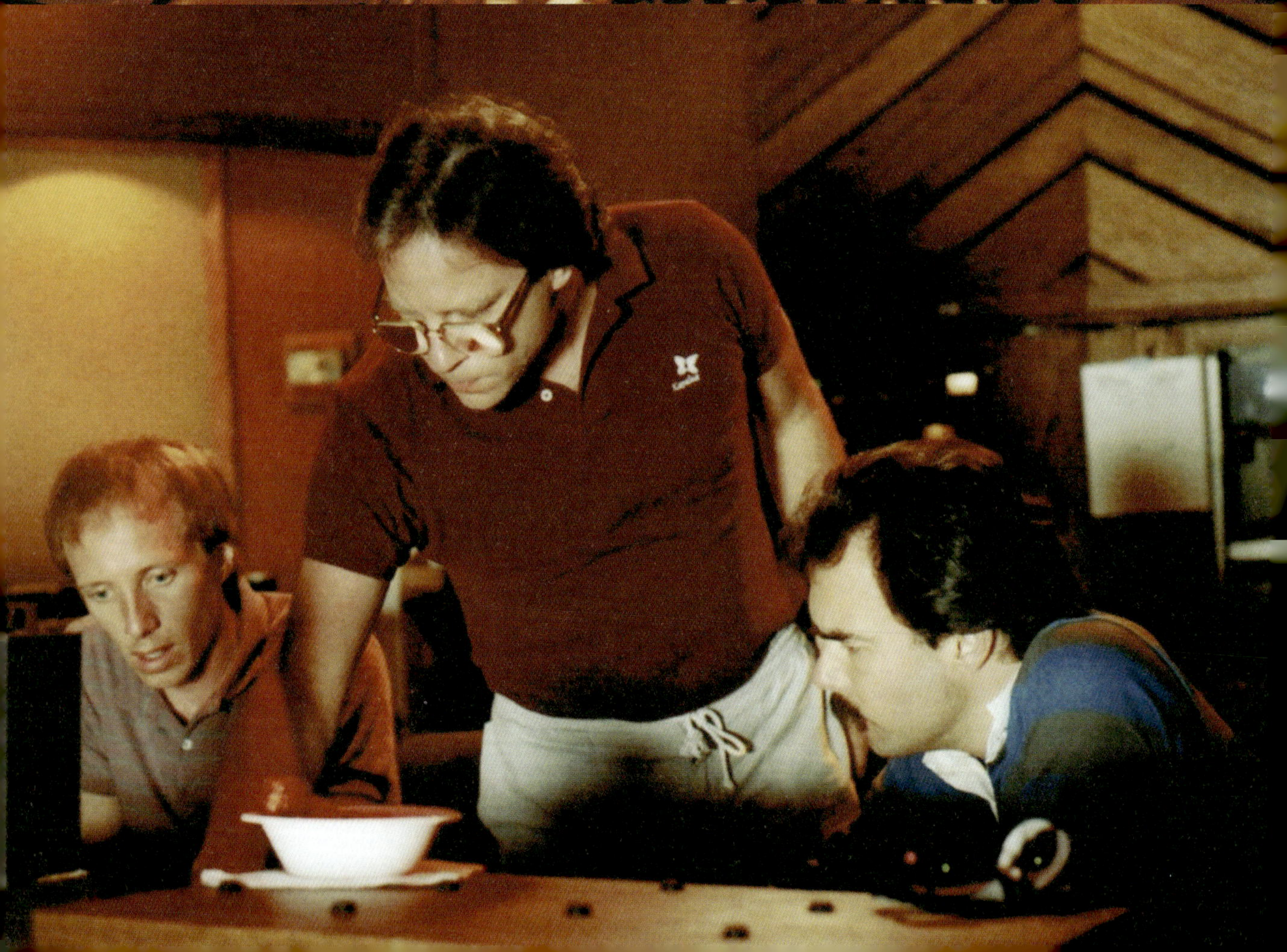

Chapter 4 At the End of the Day

With principal photography now wrapped, the process of cleaning up and moving everything out of the Wampum Mine would begin. "We were picking up cable for, like, a whole week. Myself and a couple of grips were driving around in golf carts and a couple of small pickup trucks picking up cable, picking up lights, picking up stuff they thought they had stricken from the set," says PA John "Flash" Williams. "What was salvageable, that wasn't destroyed by zombies, was cleaned up and sent back. We were returning props and returning stuff that was loaned to the production."

Location manager, Jim Bruwelheide, was also very busy at this time. "Throughout the post-production phase, it was basically dealing with returning rental equipment, things of that nature that was used during production, such as tables and chairs, golf carts, office furniture," says Bruwelheide. "Also working with the sound department; they would have to go through and pick up 'wild track' of different events that occurred throughout the filming process, such as gun fire in the mine. We would have to go out into the mine with machine guns and AK-47s, and they would record the sound of that to lay into the audio edit track during final production. So that was fun, because I would take them out into portions of the mine and the audio guys would get everything set up and the arms experts would be there and they'd let me fire the guns. So it was kind of cool."

Meanwhile, set decorator Jan Pascale, who had dealt with all of the real human organs used during the production, was busy making sure that they would be given to a place more befitting. "From what I remember, I think we actually donated them to biology labs and stuff at the end. I sort of, you know, it was a long time ago, but I sort of remember that, that we wanted it to go to a place where it would actually be used in the manner in which it was intended," says Pascale. "In hindsight I feel sort of guilty because there were these poor people that donated their bodies to science and they ended up in a zombie movie. [laughs] Their brains, you know, were not being used so scientifically."

There were bustling scenes inside the mine as the production packed up and shipped out. Wardrobe was being trucked to Carnegie Mellon, special make-up effects was being sent back to Tom Savini's house, and accounting and editing were being transported to Laurel's offices at 247 Fort Pitt Boulevard, in downtown Pittsburgh.

By the weekend, there would be what was humorously labeled in a memo by production manager Zilla Clinton as "The Grand Laurel-Day Garage Sale & Flea Market At Wampum", a chance for crew to purchase any leftover items from the production. "In general they will sell basically leftover props, materials, disposable lighting equipment such as gel or possibly extension cords, things of that nature," says Jim Bruwelheide. "Sometimes lumber, through the scenic department, or some tools. So yeah, things were sold or auctioned off. Sometimes things had a way [laughs] of just walking away, too, at the end of the film."

While those involved with the production were responsible for cleaning up after themselves, interestingly enough, some things would be left behind, including numerous fake blood stains on the mine floors. "They were there for years, especially in the area where they had the old laboratory set up and everything," says PA and mine employee Mike Butera. "Those were on the floors and stuff for years afterwards."

"I know that the storage facility up there, the Wampum Mine, kept the corral. They used it as a tourist attraction. I don't think it's still there, but I think for a good three, four years, five years after that movie it was still up there," says PA John "Flash" Williams. "They kept that one section and had it just sort of bolted into a wall with a sign on it, 'On this site in 1984 Laurel-Day productions made the now infamous *Day of the Dead*,' or something like that."

Now that the mine was cleared out and everyone had returned to their normal lives, or moved onto other projects, official post-production work would begin on the film, and at the heart of that work was editor, Pat Buba. "After shooting was finished we went to Fort Pitt Boulevard, to George's [Romero] office at 247, and set up the editing rooms there, and George and Christine went to Florida," says Buba. "Because I remember finishing the very first cut of the film, when I put together all the scenes, and calling George in Florida and telling him the first cut was done. I can't remember how soon that was after finishing. Then George came back and then we started working together on it."

Looking back on that period brings back fond memories of his beloved hometown for the editor. "I moved the editing room into what was George's big

Above: John Sutton (in glasses) and John Harrison mixing the score for the film in Los Angeles. **Below:** Bill Smith, John Sutton and John Harrison mixing the *Day* score at Los Angeles' Studio Sound Recorders. (Photos courtesy of John Harrison.)

office at 247, which is the front office, which had those huge floor-to-ceiling windows overlooking the rivers," recalls Buba. "So I would sit there and, as soon as the sun would go down, I could open the window blinds and just look at the incredible lights of the city and watch the rivers go by as I was editing. He still had his dubbing room, projection room, in the back. I remember we did a cut, did a real quick temp mix on it – we just threw it up and screened it for the first time. It was the first time we saw it all together – that was fun."

For *Day of the Dead*, Buba brought in some help to make sure the editing process went a little more smoothly than it had in the past. "I brought in an assistant from New York, Kristine Bulakowski, because previous to that trims and outs for George weren't, when he edited on films, necessarily organized," says Buba. "So I'm sure that they were put away, reconstituted, and put back in their original boxes. I have no idea what happened to those boxes now."

Those trims and outs that Buba makes reference to are of interest because, unlike *Dawn of the Dead*, which had several different versions and numerous deleted scenes, *Day of the Dead* did not. In Paul Gagne's book *The Zombies That Ate Pittsburgh*, though, there is a quote from producer Richard Rubinstein in which he mentions the original cut of *Day of the Dead* being two hours and six minutes long. If that is accurate, then what was in those scenes? The final cut of the film clocks in at around one hour and 41 minutes. That's 25 minutes worth of missing footage!

"I think when he [Rubinstein] refers to that 2:06 cut, I think that was a very loose form cut that probably wasn't even contemplated," says Mike Gornick, who served as post-production supervisor as well. "I mean, part of Pat's style was to let scenes play in terms of the breadth of a scene, quite often."

Gornick's recollection is probably accurate, as Buba himself all but says the same thing. "I can't remember too many deleted scenes, per se," recalls Buba. "A lot of it probably was more by trimming and cutting down some of the original ones . . . I can't remember too many scenes that were just totally discarded."

Buba and Gornick had known one another for years and worked together previously during the editing on both *Knightriders* and *Creepshow*, so while there was a great deal of familiarity between the two, there was also that classic tug of war regarding getting the film finished as quickly as possible. "Mike was post-production supervisor. So as with any post-production supervisor, editor you have a relationship that's built out of mistrust, [*laughs*] in a lot of ways, but that wasn't particular to Mike," admits Buba. "Editors always push post supervisors as far as they can get, and post supervisors always kind of lie to editors, I think."

Buba also remembers what could have been a disastrous turn of events during the editing – all because of the call of nature. "We had to turn out a reel to the negative cutter and I left my cutting room to go to the bathroom, and as I came out Mike Gornick was calling me, just beckoning with his finger," says Buba. "We went into the editing room and the torque motors, a splice had opened up on an editing machine, and the torque motors were still spinning and it had chewed up about, I don't know, 60 feet of film. And there was no record of it. I mean, it's not like now where you have a backup on digital copy and just go back to the latest cut . . . we had to try to figure out what shots were in there, we had no copy of it. I had to go through and figure out in my mind what kind of shots were in there. We had to order reprints of the work print and get it back and I had to re-cut that sequence by memory . . . that was not a fun day, but we got through it."

And getting through it would not be the easiest thing in the world. In fact, it was a painstaking process that required a team effort, you might say. "One of my assistants actually went through the entire room and picked pieces out of the walls," says Buba. "They had this kind of sound-proof tile kind of walls, and pieces of film were stuck in the walls because the thing had spun so fast. John Bick [an editing assistant] was going through and pulling them out by tweezers and he would sit there for hours and hours, like a jigsaw puzzle, putting pieces back together so we'd have some reference to a latent number or to a shot to be able to order a reprint. And I remember, too, it was right in the middle of a reel and it was an action sequence, it wasn't, like, one shot, it was a ton of shots in it. And we had to go back and try to re-cut it by memory."

Another interesting and unique facet of *Day of the Dead*, which was different from previous Romero films, was the use, or lack thereof, of temp music during the editing. Romero would always use some kind of a temp score to build some sort of rhythm, usually from library or "needle drop" cues. "It was different than the other films I've done with George, where temp music is a really big part of it and usually he did his own temp scores," says Buba. "George was writing another script at the time, I think, and that's why he was in Florida. Also we knew that John Harrison was gonna do the music, and so I didn't do a lot of temping on the first pass. What happened was John moved into the basement, the very first floor of 247, and set up his synthesizers down there, and I was on the fifth floor. I would do a scene and take it down on the elevator and John would come up and look at it, and he would start doing some temp music right there. And then we started using his temp stuff."

After principal photography wrapped, John Harrison returned to Los Angeles for about two months and began composing and sketching out ideas for the score. "Then I moved back to Pittsburgh, came back home to Pittsburgh in late winter, I think it was March. I spent all of March down in the basement of 247 Fort Pitt Boulevard writing the score with George [Romero]," recalls Harrison. "And while George and Pat [Buba] were cutting upstairs I would be downstairs writing to the cuts that they would send

Above: Black and white shot of Hendry Street in downtown Fort Myers, before the matte photography was added. (Courtesy of Mitchell Lipsiner.) **Below:** Completed matte shot by Jim Danforth from the finished film, showing the devastation of the city. (© 1985 Dead Films, Inc.)

me, that they would leave under the door. We didn't have the internet . . . [*laughs*] they would send me down tapes and I would work on them, then I'd bring

Above and below: Editor Pat Buba at work – with George Romero looking on. *Day* was edited at 247 Fort Pitt Boulevard – Romero's long-time office in downtown Pittsburgh. (© 1985 *Evening Magazine-Pittsburgh*.)

the stuff upstairs and I would play it and we would lay it up against the picture, make changes, see what worked, what didn't. And then once we had locked the picture I locked the score, I came back out to California, back out here, and I recorded it and then we brought it onto the stage and mixed it."

And, much like Buba's account of the editing, Harrison says that working with Romero on the score was a very creative and collaborative process. "I had all that time where I was actually composing the score while he was cutting the movie, so we could try it out. And in certain cases we could make the cut work better with the music, and in other cases I would change the music to work better with the cut," says Harrison. "That's a process that composers and directors don't often have. And a lot of directors don't want to do that, because they don't know anything about music and they're intimidated by it, but not George."

Harrison collaborated with Buba as well, especially when it came to working in a musical cue very familiar and beloved to fans of *Dawn of the Dead*. During scene 48, when Logan admonishes the "Beef Treats" zombie, just before he leaves the experimentation room, Harrison would weave "The Gonk" theme into the score. "John and I we knew we were gonna work that in somewhere, and we had to be careful about it," says Buba. "We knew while we were even shooting the movie – he said, 'I'm gonna put that in somewhere!' And we found the perfect spot."

Harrison would also be heavily involved in producing the soundtrack album that accompanied the release of the film. "What I did with that was, I had my friend and partner from my band years, John Sutton, produce the album," says Harrison. "And what we did was we recorded it all in the studio out here in Los Angeles and then we took it over to [post-production company] Todd A-O and we mixed it into the movie. Then John and I went back into the studio and I had this idea, which I had done on *Creepshow*, to take . . . instead of doing just cuts, cues, I would put together a suite of all the major pieces of music. So we went back into the studio and we created all the segues and mixed it together all in one piece and that's how it came out."

The soundtrack album would be split in two parts, with side B containing the work of John Harrison. "The Dead Suite" was just under twenty minutes of instrumental music that Harrison had scored for the film, and the music produced was definitely a product of its time. "The gear that I had at the time, it has a sort of eighties feel to it in terms of style and sound," recalls Harrison. "John Sutton was really a great producer on that, we had a wonderful engineer. I had to play all of it; we didn't have any musicians except for the guitarist and some percussion guys I brought in. It was a long, long recording session. It took several weeks."

Side A contained five separate tracks, three of which were original tracks created for the soundtrack album: "The World Inside Your Eyes" and "If Tomorrow Comes" were ballads, while "The Dead Walk" was instrumental. The man most responsible for this side of the album was Tom Cossie, whose real name is Tom Surman. Surman began using the name Cossie because he was referred to as "Cosmo" by his friends, named after the *Beetle Bailey* cartoon character Private Cosmo, who wore sunglasses and was known as a "shady entrepreneur". Cossie was a record producer from Pittsburgh who had known Harrison from his days playing live. Cossie had been vice president of RCA Records, and in the late 1970s gained notoriety for discovering the disco group Chic, who had hits such as "Dance, Dance, Dance" and "Le Freak". With the two of them having known each other for a while, Harrison took the soundtrack to Cossie, looking for a distribution deal. "At the time I had an independently distributed label, Saturn, which was distributed throughout the United States through maybe twelve, fourteen different independent distributors," recalls Cossie. "And I said, 'Yeah, I'd be more than happy to work with you on this.' So we used a lot of his background music as core music, and at the time I was working with a guy named Sputzy [Jim Sparacino], we had a band called Modern Man in Pittsburgh that I produced – Jimmy Blazer and a couple of really outstanding musicians, I think, were in that band. Sputzy was the lead singer and I said, 'Hey, this sounds like an interesting project.'"

"He had this idea, he knew Sputzy and his band, and they were in the studio listening to my music and Sputzy started ripping off some lyrics and I think the Granatis were a part of that, too, although it wasn't the Granati band," says John Harrison. "But anyway, then they did those couple of cuts with the songs, 'The World Inside Your Eyes' being one of them. They took my melodies, my music, and then put the lyrics on top of them. And then in 'The World Inside Your Eyes' they actually did them, they did a remake of my stuff with their band."

"Harrison, I give a lot of credit to him, as far as orchestrating, pretty much, the core of the soundtrack," admits Cossie. "What we did then was took the roots and the progressions and stuff and built the rest of the album around that. I would give a lot of the credit to him."

The gentleman that both Harrison and Cossie refer to as "Sputzy" is Jim Sparacino, who was a local musician and at the time lead singer of a dance band called Modern Man. Sparacino employed an interesting process while writing songs for the soundtrack. Cossie gave Sparacino the soundtrack featuring all of Harrison's music, along with a section of the script – the scene where Sarah and John have their philosophical talk at "The Ritz". From there Sparacino began writing the first song, "The World Inside Your Eyes", a process that would take close to a month to complete. "What happened was, as we were going through all this stuff, Tom [Cossie] and I talked about I would write the songs, which was funny because there was a title I had in my mind, 'The World Inside Your Eyes,'" remembers Sparacino. "He called me about that tune and he said, 'Did you ever finish that?' and I was like, 'No,' and he said, 'Well, here's what I'm going to do. I've got some of the soundtrack and I want you to write a song around it. I don't want it to sound like the soundtrack, but I want it to be close enough where it doesn't sound like it's completely different.' Okay, that's hard to do." Sparacino worked diligently trying to fulfill Cossie's request, despite the challenges involved. "I sat for days trying to make it sound like it, but not a rip-off. I didn't want to rip-off John Harrison's music, but we did give him credit," says Sparacino. "So what I did was I took part of that

Above: Rhodes' death sequence, as seen – and edited – through the Moviola viewfinder. (© 1985 *Evening Magazine-Pittsburgh*.)

soundtrack, and then I took about eight bars of it and I wrote the rest of the song around it."

Sparacino and his band Modern Man would go into a local studio, Jeree Studios, to record "The World Inside Your Eyes". During his time in the studio, Sparacino was inspired to have the song be a duet, and it was there that he would find the perfect singing partner. "Delilah was also on [label] Saturn Records. I know her first name is Bea, but I can't remember her real last name," says Sparacino. "She and her husband had a band called Samson and Delilah. They were a soul act in town and they ended up being a gospel group. Bea was one of my favorites, I loved the way the woman sang; she's so soulful. I was in the studio with them, I used to do some producing for Tom [Cossie], and I was in the studio with them and I just loved her voice. So my concept with Tom was, 'Why don't we do this as a duet? Let's go back and forth – if it's going to be a guy and girl in the movie, why don't we do the same thing in the song?' And he loved the idea, so we got Bea and that's how she got involved. I'm almost positive that was my idea."

After finishing "The World Inside Your Eyes", Cossie had keyboard player Jim Blazer come up with a second song, "The Dead Walk", which was an instrumental dance track. After that, Sparacino figured that he had completed the job, but he was in for a little surprise. After returning from a trip to New York, Cossie called Sparacino to let him know that "The World Inside Your Eyes" was indeed going to be used in the film. "And then he says, 'But we have to have one more song for the album and it may get in the movie,' I said, 'Okay, great,'" remembers Sparacino. "Now that was probably, I'm going to say some time mid-morning to early afternoon, something like that. Well, a little later about 5:30 or 6:00, Tom calls and says, 'What time can I meet you there?' I'm saying, 'Where?' He says, 'The studio in

Beaver Falls.' I said, 'For what?' He said, 'Well, we have to record this.' 'Record what?' 'Well, we need another song. I need it by tomorrow morning. I've got to have this out to New York for those guys by tomorrow morning.' I was like, 'Are you kidding me? It's now 5:00. You want to go into the studio, 6:00, 7:00 at night?' You know what I mean? Anyway, that's how the other one came about."

The other song was "If Tomorrow Comes" and, in writing it, Sparacino would once again draw from the script pages he'd read numerous times when working on the lyrics for "The World Inside Your Eyes". "The thought about that scene in my mind went to, you want to do it this way, you want to do it this way, but it ain't up to either of *you*. It's up to God; you can't do anything without him anyway. So, that hints [at] the line, 'If tomorrow comes, thy will be done, if tomorrow comes.' We went that night and recorded it and it was back in New York the next day – Tom said, 'Got on the album.' [*laughs*] That song was literally written . . . I called [Jim] Blazer and said to him, 'Write a track. I don't care how long it is, make it three minutes or so, but I don't care how long the verses are, I don't care if there's a chorus, I don't care if there's a bridge, I don't care what it is. Write a three-minute track and I'll see you in an hour.' And literally that song was written, recorded, and in the mail in less than twelve hours."

Above: One of several sets that had to be struck after production ended, "The Ritz". (Courtesy of Richard Alvarez.)

"'If Tomorrow Comes' is one of the ones that really sort of sticks out in my mind – Sputzy sang it," says Cossie. "I still get goose bumps when I hear the song, it's just great."

"Tom picked me up and I'm throwing words together. I'm trying to think of that whole scenario, you know, of what would happen if it's only you, it's only me, and all that's left is destiny. You know what I mean?" says Sparacino. "Wrote it on the way up, got there. Blazer met us there, he starts doing tracks; I'm listening to the tracks still trying to write words and melody. It was a cluster, is what it was."

Strangely, when "The World Inside Your Eyes" plays at the end of the film, Sparacino's voice has been removed, leaving only Delilah's intact. I asked Harrison, Cossie, and Sparacino about this and – as with so many subjects relating to the film – got a range of different answers.

"That was Tom's [Cossie] call. We had agreed to put one of the songs at the end of the movie and that was the one that he gave us," says Harrison. "I can't give you a good answer to that. I think that was really just Cossie's decision."

"They just thought that they wanted to just have a female vocalist on the end. So, I said, 'Well, you

Above: Some of the junk and clutter near the corral set that had to be cleared out after production wrapped in the mine. (Courtesy of George Demick.)

know, that's not the way it was recorded.' But the thing is, when you do a soundtrack album and you come in after the fact, not from the beginning, you have really no negotiating rights for making any demands," says Cossie. "We had no demands, let me put it that way. And nor were we in a position to demand anything. So when they wanted to do that I said, 'Well, hey, if that's what you feel's gonna help you . . .' I don't know."

"I have no idea," says Sparacino. "It's my luck."

The soundtrack would be released on vinyl, along with a cassette tape version. There would also be a 45 single release of "The World Inside Your Eyes", featuring "The Dead Walk" on the B-side. The soundtrack was publicized via a full-page advertisement in the October 1985 issue of *Fangoria* magazine, where you could send in a check or money order for only $9.98, plus $2.00 postage, and receive either the vinyl or cassette version, plus the 45 single.

"I think we did about 10,000 albums. All configurations combined between the vinyl, the cassette," recalls Cossie. "That's a combination of everything. And matter of fact, the actual manufacturing . . . I know we did that many jacket, labels, and stuff. What I probably did . . . we probably did [closer] to maybe 4,000 to 5,000 units, to be honest with you. Because I had a lot of paper backup on the stuff, so they weren't all manufactured. With soundtrack albums like this, unless it's a huge movie and unless you can derive a major hit single from it, soundtrack albums really don't sell that well."

Looking back at the music and the work he did on it, John Harrison is pleased with how it came out. "I love the theme, the opening theme," says Harrison. "The whole opening piece of music I like a lot."

Other than the opening theme, the music that ranks at the top of Harrison's list accompanies the scene when Sarah and John have their heartfelt talk at "The Ritz". "That probably is my – if not my favorite – that's the second part of it," says Harrison. "It's a recapitulation of the theme, of the music, but it's slowed down and it has a different melody over top of it."

One thing that took Harrison by surprise was the criticism leveled at his score by fans, who claimed that it didn't emphasize the horrific elements in the film. "I guess they wanted a real kind of 'horror' score, and *Day* is not," says Harrison. *"Day* has melodies and romantic themes and stuff like that, which George [Romero] and I really wanted to use to kind of lessen the horror of it, make it much more . . . really get into the drama of the story that George is trying to tell. But

Above: Cletus Anderson's fantastic corral set was dismantled after filming wrapped. (Courtesy of George Demick.)

some people didn't like that. Some people wanted it to be really just in-your-face horror music."

Luckily for Harrison, the one person who mattered most thought very highly of his score. "The music was, I thought, sensational," says George Romero.

Another important aspect of post production was the completion of the matte photography work involving the deserted city. Even though David Garber and John Green are credited with the work, it was actually Jim Danforth who would create the matte painting featured in the film's opening moments after being contracted out by Garber/Green. Danforth was a longtime veteran visual effects artist who had worked on such classic titles as *The Outer Limits, Clash of the Titans, Willy Wonka and the Chocolate Factory, The Thing* (1982 version), and *Creepshow*, to name a few. "They sent me the negative and said, 'Paint in the rest of the city that wasn't there. We want the city to be bigger,'" says Danforth. "Then they said, 'Oh, also, we need a shot with no zombies.' There were zombies walking down the street, so they had the actors in the zombie costumes and zombie make-up on this film that they gave me and some of the buildings from the town, wherever they shot it, Florida I think. Then they realized, I guess, that they didn't get the shot, which would have been so easy to shoot, with no zombies. So, I had to paint out, for one second cut, paint out the end of the street, just paint an empty street to cover up the zombies that were there. That was sort of it."

And while this was a fairly simple and uncomplicated assignment, it wasn't without its issues. "The only really hard thing was that the shot had a lot of tall palm trees with waving fronds, and they were up against the sky, which I had to repaint, and I didn't want to have totally painted palm trees, I thought that would just look stiff," recalls Danforth. "So I painted around the palm trees so that I could have fronds up against the sky that became the matte edge and then within that I scraped away the painting off the glass so that I could see the projection of the moving fronds behind that. And then just by sort of making little, oh I don't know, dotted lines you might say, or just chunks, cutting chunks in the painting and so on, we just lit enough of the waving fronds through around near the edges, that it didn't look like a sharp edge and seemed to get away with it. It's not something that I would recommend, but it worked in that case."

The man who actually shot the plate for Garber/Green during this scene was director of photography, Mitchell Lipsiner, who found out firsthand the penny-pinching nature of the production. "One of the issues that we had was I had an argument with the special effects people," recalls Lipsiner. "They had insisted that we use the camera that I used. I had requested a different camera for a steadier image and they said,

'No, your Arriflex will be fine.' We shot it with an Arri III and I remember when they said that they blew it up there was some movement in it . . . and, 'Okay, well I told you so.'"

"The Arri III is a good camera, it just wasn't designed to do that kind of stuff," says Danforth. "I don't recall that the Arri III has registration pins and I wouldn't use that camera." Registration pins are tiny metal rods that go through the perforation of the film, which help to align the film in an exact position, in turn keeping the image steady and preventing movement within the frame. Today it's not as much of an issue, because technology allows an electronic means of handling this. "I never watched Garber/Green working by themselves, so I don't know what they did, but I suspect they didn't bother to do any of that," says Danforth. "And what you're telling me about using the wrong camera sort of substantiates that, but no, I don't remember noticing any problems. But on the other hand, there was no point in my paying too much attention to it because there wasn't anything I could do about it."

I went back and asked Lipsiner if he recalled whose decision it was to use the Arriflex III camera for the matte shots, and he said that it was not Garber/Green, but was most likely whoever was pulling the mattes. Regardless of who made the decision, it didn't hamper the final product. Danforth's work looks fantastic and very convincing in the film.

As previously mentioned, the post-production supervisor on *Day of the Dead* was Michael Gornick, who had served in the same capacity on *Creepshow, Knightriders, Dawn of the Dead,* and *Martin*. This time around, though, things weren't quite the same, as Gornick was spending more time in New York handling business for Laurel Entertainment. "This was a little different, because George [Romero] wasn't intimately involved with it. I was oftentimes in New York with my new duties with Laurel Entertainment, and so I didn't watch so much or I didn't witness so much the active cutting that I had in the past," recalls Gornick. "But once that was accomplished, or once we had done sections, or we were going through the scoring and so forth, then it became my duties back in New York, in terms of application of sound, answer prints, and so forth – my typical role."

In the latter part of April 1985 Richard Rubinstein requested that Gornick personally carry the conformed negative rolls from New York to Los Angeles to Technicolor. To assist him with this task, Gornick turned to his former assistant cameraman, Tom Dubensky, who remembers how they both avoided a total disaster during transit. "So we fly to New York and we get to Technicolor and all the reels were cut except reel one, because they just got the title section,

Above: Towards the end of filming, poster art was already beginning to appear on set. (Courtesy of George Demick.)

they hadn't spliced it in yet. So I helped Mike splice it into the work print, and then he took reels two through ten to California, and I stayed behind and then got reel one the next day, and flew out and met him in LA," remembers Dubensky. "Mike had one of those collapsible portable dolly carts, like the kind people would put their suitcases on to roll around, and so that's what he put the nine rolls of conformed negative of *Day of the Dead* onto. We're going down 9th Avenue and it was, 'Oh, here it is. Here's the movie.' 'Cause we're walking down 9th Avenue and we were crossing the street and going over the curb in New York, not known for its smooth streets, where it was a bumpy street, and we hit a rut and suddenly all the boxes started tipping over and the one started sliding off. He stopped and I grabbed it and we put it back securely on the dolly, like 'Gee whiz', if that reel would have fallen off, rolled across the street, it would have been a $3.5 million movie right on the streets of New York."

As Laurel-Day, Inc.'s post-production neared its conclusion, it would be United Film Distribution Company's turn to spring into action, as the marketing and release of the film approached. For the filmmakers, it was a chance to simply sit back and see what the reception to all their hard work would be from fans and critics.

"When you put the music on and you put your sound effects on, I actually think it's not a bad movie for $3.2 million," says David Ball. "That's what we spent, we spent $3.2 million."

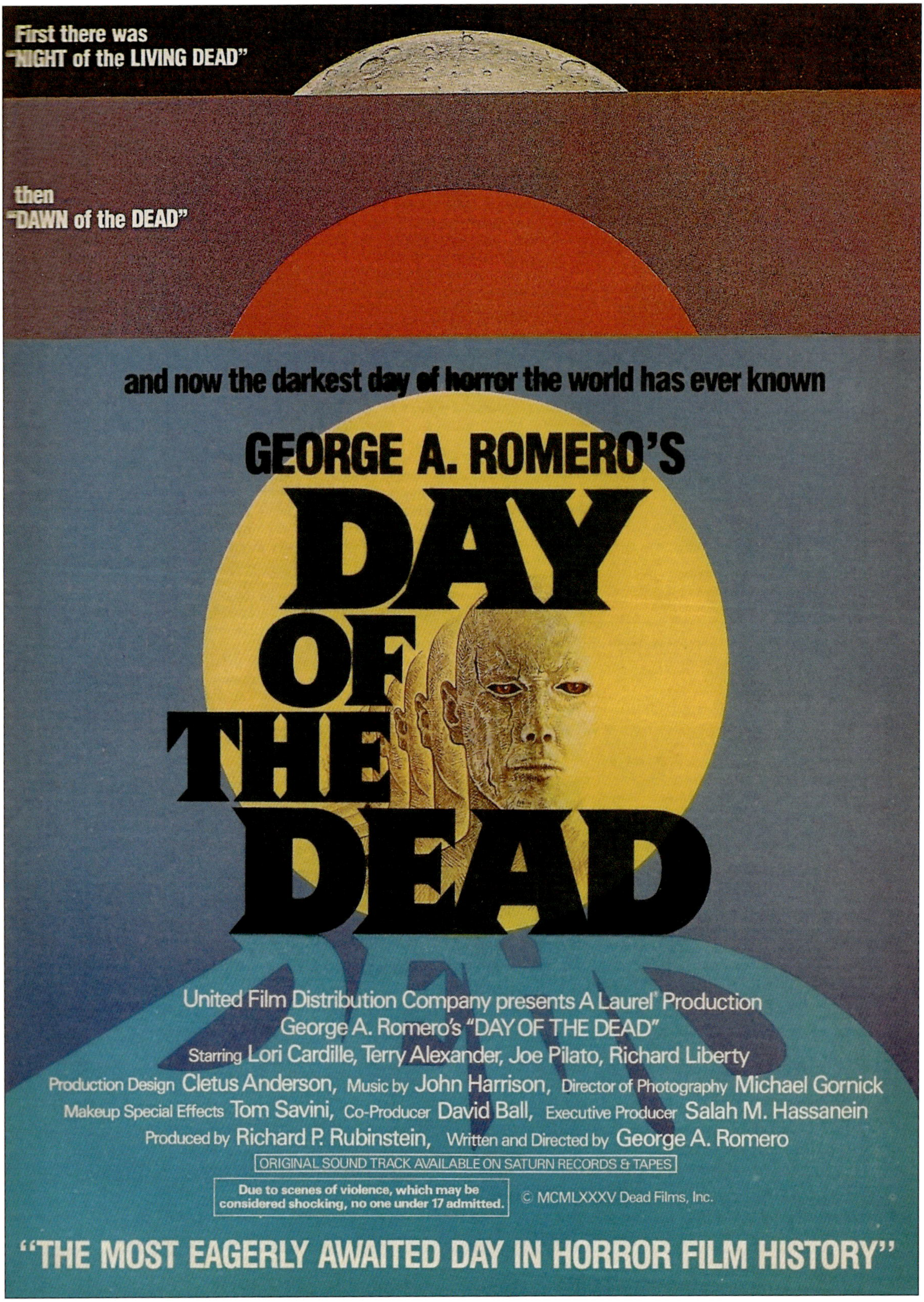
First there was
"NIGHT of the LIVING DEAD"
then
"DAWN of the DEAD"
and now the darkest day of horror the world has ever known
GEORGE A. ROMERO'S
DAY OF THE DEAD
United Film Distribution Company presents A Laurel® Production
George A. Romero's "DAY OF THE DEAD"
Starring Lori Cardille, Terry Alexander, Joe Pilato, Richard Liberty
Production Design Cletus Anderson, Music by John Harrison, Director of Photography Michael Gornick
Makeup Special Effects Tom Savini, Co-Producer David Ball, Executive Producer Salah M. Hassanein
Produced by Richard P. Rubinstein, Written and Directed by George A. Romero
ORIGINAL SOUND TRACK AVAILABLE ON SATURN RECORDS & TAPES
Due to scenes of violence, which may be considered shocking, no one under 17 admitted.
© MCMLXXXV Dead Films, Inc.
"THE MOST EAGERLY AWAITED DAY IN HORROR FILM HISTORY"

Chapter 5 The Light of Day

Long before the summer of 1985 rolled around, fans were very aware of the upcoming release of *Day of the Dead*. Magazines such as *Fangoria* regularly reminded readers of the forthcoming magnum opus from George Romero and Tom Savini. A perfect example of this is the July 1984 issue of *Fangoria*, which featured a set report for *Friday the 13th: The Final Chapter*. Editor Robert "Uncle Bob" Martin opened the article by immediately asking Tom Savini about the production green light being given for *Day of the Dead*.

The horror magazine offered valuable support to the movies that Romero and company were cranking out with United Film Distribution Company at the time, and this film would be no different. "The thing is, there was a relationship where people associated me with Savini, and it's totally justified in that Savini was really responsible for *Fangoria* not folding in the first couple of years. It was not conceived as a horror film magazine at all, and there just happened to be an article about Tom Savini in issue number one, which otherwise was given over to just boring, light fantasy stuff. And the readers, those few people who bought *Fangoria* number one, responded very well to Tom Savini," confesses Martin. "*Day of the Dead* . . . of course, since *Dawn of the Dead* put the magazine on the map, with that Tom Savini coverage in issue number one, it was absolutely necessary for us to cover it and to be as nice to George [Romero] as possible, 'cause we owed our existence to him, pretty much, him and Tom."

As mentioned briefly at the end of Chapter One, one of the earliest forms of marketing for *Day of the Dead* appeared in May 1983, when an early version of the US one-sheet art would be featured in the 26th International Film Annual edition of *Variety* magazine. The artist who created the indelible artwork is a gentleman named Bill Spewak, who worked for Charles Schlaifer & Company, a New York advertising agency that specialized in motion pictures, as well as television. Spewak had created campaigns for numerous other films, ranging from the Robert Redford and Barbra Streisand classic *The Way We Were* to the notorious exploitation romp *Mother's Day*. "Well, thinking about *Night of the Living Dead*, *Dawn of the Dead* . . . and I just had a feeling of marching zombies, [*laughs*] and how to do it [in a way] that it doesn't offend graphically. That's pretty much it," recalls Spewak. "I don't know if I arrived at that immediately, but just maybe playing around with a pencil and a tissue pad, it seemed kind of overpowering at the time as an idea. So that was it!"

From there Spewak turned the design over to an illustrator at Joe Mendola Studios in New York, with an important mandate that the art not be offensive. "The trick was not to be too obvious and too disgusting. All you could do was stylize it," says Spewak. "So I had to go through my illustrator books and choose an illustrator that I think could possibly, kind of semi abstract the situation. And then I would have samples of the illustrator sent over and look at his samples, or look at their samples, 'cause there were a few of them. And then choose one and explain the whole thing. Usually a rep comes over, but in this case I think both of them came over, and we kicked that around a little bit and told them exactly how I felt it should be, and then the illustrator would do a pre-painting sketch. And then it would be kicked around again at the agency and go on from there, and they would do a finish and that would take probably under a week. And that was pretty much it."

During our talk, Spewak said he thought the illustrator who would have done this work, the fleshing out of his design, was a gentleman named Hector Garrido, who was well known for his covers for *The Hardy Boys* and *Nancy Drew* novels, among others. I contacted Mr. Garrido, but he had no recollection of ever working on the poster art for the film. Whoever was responsible, their job was to illustrate those "marching zombies" inside the bright yellow sun, while Spewak turned his attention to the logo's typeface.

The original artwork that appeared in that May 1983 issue of *Variety* would have some very slight differences from the finished poster design in 1985. The iconic poster art features the moon at the top with the words, "First there was Night of the Living Dead," then below that, the sunrise dawning in the middle with the words, "Then Dawn of the Dead," and finally, the lower half featuring the sun with a zombie face in the center, with other zombie heads following behind it, with the words, "And now George A. Romero's *Day of the Dead*." Some of the slight differences included the shape of the zombie's nose, its lips, and its ear. There were also more zombie heads trailing behind the lead zombie's face, and the shading on half of its face was much darker as well. The word "Dead" in the main title didn't cast a large shadow, and the famous tag line of "the darkest day of horror the world has ever known" wasn't part of the design yet – that would come two years later, after the creation of the teaser trailer.

Left: Poster art advertisement in *Starlog* magazine issue #100, November 1985.

205

Above: Soundtrack album advertisement in *Fangoria* magazine issue #48, October 1985.

"Well, obviously we had this tremendous brand of *Night of the Living Dead* and *Dawn of the Dead* that we were building upon, and obviously concurrent with that is even George Romero's brand equity," says Terry Powers, who was associate director of national advertising for United Film Distribution Company. "So we were really capitalizing on the awareness within that audience of – here is the next chapter in his trilogy. And obviously the promise of everything that you loved in the first two is now bigger, better, and bolder."

This artwork would be used for the teaser poster and then for the final one sheet, which were basically identical, except for a few minor changes. The teaser poster would not feature the tag line about "the darkest day of horror the world has ever known", there was no disclaimer about the shocking violence contained in the film, and the coloring was slightly different compared to the final one sheet. The teaser poster also stated at the bottom, inside the white bordering, "Coming to a Theater Near You."

Powers worked with Genero Printers in New York to produce the one-sheet posters, as well as the press kits, for theater managers to order through one of the movie advertising distributors. He estimates that perhaps 5,000 one sheets would have been printed for the film. "There were two big companies at the time: [Donald L.] Velde and National Screen Service," says Powers. "So instead of being the distribution house yourself you shipped everything to one of those two companies; Velde's business is long gone now. And then I, as a theater manager in Savannah, GA, would say, 'Okay, listen I've got a date that I'm gonna get *Day of the Dead* on October 31st. So here I am, a month out I'm gonna start playing that trailer. So I'm gonna call Velde and I'm gonna get a set of ad slicks, I'm gonna get a set of two or three one sheets, and I'm going to get the 35mm trailer. And I'm going to get that shipped to my theater.' And in most cases it was shipped with the prints – not with the actual print of the movie – but with the next time they got a delivery from the film exchange."

The theatrical trailers and television advertisements created for the release of the film were handled by Barry Schoor and Ed Glass, who ran their own company specializing in movie trailers. Not only did they create the trailers and TV spots, they also created the ten-second long United Film Distribution Company logo that appears before the opening of the film. Schoor wrote the trailers and TV spots and Glass cut and edited the final versions. They would also work with a company called The Optical House, who handled the graphics featured in the advertisements. The tag line "The most eagerly awaited day in horror film history", which was featured in the trailer – and later in a print ad for the film in issue number 100 of *Starlog* magazine – was from Barry Schoor.

When it came to finding a narrator for the trailers and spots, Glass and Schoor turned to an actor they'd worked with many times in the past, Adolph Caesar, who was nominated for an Academy Award for his role in *A Soldier's Story*, as well as appearing in Steven Spielberg's *The Color Purple*. Caesar, known for his commanding voice, was no stranger to narrating horror and exploitation film trailers. He can be heard in ads for such well-known titles as *Blacula, Dr. Butcher MD, Mother's Day, Sleepaway Camp, A Nightmare on Elm Street,* and Romero's *Dawn of the Dead*. "He was a consummate professional actor and narrator and he knew exactly how it should sound," says Schoor. "He needed virtually no direction except perhaps on timings, if some things had to fit. Adolph was one of a kind and, as I say, a consummate professional."

One trailer that Glass and Schoor did not create for *Day of the Dead* is the one of the zombie eating popcorn while watching the film in a movie theater. Most likely it was created by Taurus Entertainment after they merged with United Film Distribution Company in 1987, later taking over complete control in 1991.

By the time the latter part of May 1985 rolled

Above: Billboard advertisement for the film outside the United Artists Twin (formerly the Rivoli Theater) in Times Square, New York City. (Courtesy of Taso Stavrakis.)

around, private screenings of the finished film were being held – mainly for cast, crew, and friends of the production, as well as members of the public who were fans of George Romero.

On May 23, 1985, the New York "premiere" of the film was held at the Eastside Cinema in Manhattan. The screening was attended by George and Christine Romero, Richard Rubinstein, Greg Nicotero, Lori Cardille, Terry Alexander, Howard Sherman, and Jarlath Conroy, to name just a few. There have been stories about the crowd booing at the end of the film, backed up by star Lori Cardille herself. One fan who was at that particular screening was Norman England, and he doesn't remember any booing at all. "People booed? I totally don't recall this!" says England. "As far as I could tell, it went over well. I had a totally amazing time."

"No, I don't remember that at all," says Jarlath Conroy. "I would have remembered if I was booed."

"I think I blocked it out," says Howard Sherman.

"No, I don't remember," admits Tom Savini. "But then I don't remember if I was even at the *Day of the Dead* premiere in New York."

According to England, there were multiple screenings that weekend, so perhaps the booing happened at another showing that Lori Cardille was present at.

At some point, around this time, there was a cast and crew screening of the picture in Pittsburgh as well. Before the start of the film, the crowd was greeted by George Romero, whose introduction was captured on camera by a CBS news team who were doing a piece on the director for the news magazine show *West 57th*. "I feel like I always have to emphasize a warning about this film," said Romero to the packed house. "There are three and a half minutes of terribly ugly things in this movie. For the most part you can see them coming, and you can close your eyes. But anyone that feels the desperate urge to flee the room is welcome to do that . . . and we'll all understand. [*laughs*] Other than that three and a half minutes, I like to say it's a great big bundle of music and laughs . . ."

Finding anyone who could remember when or where this screening took place has been similar to my search for the call sheets – an *Indiana Jones* adventure! "I don't remember us ever having premieres," says Nick Mastandrea. "Did we have premieres?" The few that could remember a screening or premiere could only recall that it was somewhere in downtown Pittsburgh. According to Tom Dubensky, the screening was held at the Bank Cinemas in downtown Pittsburgh.

One person who does remember the Pittsburgh premiere, only because of his memorable night the previous evening, is Rick Granati. Granati and his brothers had previously toured with legendary rock group Van Halen and had remained close with the band ever since. The night before the premiere, Granati would learn of big news in the rock'n'roll universe before anyone else. "When they did the premiere, it's so funny, this is the God's truth too – Eddie Van Halen was in town because his wife [Valerie Bertinelli] was making a movie and he called and said, 'Hey, I can come out for a couple of hours,'" remembers Granati. "So, man, I flew from Beaver Falls to Pittsburgh and I got there in record time, picked him up, got him back down here. He said, 'Hey, keep it quiet. I just want to hang with you guys.' So he gets here and one of the first things he tells us is that he and Alex [Van Halen] just fired David Lee Roth and nobody in the world knew it."

On June 19, 1985, George Romero would officially break ties with Laurel Entertainment by leaving the company. The idea of concentrating more and more on the wellbeing of Laurel's small screen baby, *Tales from the Darkside*, simply did not appeal to Romero. "The thing with Laurel, Richard [Rubinstein] wanted to do more television and, you know, I wanted to do features. It was just sort of a natural break," says Romero. "My whole reason for leaving was purely about a business strategy. I just wanted to make features, I wasn't interested so much in TV."

Romero's leaving, though, would have unintended ramifications for his adopted hometown of Pittsburgh and some of the crew members who worked there. "I just imagined that George could be part of a writing team, a producing team that could go on and produce a series that might bring employment and might create a substantial industry in Pittsburgh over the next twenty years!" says Mike Gornick. "He sort of abandoned that. That project fell back to New York, which marked the death knell for Pittsburgh in terms of a facility."

On July 3, 1985, United Film Distribution Company gave *Day of the Dead* a very limited release beginning in New York. It was a regional release, similar to *Dawn of the Dead*'s. By July 19, UFDC would open the film wider in more theaters, and then move their limited number of film prints regionally across the country. UFDC had what were called film exchanges, and these exchanges would store prints of their movies that would be sent out to various territories across the nation. "When I say Atlanta it includes Savannah, all of the Atlanta exchange, the whole state of Georgia," recalls Richard Hassanein, of UFDC. "You used to have the Atlanta exchange, you had the Jacksonville exchange for Florida, you had an exchange for New Orleans which was Alabama, Mississippi, Louisiana. Then you had an exchange for Dallas which was Texas and Oklahoma."

"So we'd open up a few of the film exchanges in the territories around those film exchanges, these were back in the days when there were a lot of film exchanges," says Terry Powers. "So you'd basically ship the prints to a depot within that exchange, and then they would go out to the individual theaters. The prints at the time were probably about $1,000 to $1,200 a print, so you can imagine, as you start making more and more of them, it becomes a very, very expensive investment."

When it comes to the subject of the number of film prints that were struck for *Day of the Dead*, once again you're dealing with a foggy subject. Depending on who you ask, you will get wildly different answers.

"I'm guessing we probably did about 600 prints, somewhere in that area," recalls Terry Powers.

"I believe it was 400 approximately," says Richard Hassanein. "But you know, once again, maybe it was 600."

In the October 1985 issue of *Cinefantastique* magazine, in an interview with Paul Gagne, Romero himself is quoted as saying that UFDC would circulate only a few hundred prints. And when I asked Michael Gornick, he estimated that only around 110 prints were struck!

According to the website *boxofficemojo.com*, the film opened its widest the weekend of July 19-21, in 168 theaters, so Gornick's estimate sounds more on the mark.

Regardless of the actual number of prints, the film was nowhere near as successful at the box office as *Dawn of the Dead* had been six years prior. Things had changed in the film business during that time, so there could have been a myriad of reasons why *Day* failed at the box office. Romero's third zombie film had competition that summer from Dan O'Bannon's *Return of the Living Dead*. Could there have been confusion by some movie goers regarding that release? In *The Zombies That Ate Pittsburgh*, that topic is discussed by Romero, who believes that was the case. Another factor was that films were getting much bigger releases, and summer blockbusters were definitely much more the norm by this point. *Rambo* opened in over 2,000 theaters, *Back to the Future* opened in nearly 1,500 theaters, *The Goonies* opened in over 1,700 theaters, and on and on. The limited number of screens, in the thick of the summer release schedule, no less, basically gave *Day* little chance of being successful. "I think, just like *Knightriders*, unfortunately even though Salah [Hassanein] owned a chain or participated in a chain – he didn't control those screens. Meaning that there's so much product being exhibited that he couldn't necessarily bump that product and put his product out," says Mike

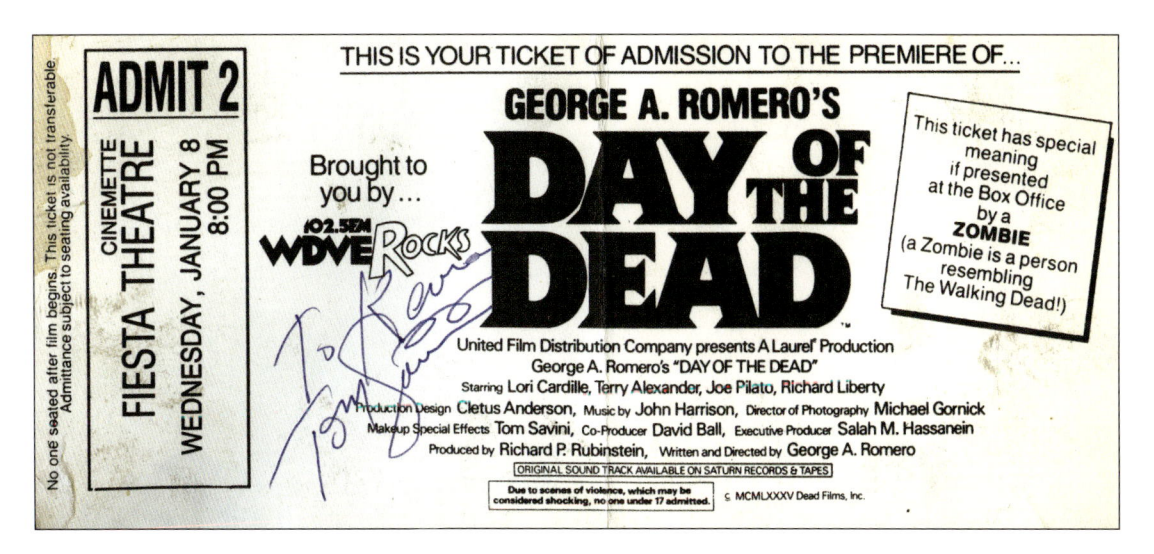

Above: Kevin Rolly's ticket for the Pittsburgh premiere at the Fiesta Theatre on January 8, 1986, which he had signed by Tom Savini. (Courtesy of Kevin Rolly.)

Gornick. "I mean, when *Knightriders* broke, you're breaking two, three theaters. It's impossible! And I think, likewise, with *Day*, even though it had a lot of ballyhoo and advance word, there weren't enough screens. You gotta make that big break."

It's more than likely that Salah Hassanein feared this outcome and thus remained adamant about not going larger with the budget for an unrated film during pre-production. "Initially, I was somewhat depressed by the fact that I thought Salah's goal was to make another significant *Dead* film," admits Mike Gornick. "But eventually I realized what he was going through in terms of [being] a businessman, that he had taken some heavy losses on *Knightriders*, in particular, in that production. *Creepshow* was a moderate success, but nothing in terms of a box-office smash, and so he couldn't recoup any monies. I think by the time he got to *Day* he realized that, and I'm sure he had his own corporate investors. He had another partner, Mr. [Marshall] Naify, who I'm sure was really the money source. Seeing it as a businessman and an investor, they were trying to be cautious and didn't want to overspend again, realized the market might have been limited."

"These guys somehow, and I don't know how, owned a company called UATC, and that company was United Artists Theater Circuit, Inc. They had 1,400, 1,500 cinemas in America," says David Ball. "The person that ran UATC, who had made it so profitable, was Salah M. Hassanein. Bob and Marshall Naify, I can only think they had some type of inheritance, because Salah Hassanein ran the entire show. The Naifys bought Todd-AO, which was a world-famous, world-renowned post-production house in Hollywood."

The men behind UATC, the Naify brothers, were sons of a Lebanese immigrant, and became billionaires through their careers in the theater and cable television industries. UATC had separate companies in the east, west, and southwest. "They had the controlling interests of all the companies combined," says Salah Hassanein.

"Salah had about 1,500 cinemas and, of course, in those days they were making money, so he then got involved in putting money into films to fill his cinemas, which was a little bit difficult and iffy, because there were certain anti-trust laws going on in America at that time," says Ball. "Salah had to stay on top of it because the anti-trust laws said that you couldn't exhibit a film that you'd invested in. And so, if you would put money into a movie, you couldn't show it in your cinema chain."

To get around this predicament, Hassanein would go straight to the source. "So what they did was they went to Rubinstein and his company was Laurel, and Laurel made all the productions for UATC under a single purpose vehicle for the film like Day of the Dead, Inc.," says Ball. "I think when we did *Creepshow* it was called Laurel-Creep. When we did *Day of the Dead* it was called Laurel-Day."

According to Salah Hassanein, though, this wasn't an issue. "There was nothing about anti-trust laws involved at all," says Hassanein.

The respect for Salah and Richard Hassanein and their business decisions, from those who worked with and for them, was pretty consistent across the board, in particular for the elder statesman. "It was Richard's show and Salah was clearly from more of the high level, 35,000-foot view. But Salah, by his nature, is involved in all of the details," says Terry Powers. "The gentleman is one of the most impressive people I've ever had the pleasure of working with. He is just

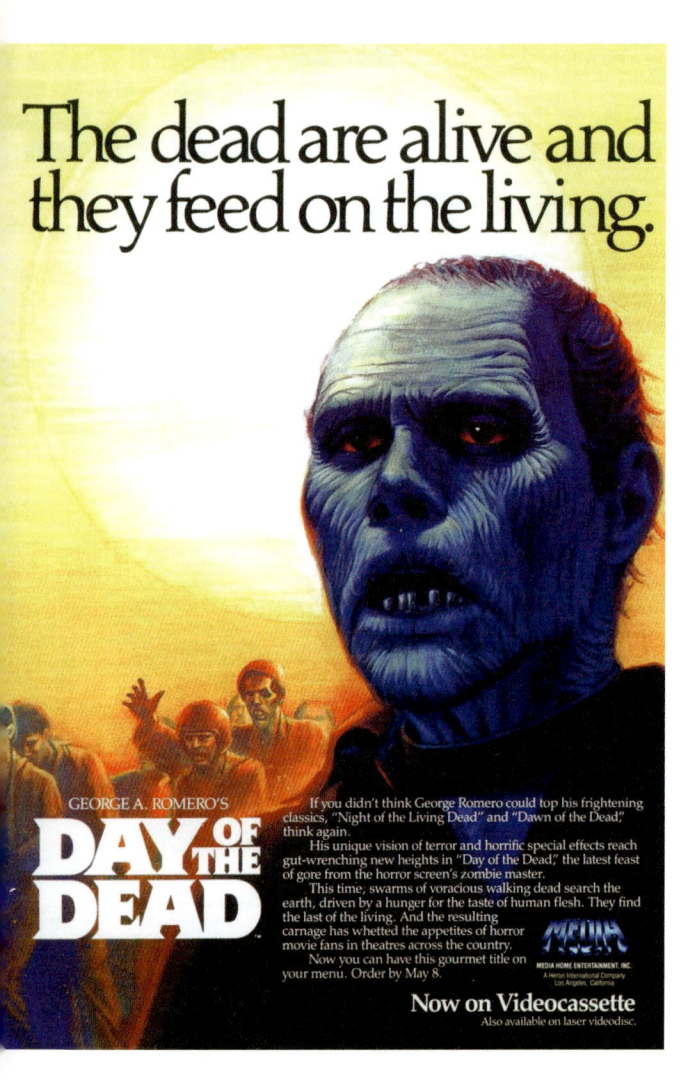

Above: Magazine advertisement for the Media Home Entertainment video release of the film in May 1986, with new artwork featuring Bub.

incredibly meticulous and incredibly smart, a wealth of information. So he was certainly involved in a lot of the decisions and certainly a lot of the approvals – especially when it came down to campaign. But, in terms of a lot of the specifics of the distribution of that film, it was left to Richard and his team."

"Excellent, a great pleasure on many levels, gentlemen," says Barry Schoor. "As business people, as creative people, as people people . . . tops."

Not everyone, however, was in agreement about the father-and-son-run film company, at least not when it came to the son. "His father is one of my gods, and it just shows that it's not always like father, like son," says David Ball. "I love Salah Hassanein to pieces. He's the hardest businessman I've ever had anything to do with. Somebody had to give Richard Hassanein a job and no one would. So his father did."

Day of the Dead would have quite a long march across the country during its theatrical run. At one point UFDC tried a new marketing ploy for the Halloween season, creating new ad slicks that featured Lori Cardille screaming as she pulls away from the wall of arms. The tag line at the top said, "The Scariest Night of the Year Now Has a *DAY* to Go Along With It."

Incredibly, the picture didn't reach Pittsburgh until January 10, 1986! It would play on six different screens in the local Pittsburgh area, including the Cinemette East Theater at Monroeville Mall, as the ad slick in the newspapers proclaimed "Filmed on Location in Pittsburgh".

Two nights before its official arrival in Pittsburgh, there was a special showing on January 8, 1986 at the Cinemette Fiesta Theater in downtown Pittsburgh. Kevin Rolly, who played a zombie in several scenes during production, was on hand and remembers seeing Joe Pilato at the theater. "I remember him, like, wearing a scarf and just kind of standing there," says Rolly. "He was pretending like it was a really *huge* deal. You know, he's this *big* star." Another zombie extra on hand that evening was Bill Waddell, who had also worked at the Wampum Mine. His evening was memorable because he won a "best-looking zombie" contest that was judged by Pilato and Tom Savini. "I won . . . gee, I don't even know what I won. I can't even remember," says Waddell. "All I remember was I got in the paper – that was the best prize of all. Because, literally, for years afterwards, people would see me and be, like, 'Man, I saw your zombie picture in the paper.' [*laughs*] For years!" Incidentally, his prize was one of the background zombie masks created by David Smith, which Waddell proudly wore for a photograph and article written about him for the *Beaver County Times* that weekend. Most likely UFDC had run out of the paper jackets they'd been giving out at other openings that featured the *Day* logo and the words "I Was a 'Zombie' at a Screening of *Day of the Dead*", so by the time the film made it to Pittsburgh, Waddell ended up with a mask signed by Savini instead.

Waddell and Rolly weren't the only zombie extras on hand this night in Pittsburgh. Steve Watkins and his buddy Geoff Burkman both made the trek from Dayton, Ohio to be a part of the evening's festivities. Watkins and Burkman worked as zombies during the Steel-eating sequence, with Burkman playing the umpire zombie. After making their way to Pittsburgh, they headed straight for a local Camelot Music that was giving out complimentary tickets to the premiere, but by the time they arrived, all of the tickets were gone. It was a depressing moment for the two, until they brainstormed a plan. "We're sitting there drinking a pop somewhere and, 'What are we gonna do? This sucks,'" recalls Watkins. "And as we're talking,

Above: Poster art for the film's UK release.

I guess, we decided, 'Wish there was somebody we could call. Who do we know that could get us a ticket?' And it was Savini, we knew Savini, he lives in Pittsburgh. Well, how in the hell are we gonna call Tom Savini? Let's look him up and see if he's in the book? We go to some random phone booth, grab the phone book and damn if there's not but one Thomas Savini listed in the Pittsburgh, PA phone book. Plugged in a quarter, dialed it up, and, 'Hey, is Tom there?' 'Yeah, this is Tom.' 'Tom Savini, you worked on *Day of the Dead*?' 'Yeah.' 'Oh my God! I can't believe this is your phone number.' I'm talking to him because [Geoff] Burkman was afraid to talk to him. And I'm, like, 'Oh my God, Tom. You gotta help us out!' and I paint the picture for him, 'We drove out from Ohio, we were zombies, do you remember?' 'Oh yeah, I remember you guys.'" After spending some time on the phone with him, explaining their dilemma, Savini agreed to help the two out. So Watkins and Burkman made their way to the Fiesta Theatre and waited outside for Savini to arrive later that evening. "Here comes Savini, and we were right there by the doors and, 'Hey, Tom! It's Steve and Geoff from Ohio.' 'Hey, come on in guys,'" says Watkins. "It was really kind of cool, because all the media guys were following him in and the cameras and the lights were going and Steve and Geoff kind of walked right on in." Later Savini signed various items of memorabilia, including a press kit and one sheet poster of the film, for Watkins and Burkman – items that to this day hold a special place in Watkins' heart. "I still have all that stuff," says Watkins. "Those are treasures never to be given up."

In the end, the US box-office totals would be slightly less than $6 million, while international totals were much better, bringing in around $28 million. But it wasn't just disappointing returns at the box office that awaited *Day of the Dead*, the critical reception was lackluster as well. In 1979, *Dawn of the Dead* was met with mostly positive reviews from a lot of the country's major critics, but *Day of the Dead* would not enjoy that same warm reception. In fact, one of the critics who was at the forefront of praising *Dawn* would be also be at the forefront of panning *Day* – Roger Ebert.

On the popular TV show *At the Movies with Gene Siskel and Roger Ebert*, both Chicago-based film critics would lambaste Romero's newest zombie flick. "I thought this movie was a real disappointment, especially after *Dawn of the Dead*, which I admired very much," said Ebert. "It lacks the high energy and the ruthless anarchy of that earlier movie and it gets bogged down in a lot of overacted speech-making and recycled special effects." Ebert's partner, Gene

Siskel, didn't disagree. "Actually, this film is like a trip to a rendering factory or a bad butcher shop," commented Siskel. "That's all you see, is just blood and guts being thrown across the floor of the garage or wherever they shot this picture. And there's really not much more to it."

In the July 3, 1985 edition of *The New York Times*, Janet Maslin, who famously walked out of *Dawn of the Dead* after the first fifteen minutes, wouldn't be much kinder, even though she did appreciate some of the acting. "*Day of the Dead* recapitulates a lot of *Dawn of the Dead* without taking the idea much further – though Mr. Romero does afford one character a subterranean 'backyard', complete with beach umbrella, that functions as one more comment on the American dream," stated Maslin. "However, there has been some progress; for one thing, the actors are getting a little better. Howard Sherman is as charming as possible playing the film's one domesticated zombie, who has been trained by the mad scientist to enjoy the works of Beethoven and Stephen King. Terry Alexander does a nice job in the enviable role of John, the helicopter pilot who alone has the power to collect the few remaining live people and whisk them away from this godforsaken hell hole. A large segment of the audience will wish this happened sooner."

Maslin's fellow New York critic, Rex Reed, also let his disapproval be known in the July 3, 1985 edition of the *New York Post*. "Romero is now old enough and rich enough to move on to better things," said Reed. "Instead, he's dragged out the poor old pooped-out creatures again, this time in vivid color so you can see the slimy corpses munching human entrails in living flesh tones. The point escapes me. The zombies are no longer scary. They're Halloween camp. All those growling extras stalking around with their eyes and tongues missing look like they're just going through the paces to pay off their union insurance."

USA Today critic, Mike Clark, wasn't too impressed either. After panning the film for most of his review, he managed to throw out a compliment about its spectacular make-up effects, only to turn right around and slap it down one last time. "To give *Dead* its due, the final reel has some punch because of Tom Savini's super effects, including one showstopper of a body getting pulled completely apart," said Clark. "Yet overall, the thrill is gone. Unless Romero can come up with a fresher spinoff – maybe something with the *Grateful* Dead – he should pack his dismembered limbs and will them to the University of Southern California's film school."

The reception on the west coast would not be much better. In the October 4, 1985 edition of the *Los Angeles Times*, reviewer Kevin Thomas joined the chorus in heaping dung upon Romero and his film. "Let's hope he's not tempted to go for a quartet, for at this point, sheer gruesomeness overwhelms his ideas and even his dynamic visuals," said Thomas. "He would, in fact, have been better off not having tried for a third installment."

Even in Romero's adopted home town of Pittsburgh, it was tough sledding for the director. In the January 10, 1986 edition of the *Pittsburgh Press*, Ed Blank was unimpressed as well. "Unhappily – and I say that because Romero is one of the film industry's real gentleman and nice guys – *Day of the Dead* is as rotten as all the cadavers that wander through it chewing up their co-stars for want of scenery," stated Blank.

Despite the mostly poor reviews, there were a few critics who still saw fit to throw some compliments Romero's way. In the September 1985 issue of *Playboy* magazine, reviewer Bruce Williamson gave the film a two and a half "bunny head" review. "What Romero's movies add to the sum of subhuman experience, of course, is overkill – plus black humor and Romero's pure boyish exuberance in exercising his considerable skills as a filmmaker," proclaimed Williamson. "The real stars of the enterprise are the special effects SWAT team, maniacal make-up artists exploring new dimensions of gore. Who'd have believed there were so many ways to tear a body limb from limb or take off a head? All a critic can offer in return is grudging admiration for *Day* as grim Grand Guignol played according to Romero's rule: either go with the joke or reach for a barf bag."

In the October 26, 1985 edition of the *Chicago Reader*, reviewer Dave Kehr would also have kind words for Romero's tale. "Beginning from a position of absolute misanthropy, Romero asks what it means to be human, and the answers are funny, horrifying, and ultimately hopeful," said Kehr.

Another positive review would come from Dan Scapperotti in the October 1985 issue of *Cinefantastique* magazine. "Romero's new film is in a class by itself, far removed from the schlock that has dampened ardor for the genre in recent years," said Scapperotti. "A well-paced, viable plot, dependent on strong characterizations, precipitates the horror elements, delivering scares at just the right time. Originality is the keynote with Romero, who has dared to plumb new avenues with such films as *Knightriders* and *Martin* despite uncertain commercial potential. *Day of the Dead* is an effective suspense thriller that complements the series with a combination of graphic horror and unforced dark humor."

And even though the *Pittsburgh Press* panned the film, the city's other major newspaper, the *Pittsburgh Post-Gazette*, would have a friendlier view in its January 10, 1986 review. "*Day of the Dead* is certainly not a film for everyone but it's above-average for the genre and, in Romero's hands, the novelty is still

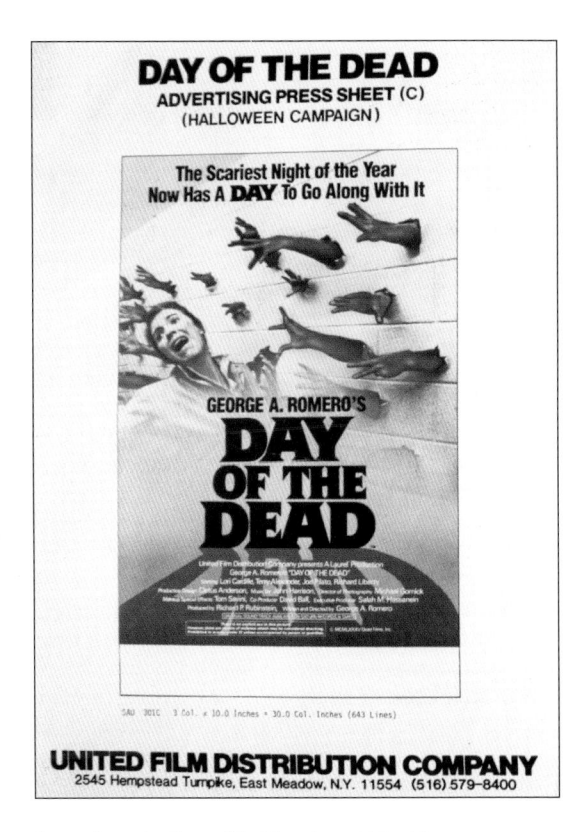

Above: Advertising press sheets and ad slicks, used by newspapers to promote the release of the film.

there," wrote film critic Marylynn Uricchio.

Surprisingly, it wasn't just the critics in the media that were tough on *Day of the Dead*. Some of the crew, especially the younger guys on the make-up effects unit, who were all tremendous fans of *Dawn of the Dead*, were let down by the film. And for the most part, a lot of that feeling comes from the fact that Romero was forced to pare down his original vision. "I was disappointed with it. I think primarily the disappointment may have stemmed because I think I'd read a portion of the original script that George had proposed to do, which was much more elaborate," admits John Vulich. "*Dawn of the Dead* is just a hard act to follow. I mean, he just really nailed it on that film." [*laughs*]

"I think if George was able to have directed the film, or make the film that he really wanted to, it'd have been really great," says Howard Berger. "I think there's things about the film I like and some things that I'm not keen on, watching it now."

"I mean, it's not a bad movie by any means," says Everett Burrell. "It just could have been so much more."

"The entire script got re-written and thrown out and a lot of the *guts* were taken away," laments Greg Nicotero. "Which is still to me, after 25 years of doing this, is still one of the hardest pills for me to ever swallow. Because the original script was so epic and so fantastic and George had such a fantastic vision."

"I actually wish the original script had been made, where Rhodes was more of a Dr. No, arch figure character," says Joe Pilato. "Because I think there would have been more latitude for nuance, but there wasn't."

The disappointment that a lot of fans felt at the time with *Day* stemmed from their love of *Dawn* and its jovial and wild tone, whereas *Day* was darker and moodier. Strangely a lot of fans who grew up loving *Night of the Living Dead* had similar feelings about *Dawn* upon its release, especially the Granati brothers. "*Dawn of the Dead*, it was like it was too modern and too . . . I don't know. It was good, it's a great film, too," says Rick Granati. "But *Night of the Living Dead* was just such a classic and it scared the living crap out of everybody."

"For me nothing measures up to the original movie, the original *Night of the Living Dead*," says Herm Granati. "That's probably my favorite horror movie of all time."

These kind of feelings carried over to the fans who grew up on *Dawn of the Dead* and weren't ready for the tone of *Day*. "It wasn't like *Dawn of the Dead*-plus, which people probably were expecting at some level," says Pat Buba.

"It's a film that has to grow on you," says George Romero. "I think everybody wanted *Dawn*. People still . . . I meet fans at these conventions and they say,

THE MAKING OF GEORGE A. ROMERO'S DAY OF THE DEAD

Above: Poster art for the film's Japanese release.

'Man, you gotta go back and do *Dawn* again.' But what I've tried to do with all the films is make them different, I mean, that makes it more fun for me. I like it that it was different. I like it that it was a little subtler. Everybody just wanted a romp, and it's a bit more thoughtful. It's darker. It's got more – I think it's got more meat on the bones."

As far as Romero is concerned, it's more than likely a television mentality that drives this way of thinking. "People tune in every fucking week for years and watch the same goddamn *CSI Miami*!" exclaims Romero. "To me that's pretty frustrating. People don't wanna try new things, you know? People don't wanna try asparagus if they're into french fries."

There were some, though, that truly appreciated what Romero had done with his third chapter, and weren't shy about expressing why. Gabe Bartalos, who had assisted Savini's effects crew briefly during pre-production, and would later come out to play a zombie at the Manor Nike Site, along with Al Magliochetti, was one such person. "I was really impressed by it. And I'll tell you, every time I re-watch it, it gets even stronger and I think that says a lot, because I went into it prepared in a sense," says Bartalos. *"Night of the Living Dead* and *Dawn of the Dead* were two very different films, but had the same potency and a very nightmarish quality achieved through two very different means, and I remember being super impressed, even as a kid. 'Wow, same guy made these and, like, delivered this disturbing, impactful thing, like, now in color, now in this pop, zam, mall kind of setting,' where, talk about a recipe to fail, and it was the opposite! It totally, you know, trucked me right in the face.

"So *Day of the Dead*, I think I was surprised by – I couldn't believe the darkness that had pervaded it; that again a third installment, completely following one and two, was its own thing. The sense of dread and claustrophobia in this inner society and what they would have grown into was, like, for the lack of scenic imagination – because it was just in this mine – where he went with it narratively showed incredible imagination, to me. That they now go out on these groups and harvest the zombies, and you've got Dr. Frankenstein doing these tests as he has been for months or years. To dream up this world, where that becomes blasé and day-to-day, is where I think he stretched, he took the visual imagination – I guess he made it more cerebral. It almost went perfectly in line with me as a young adult growing. In the beginning give me stark nightmare, that's how my brain works. Young teenager, make it in Technicolor and splatter it in my face. Then when you're a little older, it's gotta hit at another level to really be progressive, and I was stunned at how he did that. It didn't miss any expectations, it landed right there. Then, true to form, as years have gone on when I revisit it, it still has this real sense of doom. Some of the characters that are played a little big seem to almost fit, like, if it was a little less it might be soap opera. The fact that it's more shows the bravado of the scenario. It's incredibly effective. Tom's [Savini] effects had hit another level; I think a lot of it was through the support of his really good crew. The carnage had evolved also; I liked that it didn't apologize, in fact it's just, 'Ah, we'll do it in a dream sequence, we'll do it in a flashback, and we'll do it for real.'"

"It's what it's supposed to be. It's dark and sort of claustrophobic and cold and grey," says Simon Manses. "I think the cave was a damn interesting venue, a really interesting venue."

"It's almost a blueprint for what a horror film should be," concludes Bartalos. "If that's what you're declaring you're making."

Of all the interviews that I conducted for this book, some of the most insightful and thoughtful comments about the reception *Day of the Dead* received, both commercially and critically, came from former *Fangoria* editor, Robert "Uncle Bob" Martin. "The thing is, to evaluate *Day of the Dead*, you've got to first evaluate the whole body of George Romero's work, and then you've got to figure out where *Day of the Dead* sits in it," says Martin. "The thing is, I think George Romero, everything he does I kind of feel . . . I feel that . . . this is hard for me to say, but I think everything that he does is a little short of what he conceives. I think his conceptions are beyond his accomplishments."

I asked Martin why he felt this was the case with Romero, and if it could have been because the director simply didn't have the financial wherewithal to see those conceptions fully realized. "I don't think it's budget. I think it's got to do with the fact that he's an idealist. I think it's got to do with obligations to make something commercial. I think that he's an art-house filmmaker, really. I think *Knightriders* is one of the 'artiest' of art films ever made," says Martin. "I think *Knightriders* is the purest of his films as far as realizing his conception and the thing about it is, it's not in any way commercial. I can't imagine any audience that would make that movie profitable for anyone. And I just think George, if he made the films he wanted to make all the time and just the films he wanted to make, he'd have next to no audience. But what audience he did have would just love the shit out of him. He would have a very tiny, very, very enthusiastic audience. And what I regret about George is that there's no way to commercially support the films he would make if he could really let go and make the movies he wants to make."

In Martin's mind, perhaps one of the biggest missteps Romero made with *Day of the Dead* was casting the military in such a villainous light. "Any kind of military aspect to a film is gonna take fun out of it, because people do care about that stuff. Everybody knows somebody who got shipped out. Everybody knows somebody who came back not 'whole' in some way," says Martin. "And so you don't want the military and zombies together, I don't think that's a good idea. But that's just a commercial consideration; it's not a filmmaking consideration. And it doesn't make it a lesser film, but commercially I don't think you want to mix the military up with your zombies unless you do it in a comedic way."

As for the filmmaker himself, looking back, George Romero considers the film to be one of his best efforts. "I don't know how to conjure that attitude again, but I know that I really like it. I like the character of it; I like the irony of it," says Romero. "I think it's very much me and, like I say, it remains my favorite of all of them."

Even though *Day of the Dead* didn't perform well at the box office, and fell flat in the eyes of most critics, it still garnered some awards for its efforts. At both the Sitges International Film Festival and the Paris Film Festival of Fantasy and Science Fiction, Lori Cardille walked away with awards for best actress for her incredible work. At the Saturn Awards, Tom Savini won for the film's amazing make-up effects.

But when it came to merchandising, not much *Day of the Dead* memorabilia was produced for the avid collector to get their hands on. Island Enterprises produced a 24 x 36" poster featuring the poster art, as well as a t-shirt with a variation of the poster art and another t-shirt featuring Bub saluting.

The video release for *Day of the Dead* arrived on May 20, 1986. It was released by Media Home Entertainment, who were well-versed in horror and exploitation films, having previously released *The Texas Chainsaw Massacre*, *Halloween*, *Maniac*, *Basket Case*, *A Nightmare on Elm Street*, and Romero's *Night of the Living Dead* and *Knightriders*.

The video box art was completely different from the original theatrical poster art. Artist Joe Chiodo, who had previously worked for Media creating the cover art for Mario Bava's *Hatchet for the Honeymoon*, would be hired to conceive the new design, which featured Bub in the foreground and a group of marching zombies in the background. "I was given photos of the film, so I just tried to fit them in to make it all look cool," says Chiodo. "I remember the art director had me put more detail in the art, as they made posters out of it, and I remember him telling me it will be blown up Mombo [large] sized!"

The video release was something that United Film Distribution Company would have preferred to hold back as long as possible, because of their love of midnight showings. But with the changing landscape of the industry, they would agree to sell the home video rights before the film was even released theatrically. According to the US Copyright Office, the deal with Heron Communications, the parent company of Media, was executed on June 20, 1985 – two weeks prior to its New York release – and later recorded on September 30, 1985.

An interesting aside to this story comes from Tom Dubensky, who says the deal was made even earlier, to boost the film's production budget. "Originally it was 2.5 million, but then Salah pre-sold the home video rights for a million, so he said, 'Okay, you have 3.5,'" says Dubensky. "When they signed the three-picture deal, it was two movies and a zombie film and the zombie was going to be, like, 2.5 million. After *Martin* and *Dawn*, 2.5 million, it's like, 'Oh geez, that's a huge budget.' But with inflation and after doing the other pictures, well, that was kind of scaled back for something like that. Of course, the other films were both rated R, so you could justify a bigger budget."

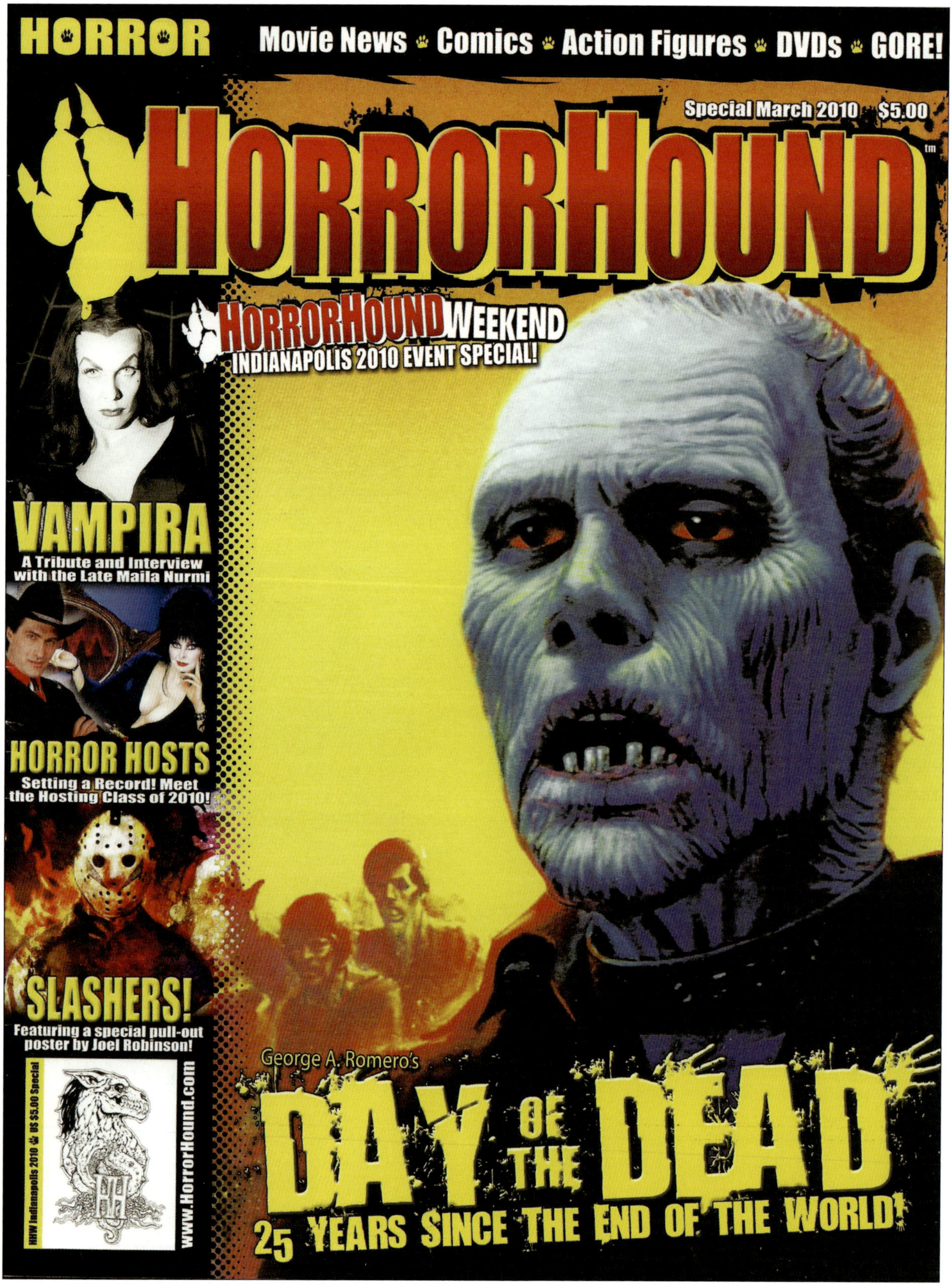
HORROR
Movie News
Comics
Action Figures
DVDs
GORE!
Special March 2010 $5.00
HORRORHOUND
HORRORHOUND WEEKEND
INDIANAPOLIS 2010 EVENT SPECIAL!
VAMPIRA
A Tribute and Interview with the Late Maila Nurmi
HORROR HOSTS
Setting a Record! Meet the Hosting Class of 2010!
SLASHERS!
Featuring a special pull-out poster by Joel Robinson!
HHW Indianapolis 2010 US $5.00 Special
www.HorrorHound.com
George A. Romero's
DAY OF THE DEAD
25 YEARS SINCE THE END OF THE WORLD!

Chapter 6 Reflecting on the Day

After *Day of the Dead*, the cast and crew, of course, all went their separate ways. Some would go on to great success, eventually moving to Hollywood and continuing to hone the craft that they learned coming up under George Romero. Pat Buba, Nick Mastandrea, John Harrison, Jan Pascale, and Greg Nicotero are just a handful of the people who've made a name for themselves in the industry and are well-respected by peers in their fields.

For others, though, having done a picture like *Day of the Dead* – or just a "horror" film, period – created obstacles for their careers that they didn't see coming. "The movie was not well received. In fact, it was like a detriment to have that movie as an actor on your résumé," confesses Lori Cardille. "I remember my agent saw it and they were just, like, going, 'Uh, yuh yuh,' you know? Really, it was not cool to be in a horror movie. If you were in a horror movie that meant that you were just, like, a washed-up, non-good actor."

"There was a period there, a long period, that I didn't negate the fact that I had done these films with George [Romero], but I didn't in any way think about them. They were just part of something that I had done," admits John Amplas. "In terms of me trying to get work, based on my work in the genre, was very difficult. I had a hell of a time."

As the years passed, some of the cast and crew would cross paths on other projects. In 1994, Lori Cardille and John Amplas would star together in Tony Buba's *No Pets*, and in 1996 Greg Nicotero and Tom Savini would appear together in a scene in the Robert Rodriguez/Quentin Tarantino vampire fest *From Dusk till Dawn*. Various *Day of the Dead* crew members – in particular the make-up effects gang – would work together on films far too numerous to list here. Some of the relationships between crew members, which started on the set of *Day of the Dead*, would last years – as is the case with Howard Berger and Greg Nicotero. They went on to form one of the most successful and respected make-up effects studios in Los Angeles, KNB EFX, eventually winning Academy Awards and Emmys for their work. "From that show, because Greg and I became such good friends, I convinced Greg to move to Los Angeles. He did and he lived at my folks' house for months and months and months," says Howard Berger. "If it wasn't for *Day of the Dead*, we certainly wouldn't have KNB, and Greg and I certainly wouldn't have ever known each other and been in business, and I don't think Greg would even be out here, probably."

Like Nicotero and Berger, John Vulich and Everett Burrell also formed their own effects company – Optic Nerve, established in the late 1980s. Optic Nerve brought the zombies back to life in Tom Savini's 1990 remake of *Night of the Living Dead*, and the company would later win three Emmys.

Across the board, nearly everyone I spoke to for this book had nothing but wonderful and very nostalgic memories of their involvement with the film. Even if they didn't actually care for the finished product – like Howard Sherman, for example – they all enjoyed walking down memory lane to discuss the experience.

What follows speaks for itself. Various cast and crew members share their thoughts about being part of this memorable film.

"You know, every day was enjoyable – it was fun," says Greg Nicotero. "That's a factor of us all being young and all getting a chance to work on the sequel to our favorite movie ever, which was *Dawn of the Dead*."

"I have really fond memories of *Day of the Dead*. I have some amazing relationships because of *Day of the Dead*," says Howard Berger. "It was a great memory, it was a blast. I laughed, I never laughed so hard. Every time we sit around and we talk about it we laugh our asses off. It's one of the few films that we did almost 30 years ago that we still remember everything."

"This was my dream, was to work on this film as a kid," says John Vulich. "This was something I was determined to do very early on, even before I got into the business, so to actually have accomplished it . . . there's, like, five or six of us that were hired to work on the film. [*laughs*] I'm sure I'm not the only person that was dreaming of working on that film. To be one of the handful of people that got the opportunity, it was certainly a very exciting and fulfilling experience, to say the least."

"It made a great impression on effects guys out in LA; when I finally did move out there, you know, 'Oh, you worked on *Day of the Dead*!' and it afforded all of us an opportunity to just do an ungodly amount of work," says Mike Trcic. "Our portfolios were so full – mine was pretty thin prior to that – just with some work I was doing at home and a couple of pieces I did at Anivision. But after *Day of the Dead*, it was, 'Well, gee, I'm going to have to cut stuff out of here to fit it in.' It was a wonderful opportunity to get to know the

Left: The cover of the March 2010 Horrorhound Weekend program was devoted to *Day of the Dead*. The convention itself welcomed members of the film's cast and crew to Indianapolis, Indiana. (© 2010 Horrorhound Weekend.)

craft, and learn more about mold making; great on-the-job training, just invaluable."

"If you look back, later on, it was a really amazing bunch of people that came together, of course nobody knew it at the time," says Dave Kindlon. "So, that was awesome . . . having worked on a Romero zombie movie . . . awesome."

"It changed my life. I mean, working for my hero George Romero – are you kidding?" says Everett Burrell. "I love that film and have huge respect for everybody involved."

"The things that were getting done and the enthusiasm . . . it was one of the best times of my life," says Rick Gonzales. "Especially working with all the guys, we'd go out for breakfast and dinner and it was like the old college-dorm sort of atmosphere. It was great."

"Well, I remember it was just a blast! It was just a lot of fun," says Tom Savini. "I remember Taso [Stavrakis] and I playing jokes on people in the jacuzzi in the hotel because there was air pumping out of there and not water. So we would go down and stay down for like ten minutes and scare people holding our breath, breathing off the valves coming in on the jacuzzi. [*laughs*] Or we would sit around the restaurant with Gary Klahr and [Joe] Pilato and all these guys, and do Danny Thomas spit takes. Somebody would purposefully drink something and wait for somebody to say something funny, then 'Spffff' and spit it out like Danny Thomas. Or in the mine, we would take golf carts and I remember almost running over Taso. He had to do a handstand on the cart and walk across the ceiling over the cart because we were ploughing into him. We all went a little berserk; call it mine fever, okay? Because we were all trapped under there, you blew your nose it came out black. But it was just us on a quest to have fun!"

"The finest experience I've ever had making a movie, is what it was," says Terry Alexander. "Because it was easy and everybody was in touch with their characters, so that makes for great magic."

"I thought it was one of my most satisfying professional jobs I've had," says Jarlath Conroy. "It's an experience that I treasure and value and remember very fondly."

"The only thing that validated my career for my children was *Day of the Dead*," says Gary Klahr. "Fans who love that movie, love your character . . . my kids are amazed by it."

"I've worked on big-budget films and that little film, *Day of the Dead*, was as professional and as organized as anything I can remember," says William Laczko.

"It was just one of those great little chapters in my life that just kind of happened," says Kevin Rolly. "It was great; it was really a tremendous experience."

"I loved the whole experience," says zombie extra and "Steel eater" Steven Godlewski. "Plus, it was really cool when walking through a video store with a date. I would pick up the movie and say, 'Hey, I'm in this movie.'"

"There are very few movies . . . I've worked on about 25 movies over the years, and there's only two or three of them that I can point to and say that I'm really proud of the final product, and *Day of the Dead* is one of them," says Norman Beck.

"The work I did on that film and other Laurel Entertainment movies [*Creepshow* and *Creepshow 2*] gave me valuable experience that I used later in my career," says Eileen Sieff. "Having to be creative and work quickly with sometimes limited resources is a good training ground."

"You know, I think the fondest memory was sort of the camaraderie of this particular group of people," says Jan Pascale. "Because we all did come from this small world; it was before the film market in Pittsburgh really exploded the way it is now. And it was this sort of intimate little family, and it was really fun to go to work every day."

"I went through the crew list and it is kind of remarkable to me that I just have a fond memory of every name I came across there," says Eileen Garrigan. "It's kind of surprising after this much time has passed, how I do have these affectionate feelings, and that we were really working as a group on that movie, and I don't know that it's really as much like that anymore."

"The more I think about it, the more I miss every one of them. I still have dreams about this kind of stuff. Yep, yep, I still have dreams about it," says Simon Manses. "There was something just very, very special about the Pittsburgh crew; very hard-working in general and very good attitudes, very good can-do attitude."

"The tone that was set by George [Romero] and how much fun it was, you couldn't wait to go in there and work," says assistant cameraman, Frank Perl. "It was just great."

"Why I think for us, especially, because we shared it, because it was the beginning of . . . it's a major part of our lives," says Katarina Wittich, referring to her husband Charles Carroll. "So, it's probably a more important thing for us than for a lot of people. It wasn't just a movie."

"That whole Romero/Laurel/Salah Hassanein thing for me is a major part of my life, and it will be a major part of my life forever," says David Ball.

"I mean, everybody that worked on that film was

Right: Magazine ad for the second Horrorhound *Day of the Dead* reunion at the March 2012 Horrorhound Weekend in Columbus, Ohio. Guests included Lori Cardille, Tim DiLeo, Taso Stavrakis, Mark Tierno, Debra Gordon and John Vulich. (© 2012 Horrorhound Weekend.)

REFLECTING ON THE DAY

THE MAKING OF GEORGE A. ROMERO'S DAY OF THE DEAD

Above: Terry Alexander, with convention assistant Renee McLamb, makes his second ever convention appearance at the Chiller Theatre Expo in New Jersey. April 2010.
Below: Panel discussion at the March 2010 Horrorhound Weekend convention. From left to right: Michael Gornick, John Harrison, George Romero, Tom Savini, Dean Gates, Terry Alexander and Greg Nicotero.

really dedicated to it. It was more of a closely knit production than *Dawn* was, because we were living in that cave and we were outside of the city, we were living in motels," recalls George Romero. "So we were our own little unit, you know, where as when we were shooting *Dawn* everybody would go home at night, but we couldn't there – so we'd all hang out at the Holiday Inn."

Clearly, nearly everyone had fond, nostalgic memories when looking back on *Day of the Dead* – nearly everyone, that is. For Michael Gornick, though, the feelings are a little more complex and somewhat bittersweet. "You know, I look at the ten-year scope of what happened to me, meaning that from '76 through '86 it was an incredible period," says Gornick. "And so, while individual moments might highlight extreme joy, satisfaction – *Martin* is one of those instances that started that ten-year cycle; the elation of making *Dawn of the Dead* and witnessing what it was to become; moving into a period of financial stability in my life, because we had signed this three-picture deal and formed a public company called Laurel Entertainment and there was high hopes. Those are all wonderful moments, so specifically *Day of the Dead* is one portion of that ten-year cycle that wasn't particularly pleasant, okay, but was kind of a natural progression

REFLECTING ON THE DAY

Above: Mark Tierno, Michael Gornick, convention assistant Renee McLamb and Terry Alexander at the 2010 Famous Monsters convention in Indianapolis, Indiana. (Photos courtesy of Lee Karr.)

of history over that ten years. It wasn't damaging. In the final analysis, over the next ten, twenty years it received note and acceptance and was a good thing for my career. It was a good experience, again, met a lot of wonderful people, but it certainly wasn't the highlight, wasn't the most enjoyable moment of my life. It marked the end of something I held precious and I can tell you no more. I like to view it not so much as a specific instance, as a tragedy, but just as one event in a series of events over ten years that marked the advent of the next ten years of my career."

Over the years, the subject of royalties has become a very sore point among some of the cast members. As was mentioned earlier in the book, an addendum was added to the cast's contracts, which has apparently prevented them from receiving residuals over the years. "It was like you give up your rights universally to anything coming down the line," says Gary Klahr. "Well, wait. You don't know what technology's about to be invented so how can you sign your rights away to something that doesn't exist? Lori [Cardille], I know, has spoken with SAG, I've spoken with SAG. They kind of agreed, but we've never seen any real residual monies. Anytime it's shown you get residuals – we don't."

The way the film was received initially upon release – both critically and at the box office – coupled with the residual situation, has left some of the cast feeling that their involvement in the series is something of a badge of honor. "Like I've always said, and I say this reverently, I don't mean this is in a negative way – we've always felt like we're the bastard godchildren of George [Romero]," says Klahr.

One way in which some of the cast has been able to earn back those residuals is through the proliferation of the convention scene. Over the years, the number of horror movie conventions has grown and, with that, so has the opportunity for actors to appear at them and make some bonus money from their work in the film. For some, who initially shied away from attending them, it has been an eye-opening experience. "With your help, finally, I went out and met fans," says John Amplas. "I entered the world of conventions and learned what a following George [Romero] has in that world, in the genre. I learned about how appreciative the fans of the genre are of the people that worked in these films – not just as actors, but as filmmakers. The fans are incredible."

"To go on these conventions – and particularly interesting for me is to have young white males come up to me and say, 'Hey man, I know all your lines, man. Some of the stuff you said really put me in a nice space and changed my direction a little bit,'" says Terry Alexander. "That for me is a great compliment as an artist and, personally, it is one of the most extraordinary things to have happened to me right now at this age."

221

Acknowledgements

Writing this book has been an incredible adventure and learning experience for me. Before undertaking this task I already knew a great deal about this film and the path it took to hitting the silver screen. But, because of the assistance of so many members of the cast and crew and others associated with the production, as well as fellow fans, I discovered even more about this film that I love so much. I owe a huge amount of gratitude to the following people for their time and their generosity by providing interviews, research material and photographs for this book, offering general assistance, or simply helping to generate early buzz for it online...

Joe Abeln; Terry Alexander (a true gentleman); Richard Alvarez; John Amplas; Barbara Anderson; Barry Anderson; Linda Arrigoni; Chad Ball; David Ball; Vini Bancalari; Mike Baronas; Gabe Bartalos; Norman Beck; Nancy Bennett [Suzich]; Howard Berger; Barbara Boyle [Frazzini]; Griffin Brohman; Jim Bruwelheide; Pat and Tony Buba; Everett Burrell; Mark Burns; Mike Butera; Charles Carroll; Rick Catizone; Glenn Charbonneau; Joe Chiodo; Zilla Clinton; Jarlath Conroy; Judith Conte; Rob Coscia; Tom Cossie [Surman]; Martin Cumiskey; Jim Danforth; Mike Deak; George Demick; Stuart Deutsch; Bill Dickhaut; Anthony "Tim" DiLeo (an unsung hero to this book); James Dudelson and Taurus Entertainment; Tom Dubensky; Brett Dunford; Olivia Dupuis and AMC TV; Enid Earle; Norman England; Michael Exler and the East Coast Horror Group; Rhoda Floyd; Greg Funk; Paul Gagne; R.J. Gallentine; David Garber; Hector Garrido; Eileen and Martin Garrigan; Dean Gates; Steven Godlewski; Susan Golomb; Rick Gonzales; Debra Gordon; Michael Gornick (there just aren't enough ways to say thanks!); David, Herm, Joey and Rick Granati; John Harrison; Salah and Richard Hassanein; Hollywood Book & Poster Company; *Horrorhound*; Todd and Laurie Householder; Tim Irr; Rick Jarrett; Jeannee Josefczyk; George Kantor; Phillip Kellams; Barry Kessler; Dave Kindlon (another unsung hero!); Gary and Carolyn Klahr; Randy Kovitz; William Laczko; Ed and Felice Lammi; Ralph Langer; Kim Liberty; Mitchell Lipsiner; Bill and Kathy Love; Al Magliochetti (yet another unsung hero!); Simon Manses; Robert "Uncle Bob" Martin; Nick Mastandrea; Bill McNulty; Bruce Miller; Jeff Monahan; Melanie Muroff; Michael Musto; Rusty Nails; Rolf Pardula; Celeste Parrendo; Jan Pascale; Frank Perl; Barbara Pflughaupt; Joe Pilato; Terry Powers; Profondo Cinema (Eric Kent and John Scott); Kevin Ritter; Robynn Roberts; Alvin and Jim Rogal; Kevin Rolly; George A. Romero (a true legend); Barbara Russell; Gene Saraceni; Tom Savini (the reason I'm a fan of this film to begin with); Barry Schoor; Christian Sellers; Deborah Sharp; Howard Sherman; Eileen Stroup [Sieff]; Richard Sieg; Theresa Skowron [Bedekovich]; Joanne Small; David Smith; Jim "Sputzy" Sparacino; Bill Spewak; R.C. Staab; Taso Stavrakis; Mark Steensland; Debbie Sudano; Steve Suehiro; Nick Tallo; Pat Tantalo; Mark Tierno; Mike Trcic; Michael Tomaso; Eliza Townsend; Joe Venegas; John Vulich; Bill Waddell; Karin Wagner; Jack Wallace; Steve Watkins; Jim Wetzel; John "Flash" Williams; Katarina Wittich; Janet Wolcutt; and Philinda Young.

I would be remiss not to send a couple of big "shout outs" to two important individuals. First is Lori Cardille-Rogal, who graciously agreed to pen a blurb for the book's back cover. Lori might be the sweetest, kindest, and most caring person I've ever met in my life, and I'm so proud to say she is my friend.

Second is Christian Stavrakis, who is my good friend and also a very talented filmmaker. Christian not only provided me with a wealth of documents and photos from the filming, that belonged to his brother, Taso, but he also designed the cover of this book. He's a very talented man and I appreciate his efforts a great deal.

I also owe an enormous, extra special thank you to Greg Nicotero for his invaluable assistance and patience in helping me make this book a reality. Having Greg pen the foreword to this book is an incredible honor. Graciously, he provided me with literally stacks of production memos, files, personal notes, and sign-in sheets for zombie extras, as well as agreeing to multiple interviews and countless email responses to my many questions. Without him and his unwavering support, this book would not have happened. I simply can't thank him enough for his incredible and endless contributions to this project. Greg, you are the man.

Finally I want to thank two people who are very special to me: first my Mom, Kay, who raised me by herself and did a great job as a single mother. Thank you, Mom, for putting up with my years of obsession with George Romero's films, and for ordering goodies for me from FantaCo Enterprises, like the *Dawn of the Dead* poster-book, which was signed by Tom Savini, and *The Zombies That Ate Pittsburgh*.

My Mom, who was a long-distance operator, is so cool that during my mid-teens she even looked up George Romero's phone number on Sanibel Island for me at work one night. What would I have done with that number? Who the heck knows? It was unlisted

ACKNOWLEDGEMENTS

anyway. But that's not the only thing my Mom did for me back then. On my fifteenth birthday she had a special *Day of the Dead* birthday cake baked for me, complete with Bub's face on it. And this was in the mid-1980s; they didn't have those fancy hi-tech ways of printing photos and logos on cakes at the time. No, she took a photo of Bub with the *Day of the Dead* logo to the bakery and they handmade this thing. And it was awesome! Thank you for everything, Mom. I love you.

Secondly, I want to thank my better half, Renee McLamb. Over the years you've proven to me what real love is all about by sacrificing your time to help me work at horror conventions with several members of the film's cast and crew, by listening to me ramble on countless times about the progress of this book, and by simply standing by me through thick and thin. You're my best friend and I love you very much.

Before closing I would like give an additional thank you to the fine folks at Plexus Publishing: Sandra Wake, Coco Wake-Porter, Tom Branton, and Laura Coulman. I owe each of you a great deal of gratitude for helping this dream of mine become reality.

Clockwise from top-left: Having fun with the wonderful Lori Cardille in a Pittsburgh coffee shop, February 2010. I was in the process of interviewing her for this book; The best birthday cake ever! In 1986 my Mom had a Savannah bakery, Gottlieb's Bakery, create this *Day of the Dead* "Bub" cake for me for my fifteenth birthday. At the time my Mom thought it was the ugliest cake she'd ever seen, but in reality she'd created a wonderful life long memory for her only child; Spending time with Greg Nicotero in his office at KNB EFX studios in Los Angeles. The special lady in the center is my Mom, Kay, who accompanied me and my better half, Renee, on vacation in southern California in December 2010; Taking in a Pirates baseball game at the beautiful PNC Park in downtown Pittsburgh, with the great Mike Gornick, August 2012. (Photos courtesy of Kay and Lee Karr.)

223

In Memoriam

Since the release of *Day of the Dead* in 1985, there have been some unfortunate losses to the group of people that helped make this film a horror classic. I was aware of some of the deaths, but others I learned about while researching this book. This section is dedicated to these people and the contributions they made to the film. There are surely many more that I'm just not aware of, but I wanted to list as many people as I could here.

Cletus Anderson – production designer

Tom Ardolino – NRBQ band member and mine zombie extra

Bruce Bahrenburg – unit publicist

Don Brockett – "splatterhead" zombie extra

Gary Brotz – Florida zombie extras casting

Overton Bernard Capps III – Wampum mine manager and zombie extra

Frank Caputo – Nike elevator masked zombie extra

Richard Golomb – still photographer

Barry Gress – make-up FX helper/Major Cooper headless corpse

William Laxson – production assistant

Richard Liberty – Dr. Logan

David Long – Fort Myers zombie extra

Ralph Marrero – Rickles

Akram Midani – Carnegie Mellon University dean of the College of Fine Arts and mine zombie extra

Terry Prince – background zombie mask designer

Bonnie Priore – make-up

Alvin Rogal – insurance

Vince Survinski – continuity zombie extra

Natalka Voslakov – make-up

Holly Wagner – Pittsburgh zombie extras casting

Roy Wetzel – zombie extra for Rhodes' death

John Wolcutt – weapons

Virginia Zimarik – Sanibel Island zombie extra

Below: With Dr. Logan himself, Richard Liberty. This photo was taken at the *Fangoria* Weekend of Horrors in Orlando, Florida, in September 2000. Sadly, just a little over three weeks later Richard would pass away from a heart attack. (Courtesy of Lee Karr.)